The Art of THE LORD OF THE RINGS™

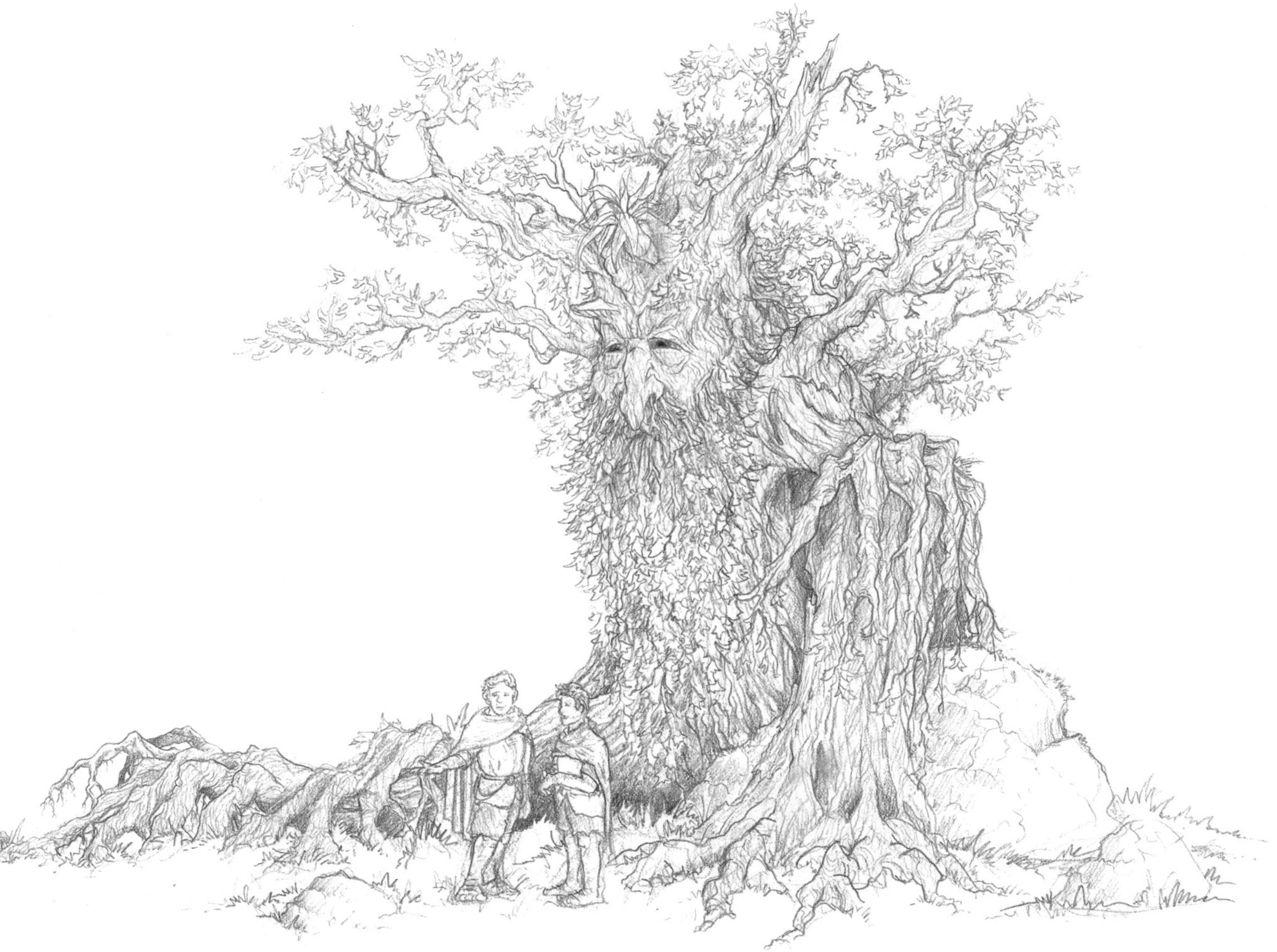

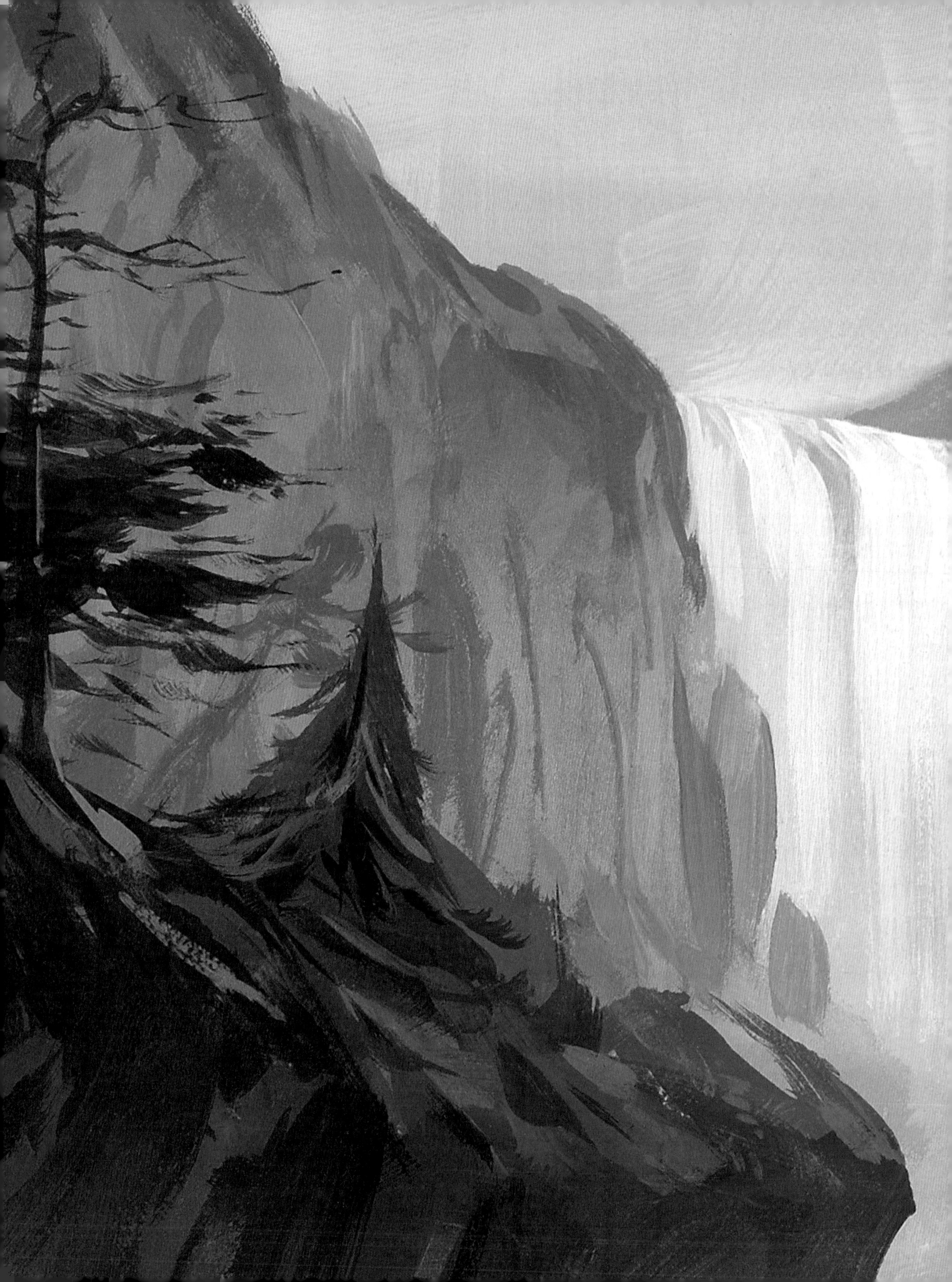

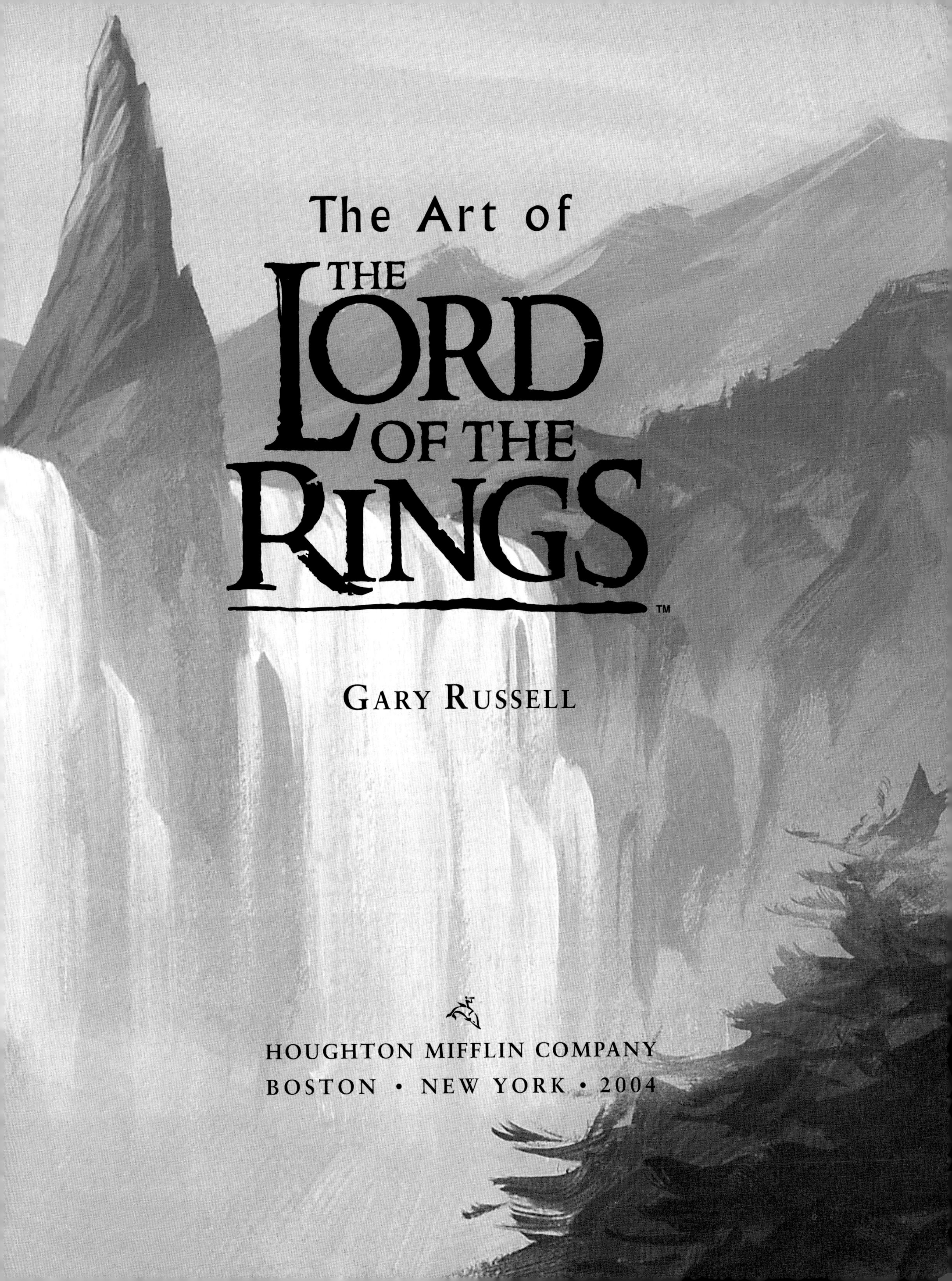

The Art of THE LORD OF THE RINGS™

GARY RUSSELL

HOUGHTON MIFFLIN COMPANY
BOSTON • NEW YORK • 2004

The Art of The Lord of the Rings is a companion to the films *The Fellowship of the Ring, The Two Towers,* and *The Return of the King.* It is published with the permission, but not the approval, of the estate of the late J.R.R. Tolkien.

Visit our Web site: www.houghtonmifflinbooks.com.

Library of Congress Cataloging-in-Publication Data is available.
ISBN 0-618-51098-2
ISBN 0-618-51083-4 (pbk.)

Printed in Italy by Rotolito Lombarda SpA
HC 10 9 8 7 6 5 4 3 2 1

Editor: Chris Smith
Layout: Terence Caven
Production: Nicole Abel

Page 1: Treebeard, pencil sketch by Daniel Falconer; pages 2/3: The Falls of Rauros, color study by Jeremy Bennett; page 6: Rivendell, color study by Paul Lasaine; page 7: The One Ring Is Lost (detail), teaser poster concept by Paul Lasaine; page 62: The Fellowship of the Ring, watercolor by Alan Lee; page 63: Lothlórien, pencil sketch by Alan Lee; page 112: The Return to Bag End, watercolor by John Howe; page 113: The Ferrymaster's Cottage, pencil sketch by John Howe; page 204: Rivendell, digital matte painting by Dylan Cole; page 205: Fireworks Dragon, digital concept by Gus Hunter.

This book is for Paul Vyse, without whom . . .

Contents

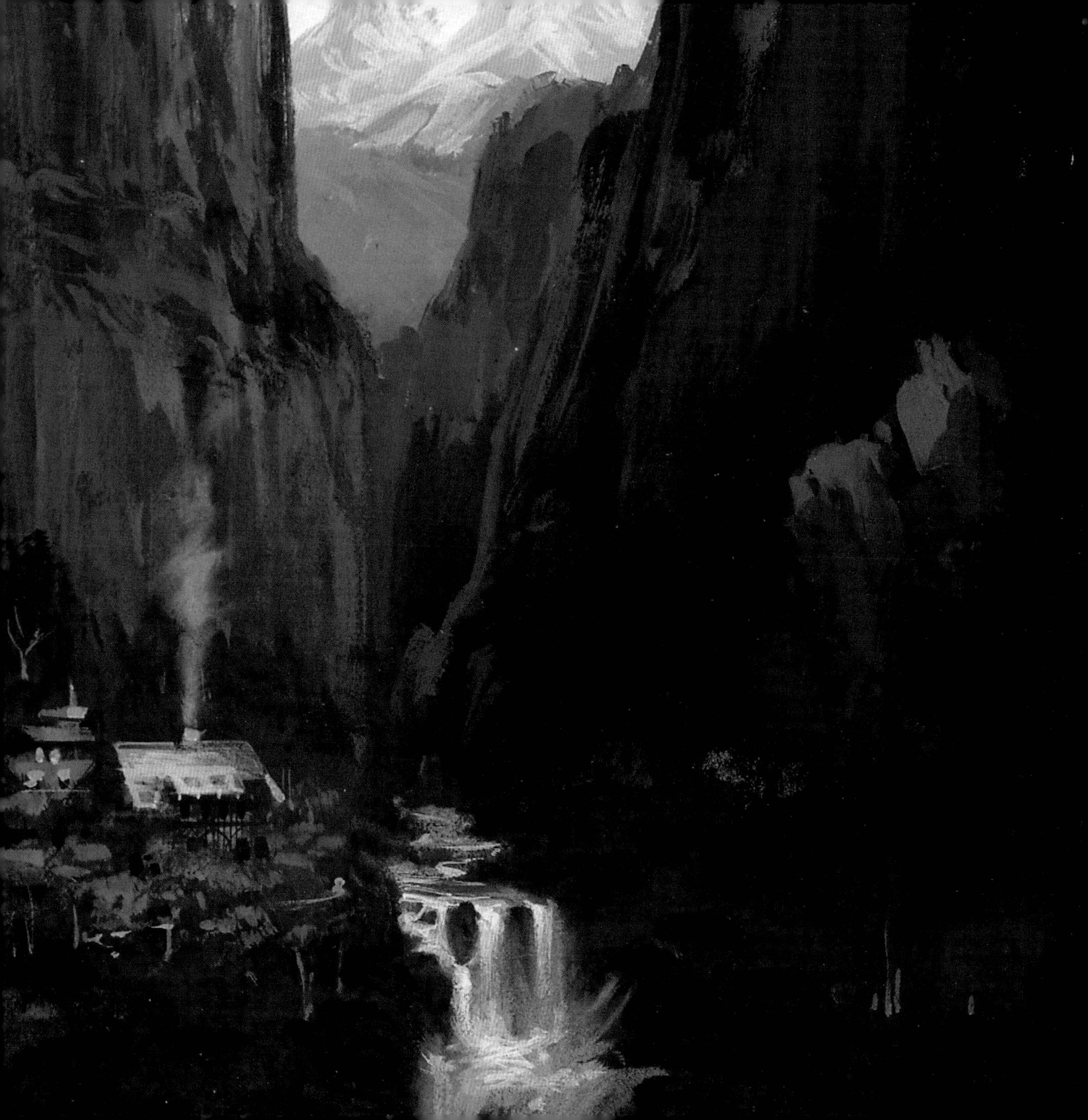

FOREWORD

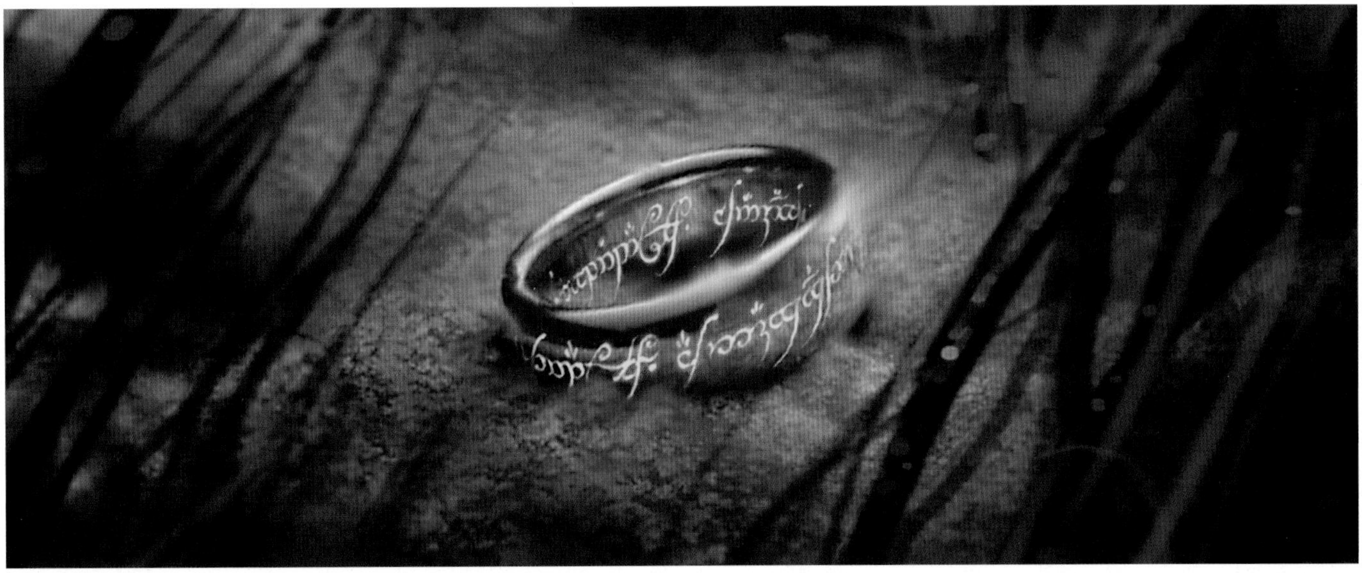

The previous three books in this series, one might be forgiven for thinking, were pretty much it. Three *Art of* books, one per film, should surely be enough for anyone.

As you can plainly see, this is not the case. A nice compilation, a true *Best of,* was always in the back of my mind when putting together the first three books. Art that might have been reproduced smaller than it deserved or had been cropped to fit on the page would get a chance for a second, better airing. So it was always my intention that the *Best of* volume would concentrate less on words and more on being a visual record of this extraordinary trilogy of movies, and the heart and soul that went into making them.

However (oh, there's always a caveat, you cry), one thing that arose very early on in the production of the books was the question of time, or lack of it. You see, each previous *Art of* book had to meet a specific deadline. That meant text and pictures all needed to be selected and sent off to be printed quite a few months before the finished volume reached the shelves. This would have been fine, if it weren't for the disheartening fact that although the book was being designed, printed, translated into many different languages, and generally made to look beautiful, down in New Zealand work continued on the films right up to the day Peter Jackson had to deliver his finished print to the studios of New Line Cinema.

And thus it was that although each book had about five hundred glorious pieces of artwork, there were hundreds more that had been drawn, painted, Photoshopped, and generally created from scratch between my finishing the book and the crew finishing the movies – art that otherwise would never see the light of day.

Thus it was that word was sent out to those kind souls who had been so accommodating to me over the past three years: "Hey, guys, we're doing it again!" This time we asked the artists to select their favorite pieces that had been previously printed, along with their favorites from the ones that had been missed because they didn't actually exist at the time.

On top of that, and I offer no apologies about this, a majority of works presented in this fourth volume are also my personal favorites. As I mentioned in earlier forewords, I am not an expert on Tolkien's work or particularly well versed in the detail of *The Lord of the Rings*. One of the reasons I took on this project was that, as a fan of great movies, I would be able to view and select these pictures on their artistic merit and visual strength, and not because I thought John Howe, Daniel Falconer, or Christian Rivers delivered a Balrog that looked most like the way I had imagined a Balrog. Before arriving in Wellington, I had never encountered the word Balrog. I just looked at, loved, and selected what I believed then, and still believe today, to be fantastic pieces of art. They could have been created for a gallery rather than for a movie, as far as I was concerned – I just fell in love with the beautiful pictures.

And so, until work begins one day on the long-awaited *The Hobbit* movie (go on, everyone, you know you want to), here is my last collection of *The Lord of the Rings* art. It's been an exciting voyage of discovery, and I'm very, very pleased to have had, through the work of the people whose art is contained herein, my eyes opened to the glorious world that Tolkien created and Peter Jackson lovingly and wonderfully enhanced.

Gary Russell
April 2004

VISUAL EFFECTS DESIGN

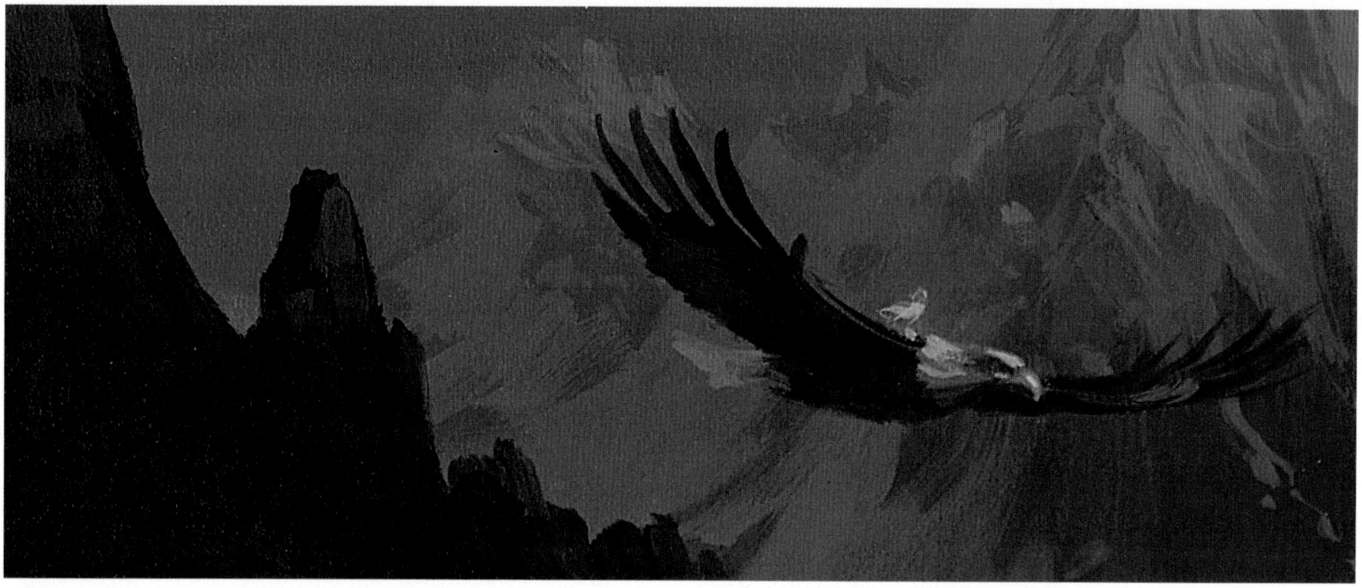

My role is purely as a visualizer. If Peter Jackson is not able to come up with an image of something he's got in his brain, he's got designers like us to help him. The art we do becomes something that can be used to show everybody else as well, almost like a trailer. Hopefully, we were hired because we had an aesthetic vision similar to Peter's, so we follow him and translate his ideas to everyone else on the show. "See this painting – that's what I want the Mines of Moria to look like," and so on. I, along with Jeremy Bennett, Gus Hunter, and the others are guides. We make significant suggestions, create as many paintings as he wants, and he picks the ones he likes.

It's not the size of the painting that matters, it's the thought that goes into it and the planning. I can do a ten-foot version of a painting just by using bigger paintbrushes and still come out with exactly the same detail as a five-incher. Usually, I can do a couple of these a day, whereas one of the big ones, because there's so much detail, can take three days, maybe four at the outside.

I often start with paint. Sometimes I'll do a little sketch first – I usually don't like to sketch that much, and if I do, it's very minimal. The Lothlórien paintings, for example, didn't have any drawings at all; I just started painting. Sometimes, if I want something specific, I'll do a few little studies first before I get into it. I might make mistakes, little tiny things, but then I've got a pretty good guide for painting the big elaborate one. At that point it's just about added details – the painting doesn't really say any more to the director than the little one does, but people like to see the big ones.

One of the ideas we went with was that the story is really like a journey back in time for Frodo and Sam. You look at the Shire, and it's almost like an old English farmhouse from the late 1800s. And as they go on their journey, every step they take, every new location they come to, is like going further back in time. Aragorn is right out of King Arthur, which puts you back in the twelfth century. Then they meet the Orcs, much further back, Medieval, Bronze Age, Iron Age stuff. All the way back until you start getting into Mordor, which is like going into an almost primordial situation with cavemen. Finally, you go all the way back to Mount Doom, where the Ring was made and forged, which almost represents the creation. So it's a neat concept for a designer; it keeps you in line.

Paul Lasaine
March 2001

"Paul and Jeremy are masters at using light and color. They have often shown me the mood of a particular moment through their use of paint. I get from them a potential flavor and tone of the lighting."

PETER JACKSON

I had read the books a few times and loved them, but more than anything I am a big fan of Alan Lee's work. To actually be working alongside him is humbling but also great fun. His wealth of emotional knowledge regarding Middle-earth is astonishing. If I have any questions, he can probably answer them.

My job as VFX art director is to take shots handed over from Peter Jackson and integrate the live action and blue-screen footage with the environments that we create for them. The geographical location, time of day, lighting, and color palette are all elements that need to be taken into consideration and carefully balanced. The job is time-consuming but ultimately satisfying.

I piece all these things together and present them to Peter for comment. If we take the Dead Marshes, for example, I might present artwork for a group of shots and give Peter a variety of options so he has more to choose from. He might say, "Well, I like that on that painting, but this I'd like to change."

I also have to take into account if there are any miniatures, decide where they will be placed in the artwork, what elements might be added to it, as far as the atmosphere, massive elements, blue screen, figures walking on the miniature, waterfalls, woods, skies, and so on.

I imagine it's unusual that I'm this involved in so many aspects of the production – but then I imagine a film that generates this much artwork is also unusual. It's rare – but I think all big-budget movies dealing responsibly with genres like this should do exactly the same.

When I first started, I was totally thrown and wondered "How on Earth are we going to do all that on film?" but I quickly realized it was a gigantic endeavor, and with so many people pulling together, I knew it would be all right in the end. Of course, I still wonder how we're going to do half the things we do, and sometimes it feels formidable and a bit terrifying.

Right now I'm doing pretty much what Paul was doing, so I can see why I was brought on in the first place, given the number of meetings that I have to attend and therefore the amount of time that I don't spend at the drawing board. When Paul was around, I had the luxury of time to develop environments, like Isengard, and I could do fifty sketches for one shot – thinking about how it might look, how the miniature of it might be composed, and so on. Now it's more of a balancing act, although in some respects it's easier because all the filming has been done and we're dealing with lots of footage that is more or less cut, so you know exactly what has to go into the final shot.

Jeremy Bennett
April 2003

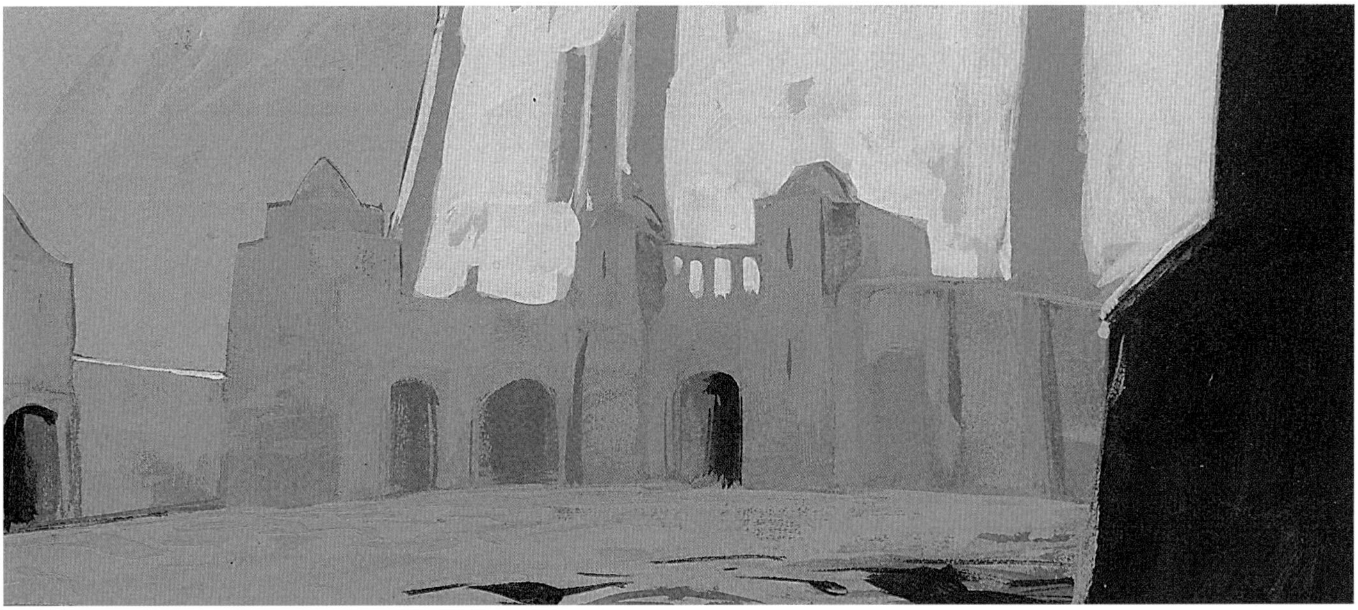

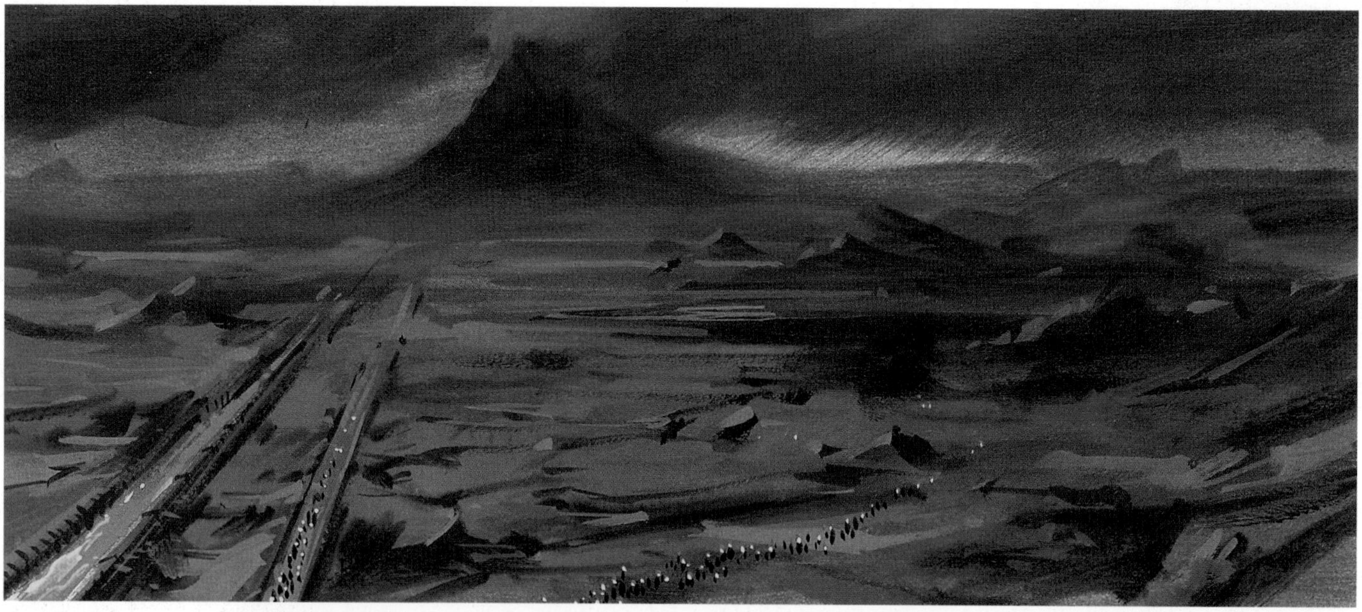

MORDOR
Barad-dûr
These three separate frames are from a long panning shot showing the Orcs swarming toward the Barad-dûr bridge during the prologue. The camera pans past them and onto the Orcs who are rebuilding Sauron's destroyed fortress. These were used as color guides, and Jeremy added the Orcs to give the digital artists a sense of scale and environment. *JB*

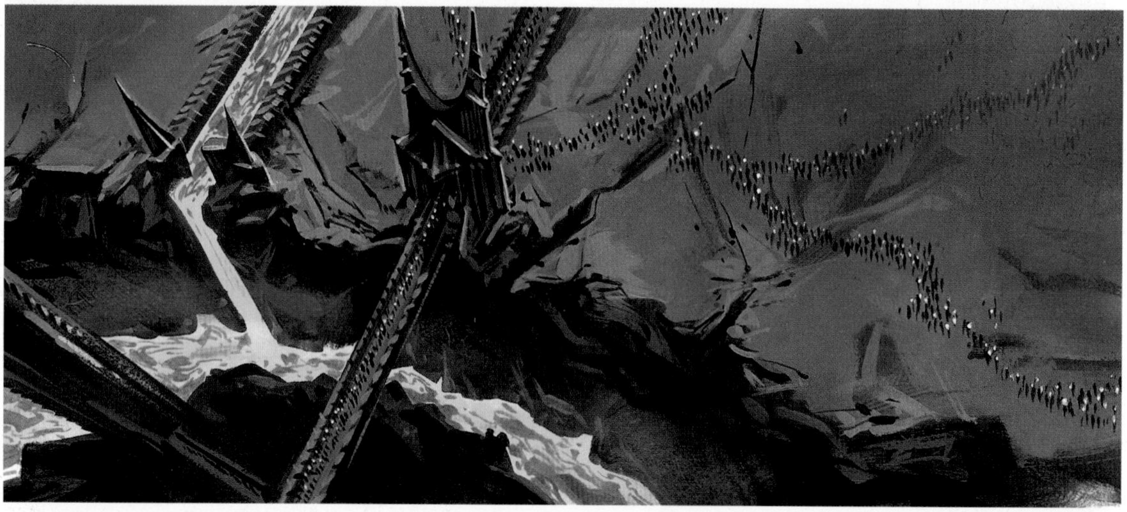

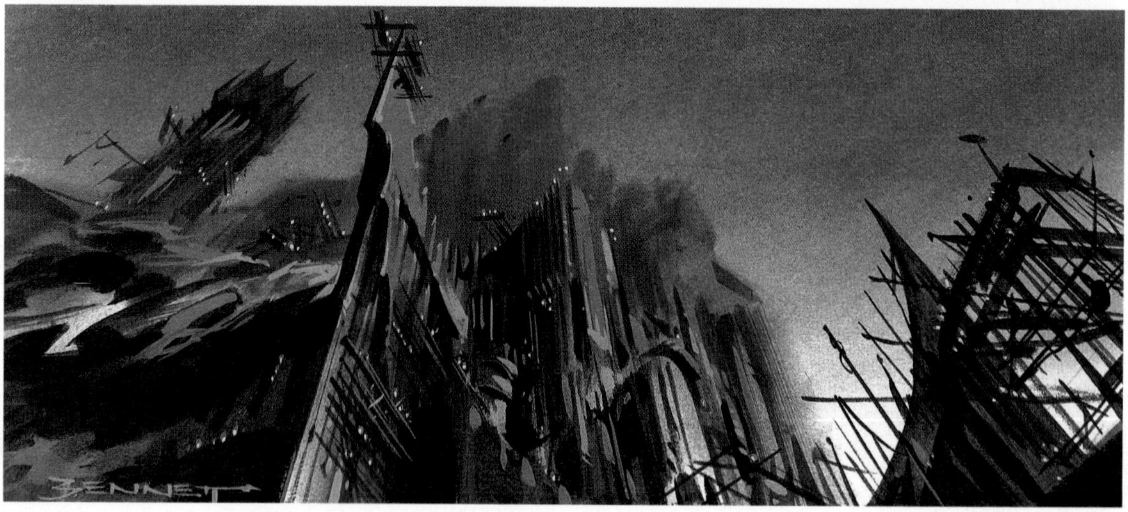

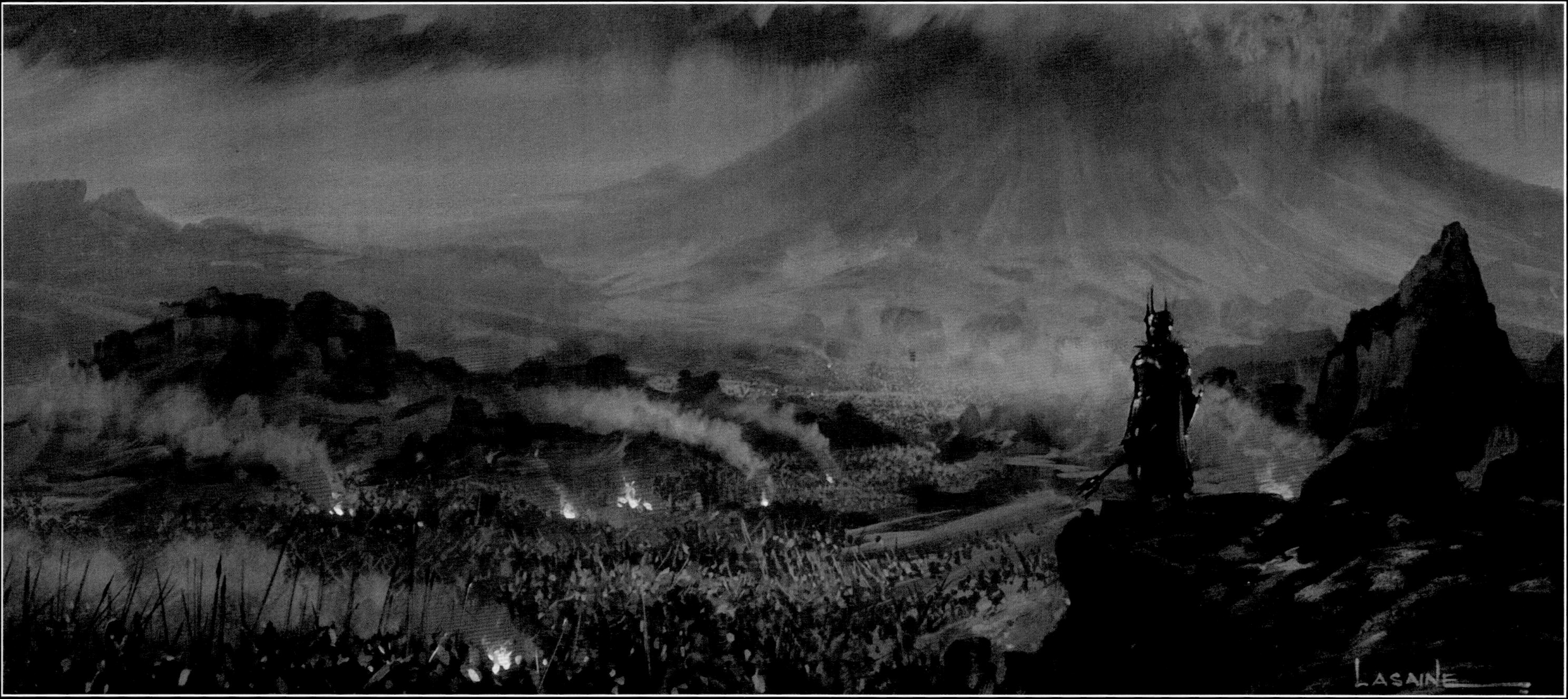

MORDOR *Battle of the Second Age*

“This conceptual image was produced as a first look at the giant battle that happens in the prologue. Here we see Sauron casting an eye over his troops. Peter Jackson wanted to get a feeling of what it might look like when you have 600,000 troops ready for war in Mordor. I used a different color palette for this one. Avoiding the harsh browns and industrial blacks of ‘our’ Mordor, this painting instead has cool grays, magentas, and a rather steely blue about it.” *PL*

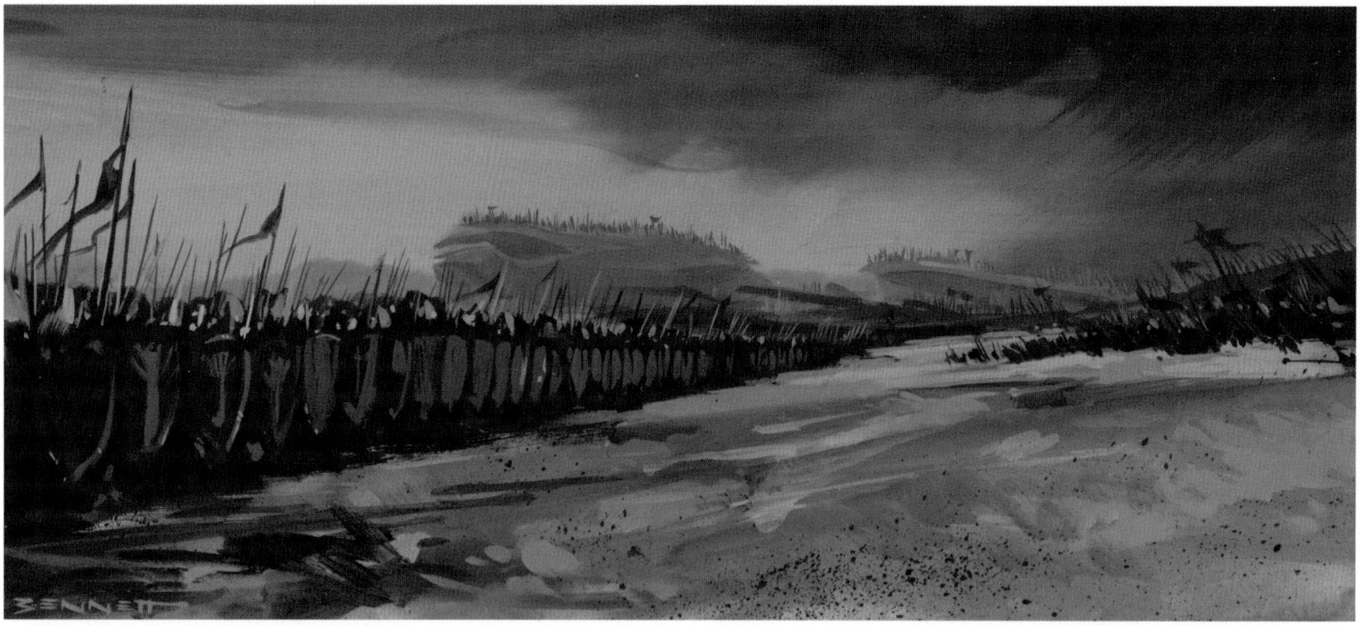

MORDOR *Gorgoroth Plain*
"This is a very early study addressing the possible look and feel of one shot from the prologue battle sequence, where the Elves line up to face the hordes of Orcs that are charging toward them."*JB*

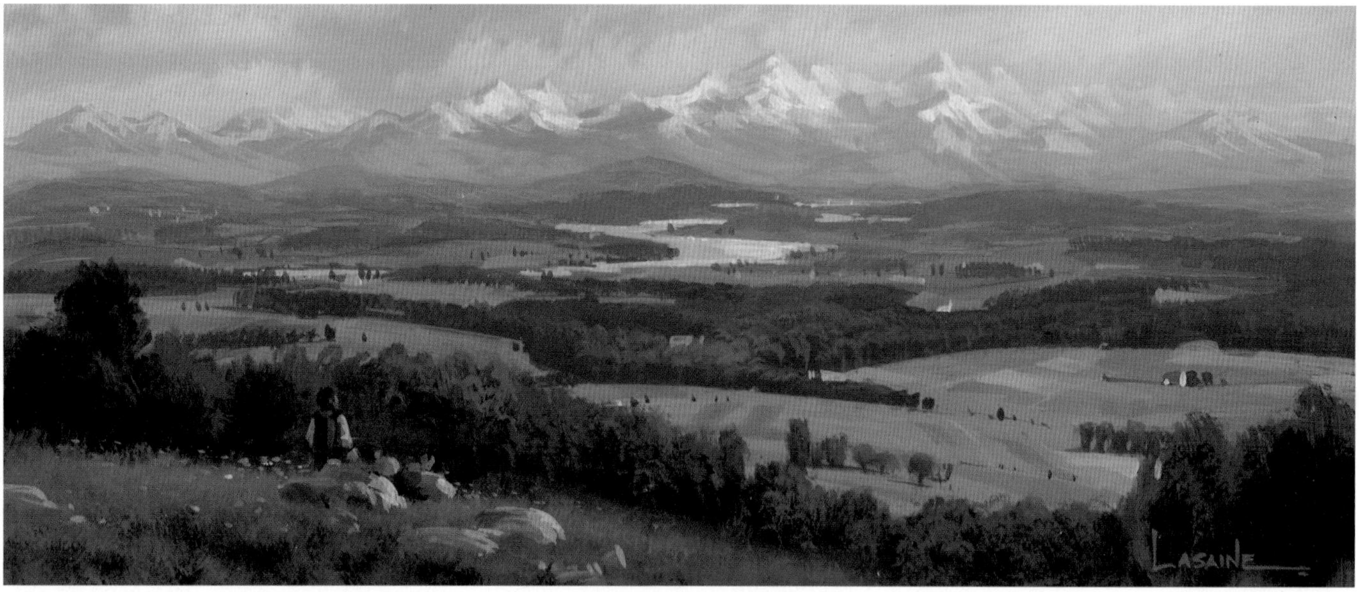

THE SHIRE *The Westfarthing*
This is one of Paul's favorite paintings, and the image of Frodo and Sam observing the landscape before them is echoed in its companion piece on page 23. The contrast is not just in what the pictures show, but in the way the colors create mood and atmosphere. *PL*

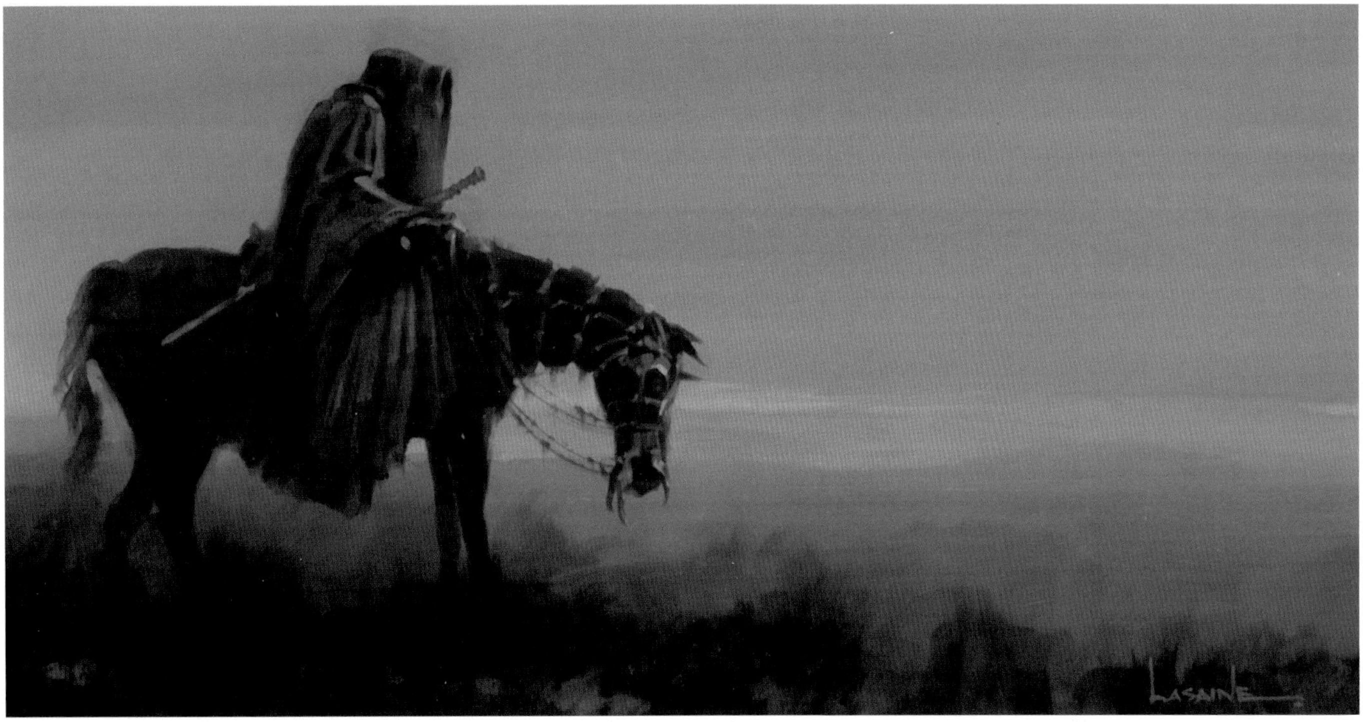

BREE ***The Black Rider***
"Peter asked me to do this illustration of one of the Black Riders to inspire the crew who were preparing to shoot the Bree sequence. I chose to depict a nonaction moment that was never intended to be in the film. I thought it would be interesting, and kind of creepy, to show a Ringwraith just patiently waiting for Frodo to put on the Ring. Almost as if to say, 'I've waited more than a thousand years . . . I'm in no hurry.'" *PL*

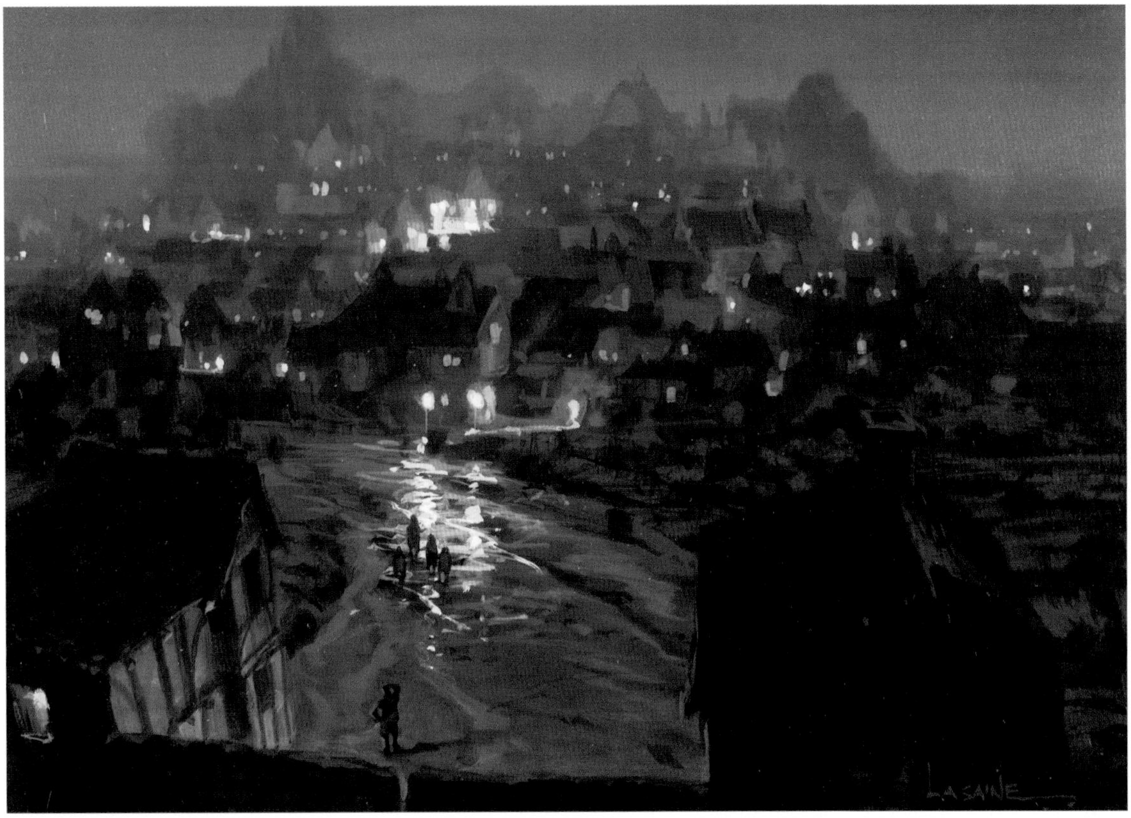

BREE GATES
Matte painting sketch
"This illustration of the establishing shot of Bree is an adaptation of a pencil sketch by Alan Lee. It was done as a guide for mood and color for the whole Bree sequence. Later it was used as the rough layout for the matte painting of the establishing shot." *PL*

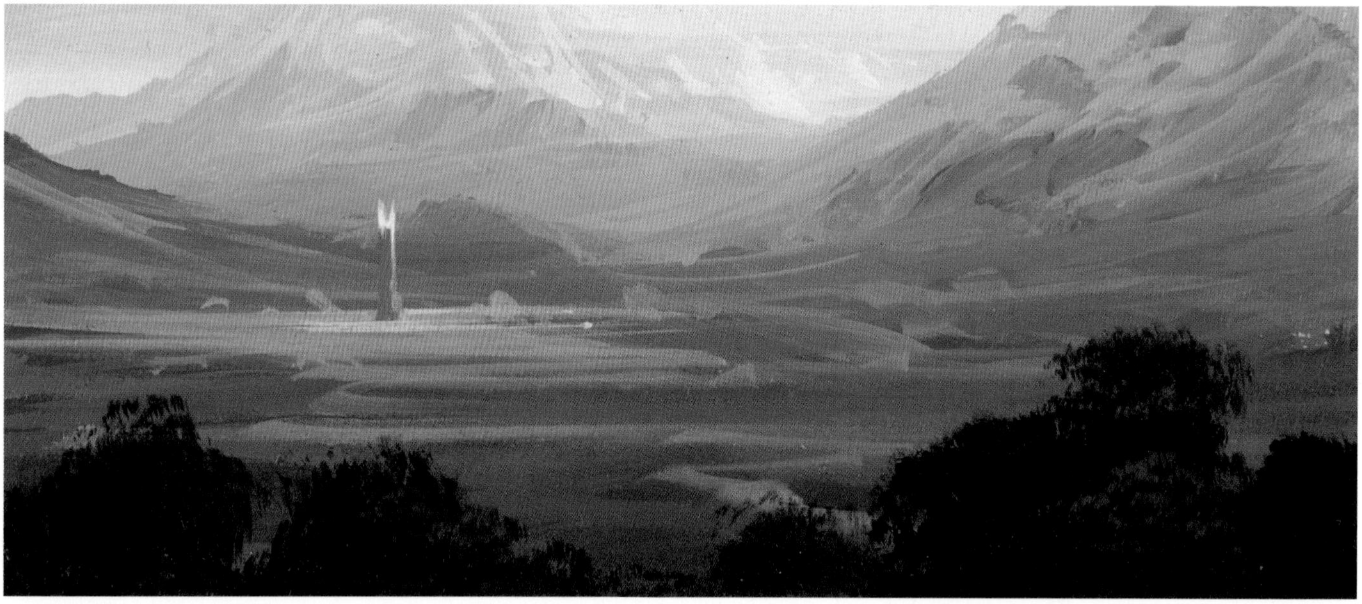

ISENGARD ***Orthanc Tower***
"This was an early design for the look of the Isengard valley – before we find out that Saruman is actually a bad guy." *PL*

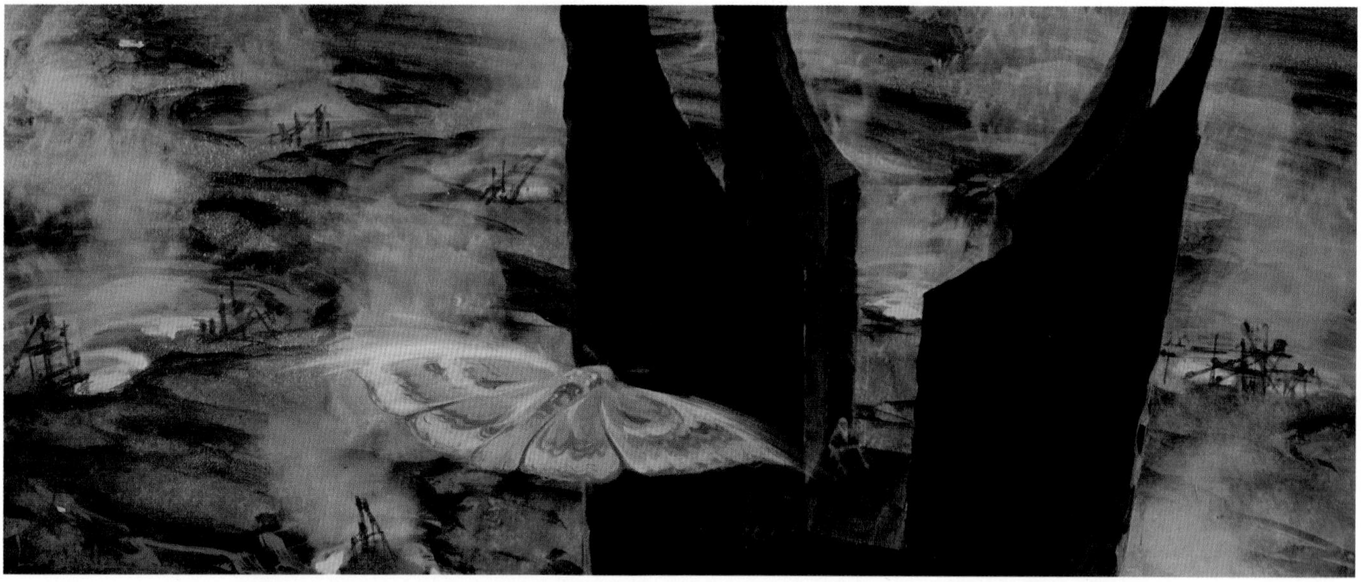

ISENGARD ***Orthanc Tower***
"This one, the Moth Shot, I call it, was done after a request from Peter. Primarily, it was to show the first time that we actually see Isengard as a destroyed, wasted Isengard. Up until then it was this beautiful forest garden. We follow this moth in a crane up over the wall, and there it is, essentially a big industrial wasteland. This was a color study, really, done before anything was actually shot. We were interested in the development of the valley. The crew actually had this with them when they filmed the location shots, so when it was time to do the final matte work, it would be exactly as Peter had intended way back when we started on this painting." *PL*

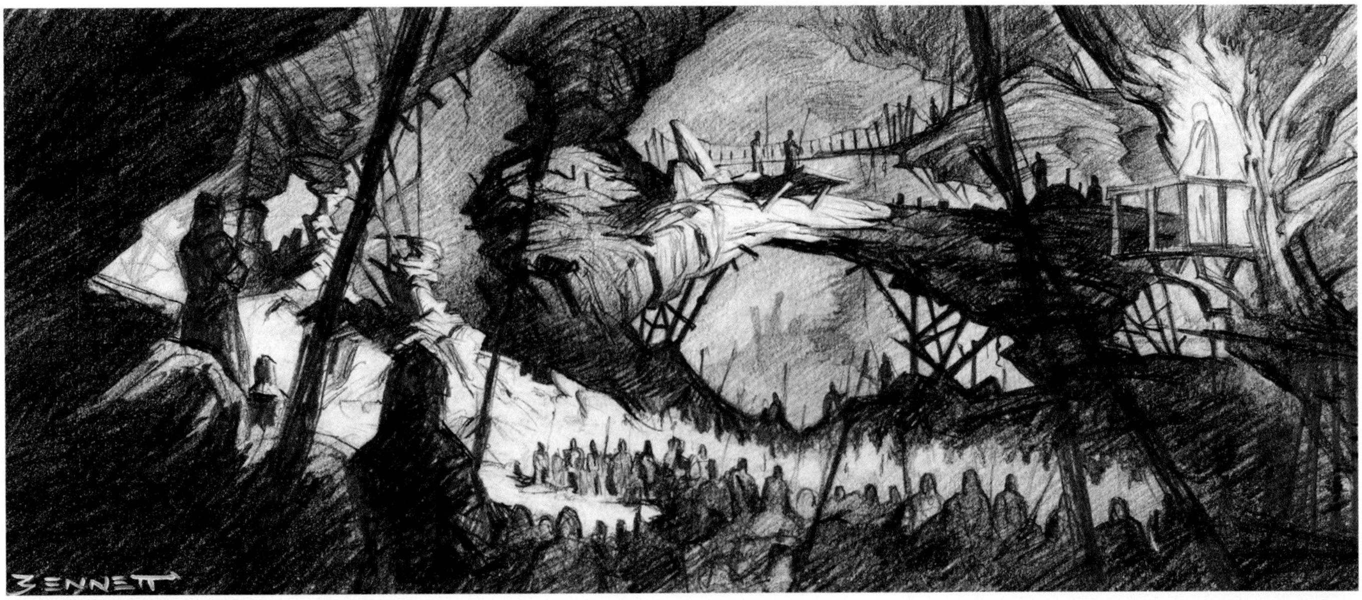

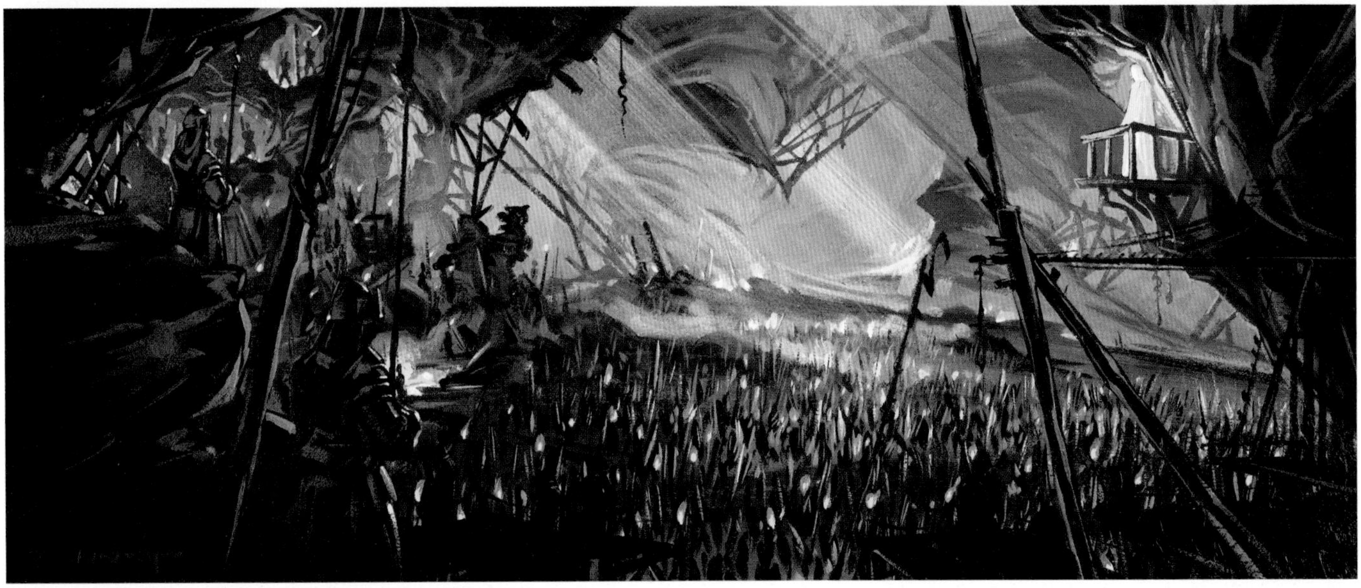

ISENGARD ***The Caverns***

The painting (above) of the Uruk-hai below Isengard was the result of about fifty sketches and compositions created to resolve foreground, background, and midground elements of the final shot. The scale of the Uruk-hai and the caverns was of some concern; thus this painting was needed to set the perspectives. The rough pencil version (top) was actually used by Alex Funke, the director of photography, for the miniature setups. He taped Jeremy's sketch onto the monitor on the miniature stage and lined up his shot against the pencils, which was very satisfying to the artist – a rare chance for the artwork to be used so literally. *JB*

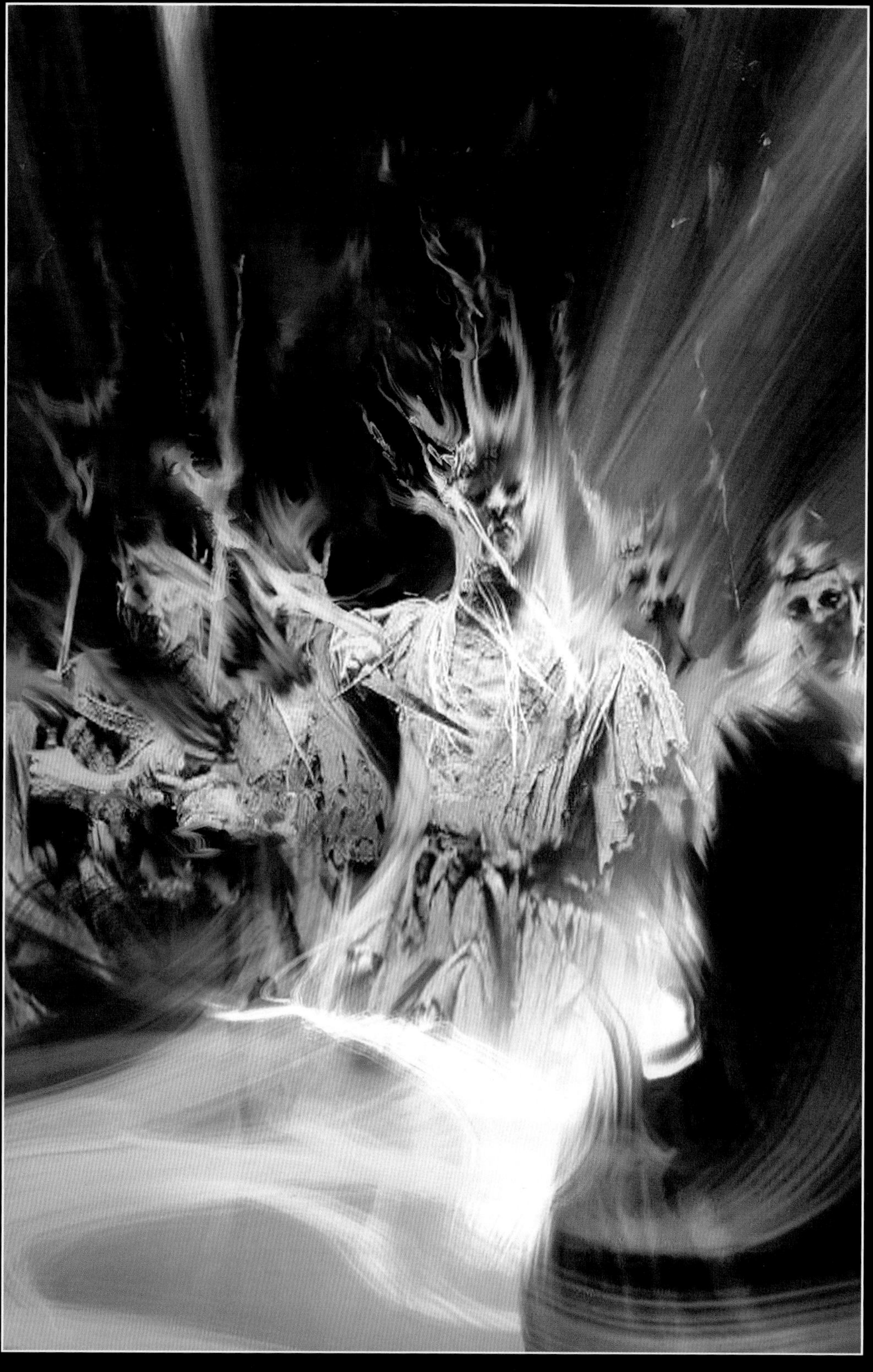

RINGWRAITHS *Wraith World concept*
"What do you see when you put on the Ring of Power? Designing what came to be known as Wraith World was an interesting design problem. We knew it had to be nightmarish, as the occupants were essentially zombies, but we wanted it to have a quality unlike nightmare sequences seen in other films. We wanted it to have an 'altered reality' about it, as though Wraith World was a parallel reality, coexisting with the real world, rather than an actual, tangible place. The look itself, I felt, needed to be not only loud, chaotic, and frightening, but also elegant and beautiful – like a ballgown in a hurricane. In this painting, I started with stills of each of the Ringwraiths shot against blue-screen. Next, I put them together in Photoshop and then distorted the hell out of them. I made quite a lot of these paintings before Peter felt I'd hit upon the right look." *PL*

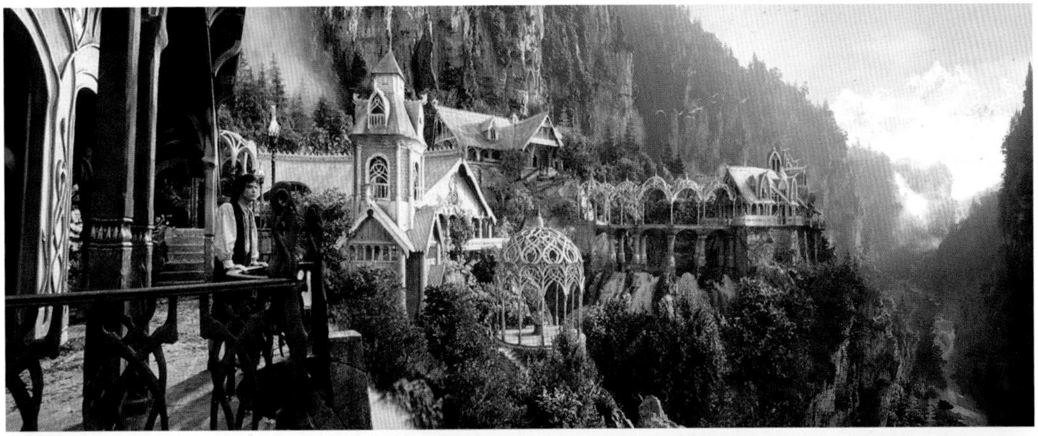

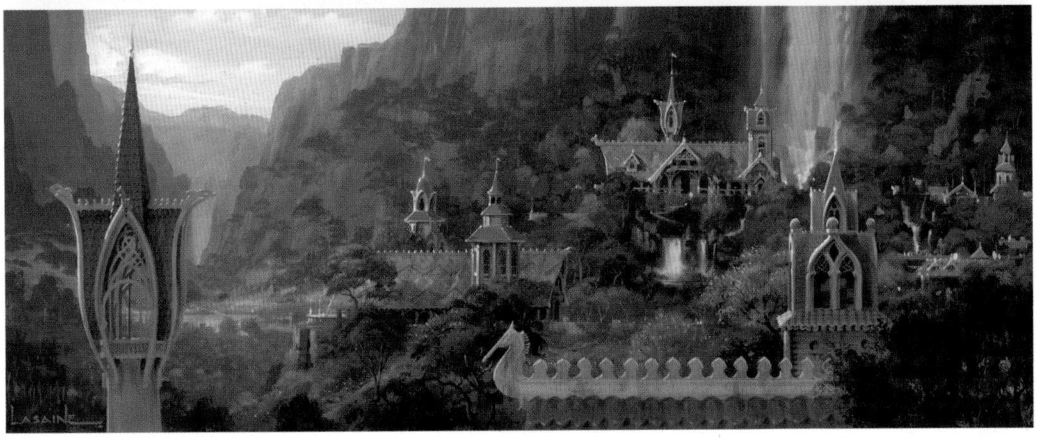

RIVENDELL
Matte painting sketch
"This is a Photoshop illustration done as a matte painting design for the scene in which Frodo sees Rivendell for the first time. At the time I did this painting, we had Alan's magnificent designs for Rivendell architecture, but we still didn't know what the landscape surrounding Rivendell would look like. We knew it had to be beautiful, but it had to be epic and magical as well. This illustration combines a still of the live-action set of Frodo on the balcony, the miniature of the Rivendell architecture, miniature trees in the midground, dozens of scenic photos taken all over New Zealand, and waterfall elements, as well as some hand-painted elements to blend everything together." *PL*

RIVENDELL *Color study*
"This is one of the earliest color studies for Rivendell and the most elaborate illustration I did for the location. After a number of preliminary sketches, I settled on this composition, which was intended to be a full 180-degree pan. At this point in its conceptualization, Rivendell was spread out like a small city. Ultimately, the final version was much more compact – like a castle." *PL*

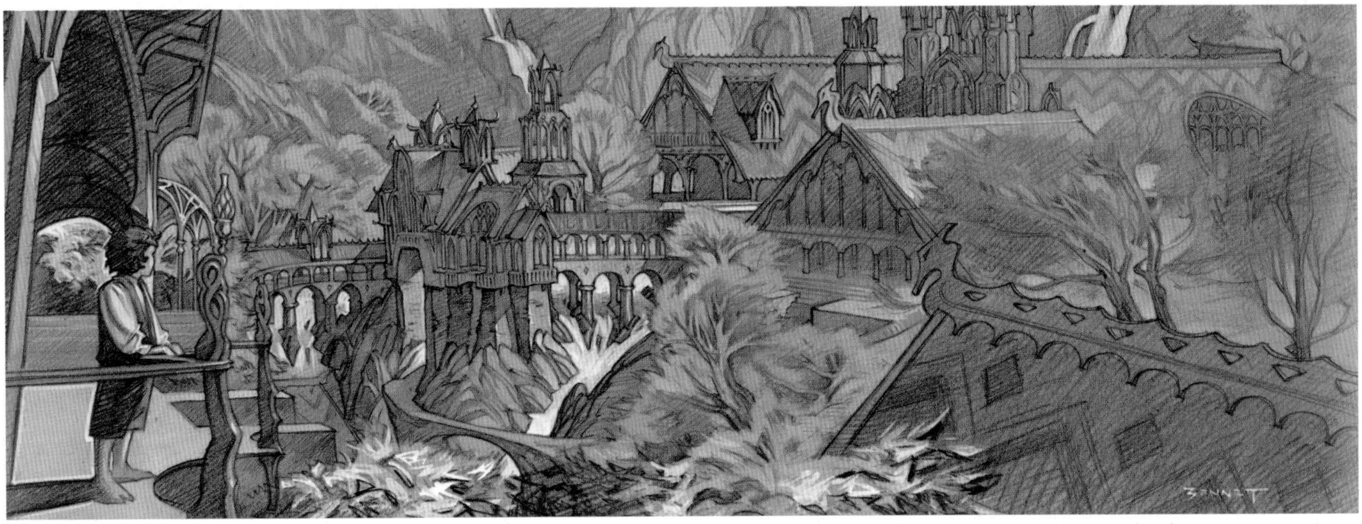

RIVENDELL *Balcony sequence*
"A proposed view from the balcony in Rivendell. One of several, this was based on the forms that Alan Lee had conceived but rearranged for the sake of the composition. This was drawn on warm yellow paper stock with highlights in white gouache." *JB*

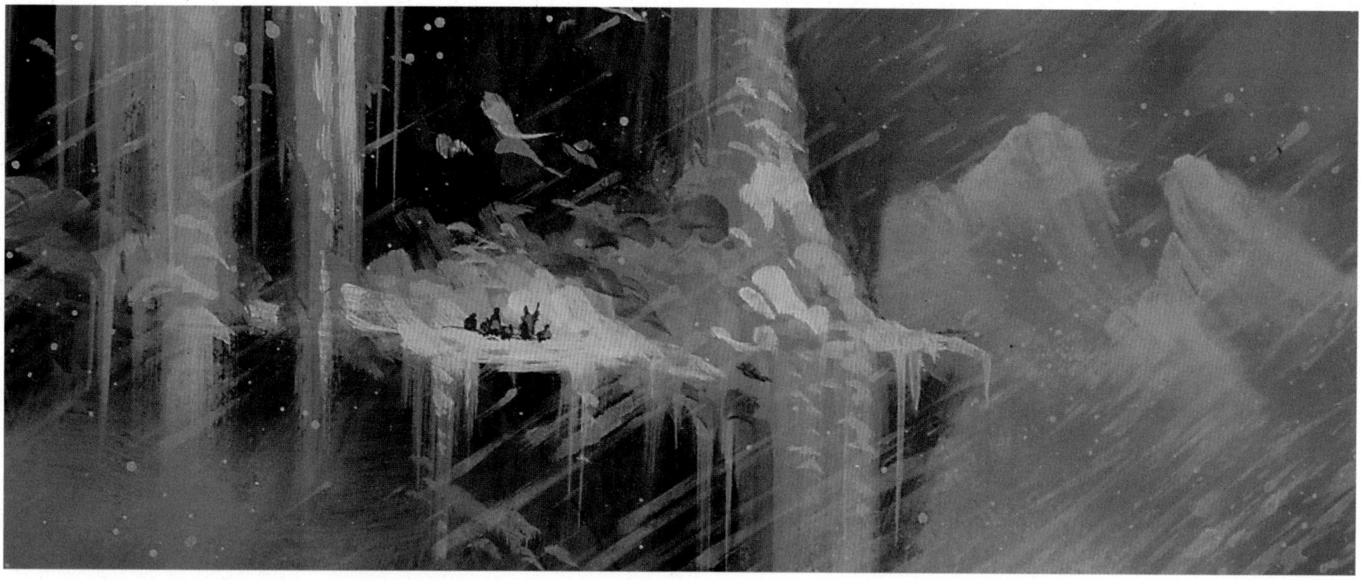

THE MISTY MOUNTAINS *Caradhras Pass*
This was one of a number of color guides that Paul produced for Peter, which captured so well how the scene should look that it became the template for the shot in the film. *PL*

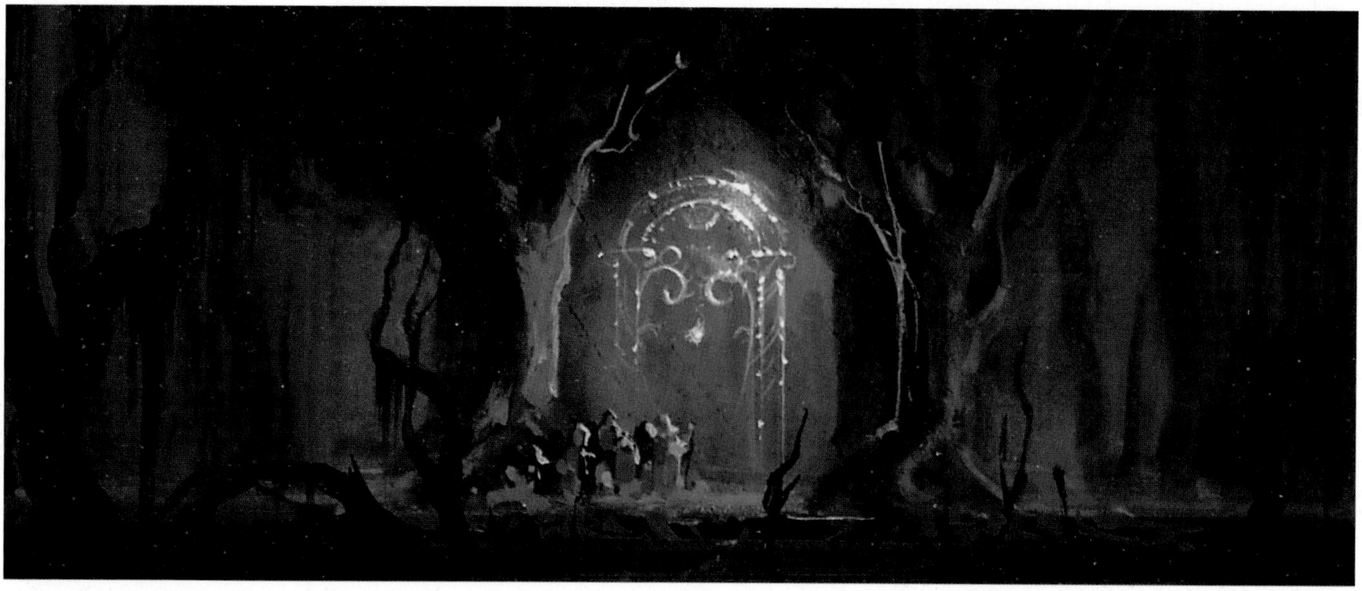

MORIA *The West-gate*
This color scheme shows how the entrance to Moria would look when lit by the all-important moonlight. The tiny figures of the Fellowship give an idea of the scale. *PL*

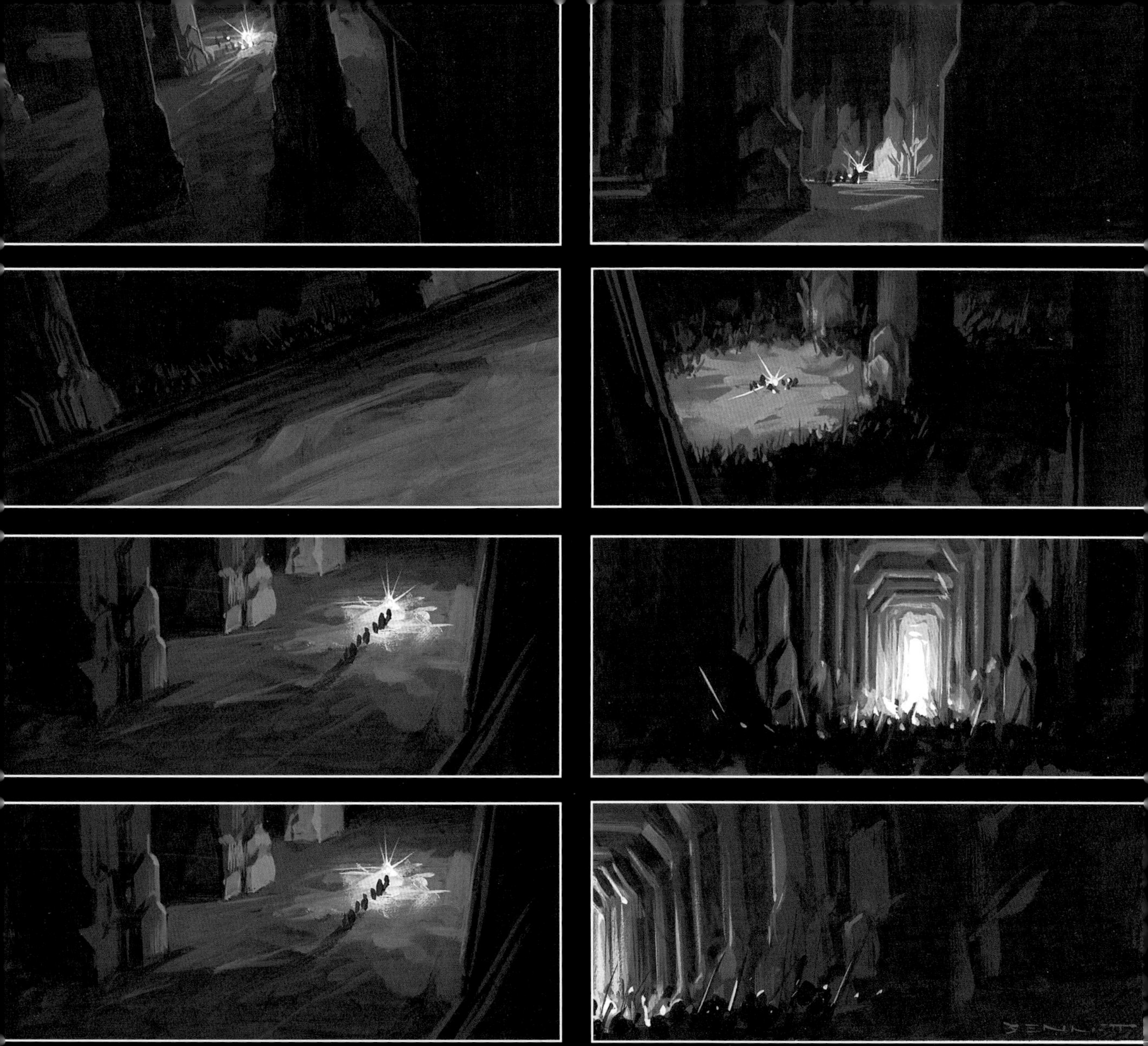

MORIA *Dwarrowdelf*

Because the Dwarrowdelf interior was almost entirely computer generated, Jeremy created the eight illustrations above that form a storyboard to the sequence, to show how the lighting would work as the Fellowship flees from Balin's Tomb and out of Dwarrowdelf itself. To the right is a more developed extrapolation of these studies, showing the Fellowship illuminated not just by Gandalf's staff but also by the flame-red glow of the approaching Balrog. *JB*

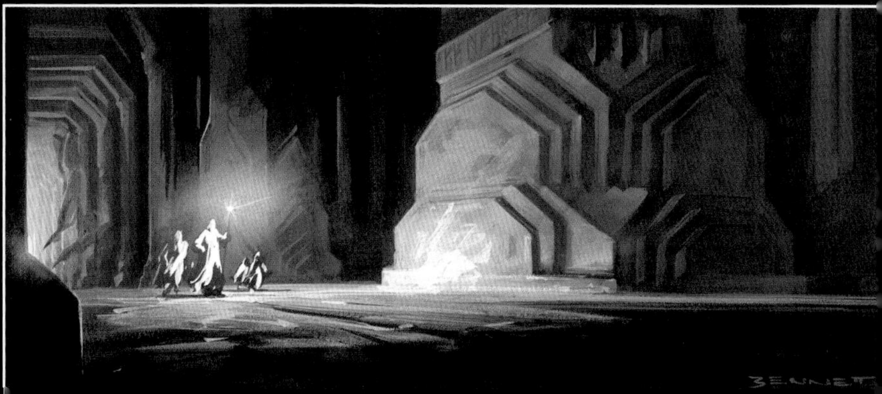

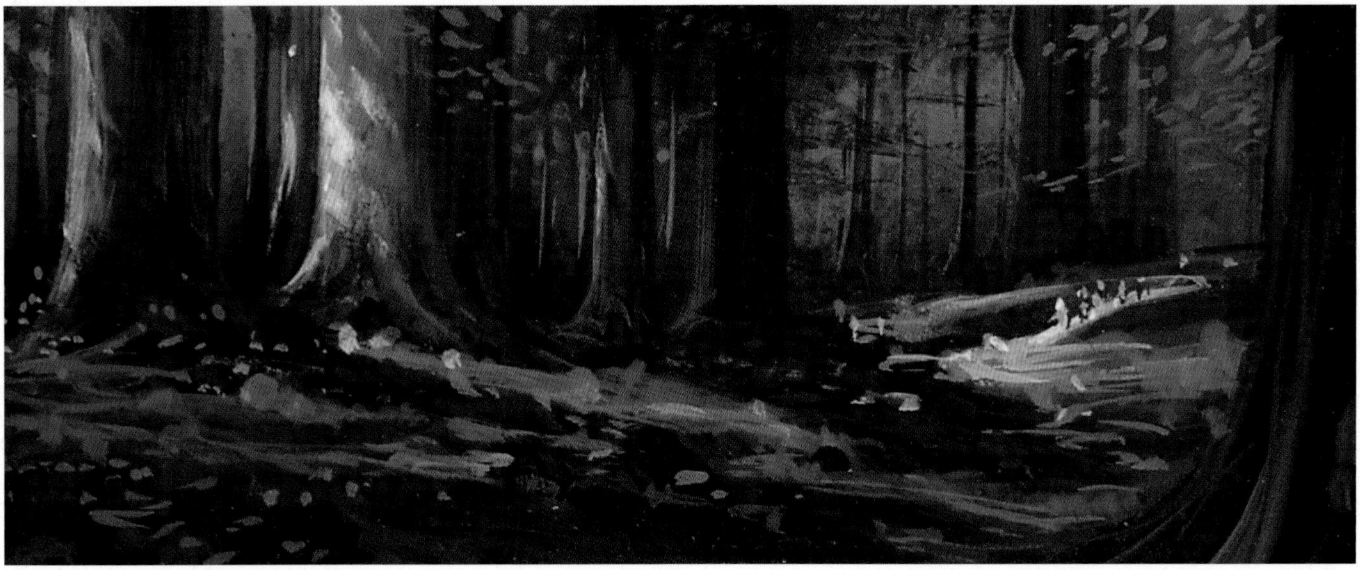

LOTHLÓRIEN *Galadriel's Glade*
"Above is a color key of the woods of Lothlórien, painted before filming began, which shows the level of light breaking through the trees." *PL*

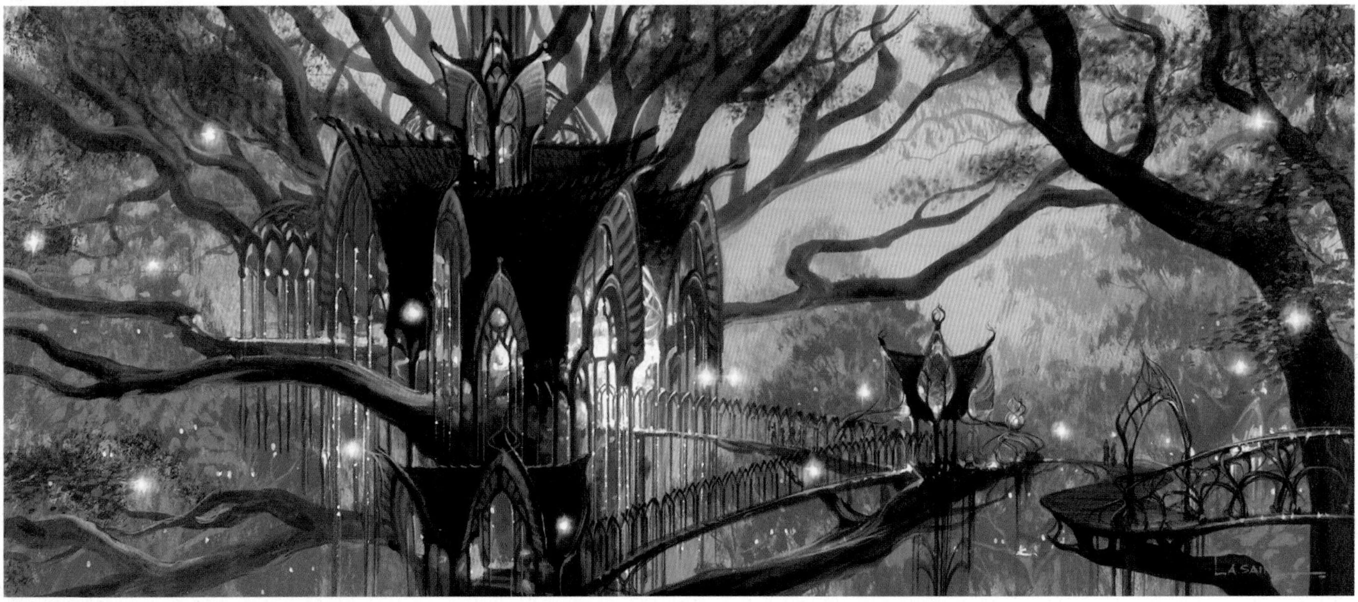

LOTHLÓRIEN *Celeborn's Chamber*
"This was the first color illustration we did for the Lothlórien location. I did it primarily as a lighting and color guide. Peter wanted Lothlórien to have a magical and ethereal look to it. I thought it would be beautiful if the architecture looked more like a chandelier than a building, so I lit it quite strongly from the inside and let the building be a light source for the surrounding environment. I carried this theory through to the other buildings in the wide view of Caras Galadhon on the next page." *PL*

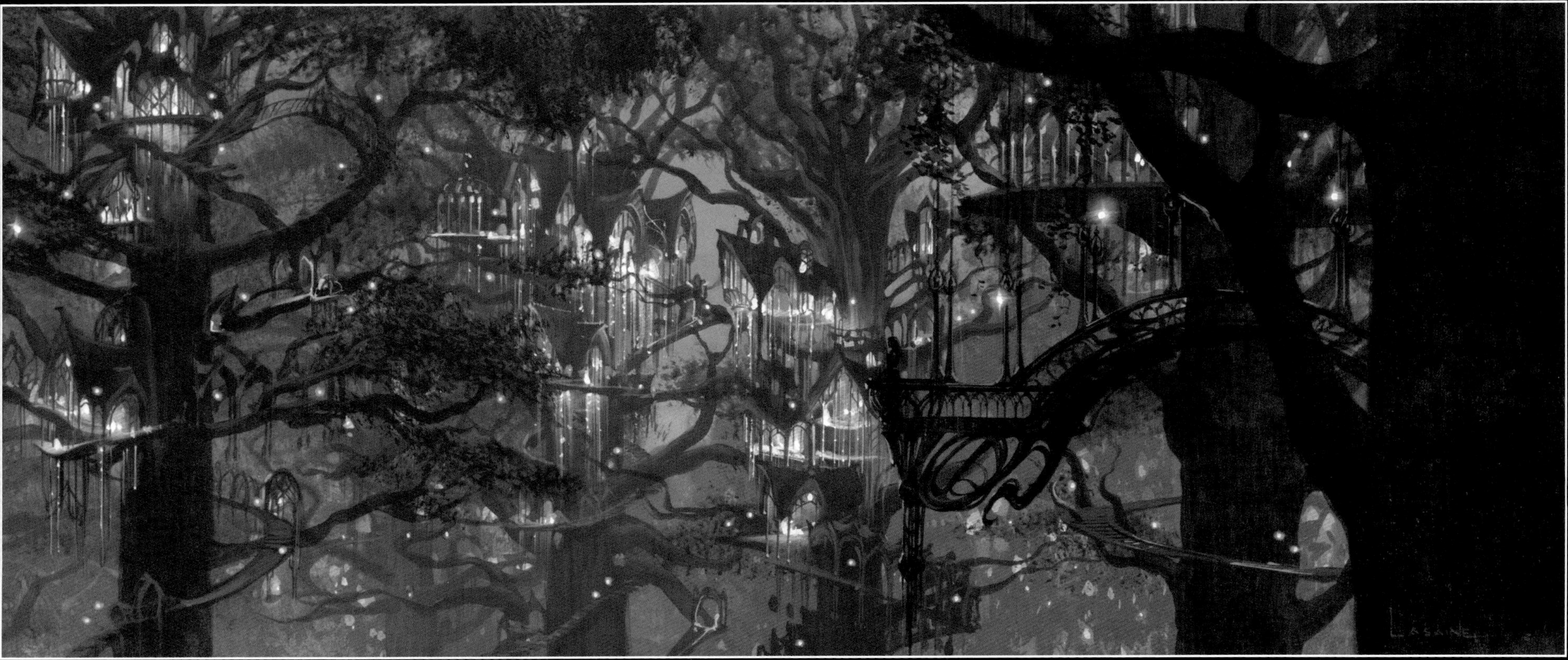

LOTHLÓRIEN ***Celeborn's Chamber***

"This is a big painting of Lothlórien, the Elven city in the trees – possibly the first one I did as a detailed exploration of the colors we might use. It's primarily based on some of Alan Lee's drawings in which he designed the architecture and even the trees themselves. From the very start, Peter Jackson had a list of shots in his head that he hoped would provide a good idea of what things would look like overall.

This kind of thing was an inspiration to him and to everybody involved. Some of Lothlórien was very abstract, conceptually, because there wasn't going to be any set built, and the actors would be working against blue-screen all the time, so a lot of these conceptual paintings were helpful to them. This was a full miniature with the characters digitally added in, as the building was too big for many shots." *PL*

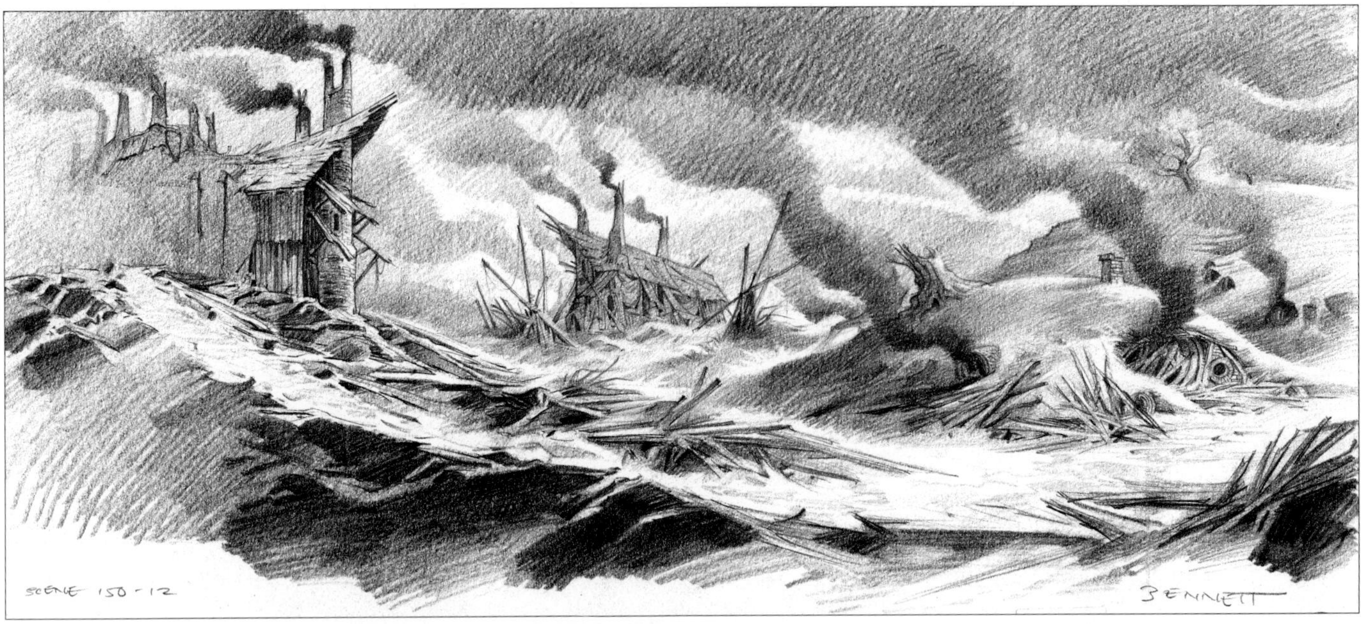

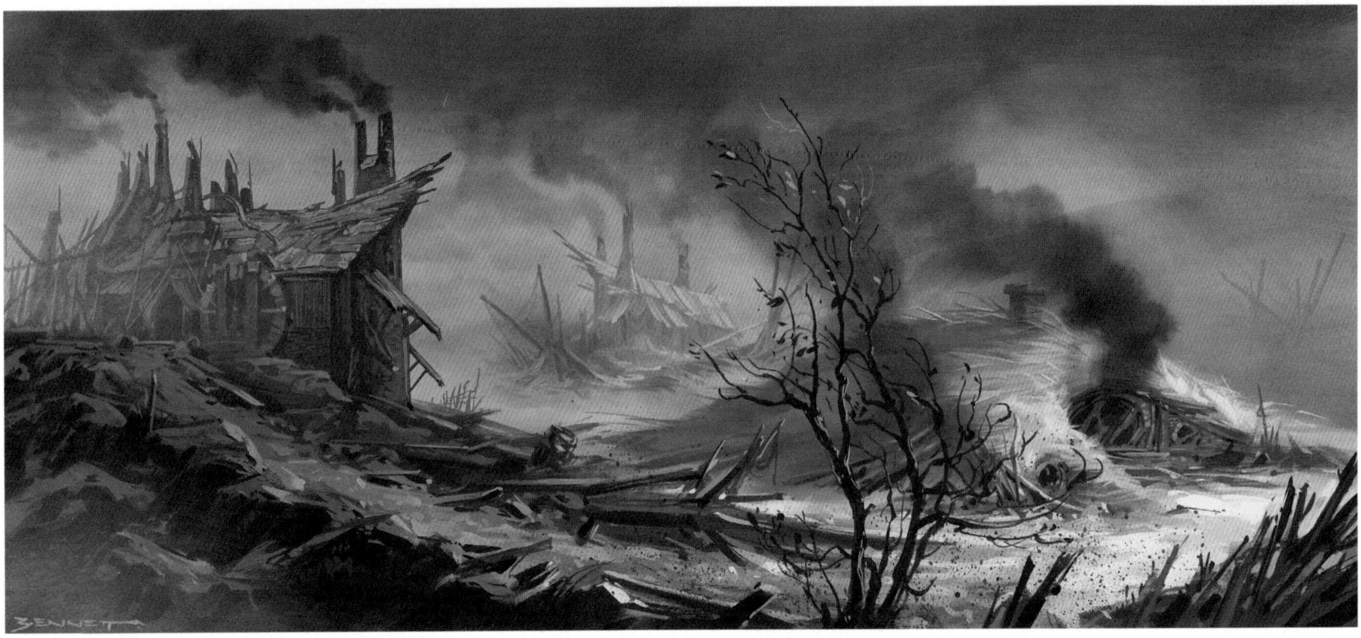

GALADRIEL'S GLADE ***Ruined Hobbiton***
The top illustration is Jeremy's first pencil take on this sequence; the lower one a full-color version. It shows the mood and color scheme intended for the scene as Frodo sees this possible future for his home. Jeremy cheated the landscape, compressing the buildings together to add to the desolation. *JB*

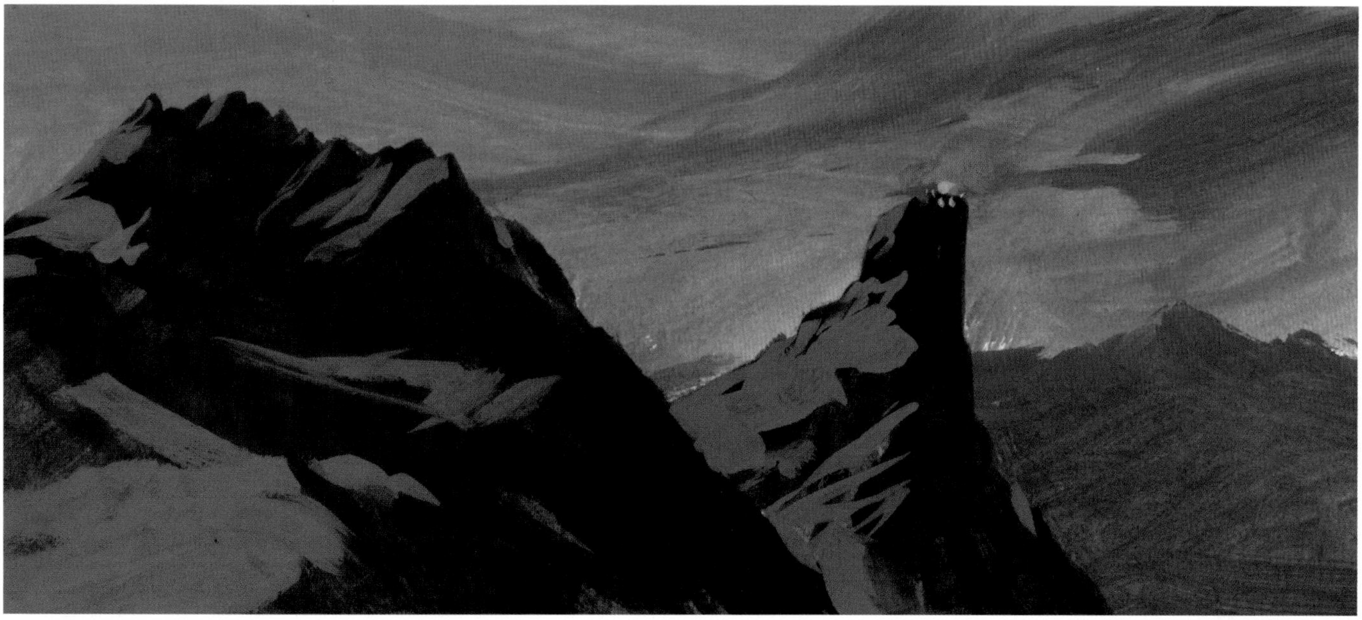

ZIRAKZIGIL *Color study*
A study of the peak of Zirakzigil environment. *JB*

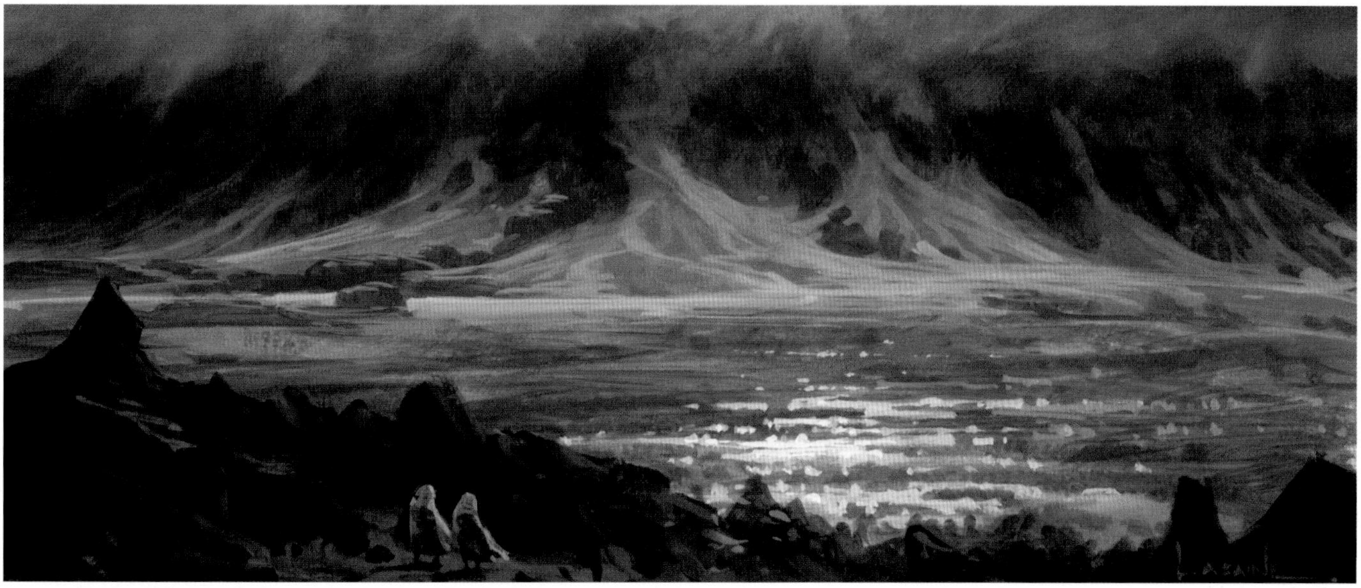

EMYN MUIL *The Dead Marshes*
"The 'echo' of the painting on page 12, this shows Sam and Frodo as they get their first view of the Mountains of Mordor. This is the point where the good guys realize that all that was once familiar is now behind them, and Mordor has begun creeping up like a cancer to take over the world. The idea of doing contrasting paintings was to provide a feeling of how far the Hobbits have journeyed into the shadows during their travels." *PL*

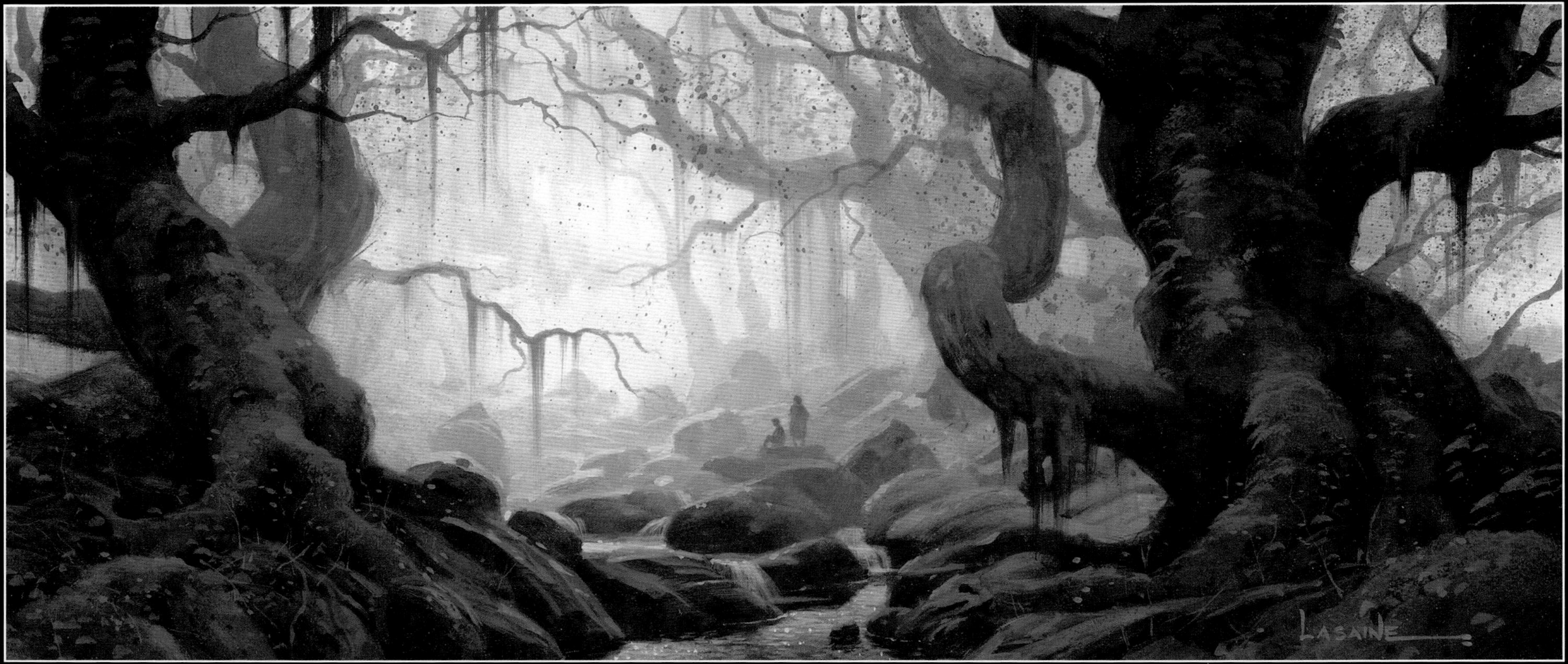

FANGORN FOREST ***Lighting study***

"I did several paintings of Fangorn Forest, but this one's my favorite. In fact, of all the work I did for these films, I think this is my best painting. Regarding the design of Fangorn, Alan Lee had already nailed the mood in his illustrations for the *Lord of the Rings* novels. I didn't feel a need to take it much further. What I tried to add, however, was a sense of a forest that had more of what I think of as 'Tolkienesque' trees. In other words, twisted and knotted – the kind of trees one might find in a New Zealand rainforest. Of course, what I ended up with was the look of a graveyard in Louisiana! Peter seemed to like it anyway." *PL*

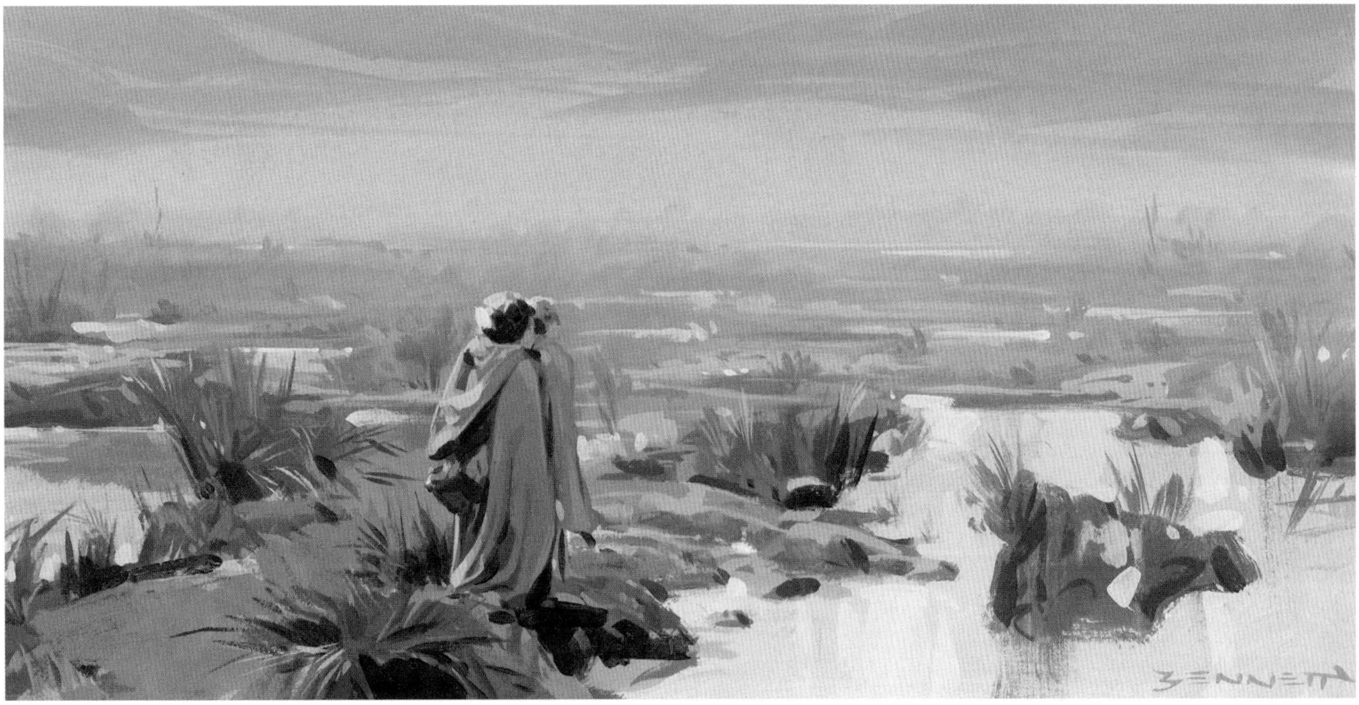

THE DEAD MARSHES *Color study*
"This was done to give some thought to the overall color palette for the marshes. Peter eventually preferred something a little brighter just to bring up the greens, so it looks a little more spooky. It probably ties in well with the spectral corpses when you see them. The idea here was to think about how much visibility you'd get around the marshes. Originally they were more claustrophobic, but Peter wanted to see four or five kilometers out into the distance so you'd really get this feeling for how large an expanse the environment was – and how easily you could become lost in there." *JB*

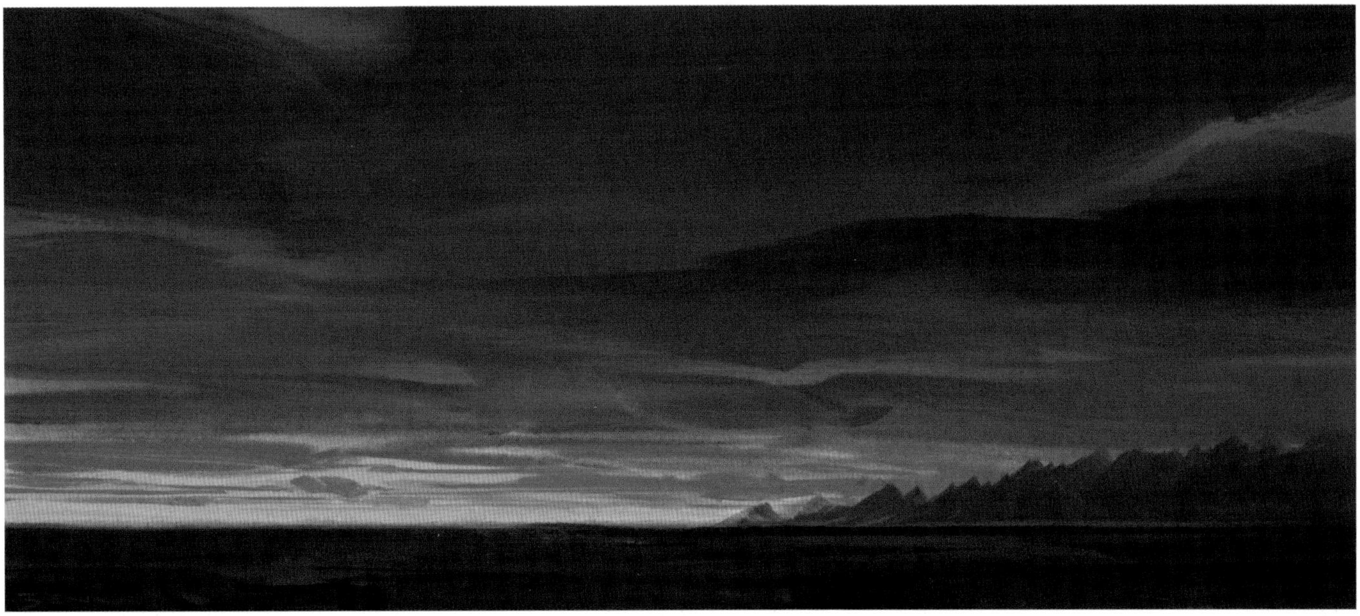

THE DEAD MARSHES *Color study*
"This is a dawn sky study of the Dead Marshes, looking toward Mordor. It was given to a scenic painter, who replicated the artwork on a canvas roughly twenty feet long." *JB*

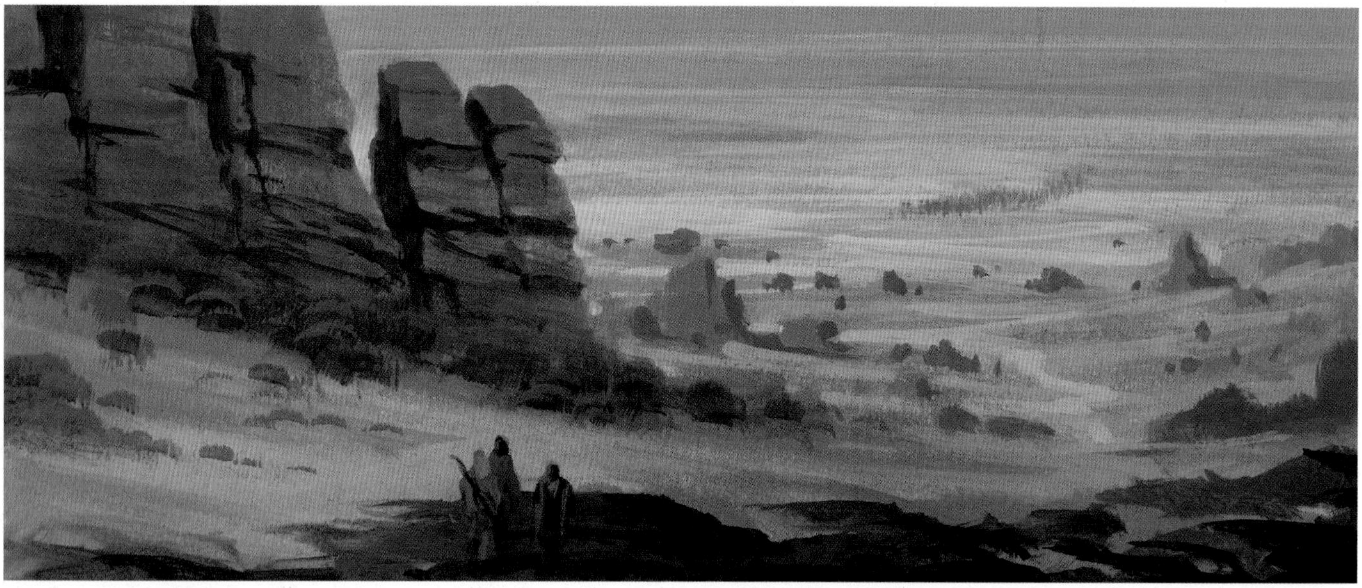

ROHAN *Eastemnet Hills*
"The color study above was done for a scene depicting Aragorn, Legolas, and Gimli tracking the band of Uruk-hai that captured Merry and Pippin at the end of *The Fellowship of the Ring*. The location, for you Tolkien fans, is the Eastemnet Hills, which lie on the easternmost border of the Plains of Rohan. Obviously, we're facing west in this scene; the Uruk-hai are heading west and north to Isengard." *PL*

EDORAS *Color study*
"This scene depicts our first glimpse of Edoras. I wanted the audience to get a sense of the dark state of affairs there, so I threw the mountain into shadow, with the exception of a small ray of light illuminating the Great Hall. This was to symbolize how Rohan was all but dead, except for the small glimmer of hope that was arriving with our heroes. For a number of reasons, however, the scene was later changed to full sun." *PL*

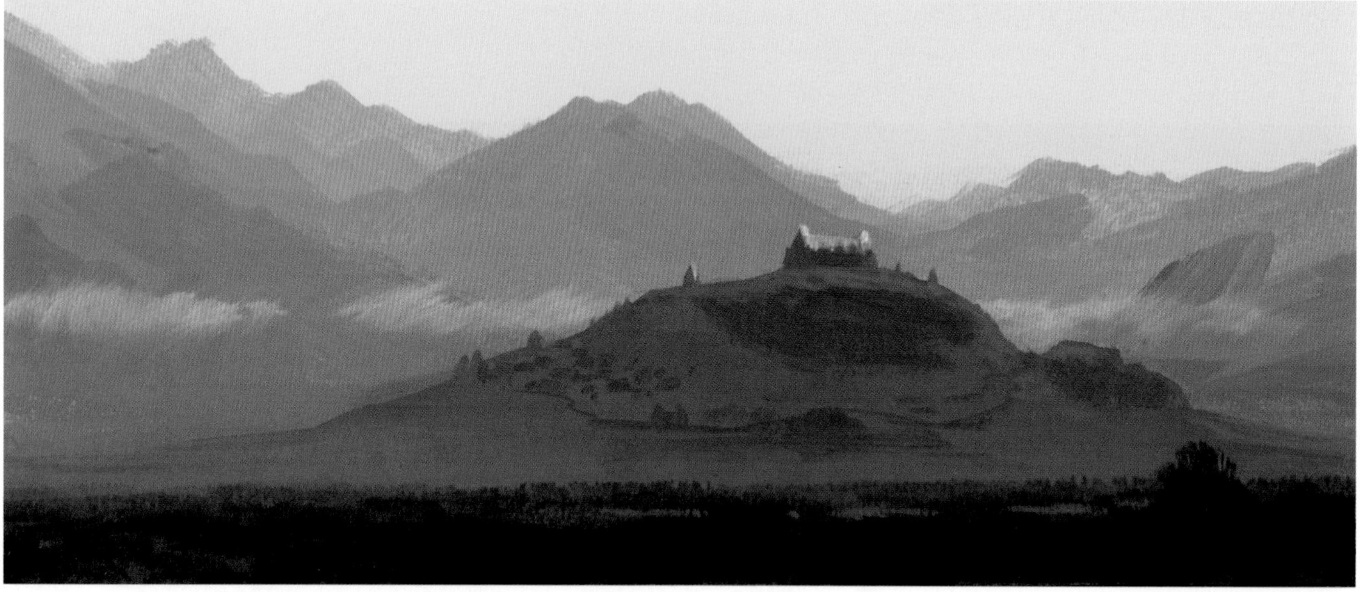

THE GOLDEN HALL *Color studies*
"These were painted from the floor plans and a couple of drawings by Alan Lee, as the Golden Hall hadn't been built at that stage. I did them for VFX effects consultant Mark Stetson. There were a couple more of these, but they were more lighting guides for the director of photography to have on set when they were lighting the environment, to give them a feel for how it could look." *JB*

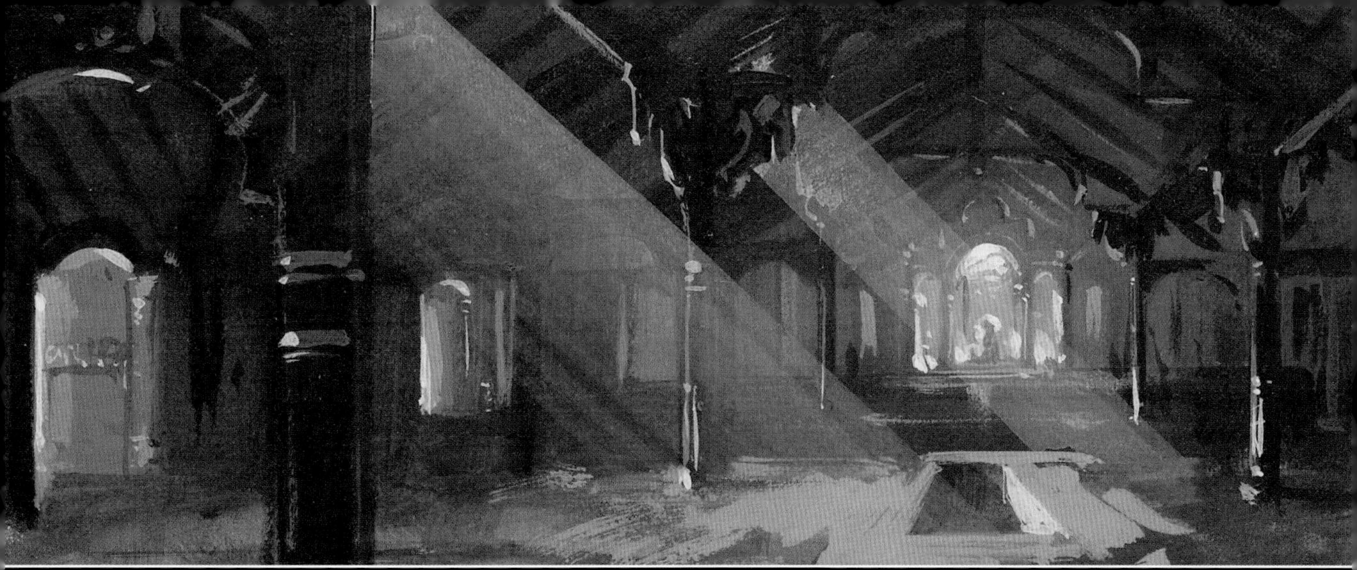

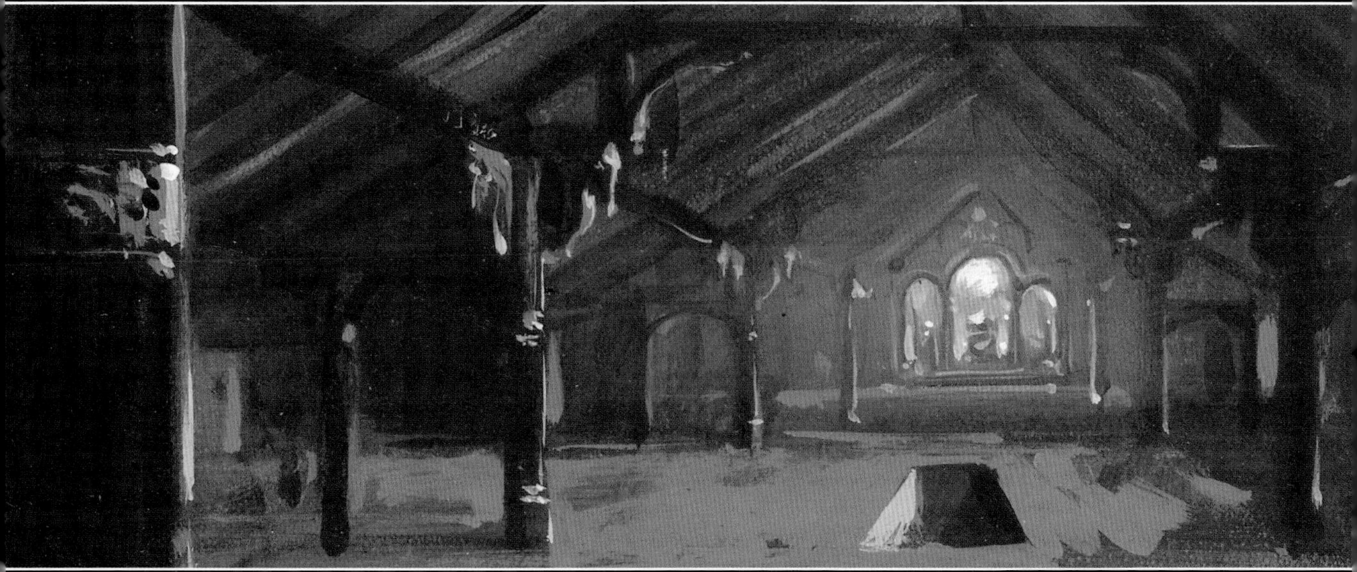

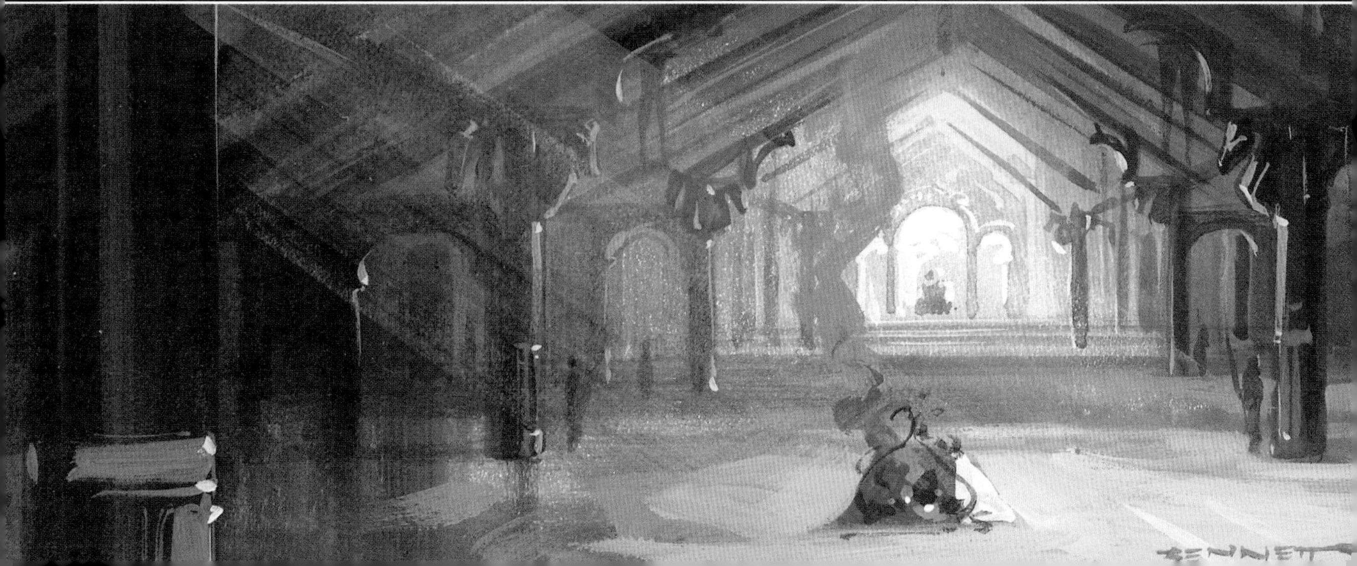
BENNETT

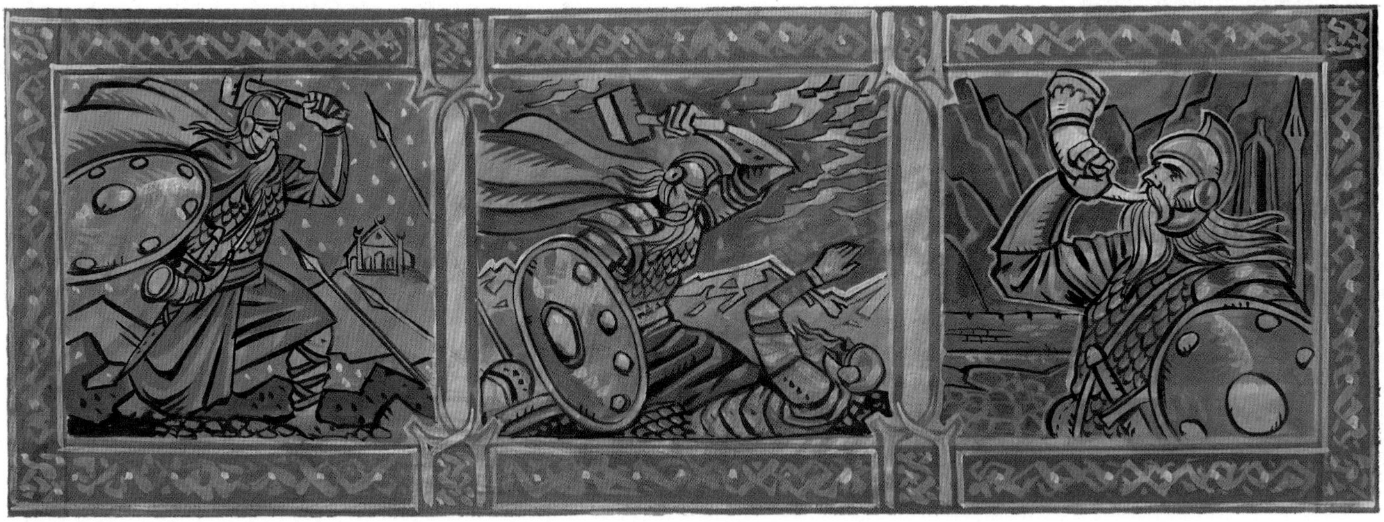

THE GOLDEN HALL TAPESTRIES *Tapestry design*

"This is a design based on reading more about the Rohan culture. It shows Helm Hammerhand, for whom Helm's Deep is named. An interesting character – totally formidable, he was found frozen dead but still standing on the Deeping Wall. It was great to go back and explore what Tolkien had written about this history and then try to recreate it. The illustration had to be quite simple to translate into a large tapestry. The borders were drawn by Shane Henson from designs by Alan Lee, and the actual painting was done by Smart Arts, a local contractor, on a roughly woven canvas. When it came back, a lot of work was done in our textile department to age it down and make it look as though it'd been hanging in a dusty hall for a few hundred years.

"It was an open brief: I could do whatever I wanted – no restrictions. With the paintings, you know exactly what an environment could look like – you've had a brief and it's up to you to realize it and get it to a stage where Peter can say, 'Yeah, that looks like what I imagined.' So in that sense it was a lot of fun." *JB*

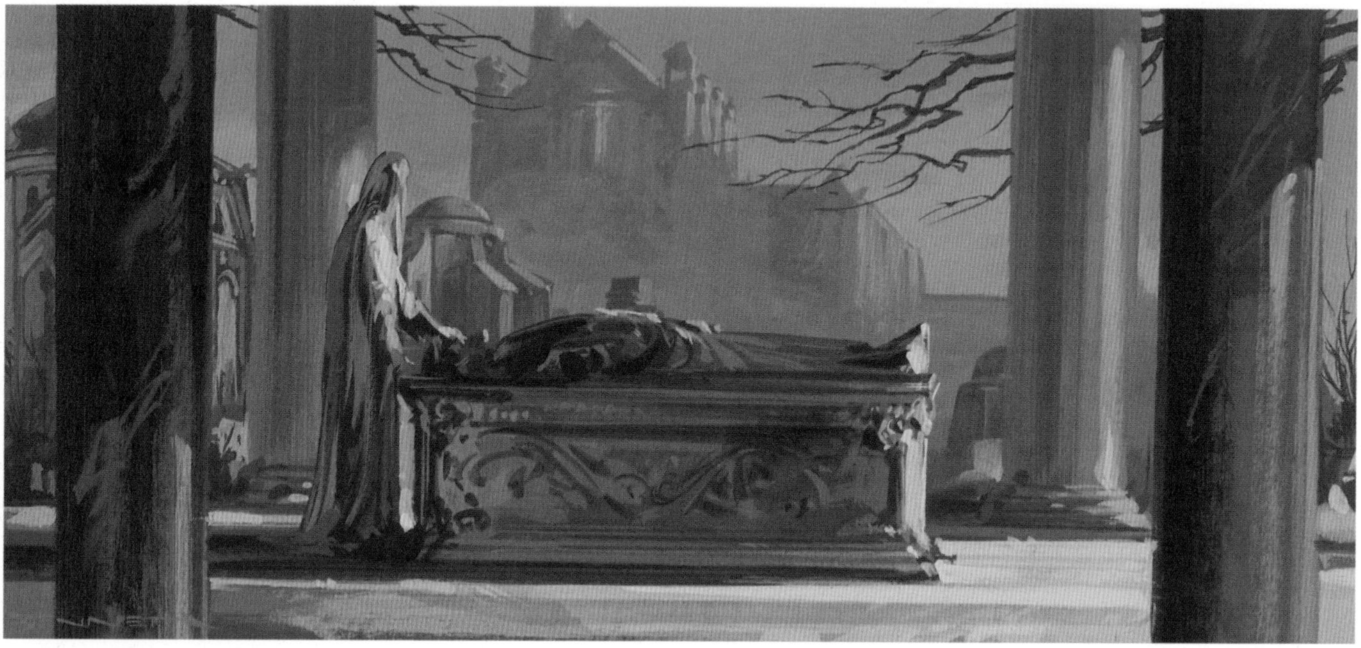

DEAD KING ARAGORN *Color study*

"The painting above was used as a rough compositional guide for miniatures as well as a lighting study for the set. Once the live-action and miniatures were shot, we combined these elements and replaced the sky to show what they might look like for post-production." *JB*

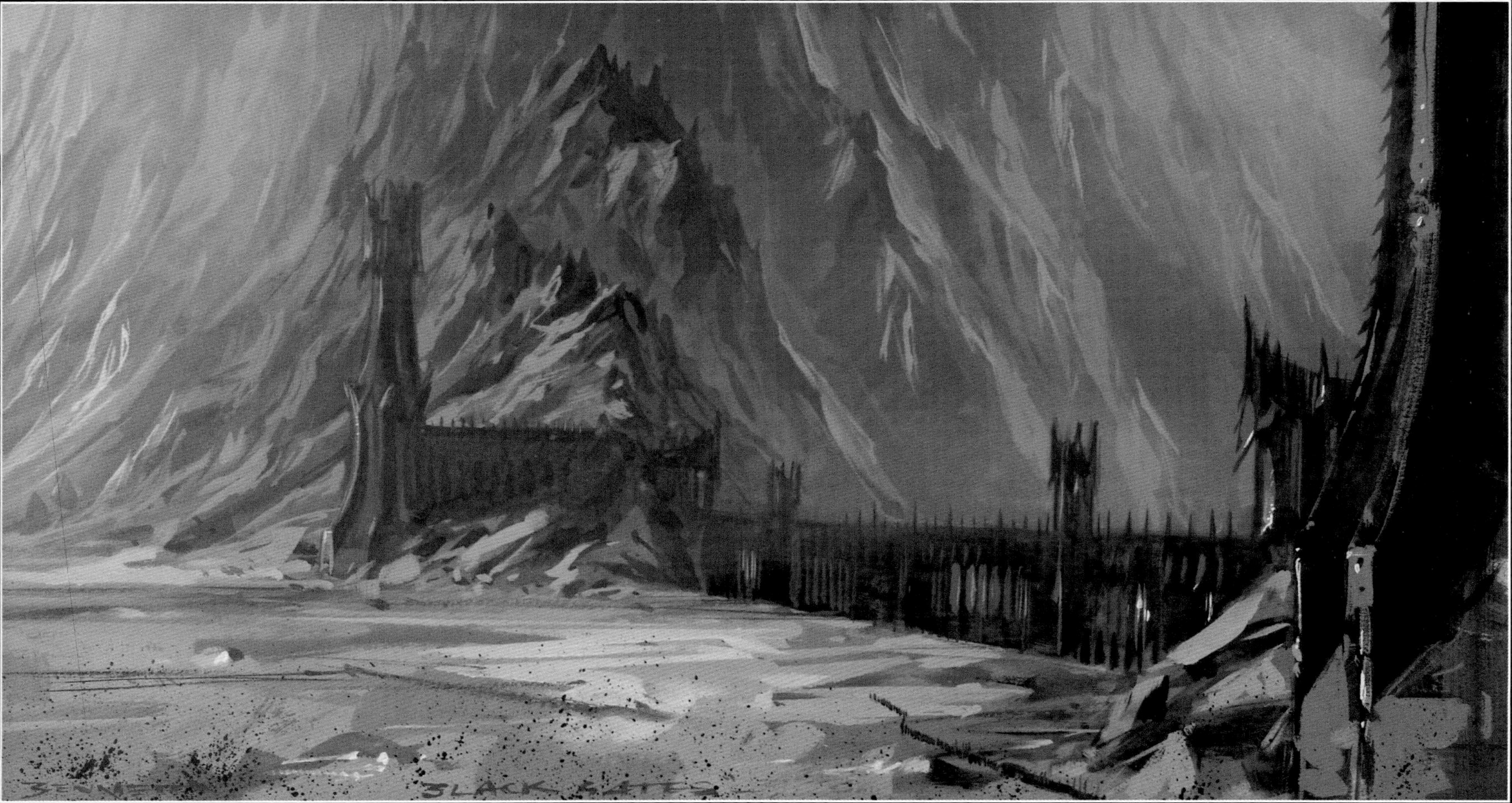

THE BLACK GATES *Lighting study*

"This early lighting study was completed for the miniatures crew, so they could use it to match the color. I always imagined the land being dead. It's as if Mordor is sucking the life out of the atmosphere, out of the air. The lighting is not flat, but it's certainly not warm, and we didn't really want to go for too brutal a look. Peter used to say he wanted it to have a sort of tobacco feel, so it's dirty, it's nasty – it's a very tricky environment to handle.

"There was so much detail in the actual gates seen in the film; they're just beautiful things. Anyway, I was blending them back into the atmosphere here – cutting the detail down – to get the feeling of depth. The Easterlings are coming in from the right so you can see the scale, see how big the Black Gates are meant to be. They're actually about seventy feet, so I cheated the scale so that the environment would look gargantuan.

"We did a lot of drawings for this, an awful lot; it's an environment that's really important to Alan Lee and me. It's the last place in Middle-earth you'd want to be – we had a very clear idea of how we wanted it to look.

"We wanted to provide a little bit of atmosphere behind the gates themselves for two reasons. First, to silhouette the gates and play up the beautiful detail there, and second to allude to the Orc camp which is behind them, to give a feeling of life and movement. This is actually for the tail end of the shot. We start right at the top of the mountains and tilt down: you have Mount Doom – or the glow of Mount Doom – off to the right-hand side, so that's a major feature in this painting. Until the later part of film three, this is as close as you're going to get to Mordor and Mount Doom itself. So it was important to us that it have a very frightening feeling – it's daylight, it's not a night shot, but it still needed to look disturbing." *JB*

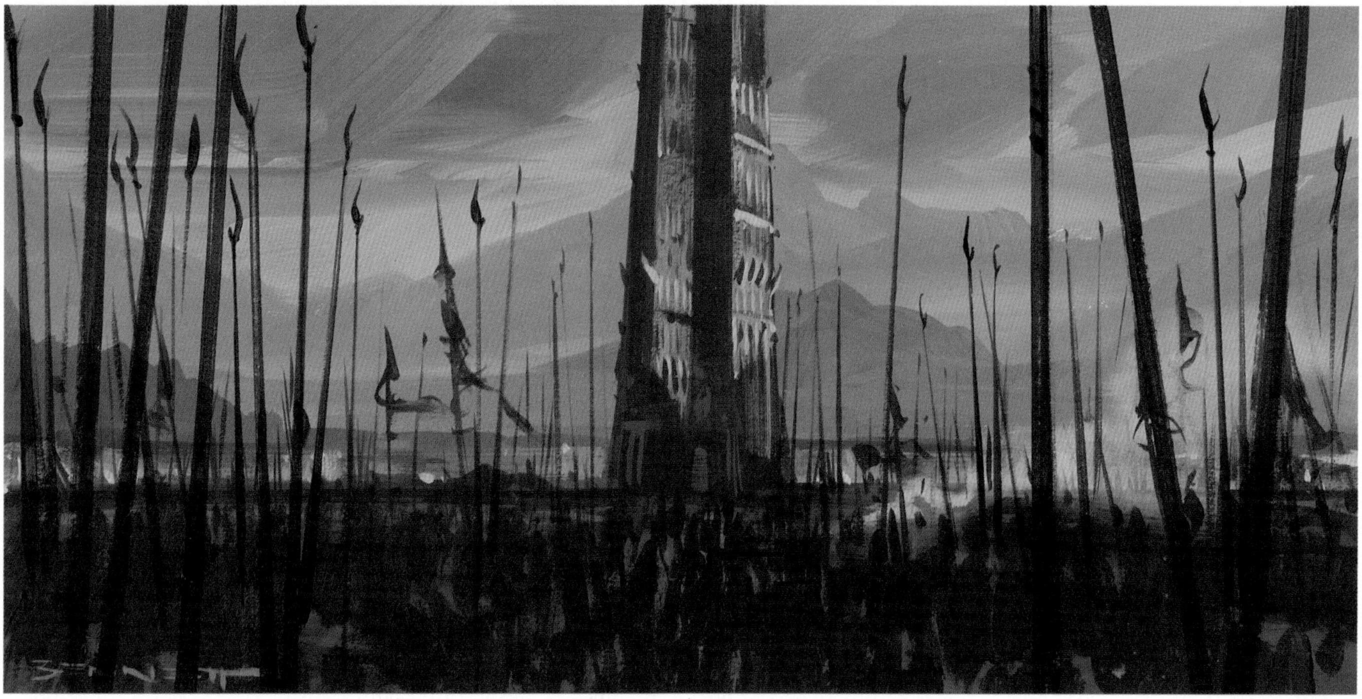

ORTHANC TOWER *Color study*
"This is the very last frame of a shot, where you pull out to reveal . . . this! We start on the balcony with Saruman and Wormtongue, and there's this elaborate pull-out from the Tower right over the sea of Uruks. This painting was really just a guide to look at pike placement and to give a general feeling of the environment behind Isengard – it's early morning light, but quite moody." *JB*

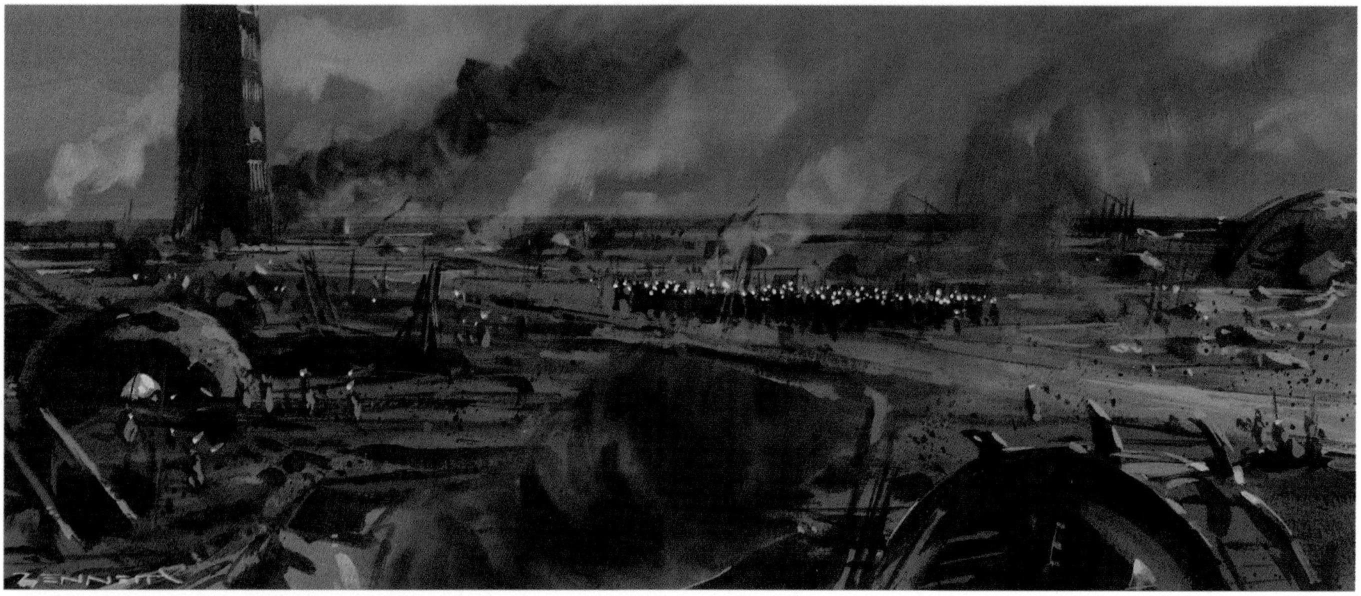

SARUMAN AND WILD MEN ***Composition and color study***
"A quick study to establish the overall composition of the shot, like the position of the Wild Men, the number of torches, and the general amount of smoke and haze. An illustration like this will be used as a fairly good guide for the compositor, who will piece the shot together." *JB*

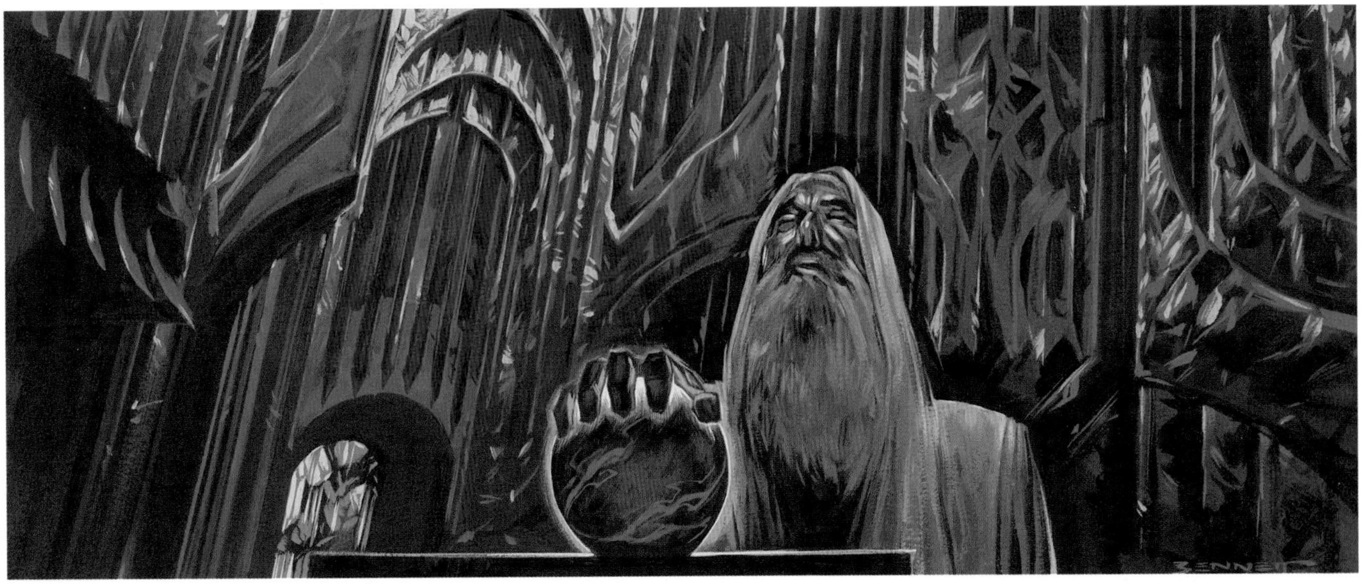

SARUMAN'S NIGHTMARE ***Concept***
"When these were done, we weren't sure that we would have a prologue sequence in *The Fellowship of the Ring* in which Sauron was revealed (we thought he might be saved for *The Return of the King*). So I wanted to hide him in the architecture in the background to such a degree that you might see the film three times and not notice anything – and someone might say, 'I think I saw something in the walls – was it Sauron's face?'

"At this point Saruman is communicating with Sauron. He thinks he has it all under control – he can use the palantír correctly – but in actual fact, Sauron has total control over him. So it's a little obvious, but I think the idea of using the sheen and the detail to suggest Sauron's presence could have been worthwhile." *JB*

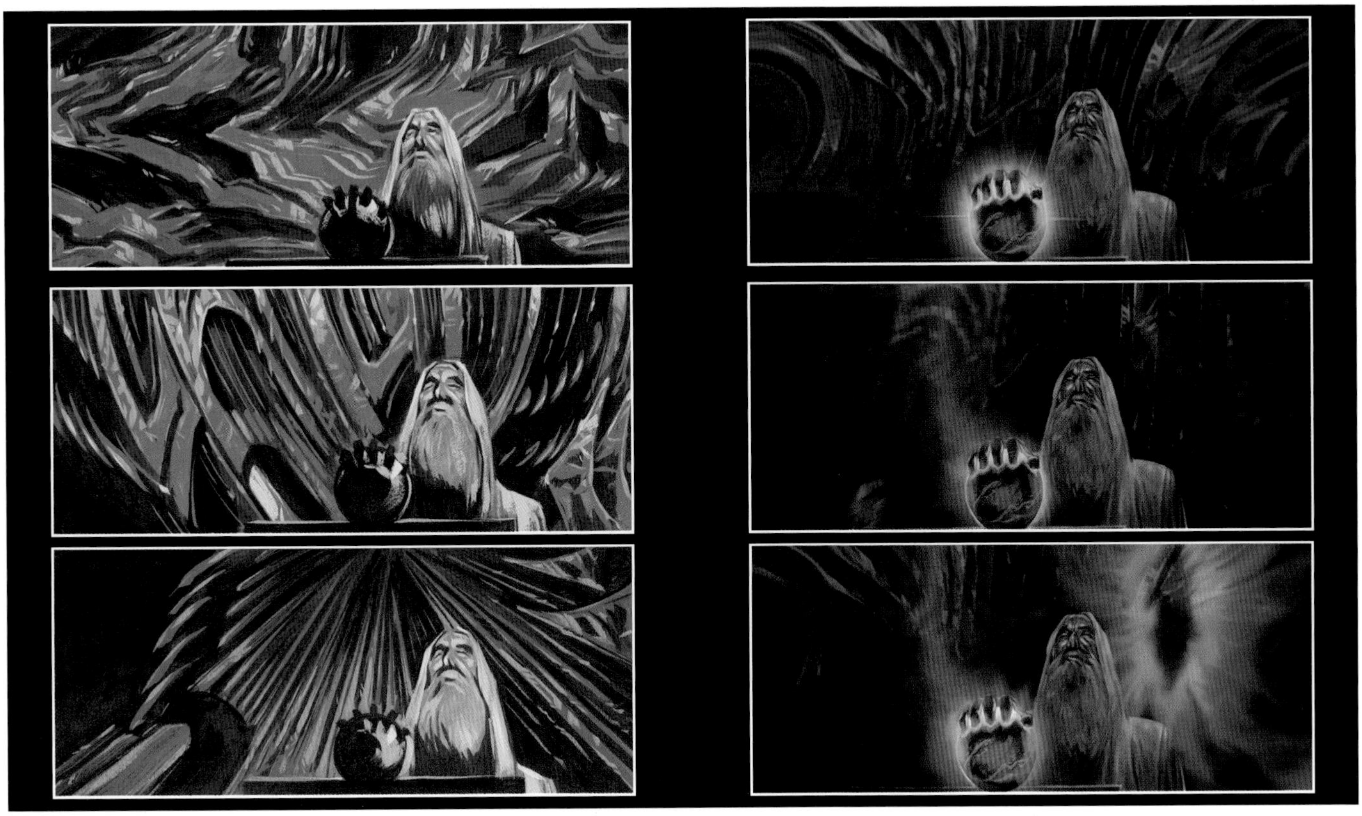

SARUMAN: THE PALANTÍR ***Digital artwork***
Gus took Jeremy's original painting, scanned it, and then did variations (above) using digital technology. *JB & GH*

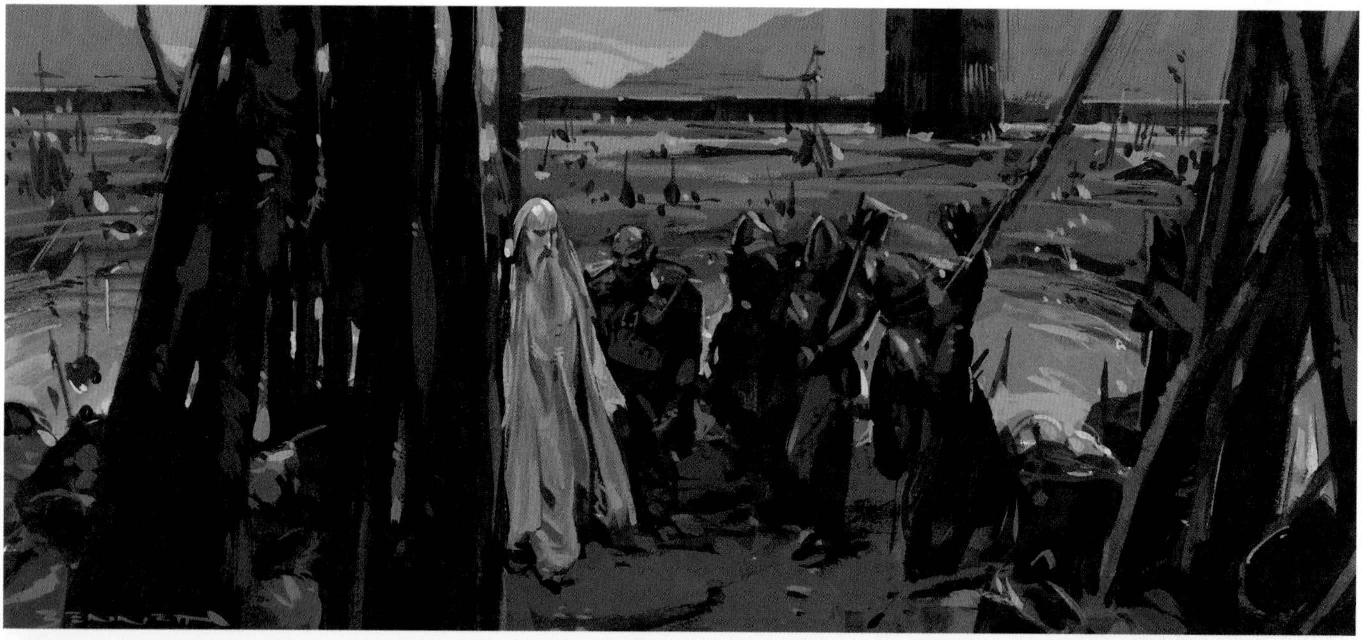

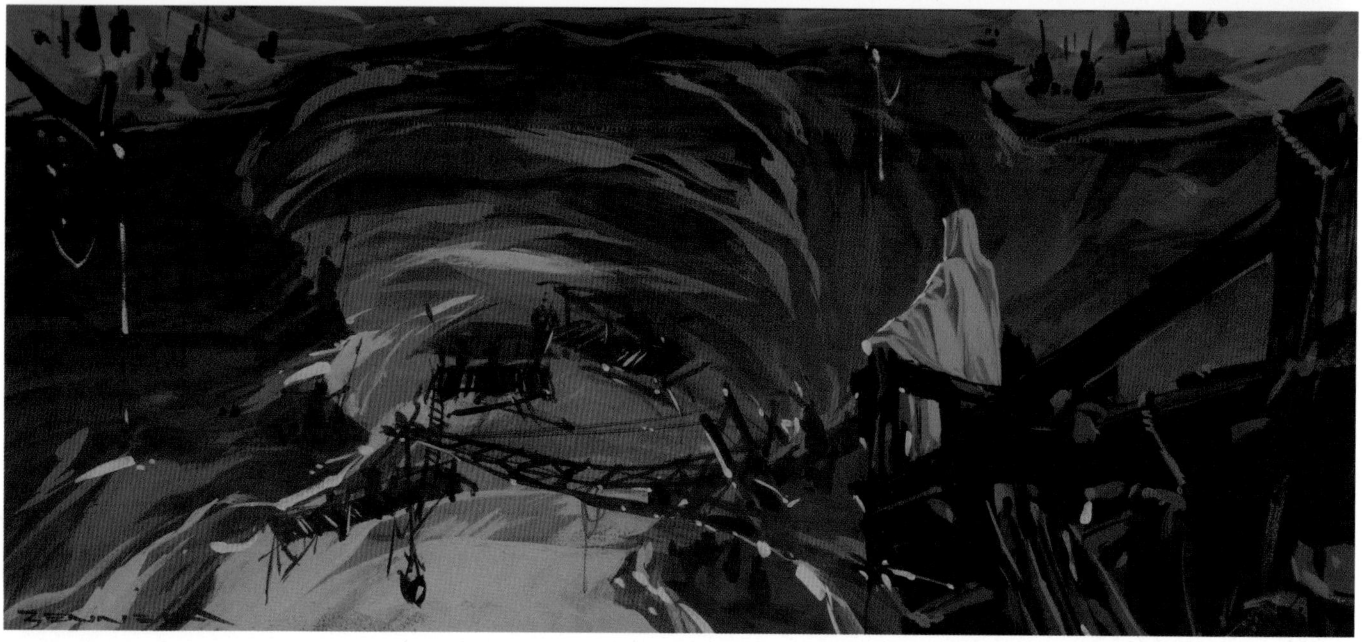

ISENGARD *Color studies*
"The artwork at the top involved designing a background for the blue-screen shot and showing the ash-covered desolation of the environment Saruman was creating, contrasted with the glow of his fires from the caverns below, more of which can be seen in the next painting." *JB*

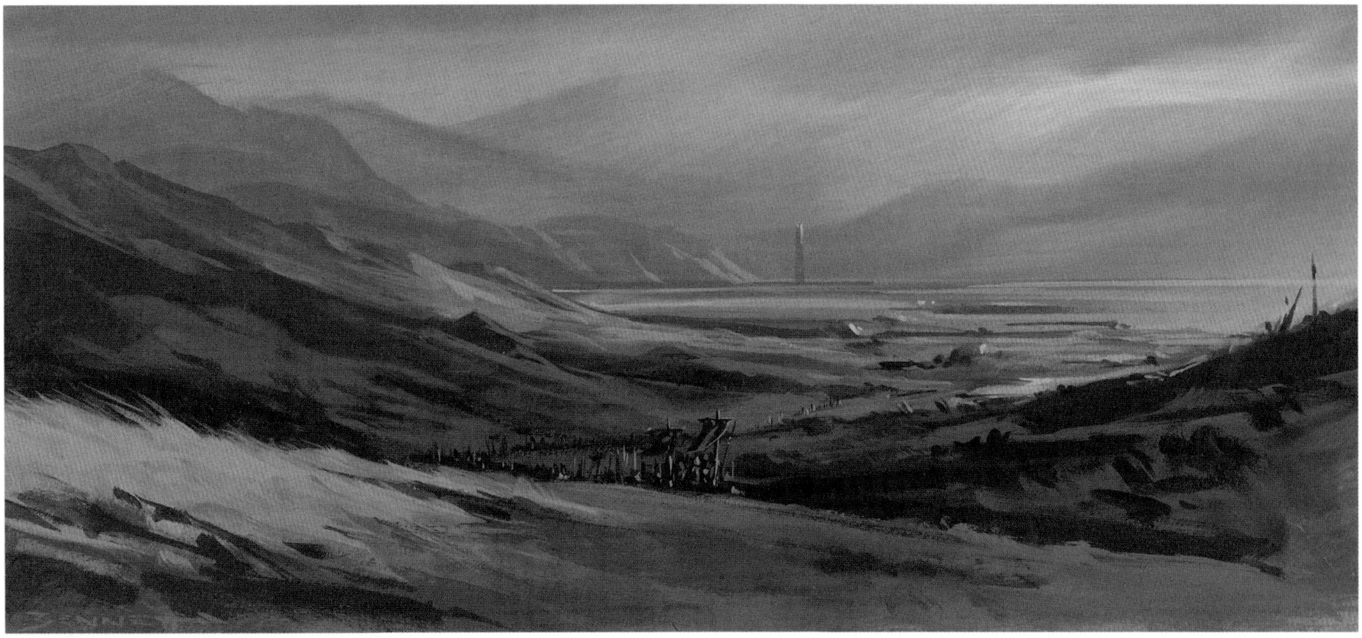

ISENGARD *Color study*
"This is a scene that I was not sure would appear in the film; it was really done just to give a feeling for what the valley might look like. At this stage the Orcs have totally deforested Isengard – I probably need to give it a lot more stumps and things in there. It's totally devastated, and I really wanted to make it look windswept, almost as if there was a squall passing through. And you have the Uruk-hai coming through into the foreground – just walking on by." *JB*

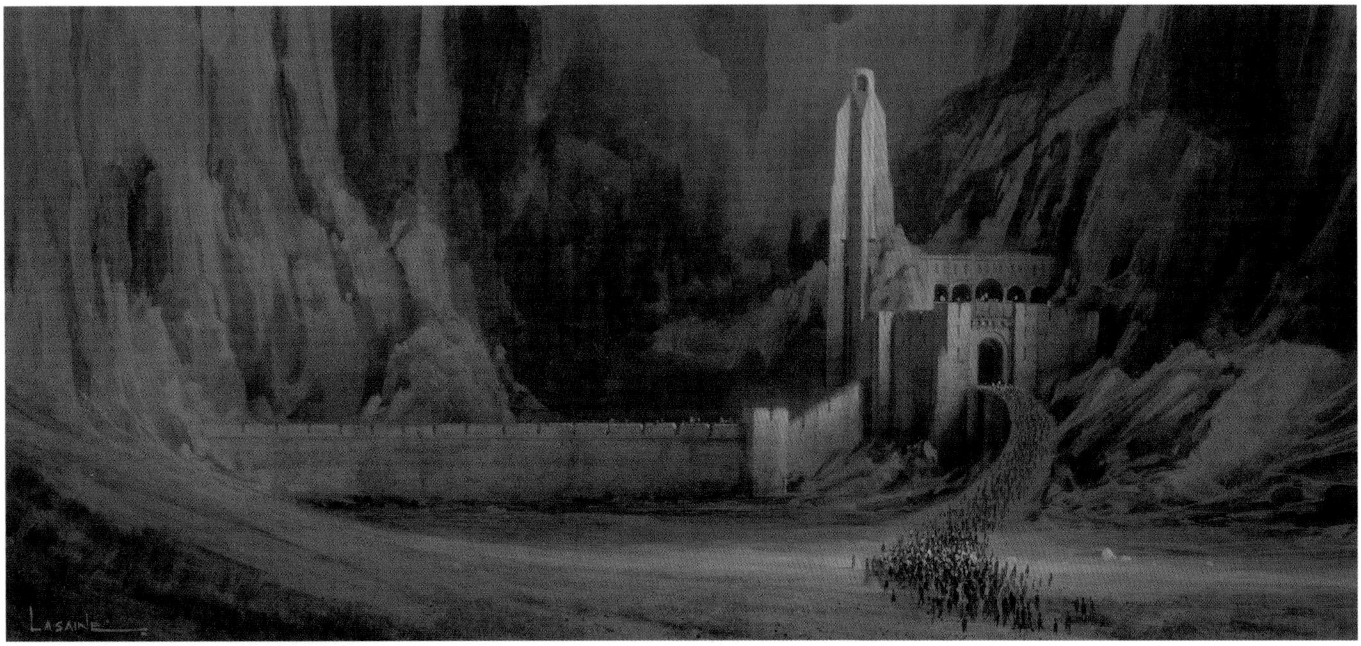

HELM'S DEEP *Color study*
"This piece was done as a lighting, mood, and color guide for the sequence in which the Rohan refugees first arrive at Helm's Deep. I went for a romantic, almost idyllic, lighting scheme. I thought it would be a nice idea to show Helm's Deep through the eyes of the refugees – a beautiful sanctuary, a welcome sight after their long and dangerous journey. It's always fun to show a citadel in its best light . . . especially when you're going to lay siege to it in the next sequence." *PL*

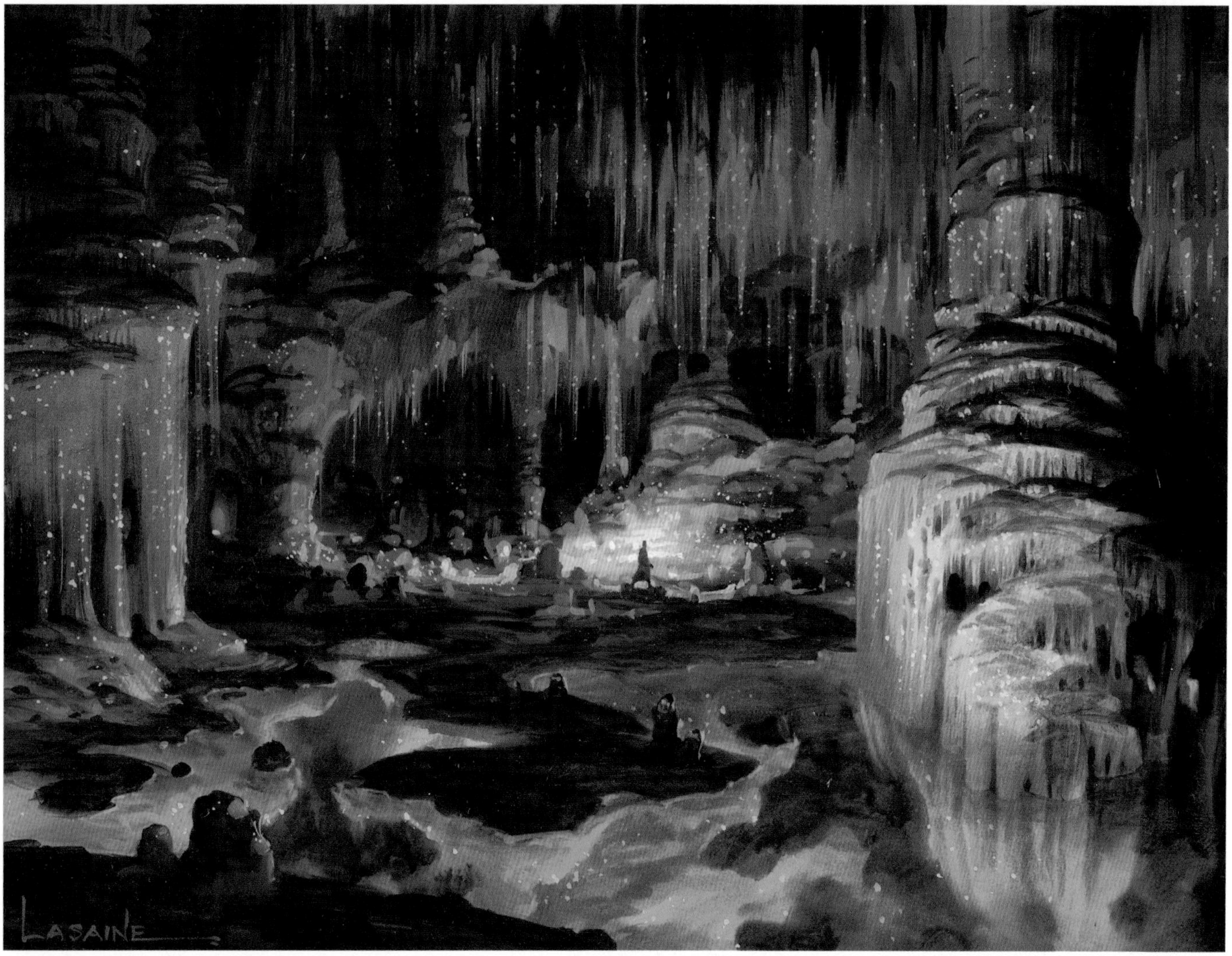

THE GLITTERING CAVES *Color study*
"This concept for the Glittering Caves was originally done for *The Return of the King,* which, early on, opened with a romantic scene between Aragorn and Arwen on the 'morning after' the battle for Helm's Deep. In that version of the script, Arwen had been present at the battle. As inspiration for this painting, I used an old set of 3D Viewmaster images from a beautiful cave complex I visited years ago in Virginia called Luray Caverns." *JB*

HENNETH ANNÛN *Color study*
"I based this painting on one of the storyboards, and as far as I know it was the first color image done for this location. In trying to establish the overall look of Ithilien, I really wanted to play up the contrast between this location and Mordor, which for Frodo and Sam was the next stop. I wanted this environment to be lush, wet, and green – almost tropical – and rather idyllic in its beauty. The last refuge on the road to Mordor." *PL*

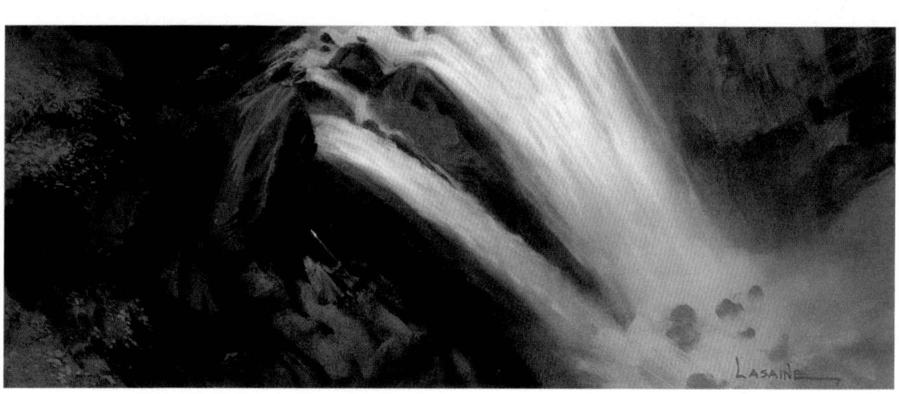

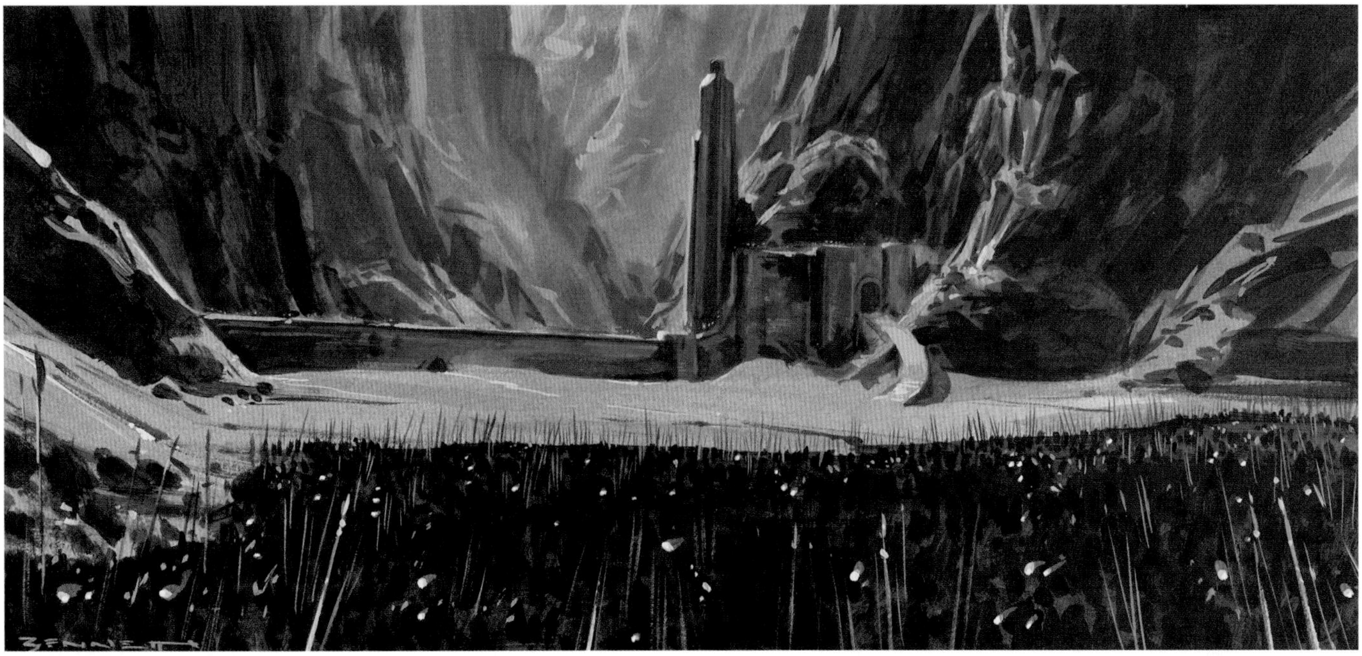

HELM'S DEEP *Color study*
"This is the end frame of a shot that starts at the head of the valley: ten thousand Uruk-hai are marching past, and the camera follows them in and reveals Helm's Deep in the distance." *JB*

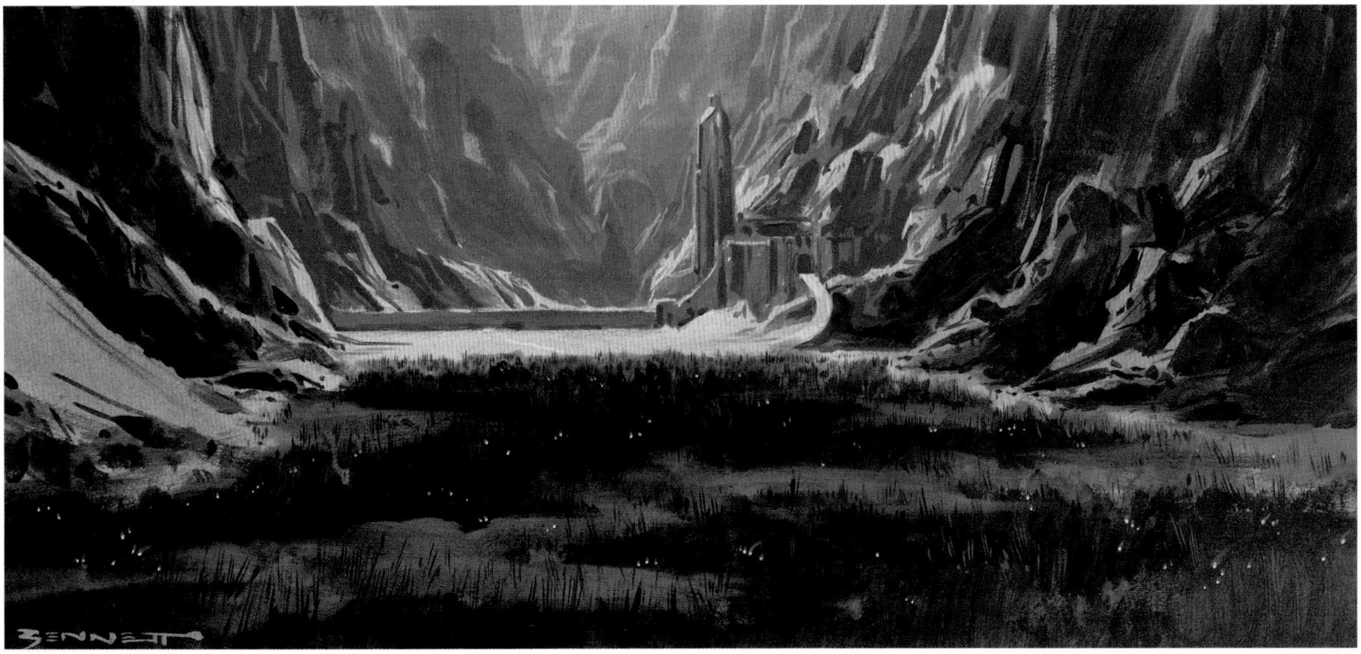

HELM'S DEEP *Color study*
"There are a lot of Uruk-hai – and you see them all. The idea here is that it's nighttime, and they're dressed in black, so you're never going to see them except for the flames of their torches. I wanted to allude to pikes against the night sky, and banners, and fire in the darkness." *JB*

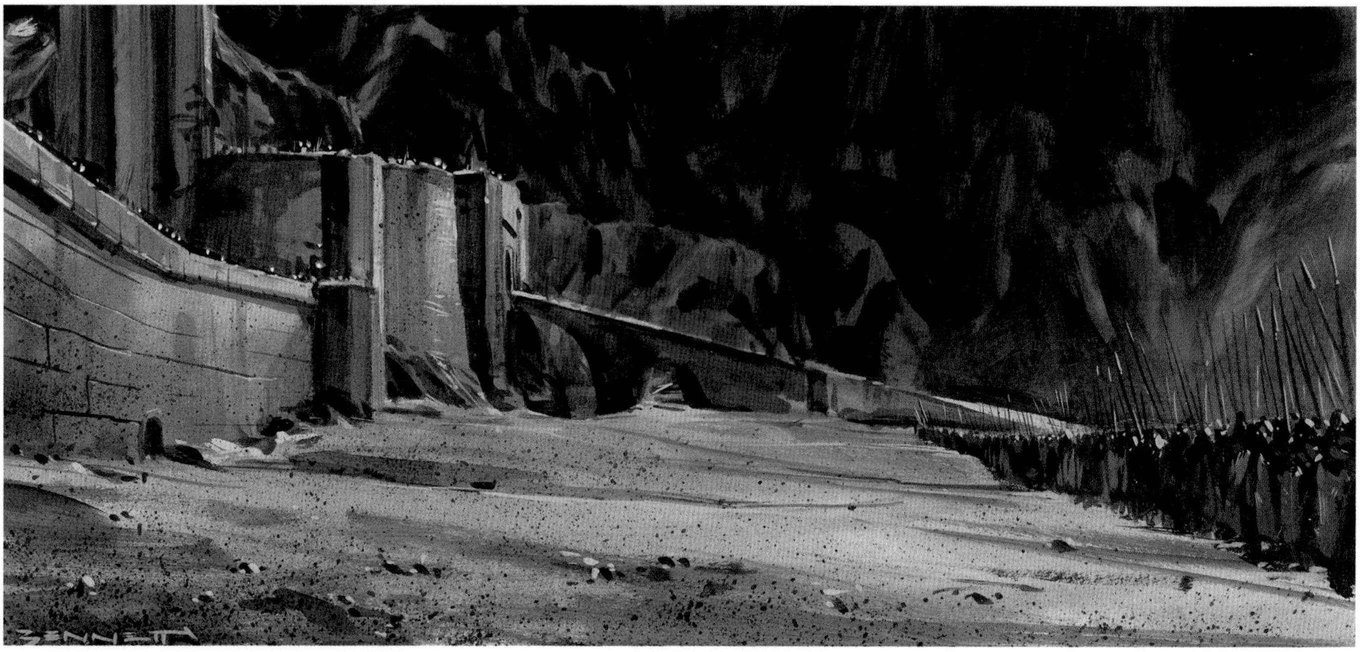

HELM'S DEEP ***Compositional study***
"This features all the characters – the Elves on the Deeping Wall, the Rohirrim up on the Hornburg itself, and the Uruk-hai – all facing off against each other. It was done – because the figures would all be CGI – to give the guys in digital an idea as to where they would be placed. Peter Jackson had specific instructions as to where they should be in the shot – just past the Causeway, just before the Causeway, higher up . . . wherever he felt they looked best. It's also to give a feeling for the overall palette as well as a sense of atmosphere. The whole environment is actually incredibly dark, and the tricky part – the challenge – was to really show off the elements we were building or adding." *JB*

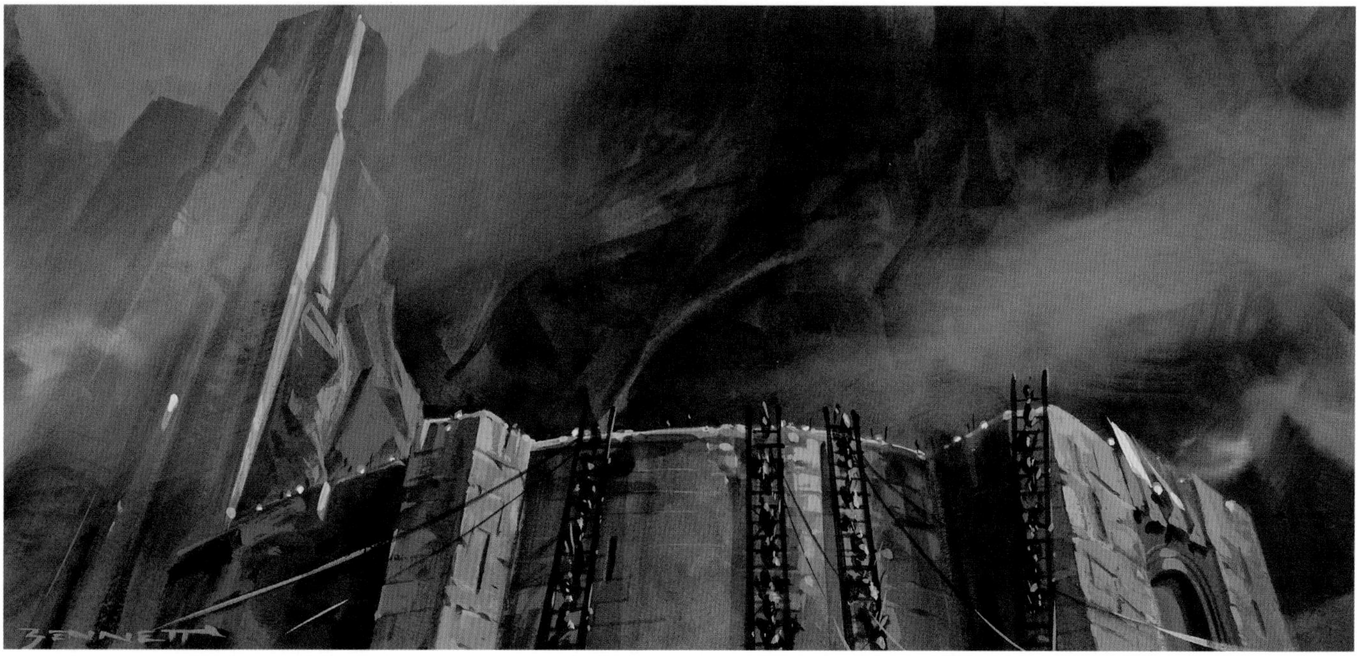

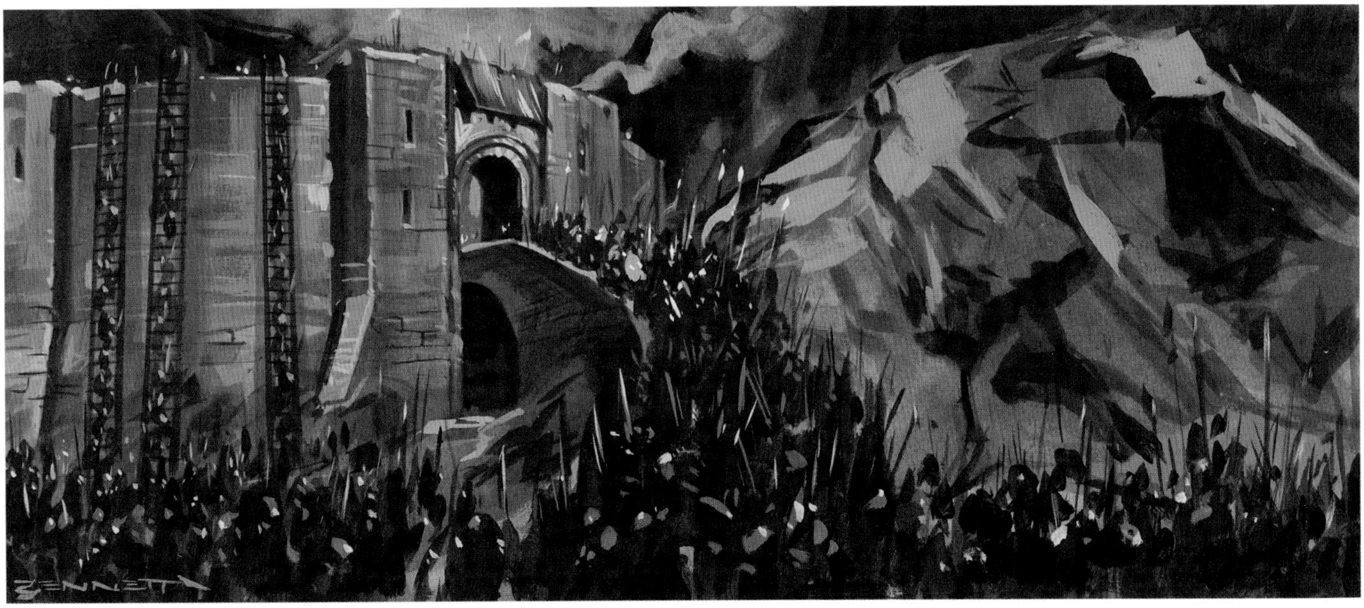

HELM'S DEEP *Color studies*
"This painting and the one at the bottom of the previous page were done for mood and atmosphere, and to establish the placement of siege ladders and the digitally created Uruk-hai storming over the walls and up the Causeway." *JB*

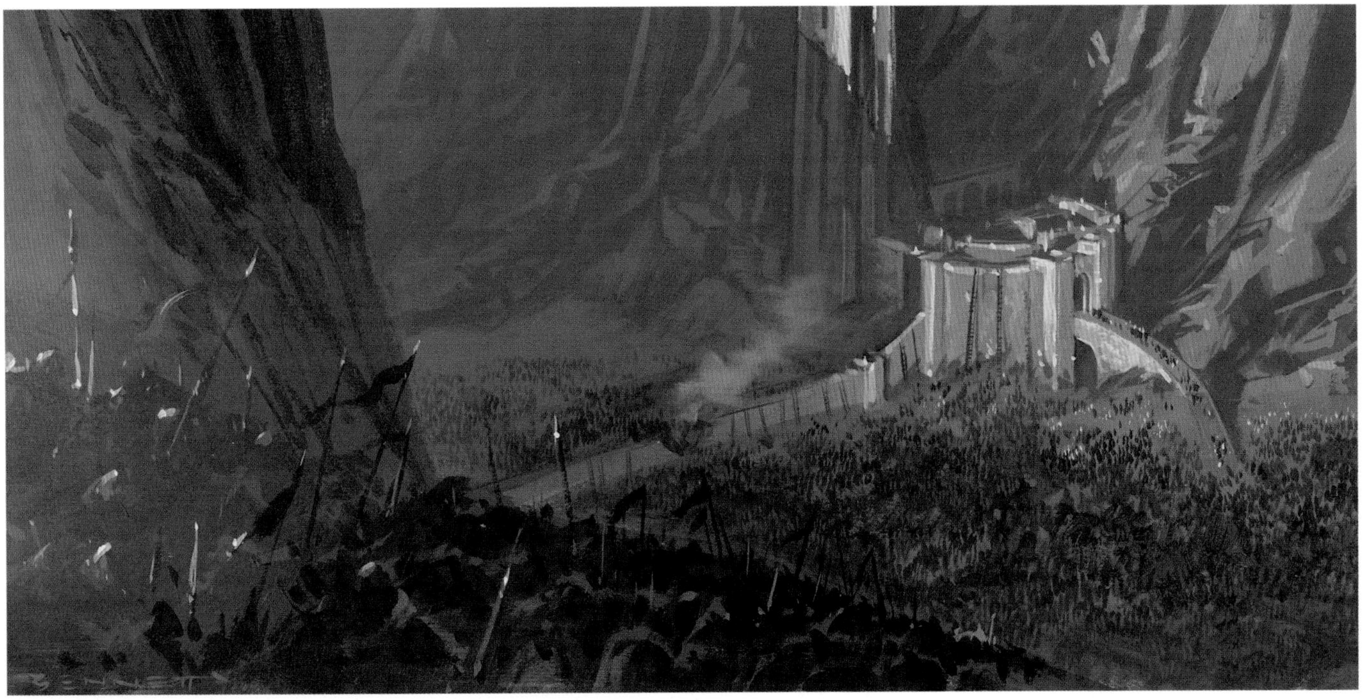

HELM'S DEEP *Color study*
"This is a color palette for the sequence in which Gandalf and the Rohirrim charge down the slope to save the day, because at this stage you have Théoden and the guys doing their final charge into the Uruk-hai. So here we're looking at the position and the angle of the Helm's Deep miniature, which will be a guide for Alex Funke to shoot it, and the amount of light that's striking it, so it's lighting stuff for them. It'll be a great shot and great sequence – actually, one of the best." *JB*

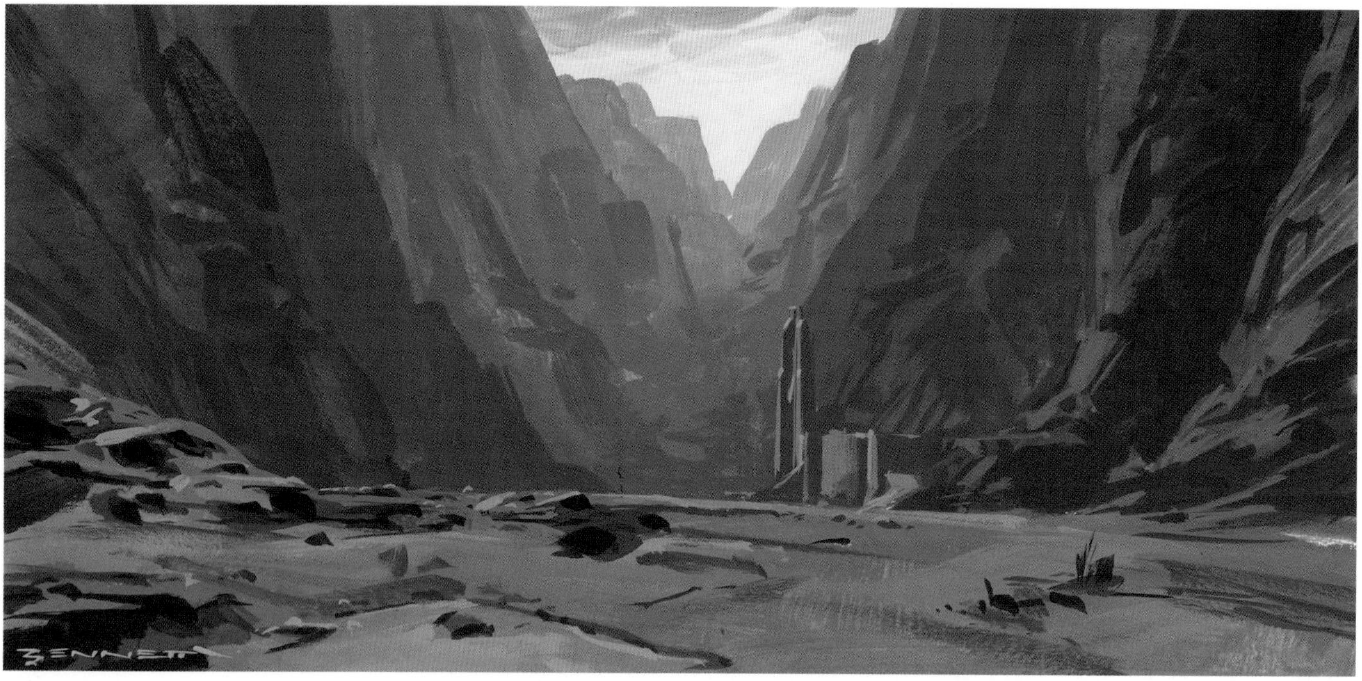

HELM'S DEEP *Color study*
"This painting was used by one of our matte painters to resolve the far end of the valley at Helm's Deep, which was seen as the Uruks were retreating toward the camera. The dawn sky can be seen in the distance."

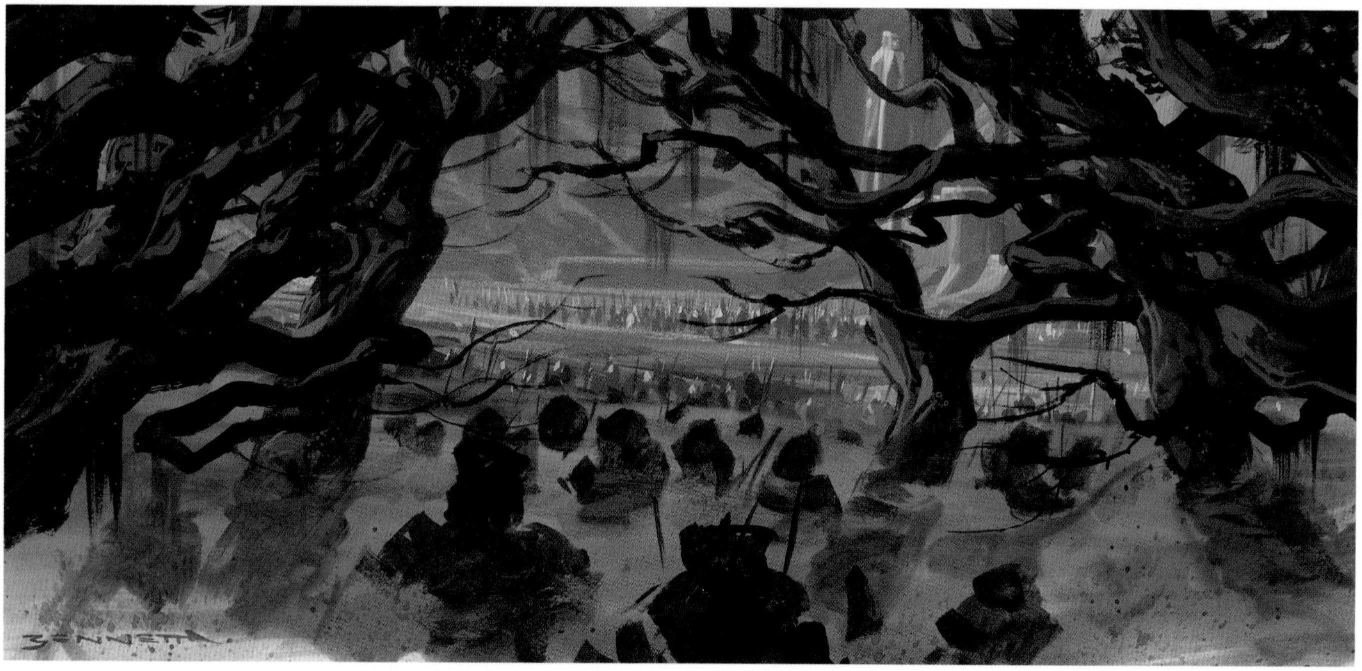

HUORNS AT HELM'S DEEP *Color study*
"This painting is a quick color study based on one of Alan Lee's drawings, with the emphasis on Helm's Deep at dawn, at the far end of the valley. In the foreground you can see the Uruks retreating into the forest. The trouble is, that forest wasn't there when they arrived . . ." *JB*

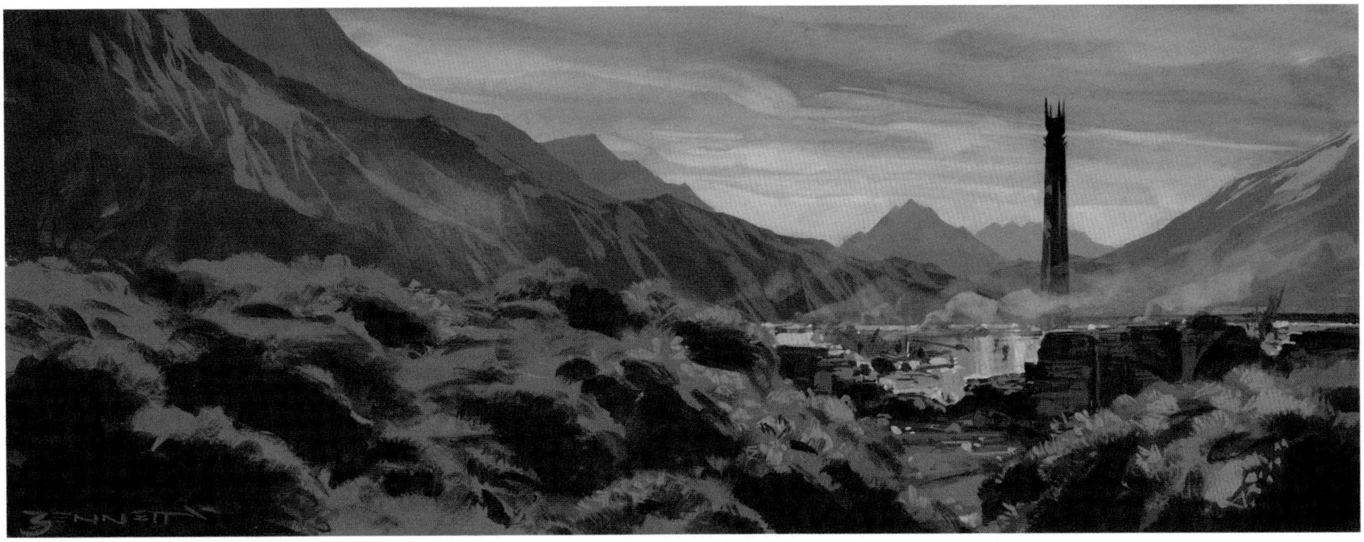

ISENGARD *Color study*
"This was a painting produced to answer any questions regarding Isengard's position in the valley at this particular time. This was used ostensibly by the matte painters to ensure continuity." *JB*

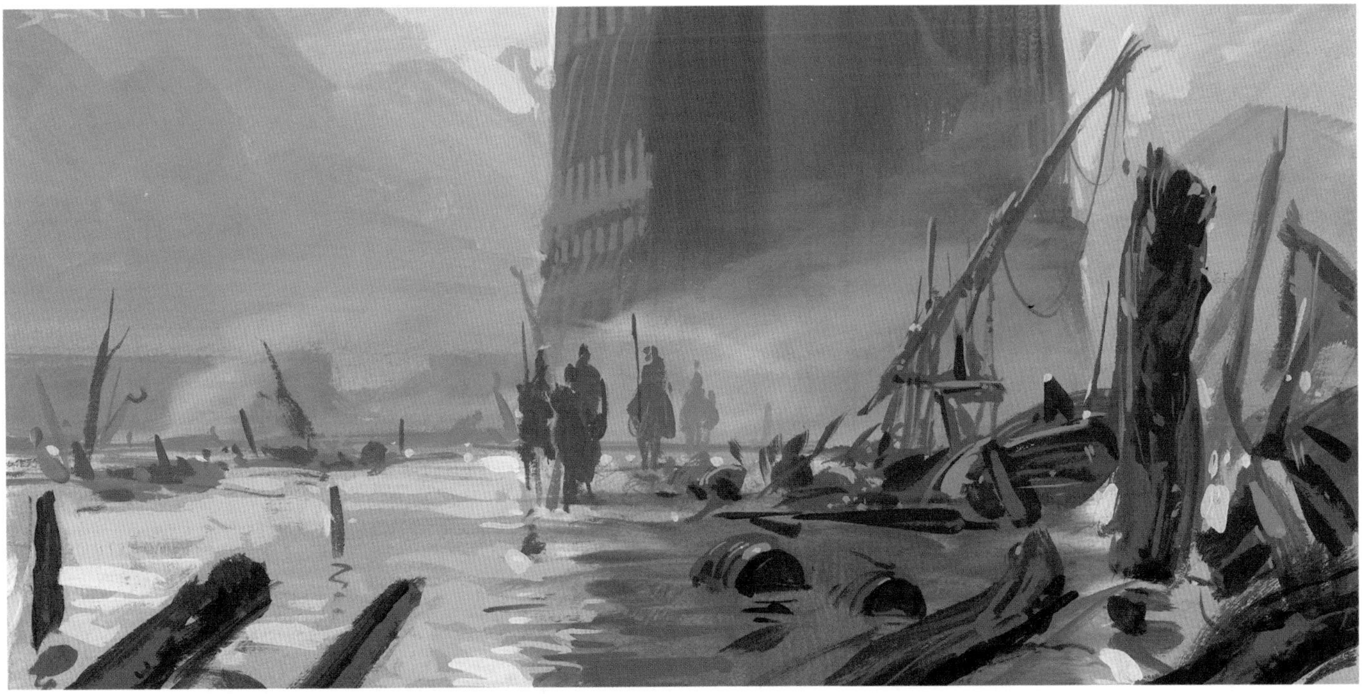

RUINED ISENGARD *Color study*
"This study shows the atmosphere, lighting, and look of the surrounding environment." *JB*

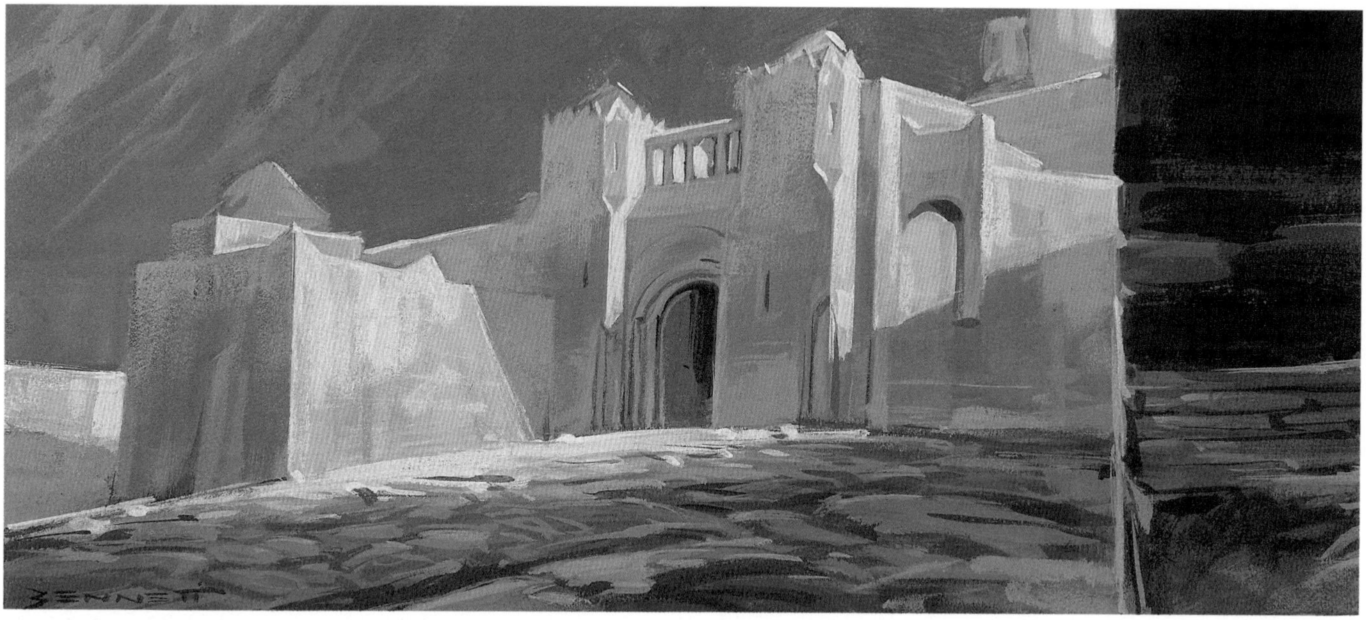

MINAS TIRITH *Color study*
"This was one of several color studies done of the second gate in Minas Tirith. I was quite happy with it as a color study; however, it ended up looking more like a view you would find in Morocco than like Romanesque Minas Tirith." *JB*

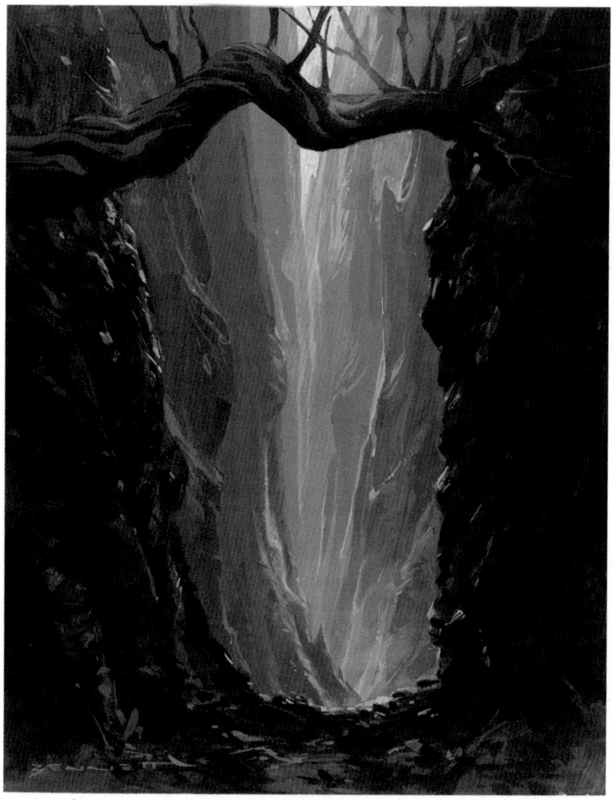

PATHS OF THE DEAD *Color study*
"This is of the Dimholt Glen, the passage to the Paths of the Dead on the top of the Dunharrow plateau. The painting was redone for Peter as he thought we needed to see the path receding away from us into the glen." *JB*

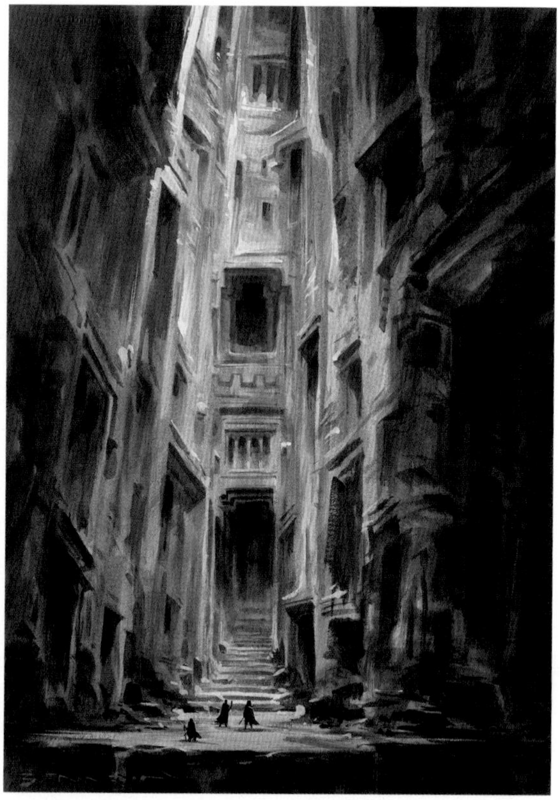

CITY OF THE DEAD *Color study*
"This is a lighting study to show how the City of the Dead might look to Aragorn, Legolas, and Gimli as they see it appear out of the rock." *JB*

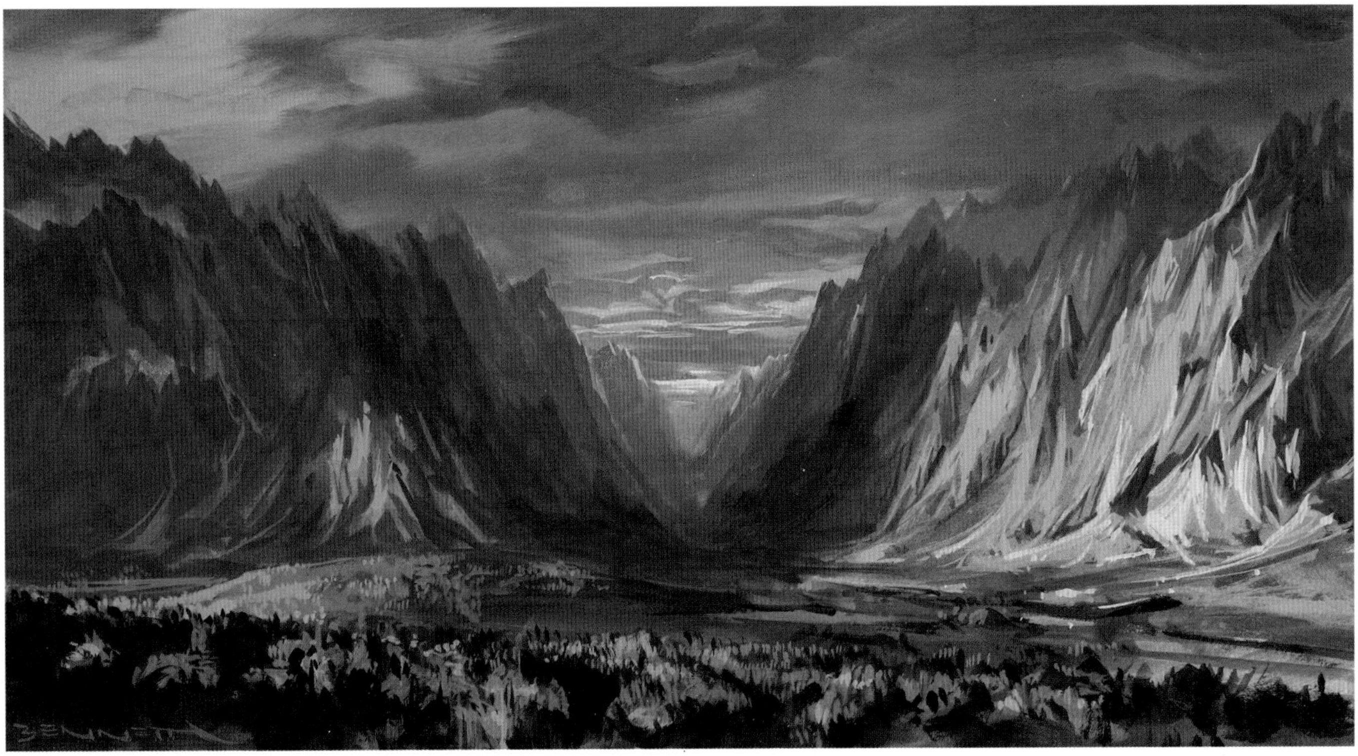

MORGUL VALE *Color study*
"An early color study of the Morgul Vale using one of Alan Lee's studies for inspiration." *JB*

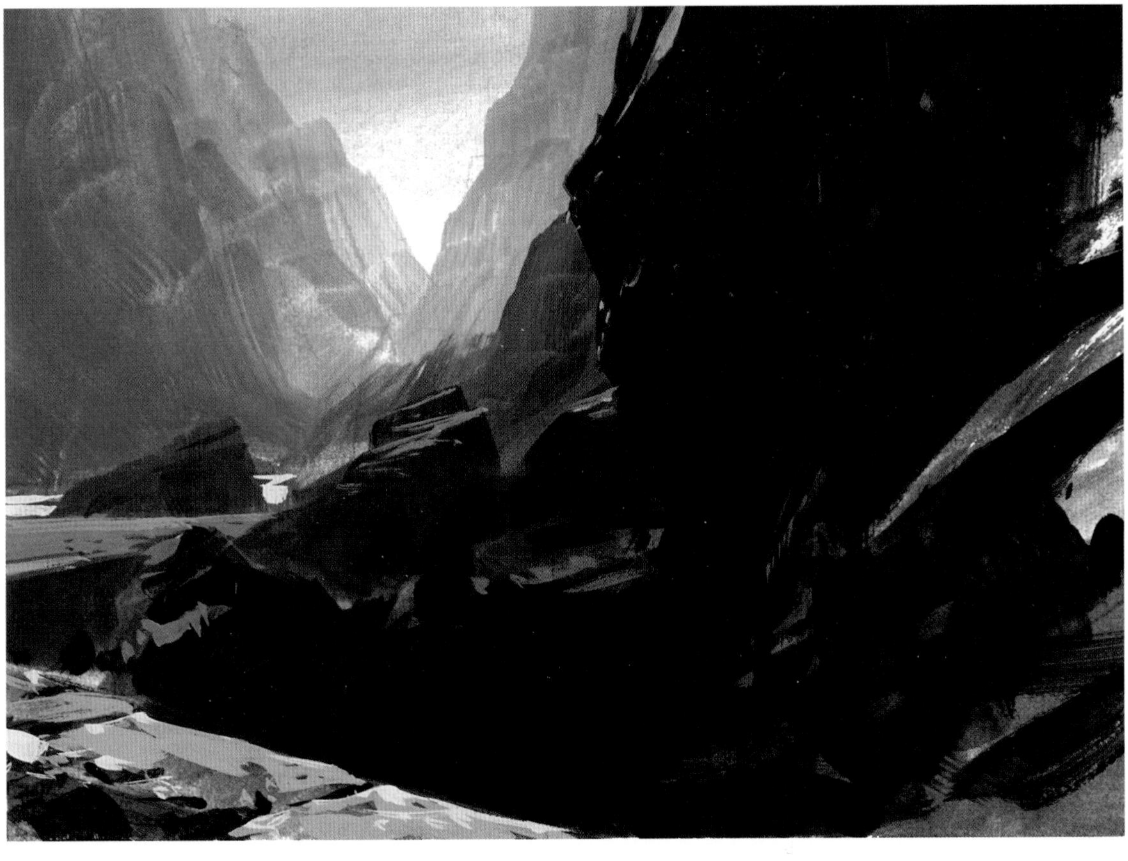

MORGUL VALE
Color study
"A view of the Morgul Vale from the gargoyles opposite Minas Morgul – basically a layout for a matte painter." *JB*

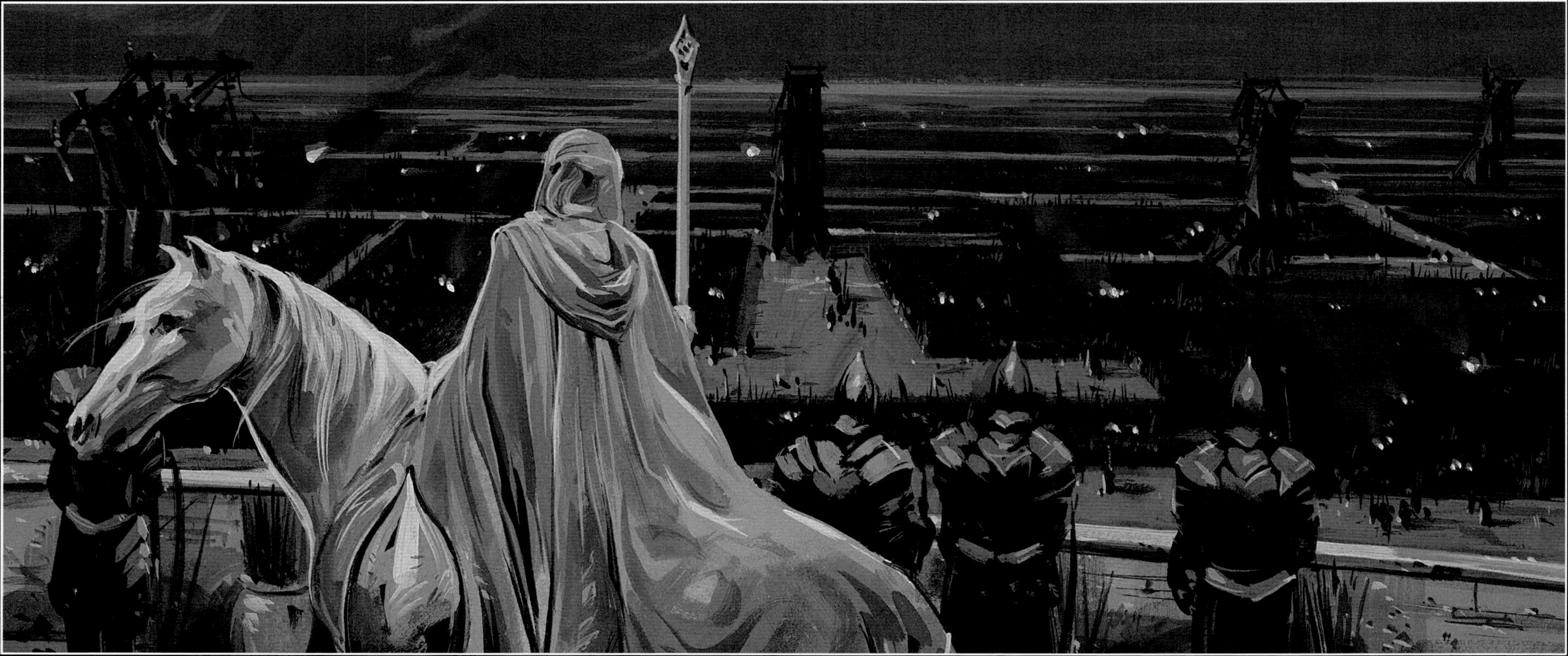

THE SIEGE OF GONDOR *Color study*
"This is the moment when Gandalf rides up onto the parapets on Shadowfax and sees the Orc formations. You've got the siege towers being pushed by four trolls each. There will also be catapults in front of them, but I haven't actually put them into this. I really wanted to introduce as much smoke as possible on the field of battle, and those are large braziers out in the distance, burning. The Orcs have torches, rather like the Uruk-hai at Helm's Deep, and I've used the smoke from them to imply ghostly silhouettes emerging

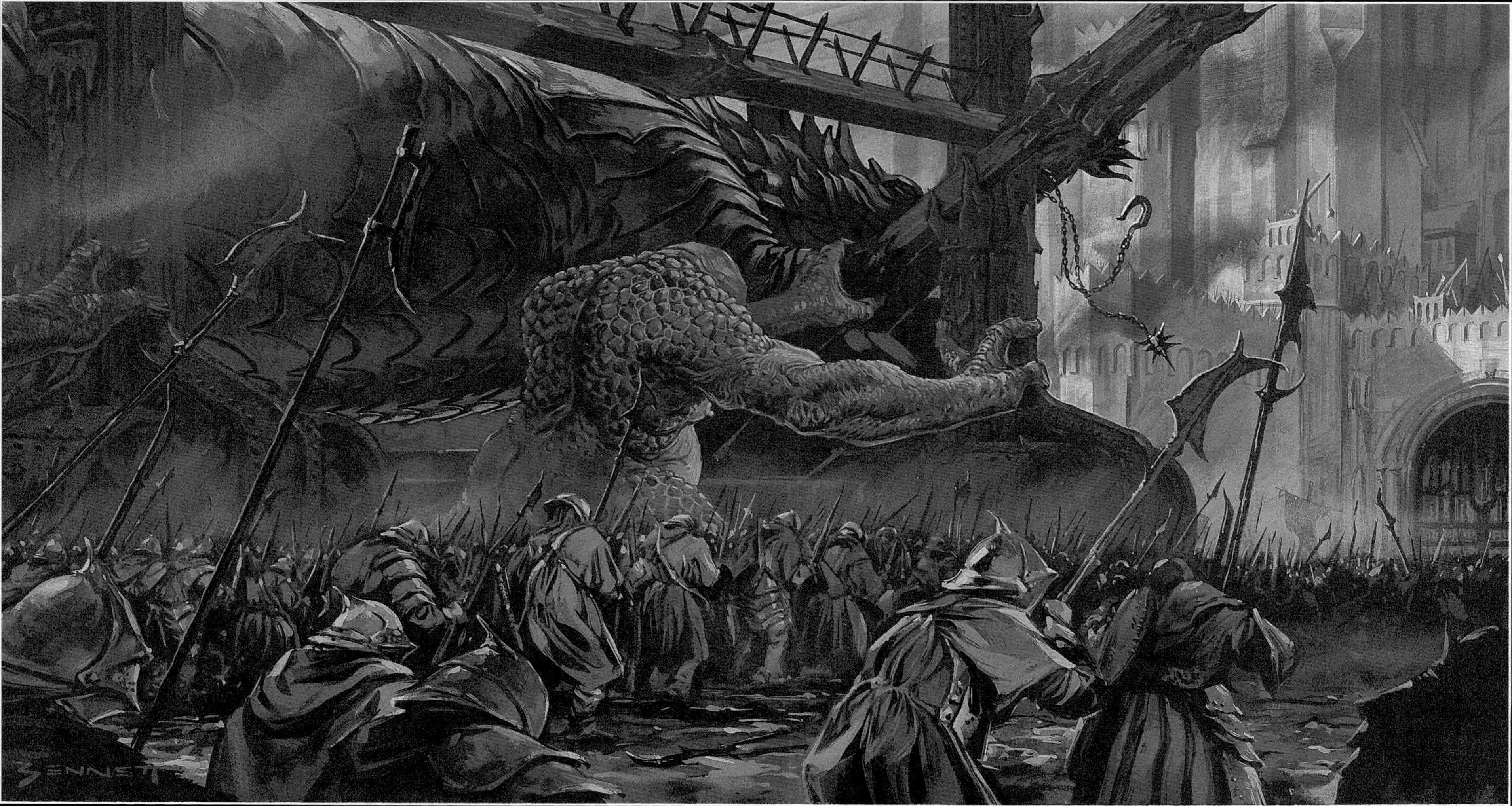

THE SIEGE OF GONDOR *Color study*
"This is pretty old now, one of the first things we did. Grond is accurate, as is Minas Tirith in the background, because they'd been made by the time I painted this. I just went and sat with a pen and paper for fifteen minutes and roughly drew what they had built, in the right positions. I was working from finished miniatures, which was great, if very unusual. But because the footage had already been shot, I had a pretty good idea as to what the Orcs in the foreground would be wearing and so on. Certainly for an image like this, it makes life a lot easier. The mountain-trolls, however, are now fully armored. I didn't know back then what they would look like, how they'd be dressed – no one did. All we knew was that they'd be a lot bigger than the cave-troll from *Fellowship*. There will be three trolls either side, and Grond will now also be pulled by the great beasts at the front – a decision that also occurred after this was painted, so I had no idea that was going to happen. But that's one of the great things about all this – they look at your paintings and it inspires them to do even more. Look at those big wheels: you get a real sense of power – you can kill half your enemy just by running them over. In the film I think you actually see Orcs

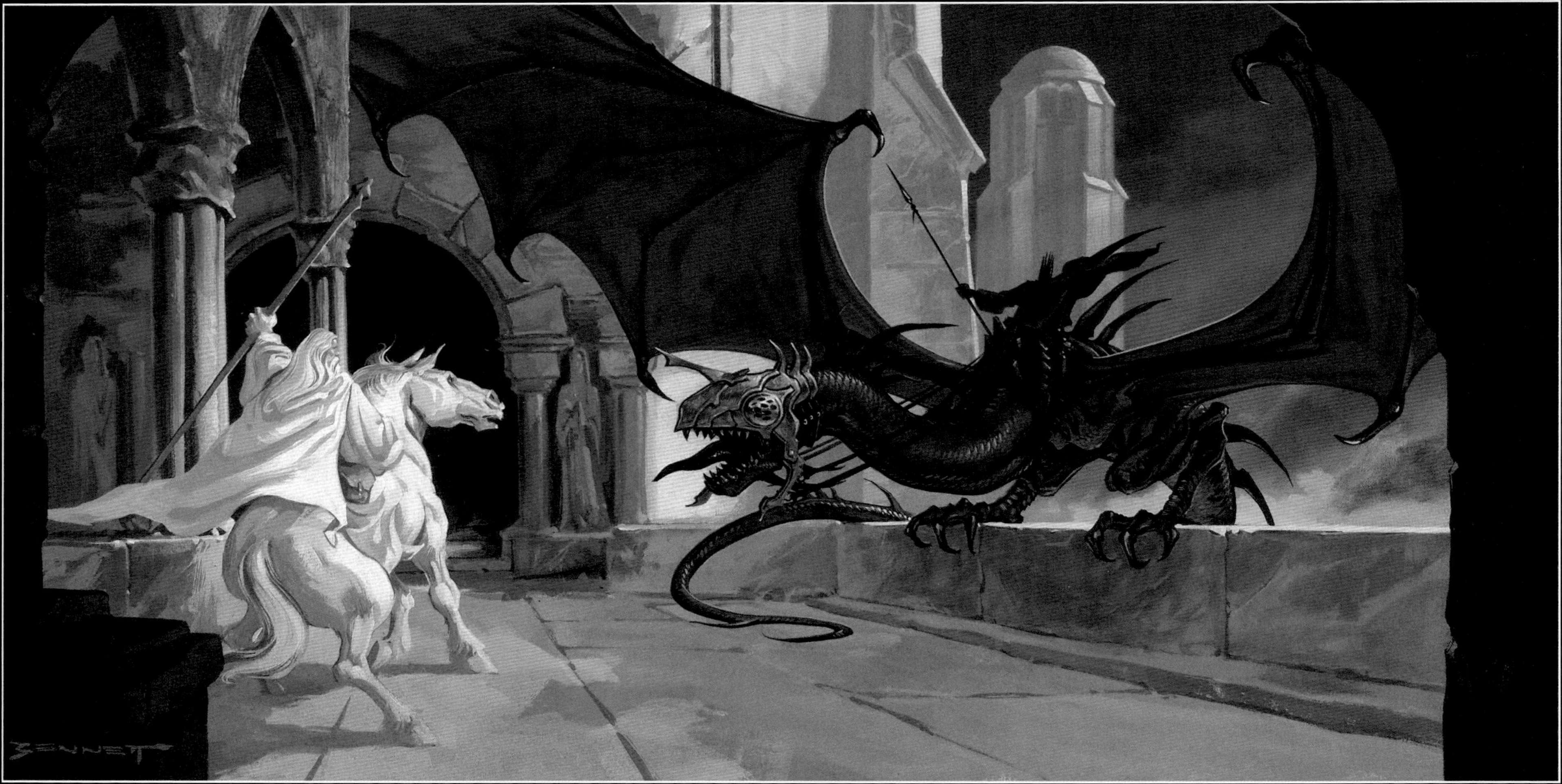

GANDALF FACES THE WITCH-KING *Color study*
"Once again this is a very old painting done from a storyboard frame. Because it is pre-shoot artwork, the Minas Tirith environment is very different in the finished shot. However, the look behind the fell beast was carried through to the finished shot. The resulting scene in the extended cut of the movie is a personal highlight." *JB*

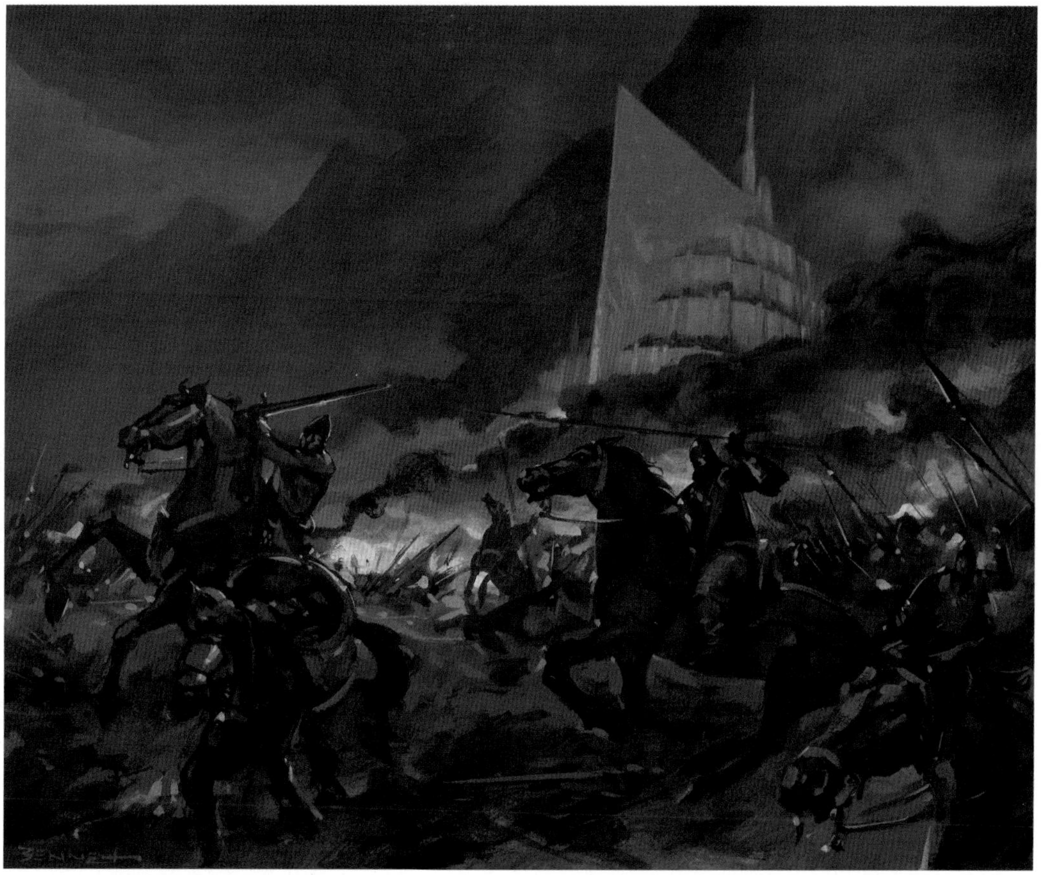

THE PELENNOR FIELDS
Color study
"At this point Sauron's forces have broken through the Great Gate of the city using Grond, and it's dawn. So this is where we see Denethor, as a flaming fireball, throw himself off the seventh tier of Minas Tirith. We follow him down, and then the Rohirrim just smash through the foreground, ripping the Orc companies apart. The battle is absolutely raging, Minas Tirith is on fire, and it's just carnage, wholesale slaughter. This was my impression of what that event might look like. I like the fact that everything, the whole landscape, is on fire, although I'm not sure whether that's how it's going to look in the end. It might look worse . . ." *JB*

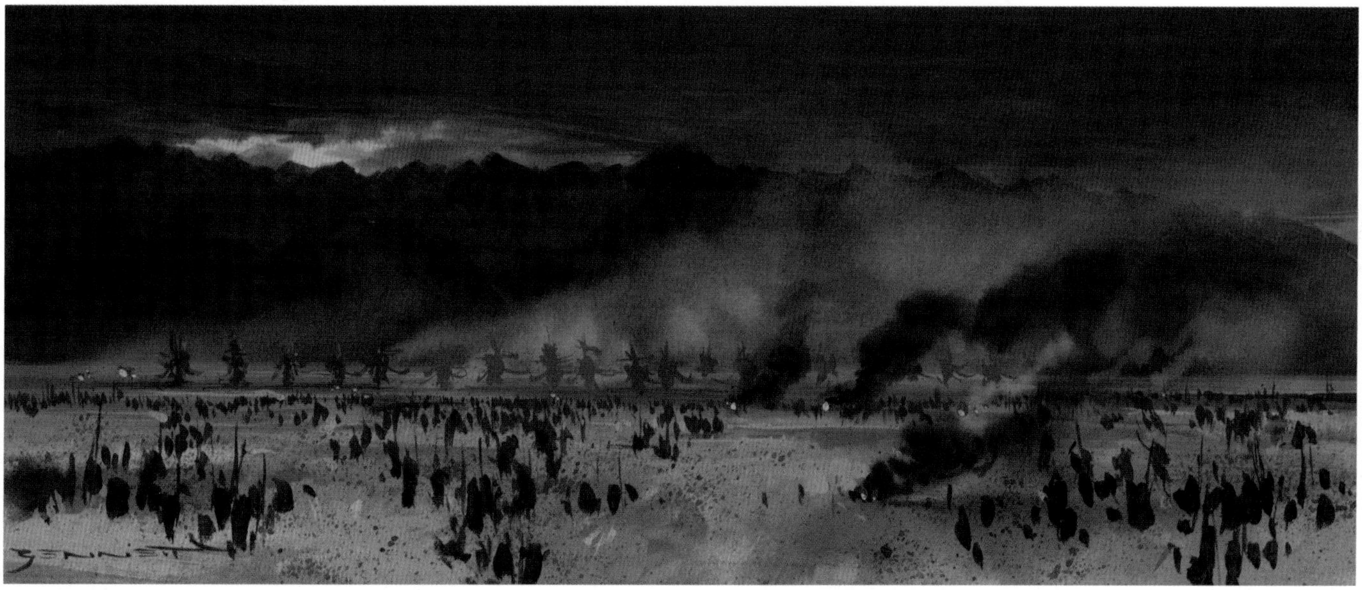

THE PELENNOR FIELDS ***Color study***
"This is a snapshot of the battle, moments before the mûmakil arrive, which was used as an idea for their appearance on the field." *JB*

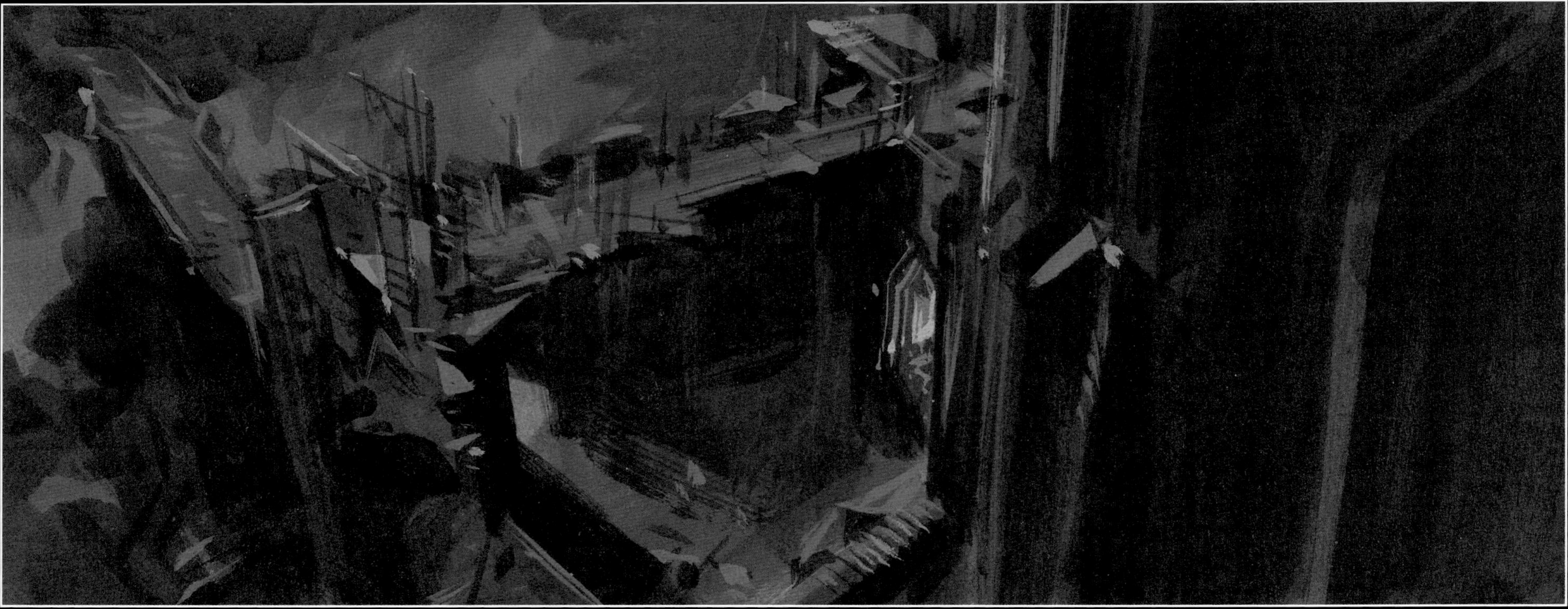

CIRITH UNGOL *Color study*
"We're looking down into the Cirith Ungol tower courtyard. There's a little bit of light coming from the doorway that Sam will enter. In the top left corner is the bridge, and halfway between is the actual entrance, so he's just come down out of Shelob's Lair and followed the Orcs and Uruk-hai that have picked up Frodo and taken him off. The miniature of this set is amazing – there's so much detail in it – and it'll be interesting to see how much of that comes across on screen. I imagine some of it will be lost, but at least you'll know it's there." *JB*

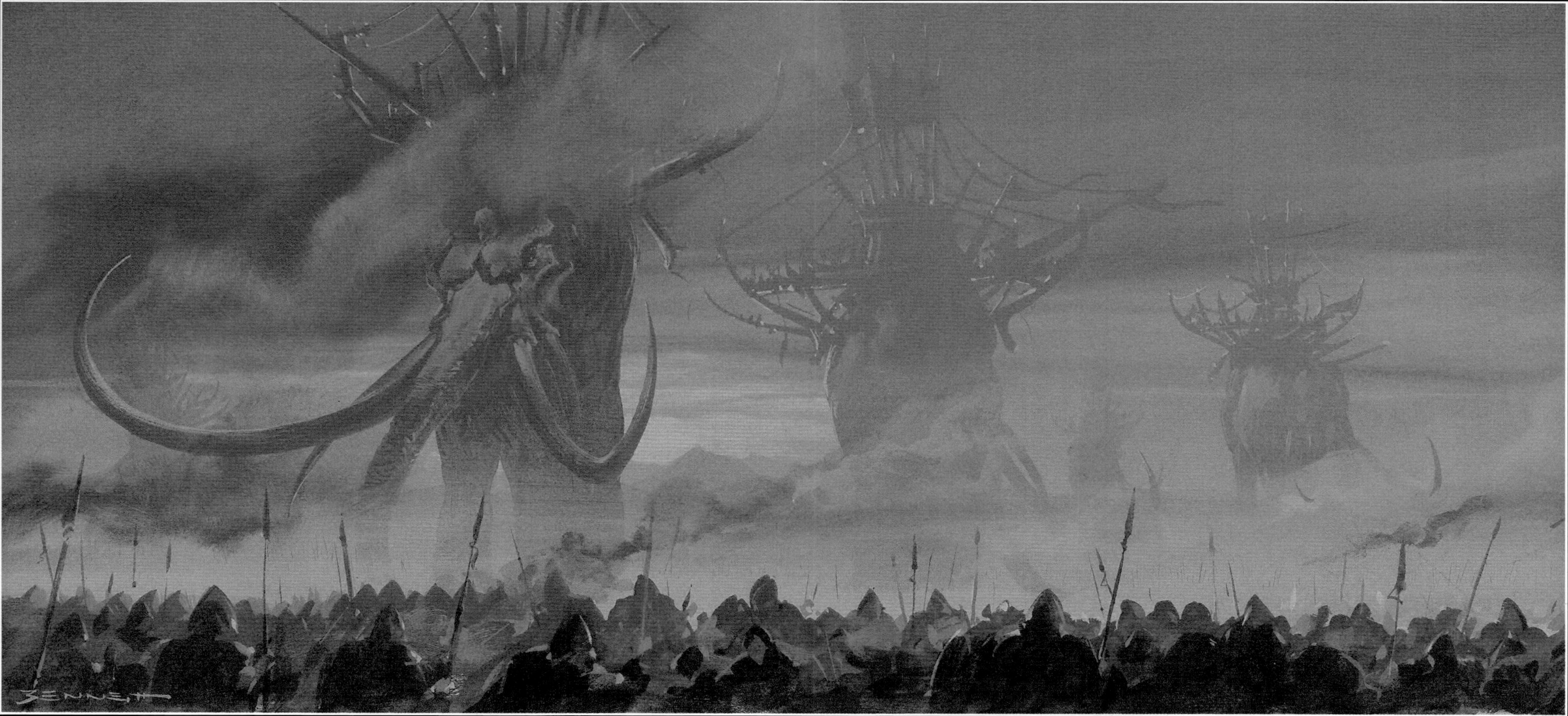

THE PELENNOR FIELDS *Color study*

"At the stage this was painted there were only six mûmakil that came through at dawn. I imagined that the Rohirrim thought they were doing pretty well in the battle – little did they know what was coming next! I think we've now got eighteen or twenty mûmakil and they come bearing these amazing creations on their backs, full of Haradrim, which are going to blow people away. But when I painted this one I was wondering what the towers on their backs going to look like? I pictured Spanish galleons. You could just imagine how confusing they would be – looking up through the mist to see these ship-like things coming across dry land. And then, out of the mist appear these Oliphaunts, fully armored, with chains slung between the tusks, armor on the legs, and they're so big! These things were truly enormous." *JB*

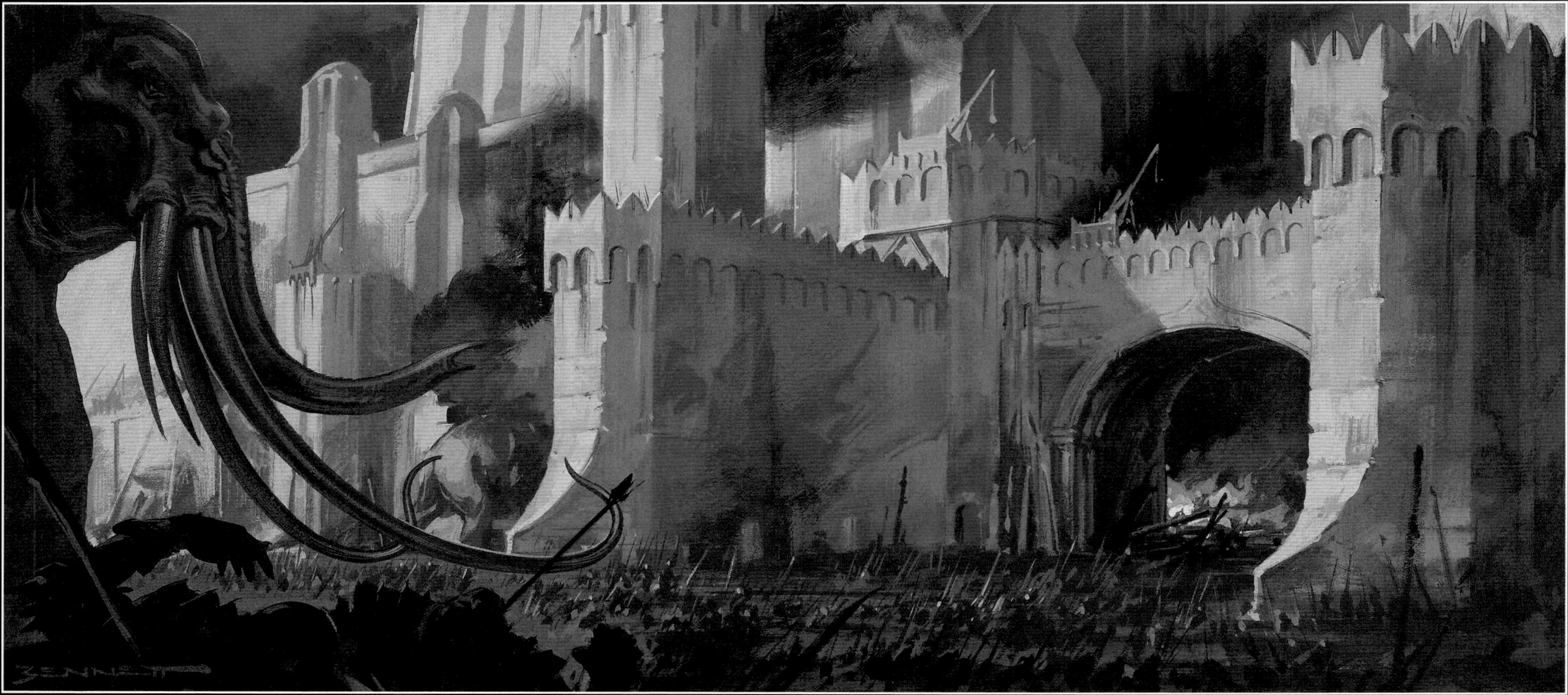

THE MÛMAKIL REACH THE GATE *Lighting study*

"Once again, this is a painting that was done quite some time ago, but Peter really liked it, and it was given to the miniature builders as the lighting guide for Minas Tirith during the siege. He loved this low side-light: it's quite dramatic. Peter enjoyed this look, but also wanted raking shadows from the siege towers and a warmer palette on the ground. He said it felt like that post-storm moment, when you've still got black clouds over in one direction, but you look the other way and the sun's coming through. So I envisioned the cloud permanently over the Pelennor Fields, with the light, signifying the end of the day, just poking through – but you can still see dark sky up at the top left-hand corner." *JB*

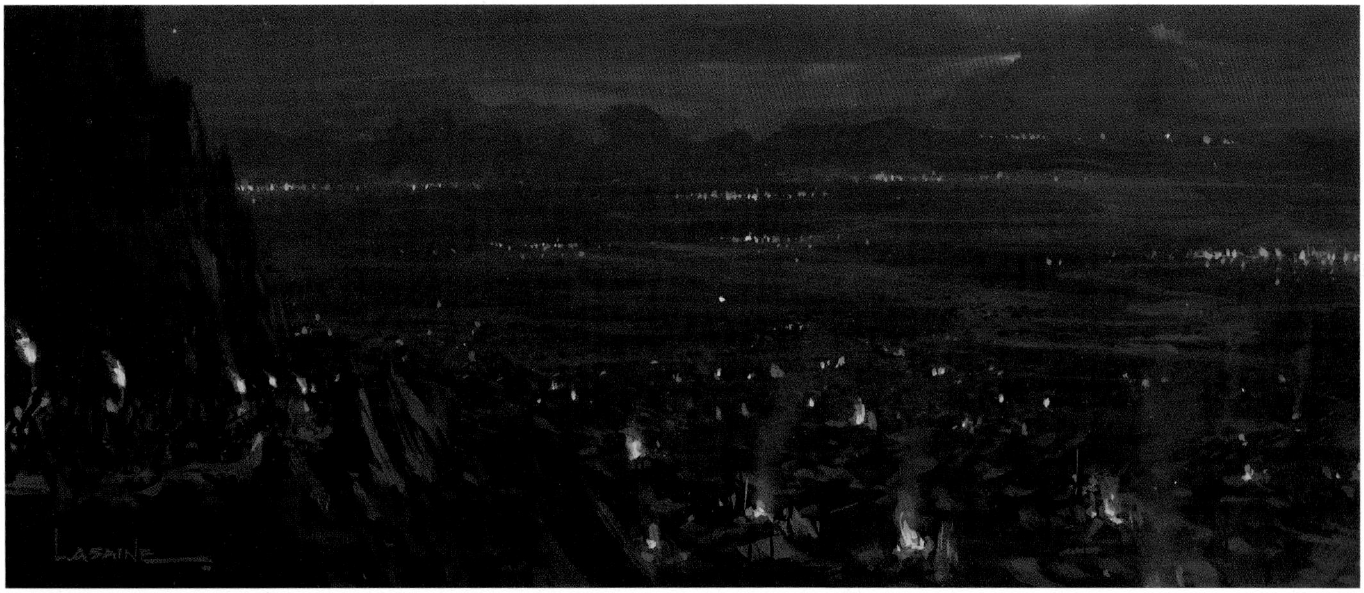

MORDOR *Color study*
"This is Sam and Frodo's first view of Mordor. The landscape is covered with thousands of Orc encampments. In trying to determine exactly what Mordor would look like, we came up with the idea that the entire land was once a massive lake of molten lava, with the surrounding mountains being the walls of an extinct volcano hundreds of miles across. Mount Doom is all that's left of the original volcano." *PL*

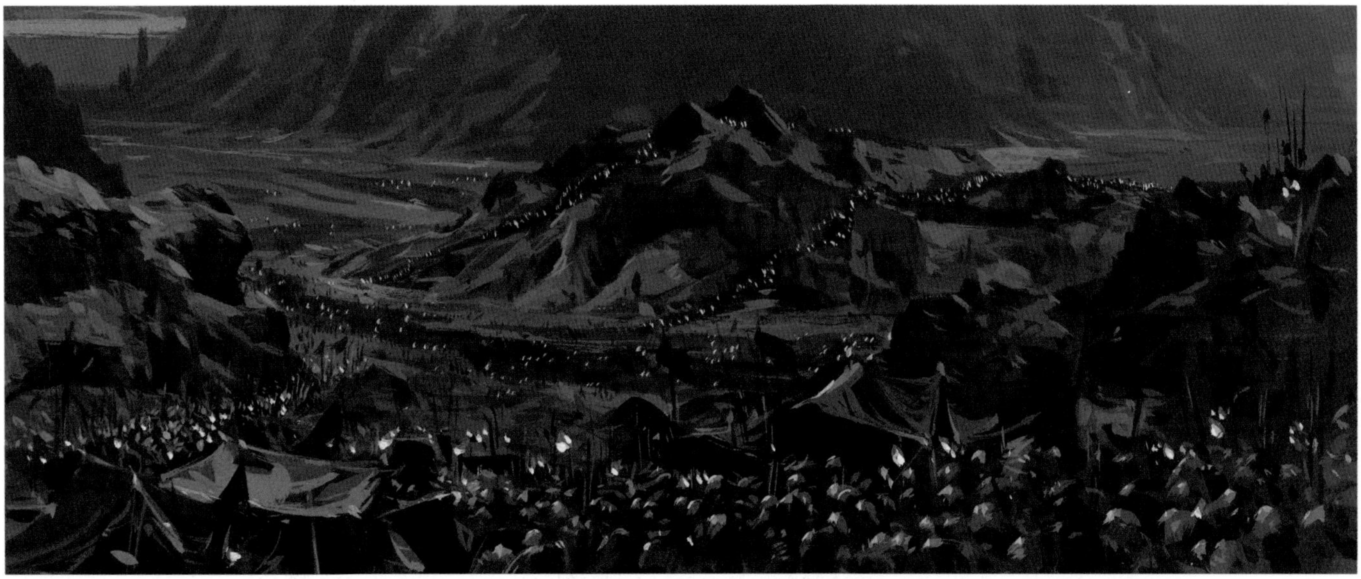

THE BLACK GATES *Color study*
"This is the last frame of a scene where you see Sam and Frodo dressed up as Orcs and was done as a color study for the matte painters. Up in the top left-hand corner you've got the Black Gates, and Mount Doom would be over to the right. When our heroes leave Cirith Ungol tower and bump into some Orcs, they get rounded up and sent off to war." *JB*

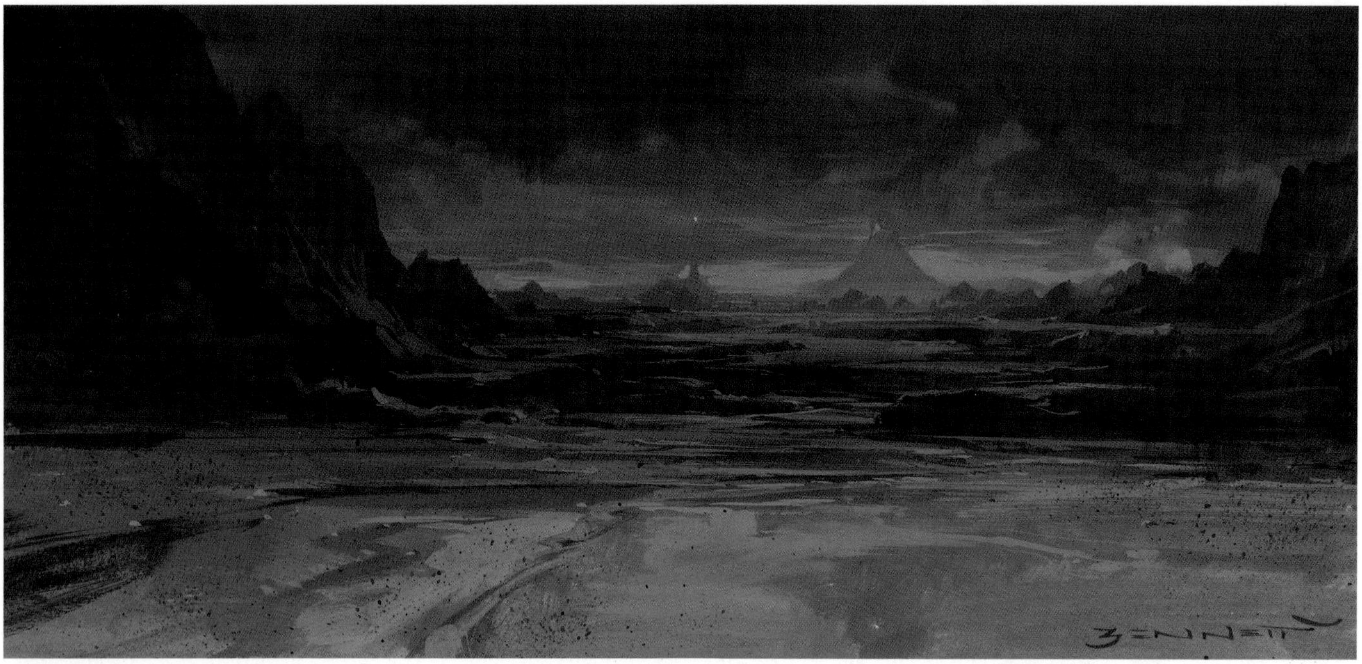

THE BLACK GATES *Color study*
"Barad-dûr and Mount Doom, as seen from just inside the Black Gates, focusing on the midground in particular." *JB*

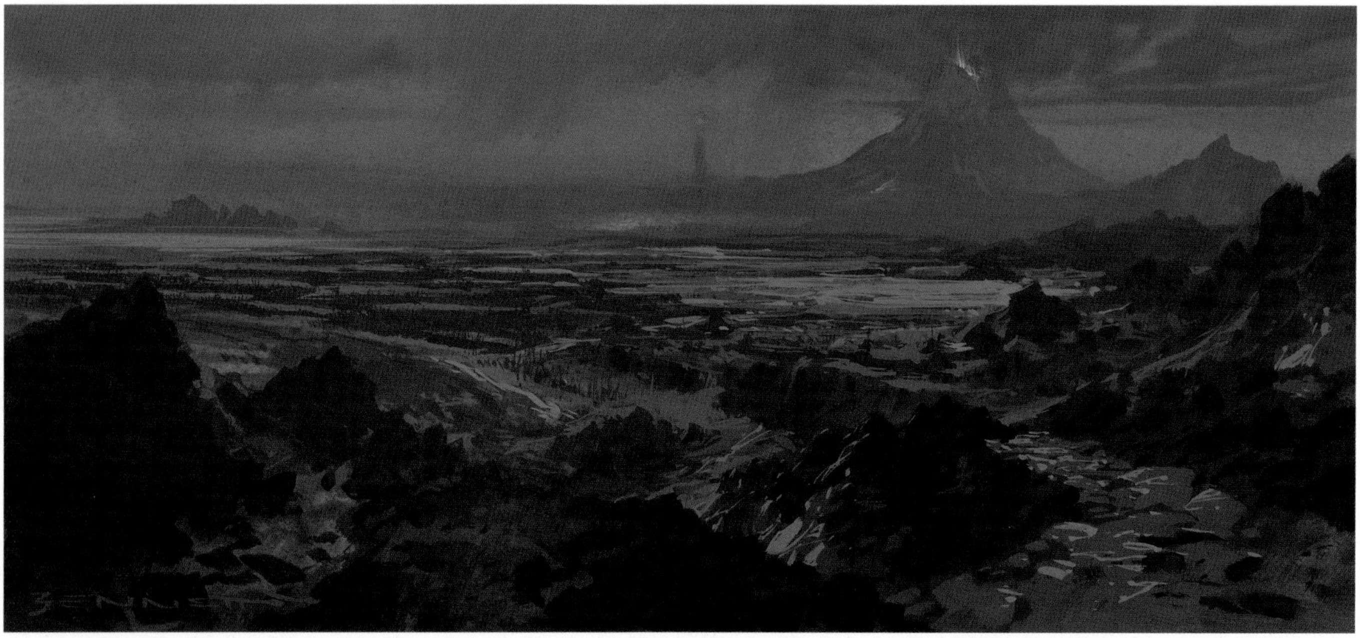

GORGOROTH PLAIN *Color study*
"This study formed the basis for a matte painting; it depicts the Orcs leaving the Gorgoroth Plain for the Black Gates, as seen by Frodo and Sam." *JB*

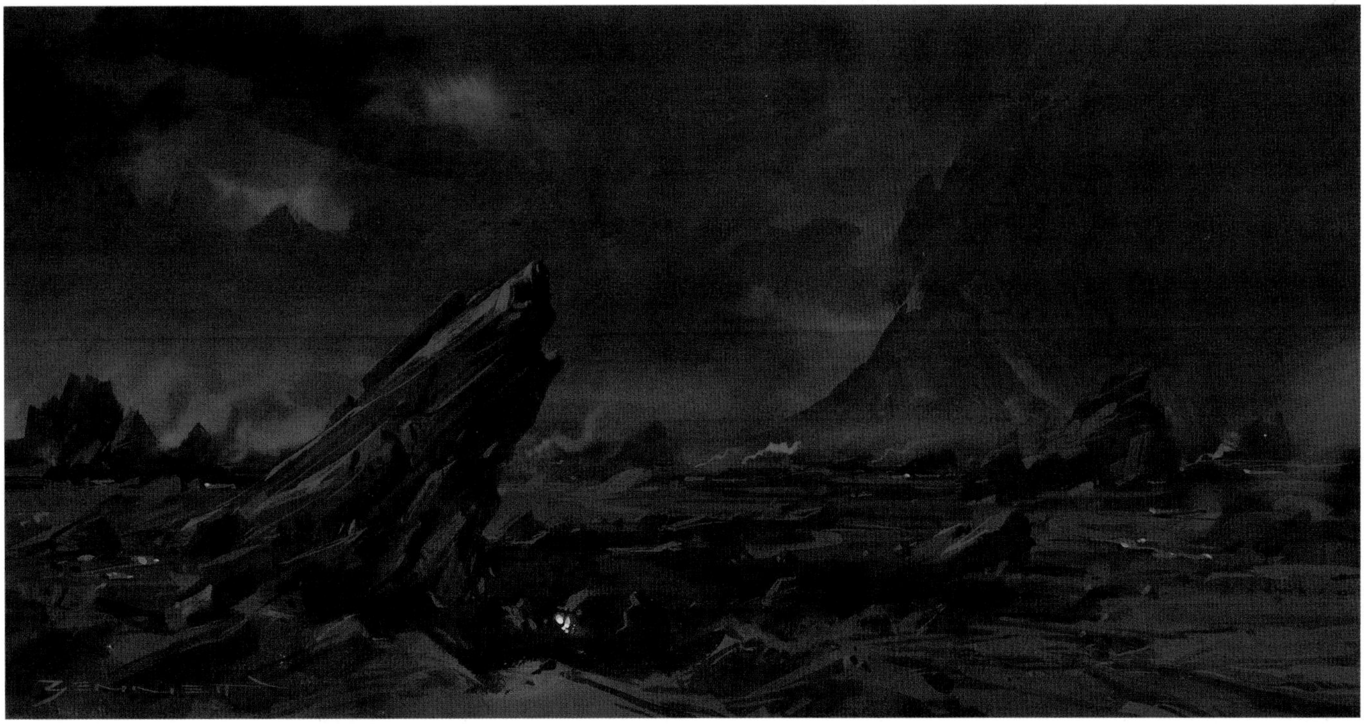

GORGOROTH PLAIN *Color study*
"I imagined Gorgoroth to be a series of cracked and shattered rocky plates, littered with grotesque rocky outcrops. These were found at Breaker Bay, on the south coast of Wellington." *JB*

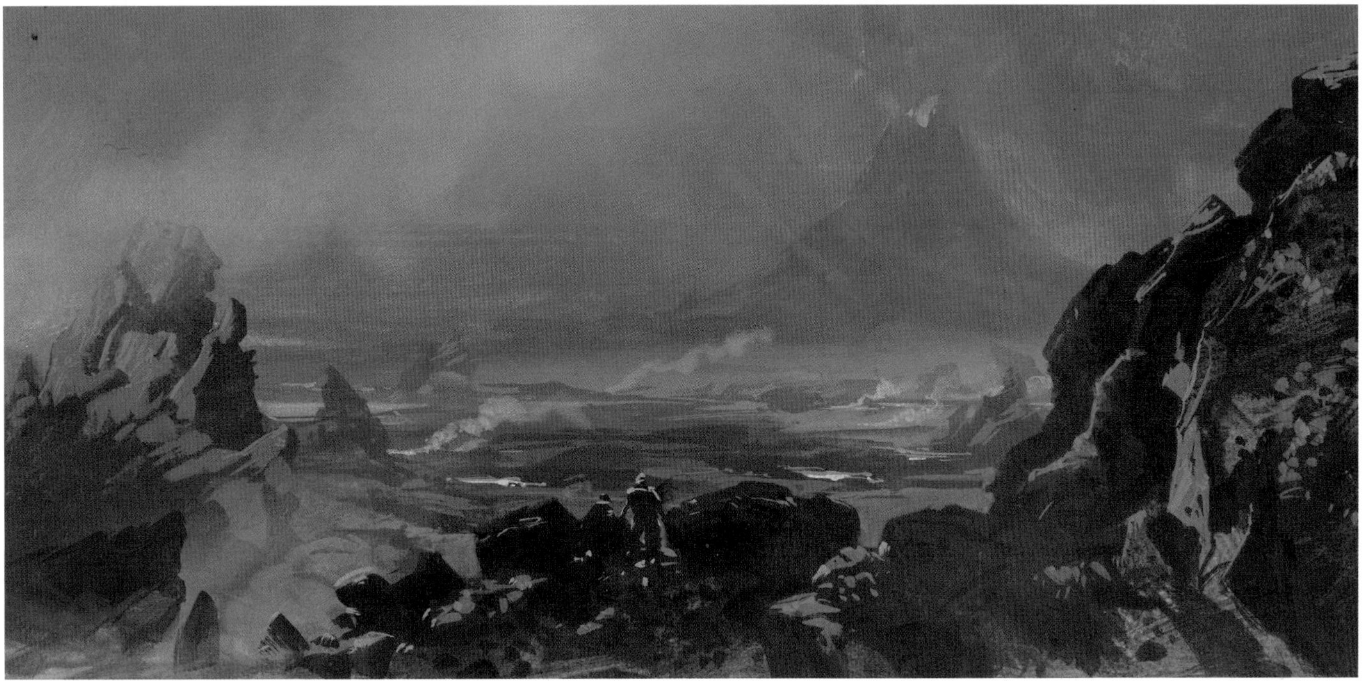

GORGOROTH PLAIN *Environment study*
"This was possibly the third painting done for this shot. It was helpful in establishing the overall color palette for the scene. But it has since changed again, and the final matte painting by Dylan Cole [see page 220] was quite different. The result, however, was worth the wait." *JB*

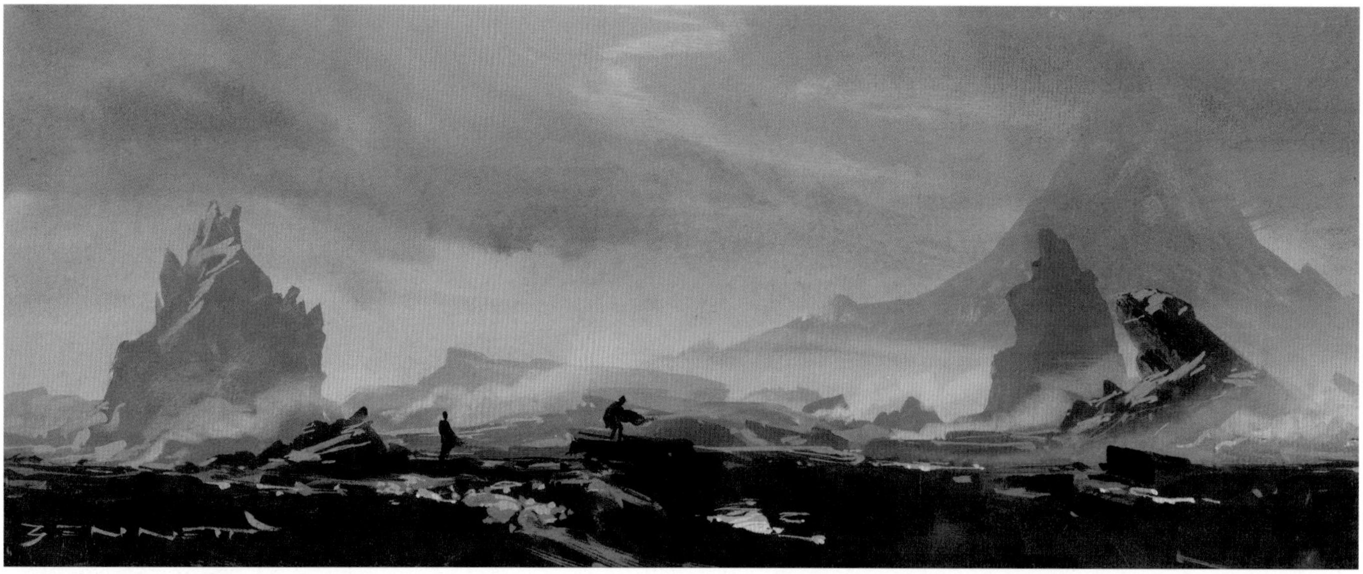

GORGOROTH PLAIN ***Color study***
"Another view of the plain, this time showing Sam and Frodo easing their way across. The scale of the task that remains to the Hobbits is here emphasized by their size relative to the environment, and Mordor is rendered unearthly through the use of mauves and purples for the lowering sky." *JB*

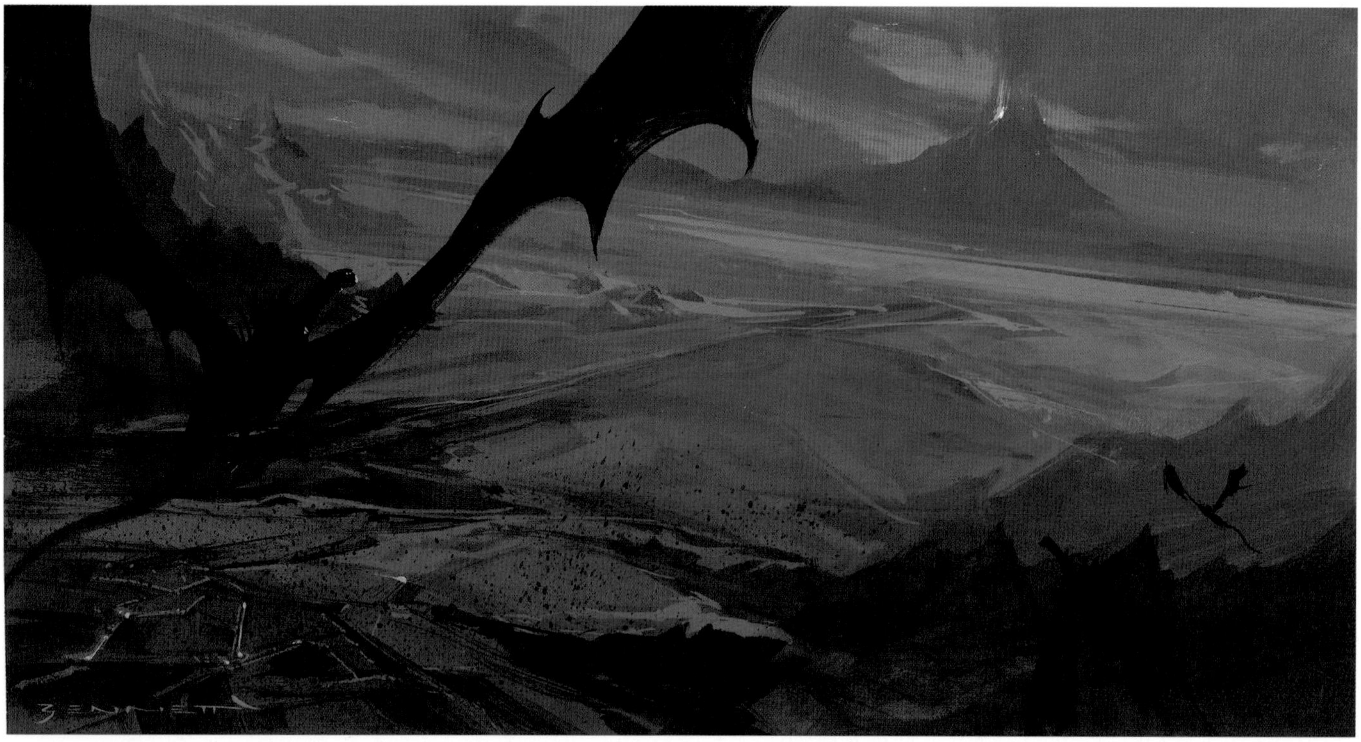

MOUNT DOOM ***Color study***
"Frodo has just put on the Ring inside the Crack of Doom, alerting Sauron and the Nazgûl to its location. Meanwhile, the battle outside the Black Gates is in full swing. This is the last frame of quite an elaborate shot starting outside the Black Gates and panning with the fell beast to Mount Doom." *JB*

MORDOR *Color study*
"This was a very early study looking at the Mordor environment and the base of Mount Doom, giving particular thought to its sulfurous atmosphere." *JB*

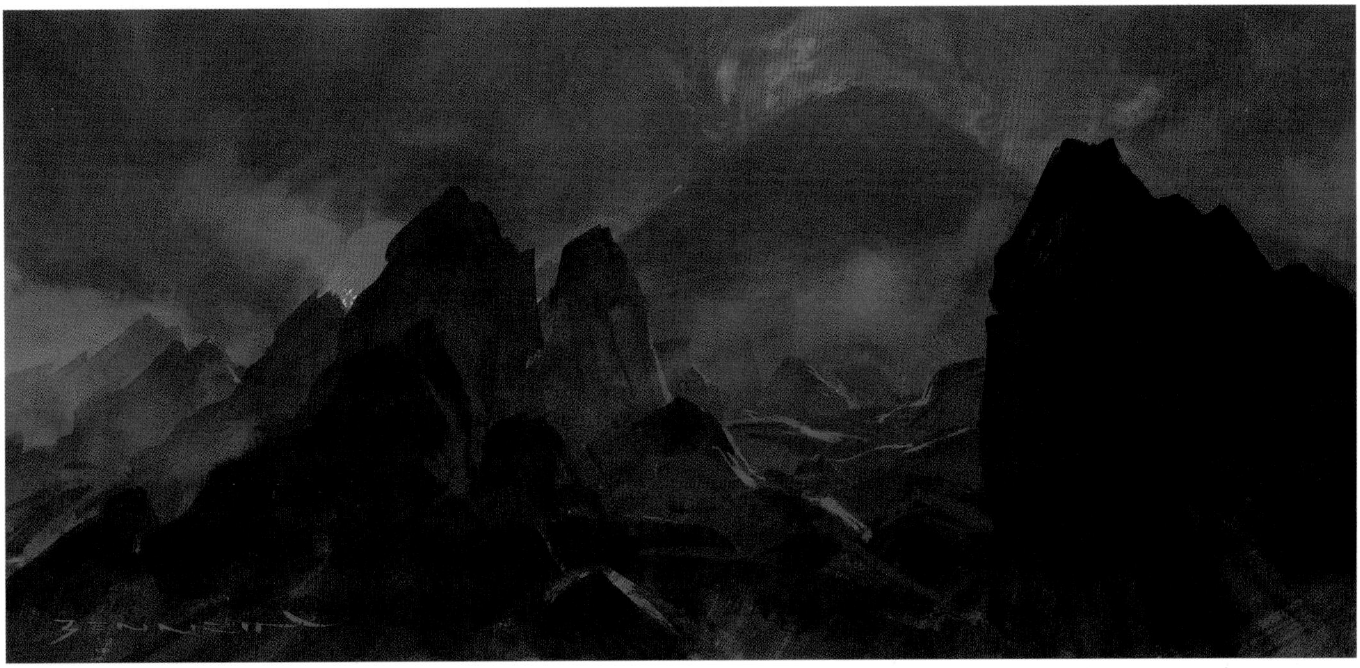

MOUNT DOOM *Color study*
"This picture is looking up at the summit of Mount Doom, with the focus this time being on the amount of mist and smoke that might be present." *JB*

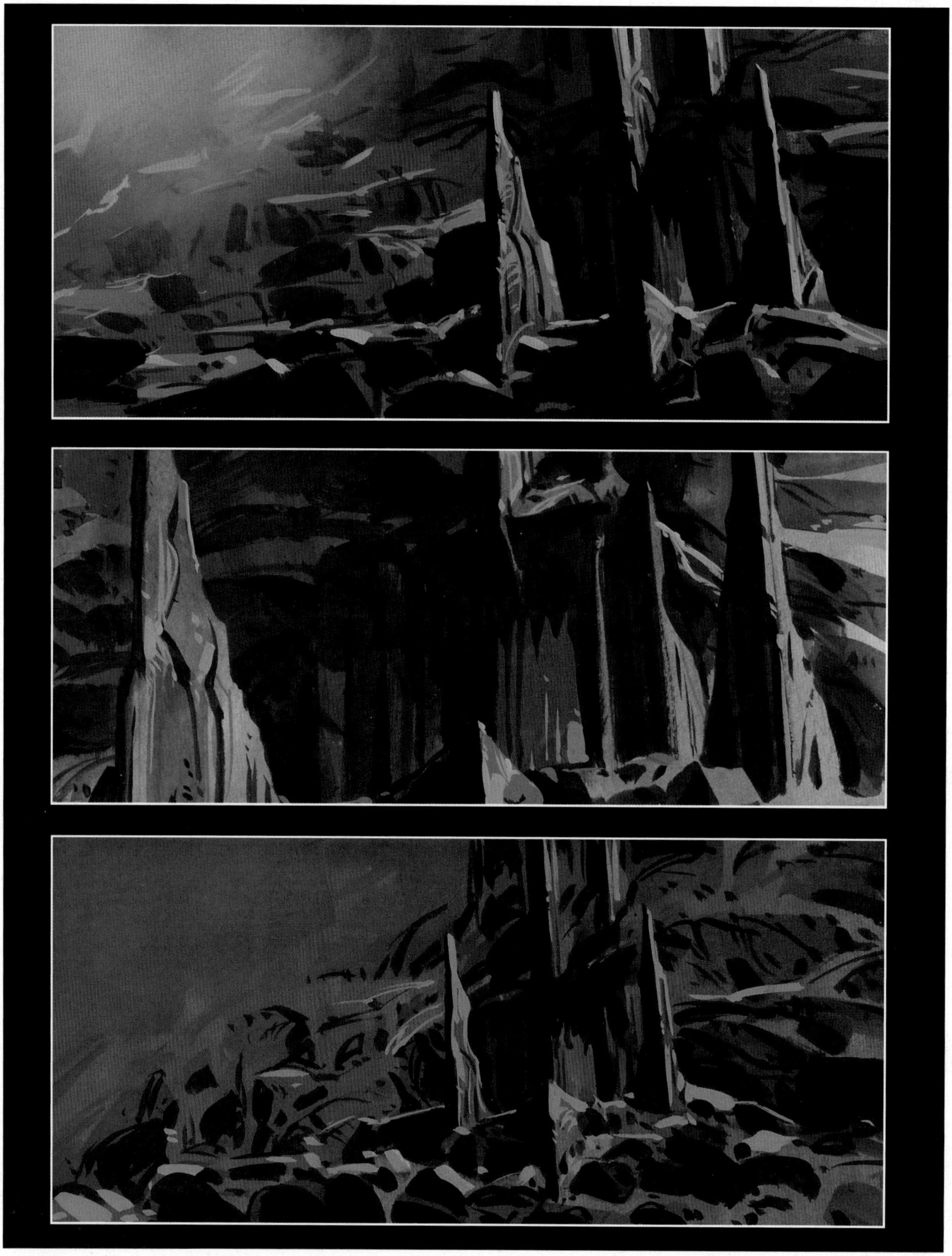

SAMMATH NAUR ***Compositional studies***
"Three studies of Sammath Naur, the entrance on the slopes of Mount Doom that leads to the Crack of Doom, exploring possible compositions for the shot in which the Eye of Sauron strikes out." *JB*

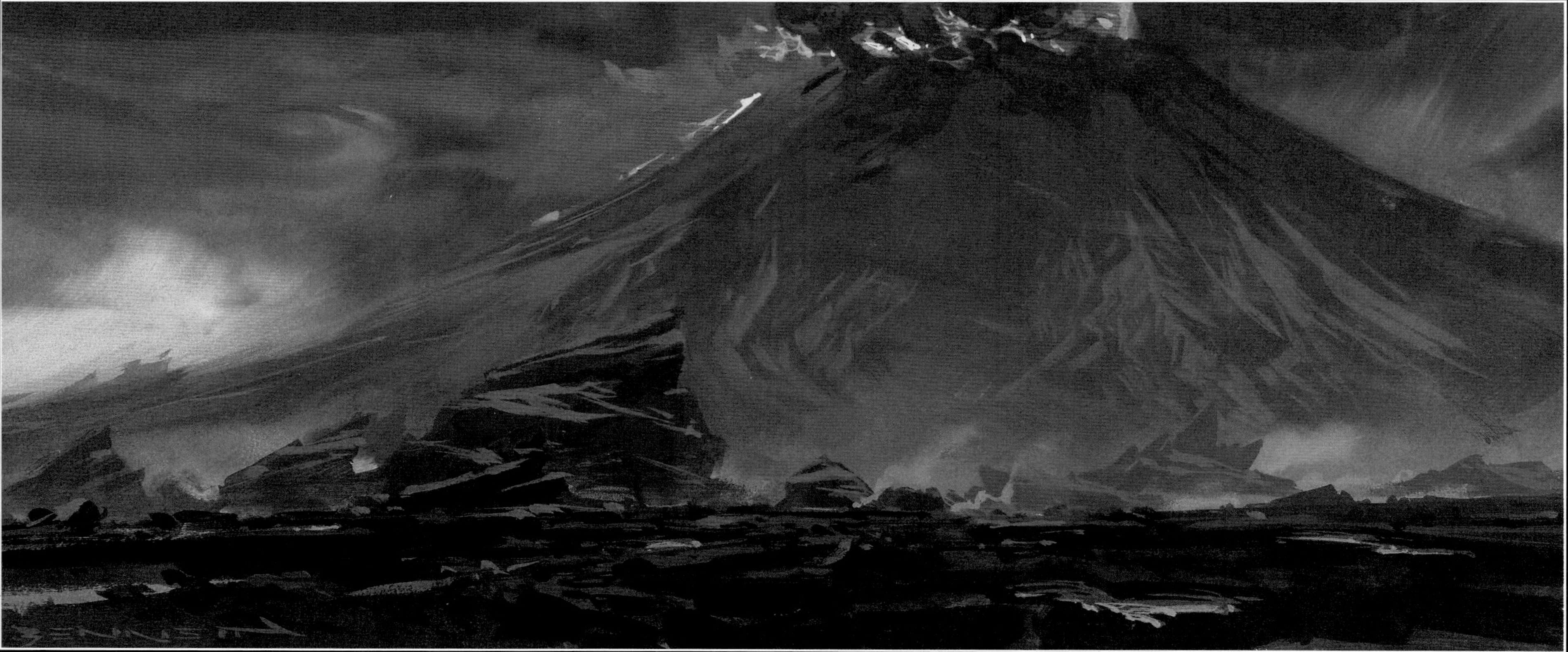

MOUNT DOOM *Color study*
"In this painting, we are looking up at Mount Doom, so the horizon line is quite low. I've introduced some quite large, quite aggressive rock shapes into the environment, with the idea that they look a lot different from the Emyn Muil – you certainly know you are in Mordor. I wanted it to look quite windswept, quite cold, quite dark, and I wanted the palette to be very cool. I've just indicated what I think we should be seeing beyond the horizon line: more rock shapes, which I wanted to push quite far away and haze out with atmosphere, adding some cracks in the ground through which we see the glow of lava." *JB*

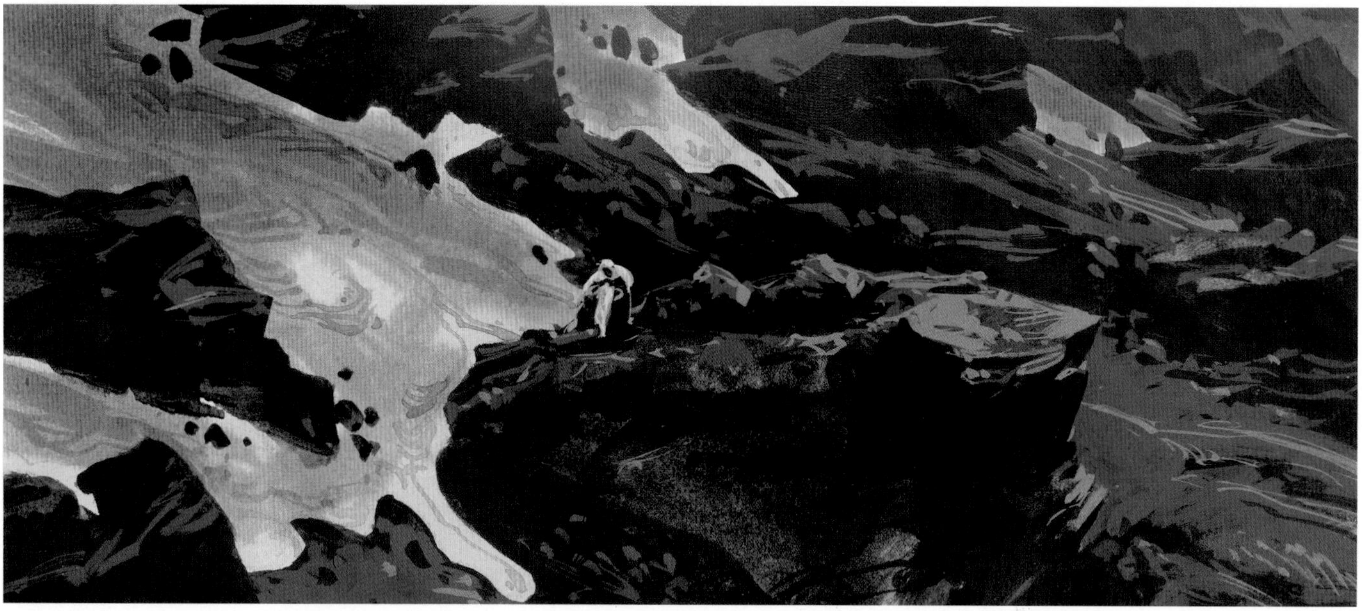

MOUNT DOOM *Color study*
"This sketch shows the lads climbing on the rock after their exit from Sammath Naur, moments before the slope is inundated in lava. This is one of my favorite studies." *JB*

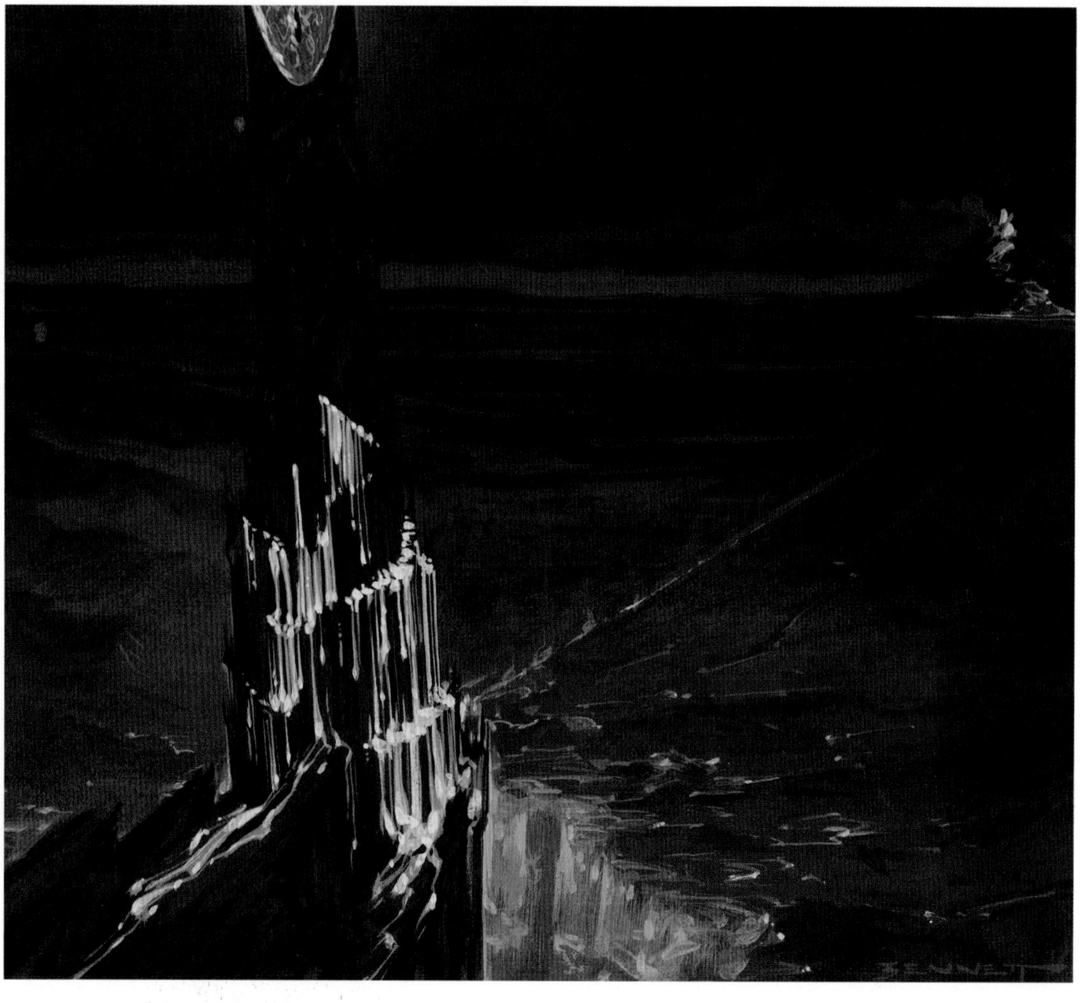

BARAD-DÛR
Color study
"This shows one of the ideas we had as to how we would bring down Barad-dûr, completely destroying it! Just imagine the lava pulse coming from Mount Doom, surging along the canal, and creating a reaction that would push the lava right up into the tower, to the point that it would start overflowing and spilling back down, rather like a candle. An old idea, but we wanted to take a look at it just to see how it might look." *JB*

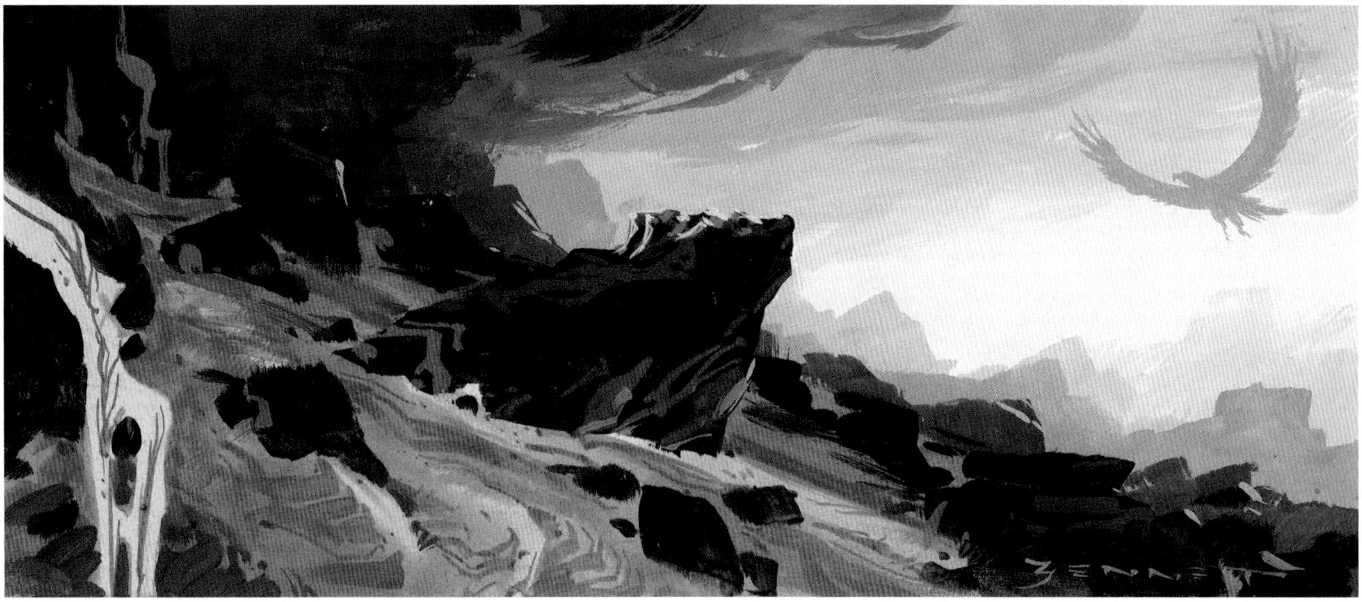

MOUNT DOOM *Color study*
"One of a number of sketches handed to the miniatures department, which was supplying the practical lava for the shots; it was also used as a guide by the compositors who pieced everything together." *JB*

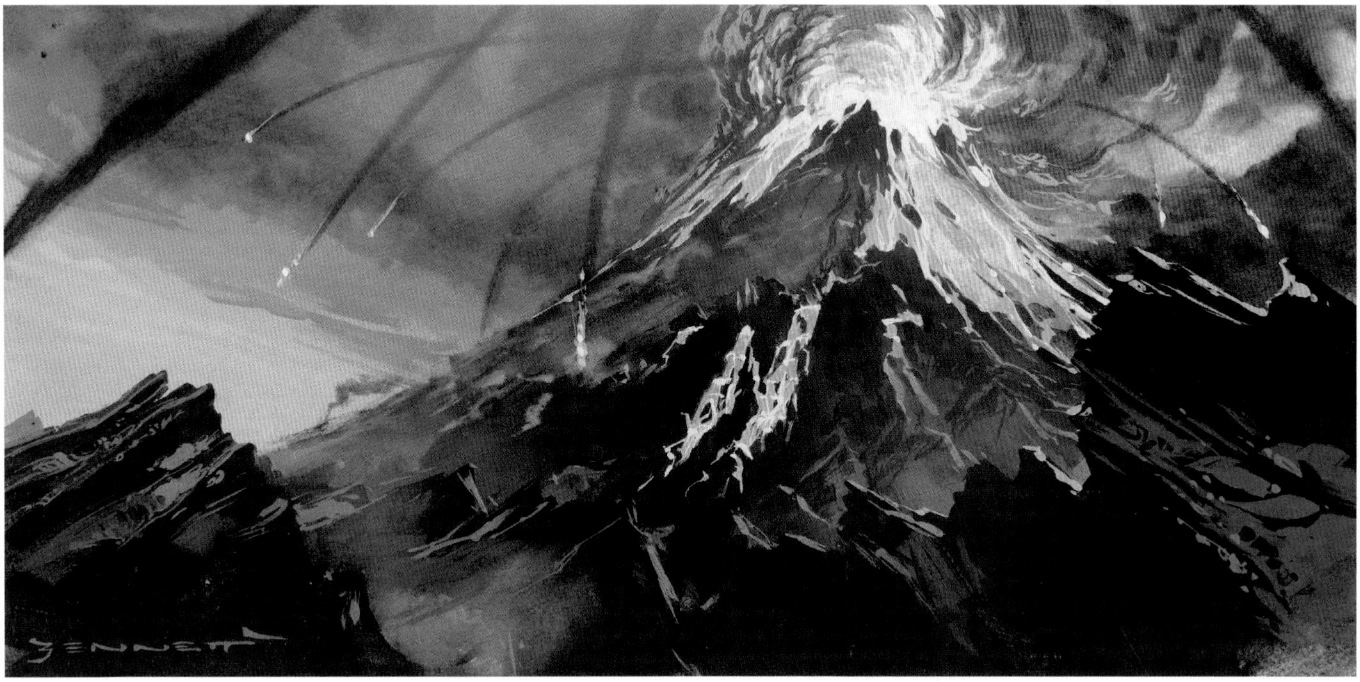

MOUNT DOOM *Color study*
"This study represents the greatest amount of destruction we'll see on Mount Doom. The lads at this stage have nowhere to run and will have to weather the firestorm." *JB*

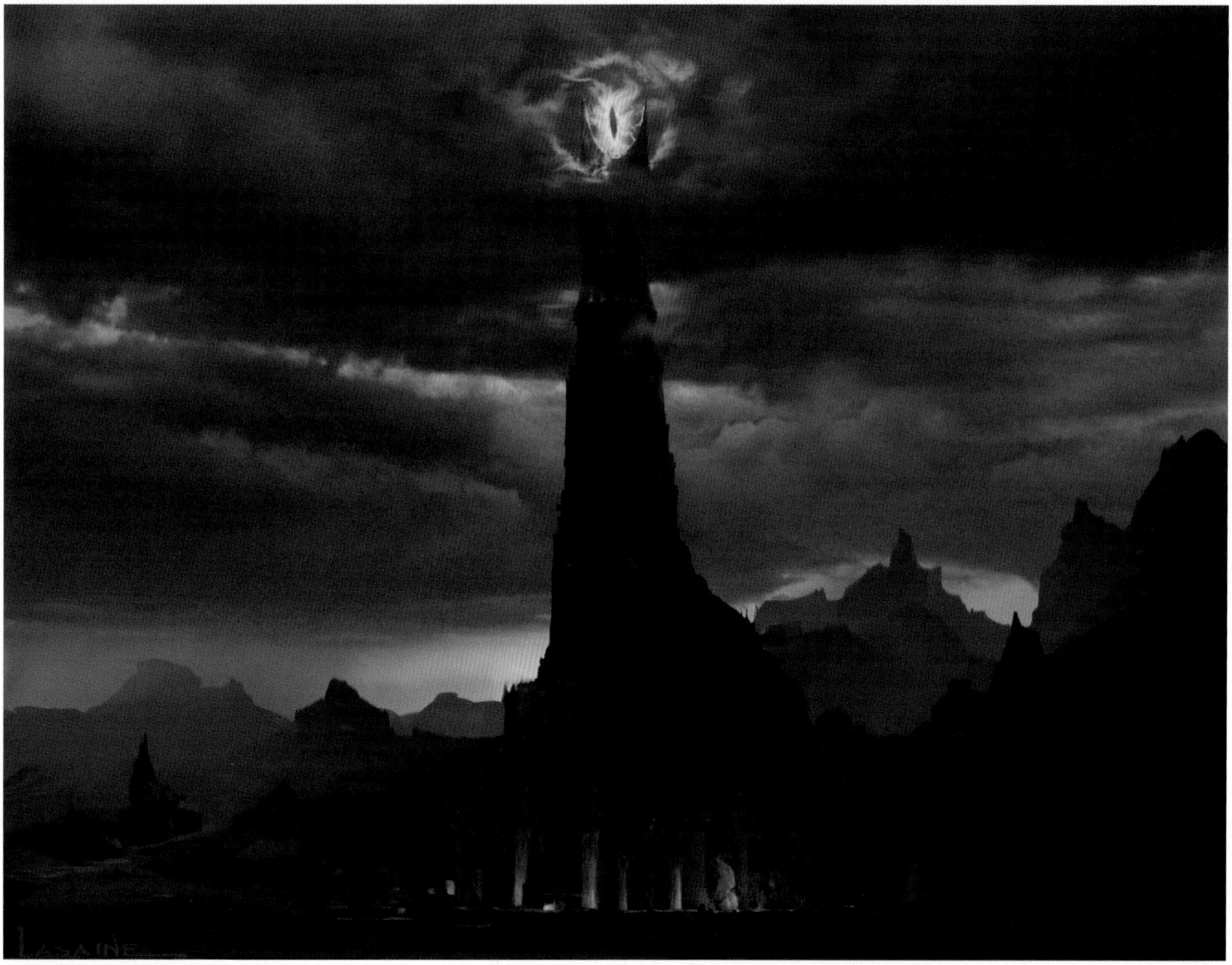

BARAD-DÛR ***Digital composite***
"This is a composite illustration utilizing miniature, photographic, and painted elements. I did this piece to show how the Barad-dûr miniature might work with the surrounding Mordor landscape. One problem we wrestled with was how to depict a three-thousand-foot-high tower when we obviously didn't have a real three-thousand-foot-high tower at our disposal. I liked the idea of emphasizing its height by punching the tower up through the bottom of the clouds." *PL*

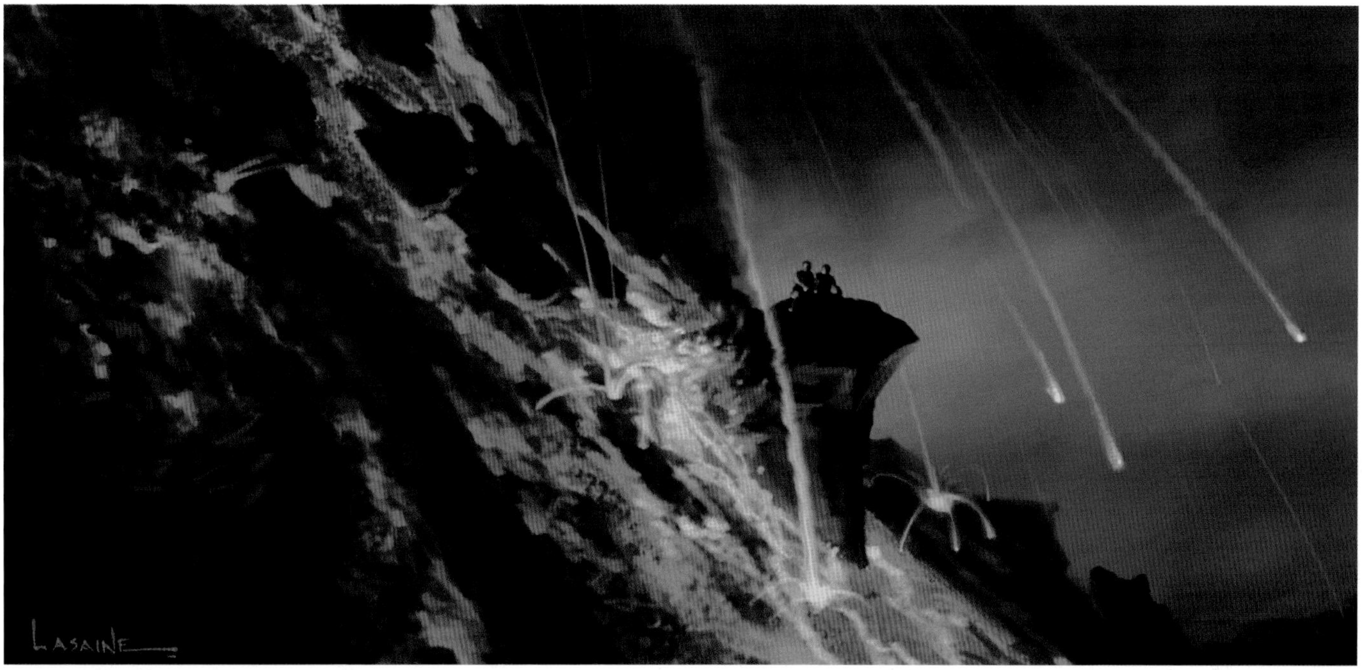

DOOMED ON MOUNT DOOM *Color study*
"This was one of my guilty pleasures, done while we were supposed to be concentrating on finishing the design for *The Fellowship of the Ring*. I just had to do at least one shot from the climax. Kind of like skipping to dessert when you haven't finished dinner yet." *PL*

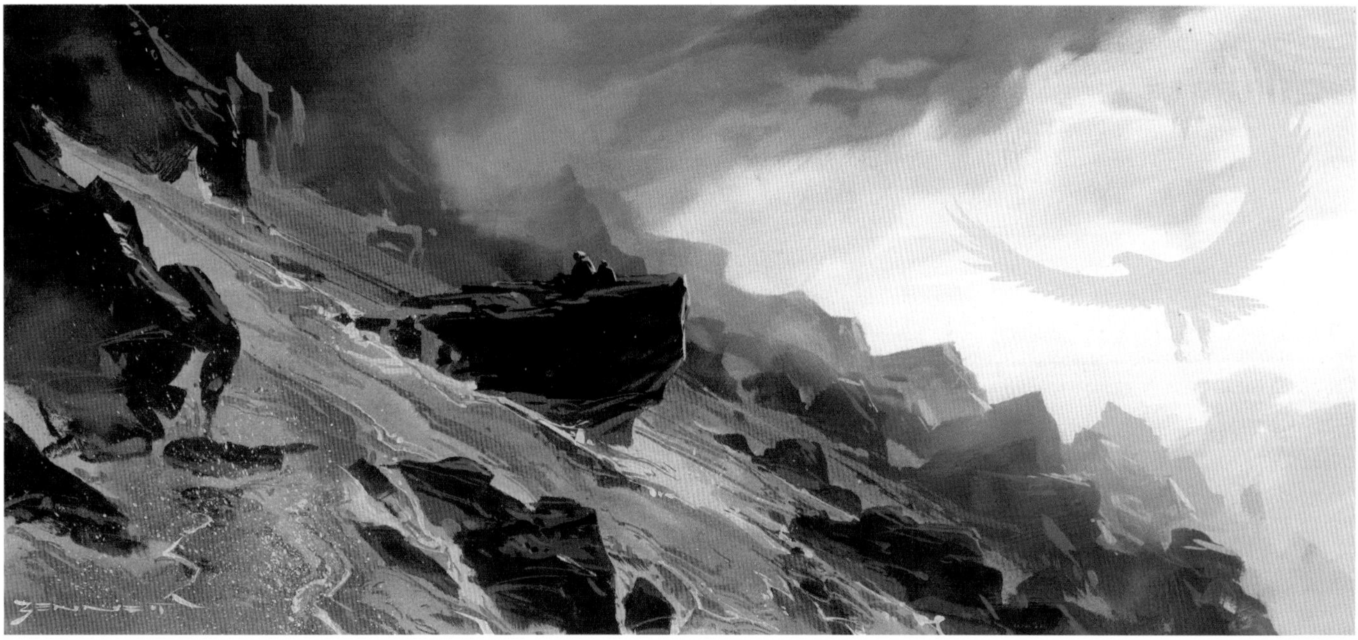

MOUNT DOOM *Color study*
"This is a more developed look at the last shot of the lava-flow sequence, in which Gandalf arrives riding Gwaihir to rescue the Hobbits. It was a study more of the sky and the backlit look of Gwaihir than of the lava. An earlier painting by John Howe was definitely the influence for this piece." *JB*

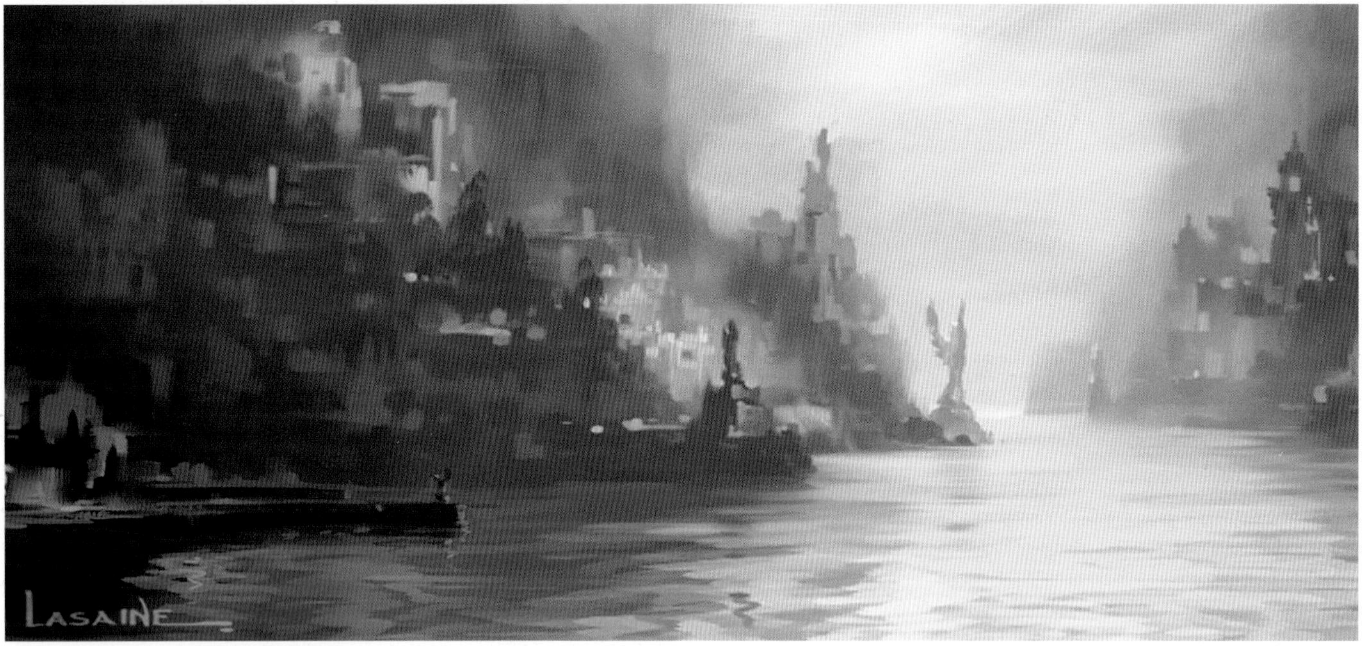

THE GREY HAVENS *Color study*
"This is a very early sketch done primarily as an atmosphere study for the location. When I did it, none of the architecture had been designed, so it was quite abstract. I was inspired by a beautiful location in southern New Zealand called Milford Sound, a fjord with soaring cliffs and breathtaking waterfalls. Here I tried to imagine Milford covered with Elven architecture." *JB*

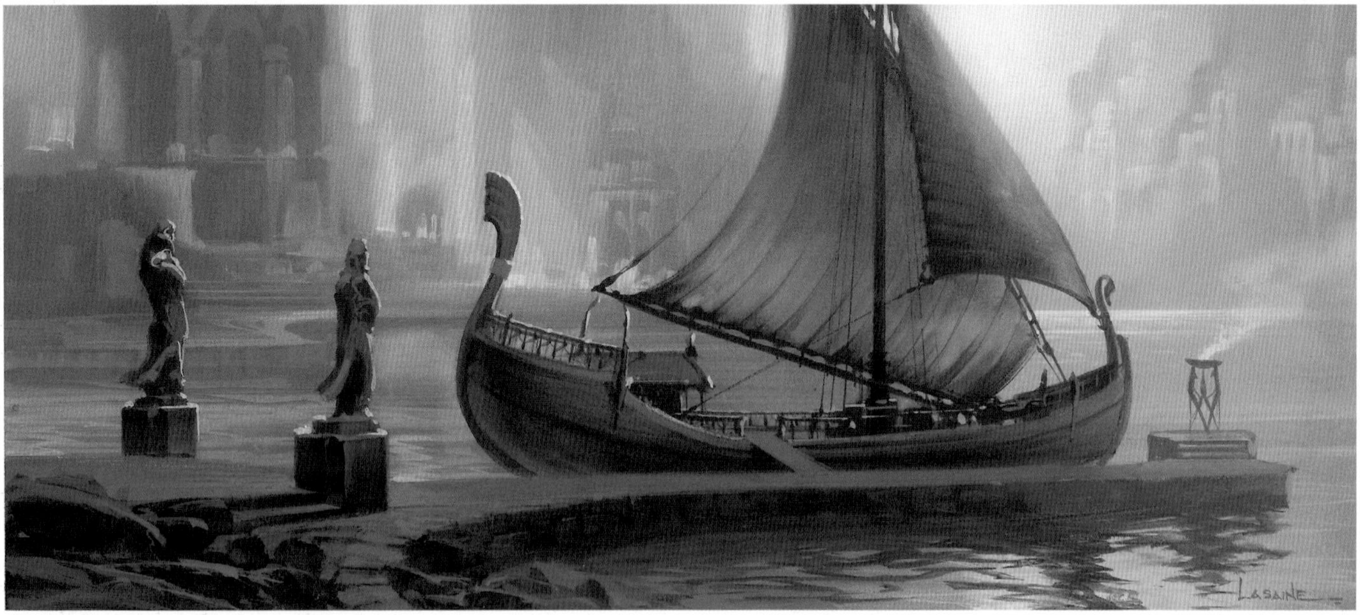

THE GREY HAVENS *Color study*
"This was done to explore what the Elven ship that carries Frodo and crew to the Undying Lands might look like. I was particularly interested in the sail design – in this version I came up with a hybrid between a Mediterranean lateen sail and a Chinese junk." *PL*

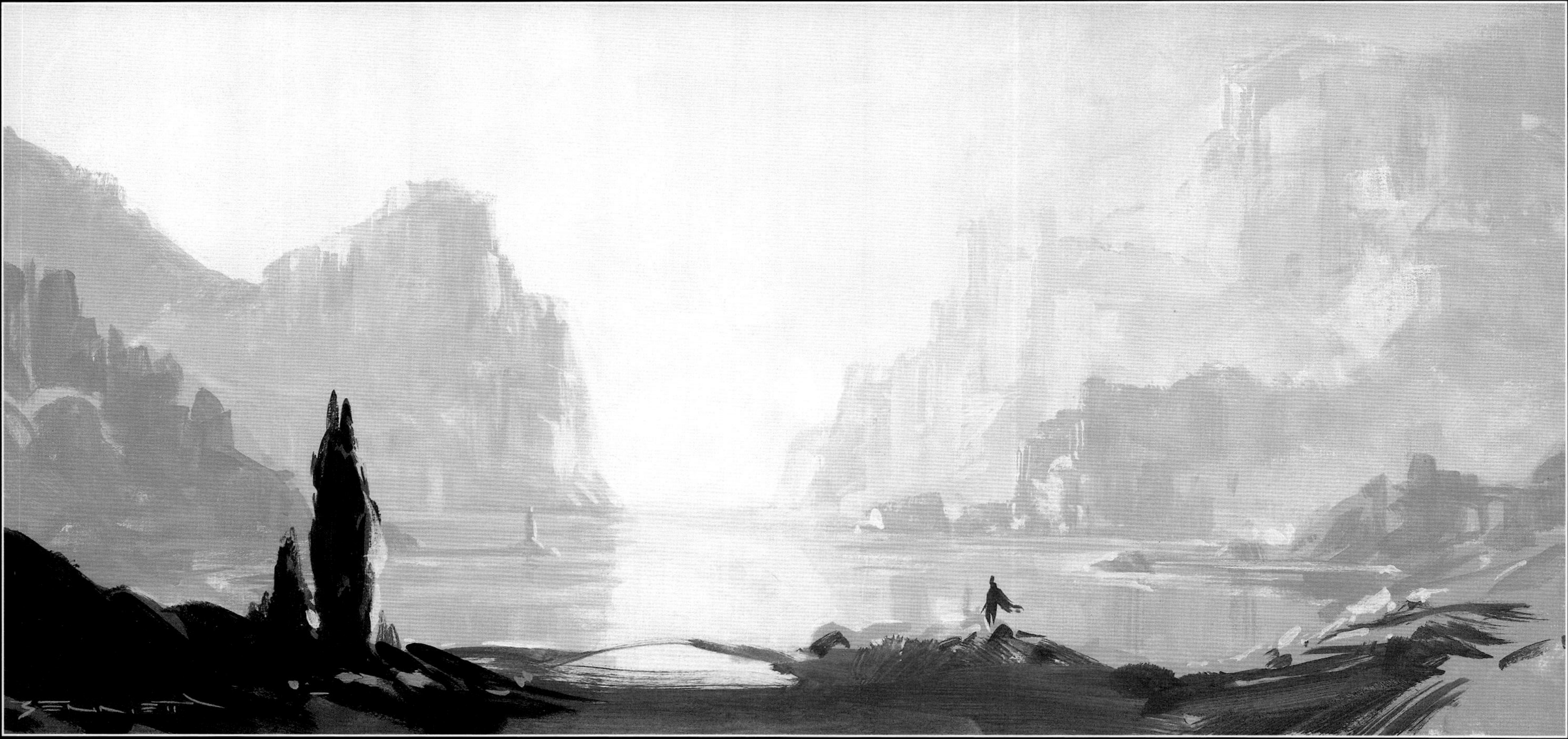

THE GREY HAVENS *Environment study*
"This explores the look of the Grey Havens, and how it should be lit, for the miniatures department. When conceiving the environment we were thinking of J.M.W. Turner, so this is my attempt to capture his masterful quality of light." *JB*

CONCEPTUAL ART: ALAN LEE

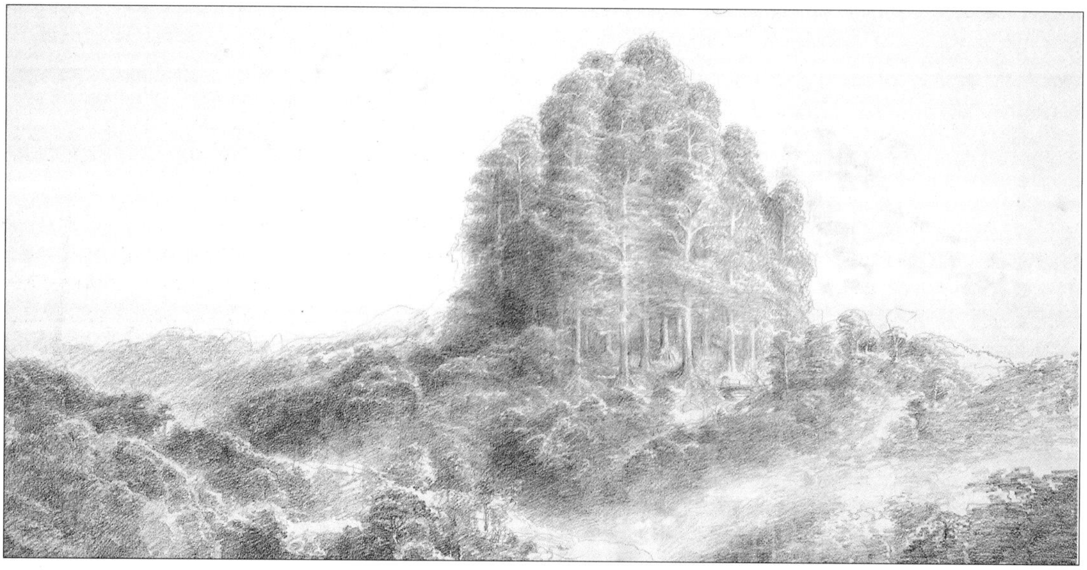

I first read *The Lord of the Rings* when I was seventeen, and it took over my life completely for a period. I didn't do many illustrations based on it until about 1990, when HarperCollins approached me about painting a celebratory edition of the work for the Tolkien centenary. There was a long period of discussion with Tolkien's family. They were concerned in particular about how the Hobbits were going to be depicted, so I did a couple of sketches, and they finally agreed to my illustrating the book. After that I got to do *The Hobbit,* too, and I became officially associated with the whole oeuvre. Despite that, I wouldn't say that I'm a huge fan – I'm not a person who reads it every year. It's obviously been an important part of my life for over a decade, and I feel I know it pretty well now, but I don't actually know the book as well as some of the people at Weta, who are true aficionados.

I think my ideas come mainly from reading the books, but also from having been thoroughly steeped as a child in Norse mythology and other areas from which Tolkien himself had drawn. In some ways, there's only one way that I can draw Orcs and Goblins, and that has to do with my cultural background, stuff that influenced me. So to a certain extent, I just have to trust my intuition, priming it with the text, and having faith that the work that comes out will reflect what other people see in it as well.

Working on the movie happened at the perfect time for me. I didn't have a contract for another book at that point, and I was ready for a change of scene. It probably was the first time in twenty years that I could actually leave Britain for an extended period without having editors screaming at me about deadlines!

I'd always thought that *The Lord of the Rings* had fantastic potential as a live-action film – I was sure it was going to happen at some point. There had been discussions with somebody else about a possible television adaptation, which was very interesting, telling the story over twelve episodes, but, like many other attempts, the ideas failed to materialize.

Part of the attraction of this film was, of course, going to New Zealand. I'd always been curious about the place; the few photographs I'd seen of it greatly impressed me. And I suppose I had this idea of it as a kind of distant version of Britain, only cleaner, with taller mountains and weirder landscapes, almost like Middle-earth!

"Alan Lee's artwork has a beauty and lyricism about it. His art captured what I hoped to capture with the films, which is a sort of graceful and gentle feeling – a poetry, I guess."

PETER JACKSON

When we got here, Weta had started doing some of the creatures. They'd done the Cave-troll, they'd done a lot of work on the Orcs and various other creatures, but they hadn't done any of the places or environments, and that became our job. Though we worked together on some of the designs, John Howe did more work on the creatures and armor. Broadly speaking, I concentrated more on the "wholesome" side of Middle-earth, while John was Sauron's chief architect. There were exceptions, though, with my work on Isengard and Cirith Ungol, and John's beautiful designs for Bag End and the Green Dragon.

Peter wanted grand and original ideas for the films and would often see a potential in our drawings that we hadn't quite grasped ourselves. He wanted the environments to be recognizably part of Tolkien's created world, and as firmly rooted in reality. I don't think that any of us ever felt we were working on a fantasy film. We were trying to create cultures and landscapes that were part of a conjectural history of our world, and everything in it had to be credible.

We tried to anticipate the kind of dramatic camera moves that are part of Peter's trademark. The sets and miniatures are never simply backgrounds. They form an integral part of the action and are another medium for Peter's amazing storytelling.

Alan Lee
June 2004

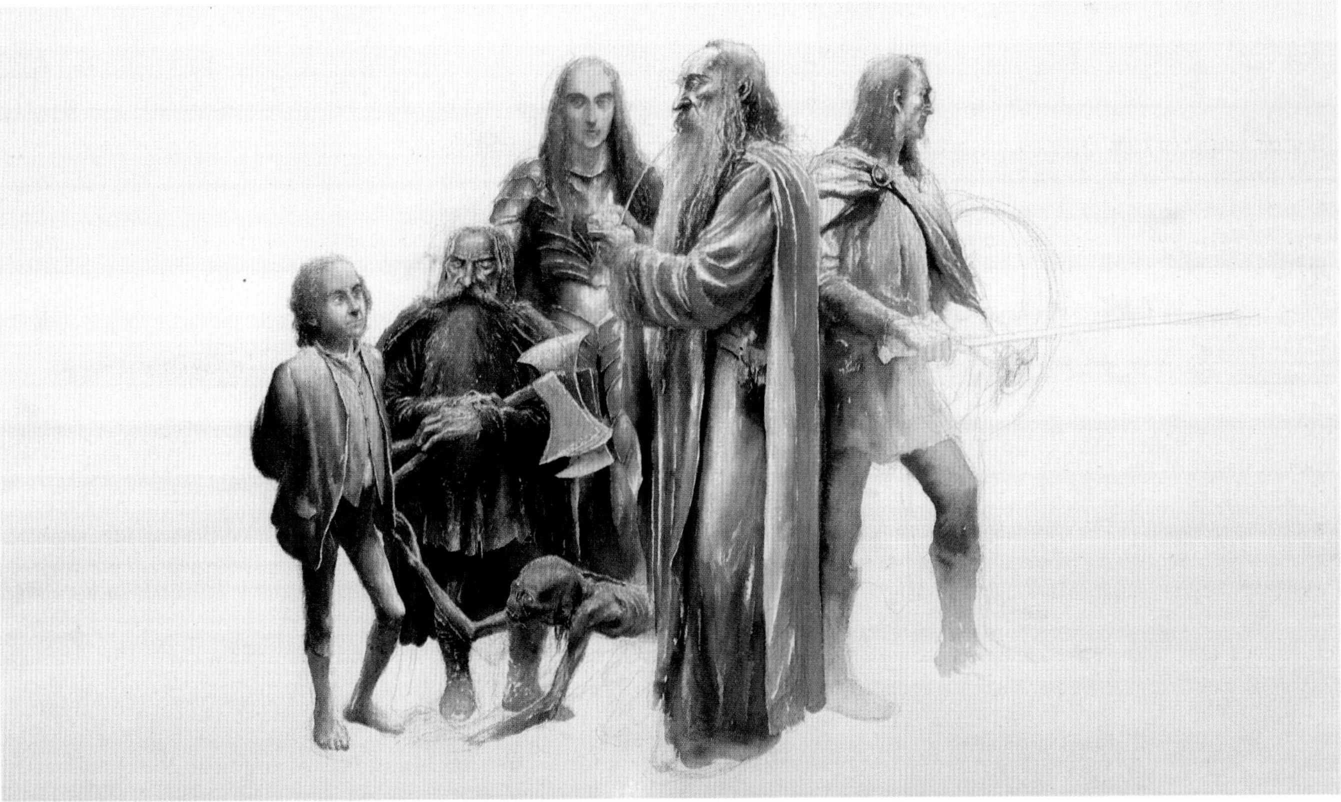

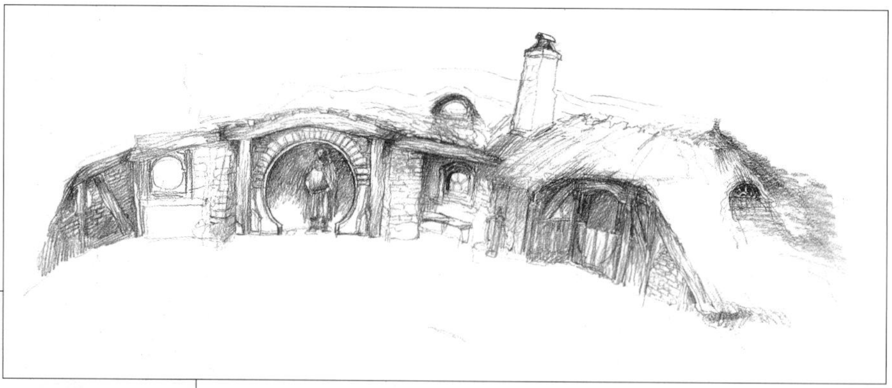

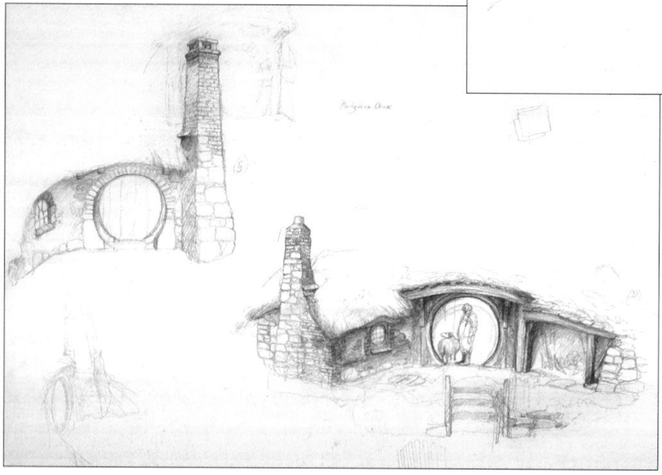

HOBBITON *Hobbit holes*
"I did about twenty-five different Hobbit dwellings to go into specific spots in the location we had chosen for Hobbiton. Apart from their round doors and windows – and the fact that they are half buried underground – the houses have the look of English vernacular architecture from different periods, suggesting that the area had been inhabited for several hundred years. I don't think any of us wanted to create startlingly new concepts for the look of Hobbiton. We wanted people who see the film to feel that they recognize it, that they really are in Middle-earth." *AL*

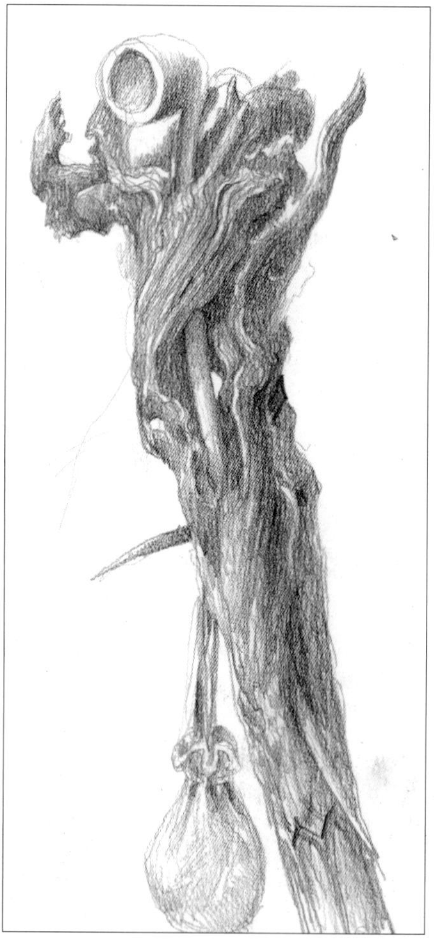

GANDALF
Staff design
"The first of Gandalf's three staffs was as versatile as the others. As well as a walking aid and a weapon, it would be a place for him to stow his pipe when he wasn't using it. It also featured a tobacco pouch, and a metal spike that could be used for cleaning the pipe, getting stones out of horses' hooves, or scratching secret signs on Hobbit doors." *AL*

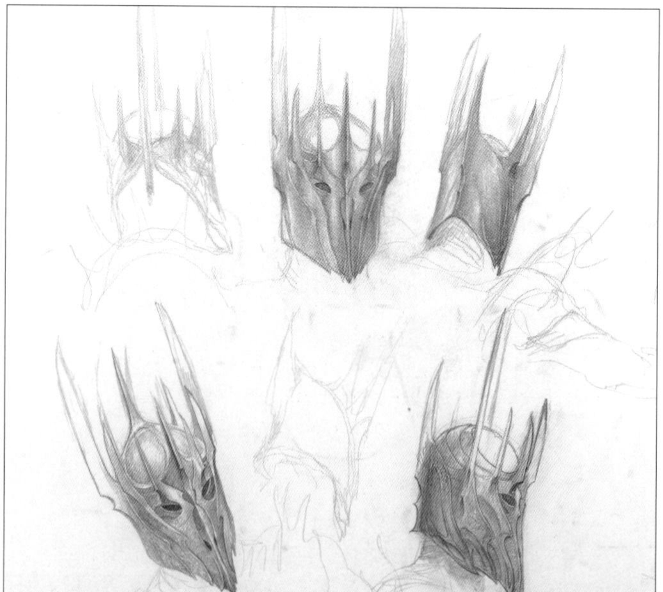

SAURON *Helmet designs*
"Sauron's suit of armor was one of the most remarkable objects that Weta produced during their work on *The Lord of the Rings*. Every inch of its etched surface was endlessly worked to create shapes that echoed the form and personality of the character within. It really looked as though it had been made by Elves who had been enslaved and tortured expressly for the purpose. I contributed these designs for the helmet, though they were taken a lot further by Peter Lyons, Warren Green, and Stu Johnson, Weta's brilliant armorers." *AL*

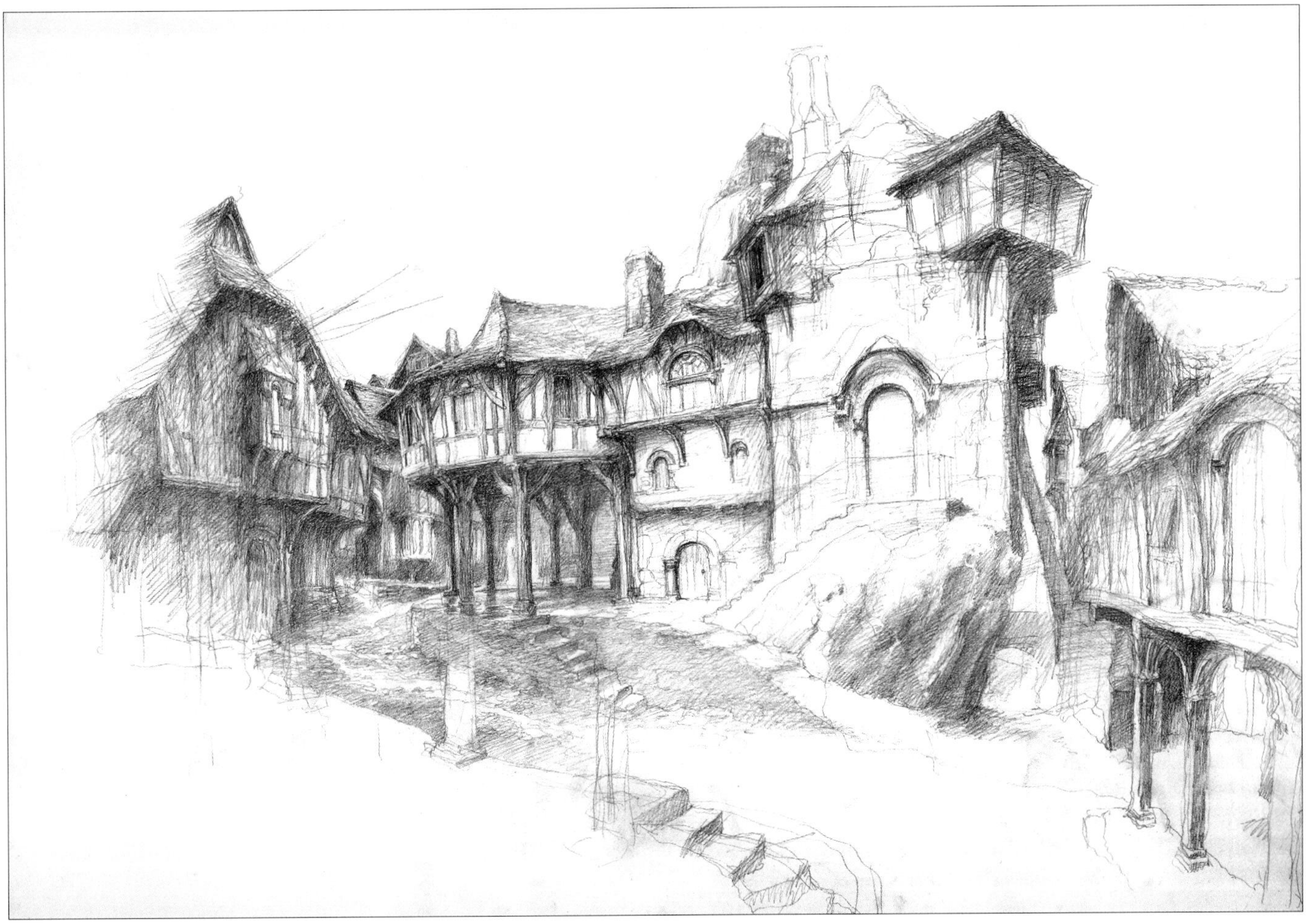

BREE *Town Square*
"This drawing was done after visiting the disused army barracks that we were going to turn into our set for the streets leading to the Prancing Pony in Bree. The barracks and administration offices were concealed behind these medieval facades, and the streets were covered by about eighteen inches of mud and gravel. I'd taken photographs of half-timbered houses in Devon when I was last there, and they served as models for the warped and crooked buildings." *AL*

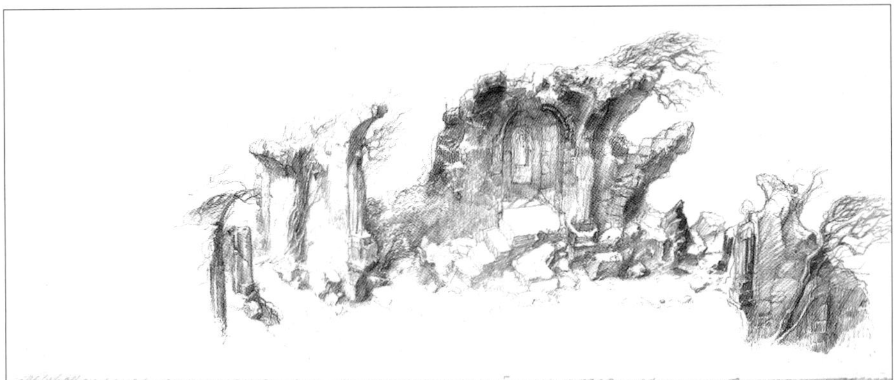

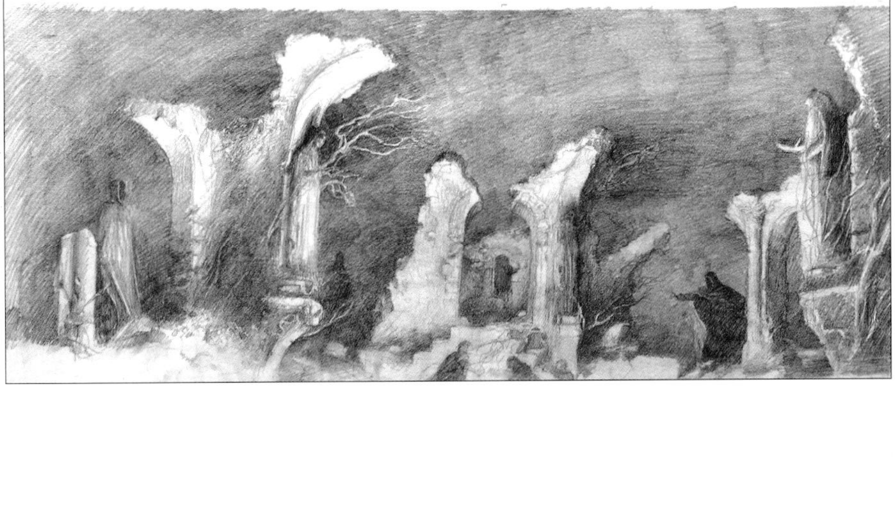

WEATHERTOP *The architecture*
"These pencil sketches show alternate day and night looks for the place, with the ruins of the Amon Sûl tower creating a distinctive silhouette and defining the environment in which the Ringwraiths will attack the Hobbits." *AL*

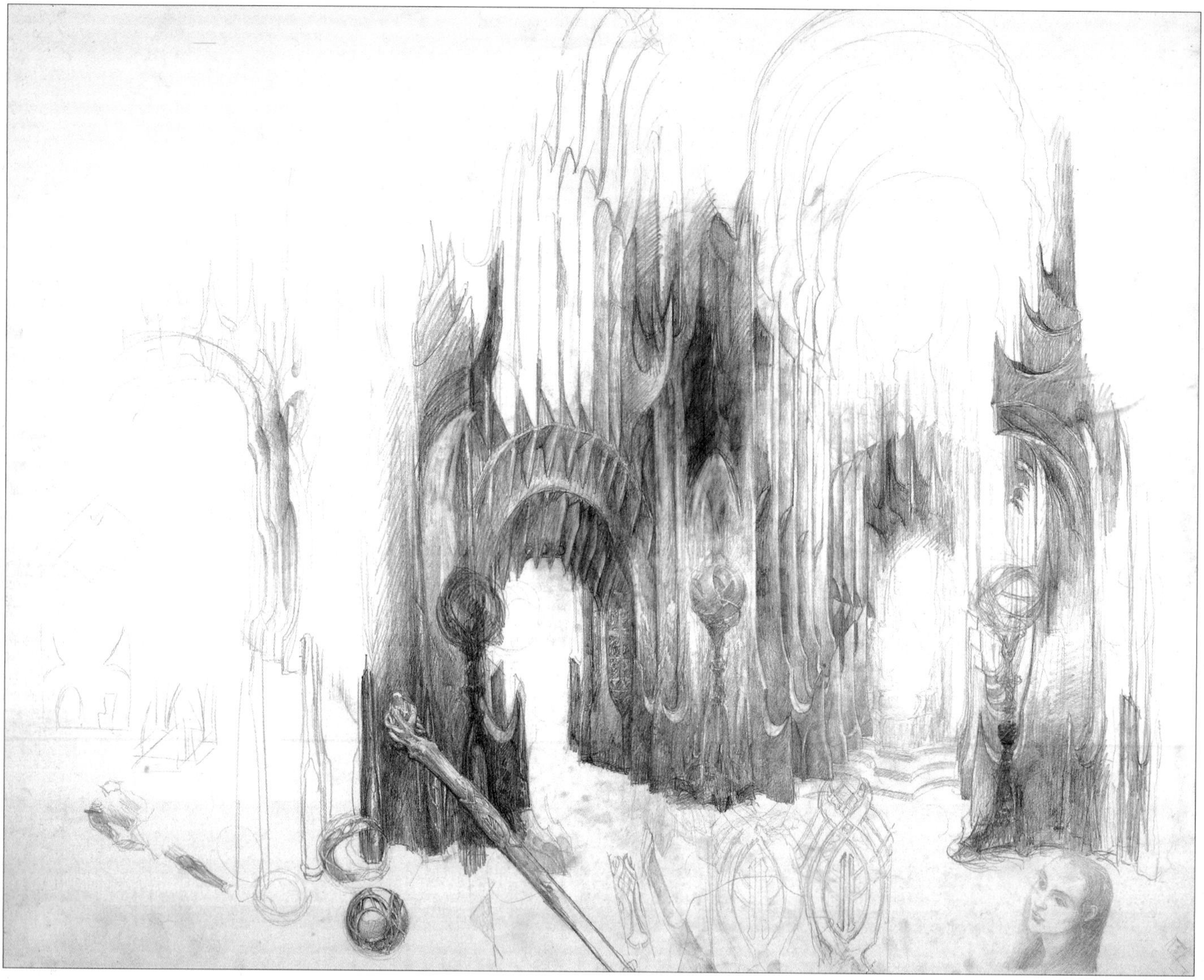

ISENGARD *Inside Orthanc Tower*
"This drawing is getting close to the look of the finished set. It was built up to about seven meters, and the rest of the interior was modeled digitally. This also shows the lamps that were made by Natalie Staniforth, a talented sculptor who came out from England to work on the project. There are some other things going on in this drawing, too: an Elf, some doodles, and Gandalf's staff. Someone may have just reminded me that we needed three different staffs for Gandalf. He loses his first one in Orthanc and the second in Moria. We looked for some pieces of wood that had the right knotted-root look, but then I drew something and it was sculpted by Brigitte Wuest – another brilliant sculptor." *AL*

ISENGARD *The Caverns*
"The drawing opposite is for the Isengard Caverns, where the Orcs are working to arm and equip an army of Uruk-hai, who have been specially created to serve Saruman. This area is briefly alluded to in the books, but Peter Jackson and Richard Taylor saw the potential for creating some stunning and dramatic set pieces. Both John Howe and I did drawings of the pits and machinery, and I made a maquette of the caverns, which served as a starting point for the miniature. The size and complexity of the miniature grew as Peter started to work out what he wanted to do with it, and I'm still trying to figure out how Alex Funke filmed some of those awe-inspiring shots." *AL*

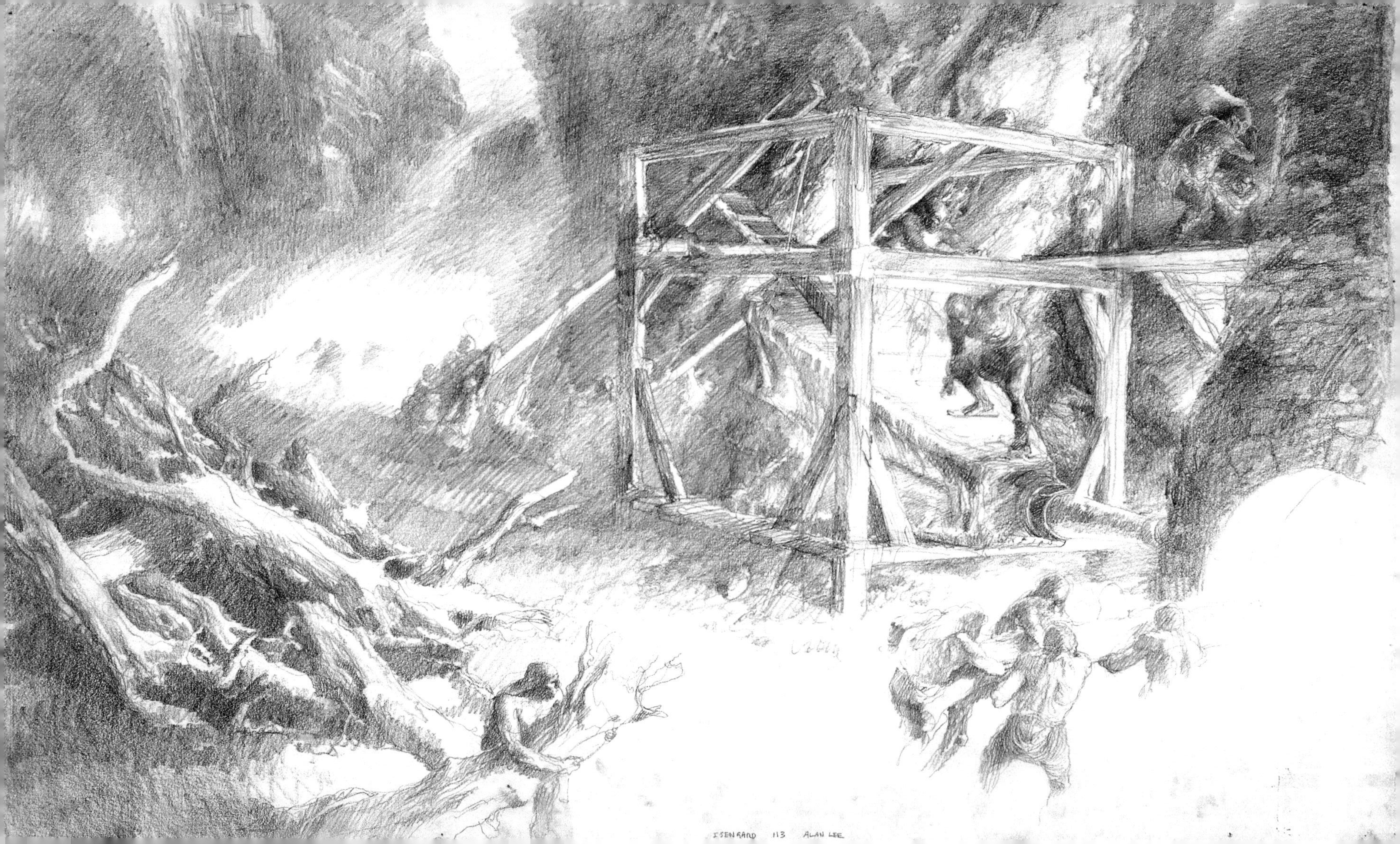
ISENGARD 113 ALAN LEE

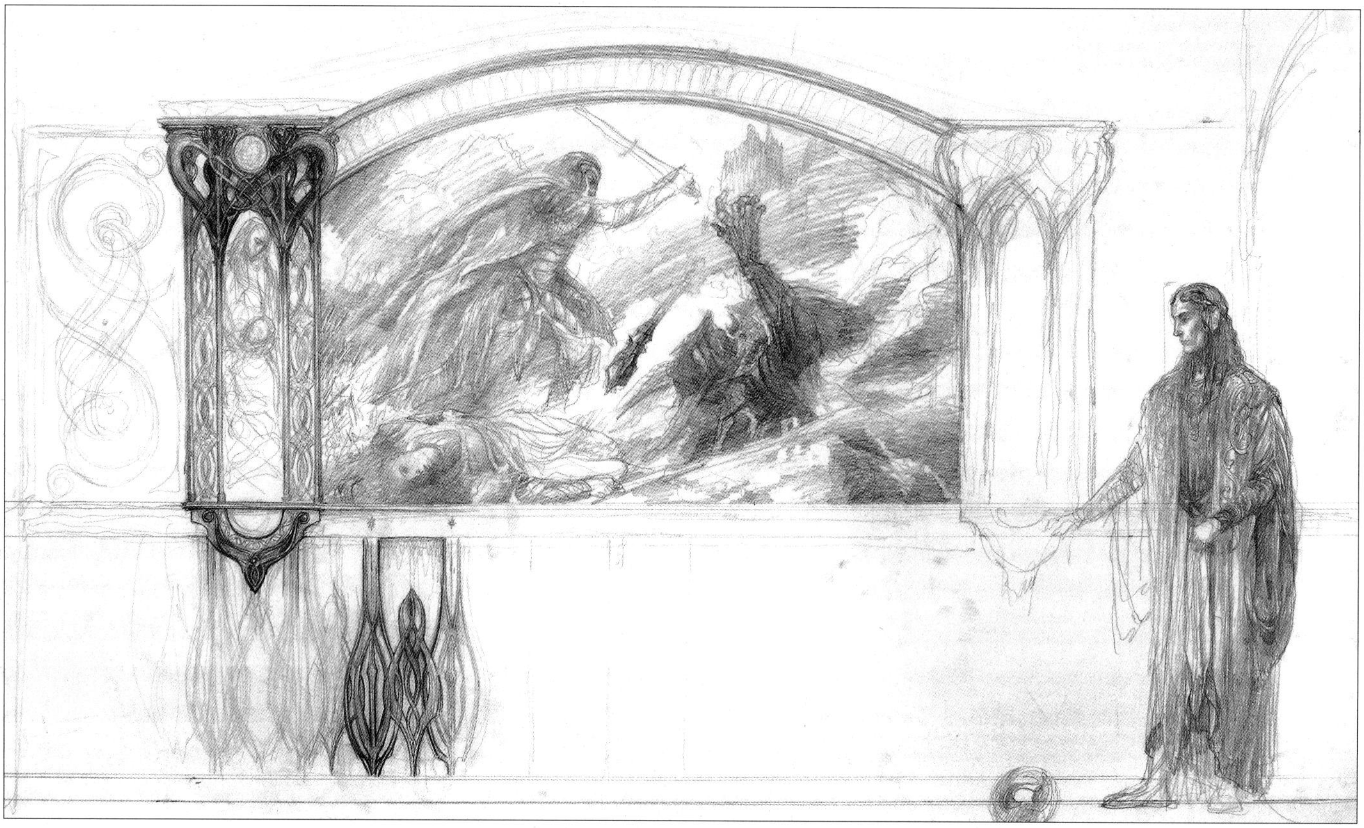

RIVENDELL *Elrond's Chamber*
"The script referred to murals or tapestries that could be used to illustrate important moments in the history of Middle-earth and, in particular, the battle of the Last Alliance and the defeat of Sauron. Rivendell, as well as being the home of the Elves, was a repository for ancient books and artifacts, including Isildur's broken sword, Narsil. Peter Jackson wanted a pictorial device to link the sword with the events we see in the prologue to *The Fellowship of the Ring*. I did this drawing before the battle scenes had been shot and changed the composition in the final painting to match them more closely." *AL*

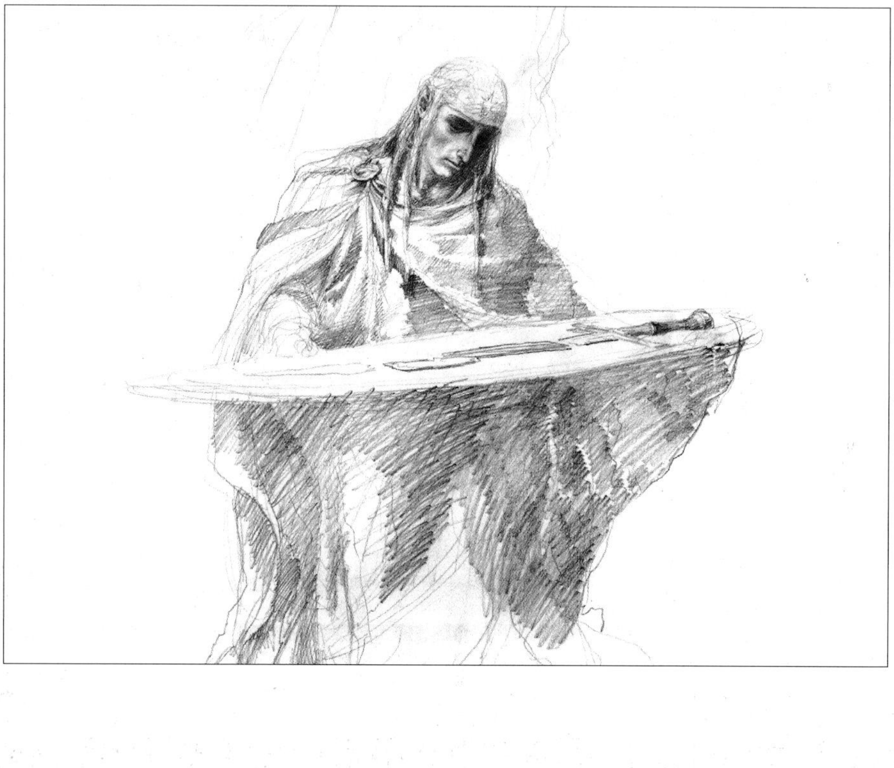

RIVENDELL *Narsil statue*
"We could have simply laid out the shards of Narsil on a tabletop, but this pietà-like statue seemed more appropriate, given the important symbolic value of the sword. Brigitte Wuest, the sculptor, did a beautiful job of turning foam and plaster into ancient and venerated wood." *AL*

RIVENDELL *Watercolor*
"This is an early conceptual illustration for Rivendell and its immediate environment. This was done before we had sculpted and scanned our ideal Rivendell valley, and long before we found the real valley that was used to create backgrounds for the final shots." *AL*

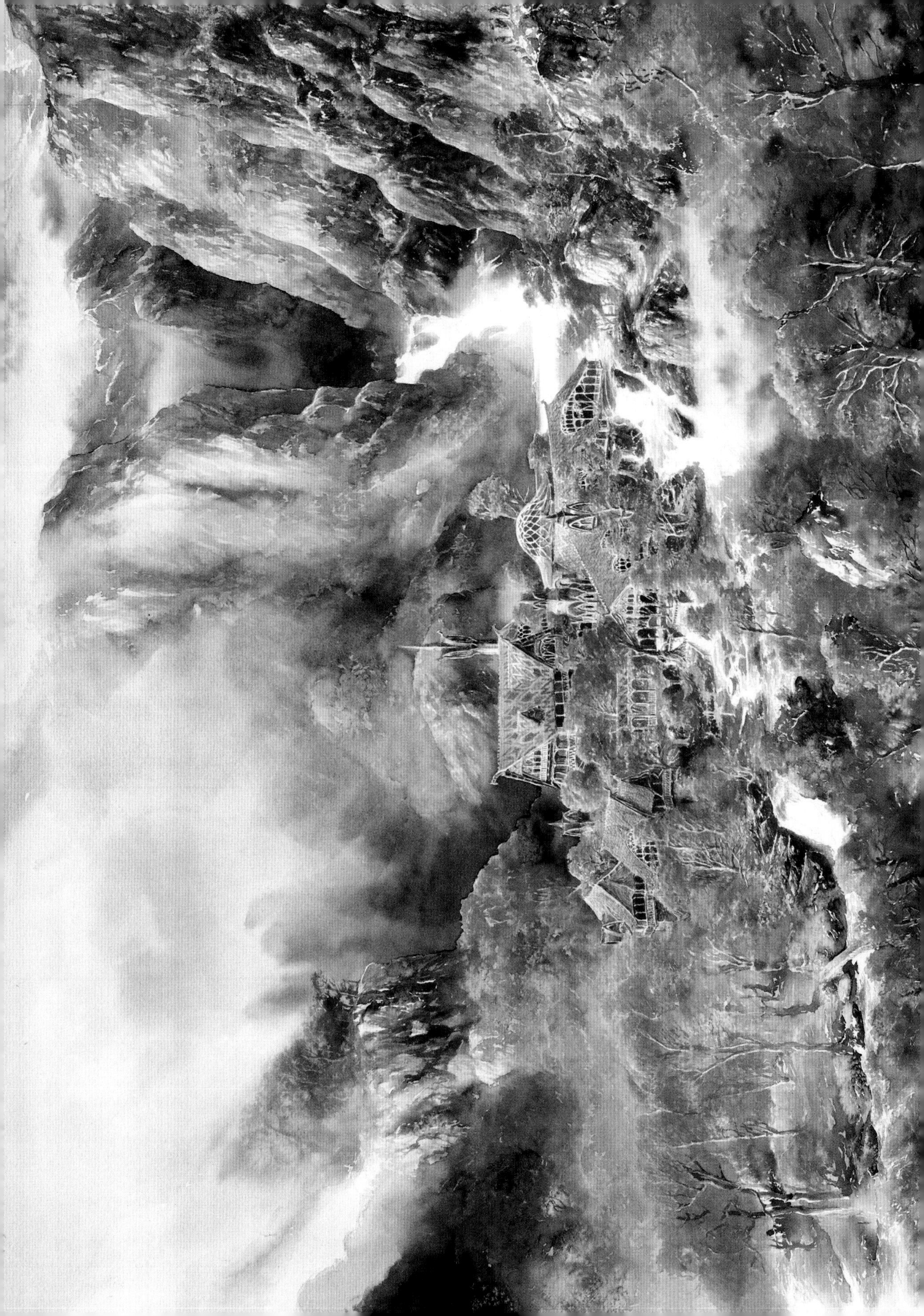

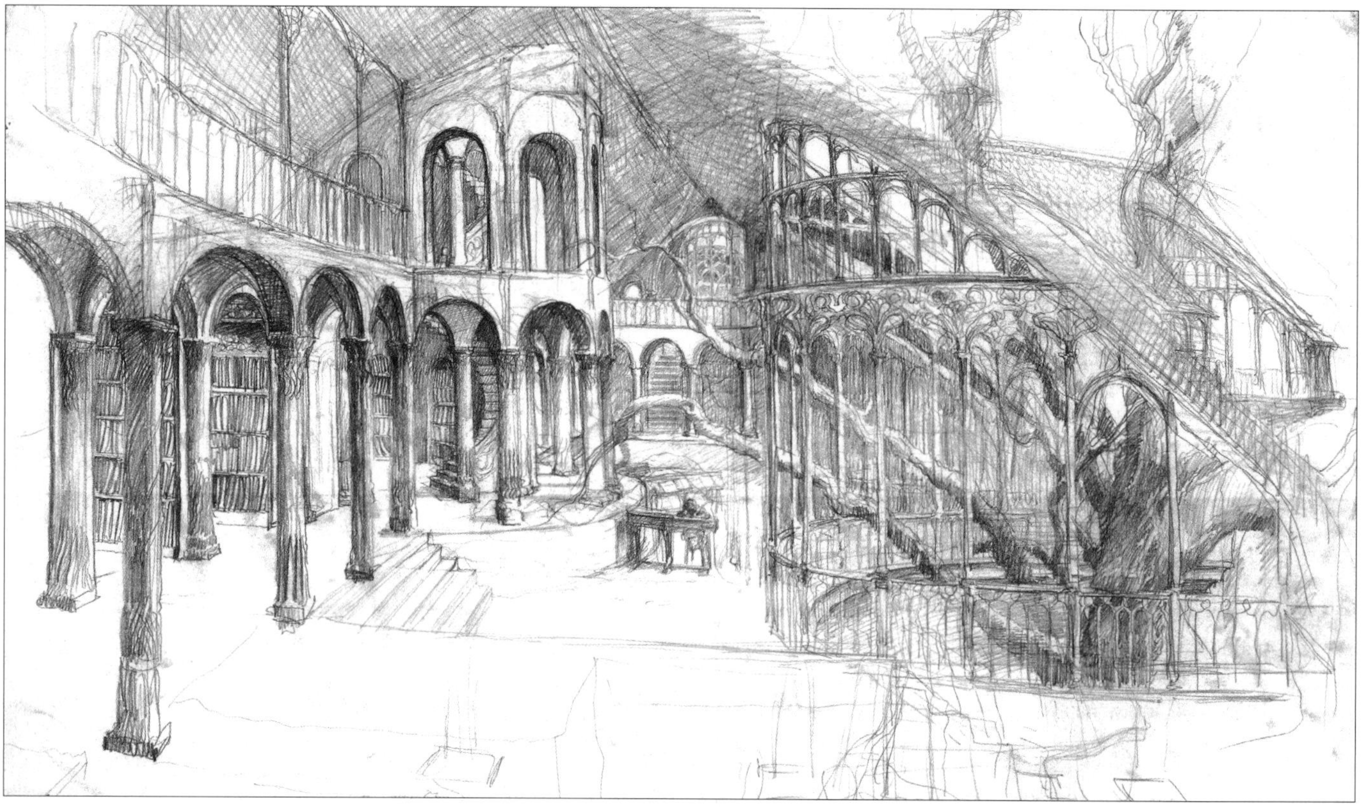

RIVENDELL *The library*
"The scene in which Bilbo is showing Frodo his book was originally going to take place in a library, but this would have been a large set just for one small scene. It was eventually shot on a porch, which was part of our large exterior set, but we used the layout of this drawing as a basis for Elrond's Chamber, which also incorporated the Council Chamber." *AL*

RIVENDELL *Council Chamber*
"The Council of Elrond scene occupies quite a few pages in the script, and Peter Jackson was keen to get as much depth and variety as possible into the background of what, for much of the time, is a series of talking-heads shots. We achieved this by combining it with the Elrond's Chamber set and a large woodland/garden area. This was used for a variety of scenes, including the reforging of Narsil. This drawing is a view from the garden, across the terrace where the Council is held, and into the interior of Elrond's building." *AL*

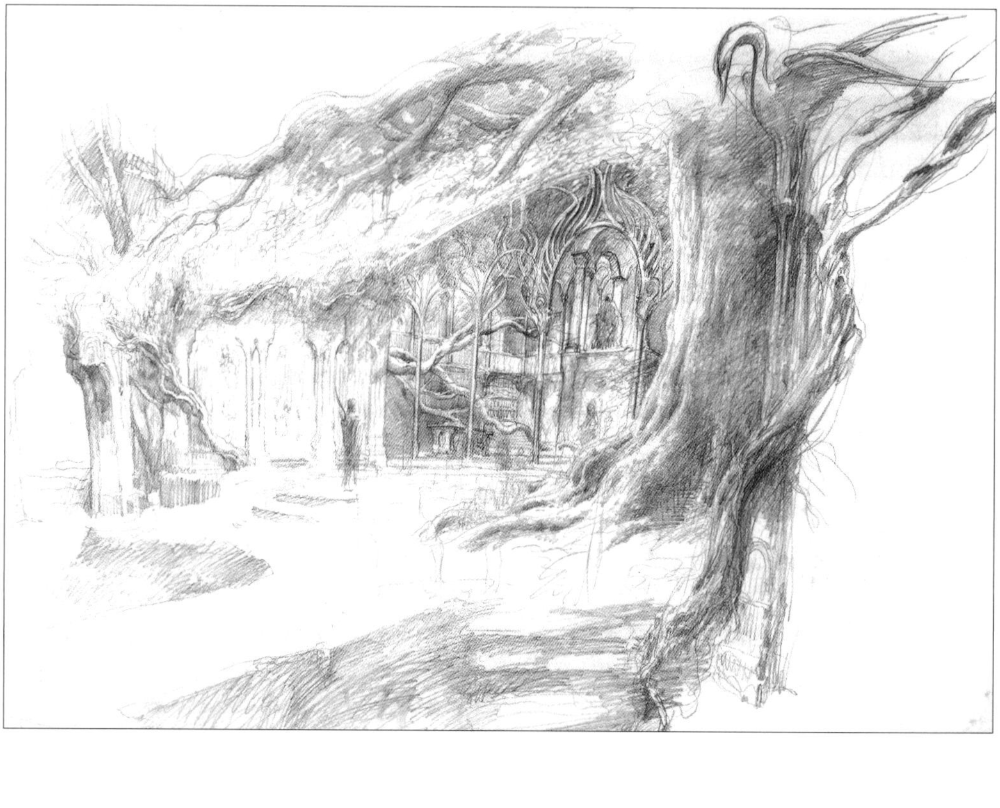

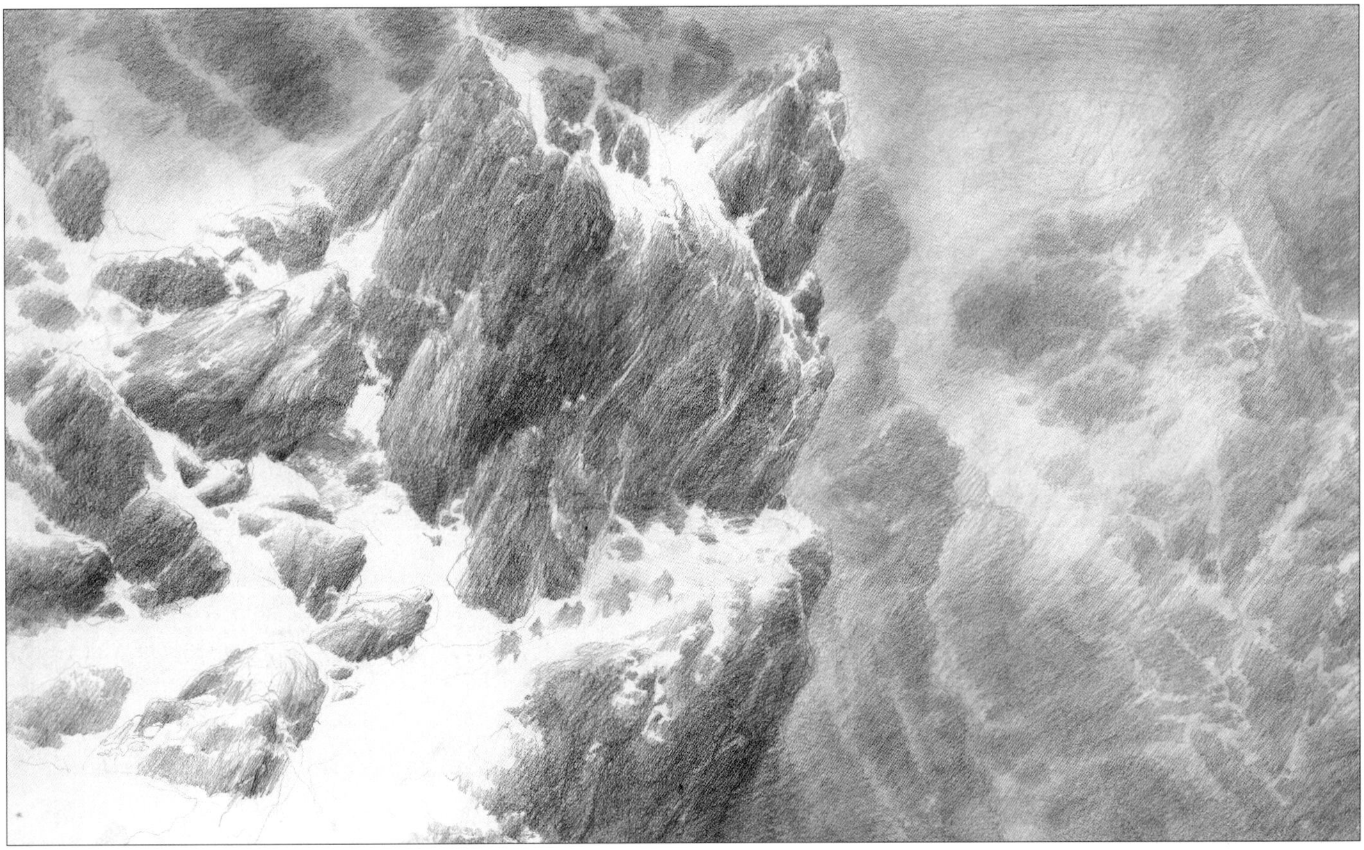

THE MISTY MOUNTAINS *The Pass of Caradhras*
"This was the first drawing I'd done of the narrow and dangerous route over the Misty Mountains, and it was a starting point for the construction of the miniature." *AL*

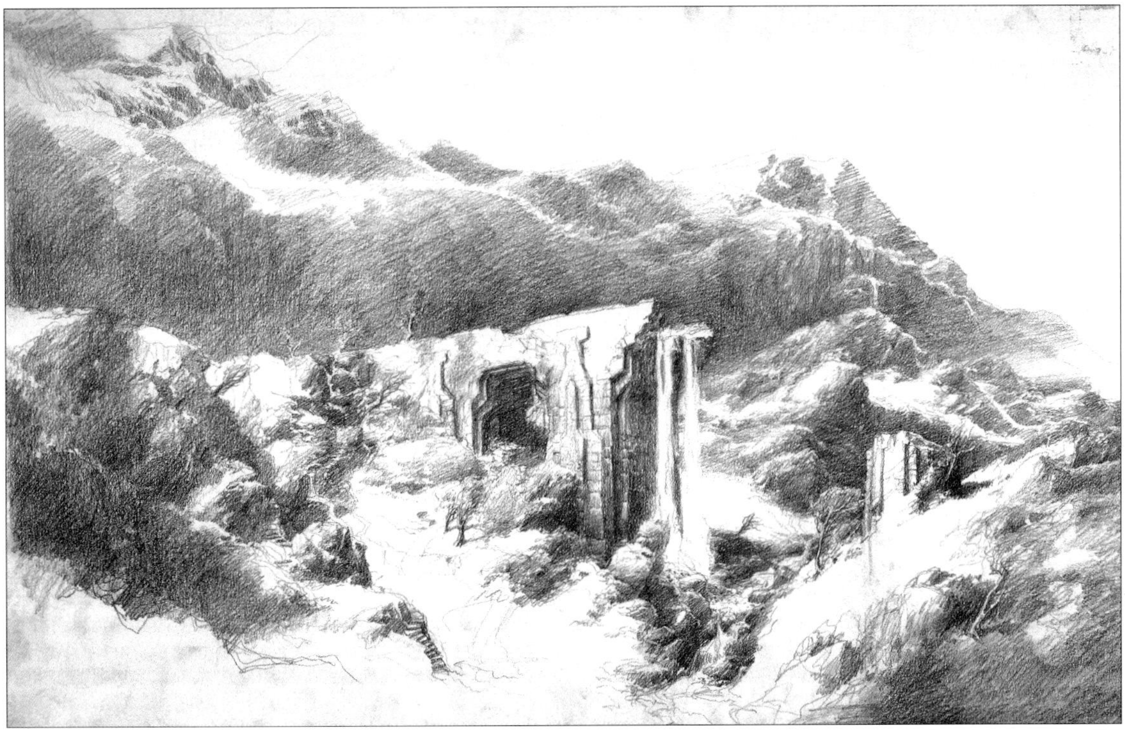

MORIA ***Exterior pencil sketch***
"The drawing to the left was used to create the miniature for the outside of Moria. There's a shot almost identical to this sketch in the final movie. It is always satisfying to know you got something pretty much right the first time." *AL*

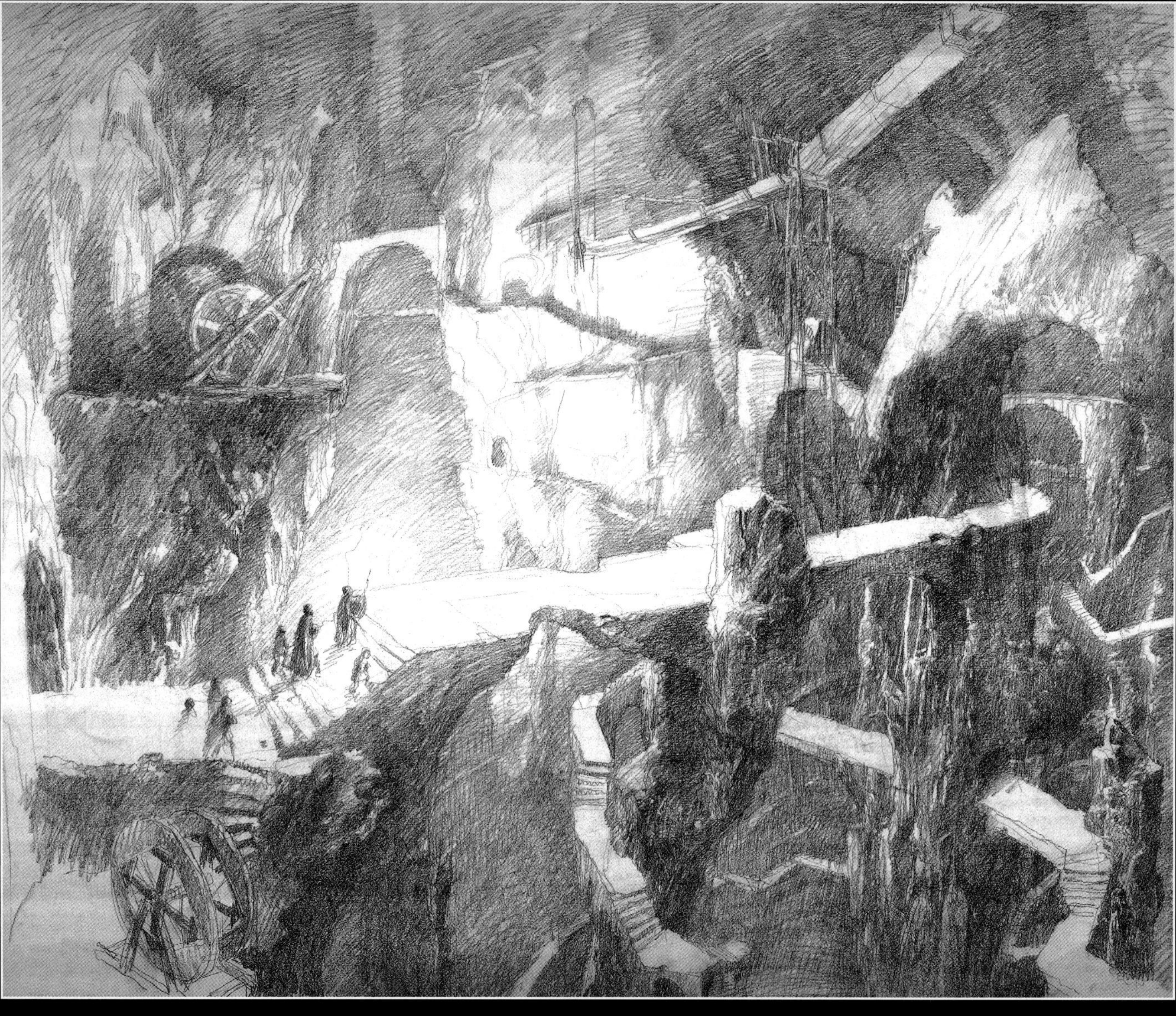

MORIA *Mine workings*
"One of my favorite drawings of the interior of Moria. This was created as a miniature and used in the shots of the Fellowship approaching the cemetery stairs." *AL*

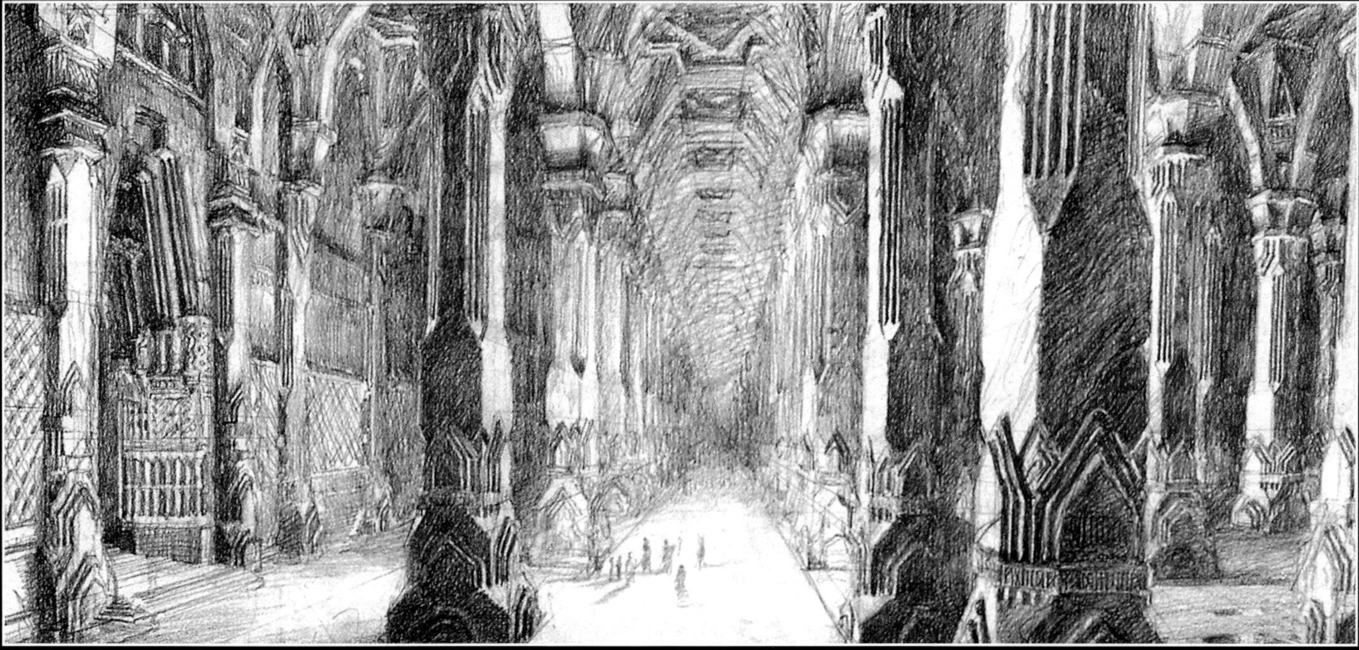

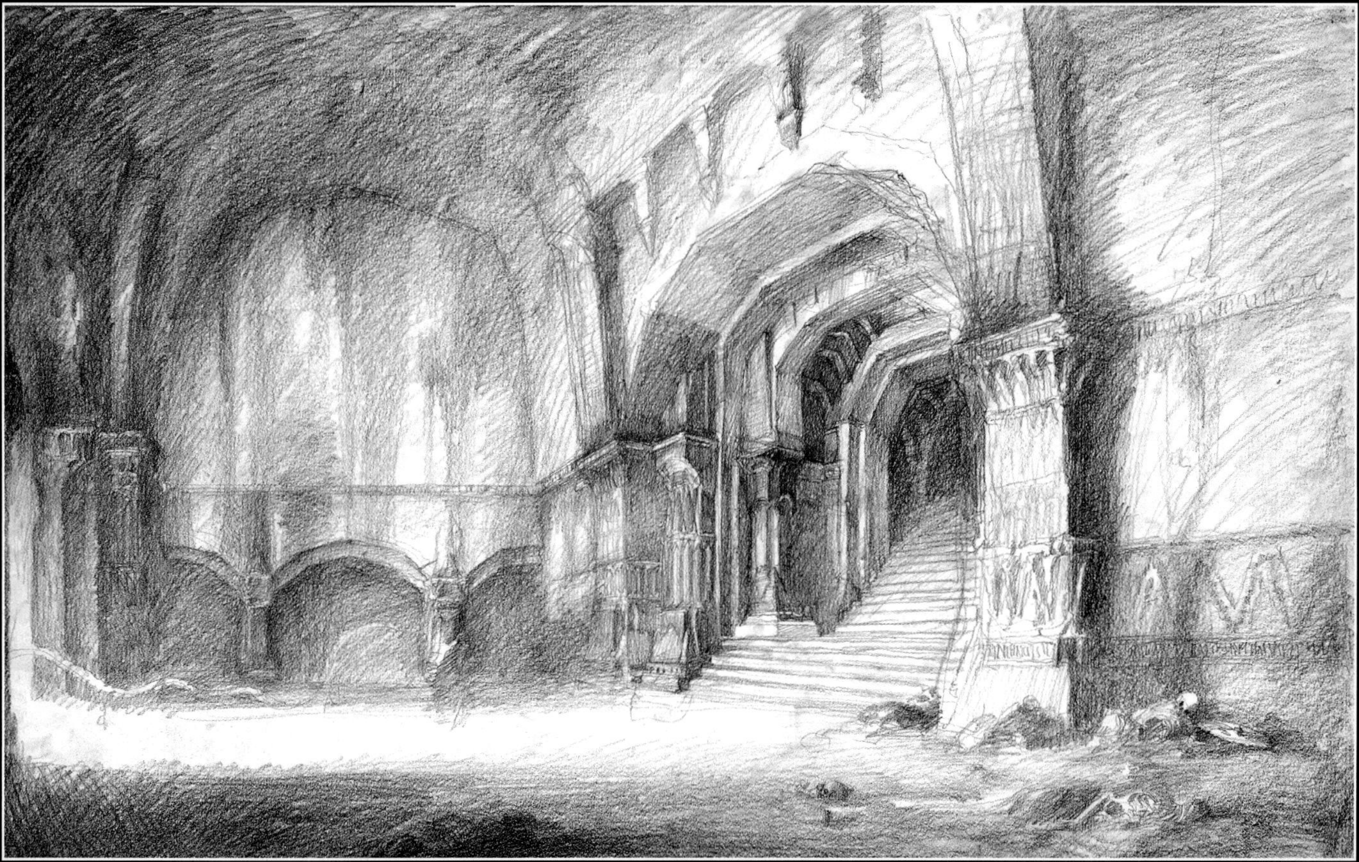

MORIA *Dwarrowdelf*
"The top picture is the Dwarrowdelf chamber, which is a mainly computer-generated environment. The lowest sections of the pillars were built for use in close-up action with the Fellowship as the Orcs pursue them. The below drawing is a design for the entrance chamber to Moria, which the Fellowship discover to be full of corpses." *AL*

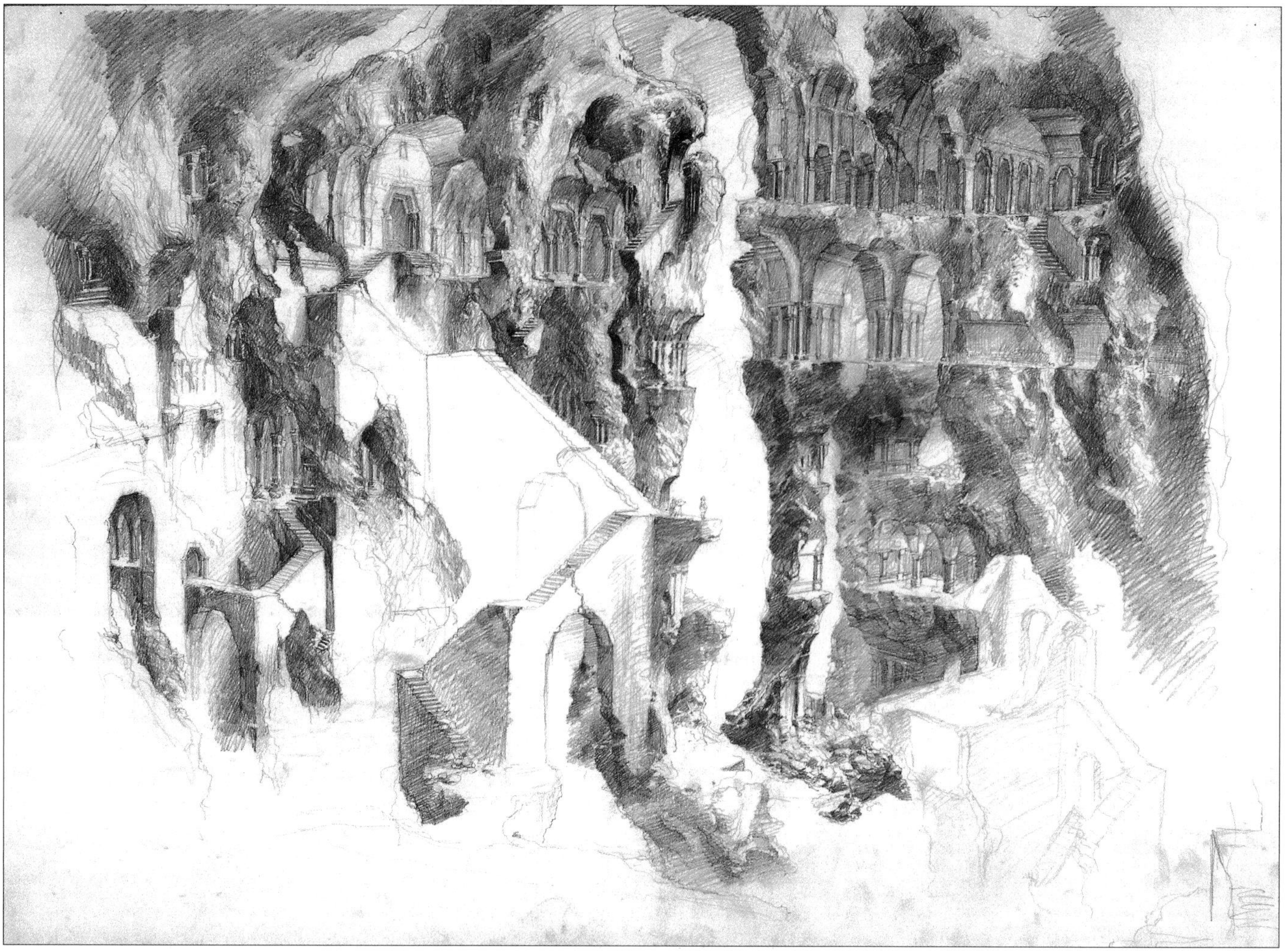

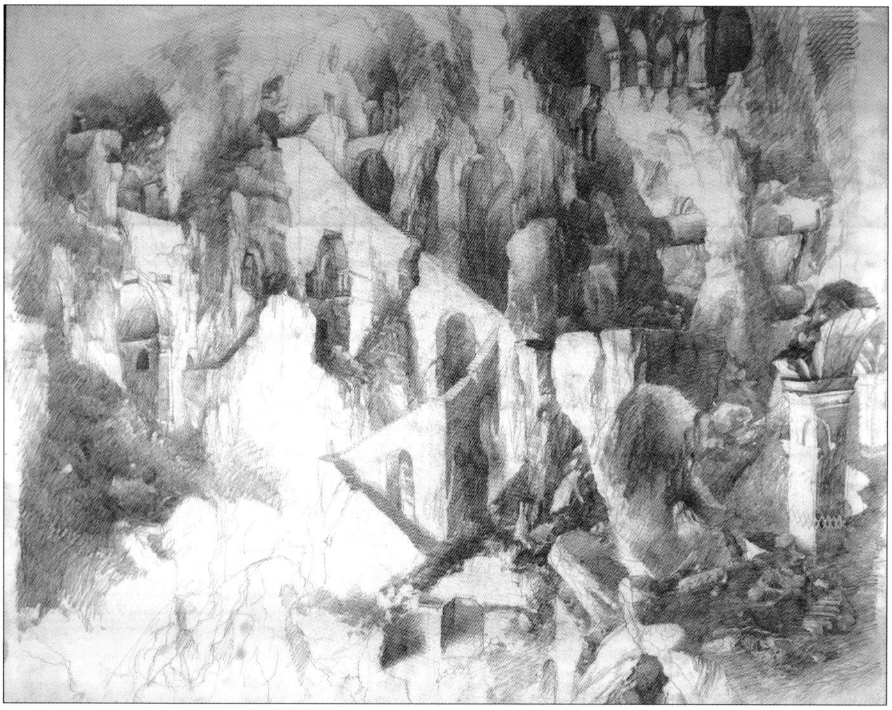

MORIA *Khazad-dûm*

"These two drawings are of the part of Moria that lies between the Dwarrowdelf chamber and the bridge where Gandalf meets the Balrog. In the book you get the impression that they descend through tunnels, but there was an opportunity here for something quite spectacular that would allow us to see more of the ruined Dwarven city and the plunging depths below it. It was built as a miniature, and Grant Major designed the set elements that were used in conjunction with it.

"Peter Jackson liked the first image so much that all the subsequent drawings, including the lower sketch, were just more detailed refinements for the model-makers." *AL*

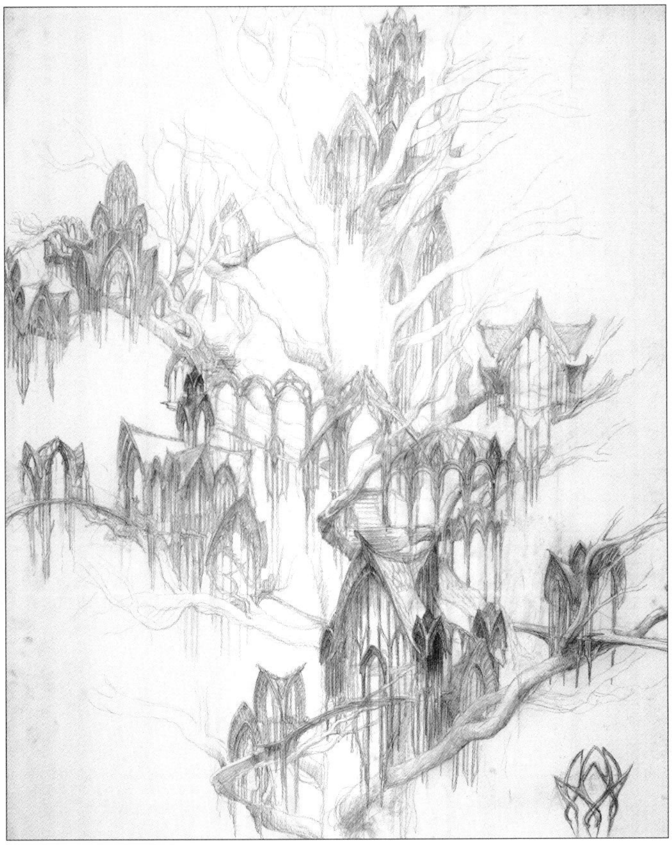

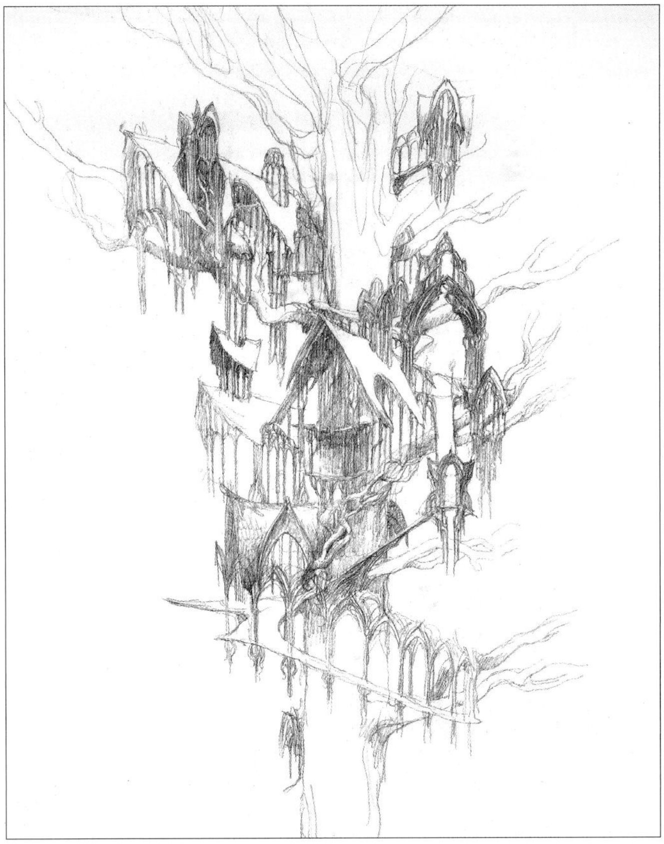

LOTHLÓRIEN *Tree concepts*
"Above are a couple of the many possibilities we offered for the dwellings in Lothlórien. The model makers, led by John Baster and Mary MacLachlan, would work directly from drawings like this, sometimes copying details as closely as possible and at other times taking them just as a starting point, which they would expand upon in a free-form way. Lothlórien, like most of the sixty-odd miniatures that were built at Weta for the trilogy, developed in quite an organic way, much as it would have in reality. There were always design maquettes, which Peter Jackson used to work out the kind of shots he'd like to get, as well as to sort out the scope and logistics of the miniatures. But the end result is due to the skill and artistry of those dedicated model makers, and later to the craft of people like the director of photography, Alex Funke, and his miniatures film unit." *AL*

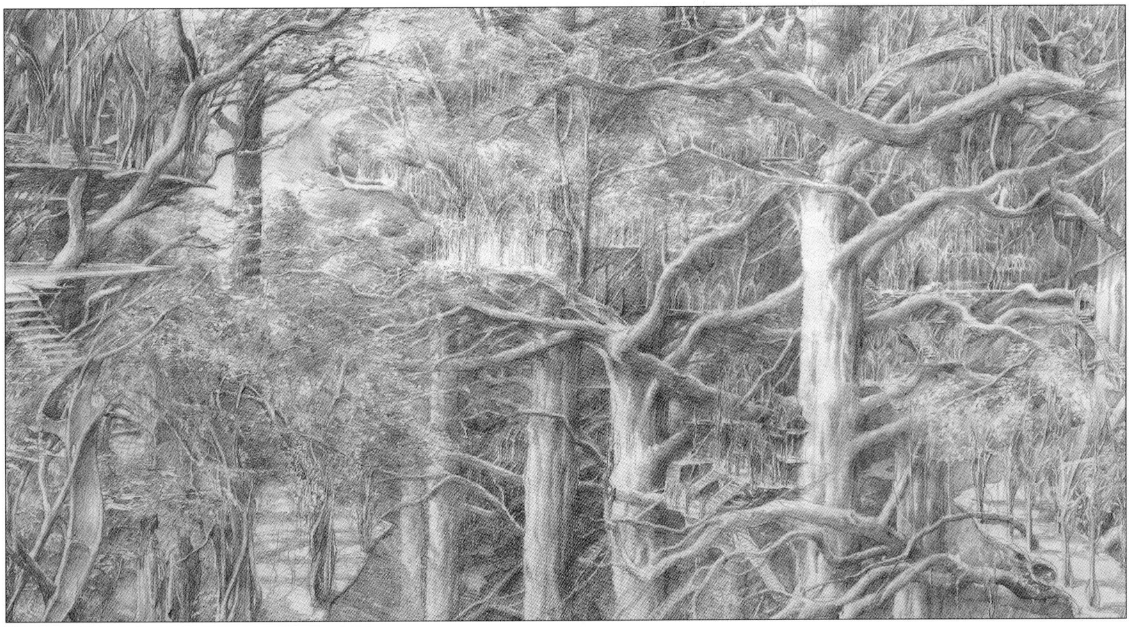

LOTHLÓRIEN
Tree concept
"This drawing is a view of the interior of the Golden Wood and was a guide for the model makers, showing how the Elven walkways were a natural and complementary extension of the mallorn trees that supported them." *AL*

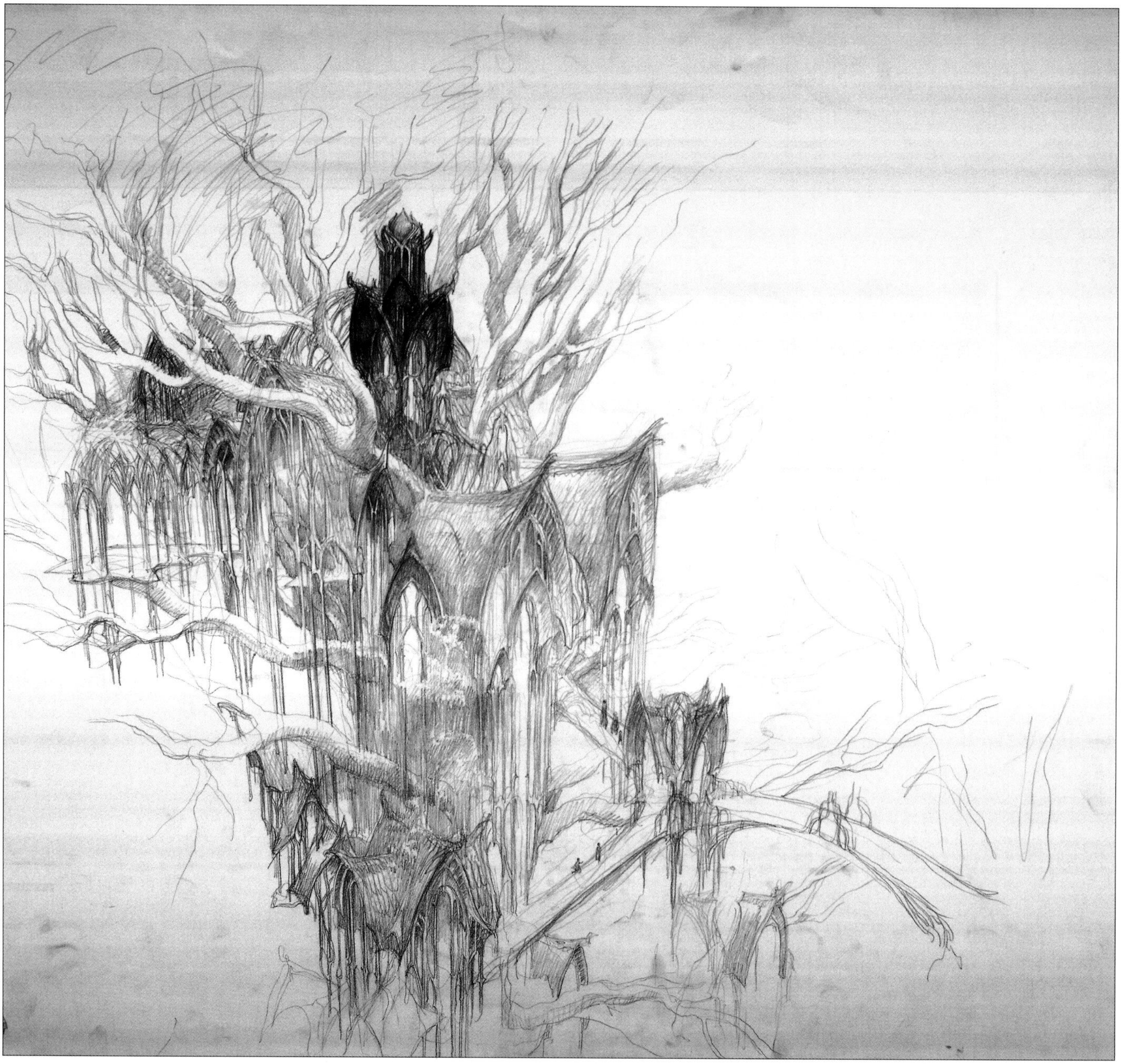

LOTHLÓRIEN ***The Palace***
"At the highest point in the Caras Galadhon miniature set is the Palace of Celeborn and Galadriel, beautifully detailed by Weta's miniaturists and dressed to camera by John Harding's team, for one of the most captivating shots in *The Fellowship of the Ring*. At this stage in the production, a fifth miniatures crew, led by David Hardberger, had joined Alex Funke, Chuck Schulman, Richard Bluck, and Brian Van't Hul, to help get through the enormous workload of all three films, and so David did the Lothlórien shots." *AL*

LOTHLÓRIEN ***Caras Galadhon***
"One part of Caras Galadhon that we didn't see in the film was the main gateway, approached via a bridge across a deep, dry moat." *AL*

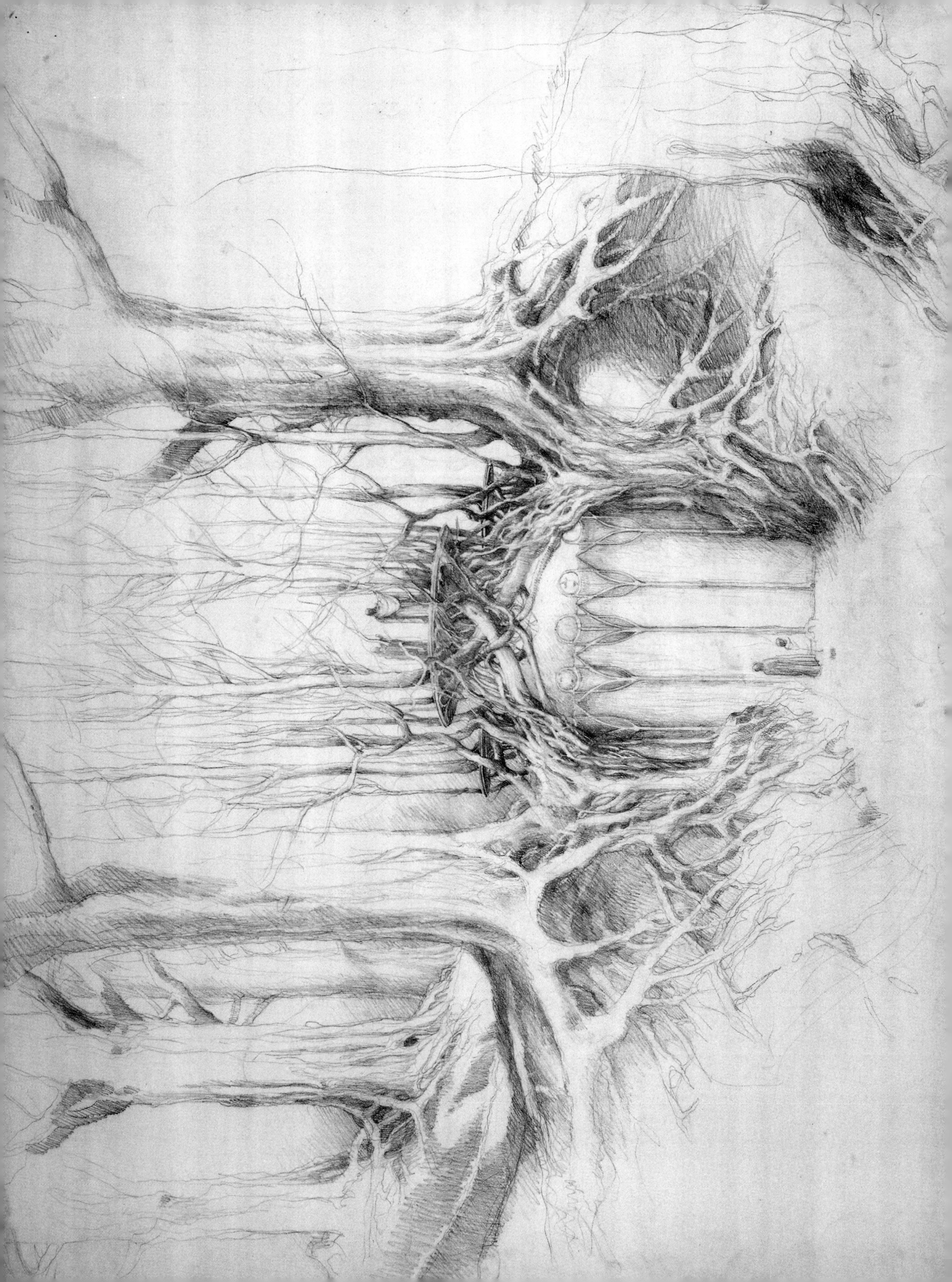

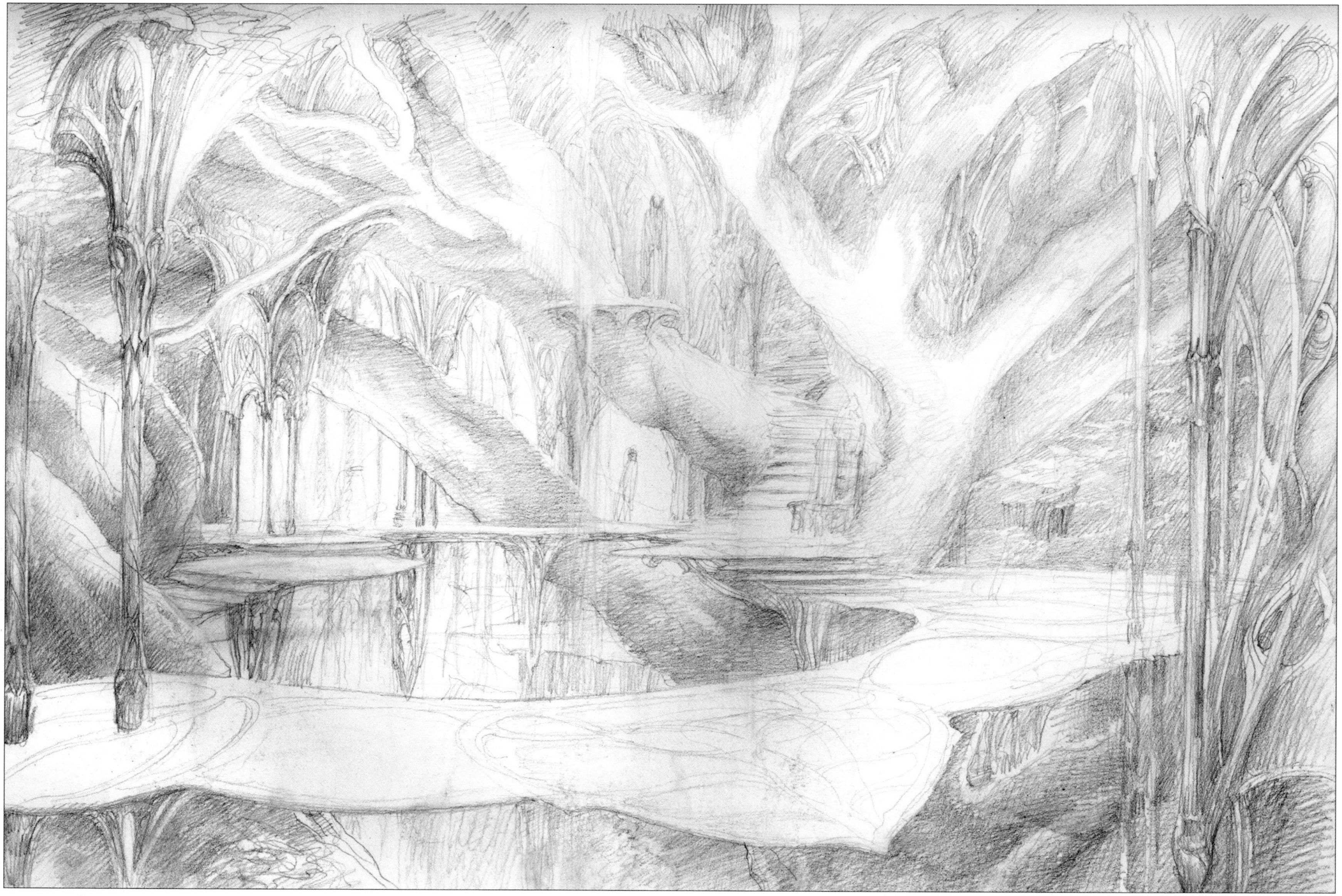

LOTHLÓRIEN *Celeborn's Chamber*
"We were getting short on time and needed an approval from Peter Jackson on the set we would be building for the scene of the Fellowship's meeting with Galadriel and Celeborn. He was shooting Mordor scenes on Mount Ruapehu at the time, so I drove up and sat in the ski-field lodge, which had become a temporary base, and drew in my sketchbook until I produced one that he liked. And this is it." *AL*

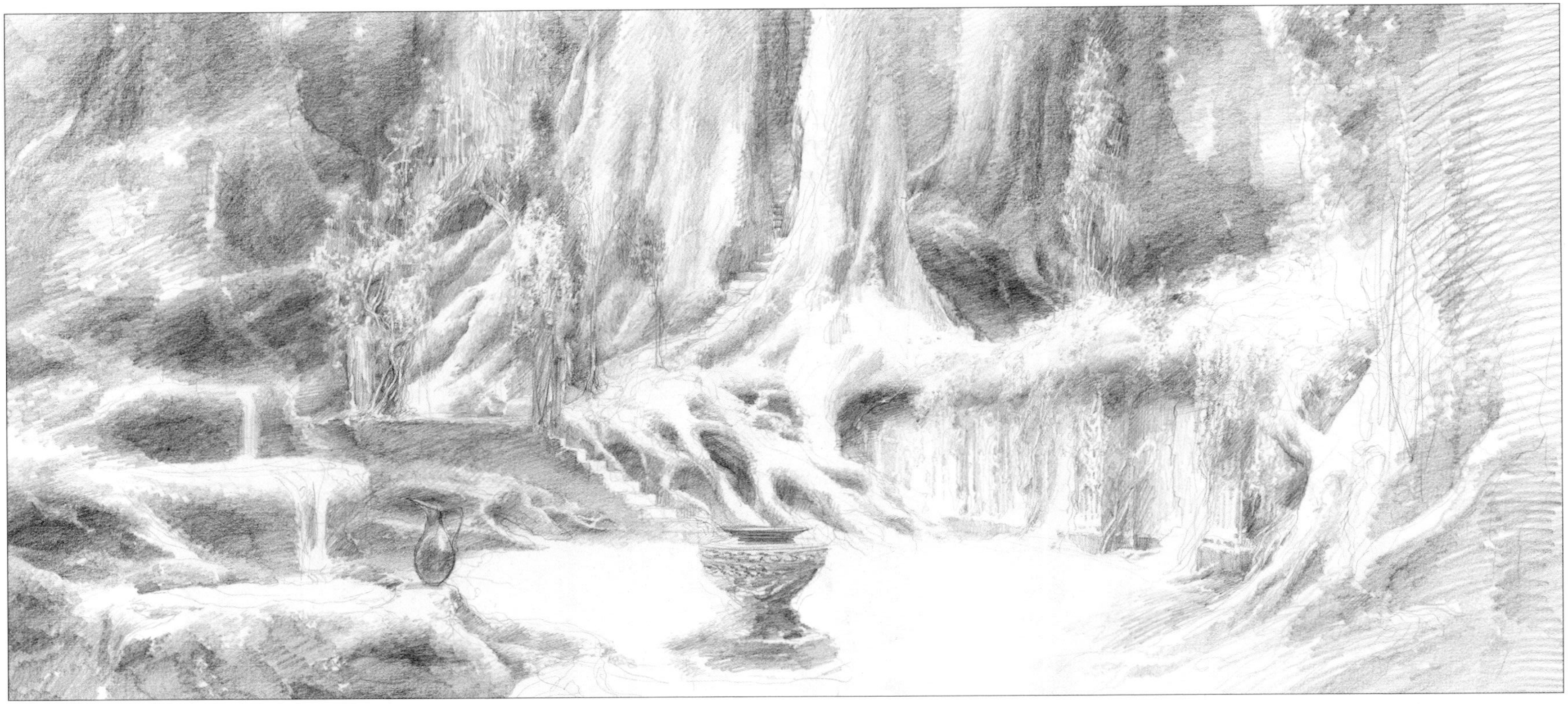

LOTHLORIEN *Galadriel's Glade*

"Peter Jackson wanted Galadriel to make an entrance that was a little more interesting than was possible with the earlier drawings I'd done for this set. So we created a mallorn tree that was split in two and a pair of statues with flaming bowls at the top of the stairs that she descends. We also made more of the spring from which she takes the water to activate her mirror. To create the detail on the bowl and jug, Gareth Jensen and I painted the design in an acid-resistant paint and sprayed over this to achieve a finish that, after etching in acid, was similar to an aquatint. We had several versions, in two different scales, as we had for most of our props. One of these was painted black below the water line so that we could get a good reflective surface. A quickly improvised starry sky, made from flashlight bulbs and a black sheet, was hung above it so that we would see something more appropriate than the studio roof reflected in it." *AL*

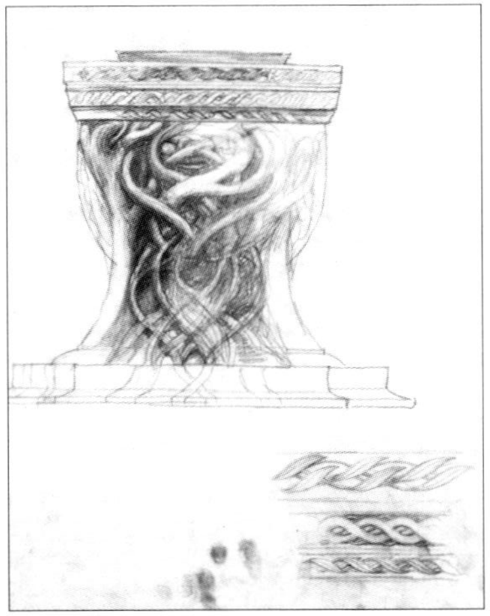

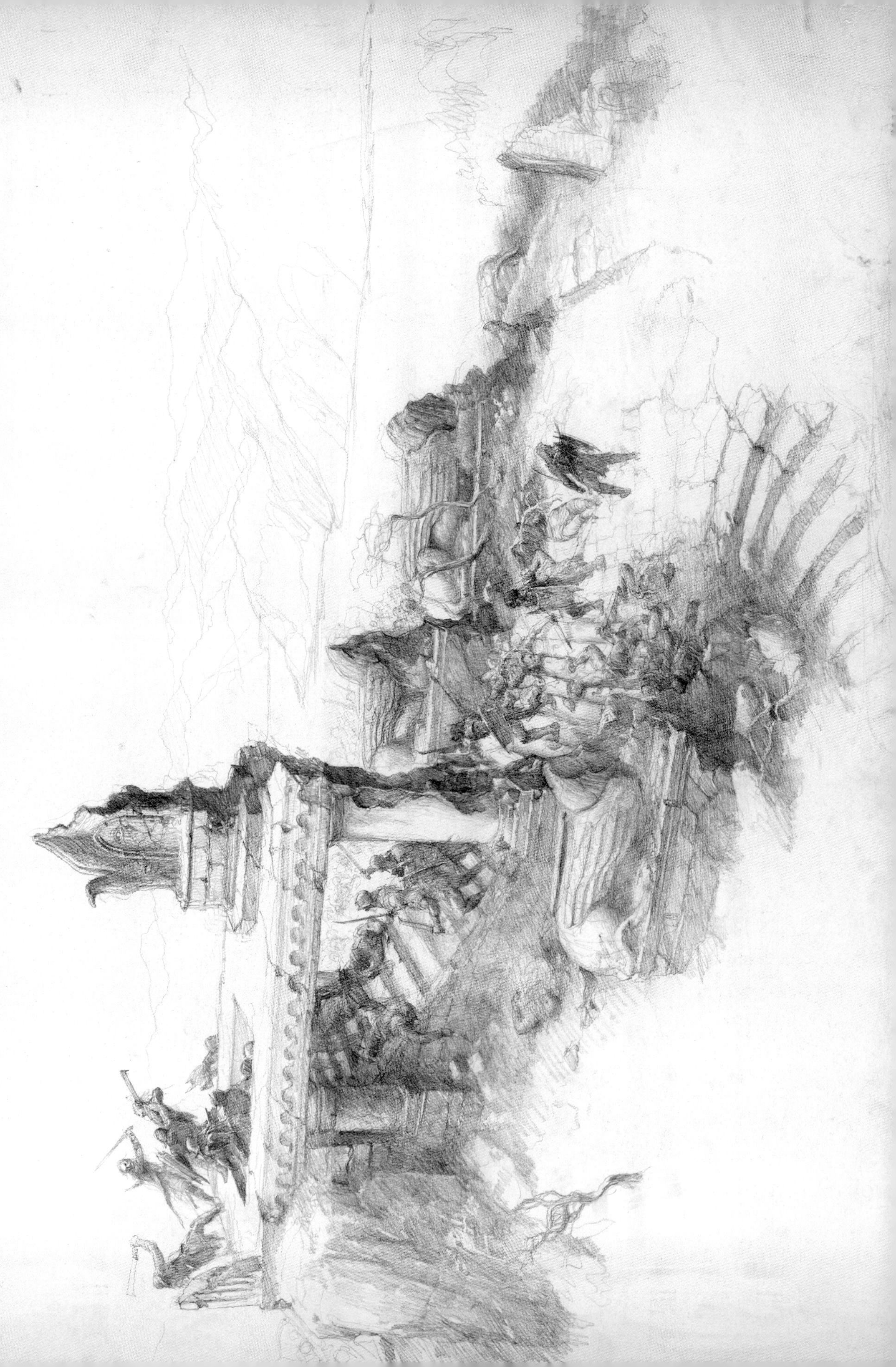

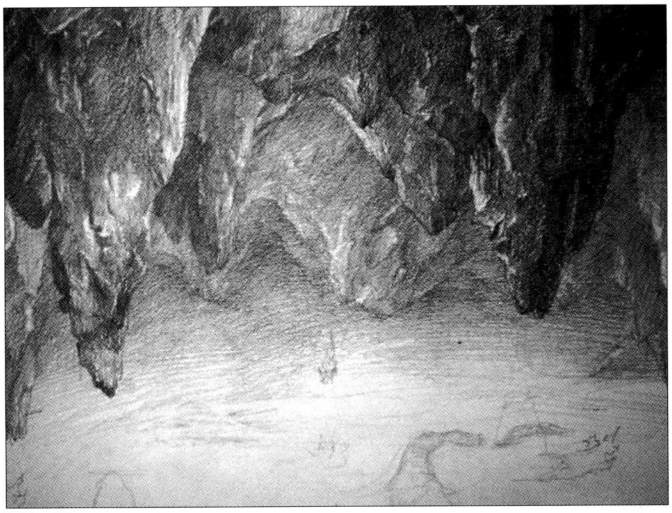

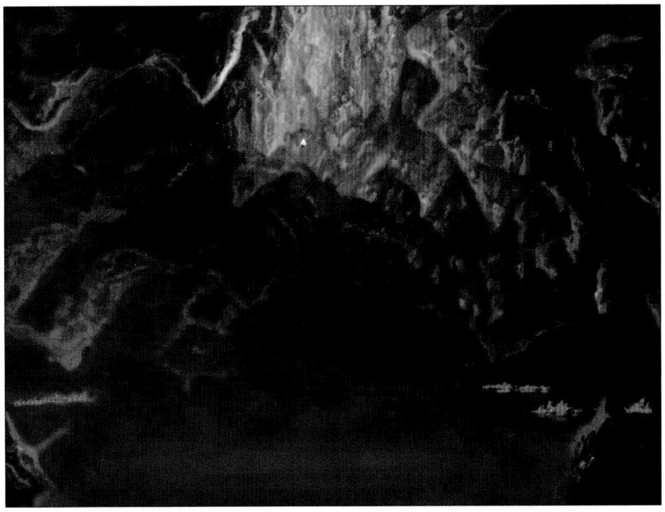

KHAZAD-DÛM *Pencil sketch and digital artwork*
"There's an amazing sequence at the beginning of *The Two Towers* in which we follow Gandalf and the Balrog down the chasm and we have a wide shot showing the Roots of the Mountains and the lake that they splash down into. I also did drawings for the Endless Stair and the nameless creatures that might have watched their progress. The drawing above left was the original idea, which was further developed in the digital study above right." *AL*

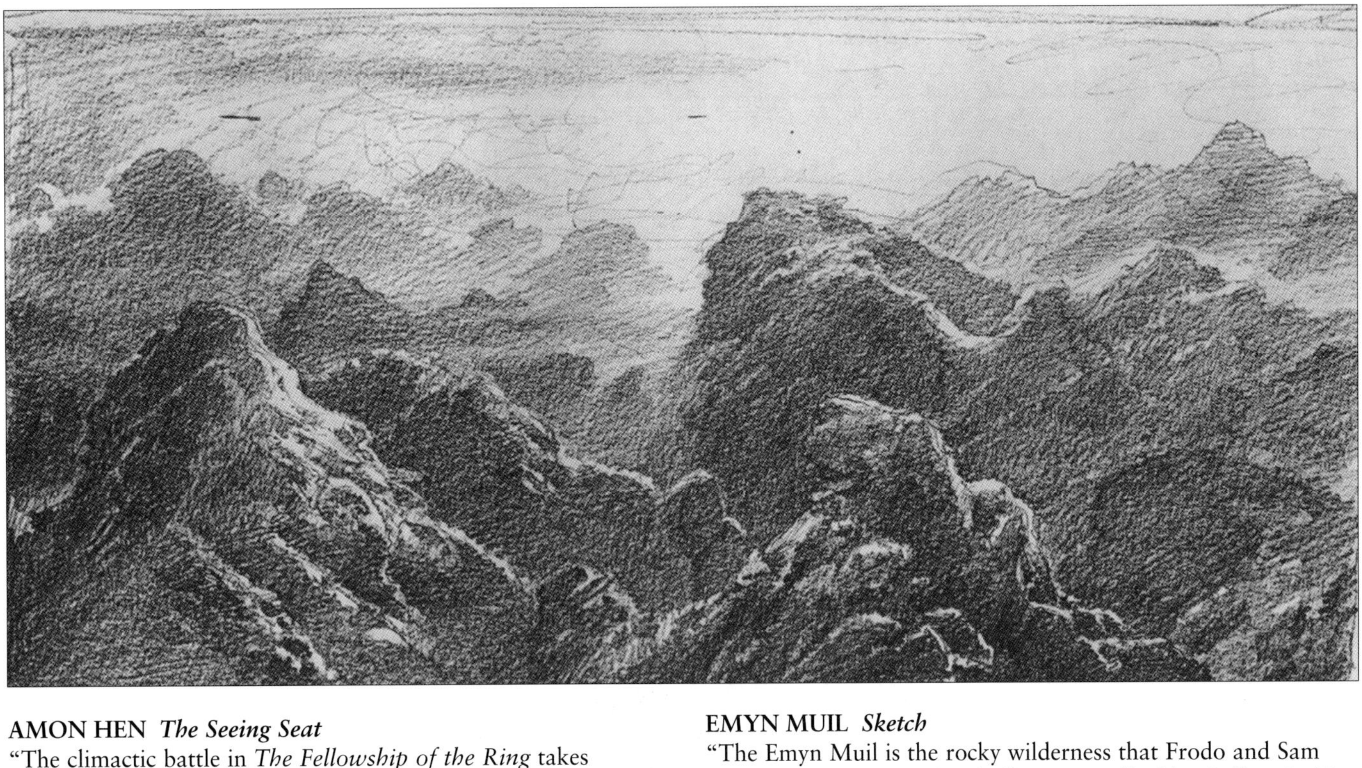

AMON HEN *The Seeing Seat*
"The climactic battle in *The Fellowship of the Ring* takes place around the ruins of Amon Hen. We wanted to create some architectural remains that would work well for Frodo's third experience of Wraith World and also provide an arena for some good action between Aragorn and our other heroes and Saruman's ferocious Uruks." *AL*

EMYN MUIL *Sketch*
"The Emyn Muil is the rocky wilderness that Frodo and Sam cross on their way to the Black Gates, stalked by Gollum." *AL*

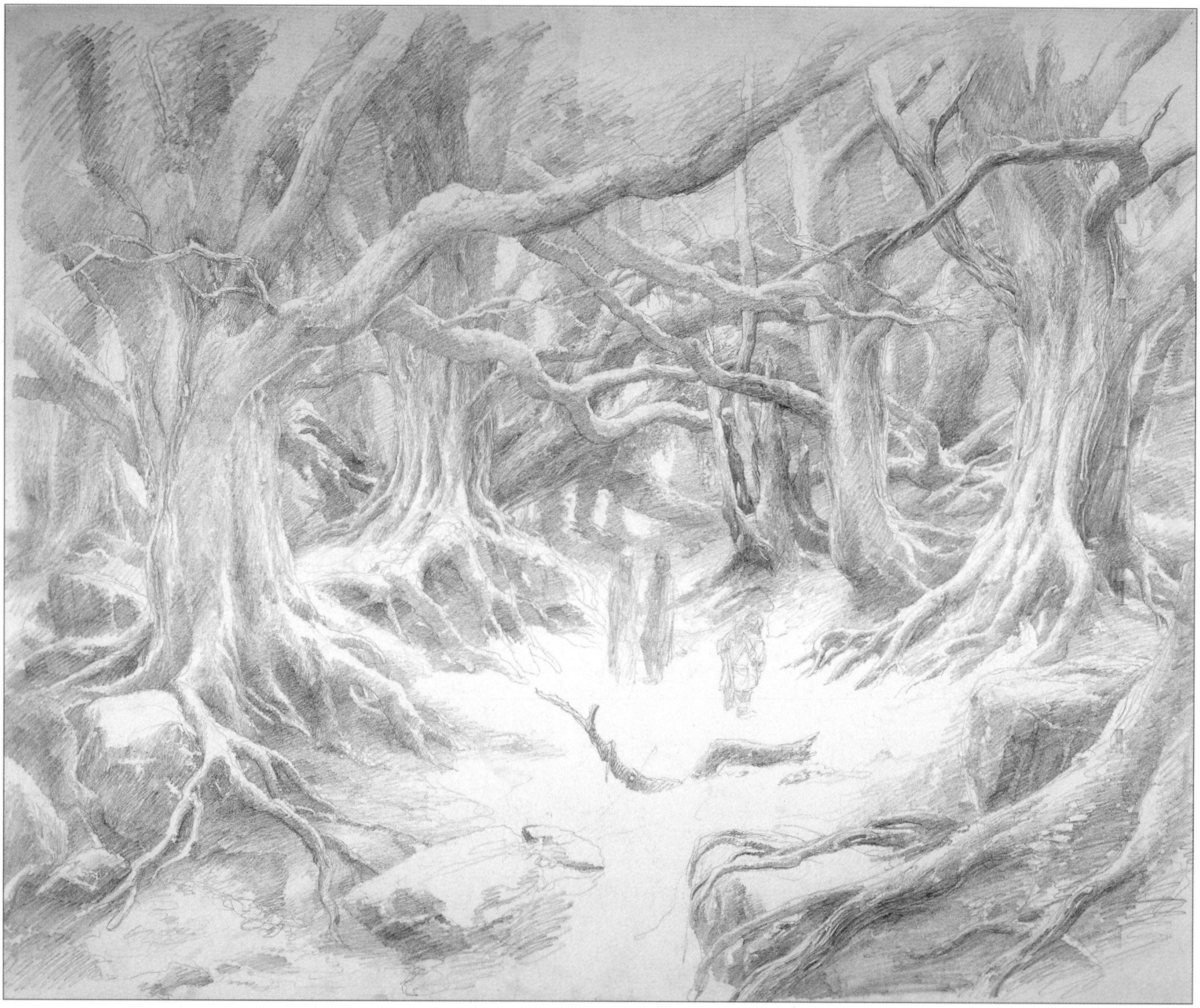

FANGORN ***Pencil sketches***
"We looked at a number of possible locations for these shots of the interior of the forest, but Brian Massey and the greens department managed to create some memorable studio sets that more than answered our needs. The pen drawing opposite was done to assist those constructing the miniature." *AL*

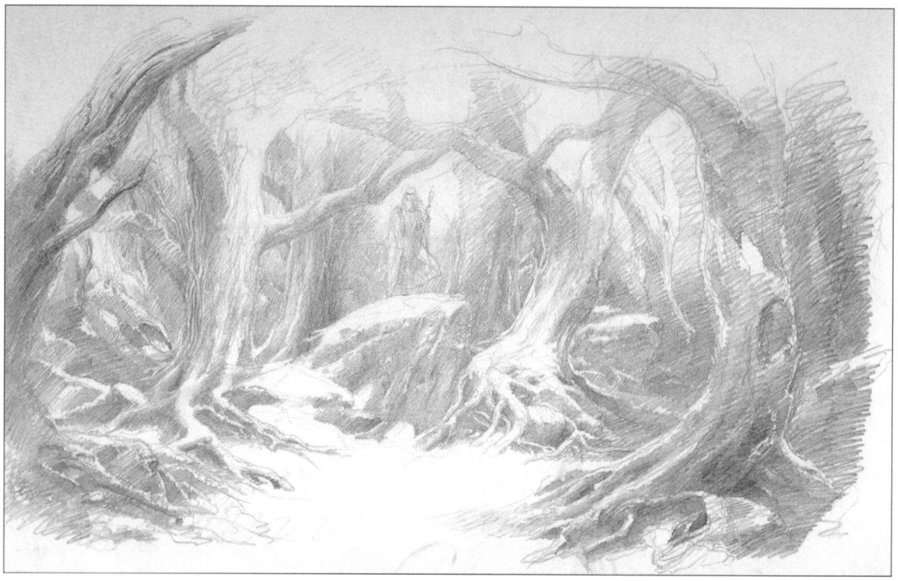

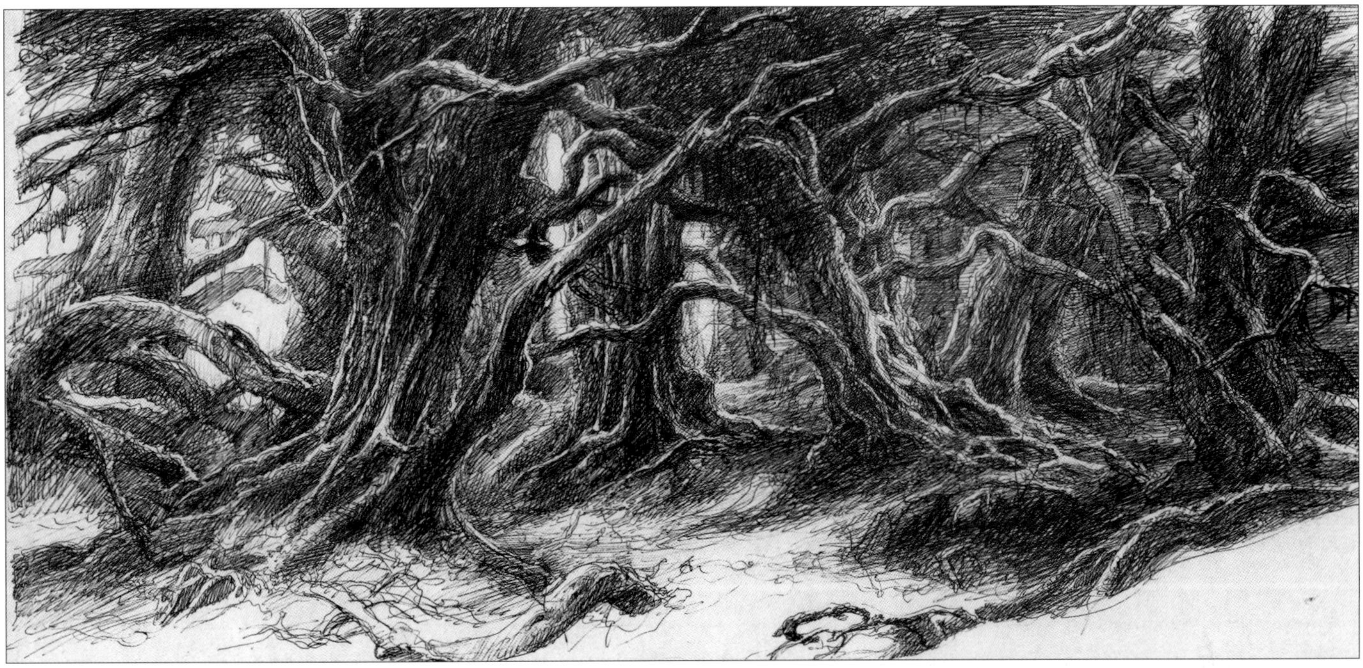

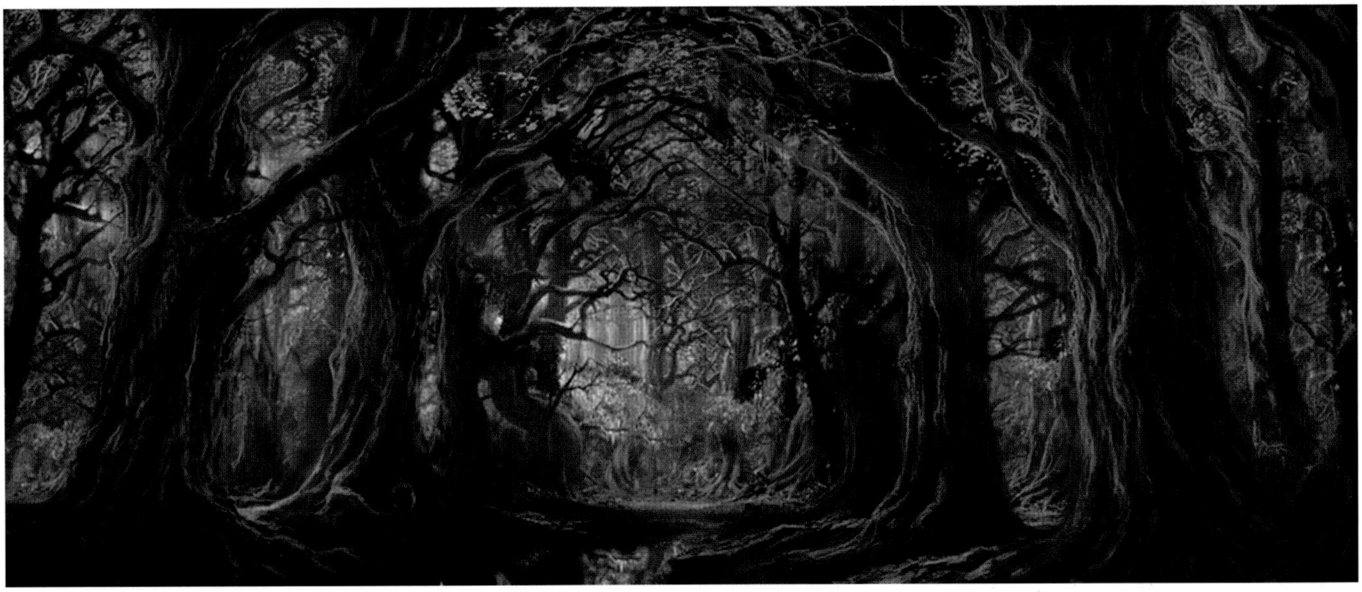

FANGORN *Color study*
"For the wide shot of Wellinghall, we extended the original set with more miniature trees and moss-covered ground. Brian Massey's greens men and women worked closely with John Harding's Weta crew on all the many Fangorn Forest miniature shots, so we were able to ensure that they matched the full-sized sets as closely as possible." *AL*

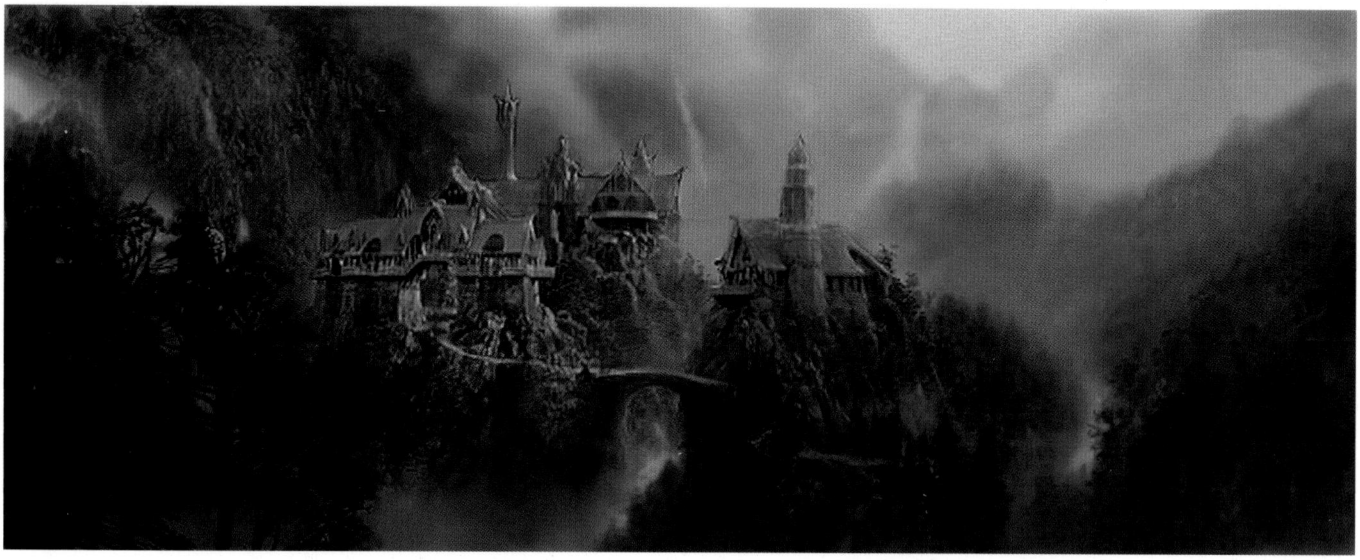

RIVENDELL ***Digital artwork***
"We sometimes tried to ease the pressure on the miniatures department by recycling film that had been shot for other scenes, or for tests, particularly when no camera movement was required. This was the case with Arwen riding back into Rivendell. This and other artwork was done to guide matte artist Yanick Dusseault and the compositors who would be placing waterfalls and trees in the environment." *AL*

EDORAS BUILDINGS
Pencil sketch and digital artwork
"We found the most wonderful location for the city of Edoras in the mountains west of Christchurch. We built the Golden Hall, the stables, and a few other buildings on the top of the hill, and a complex of buildings around the gatehouse at the bottom. The wall and the rest of the city were created digitally by Cory Bedwell and others in post-production. I did the drawing below as a guide." *AL*

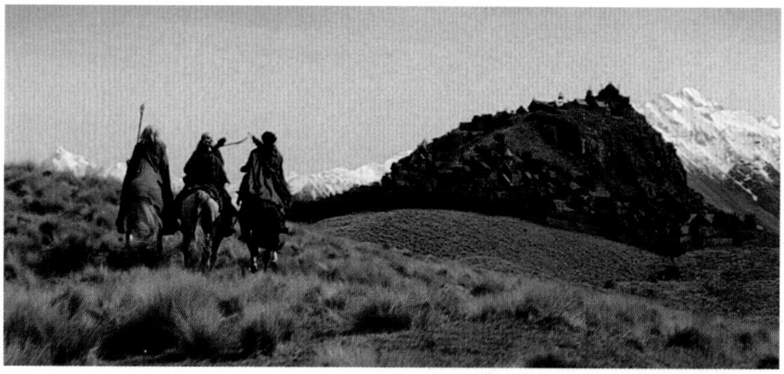

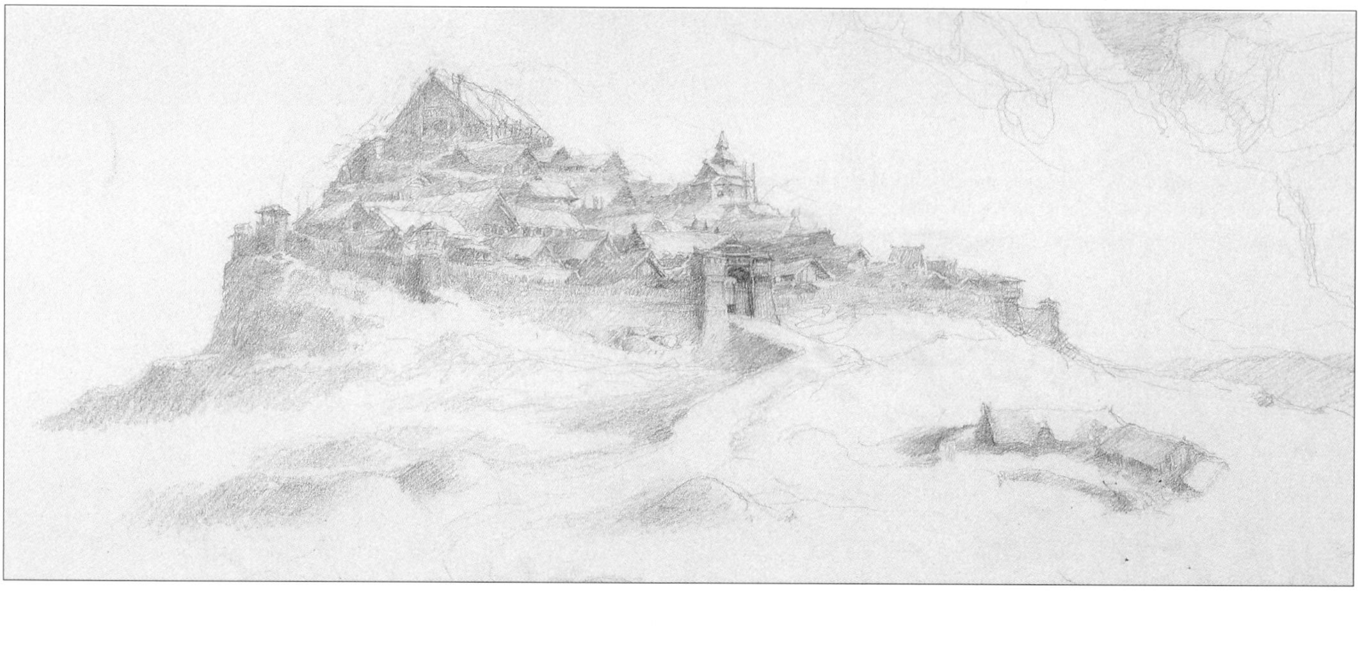

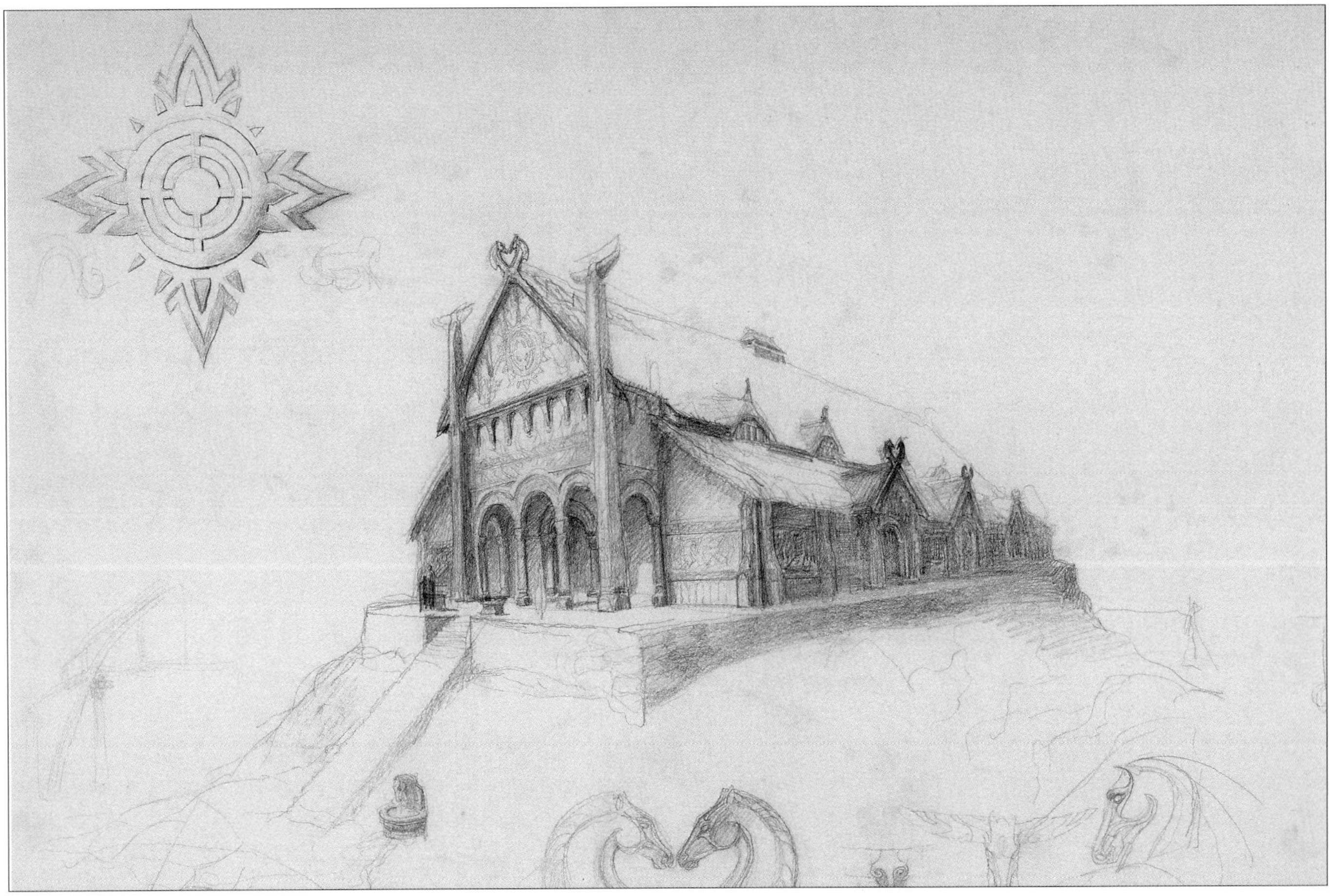

THE GOLDEN HALL ***Pencil sketch***
"The buildings of Rohan are wooden and based loosely on our idea of structures that would have existed in northern Europe during the Dark Ages. The description of Hrothgar's Hall, Heorot, in the Anglo-Saxon poem *Beowulf* was probably as useful as Tolkien's own words in evoking the kind of place we wanted to create. We wanted it to feel ancient and strong, bound with iron and heavily decorated. We adopted the sunburst motif as something that felt appropriate for a plains-dwelling, seminomadic people, and, of course, we used lots of carvings of horses on gables and gateways." *AL*

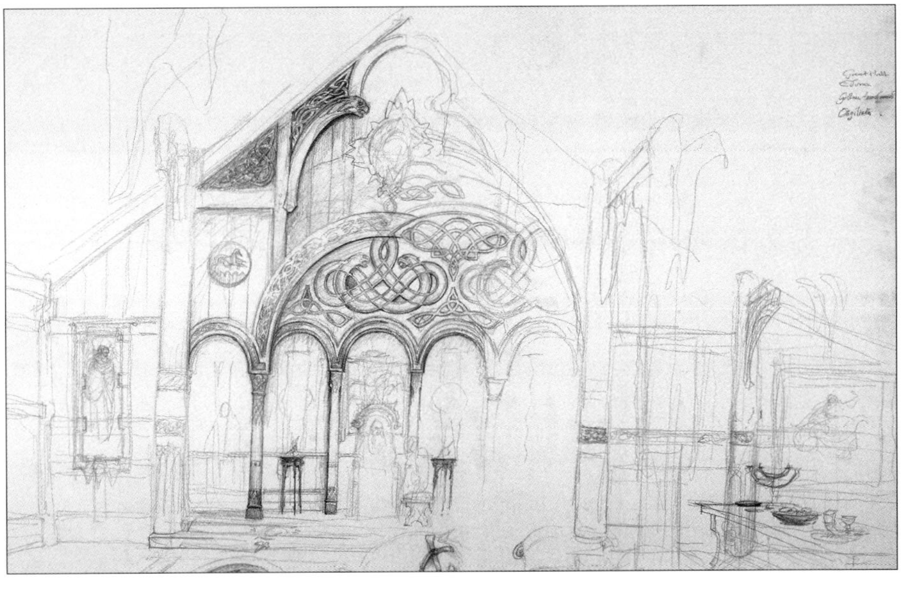

THE GOLDEN HALL ***Pencil sketch***
"I did a large number of drawings of this interior, covering it from every angle. We wanted to make it as rich and as authentic as possible. Helen Strevens did a great job on all the drafting, and we consulted books on barn construction to make all the timber-work believable. For all its richness we wanted the first impression to be quite somber, to reflect the state of decay that Saruman and Wormtongue had engendered." *AL*

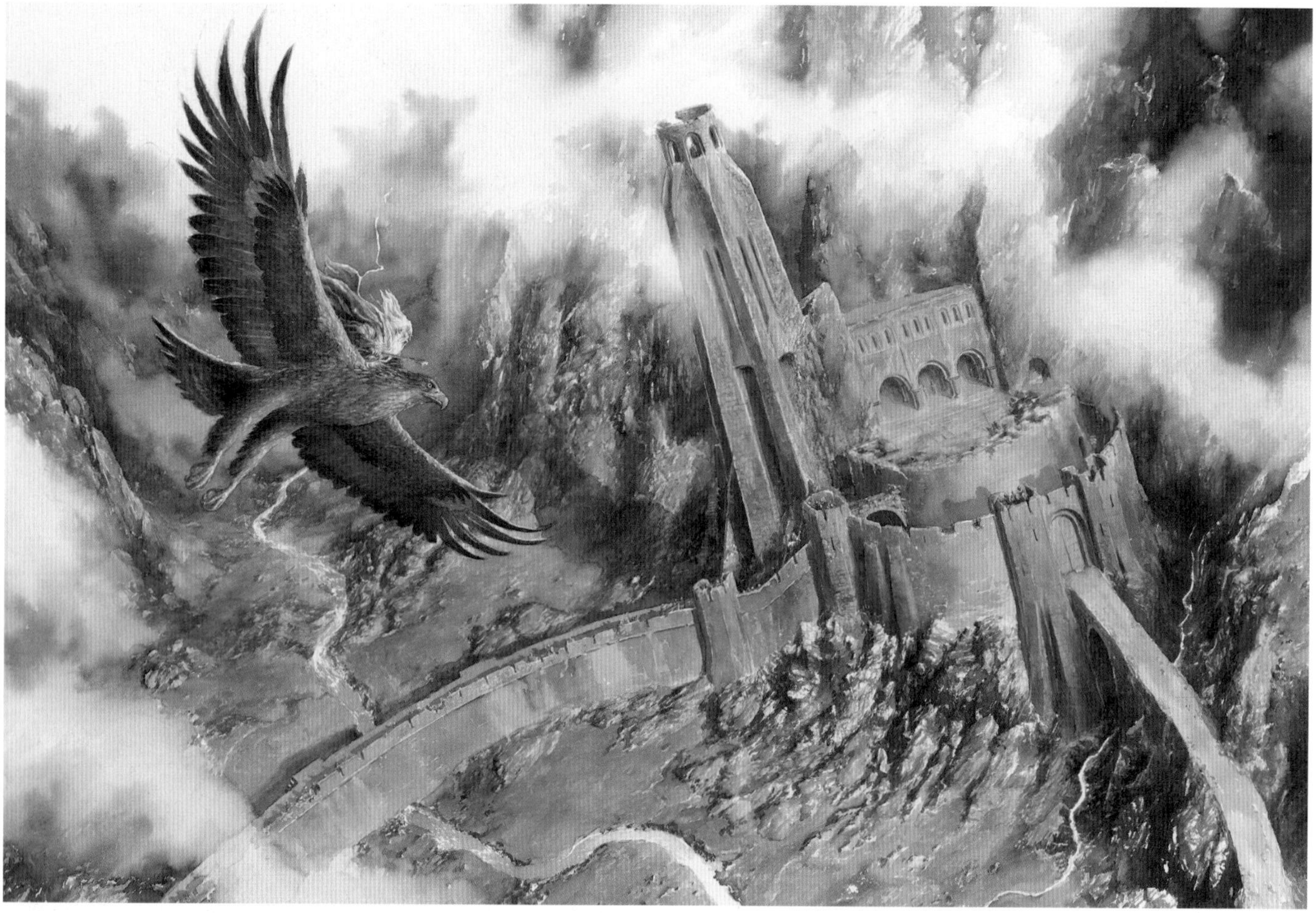

HELMS DEEP *Watercolor*
"Peter Jackson was keen to start work on the miniature of Helm's Deep as soon as possible. I did many drawings and this painting soon after arriving in New Zealand in January 1998. I think that one of the reasons the final battle, and the events leading to it, in *The Two Towers* work so well is that, throughout the action, you know exactly where you are in that environment. With Richard Taylor's team on the miniatures and Grant Major and Dan Hennah on the sets cooperating very closely, Peter managed to create a seamless and logical flow in all the many scenes in that dramatic climax." *AL*

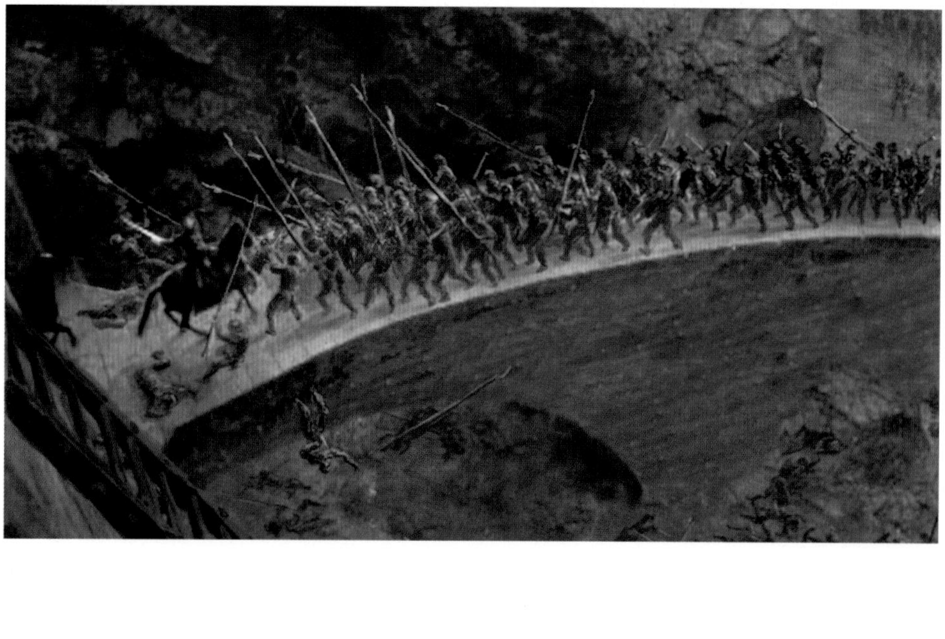

HELM'S DEEP CAUSEWAY
Digital artwork
"This image is a guide for the digital artists combining the shots in the dawn charge sequence, and for the placement of the massive digitally created Uruk-hai soldiers." *AL*

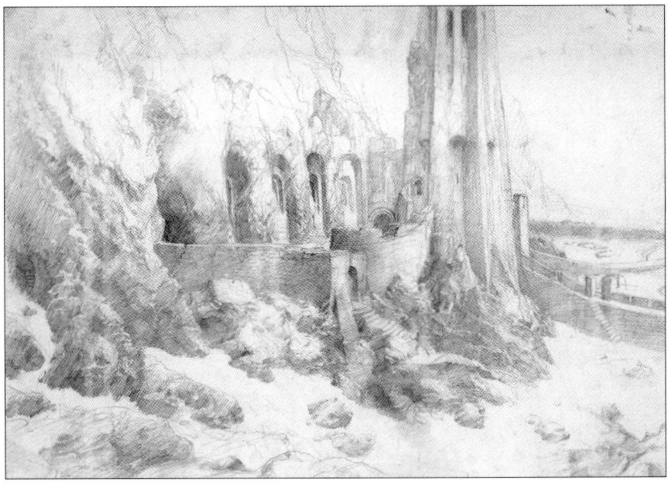

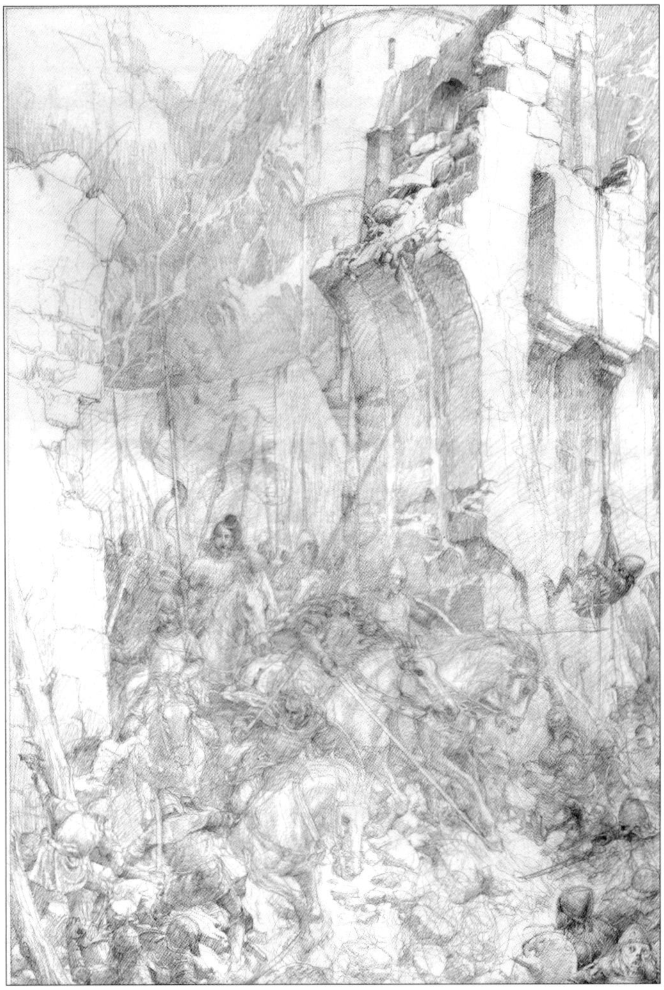

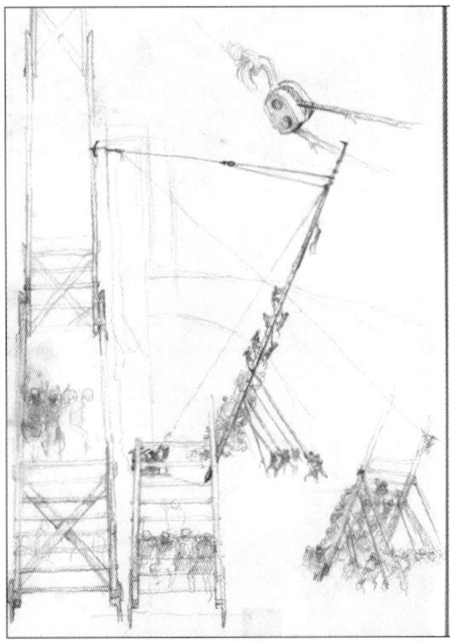

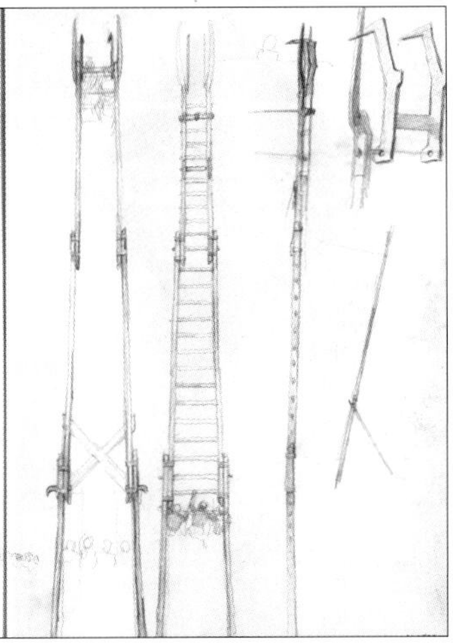

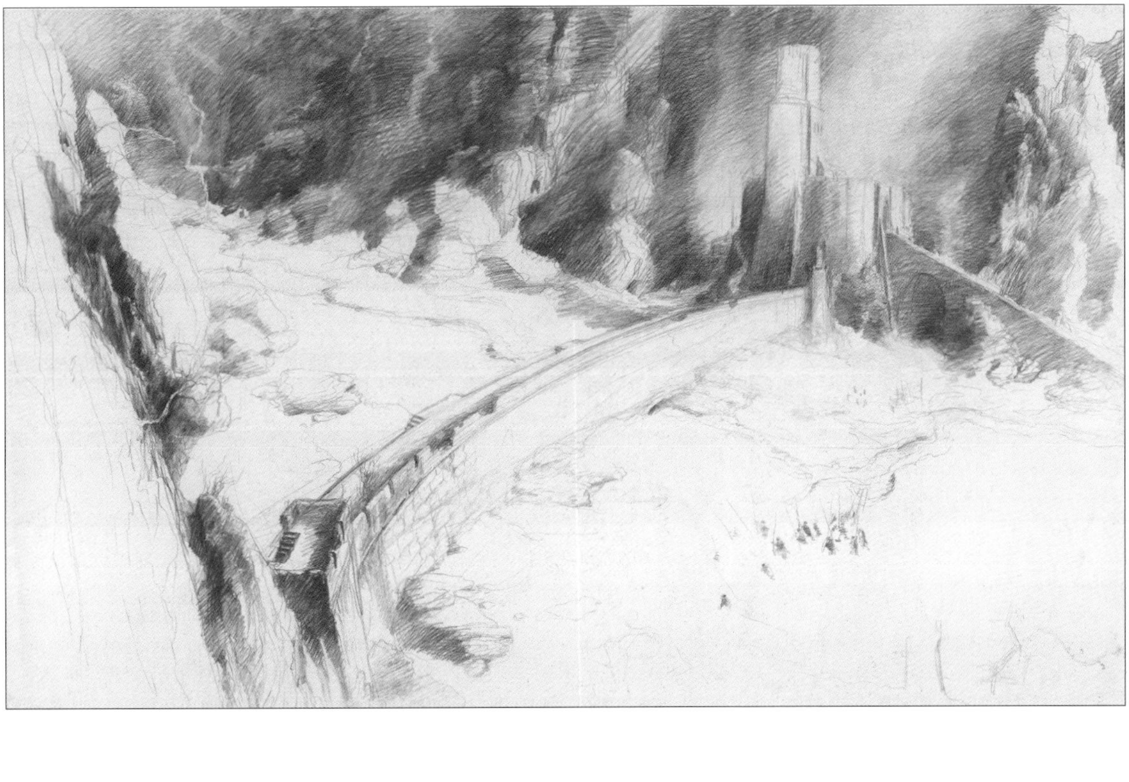

HELM'S DEEP
Pencil sketches
"These images are a selection of the many drawings that I produced, which provided Peter with views of the fortress from different angles and at different stages of the assault." *AL*

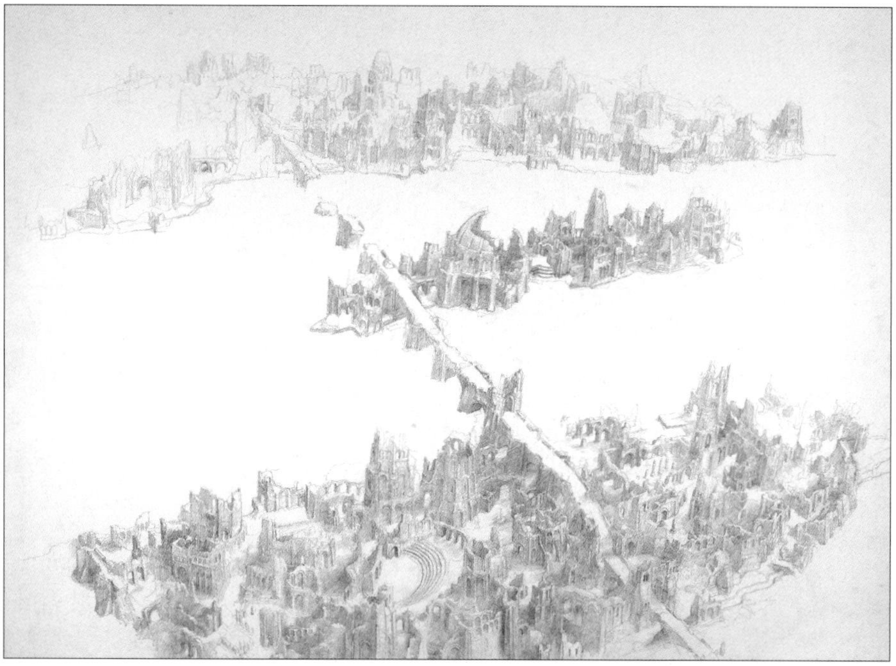

OSGILIATH ***Pencil sketch***

"Osgiliath was one of the most enjoyable sets to work on. We had a lot of existing pieces of masonry left over from some of our earlier sets and added new designs to make the ruins as rich and complex as possible. I thought that the river might have become choked in places and flooded some areas of the city – which adds to the interest. The bird's-eye view shows the broken bridges and an island, somewhat inspired by the Ile de la Cité in Paris, which contains a large cathedral-like building. We know that Osgiliath had once housed one of the palantíri, which had been lost when the tower it was kept in collapsed, so it could be that building." *AL*

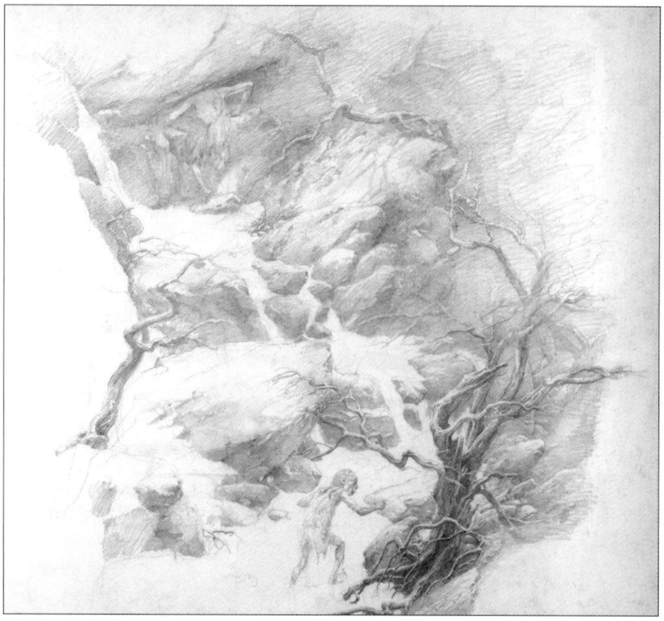

GOLLUM'S CAVE
Pencil sketch

"I did this drawing as a guide for the set builders showing the scene in which Sméagol undergoes his transformation in *The Return of the King*. The creature staggers through a rocky landscape as he makes his way toward his eventual home in the Misty Mountains." *AL*

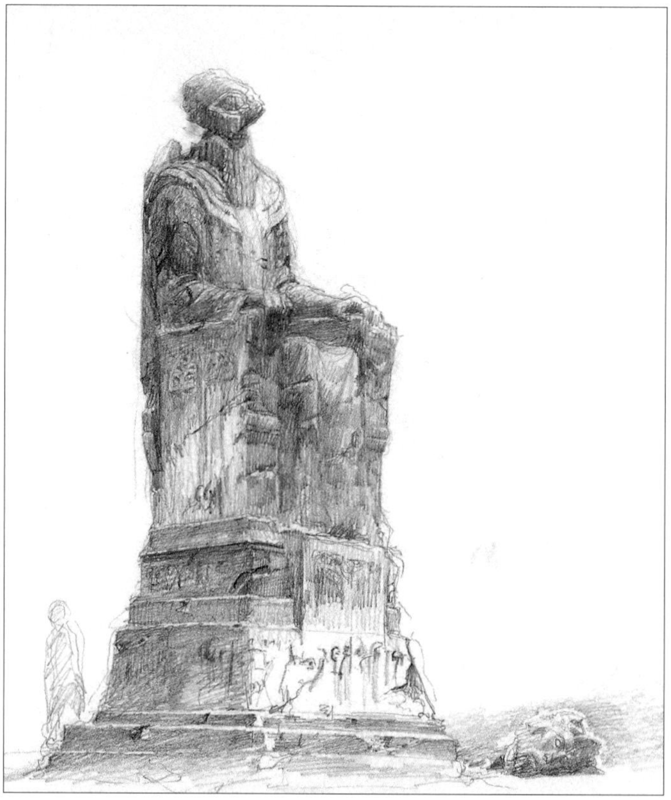

ITHILIEN *Pencil sketch*

"The desecrated statue of a former ruler of Gondor marks the crossroads between Osgiliath and Minas Morgul, and between Harad and Ithilien. The ray of sunlight piercing the gloomy cloud that covers Mordor and its immediate surroundings, to illuminate the wreath of flowers that have grown over the statue's fallen head, is a powerful symbol of hope in the book and an image that we all wanted to capture." *AL*

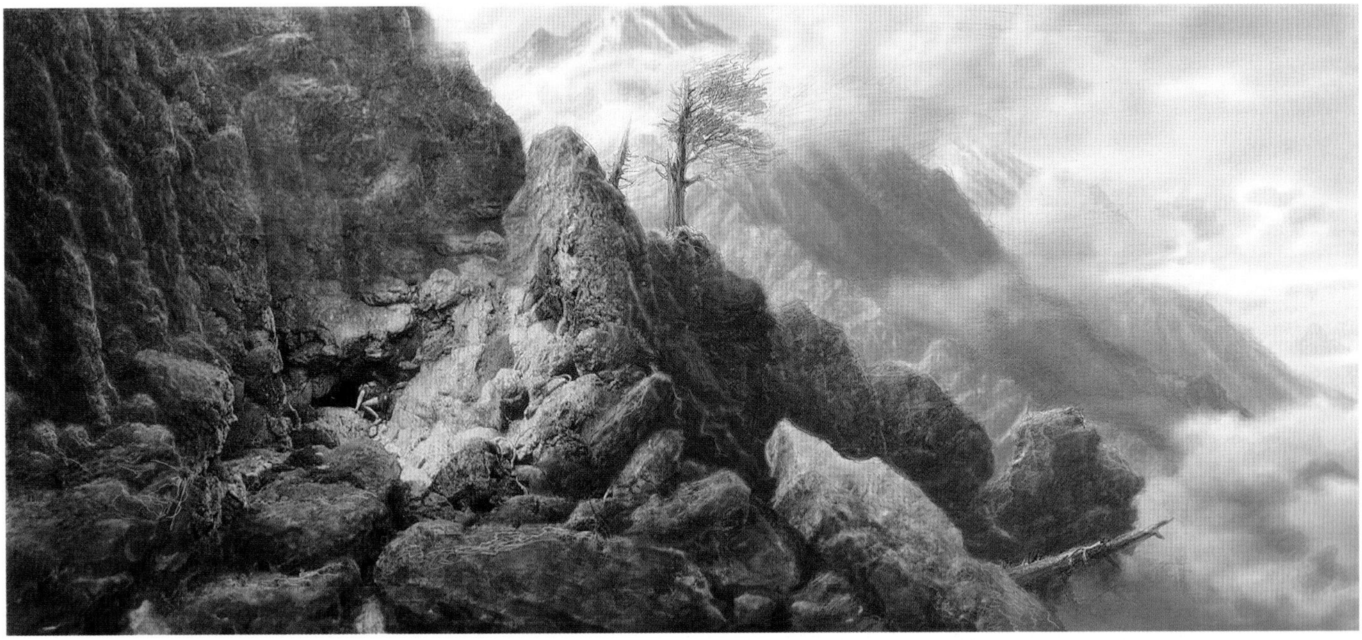

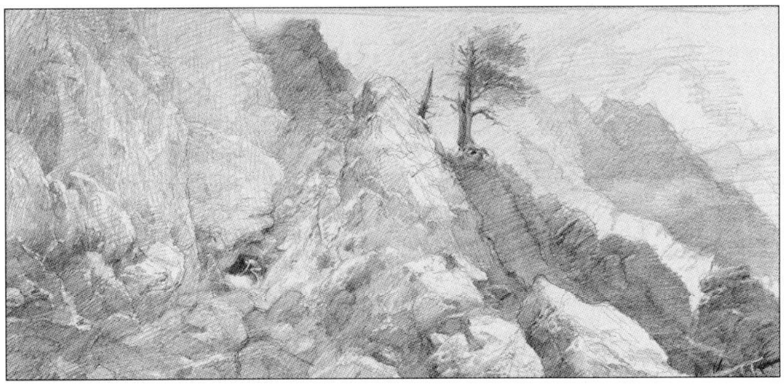

THE MISTY MOUNTAINS ***Pencil sketch and digital artwork***
"We had made a compact but quite effective set for those wonderful scenes at the beginning of *The Return of the King* in which Sméagol slowly changes into Gollum, and Peter wanted a wide shot in which we see the wretched creature crawling into his cave. The original shot was scaled down in frame, and Yanick Dusseault provided his lovely matte painting – based on my original sketch – to complete the picture." *AL*

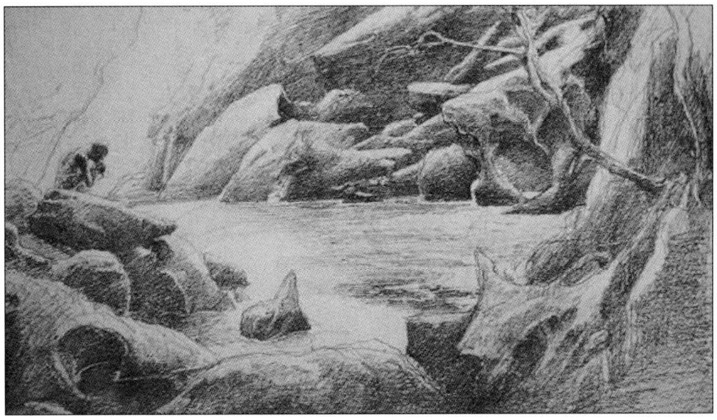

THE FORBIDDEN POOL ***Pencil sketch***
"We built the set for the pool and the interior of the cave in the same studio so that they could share the waterfall that Ed Mulholland's construction crew made for us. In the final shots more water was added to the scene to make it feel more natural." *AL*

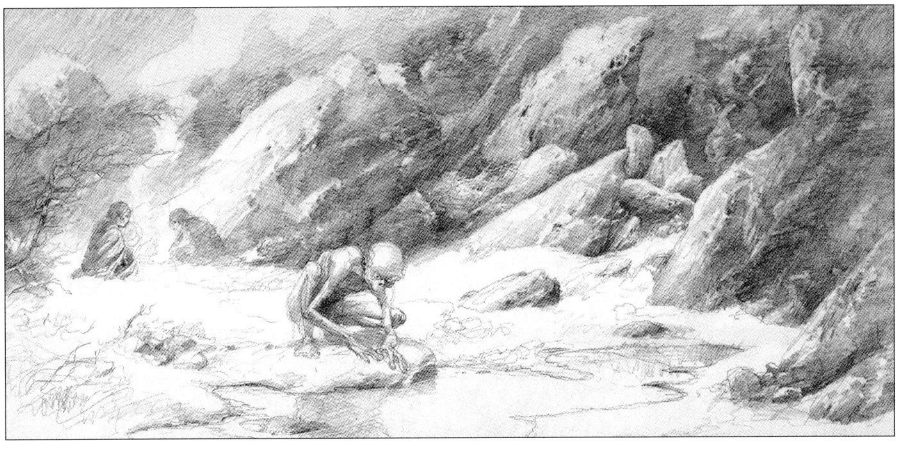

MORGUL VALE ***Sketch***
"We built a small set for the scene, in the shadow of the Morgul Vale, where Gollum has a conversation with his reflected image in a pool of water while Sam and Frodo sleep. The drawing to the left shows the tangled gorse bushes that Peter Jackson wanted, to make their campsite less visible. It looked like a simple set, but the small team of greens people, as well as Grant Major and I, having worked through the night, were just applying the finishing touches when the crew arrived to shoot it the following morning." *AL*

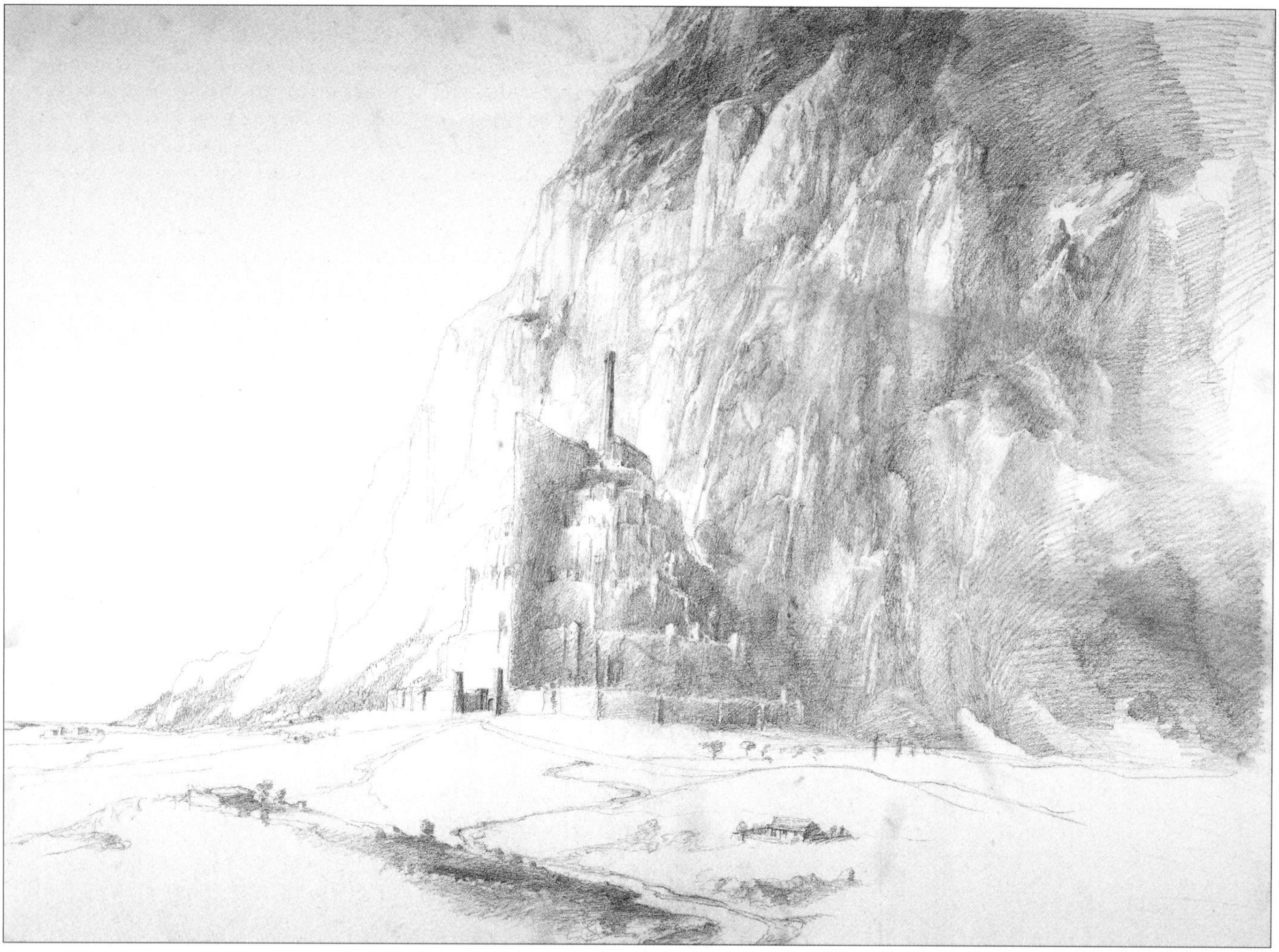

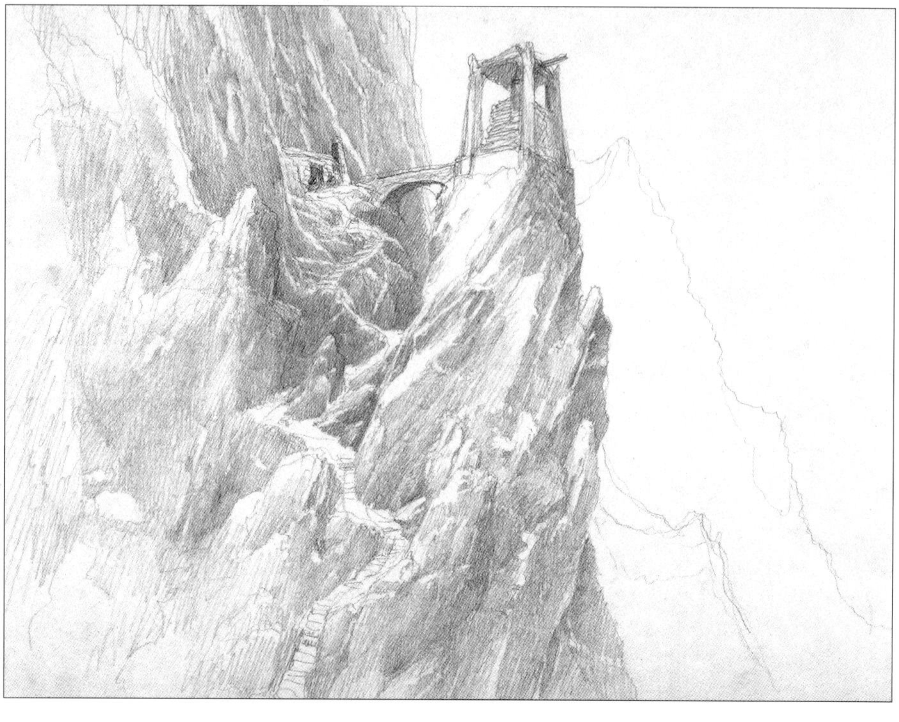

MINAS TIRITH *Pencil sketch*
"This is the beacon, which sits high up on the cliffs above Minas Tirith. Pippin is dispatched by Gandalf to light the fire, and we see him climbing up the pillar of rock and fiddling with the oil lamp that hangs at the top, ready to ignite the fire-wood and warn Gondor's allies that they should hurry to her aid. There is a roof over the structure simply because, as the beacon would have been lit so rarely, the occasional burned roof would be considered expendable, while a pile of wet timber would be completely useless." *AL*

MINAS TIRITH ***Pencil sketch***

"This drawing is a look at the city and the surrounding area. We originally built a large piece of cliff behind our 1/72nd-scale miniature, but it proved too big to move into the miniature stage and so was reused for other areas of Middle-earth rock. The miniature of Minas Tirith was built over the course of several months by Richard Taylor's dedicated team of craftspeople, with John Baster and Mary MacLachlan playing leading roles, as usual. This was well before the art department, which was going to be building the sets, had really been established, and before we knew in detail what was going to be happening in that particular part of Middle-earth. But we knew that there would be a number of very important scenes played out there, and that Peter Jackson, with his love of miniatures, would be using it extensively; so the structure, though only at 1/72nd-scale, would have to stand up to very close scrutiny.

"There were sections built at 1/14th-scale for some close-up shots, most notably the Court of the Kings itself and the surrounding buildings, and these were some of the most beautifully finished and convincing miniatures that were made for the trilogy." *AL*

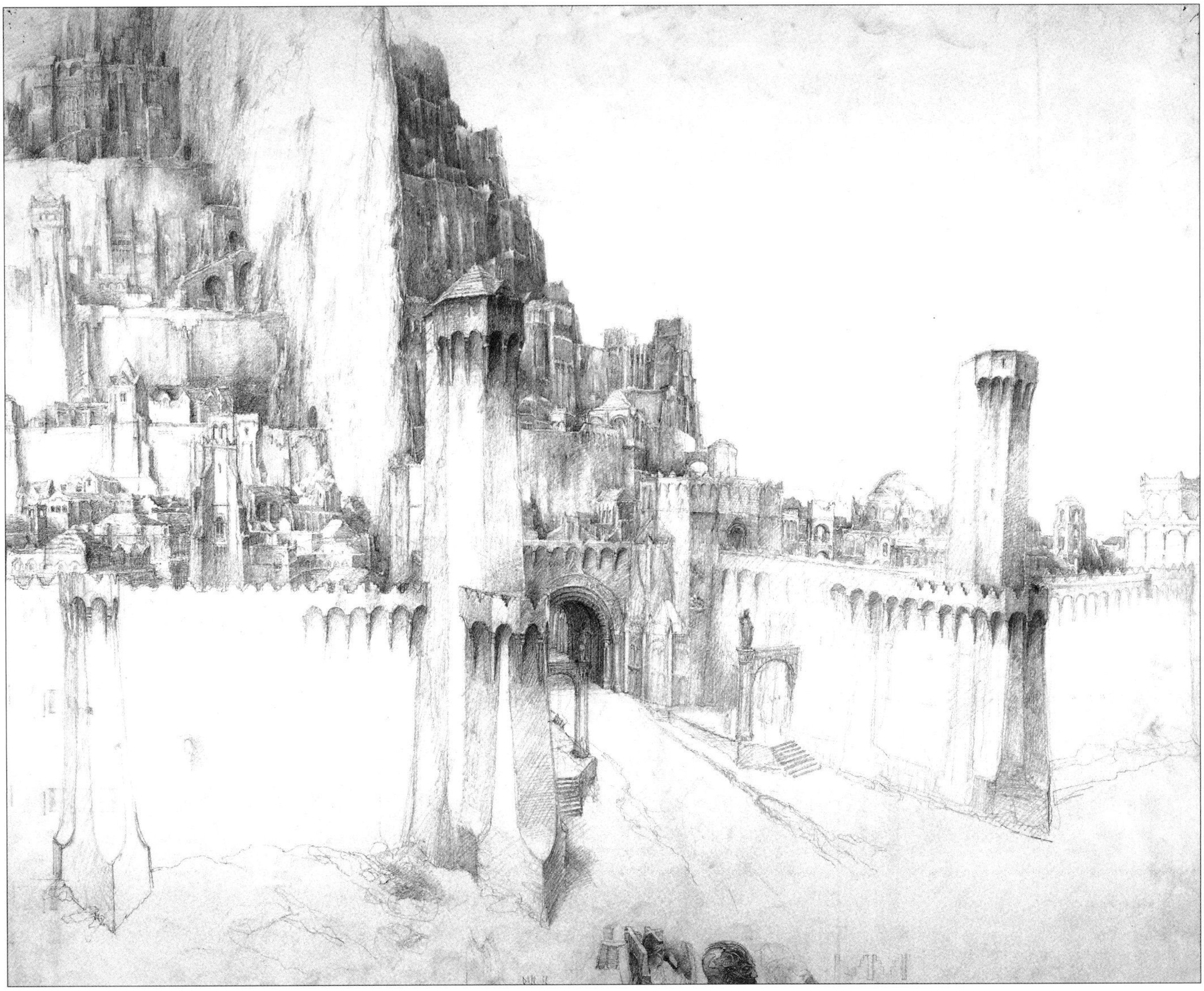

MINAS TIRITH ***Pencil sketch***

"Tolkien's description of Minas Tirith in *The Lord of the Rings* established a few basic facts that we did not wish to alter in our version. I had drawn the city before but not in great detail, and there was a huge amount that would have to be added to make it credible as the capital city of an ancient culture. I took the layout and dimensions that Tolkien had indicated and made a small maquette so that Peter Jackson could see the overall shape. Once we were happy with that, I began to explore the city in greater detail.

"I started with this view of the main gate protected by its bastions and towers and also indicated the seven tiers of the city rising up behind it, with the huge pier of rock that bisected the city and also formed the foundations of the Court of the Kings seven hundred feet above." *AL*

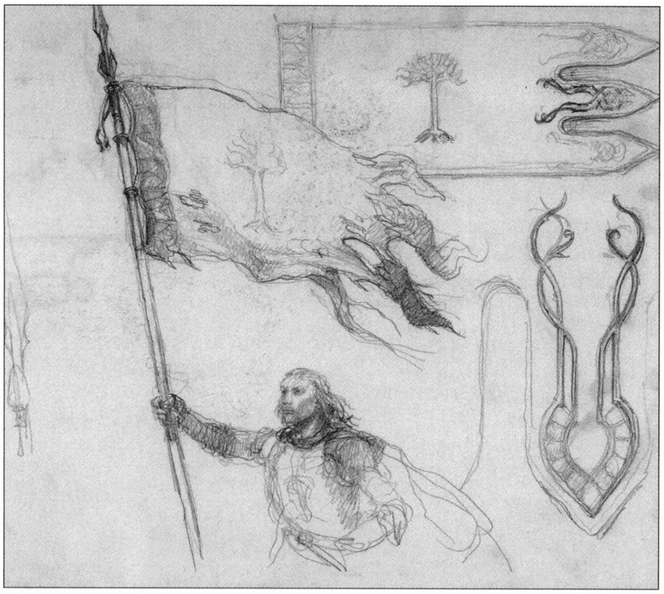

GONDORIAN BANNER ***Pencil sketch***
"We made a lot of flags and banners for Gondor and all the other cultures, and this rather battle-worn one was done as a potential design for Aragorn's flag." *AL*

MINAS TIRITH ***Pencil sketch***
"I did a series of drawings following the road that winds through Minas Tirith, as a way of exploring the look of the city from street level." *AL*

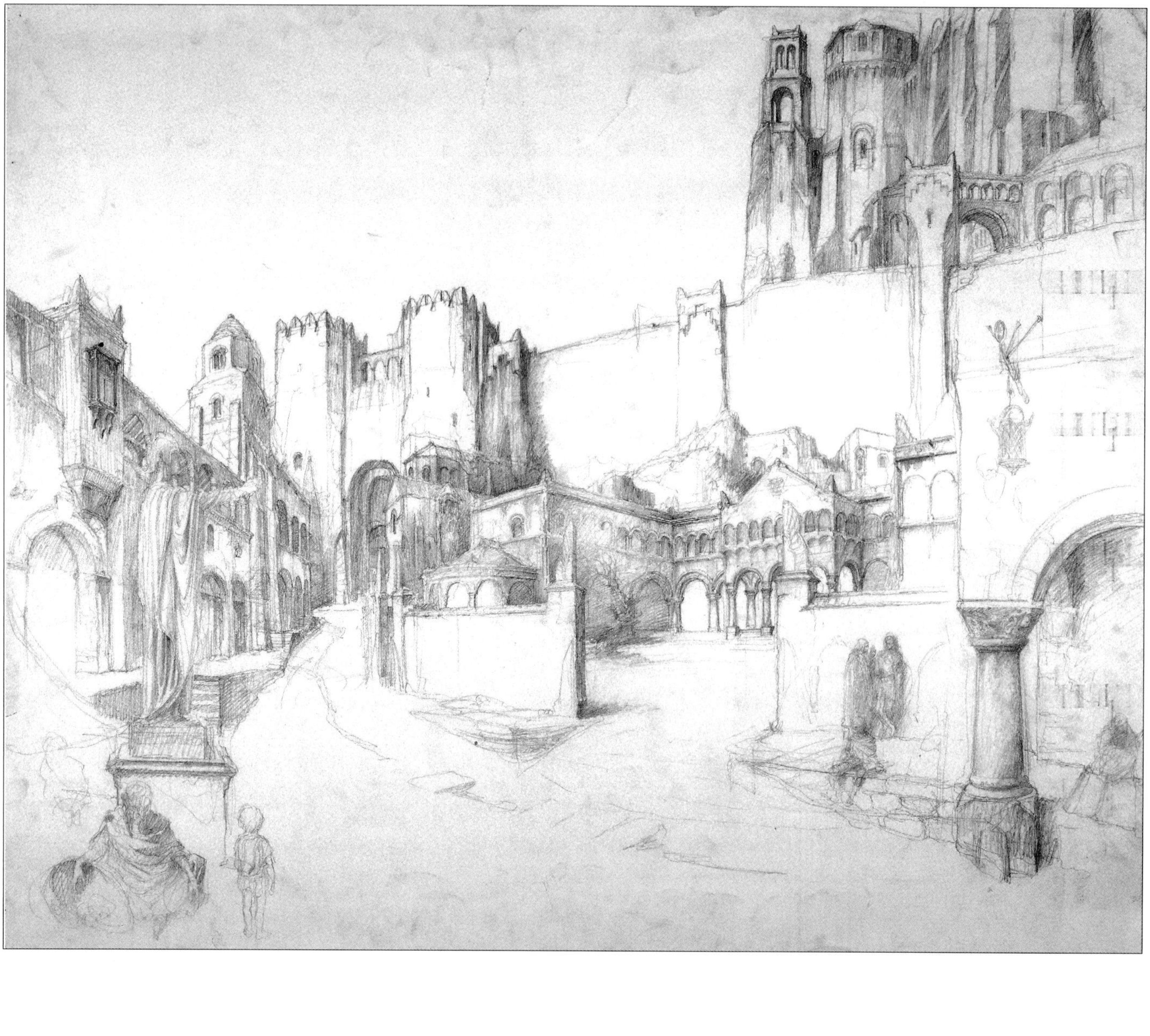

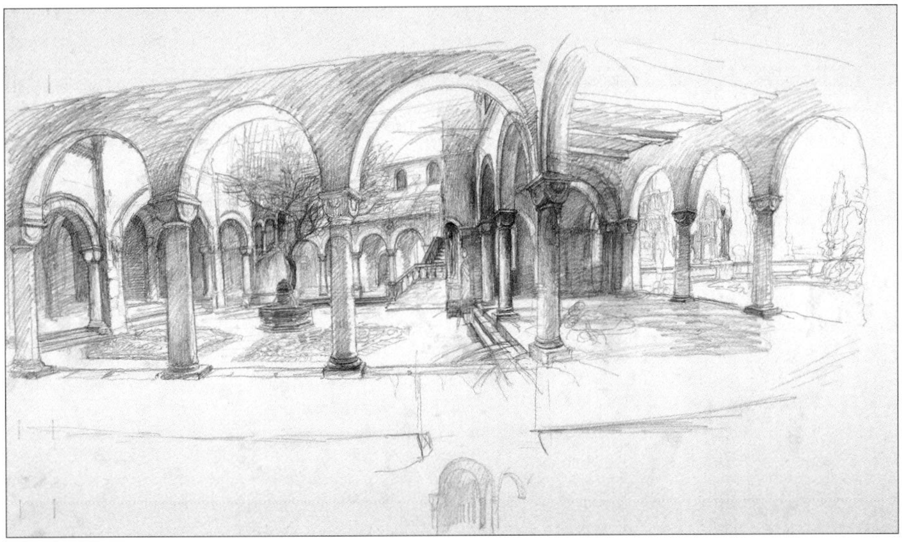

MINAS TIRITH ***Pencil sketch***
"The Houses of Healing are set around a courtyard and have a peaceful, monastic air of seclusion and retreat, though we wanted them also to feel, in the aftermath of the battle for Minas Tirith, like a Crimean field hospital, overflowing with wounded survivors." *AL*

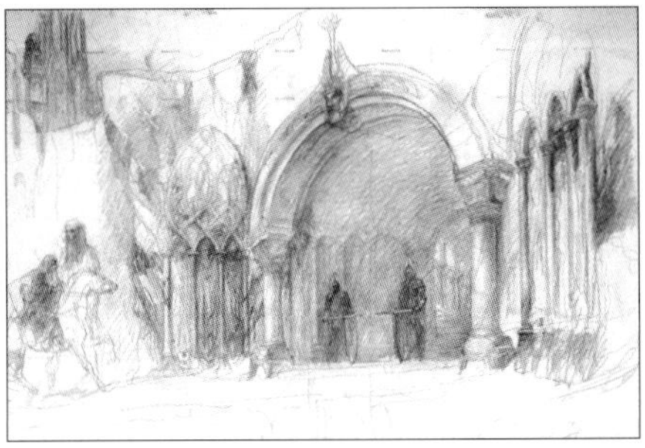

MINAS TIRITH ***Pencil sketch***
"After a steep climb, and dozens of drawings, we finally reached the seventh gate." *AL*

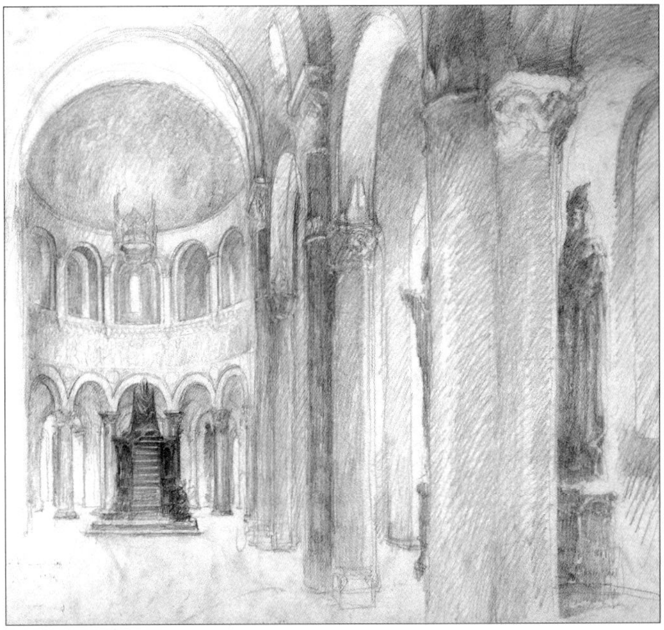

MINAS TIRITH ***Pencil sketch***
"The interior of the Court of the Kings, showing the pillars and arches, some of the statues that line the aisles, and the huge crown that hangs from the ceiling above the empty throne – and the Steward's chair that sits at its base. This set was one of the last to be built during principal photography, and it was one of the most frenetically busy periods for the art department, as well as for everybody else. Dan Hennah, Grant Major, and I spent a lot of time on this particular set because for some of our heroes it was to be a final destination, and it needed to be a worthy home for Aragorn and Arwen, as well as an atmospheric setting for our first encounter with Denethor." *AL*

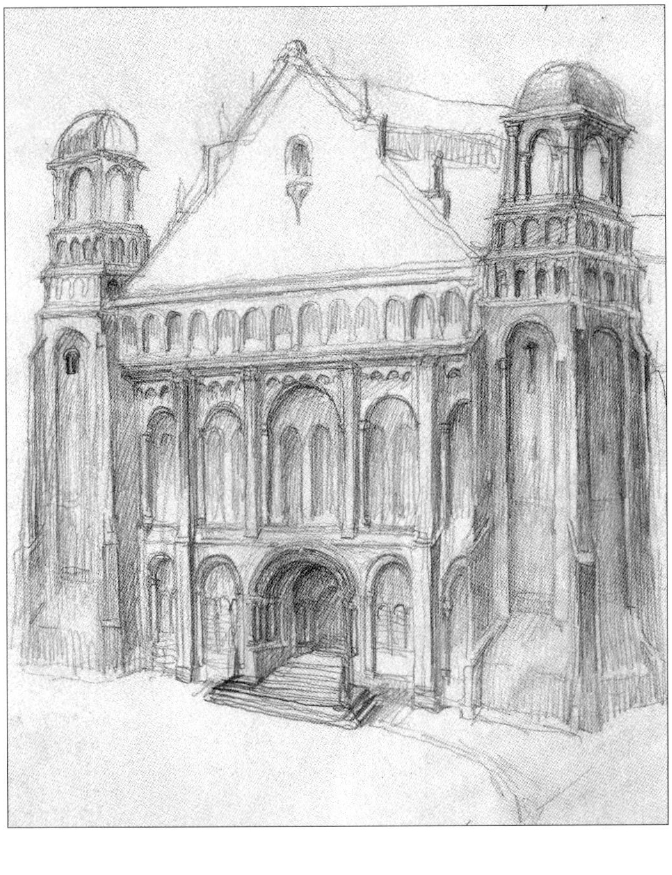

COURT OF THE KINGS ***Pencil sketch***
"This was built as a miniature, at $\frac{1}{72}$nd-scale as part of the whole city, and at $\frac{1}{14}$th-scale for the close-up set extension work for the scenes that take place on the upper level of Minas Tirith." *AL*

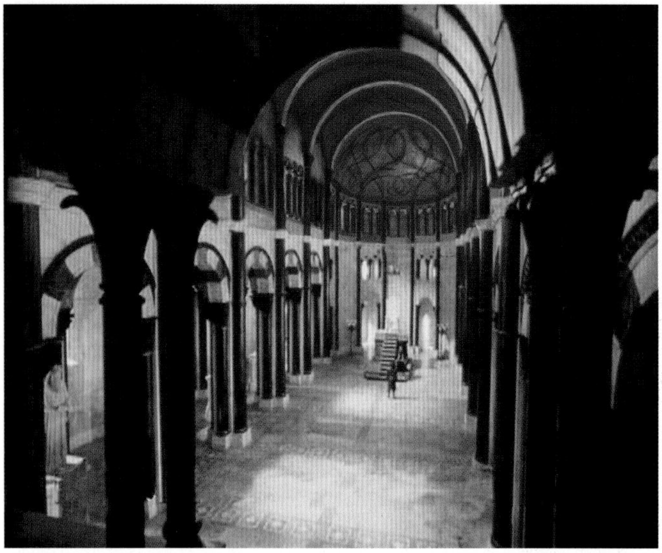

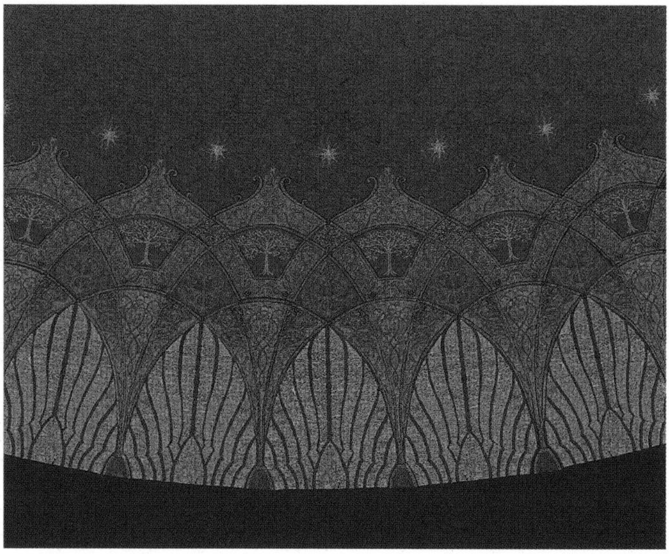

MINAS TIRITH *The Court of the Kings*
"This set was almost the same width as the building that contained it, and holes had to be made in the sides of the studio – which was a warehouse on Wellington's docks – so that lights could be positioned outside to shine through the windows. We spent a lot of time on the set, trying to make it as austerely beautiful as possible, but we knew that in order to make an impression it would need to be at least twice as high, and that would have to be achieved with a CGI extension. I had always imagined that we would have a clerestory above the aisle, but what I really wanted was a mosaic-covered domed roof at the far end. So along with the artwork, I provided this Photoshop mosaic to Brian Samuels at Weta Digital, who was building, texturing, lighting, and composing the final shots." *AL*

MINAS TIRITH *The Hallows*
"I was looking forward to seeing some shots focusing on the Hallows at the back of Minas Tirith. We see a lot of the city from other angles, and as I was quite happy with the way the miniature looked in that area, I was pleased that Peter Jackson wanted to take us there in the extended DVD edition. The little technological revolution that I'd been undergoing through post-production on these films had led me to switch to digital cameras, and I was able to take these pictures of the miniature, roughly tile them together, and drop in a background from our scenic shoot, within the space of a couple of hours." *AL*

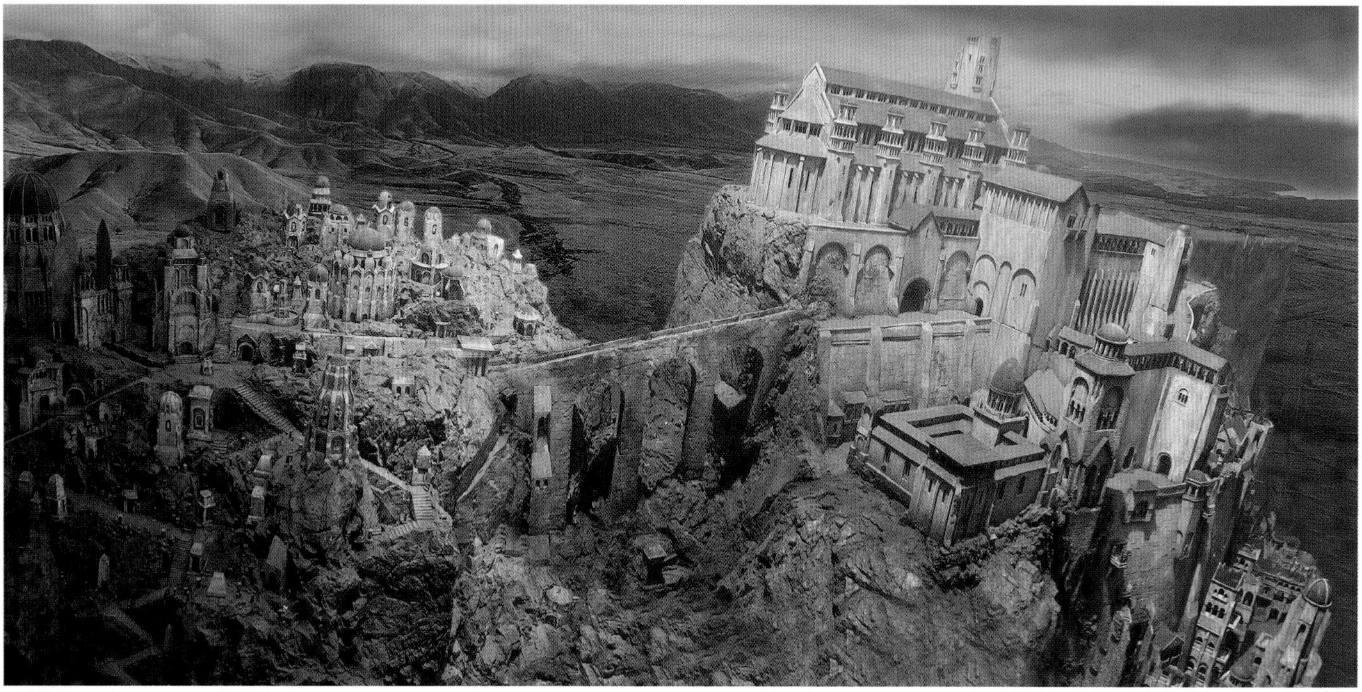

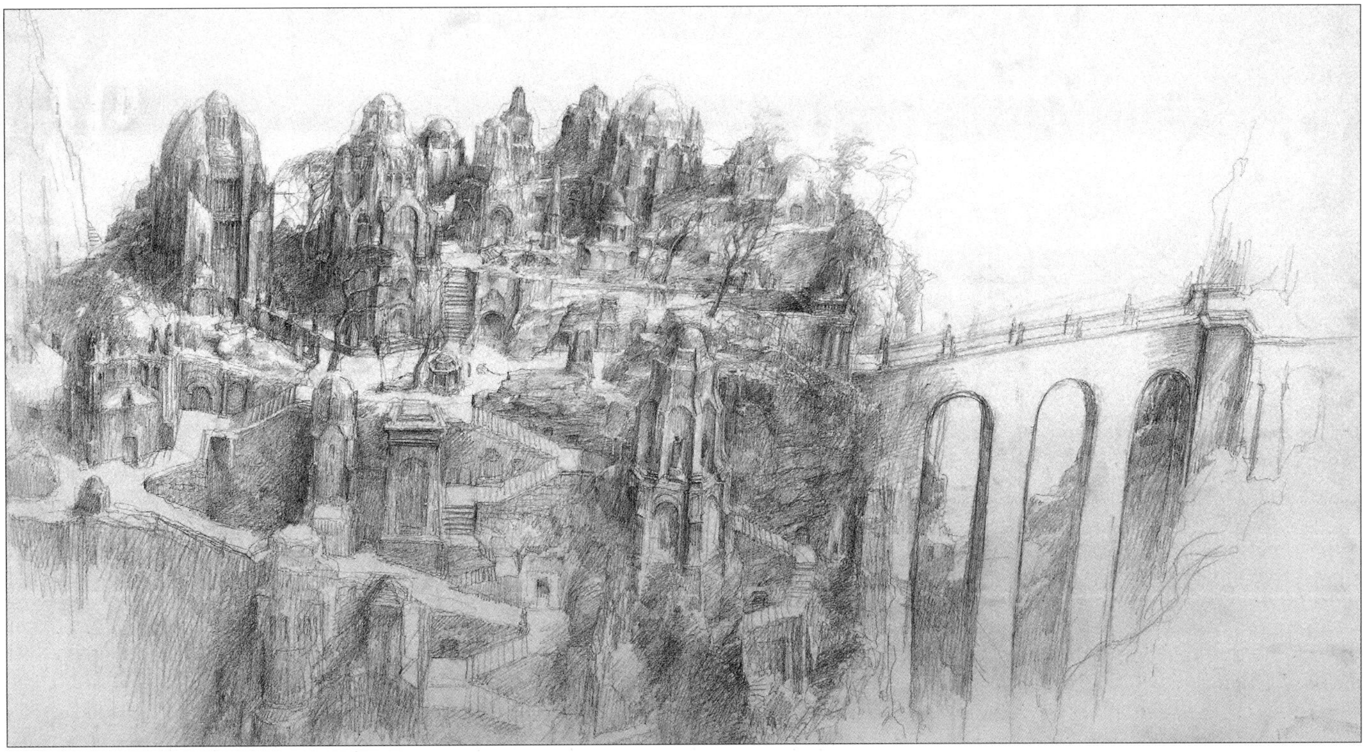

MINAS TIRITH ***Pencil sketch***
"The Hallows lie at the rear of the Court of the Kings, below the towering slopes of Mount Mindolluin. John Baster and Mary MacLachlan were able to take drawings like this and produce a highly detailed three-dimensional replica. At the left in the drawing you can see the ramp leading down to the entrance to the Stewards' Tomb." *AL*

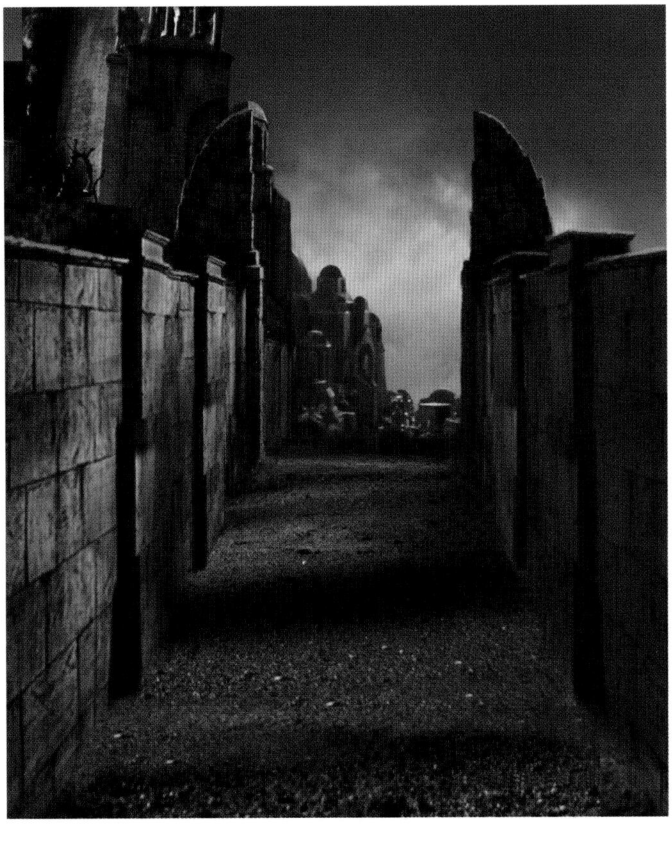

MINAS TIRITH
The Stewards' Tomb
"The Stewards' Tomb needed a set extension for shots where we were looking back through the opened door, and I was able to save a few hours of the matte painters' precious time by doing the artwork at a sufficiently high resolution that it could be used as it was." *AL*

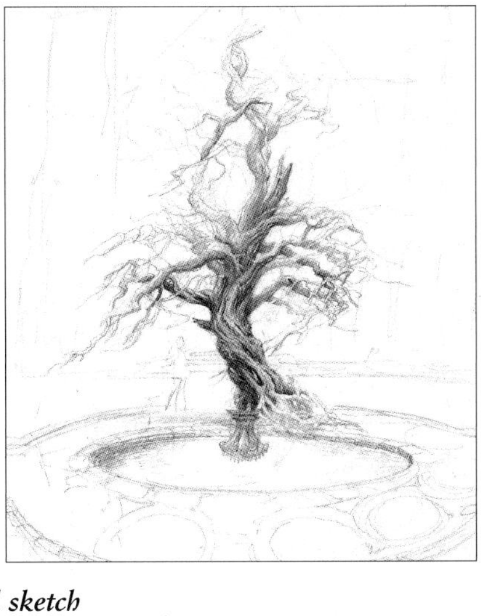

MINAS TIRITH ***Pencil sketch***
"One of several versions of the White Tree of Gondor. This was to be seen in both its dead and its rejuvenated state. I treasure a lovely memory of seeing Brian Massey's tree with four set dressers perched in it like birds, attaching thousands of blossoms to its dead twigs. I know that in the book the White Tree is replaced by a sapling that Aragorn finds on the slopes of Mount Mindolluin, but at this stage in the film allowing the new king to go for a stroll in the mountains wouldn't have been making the best use of his time – and seeing the Tree reborn is such a beautiful moment." *AL*

DUNHARROW ***Pencil sketch***
"This is a design for the look of Théoden's tent and the way it was situated at Dunharrow. It's quite close to the final result." *AL*

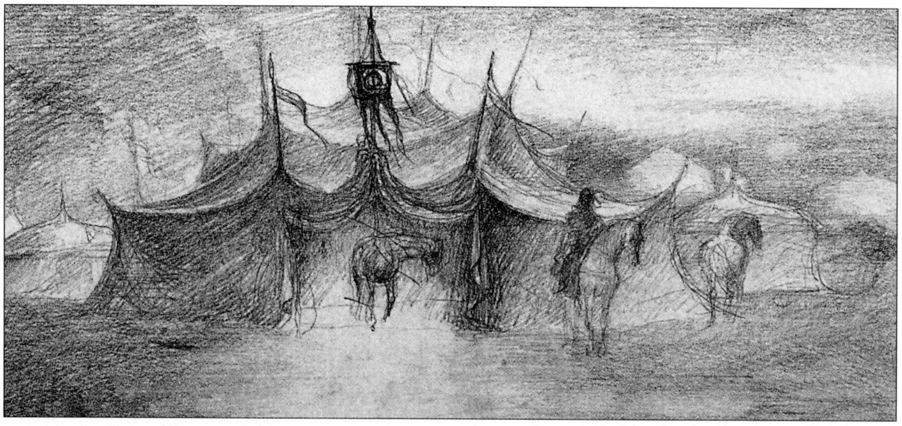

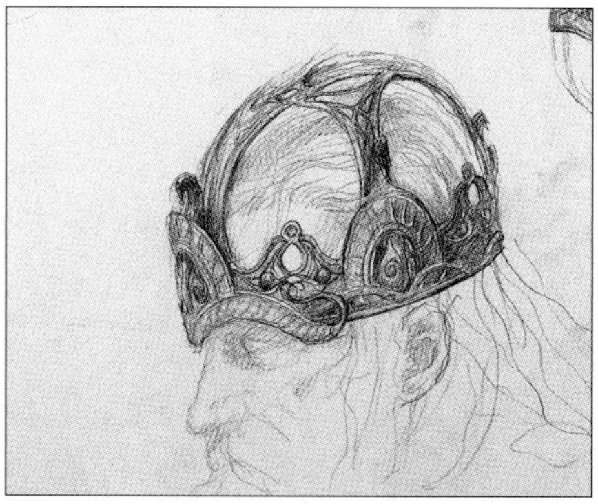

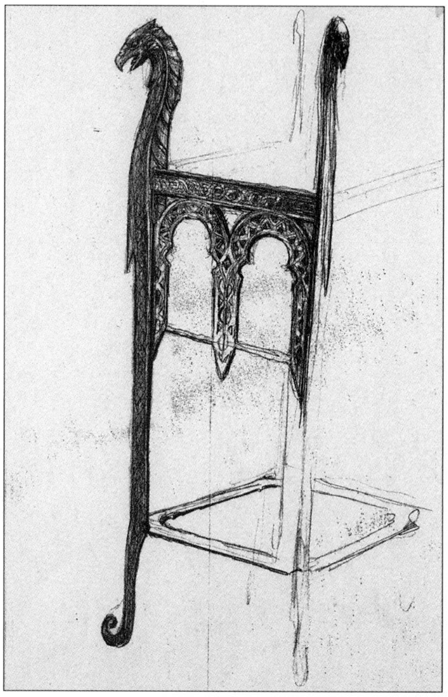

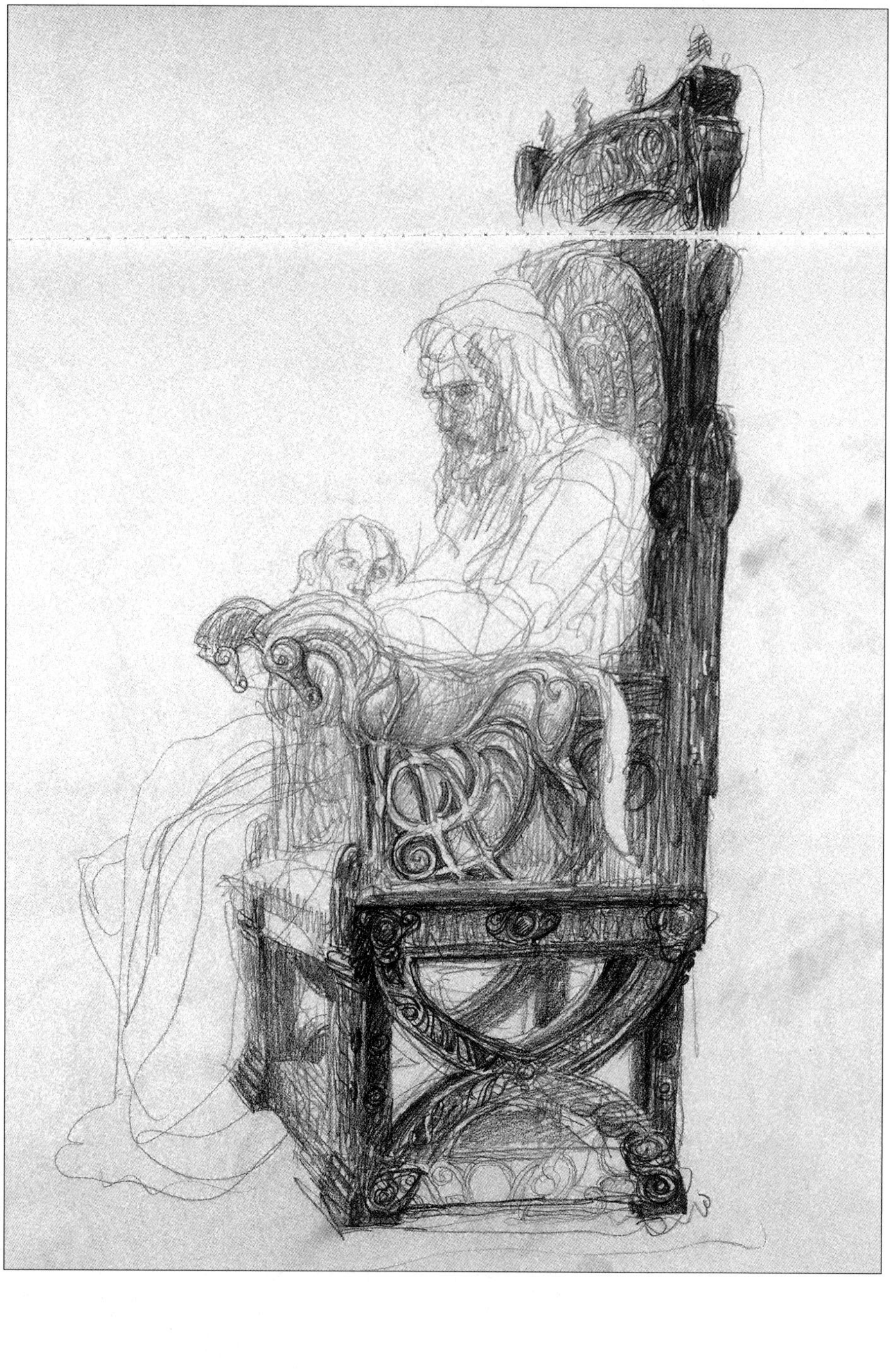

THÉODEN
Crown, throne, and weapons stand
"I did some drawings of crowns for Jasmine Watson when she and Ngila Dickson were working on Théoden's costume. The throne had to have quite a powerful presence as well, in contrast to the wretched condition that Théoden is in when we first see him. The carpenters took great pleasure and pride in their work, and this is a fine example of their craftsmanship.

"We also needed a place for visitors to leave their weapons, and this weapons stand was positioned outside the Golden Hall." *AL*

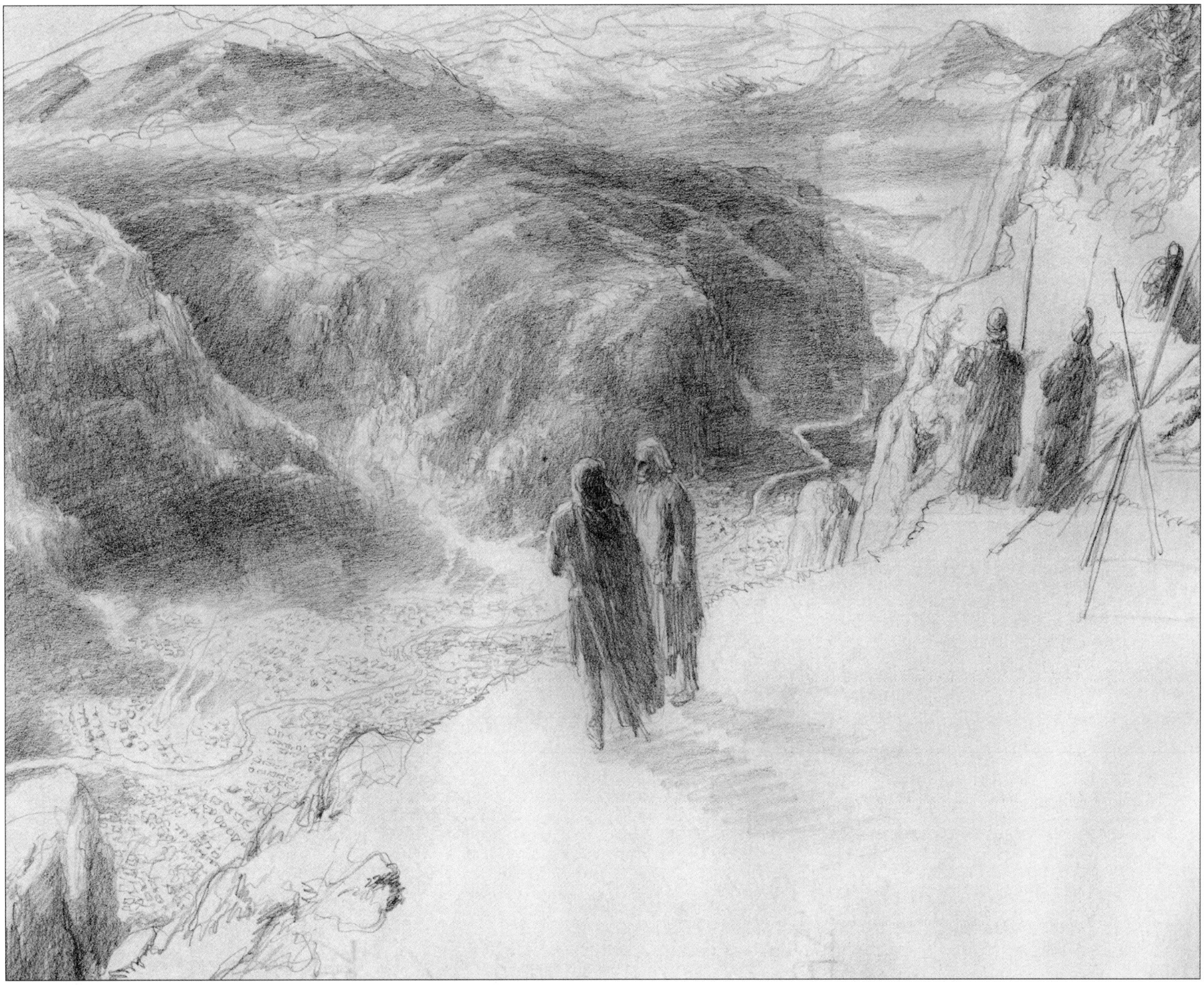

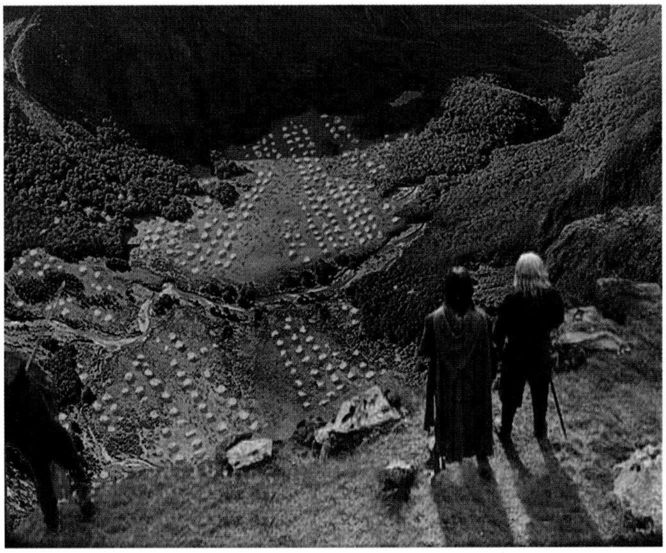

DUNHARROW ***Pencil sketch and digital artwork***

"We had the good fortune to be able to work with the excellent landscape photographer Craig Potton on some of our scenic shoots. He had worked a lot with a helicopter pilot from Queenstown, Alfie Speight, whose knowledge of the South Island made him a vital part of any recon or aerial shoot that we wished to undertake. During post-production on *The Return of the King*, it became obvious that we would need to expand our stills library with photos taken specifically for shots that Weta Digital would be working on, as well as looking out for rocky mountainsides and other elements that would be useful for matte painters and compositors. One of the environments that we needed a background for was the Dunharrow plateau, and we chanced upon the perfect place, with all the right ingredients. Alfie hovered at the top of the cliff, rotating the chopper in time with Craig's careful tiling, so we were able to return with a complete environment that needed very little manipulation, beyond filling the valley floor with six thousand horsemen and their tents." *AL*

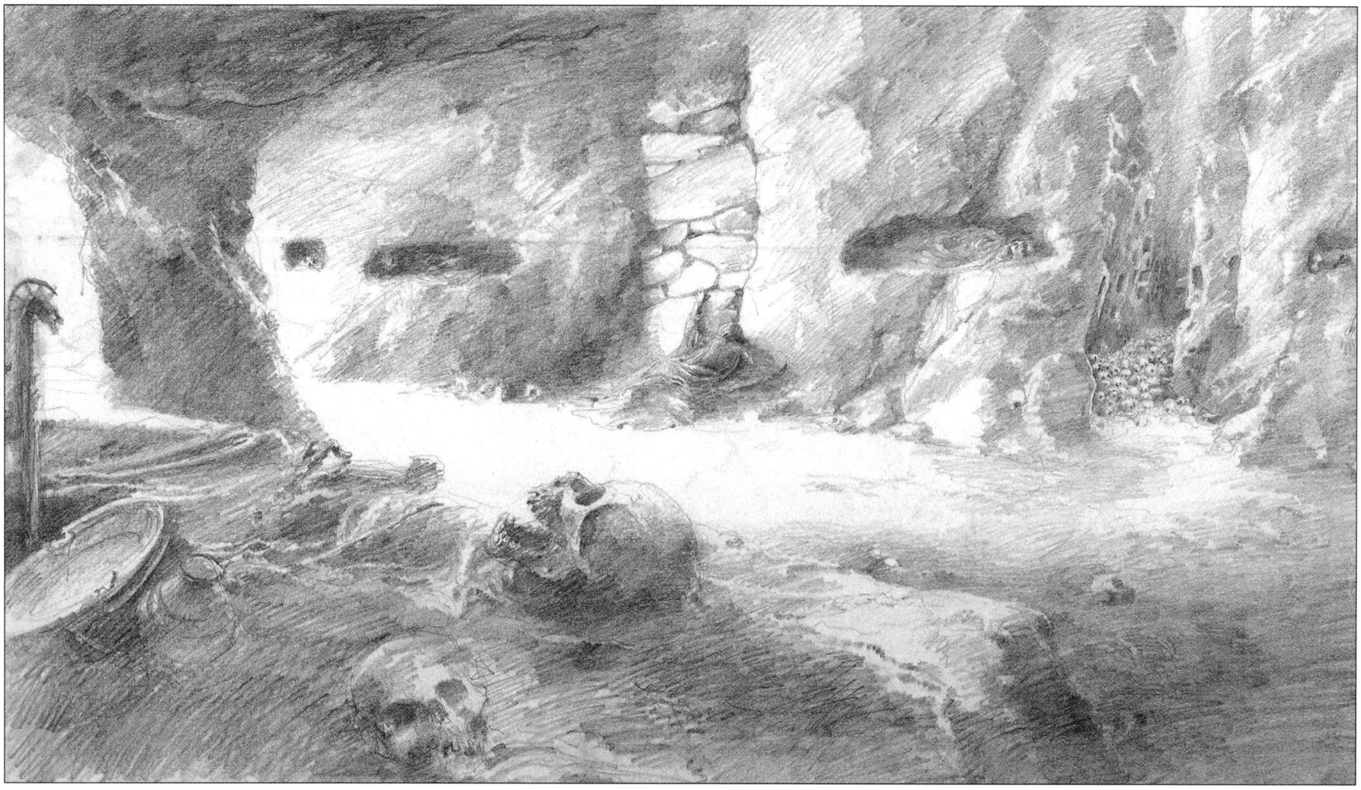

PATHS OF THE DEAD ***Pencil sketch***
"Inside the passage we become aware that we are in a catacombs with the remains of ancient corpses laid out among their grave-goods in coffin-sized niches in the walls, and the figure that Tolkien refers to – dead in the act of struggling to enter a tomb or escape some unknown terror – can be seen to one side." *AL*

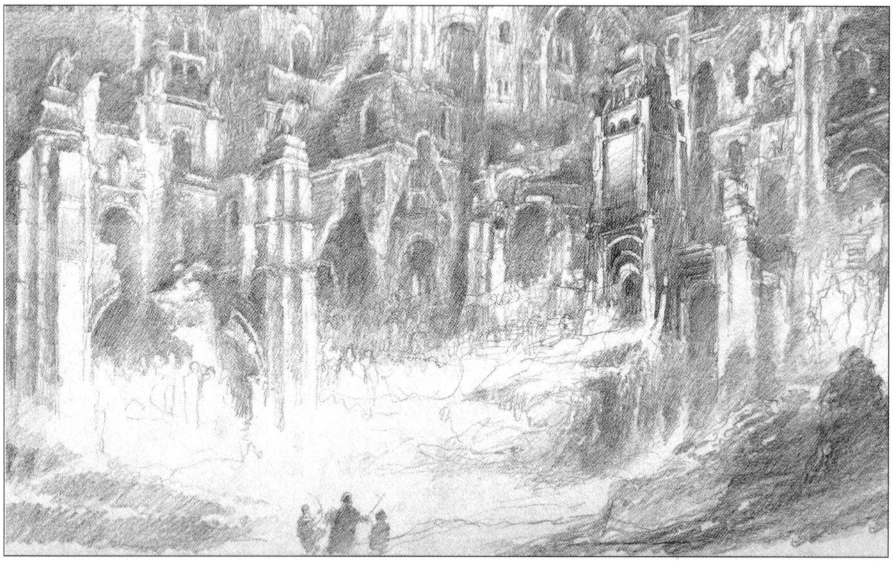

CITY OF THE DEAD ***Pencil sketch***
"Aragorn, Gimli, and Legolas, on their route through the mountain, enter a huge open space that has these more formal architectural elements, as well as a concentration of the catacomb-like rock tombs. Then, as the King of the Dead and his army emerge, we realize that there is also a ghost city clinging to the sides of the cavern and the chasm that runs through it." *AL*

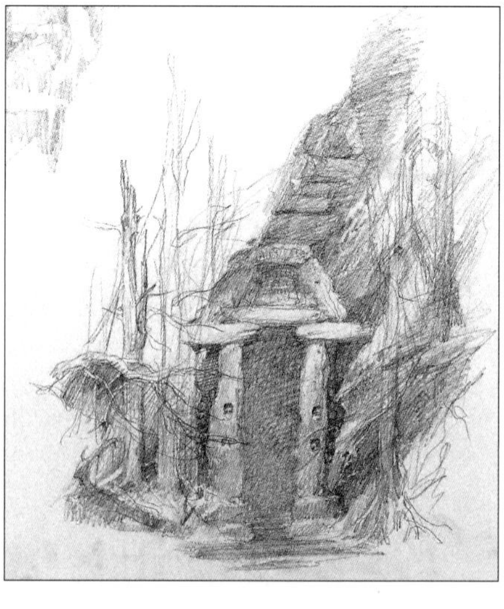

PATHS OF THE DEAD ***Pencil sketch***
"This is the gateway to the Paths of the Dead. Skulls are piled up between the slabs of rock and the walls of the ravine as well as in the niches in the door columns. We wanted some kind of inscription on the lintel above the doorway and, partly because I was unsure what language to use and partly because I like the idea that Middle-earth has some areas of its history that no one has thoroughly explored, I devised a few vaguely prehistoric pictographs that looked ominous and shamanistic." *AL*

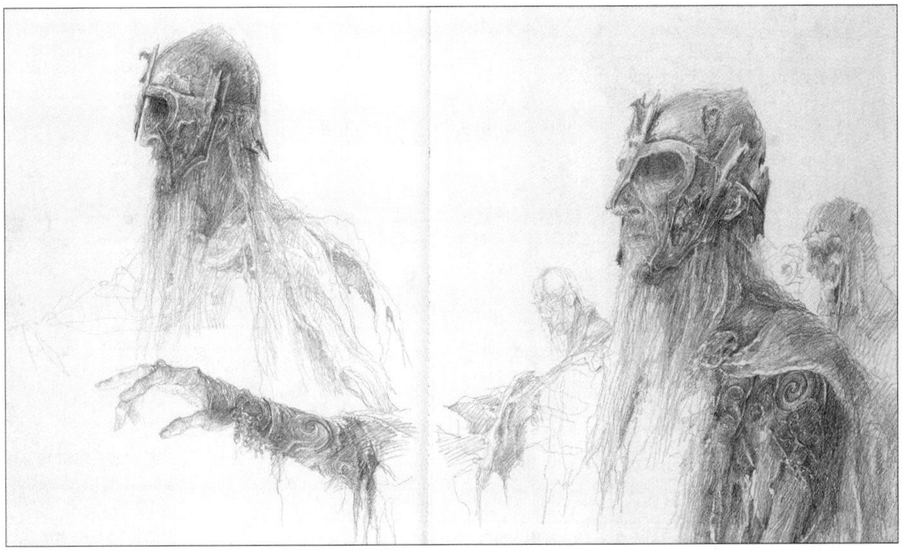

KING OF THE DEAD *Pencil sketch*
"In these sketches I was thinking about the King of the Dead's helmet and his general look. One idea we had was to have the helmet partly rotted away to show something of the inside of his face as the flesh had rotted in the same place. Although the King of the Dead was an actor in a prosthetic, he had digital insides and a digital rotting skull, and we see both at once; sometimes the skull will be more prominent and at other times the actor's prosthetic exterior, depending on how angry he is at any given moment." *AL*

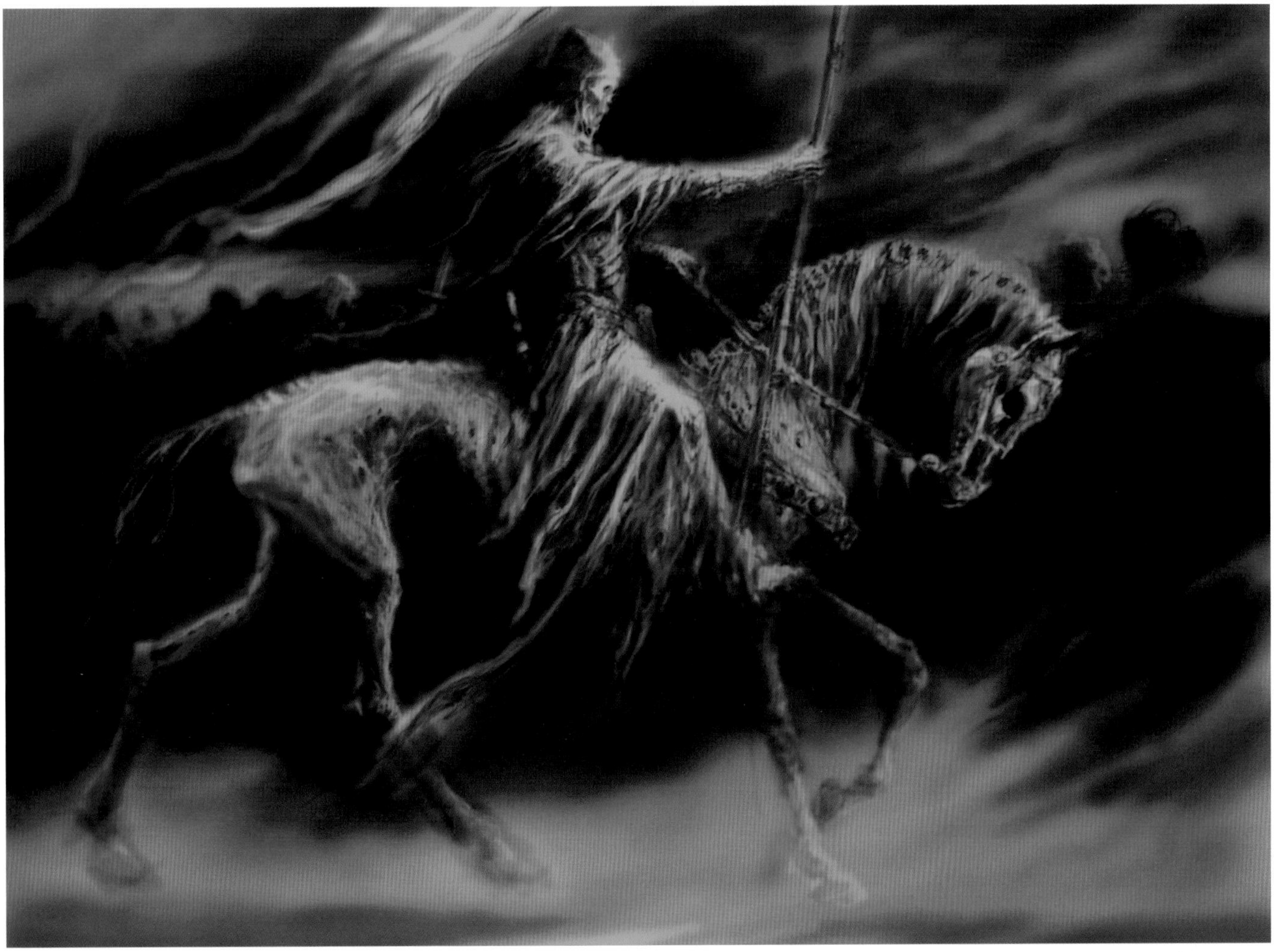

ARMY OF THE DEAD *Digital artwork*
"Peter Jackson mentioned, quite casually, that it would be good to see the occasional horseman among our dead warriors, so I produced this. There was some talk about simple ways of reproducing this effect in what might be only a fleeting shot, but the ever-optimistic Matt Aitken at Weta Digital was confident that it would be easier than it looked to model as a CG creature, so we went ahead with it." *AL*

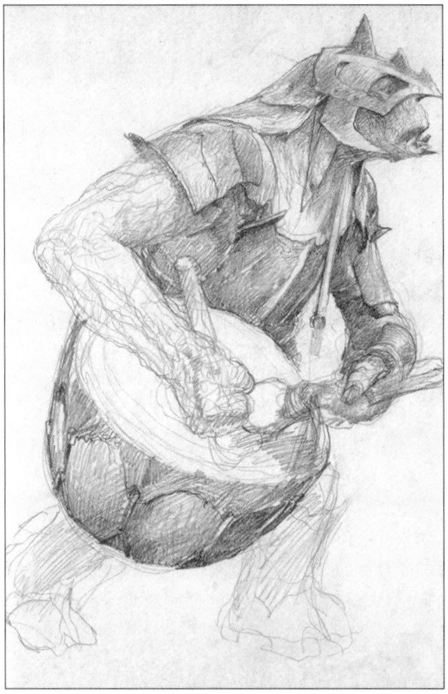

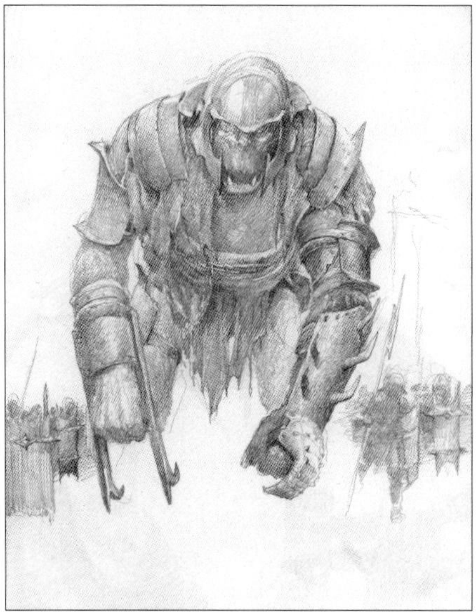

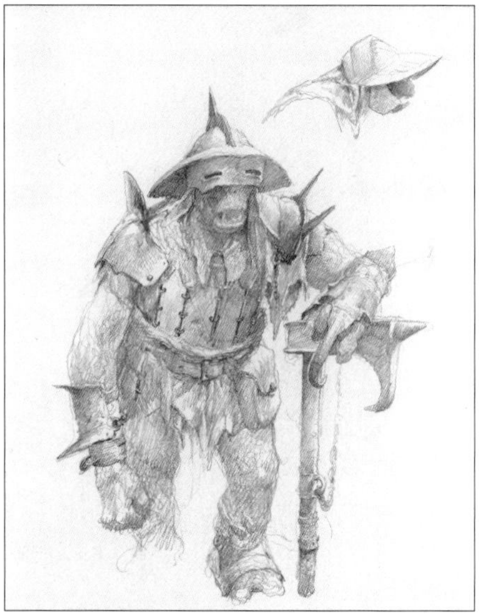

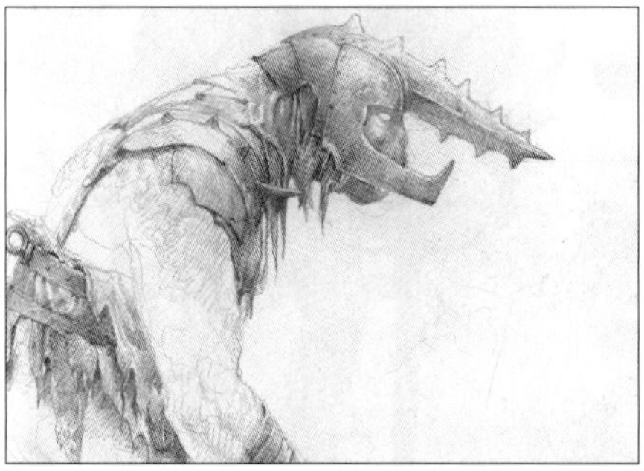

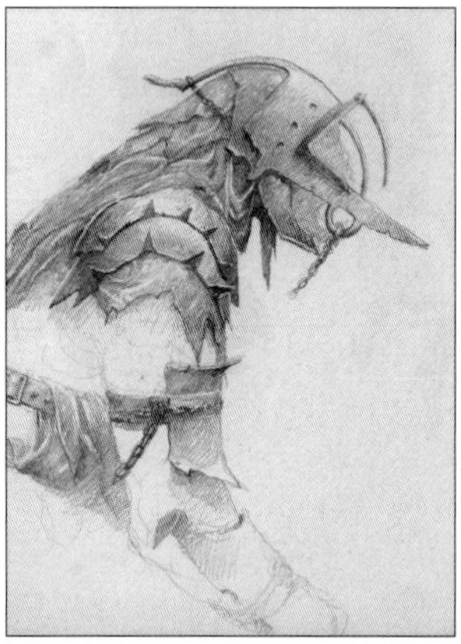

THE SIEGE OF GONDOR ***Pencil sketches***
"It was that time of year again . . . The trolls, which we had adapted from our original Moria Cave-troll into the trolls we see opening the Black Gate in *The Two Towers,* needed to be shifted up a gear or two to appear in *The Return of the King.* I hadn't been involved in the creation of the first troll, but I'd added the harness and blinkered helmets for the first upgrade and also did a few drawings for the second. We settled on five variants for use at different stages in the battle, including the one that confronts Aragorn toward the end of the film." *AL*

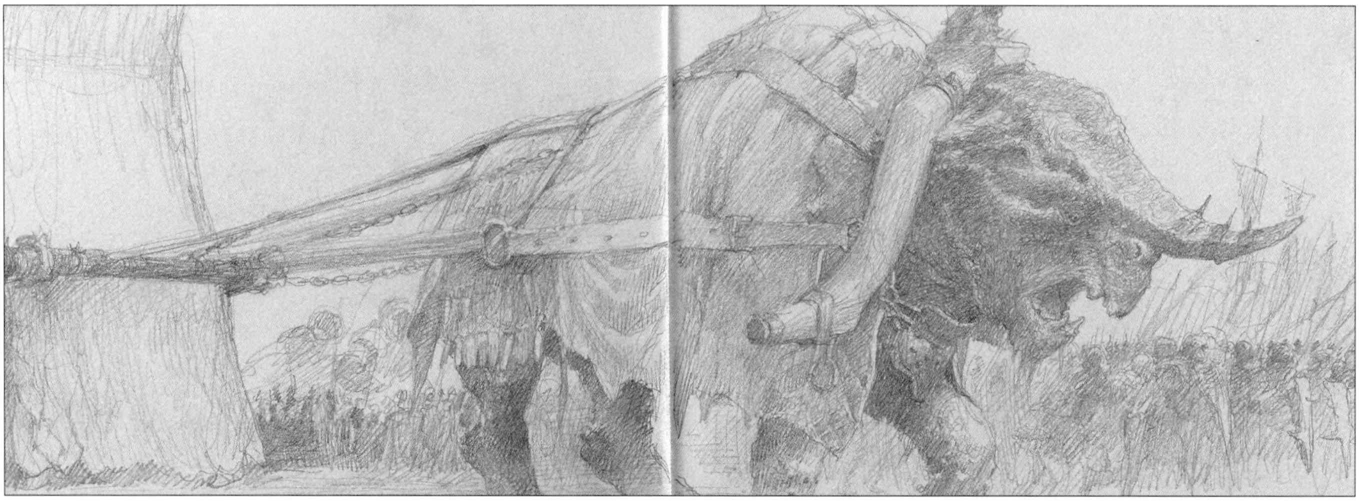

THE SIEGE OF GONDOR ***Pencil sketch***
"Because we have only one totally new monster, Shelob, in *The Return of the King*, I thought there might be an opportunity to put something else onto the Pelennor Fields, which would be a bit of a surprise. So I did this drawing of the great beast that would be pulling the siege engines and/or Grond across the fields. Then, just recently, I was looking back over some of John Howe's stuff and realized that he'd created a similar creature [see page 132] back when he was working on the project, but his had two fearsome-looking horns rather than my monosaurus look. I think my beast is halfway between a dinosaur and a huge great ox." *AL*

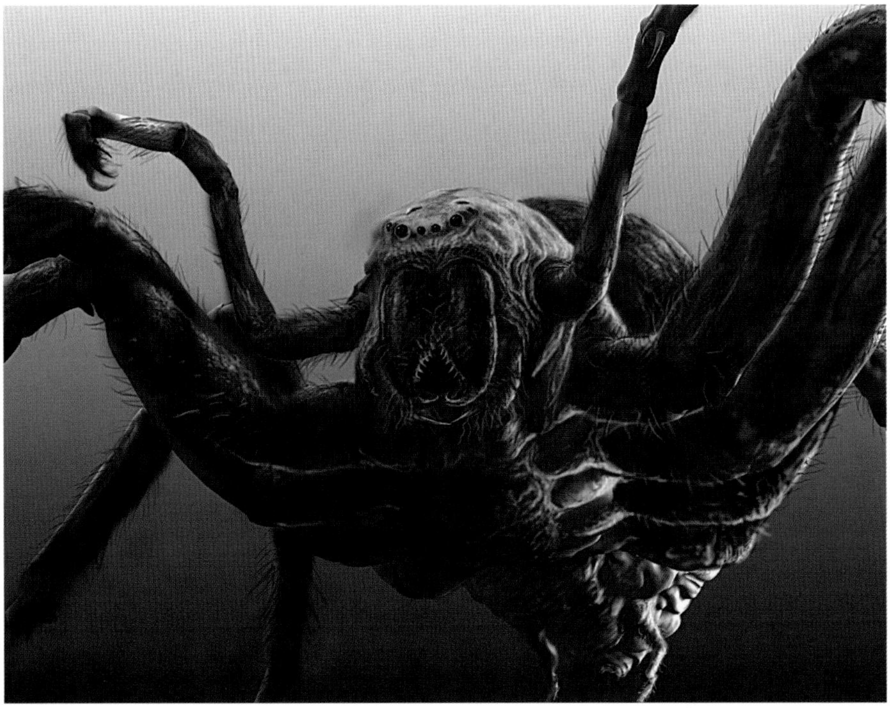

SHELOB'S LAIR *Digital artwork*
"This is one of several studies I did when we were working on the redesign of this character. A partially finished gray-scale image was sent from Matt Aitken's model department, and I worked on top of this, experimenting with some different looks. I don't think anyone who worked on Shelob quite managed to capture what Peter Jackson was actually after until he had attacked it himself with a handful of Plasticine." *AL*

SHELOB'S LAIR *Pencil sketch*
"The drawing below is Frodo in Shelob's tunnel, making his way along the passageway, with Shelob just emerging from another hole higher up. We see just her legs and body starting to pull out of this hole before the scene where she finally attacks him." *AL*

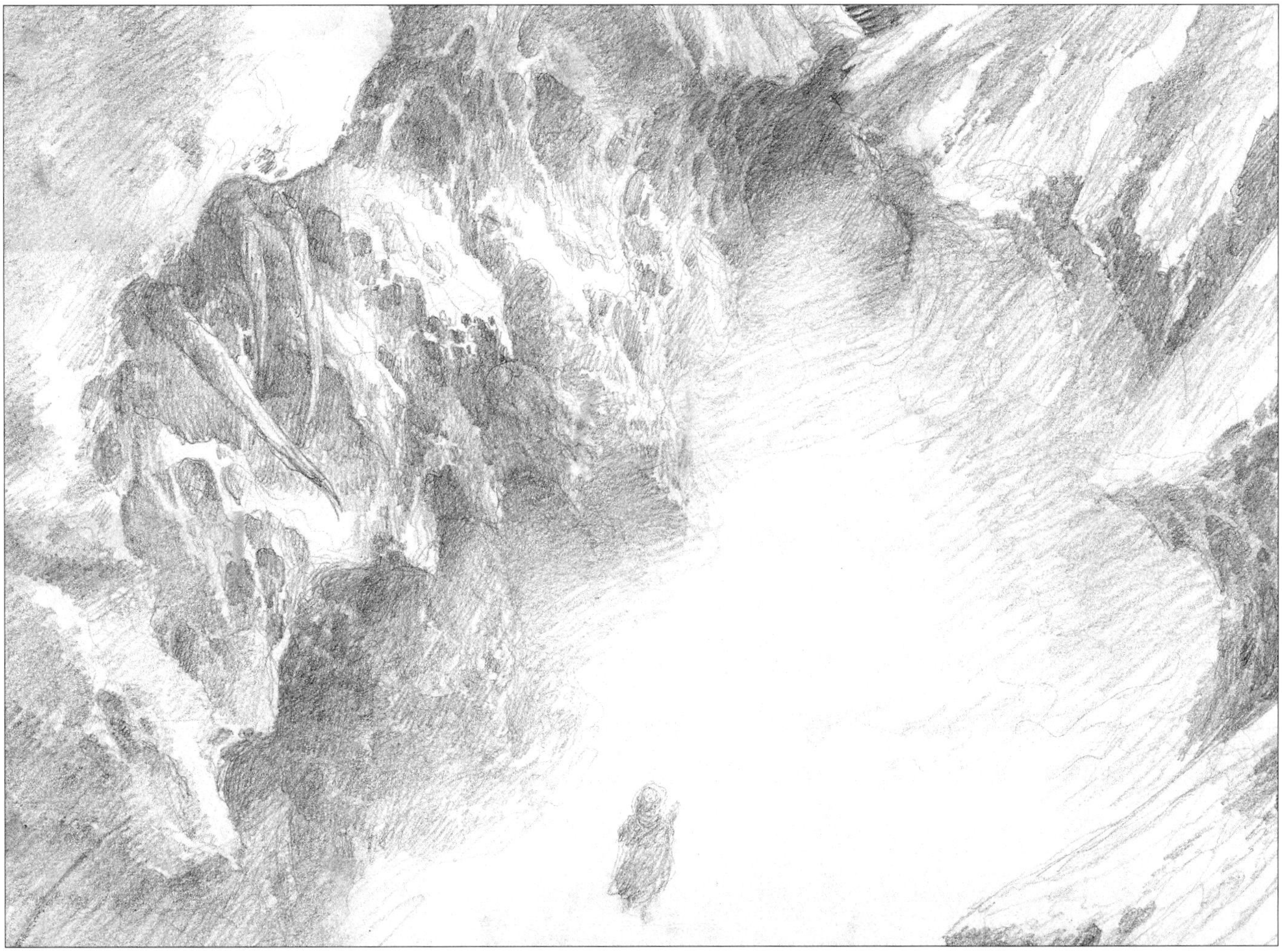

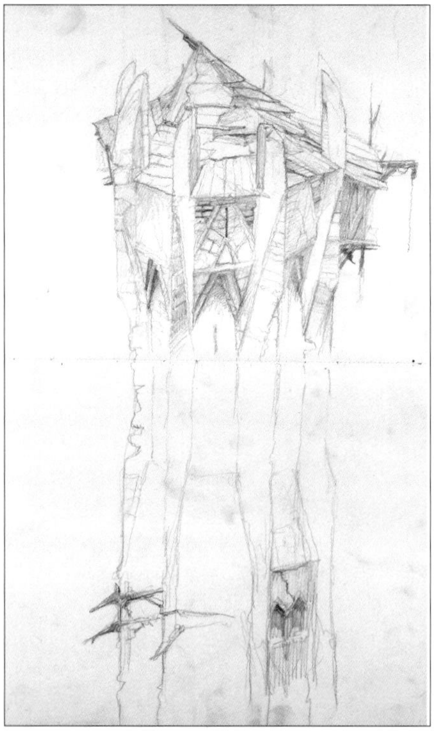

CIRITH UNGOL *Pencil sketch*
"This is of the top of the miniature and shows how a Númenórean structure might have been adapted by the Orcs that later captured and inhabited it. So it's got these large pieces of metal that help to hold the crumbling structure together but also serve to remind us that we're in a pretty evil place." *AL*

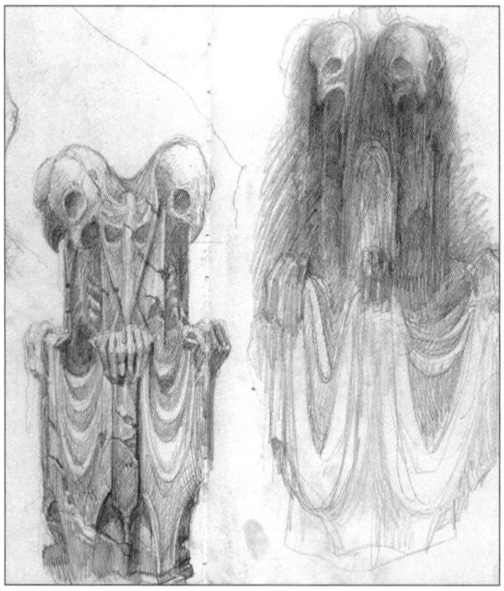

CIRITH UNGOL WATCHERS
Pencil sketches
"John Howe's drawings of the Watchers had quite a disturbing look to them, and I tried to keep that bird-skull look in these designs for the final sculptures." *AL*

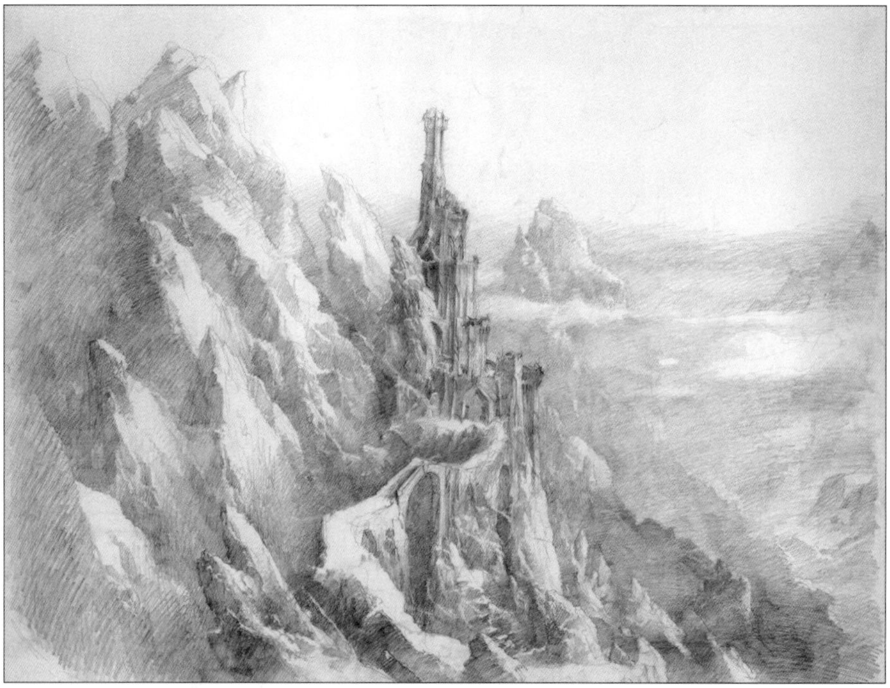

CIRITH UNGOL *Pencil sketch*
"I did this drawing, together with a Plasticine maquette, as an overall look for the miniature, and followed it with more detailed drawings. We were able to work on the sets at the same time that the miniature was being constructed, so an idea for one could quickly be applied to the other." *AL*

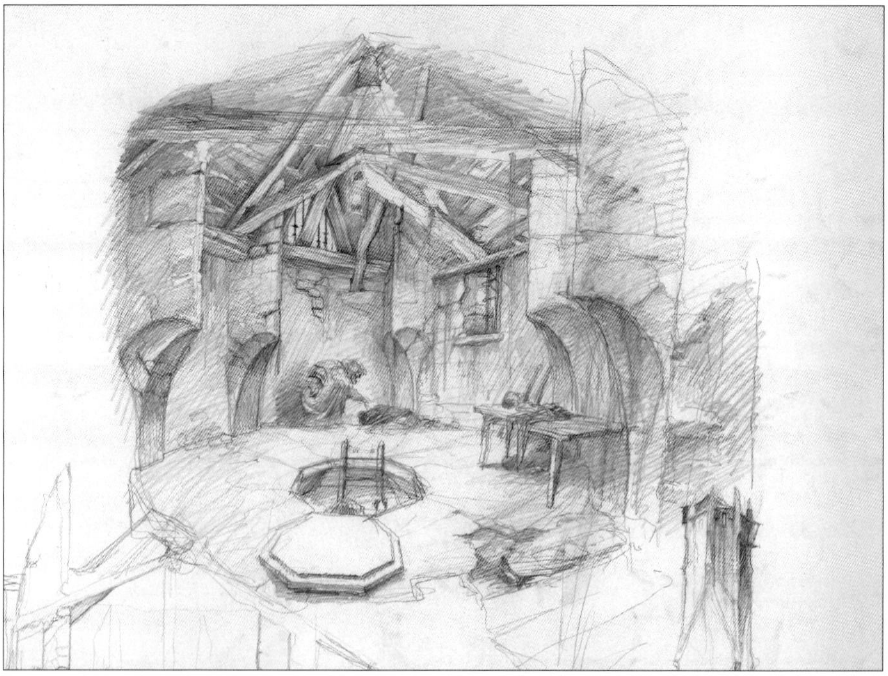

CIRITH UNGOL *Pencil sketch*
"This is the room at the top of the Cirith Ungol tower, where Frodo has been taken by the Orcs. We can just see Sam climbing up the ladder to rescue him. This set was built separately, but the interior of the tower below the trapdoor was part of the main set and offered more stunt opportunities." *AL*

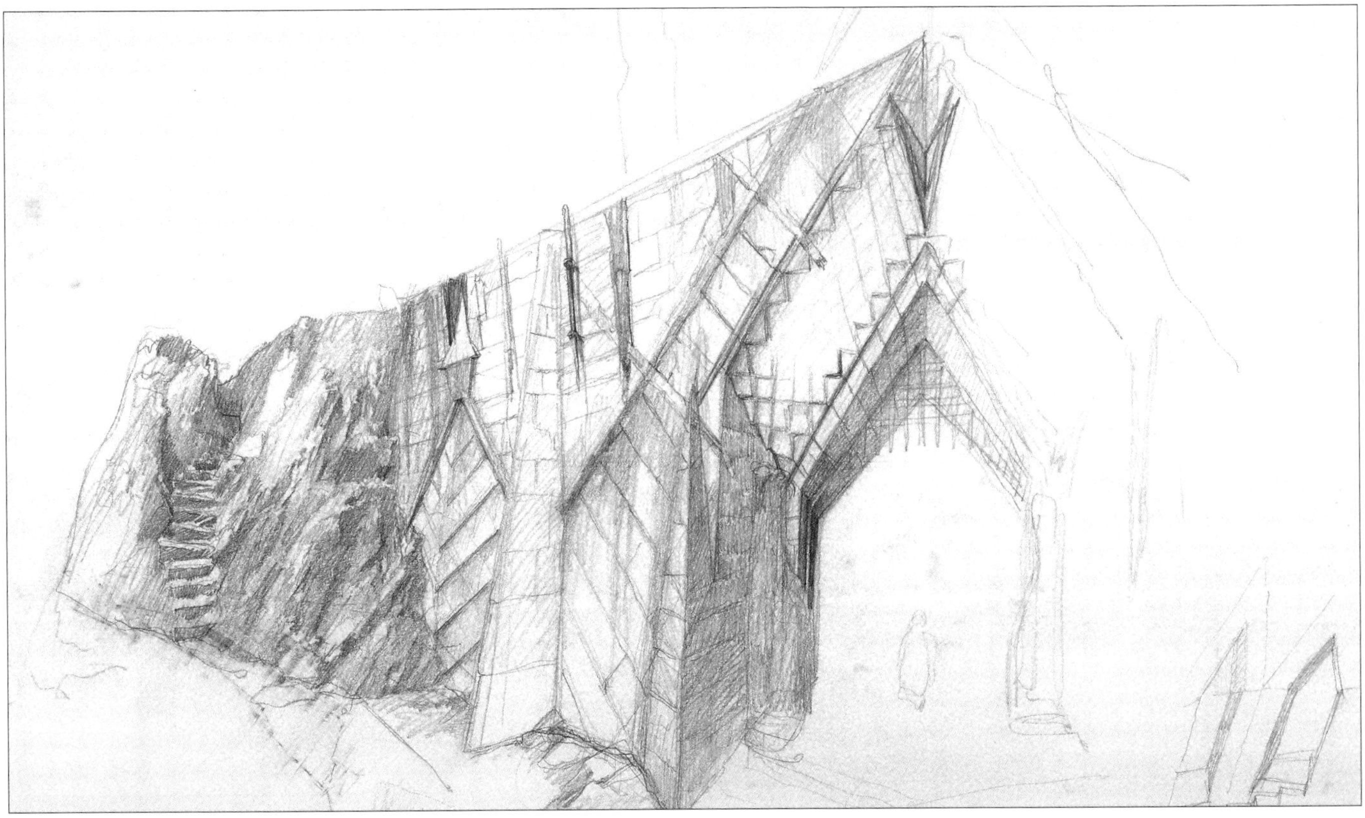

CIRITH UNGOL *Pencil sketch*
"This shows the gateway through which Sam passes on his mission to rescue Frodo, together with some of the unusual stonework that makes this fortress distinctive. The basic fabric of the walls themselves would have been created by Gondorians rather than Orcs, but they added the rusty ironwork and crude huts. The Gondorians, however, must have been affected by their proximity to Mordor, because it would have been quite a frightening place, even without the Orcish additions." *AL*

THE PELENNOR FIELDS *Digital artwork*
"Complex animation shots, like the one in which fell beasts dive-bomb Minas Tirith, involve a lot of planning. To aid this process, I had made a map covering everything between the White Mountains and the far edge of the Mordor mountains. This was turned into a simple 3D model by Eric Saindon, which Christian Rivers and Richard Moore used to stage their previsualizations. When this was complete and Peter Jackson had approved the animation, I assembled frames from it and created this art, which would cover the background for the whole shot. Dylan Cole then used it as the basis for his matte painting [see page 220]. I didn't show the layers of cloud that the Nazgûl would fly through in this artwork, which is less about the finished look of the shot and more about the basic anatomy of the landscape." *AL*

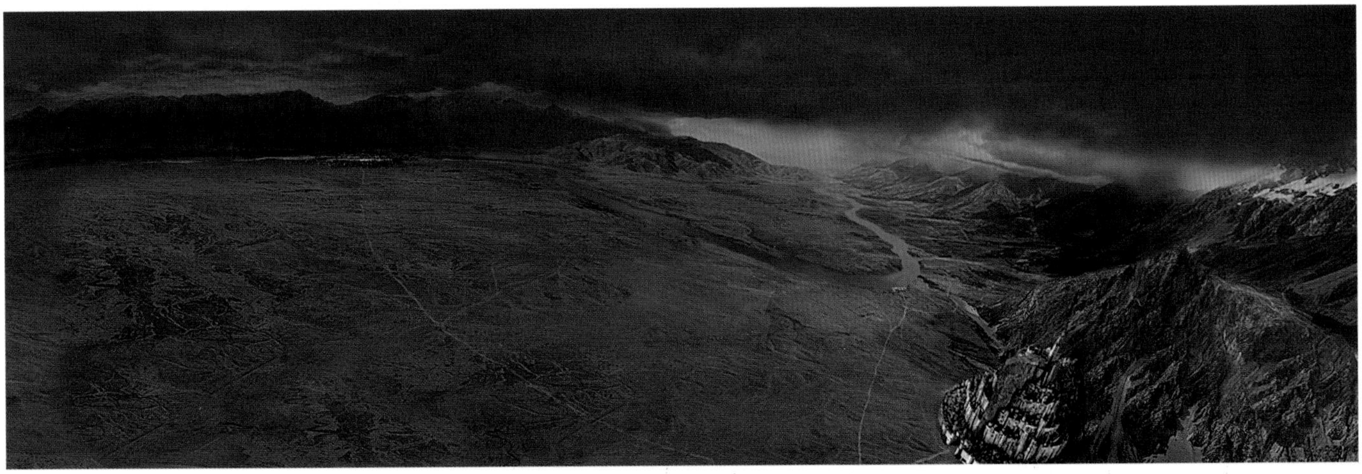

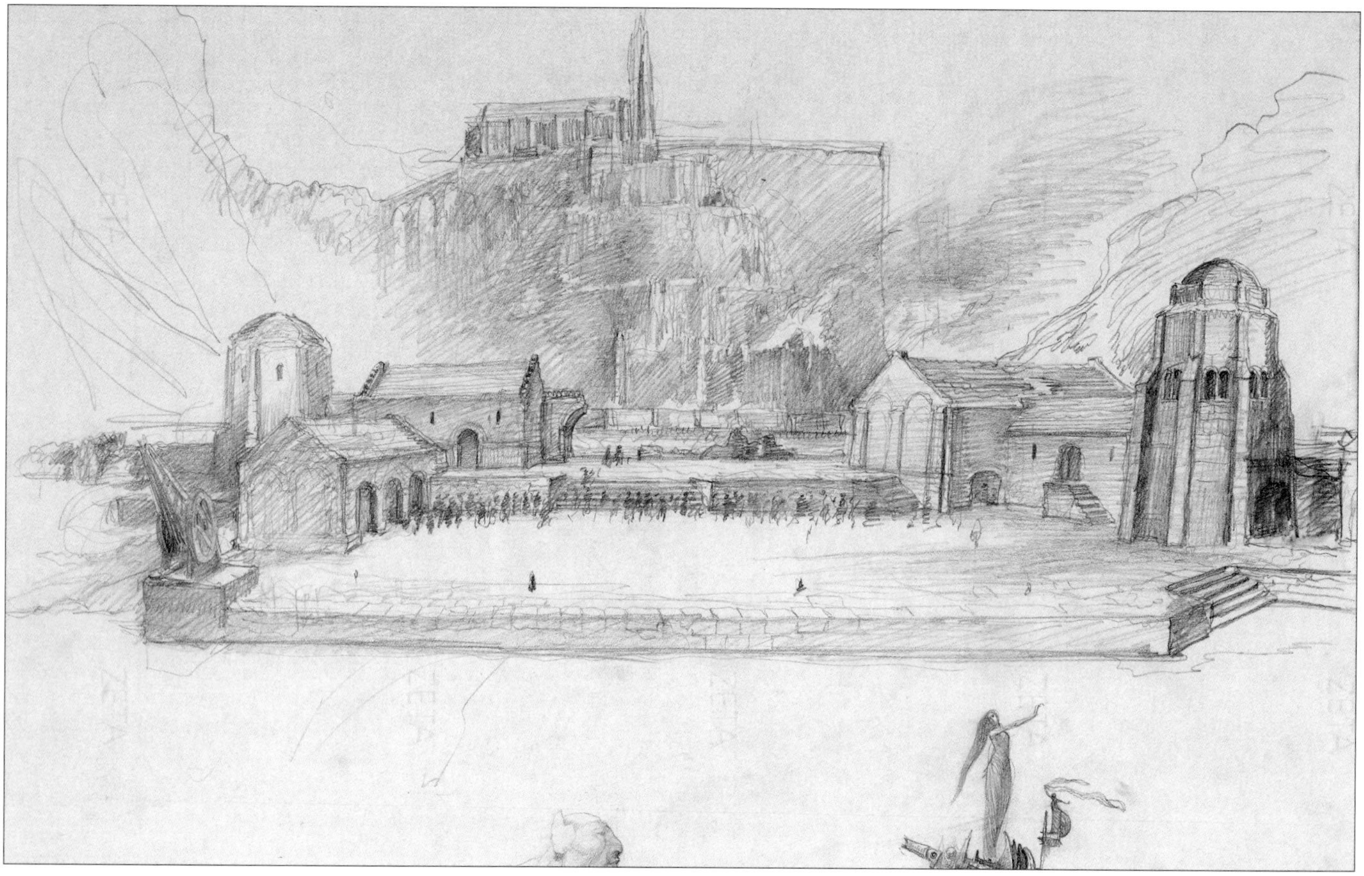

MINAS TIRITH DOCKS *Pencil sketch*
"I had done some fairly generalized and vague drawings of the docks at Minas Tirith during principal photography, but I didn't take the design any further at that stage because we just needed some flagstones for Aragorn to jump onto and then run across. Over the next three years the question of what the docks actually looked like would occasionally be asked, but there was usually something more pressing to be thinking about. I finally did this drawing during post-production on *The Return of the King,* when work on the Pelennor Fields battle had gotten to the point that we more or less knew what was going to be happening in that particular area. Weta turned it into an exquisite miniature, the last one they were to make for the trilogy." *AL*

CORSAIRS *Pencil sketch*
"I had no idea what Middle-earth pirates should look like, but I imagined that they might have the same attachment to pillaged finery and body decoration that we associate with historical pirates and other renegades. Bob Buck of the wardrobe department took the costumes a lot further, and make-up had a lot of fun with them, too. I was pleased to see that some of the crew who hadn't made the grade as Rohan or Gondorian warriors finally had the opportunity to make a brief and grisly appearance on screen." *AL*

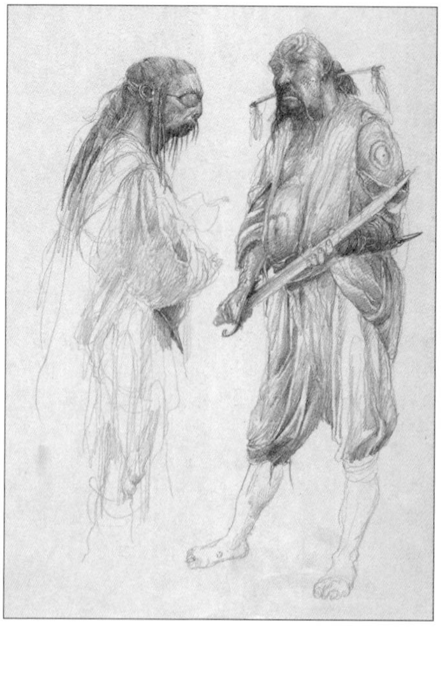

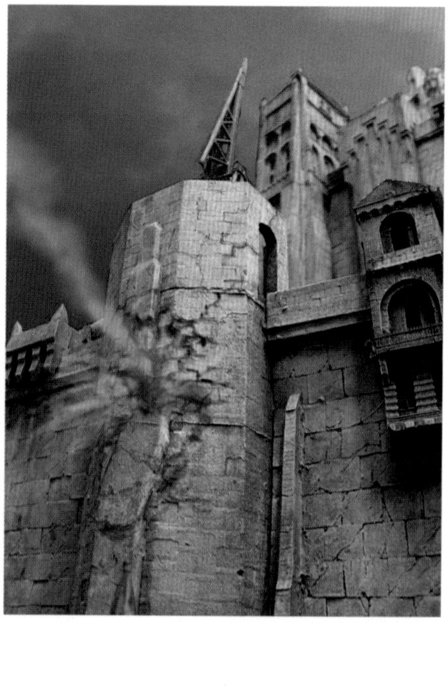

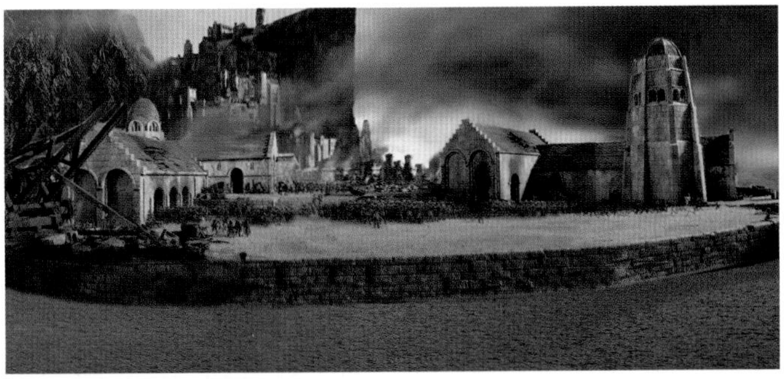

ARMY OF THE DEAD AT MINAS TIRITH DOCKS
Digital artwork
"A complex shot, involving three separate miniatures (if you count the ships as one): computer-generated water, scenic background, massive Orcs and mûkakil, and blue-screen Orcs. Other versions of this shot had been previsualized, but Peter Jackson wanted to use a move on the docks minature as the basic component. I was happy with the look of the miniature, which was probably the last one built by Weta for the trilogy. It was also one of the smallest they had created, and beautifully detailed." *AL*

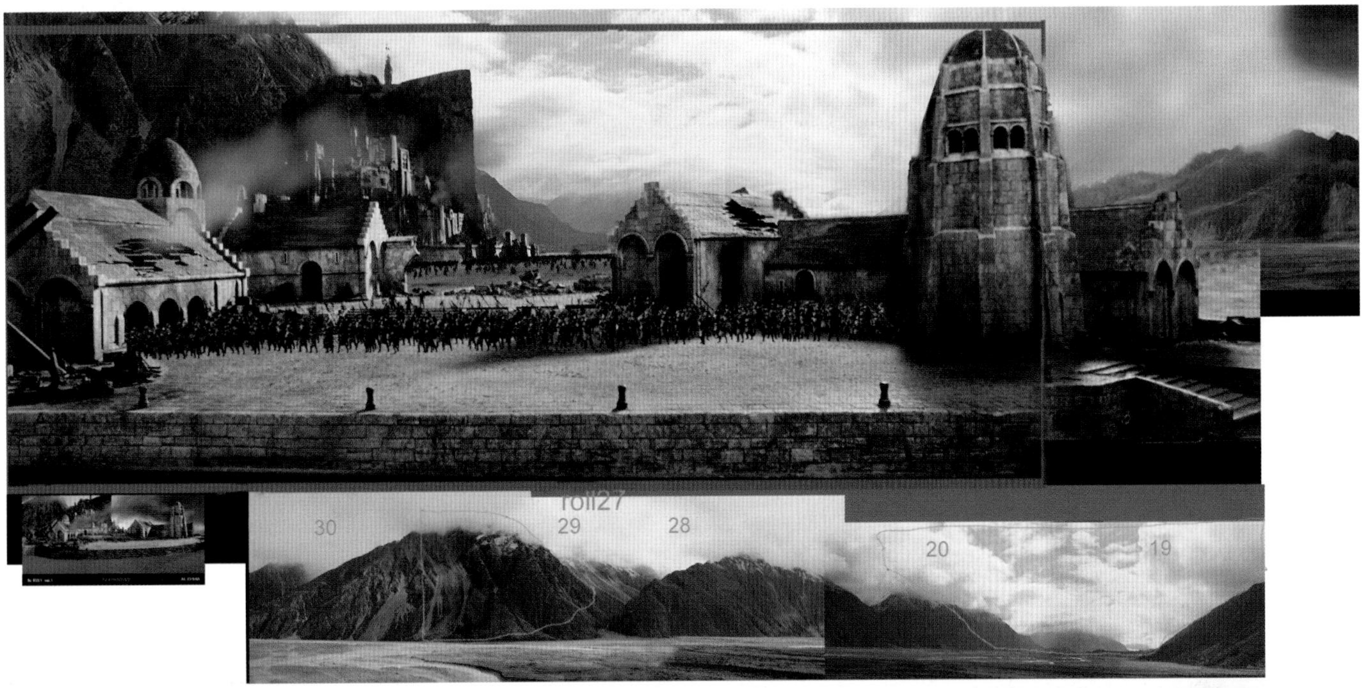

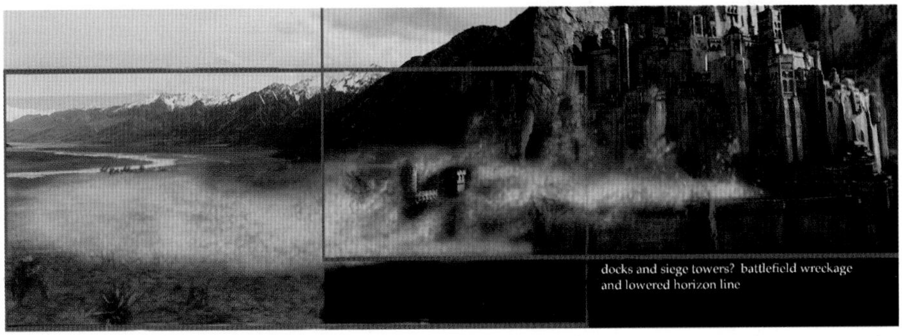

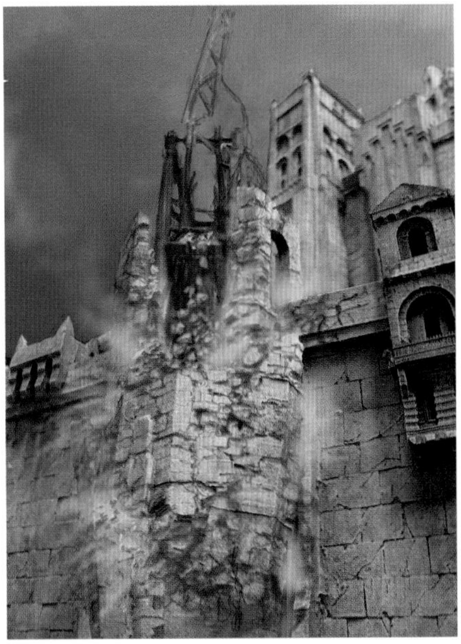

MINAS TIRITH *Digital artwork*
"Peter Jackson wanted to see some shots of boulders fired from Orc catapults destroying bits of the city, so I offered a few examples. These (left and opposite) show what might happen if one of the towers supporting a trebuchet received a direct hit." *AL*

ARMY OF THE DEAD AT MINAS TIRITH DOCKS *Digital artwork*
"I have included this as an example of the way we adapted scenic stills for use in the backgrounds of a high proportion of the shots in *The Return of the King*. Although these are frequently replaced by matte paintings, it is very useful to be able to get a background in place at an early stage in the development of a shot. The red rectangles show the first and last frames." *AL*

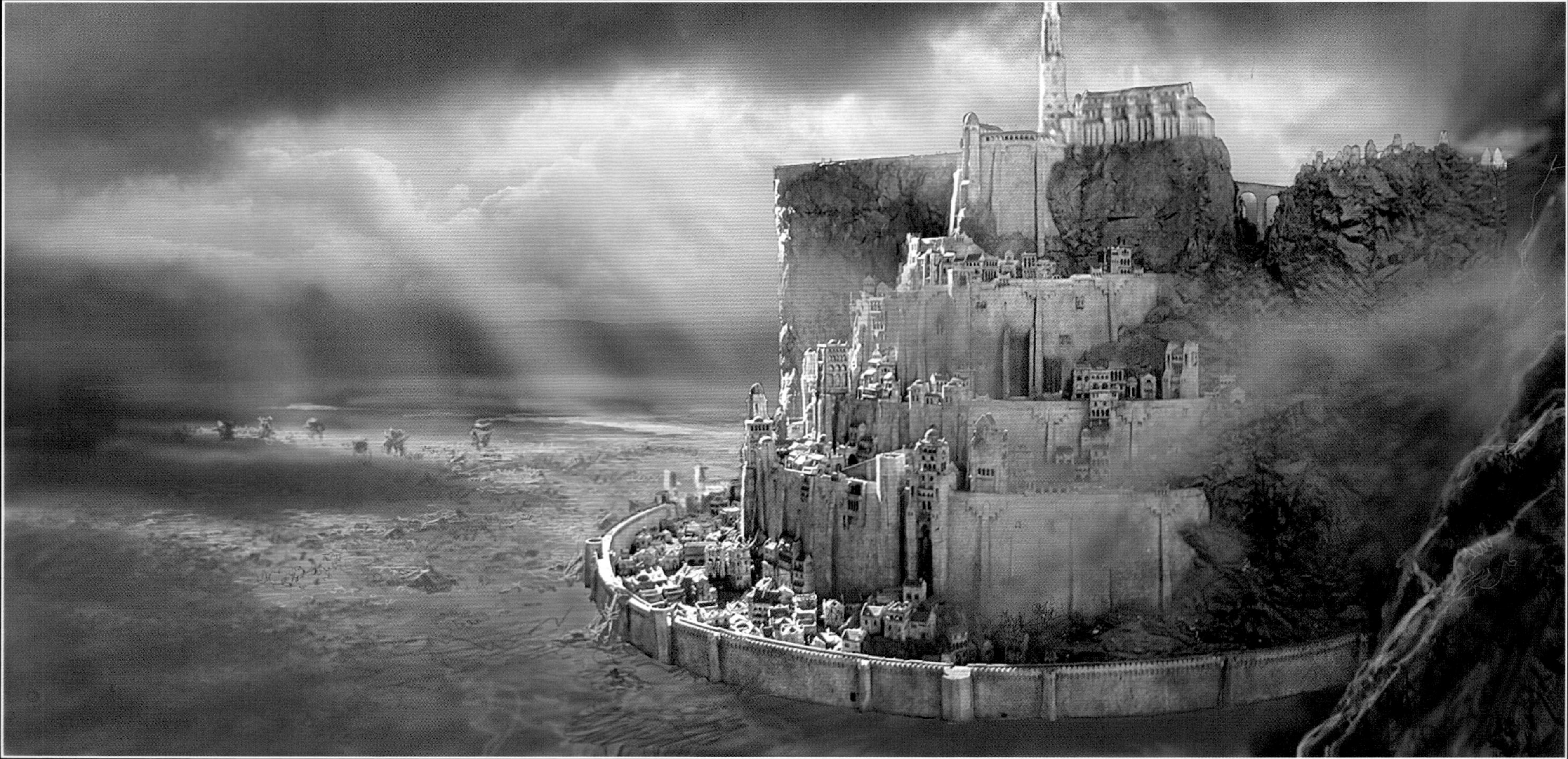

MINAS TIRITH *Digital artwork*
"Alex Funke threw light on the miniature so that I could get a digital photograph for this artwork, showing the aftermath of the battle as sunlight breaks through the covering of dark cloud." *AL*

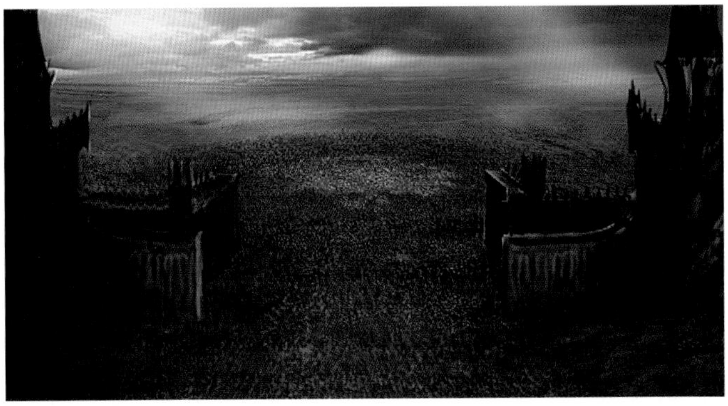

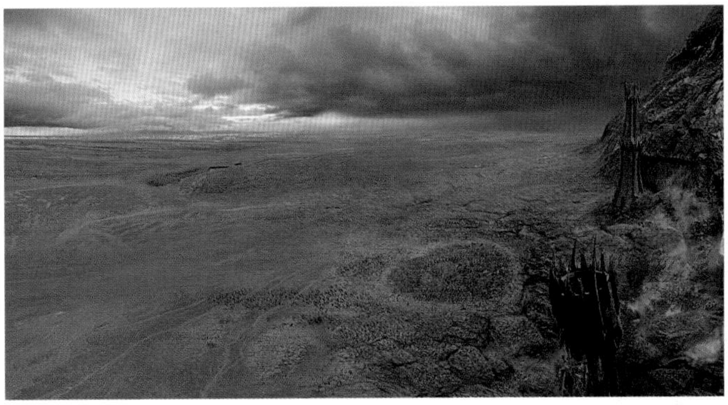

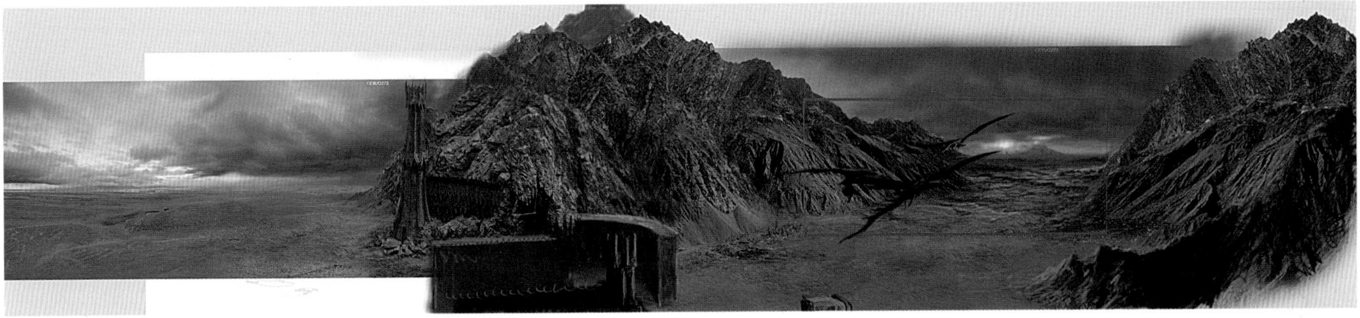

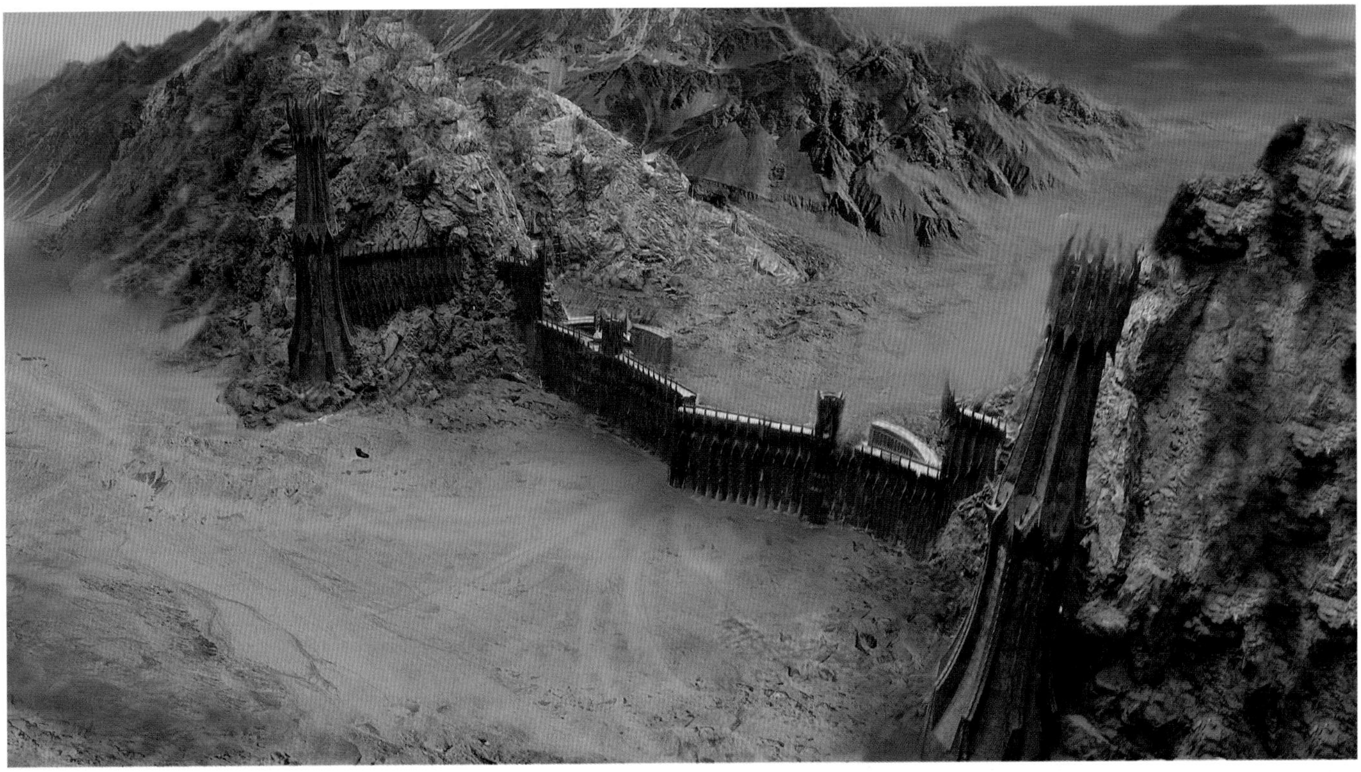

THE BLACK GATES ***Digital artwork***
"The expanse of barren land that stretches between the Black Gates and the Dead Marshes and Emyn Muil was put together from stills taken on a scenic shoot that Paul Lasaine and Craig Potton had conducted in 2000. Dylan Cole did a great job with the final matte paintings for all these Black Gates shots." *AL*

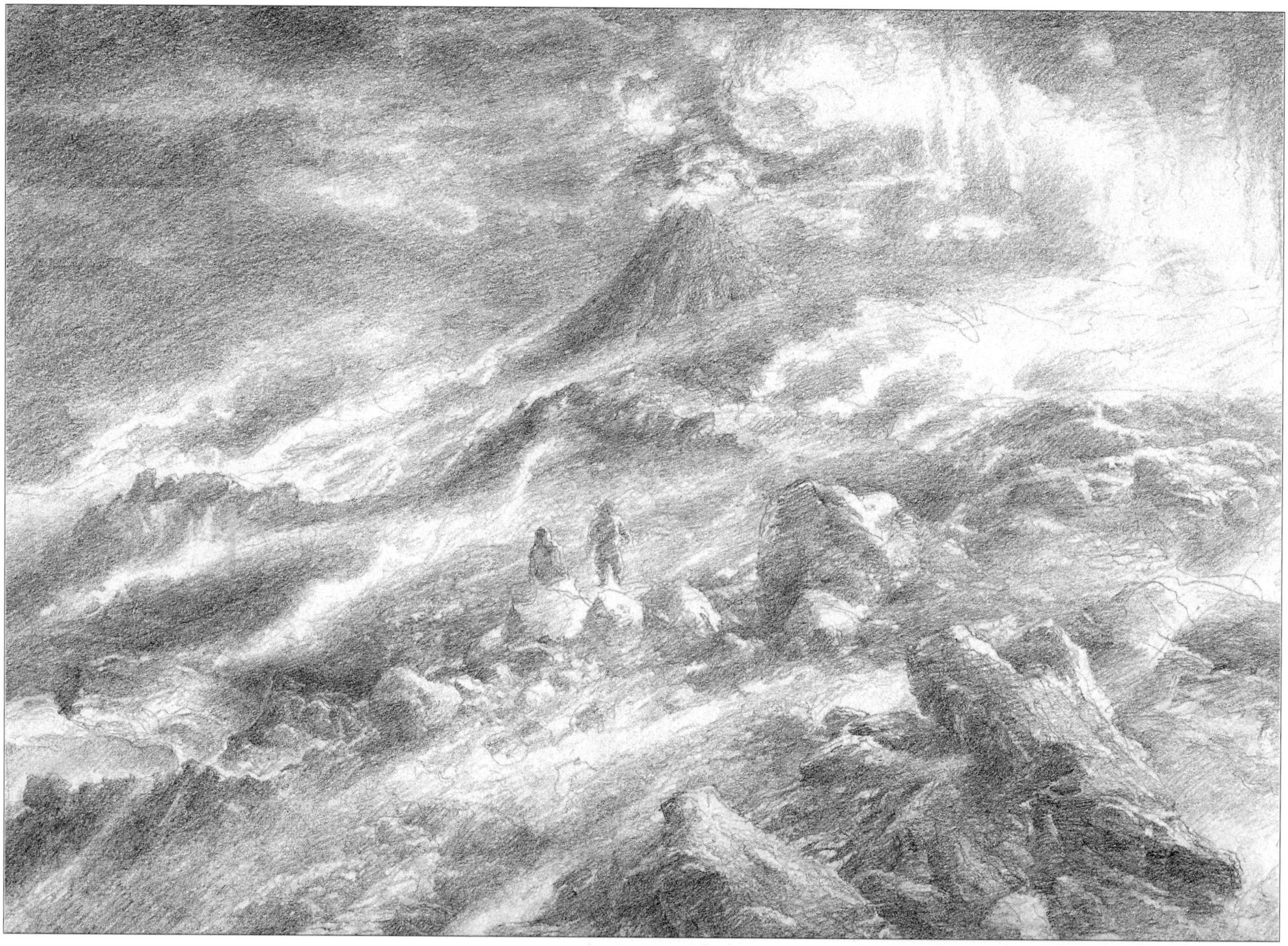

MORDOR
Pencil sketch and digital artwork
"This is a drawing I did quite some time ago of Sam and Frodo trekking across Mordor toward Mount Doom. It was based on a location shot, and I was just seeing what we would need to add to it to make it into a more dramatic environment. Paul Lasaine and Jeremy Bennett did quite a lot of work on this environment as well – in fact, everyone had a go at it. One of the features that kept coming up is the steaming vents from a bubbling lake of lava that lies just beneath the surface and that we see through cracks. You feel the whole landscape is very insubstantial and ready to go off at any time, which of course it will do at the end of the film." *AL*

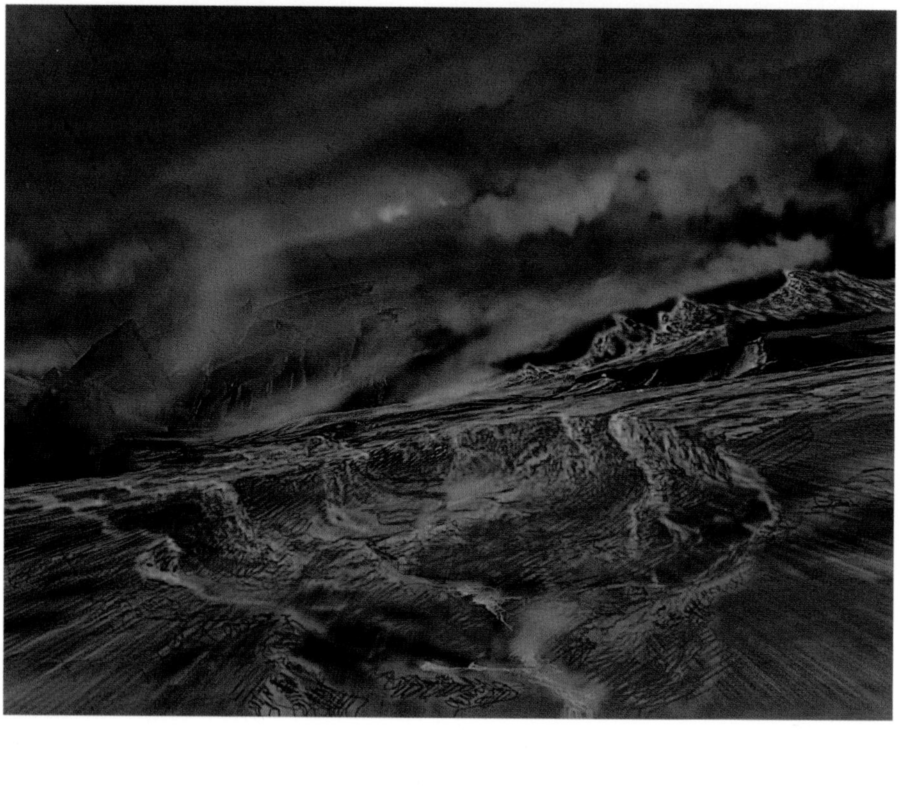

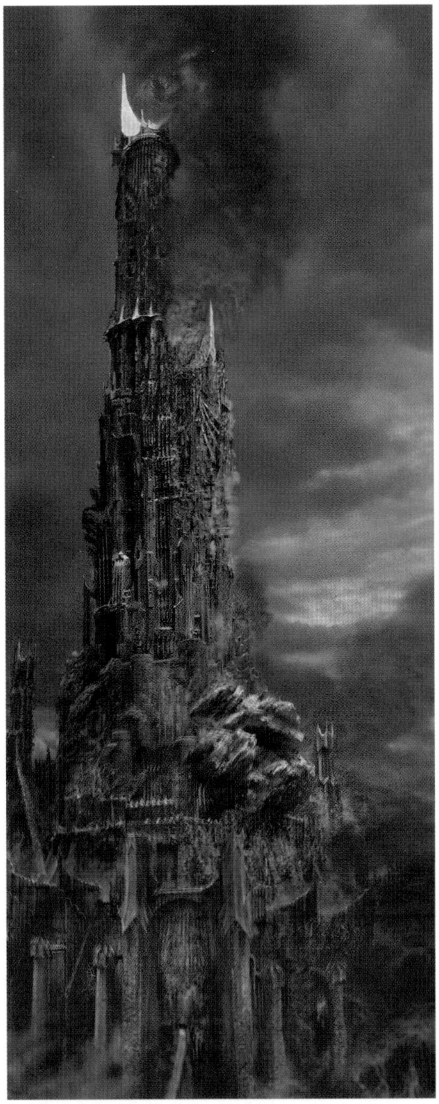

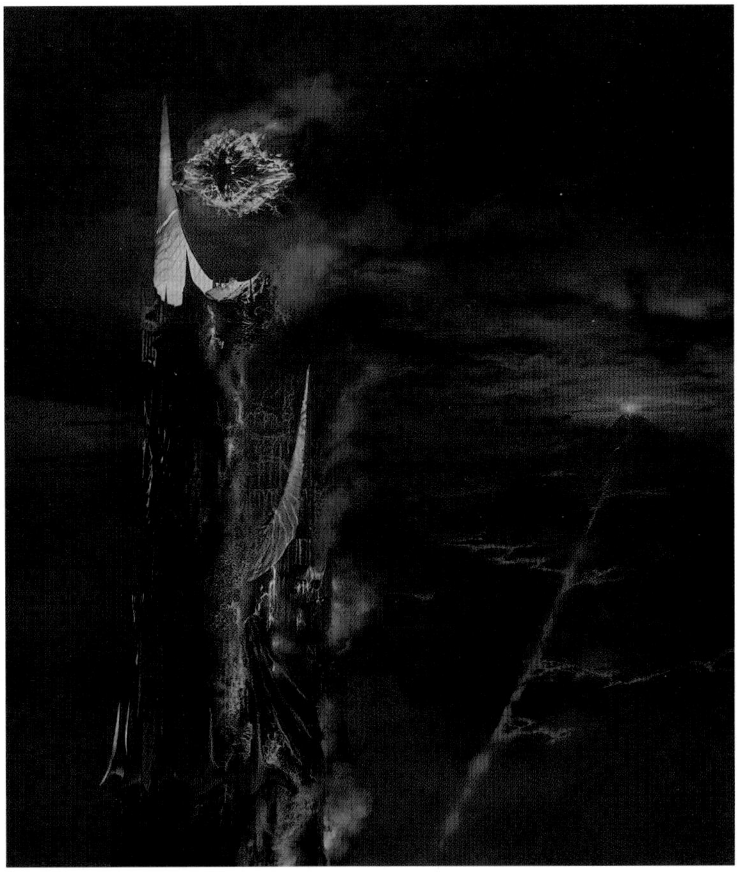

BARAD-DÛR *Digital artwork*
"Gray Horsfield at Weta Digital jumped at the chance to construct, and then destroy, Barad-dûr and the surrounding environment. A digital version of the miniature was painstakingly built, while Gray invested a huge amount of time and energy writing the code that would bring it down. I thought that it might be destroyed, along with Mordor and the Black Gate, in the course of one long camera move, but wiser counsel prevailed." *AL*

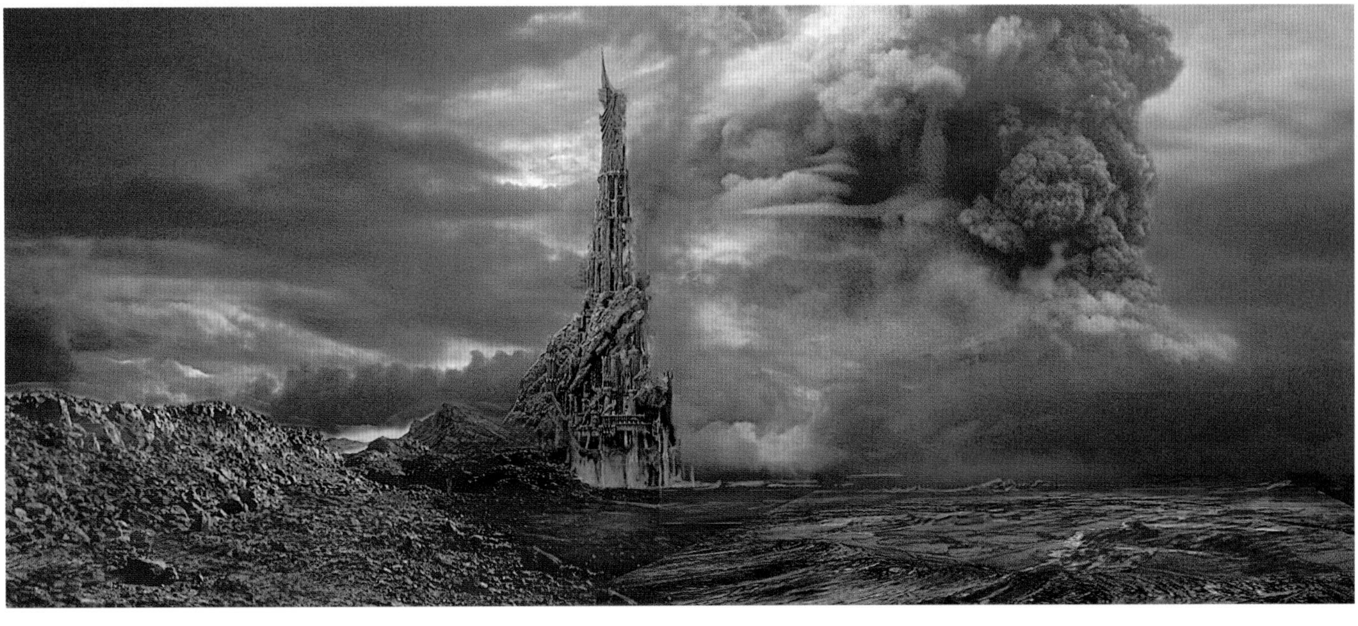

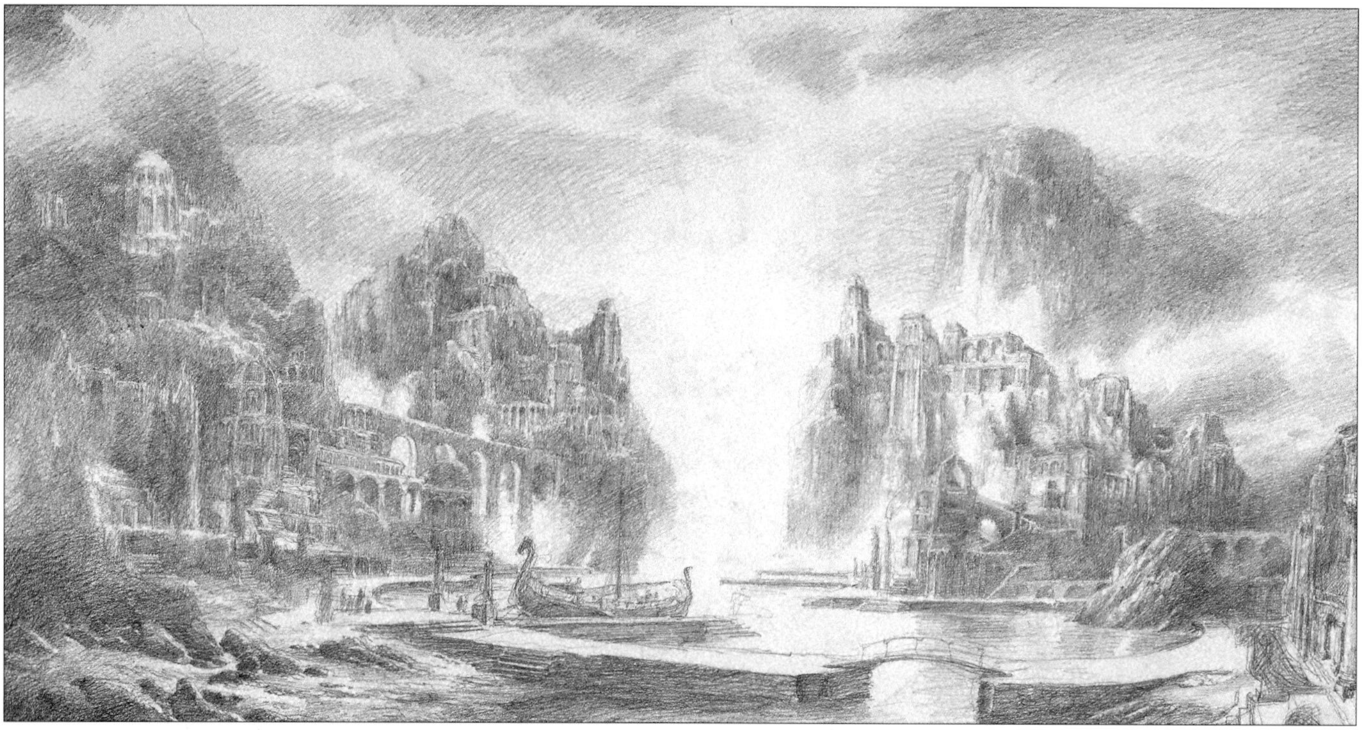

THE GREY HAVENS ***Pencil sketch***
"This is an early drawing of the Grey Havens, which was shown to the actors as an indication of what they would be looking at when the blue-screen was replaced in the finished scene. Although it would be another two years before this particular miniature was built and shot, Peter Jackson kept referring back to this drawing and the construction of the miniature reflected that." *AL*

THE GREY HAVENS
Pencil sketch
"This is another view of the Grey Havens, showing the miniature version of the dock and its surroundings, as well as a wider view of the whole area. There is something fjord-like in the landscape, but the architecture, and the light that will suffuse it, has a soft Mediterranean quality. We looked at paintings by J. M. W. Turner and Claude Lorrain as inspiration for the serene and poignant atmosphere for these scenes, as well as dreamy anticipations of our own future journeys." *AL*

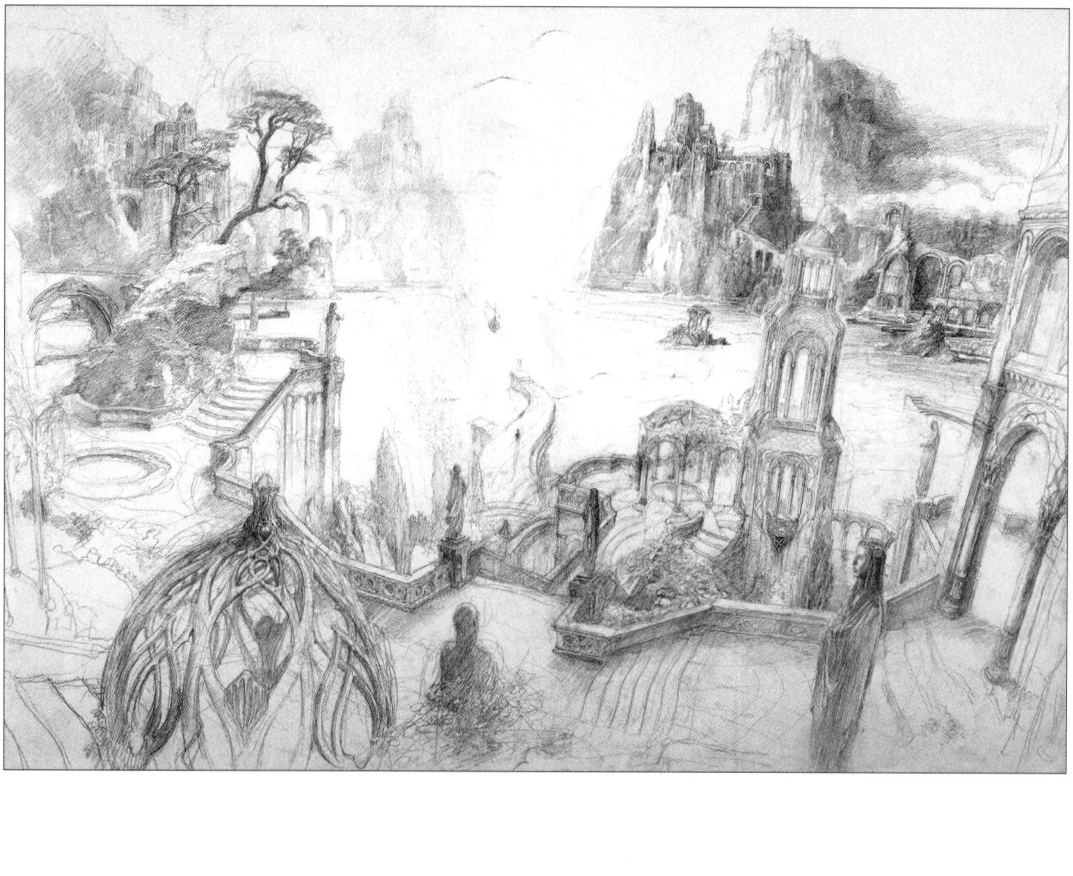

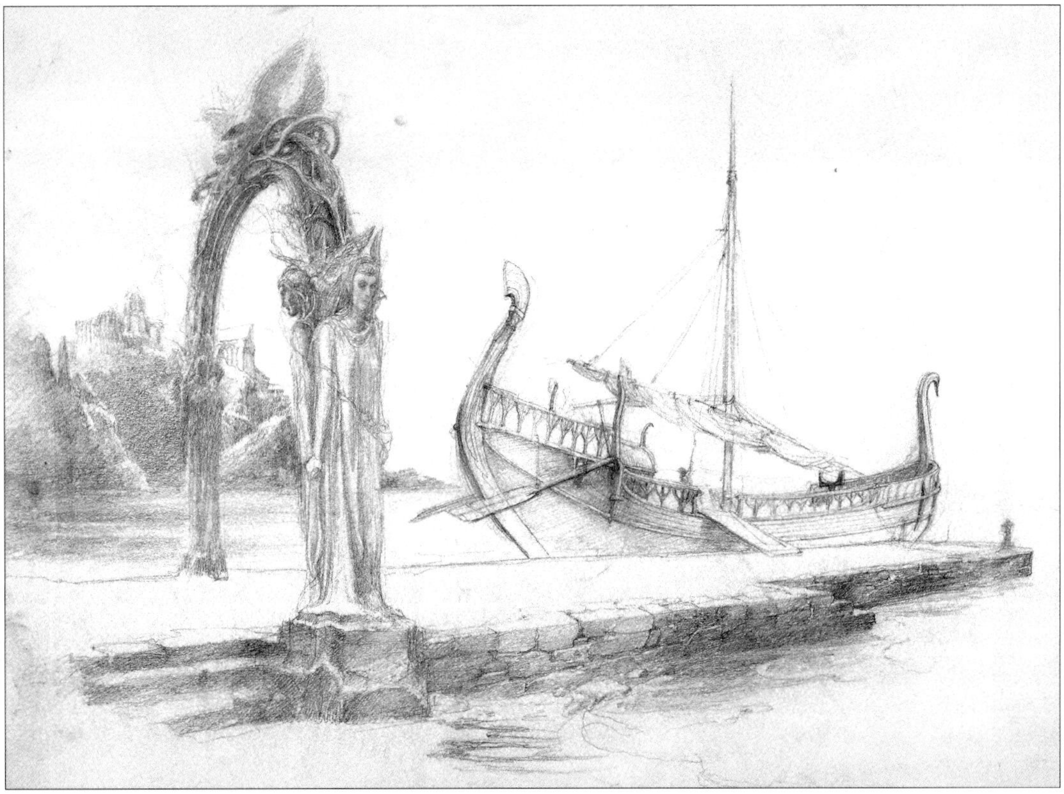

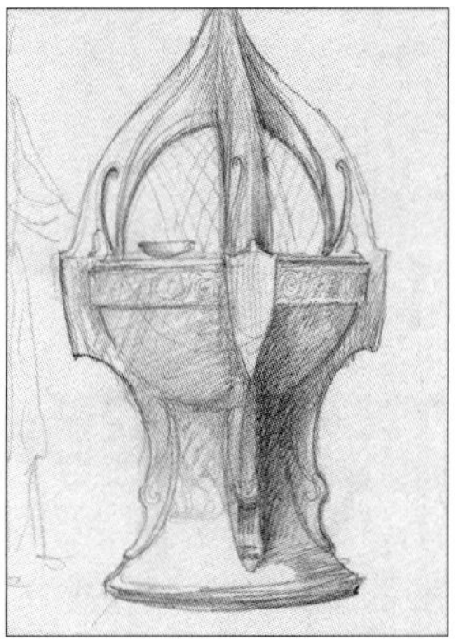

THE GREY HAVENS
Pencil sketch
"This is the fountain that the remaining Fellowship walk past on their way down to the dock. Tolkien describes them passing through a garden before arriving at the boat, so we made a pleasant little departure lounge." *AL*

THE GREY HAVENS *Pencil sketch*
"The Elven boat that waits at the dock to make the final voyage to Valinor was built as a large-scale miniature and is one of the most beautiful objects that Weta made for the film. John Baster has a passion for sailing and a deep knowledge of boat-building, so he was eager to devote his time and skills to creating it." *AL*

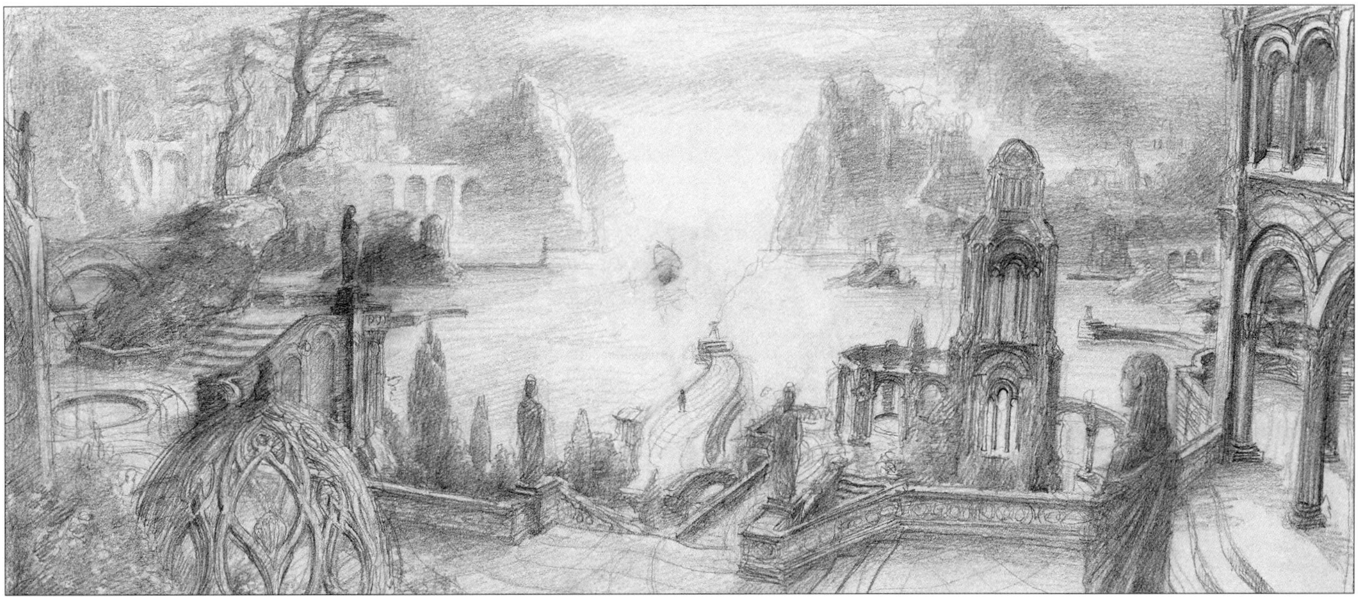

THE GREY HAVENS *Pencil sketch*
"This is a design for the last shots in this sequence, in which the remaining Hobbits watch the ship depart. This turned out to be a more complex environment than I'd pictured when reading the books, but the epic nature of everything our heroes had been through, as well as the width of the cinema sceeen, called out for something grander than just a garden and a dock." *AL*

CONCEPTUAL ART: JOHN HOWE

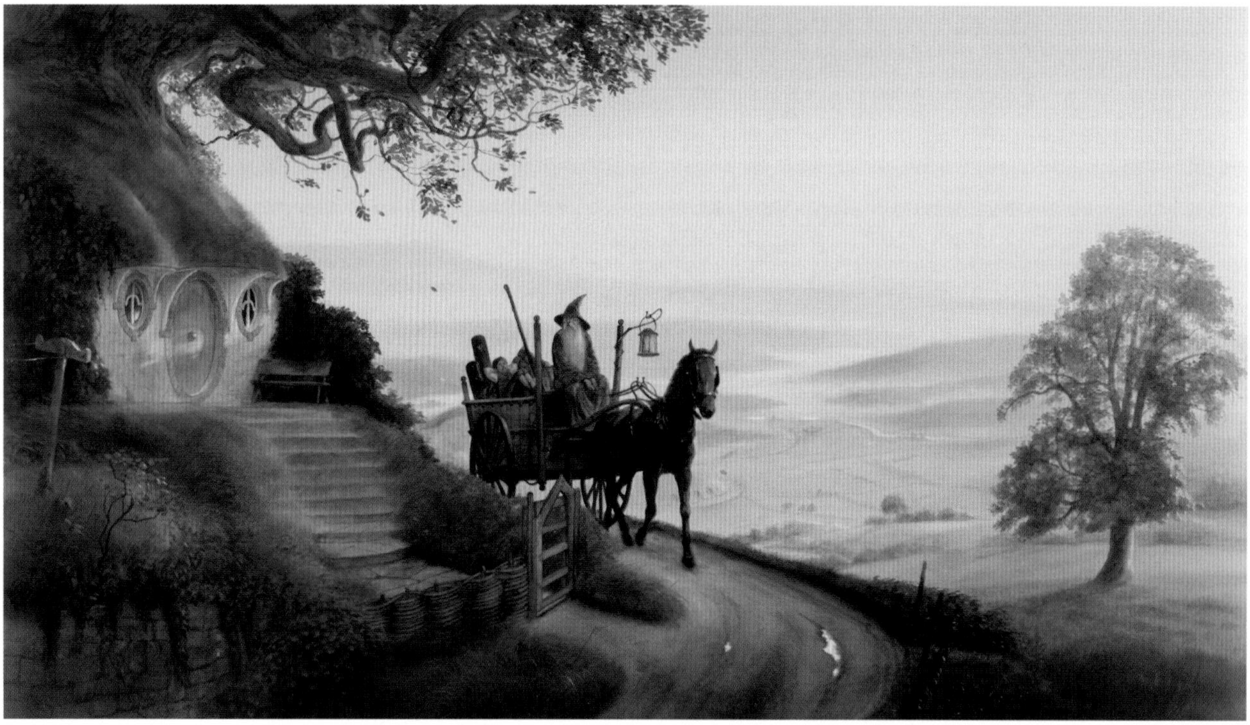

When I arrived in New Zealand, Peter Jackson's first words concerning the conceptual task at hand were: "If you guys can draw it, we can build it." The finest words for an illustrator's ears when on the threshold of a journey across Middle-earth.

I first met Alan Lee at 30,000 feet over the South Pacific. I had written to him when I was in high school, my courage primed by a copy of *Faeries*. (I had written to co-artist Brian Froud at the same time; he never replied either!) It was a memorable meeting, followed by an even more memorable arrival in New Zealand: I was so relieved to get all my armor and weapons through customs that I forgot my more mundane suitcase and nearly made us both miss the connecting flight to Wellington. (I, of course, swore Alan to secrecy about this embarrassing incident, but he, of course, paid no attention to this promise. No matter, I have stories on him, notably involving helicopters, cameras, and orange juice. . .)

Alan and I made no campaign maps; there was no carving up of Middle-earth into walled kingdoms into which the other was not welcome to draw his way. Our approach was more that of two wandering sketchbook artists, occasionally on the same road but more often than not roving far afield. Initially, we stayed a few weeks in the Shire, but then Alan entered the Mines of Moria, I went over the Misty Mountains via Zirakzigil, and then directly down the Anduin past the Argonath, to Amon Hen and beyond.

Encouraged by the very nature of Frodo's journey, we ended up being location scouts of the imagination, not leaning out of helicopters but wandering the winding paths of inspiration. I'm still surprised by the ambulatory nature of it all. Designing Bag End was more akin to wandering through a real house, rapping on half-opened doors and occasionally calling "Anybody home?" than to creating a film set. Climbing Mount Doom to Sammath Naur had all the trappings of an alpine expedition.

I had never really done pencil drawings as finished artwork

"John Howe is a master of capturing exciting moments. His artwork is almost like looking at a freeze frame from the movie. His style is what you'd expect to actually film with the camera."

PETER JACKSON

before. Sketches for me are often little more than unwelcome obligations prior to beginning a color piece. In Peter Jackson's Middle-earth, however, pencil on paper was the chosen medium: the best way to quickly convey ideas and designs. Now that I think about it, in the digitally enhanced world of modern film-making, our department was probably also the cheapest and undeniably the lowest-tech of them all – just a big stack of drawing paper and a few boxes of pencils.

A very large sheet of drawing paper and a 3- or 4-B pencil is the perfect combination of elements for conceptual work. Concept sketches are glorified doodles, and the time needed to actually cover a large sheet of paper with graphite affords the luxury of letting your mind follow the tip of the pencil rather than telling it where to go. Also, the incidental nature of the drawings freed me from the necessity of rendering something publishable (it seems to me a lot of concept art is done with one eye on the script and the other on potential *Art of* books) so upon arriving at the edge of a sheet, I added another until the drawings ended up several yards long or high.

Sketching out imaginary landscapes and locations requires a certain cadence, quick enough to warrant your salary, but sufficiently pedestrian to allow the ideas you discover on the way to help you plot the path ahead.

All the energy bottled up in these illustrations could achieve only a theoretical release. Any static image could only suggest movement, could only hint at depth and drama, relying on the spectator to complete the scene. Thus it seemed somehow perfectly natural to be involved in a process by which that could be accomplished. Computer technology has freed creativity from all the annoying hurdles of physical effects, and the route from imagination to the screen has never been more direct. Nonetheless, it was quite a trip.

John Howe
June 2004

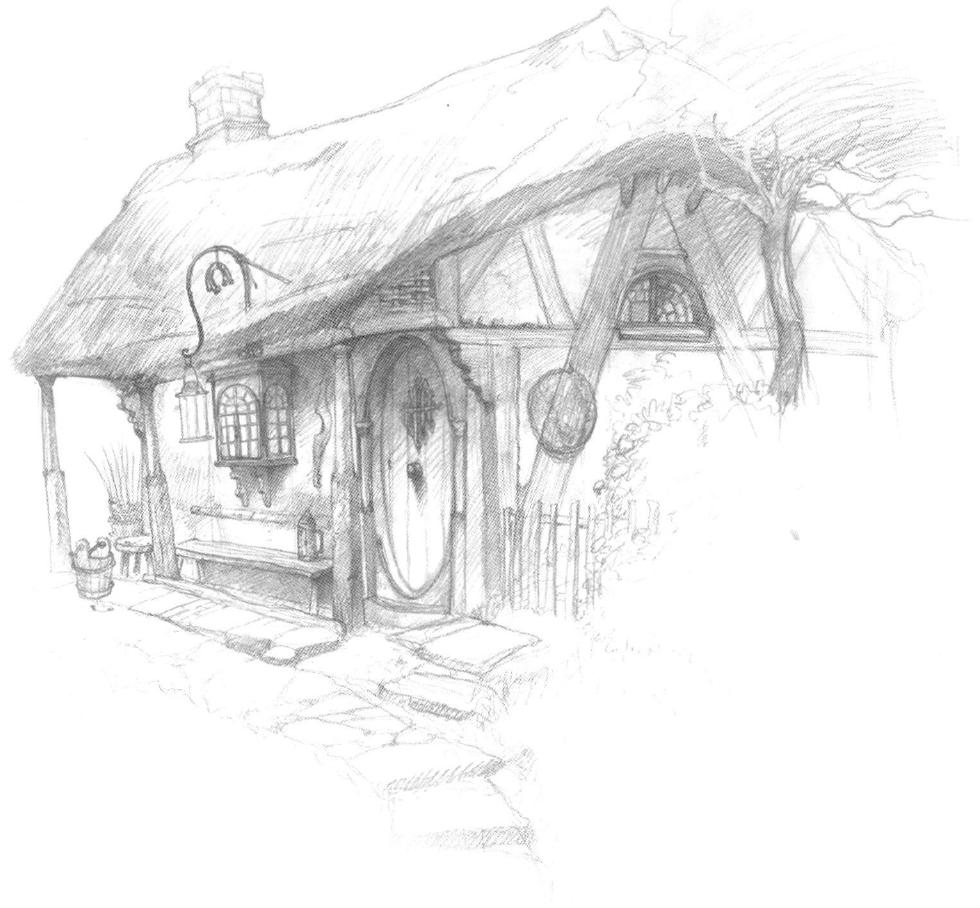

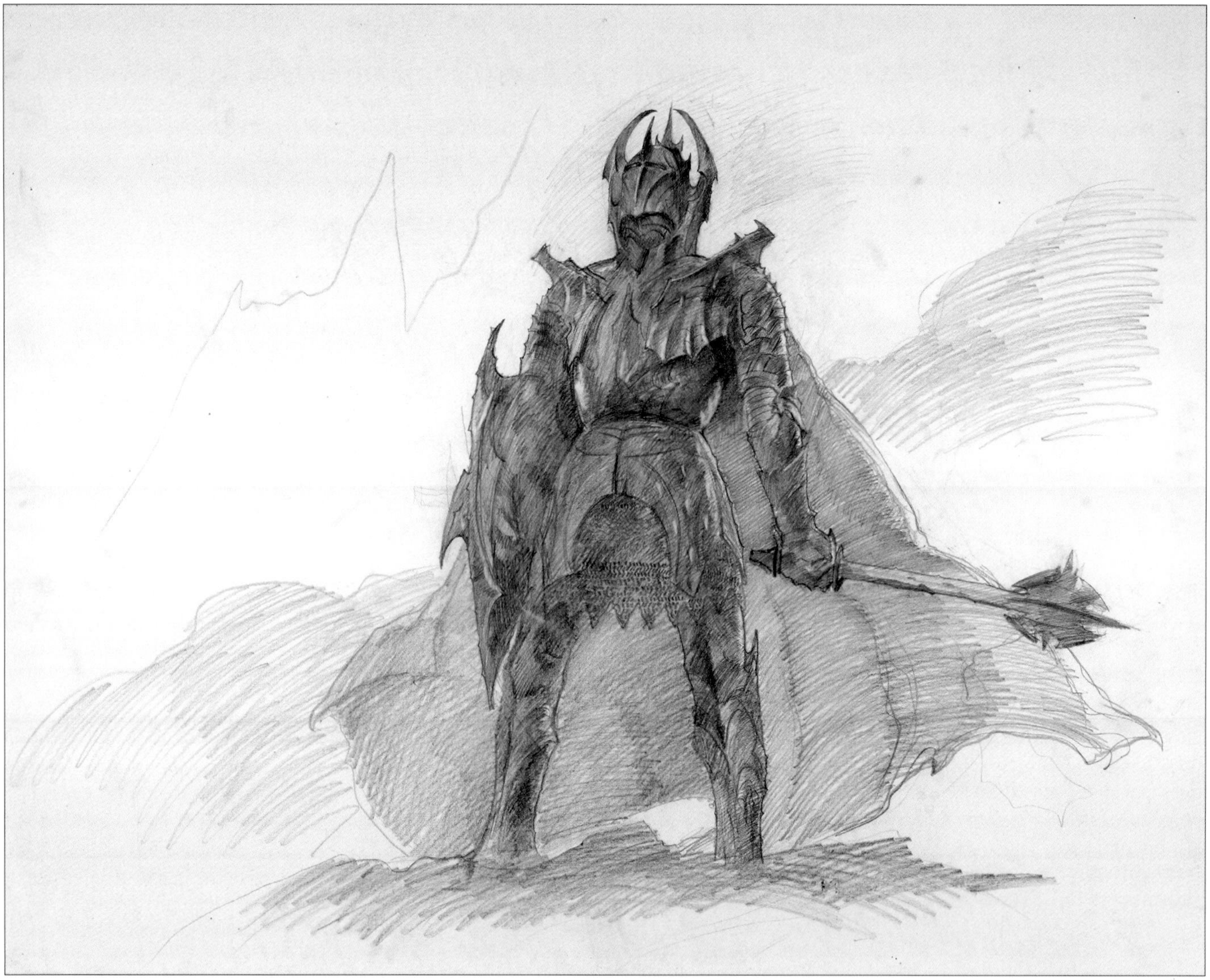

SAURON ***Pencil sketch***
"This was done a long time before we started filming. It's one of my earliest ideas for Sauron and his armor – I wanted to devise an armor that would work, that the Dark Lord could actually wear and have battles in but still be very spiky, extravagant, and Gothic." *JH*

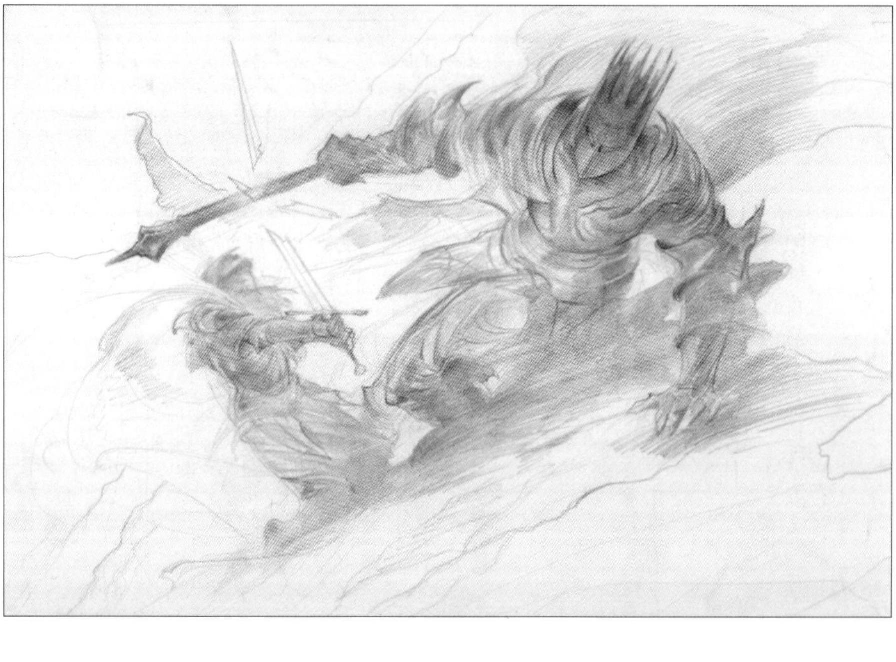

RIVENDELL TAPESTRY
Pencil sketch
"I find it hard to trade the assets of movement for qualities of decoration; thus there is rather too much action here for a real tapestry." *JH*

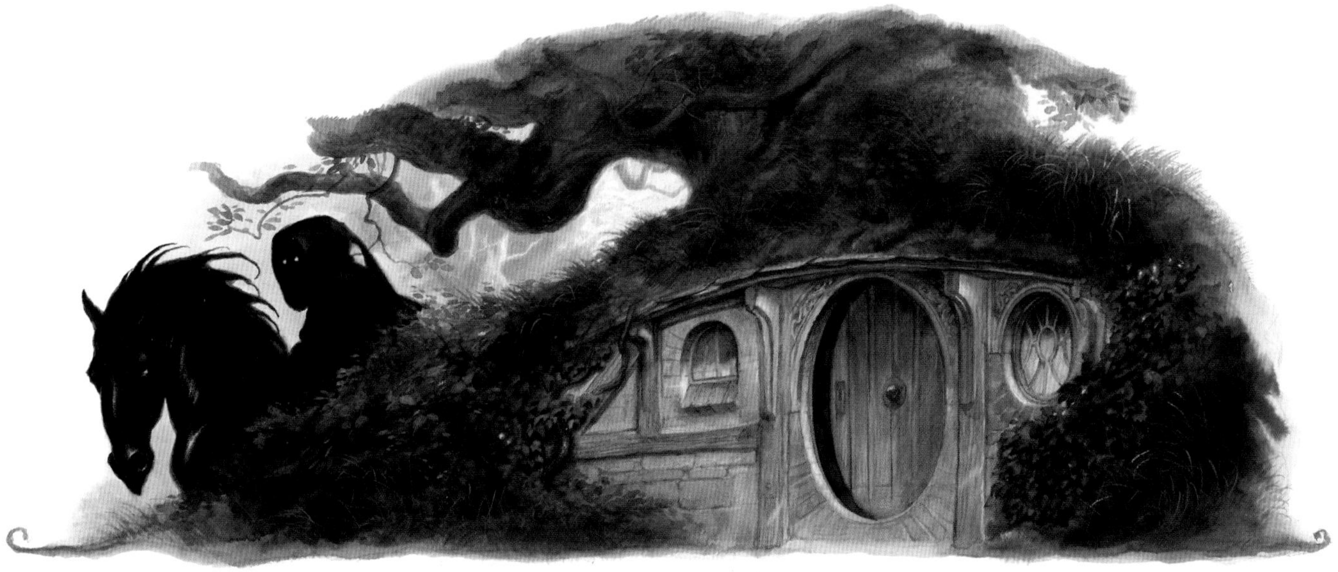

HOBBITON *Bag End*
"This painting was designed as a logo. I think I did this halfway through the project – Peter Jackson wanted a letterhead with calligraphy across the bottom of it. That's why the Black Rider is kind of cartoonish. He's not really like that in the film, of course. It's just to give some general idea of two central motifs in the first movie." *JH*

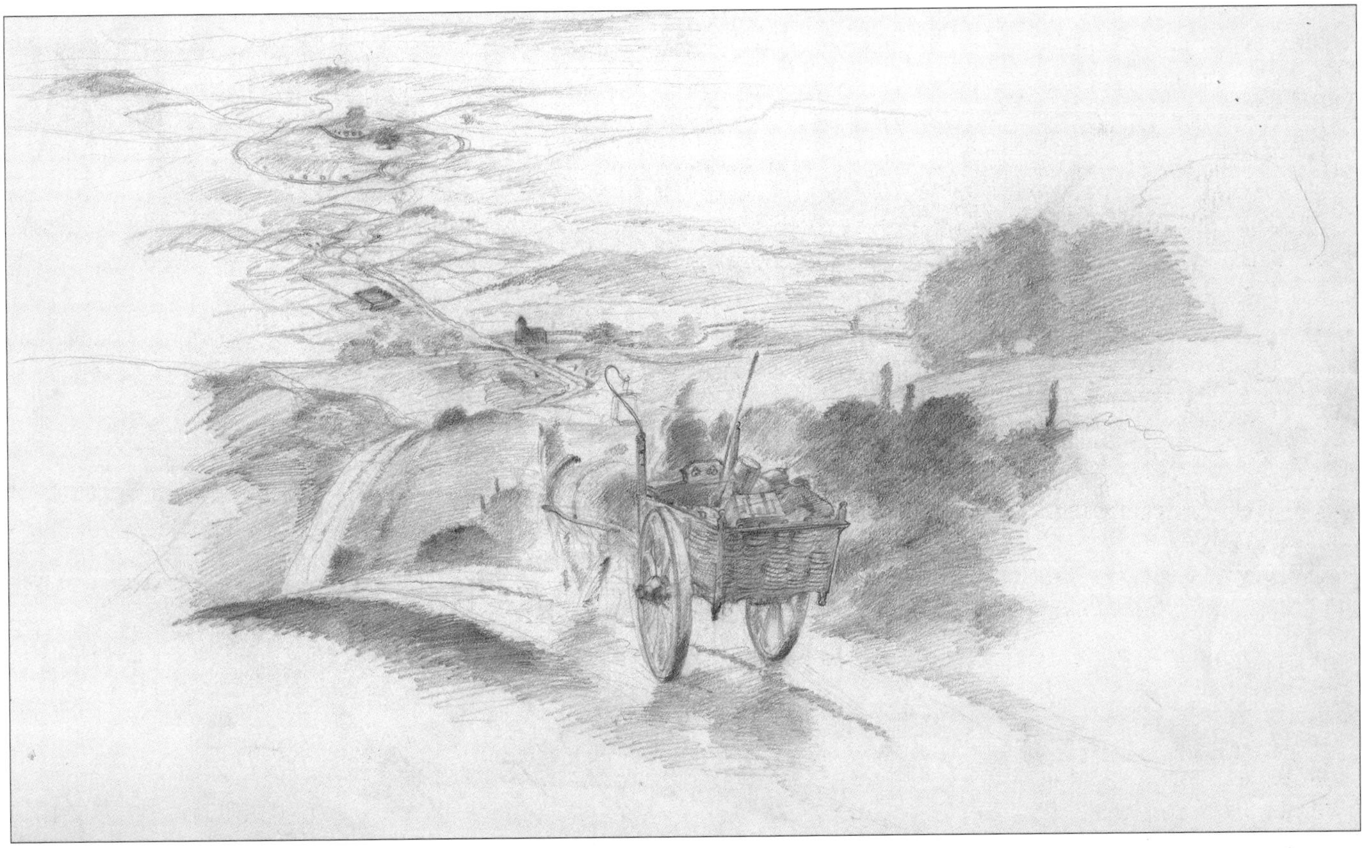

HOBBITON *Bag End*
"Gandalf arrives in Hobbiton. A sketch done long before the actual location was found." *JH*

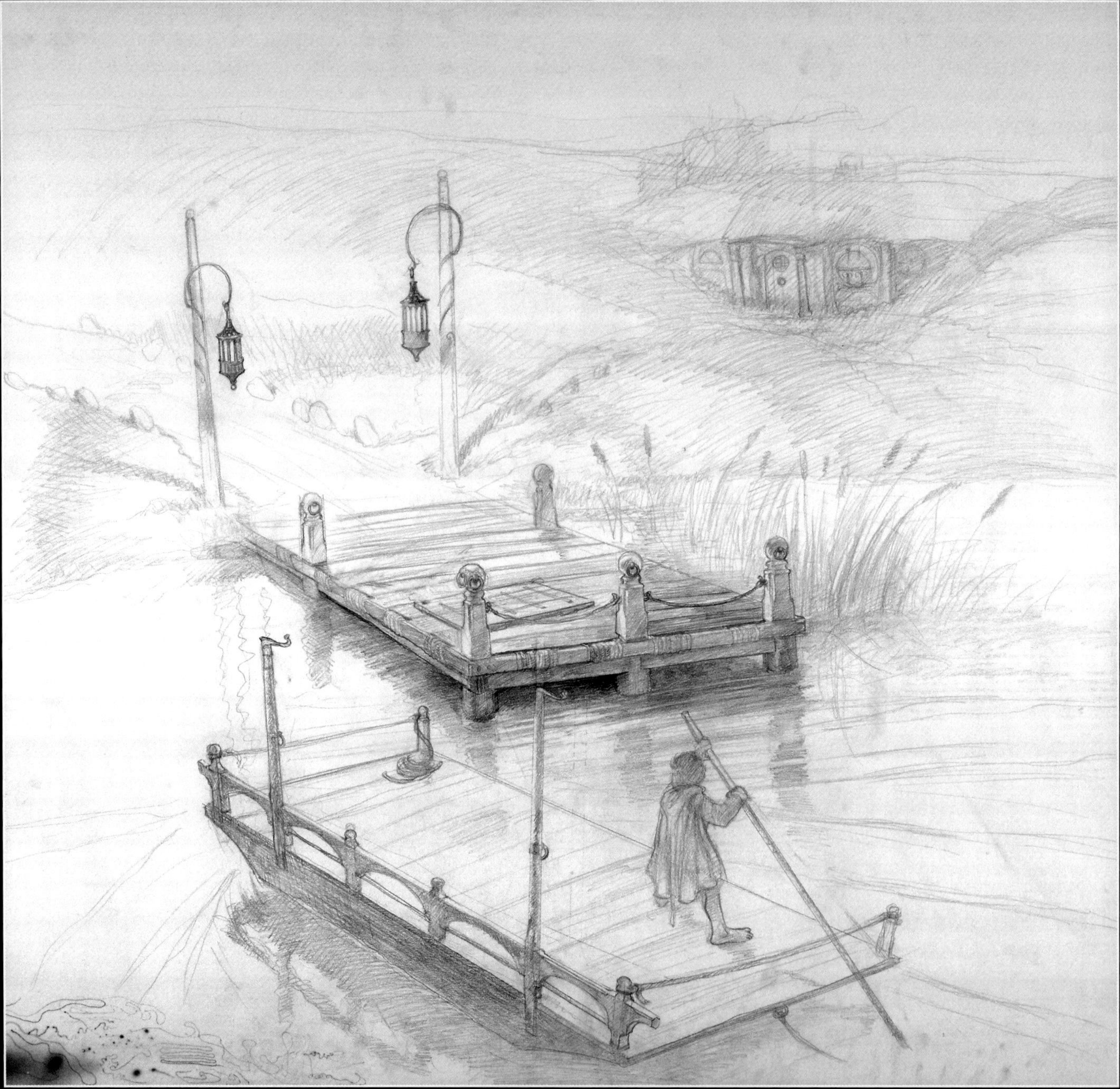

HOBBITON *Bucklebury Ferry*
"Just down from the Ferrymaster's cottage, which appears on page 113, we have the Bucklebury Ferry, which the Hobbits use to escape the pursuing Ringwraiths." *JH*

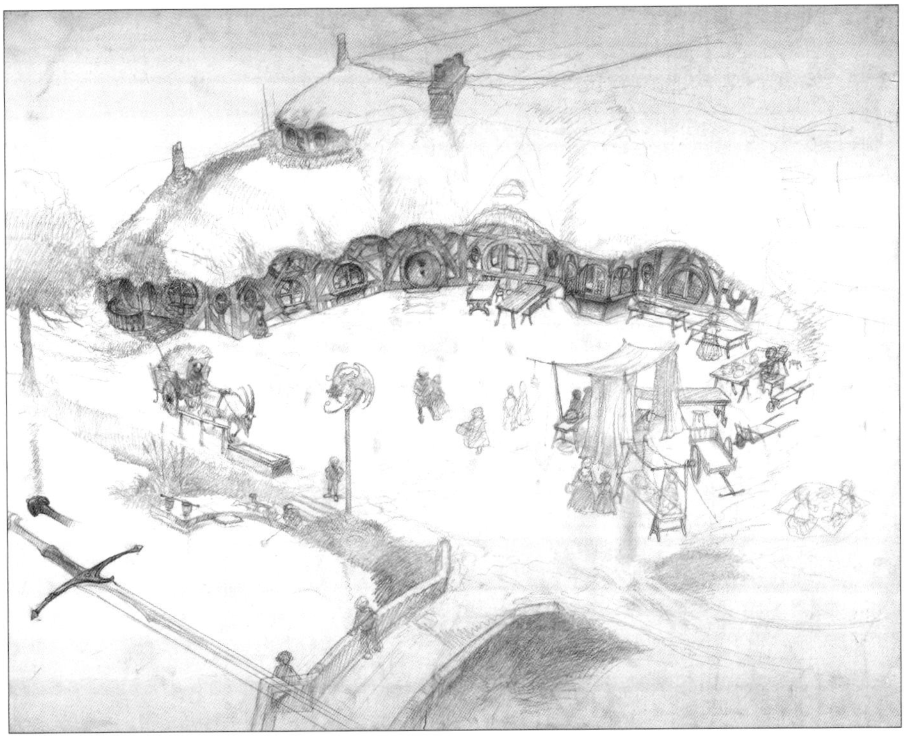

HOBBITON ***The Green Dragon***
"The Green Dragon Inn is a Hobbit pub. I've never seen a real country pub. We don't have them in Switzerland. The Green Dragon was intended to be a rambling one, which would be a Hobbit hole that had been built up from a bank into an actual building and become an inn, a meeting place. It's really the only place they socialize in great numbers. The idea was to have a market square out front. When these pictures were drawn, I believe we had already chosen the location, because I added that water down in the front." *JH*

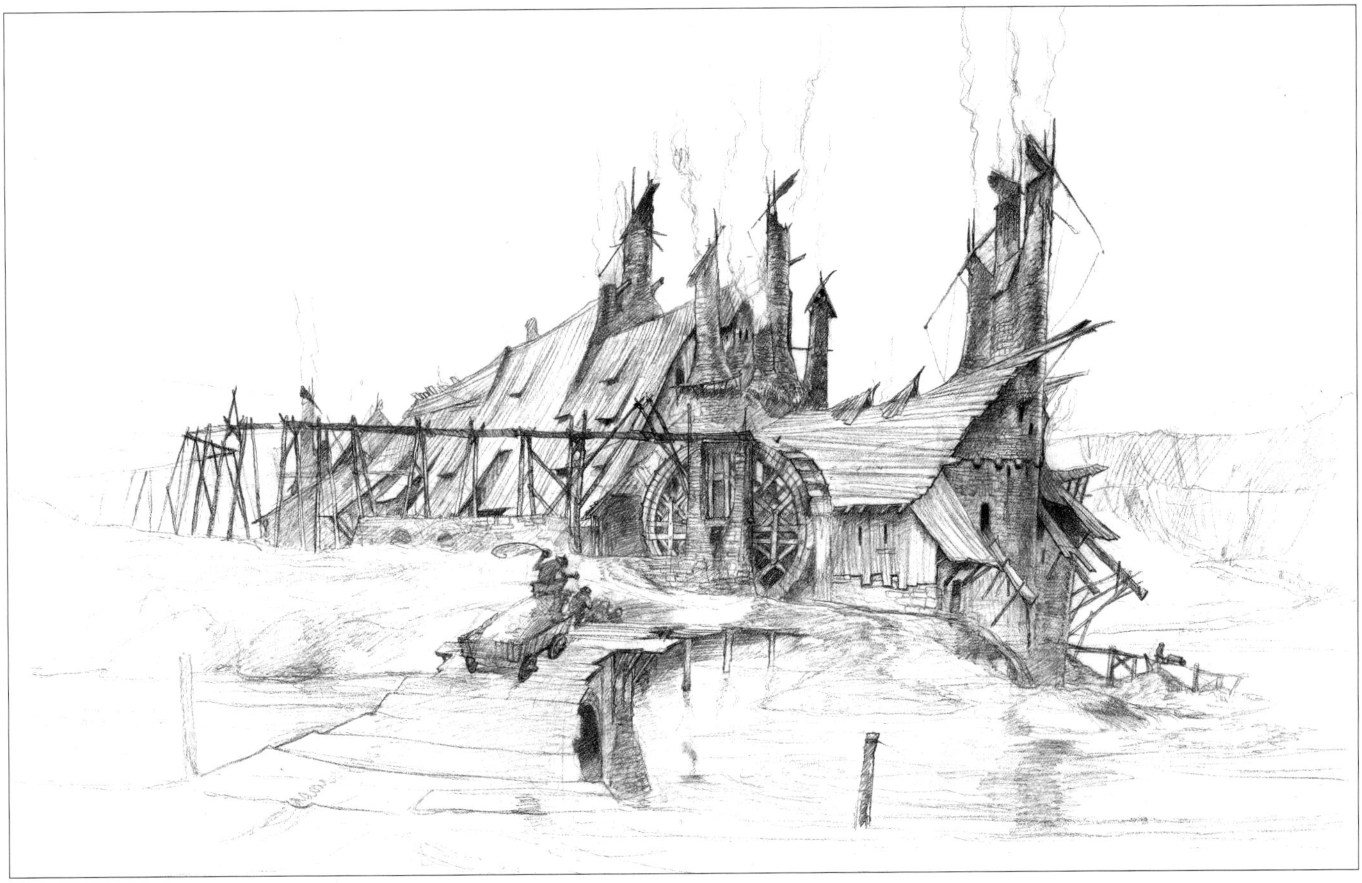

GALADRIEL'S GLADE ***Ruined Hobbiton***
"Here is a vision of the Shire being destroyed. They built the miniature straight from this. And they built that crazy hill with all the pipes and that sort of mad, hellish mill." *JH*

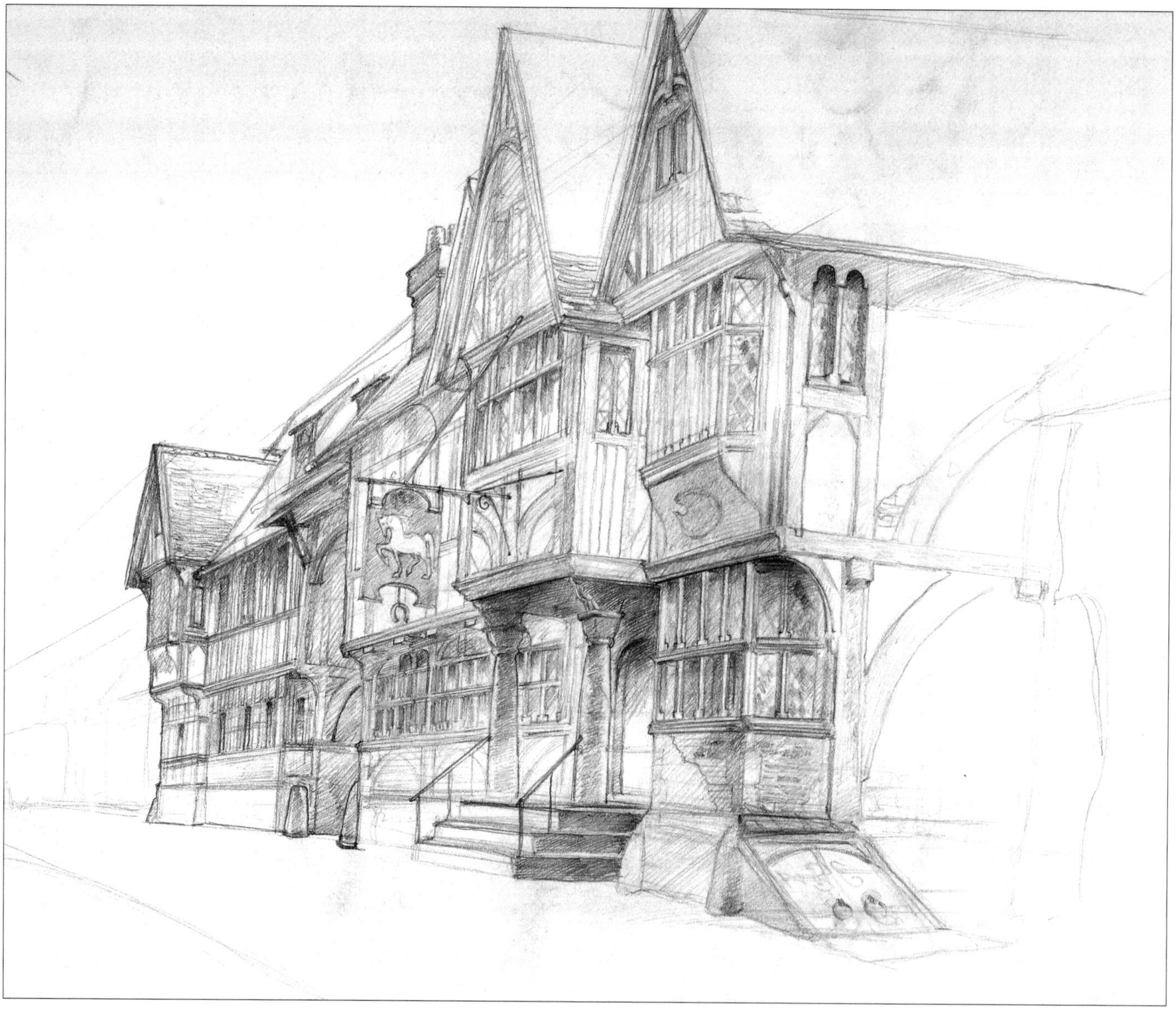

BREE ***The Prancing Pony***
"The version of the Prancing Pony above was very grandiose but ended up being much humbler in the film. I wanted to make it as intimidating as possible, absolutely huge, but I'm not quite sure that my version exactly fits the mood." *JH*

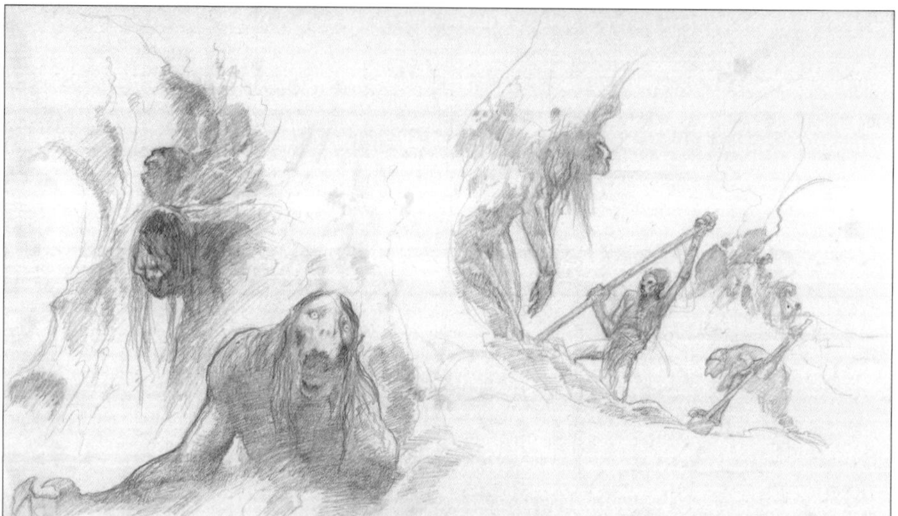

ISENGARD ***The Birthing Pits***
"There were lengthy discussions about how Saruman actually creates his Uruks. In the end, they were prized out of a slimy earthen womb, fully grown." *JH*

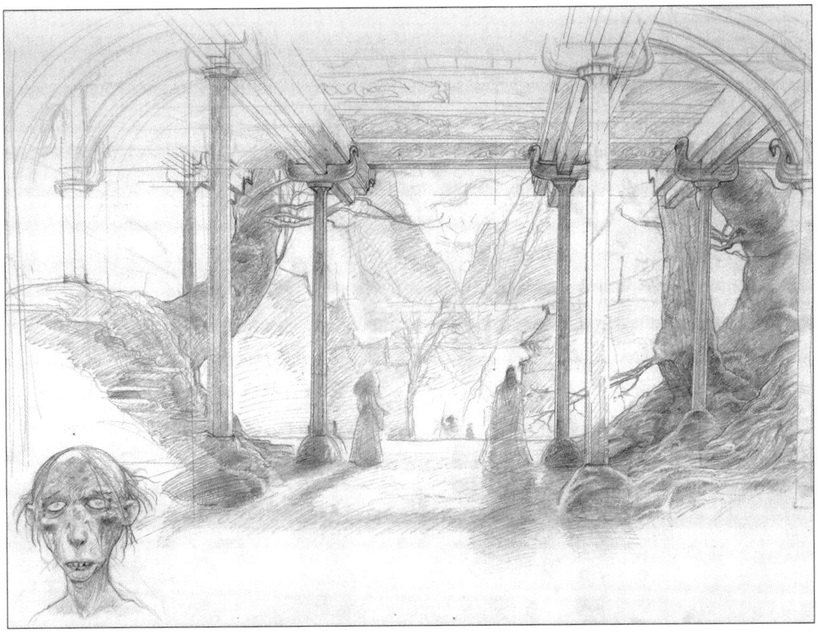

RIVENDELL *Architecture*
"How do you design architecture built by a race of immortals whose beauty and grace is almost beyond imagining? Well, of course, you can't, but we did give it our best try. The natural elegance of Art Nouveau provided inspiration to let our pencils wander freely, tempering the energy of line and curve with the melancholy of a civilization preparing to leave the world behind them. All very poetic.

"So how the devil Gollum ended up on the same page, I can't imagine." *JH*

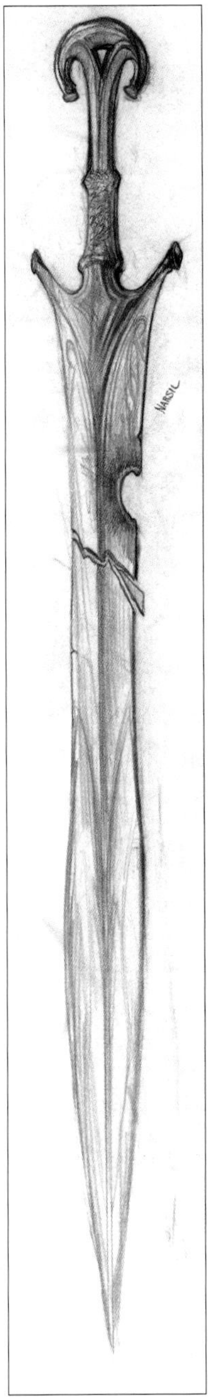

RIVENDELL *Narsil*
"An early idea for Narsil. Note the indentation made when Sauron's ring finger was lopped off at the end of the Second Age." *JH*

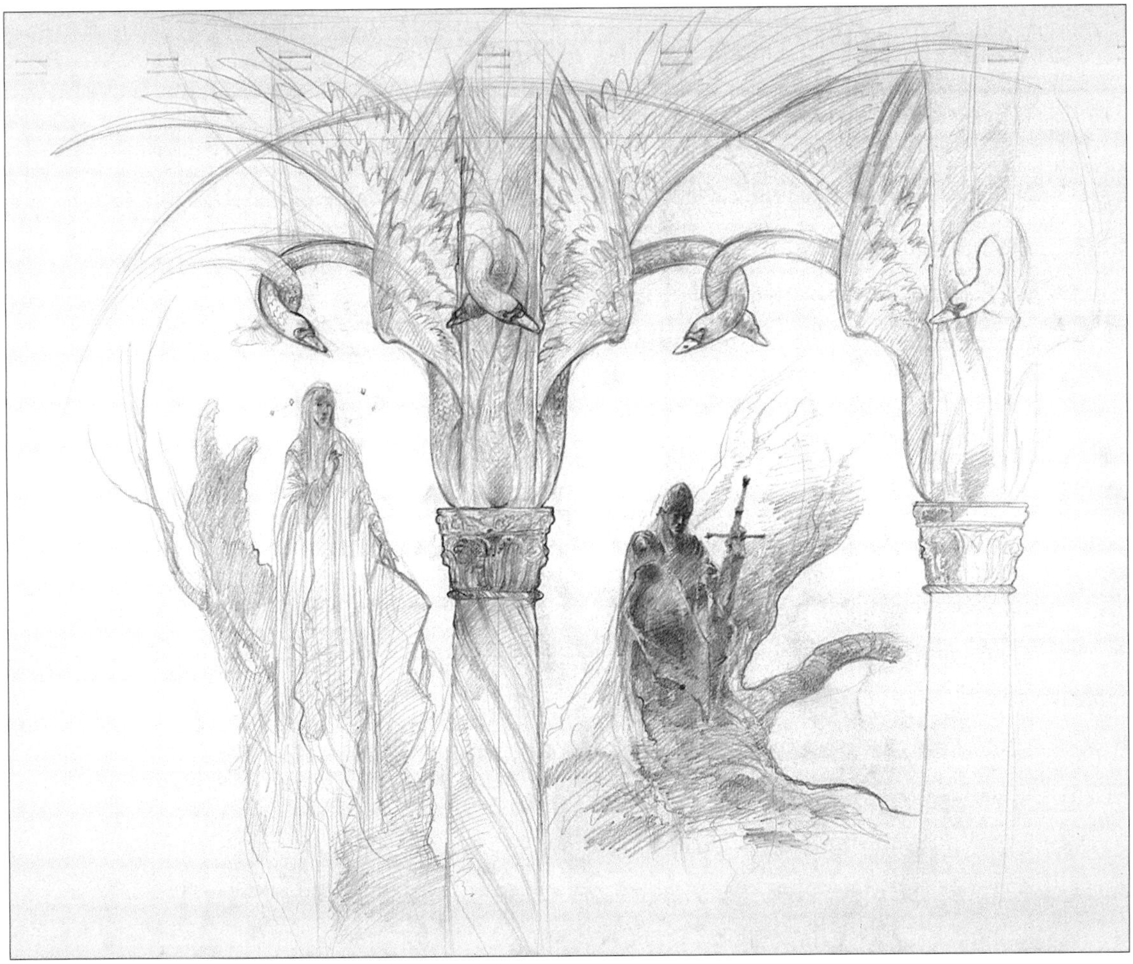

RIVENDELL *Statues*
"While Alan was wandering through the rooms of Rivendell, I was scouting out the gardens and the valley itself. I had imagined Gandalf giving Frodo a tour around the grounds." *JH*

ZIRAKZIGIL ***Pencil sketches***
"Zirakzigil is one of the Misty Mountains that rise above Moria, upon which the Dwarves built an observation tower, the culmination of the Endless Stair. It had to feel precarious and lofty: imagine going up all those steps only to emerge on some pleasant flat terrace. The top is weathered and broken to allow Gandalf and the Balrog to emerge – I couldn't imagine the Dwarves actually sunning themselves at the top on pleasant days, but rather peering through slit windows at the world below." *JH*

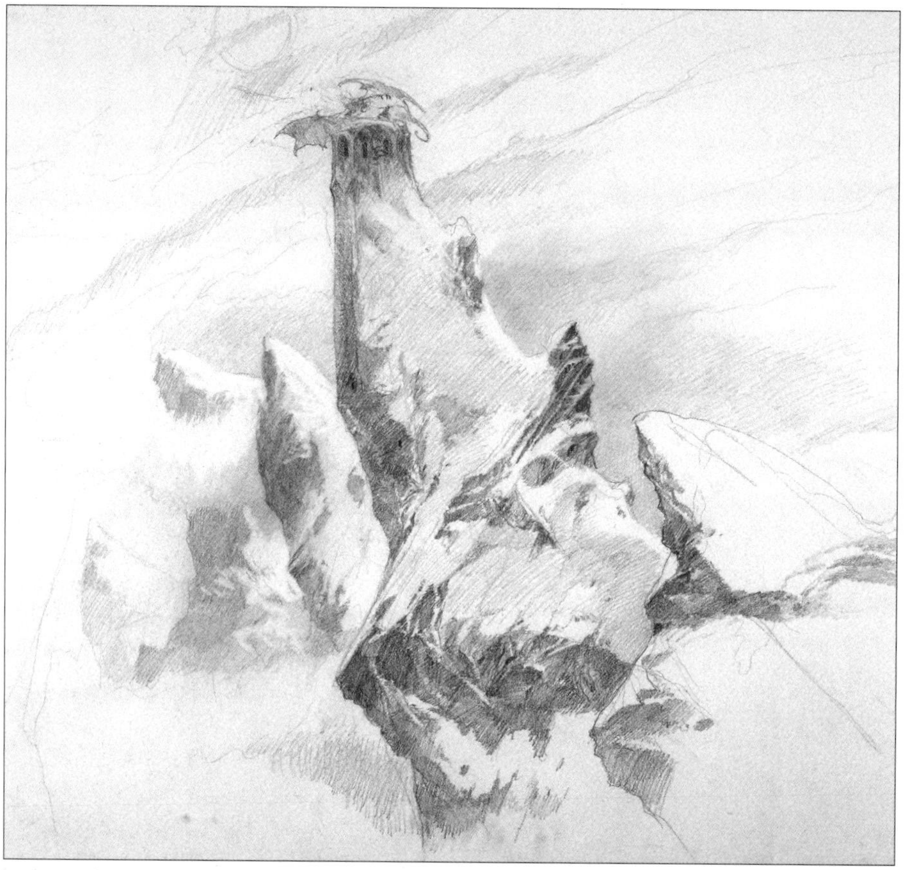

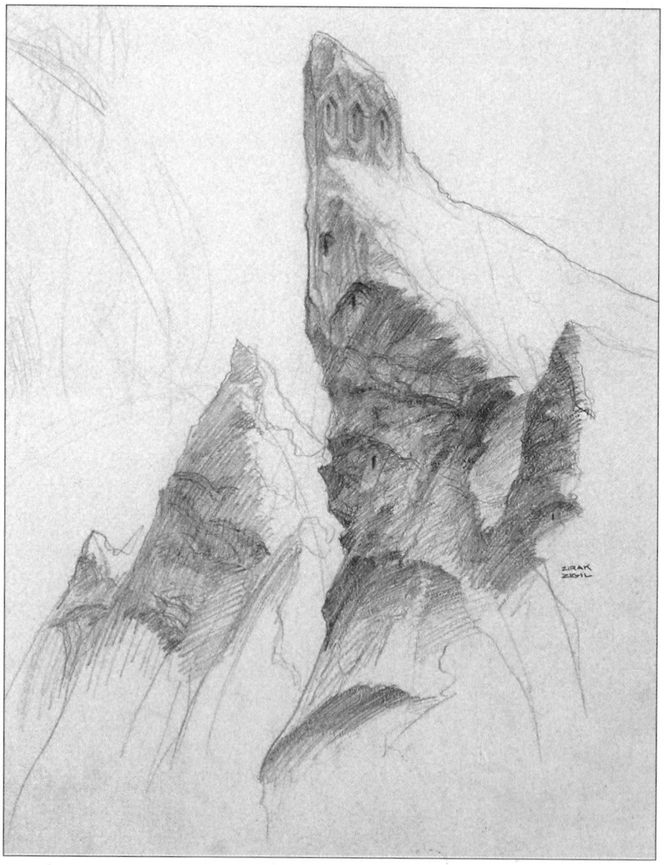

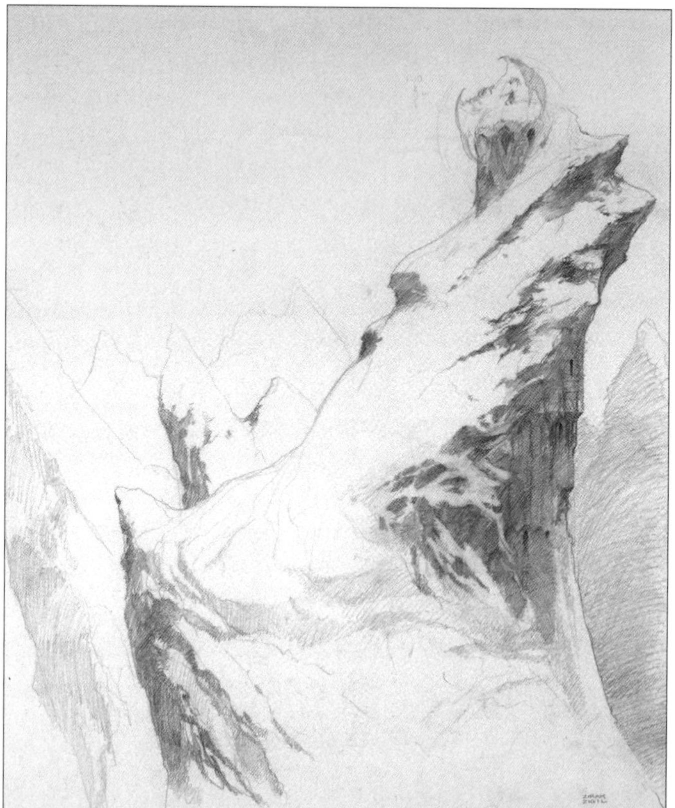

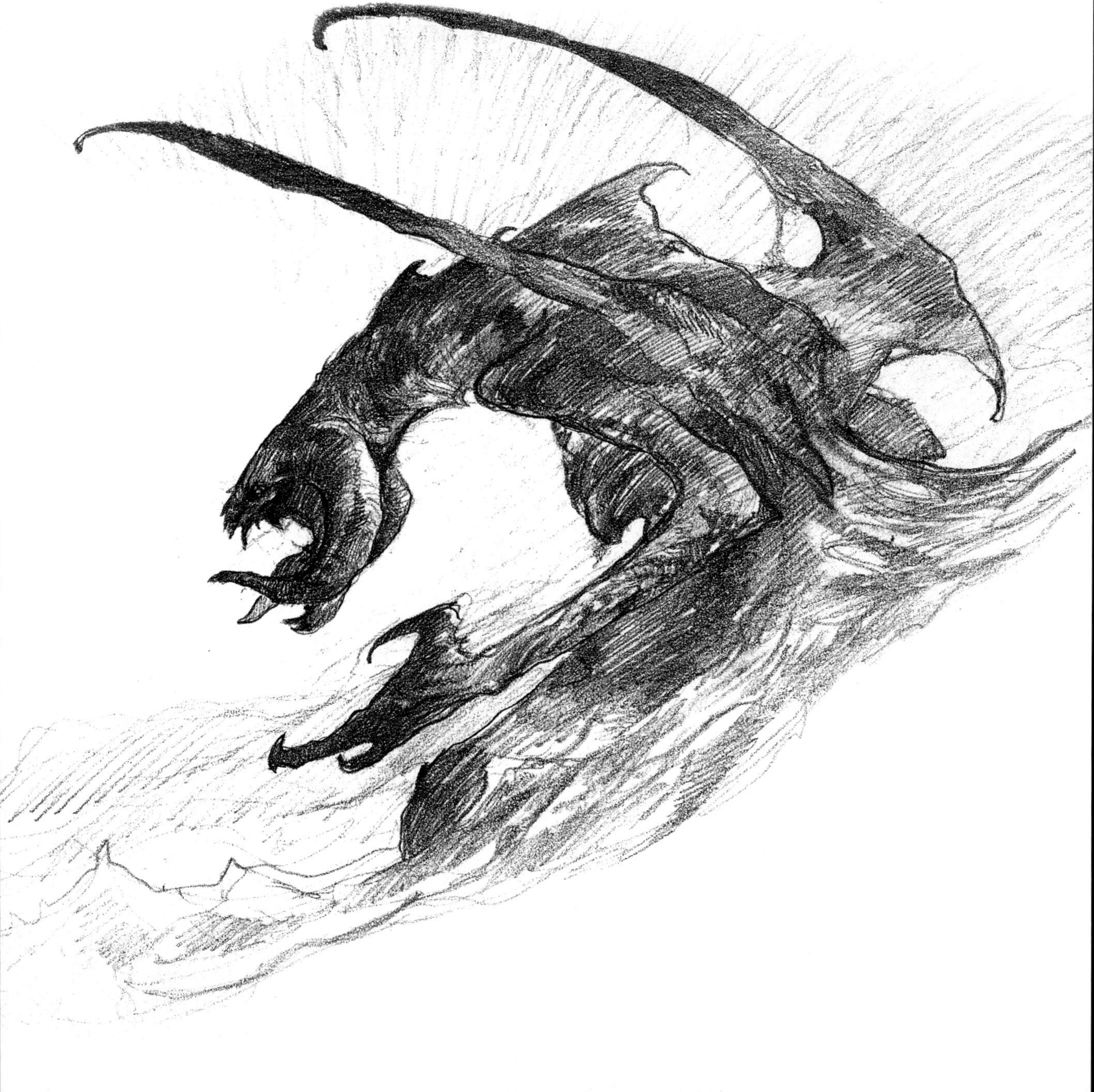

THE BALROG *Pencil sketch*

"The sequence in which Gandalf falls with the Balrog is one of my absolute favorites in the story. The Balrog turns into a 'creature of slime' before crawling back up the Endless Stair to reignite on Zirakzigil. Once his fire is extinguished, I imagined him as skeletal, diminished." *JH*

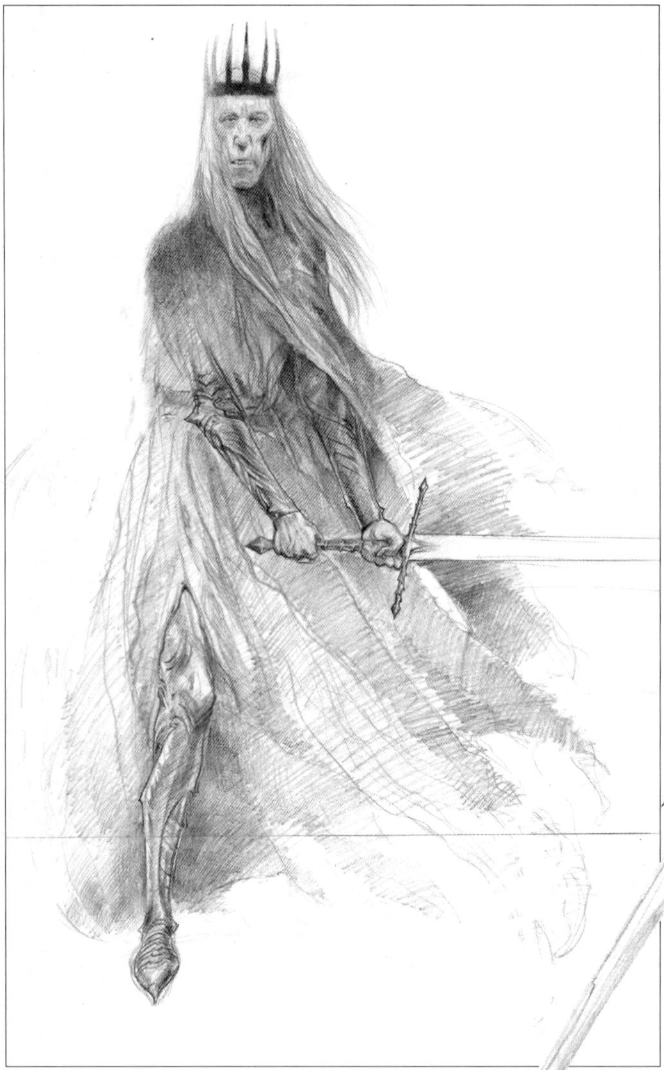

RINGWRAITH AND HORSE ***Pencil sketches***
"These are a couple of pictures of the Witch-king and a wraith horse. The idea at one point was to have the horses created digitally, so there was the full excitement of designing something completely new – but in the end it turned out that to have a real horse was much more economical." *JH*

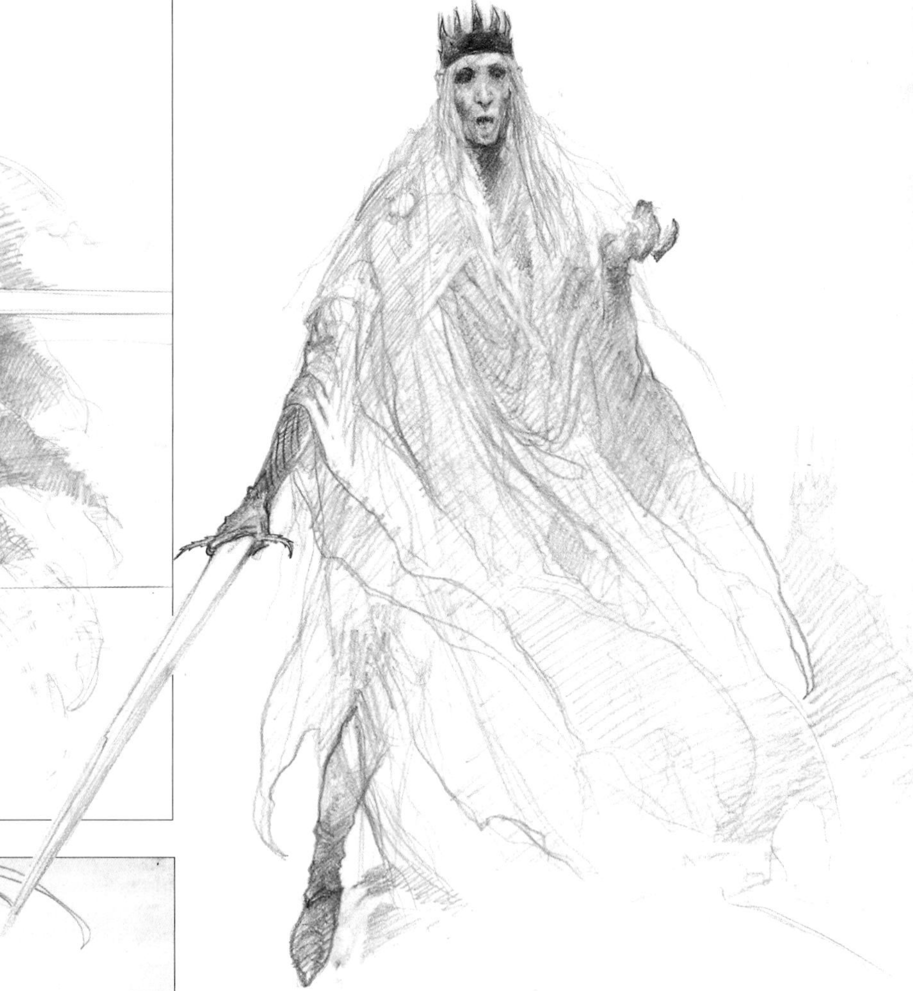

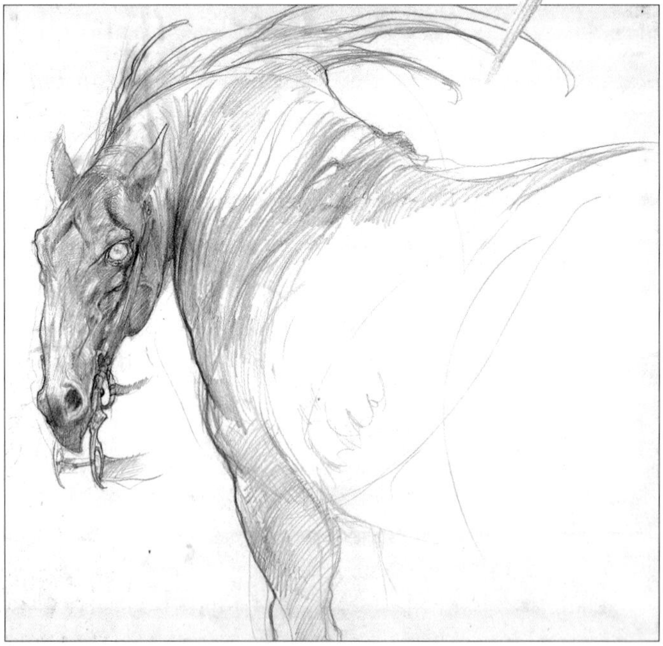

AMON HEN ***Frodo faces the Witch-king at Amon Hen***
"'Is nothing sacred!?' I hollered, when Peter asked for a color illustration of Frodo battling the Witch-king on Amon Hen. Actually, I didn't do that; I probably said, 'Sure Pete, no problem!' and went off to nurse my bruised and battered sense of ethics in a corner. It was often hard coming to terms with the changes the script required, especially if the script called for Sam to lasso the fell beast and Frodo to tempt the Witch-king close enough to stick him with Sting. Fortunately this was very early on in the project, and the script evolved a lot, thus the scene never was."

"The Seeing Seat here is just the top of a huge design iceberg, including an abandoned fortress with stairs and terraces stretching back down to Parth Galen. During the design process, the urge to wander off from Amon Hen to Amon Lhaw, and around the shores of Nen Hithoel, sketching on the way, was very hard to resist." *JH*

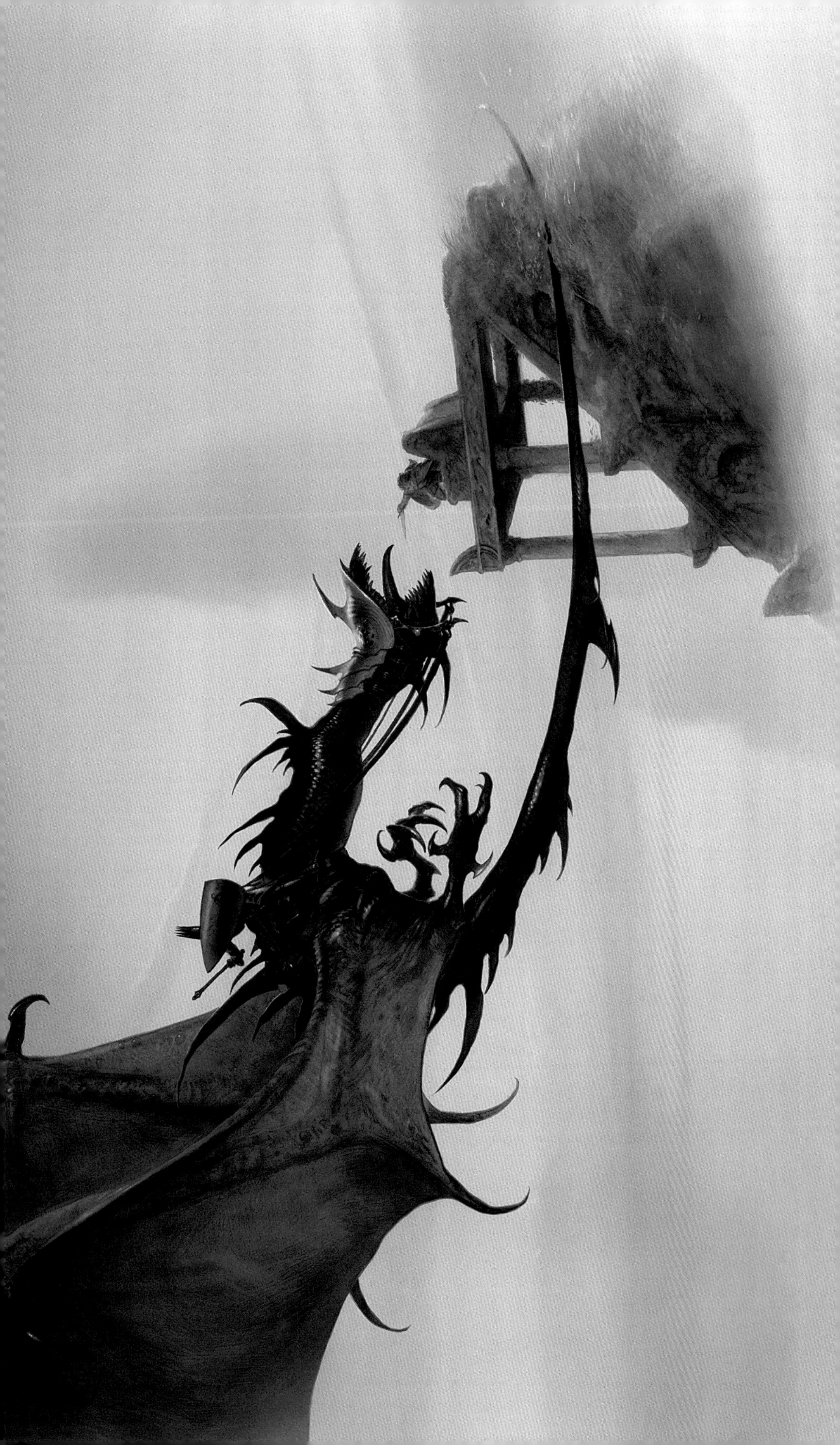

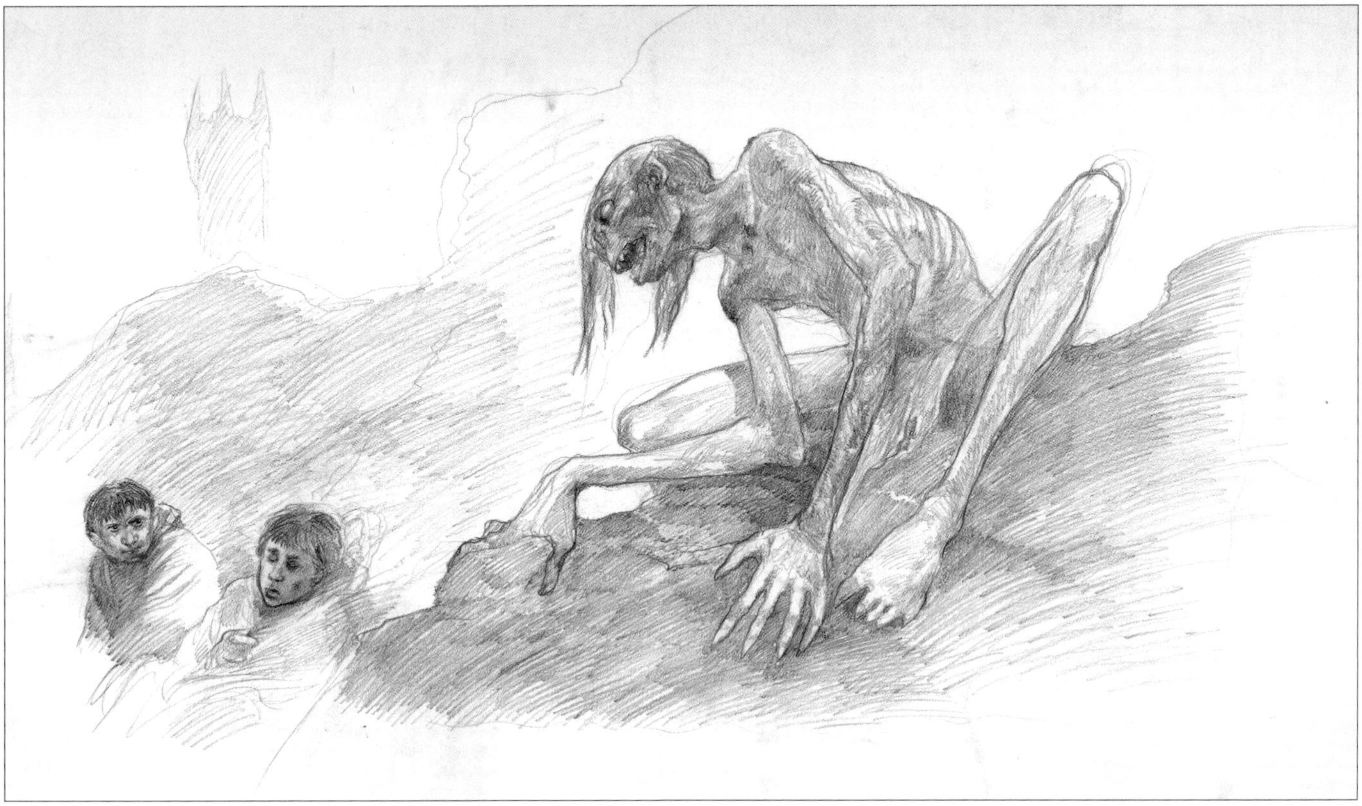

GOLLUM *Pencil sketch*

"What's in any image? Assuredly, what you endeavor to put in, yet undoubtedly you put in many other things without knowing you are doing so. The most important, intimate, and powerful ingredients in any image seem to come from the spectator. As the vital essence of Gollum is Andy Serkis's creation, so this drawing is largely his doing, even though it was done long before the actor was chosen. Since it's one of a series of doodles done in spare moments gleaned from time spent conceptualizing locations, I didn't see anything special in it, but Andy did, and it became one of the cornerstones of his interpretation of Gollum. So what's in there? Well, whatever Andy saw, he brought with him, but déjà vu always needs a nudge." *JH*

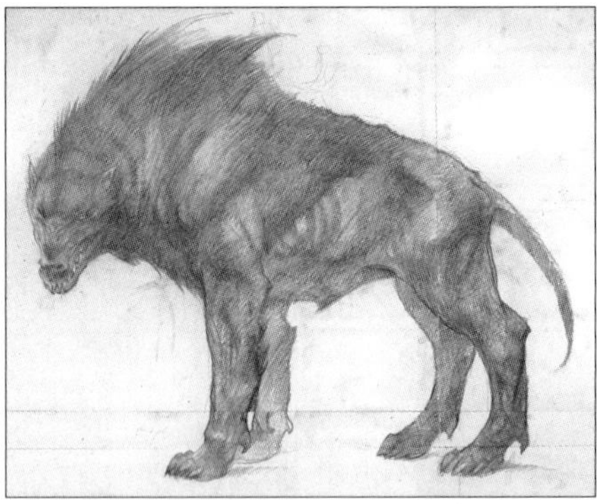

WARG *Pencil sketch*

"I thought wolves should be the starting point for the wargs, which, in the film, are simply large predators, rather than the evil phantasms of the books. This was as far as I got." *JH*

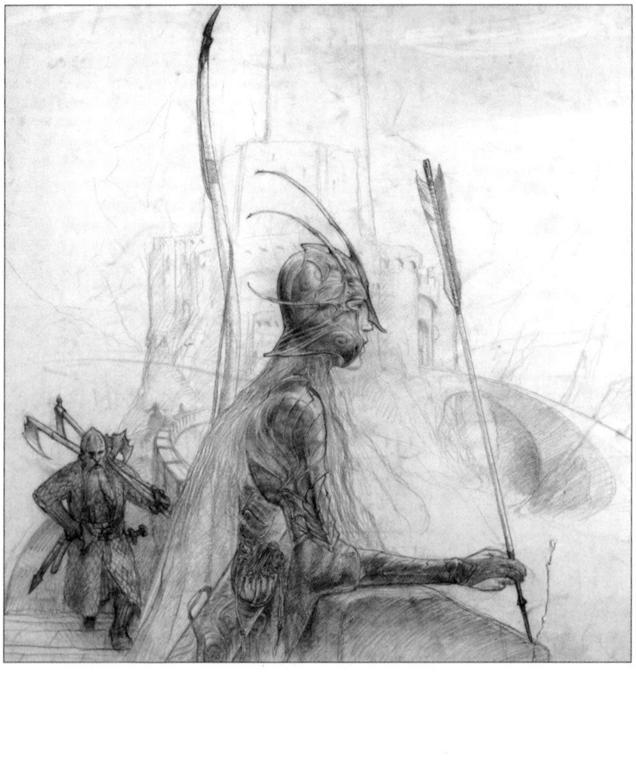

HELM'S DEEP
Pencil sketch

"What started as a doodle for a piece of Elven armor ended up as a full study of Legolas and Gimli on the Deeping Wall. I thought that Legolas should have a full suit of slim and intricately tooled armor, whether he wore it all the time or not. But such is the disparity between heroes and extras – the Elves in full armor are cut down to a man (well, to an Elf), whereas Legolas, bareheaded, comes through unscathed." *JH*

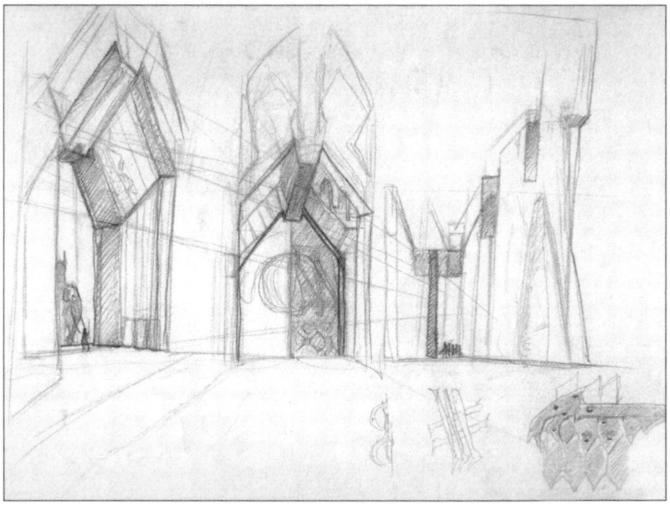

THE BLACK GATES ***Pencil sketches***

"Númenórean architecture is quite arrogant, really, but with supple lines inherited from their maritime past, which break up the bulkiness of the structures. Only a lack of time stopped me from exploring this avenue all the way back to Númenor itself.

"I am not a huge fan of 'designer's dream' architecture and cities. Too many created fantasy realms look as if they are the work of one architect (which is evidently true, but beside the point), a fault born of our contemporary desire to design novel cities and environments, forgetting that any urban area is as much a product of chance as of design. I'm influenced as much by the terrain, the materials used, as by the draftsman's pencil. I tried to bring this to mind when imagining these great structures." *JH*

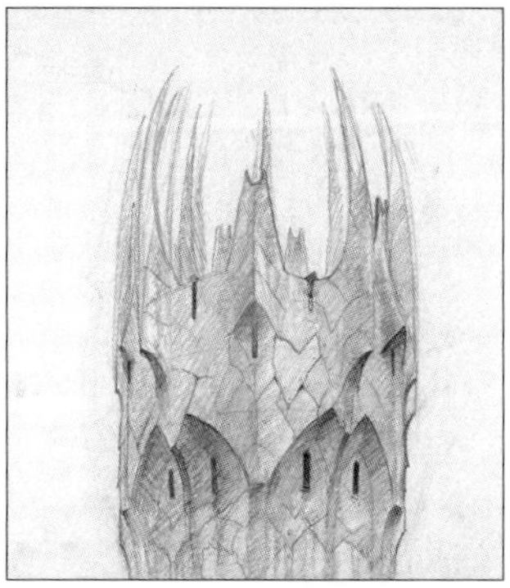

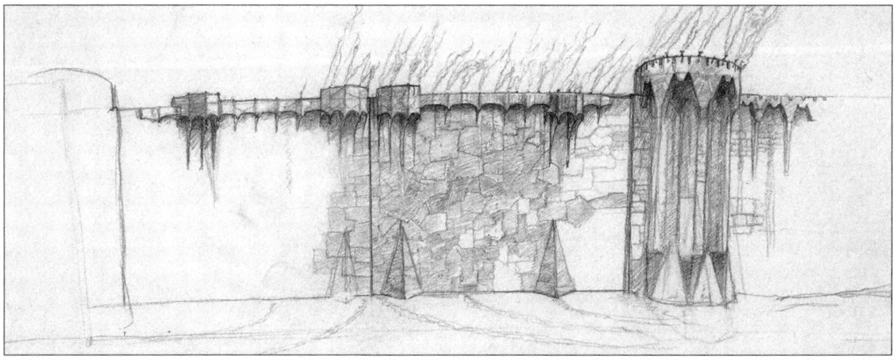

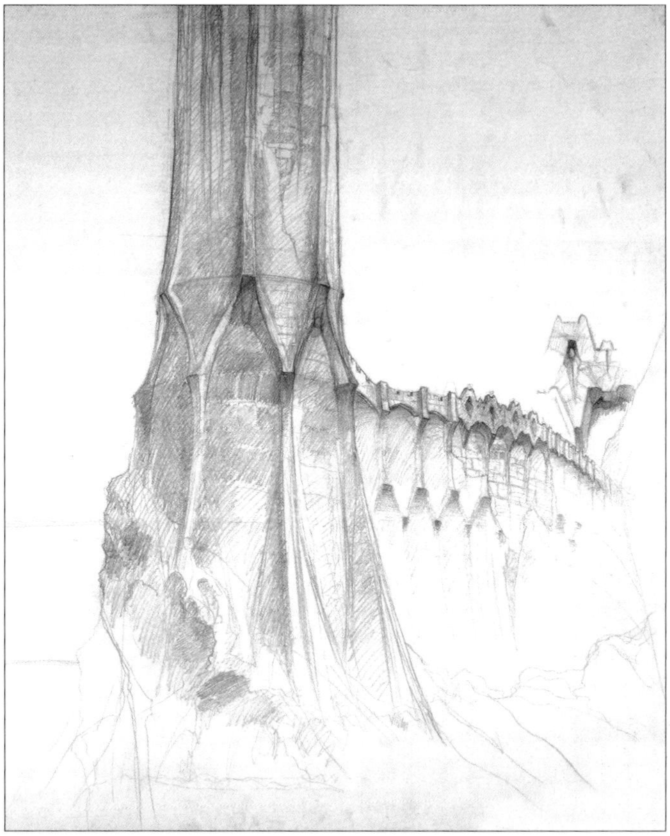

THE BLACK GATES ***Pencil sketches***

"One of the ideas we touched on was to develop a well-defined style for Númenórean architecture, which constitutes the foundations of many of the larger structures in Middle-earth. The Black Gates are Númenórean, repaired and enhanced by Sauron.

"Sauron's 'embellishments' on existing structures, as well as the architecture he creates, are wrong in every sense. He is trying to capture something – humanity – he no longer possesses. Sauron's architectural forays fall on the sinister side of 'neo-gothic.' Height for height, spikiness taken to needle sharpness, and, above all, repetition of motifs ad infinitum. Much of his architecture is in metal, riveted to stone foundations, like a mad gardener grafting extra prickles onto a rose and neglecting the flowers themselves. It is an attempt to capture all the attractiveness of human craftsmanship in an industrial manner. Above all, it is disproportioned, too tall, too sharply edged, inhuman." *JH*

THE GLITTERING CAVES
Pencil sketches
"Caverns are frustrating things to draw. They are a catalogue of subterranean marvels – assuredly most exquisite to behold, but not exactly stimulating to conceptualize. The smaller picture below shows the mouth of the major caves. A wide opening, not some discreet passage, seemed to convey the weight of the mountain more dramatically." *JH*

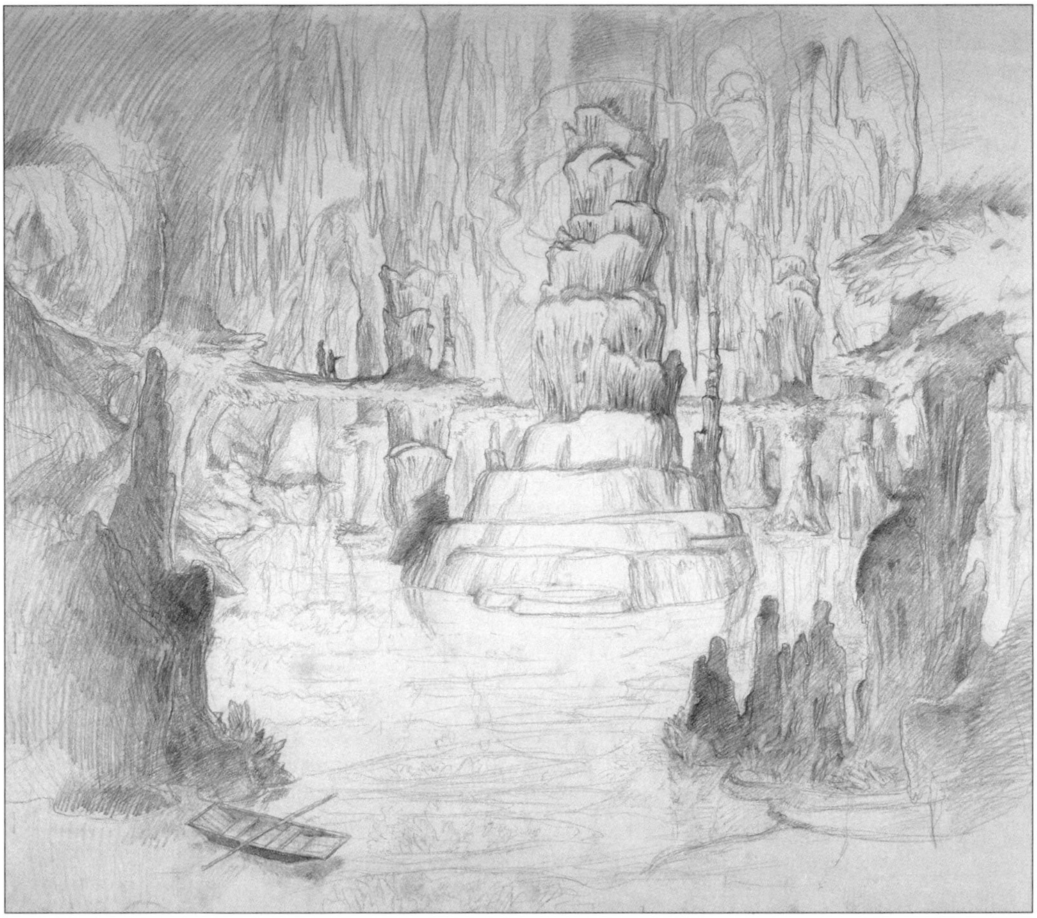

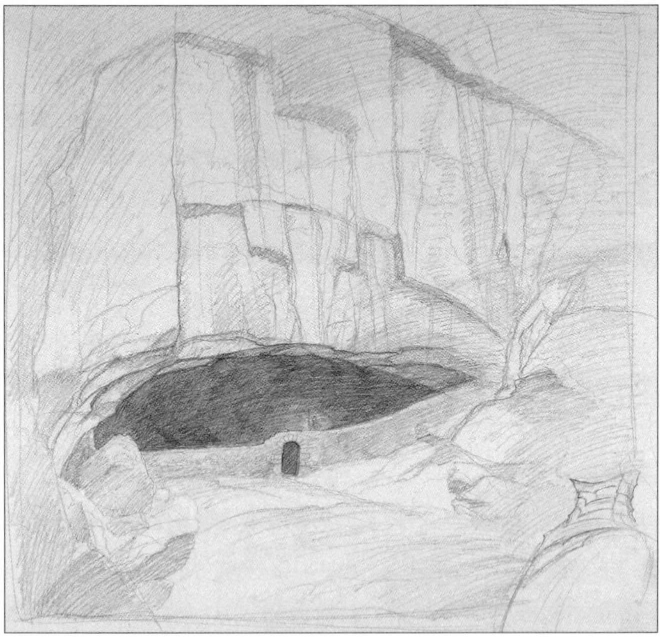

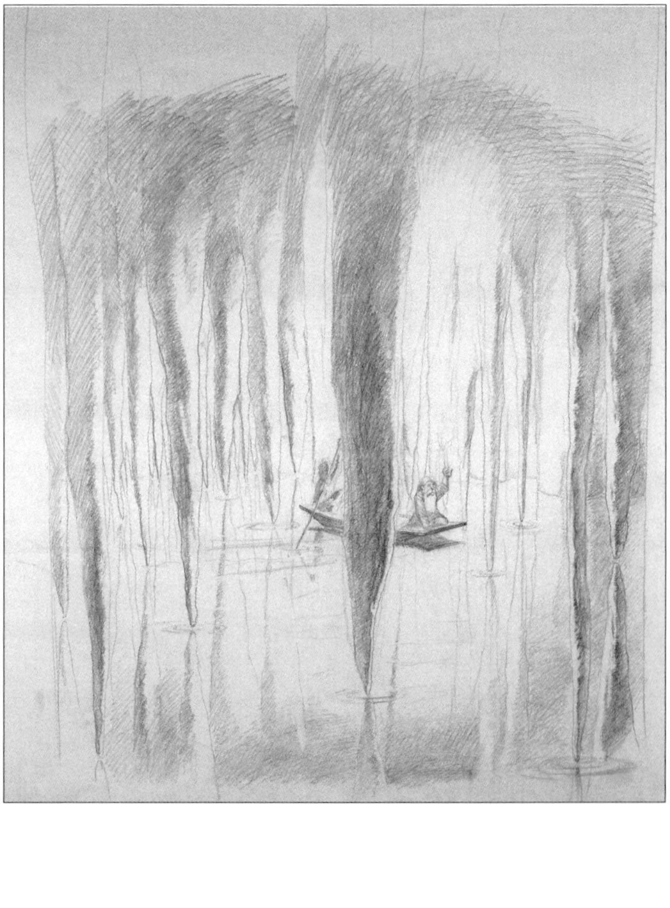

THE GLITTERING CAVES ***Pencil sketch***
"To the right we have Legolas and Gimli exploring the Glittering Caves. All the stalactites just brush the surface of the water. I wanted to create the feeling of an inverted mineral forest – something that would be pleasing to both of them." *JH*

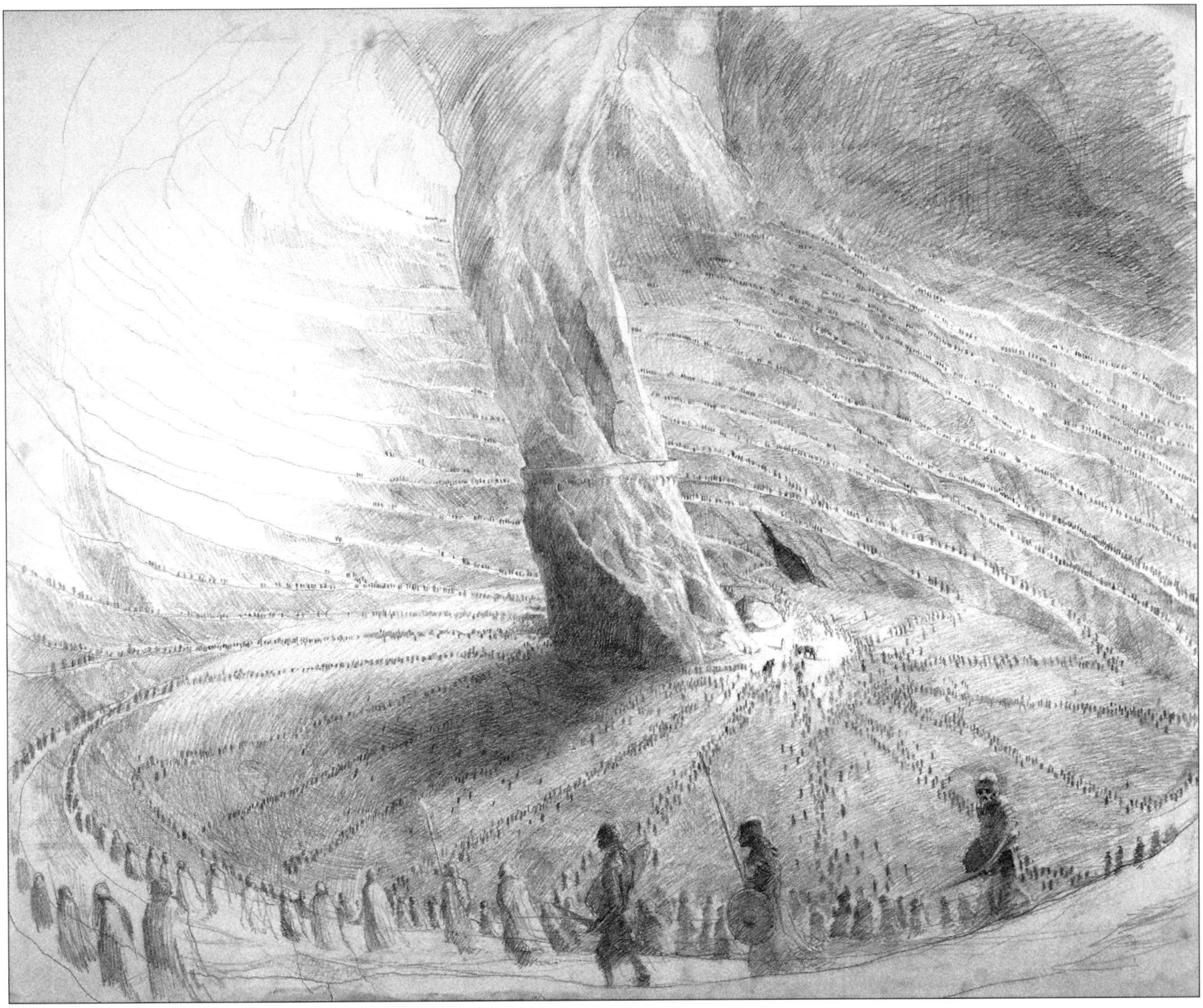

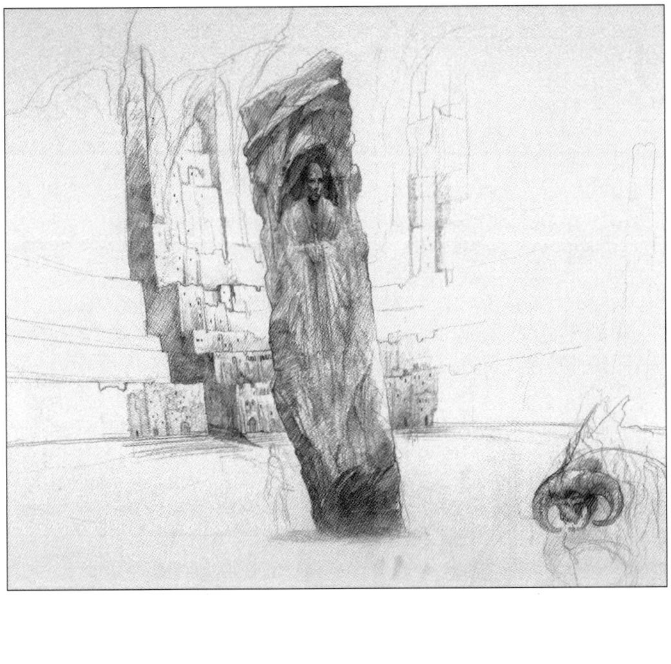

PATHS OF THE DEAD ***Pencil sketch***
"The arrival of the Army of the Dead. Huge amphitheater with a central column. The army comes out of passageways and slowly winds down the paths to the floor of the cavern. I wanted it to feel like being in the center of a slow-motion whirlpool, as disorienting as possible." *JH*

PATHS OF THE DEAD ***Pencil sketch***
"The central column of the amphitheater where the army appears. At one point Peter Jackson wanted to see an underground city." *JH*

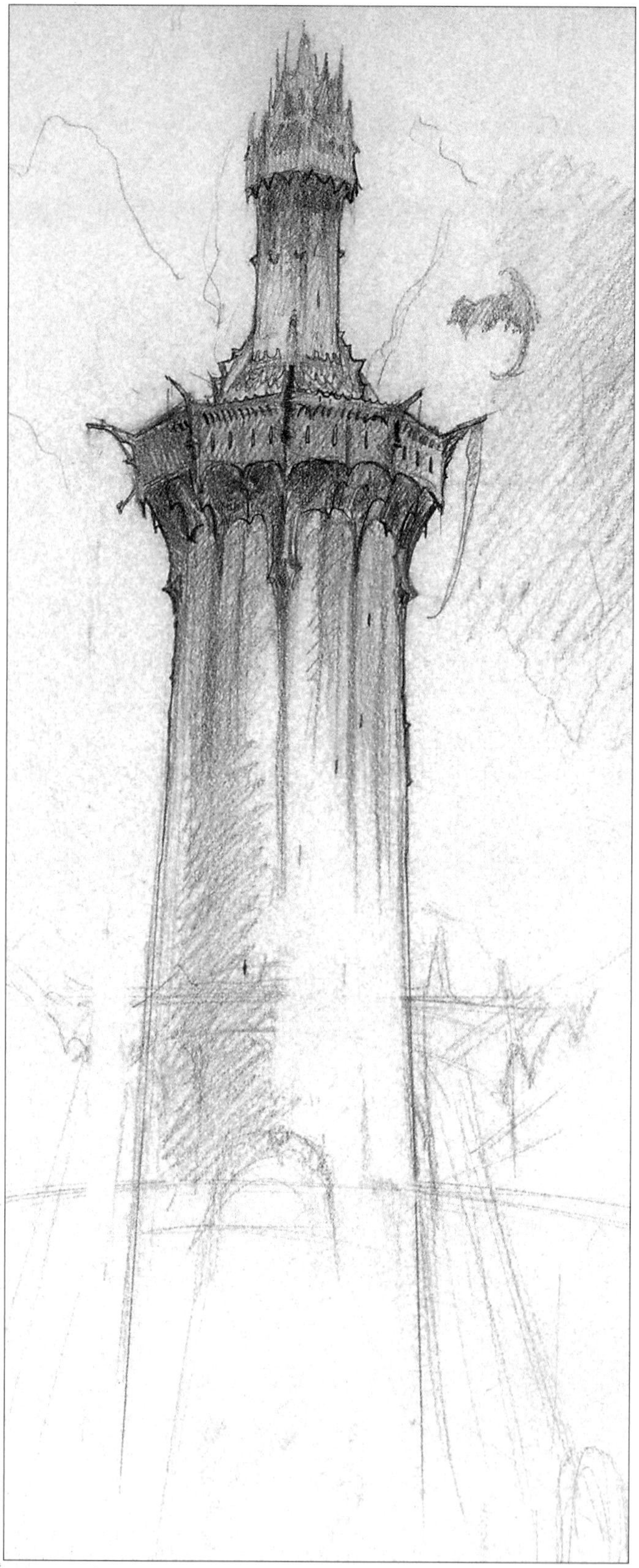

MINAS MORGUL *Pencil sketch*
"The Tower of the Moon, with the aviary of the fell beasts atop it." *JH*

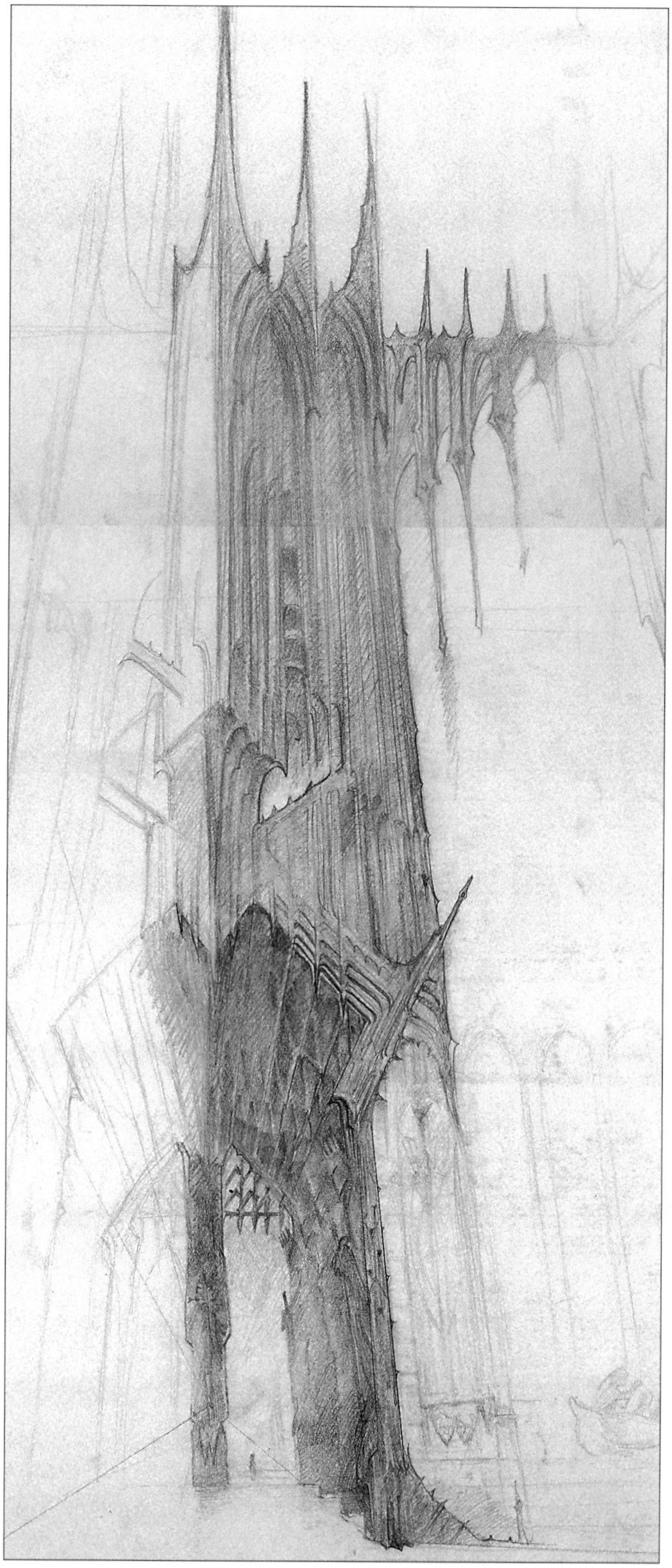

MINAS MORGUL *Pencil sketch*
"This is an early version of the main gate of Minas Morgul. As it was once the sister city of Minas Tirith, there are still traces of the same architecture, but all of this has been 'redecorated' by the most recent occupants." *JH*

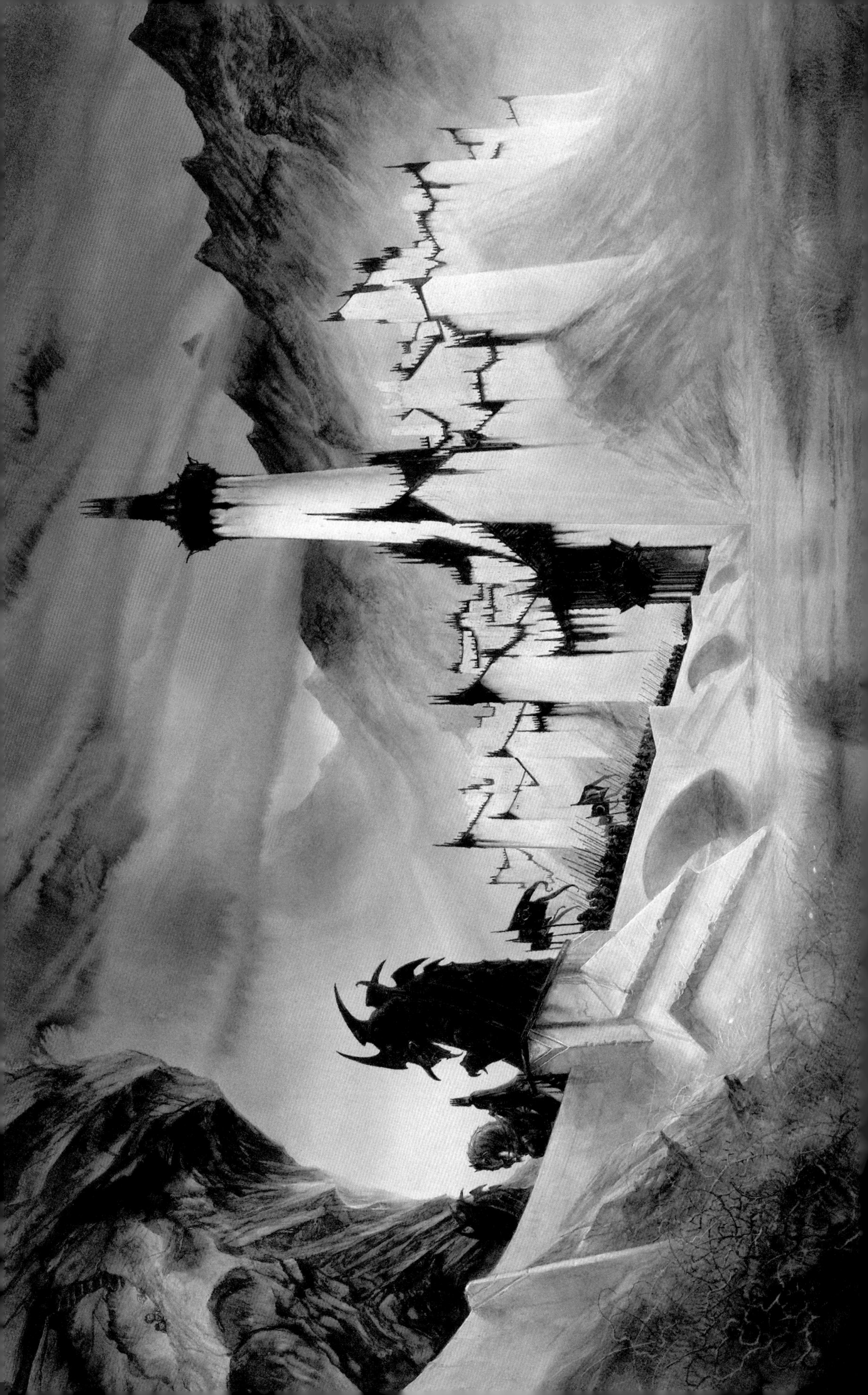

MINAS MORGUL ***Pencil sketch***
"A sketch of one of the Morgul statues. I liked the idea that these statues, designed to intimidate and keep enemies away, would be carved in the likeness of the most fearsome creature in all Middle-earth, so I came up with a stylized Balrog. Better than any 'Beware of the Dog' sign. And yes, those are wings." *JH*

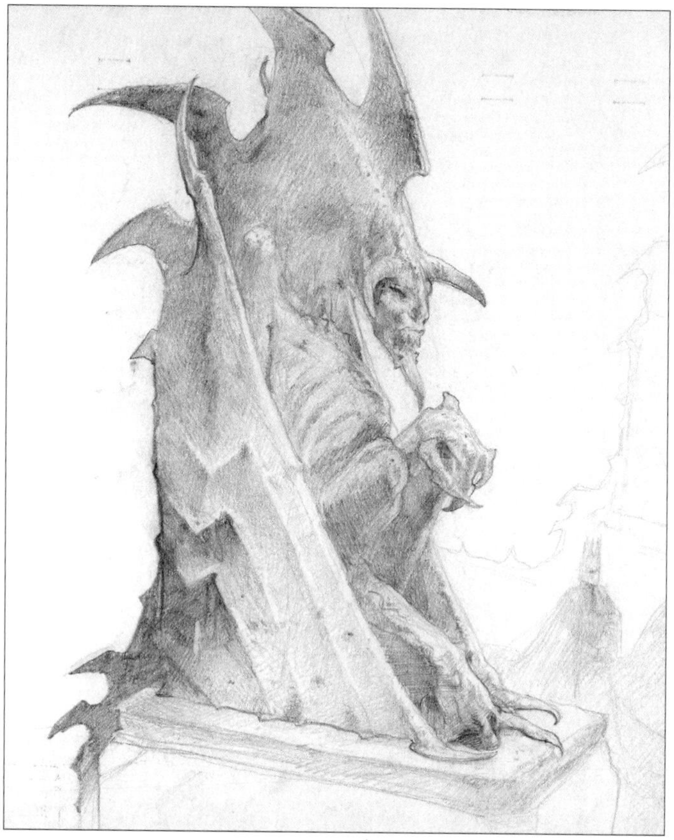

MINAS MORGUL
Pencil sketch
"I believe that Tolkien's Minas Morgul had steps leading down from the front gate, which, while it did give the opportunity for a rather more stately entrance, was not exactly convenient for armies issuing forth." *JH*

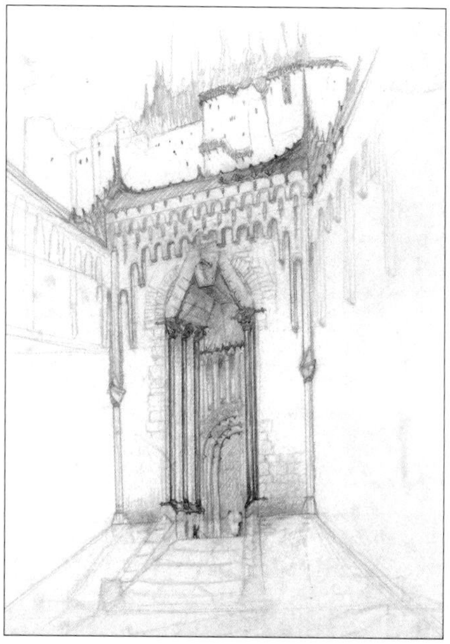

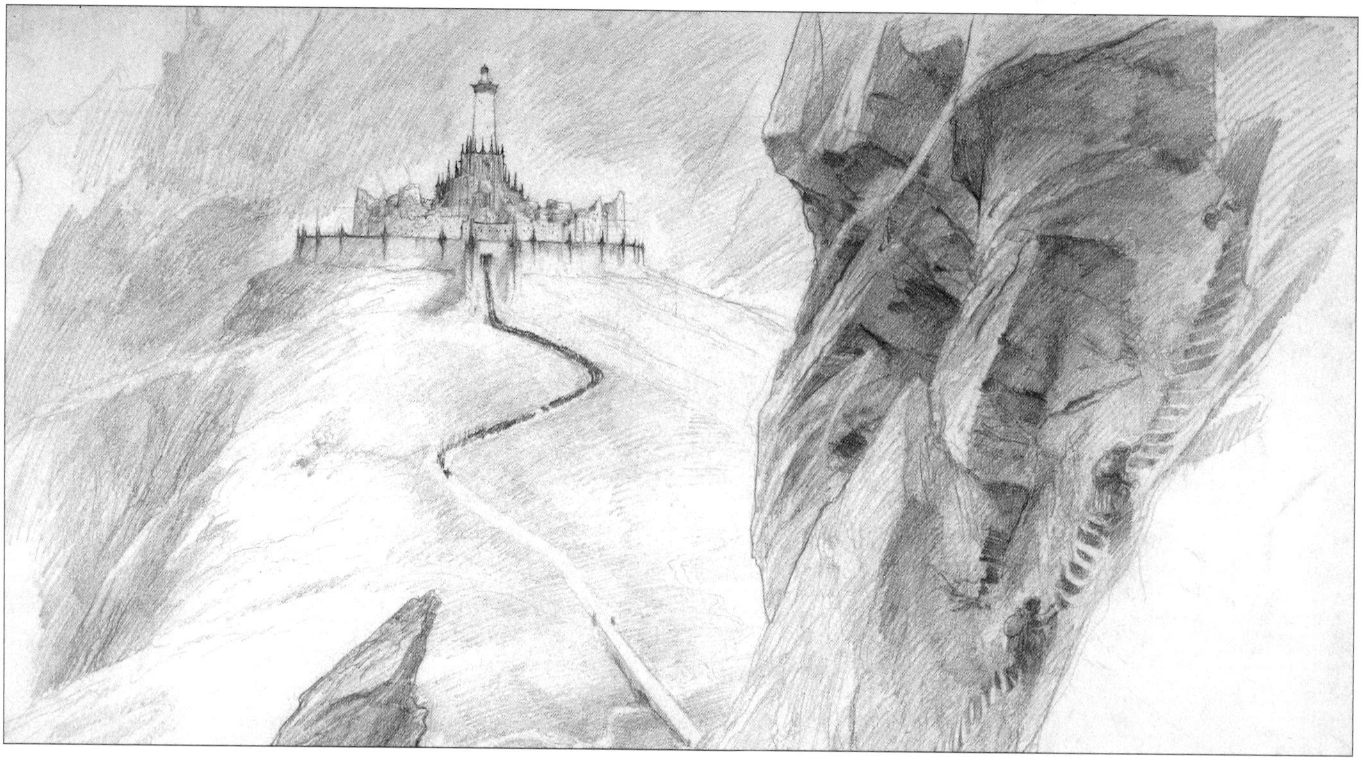

MINAS MORGUL
Pencil sketch
"An early version of Minas Morgul, which was closer to the description in Tolkien's text. However, Peter felt it was too far away from the Endless Stair." *JH*

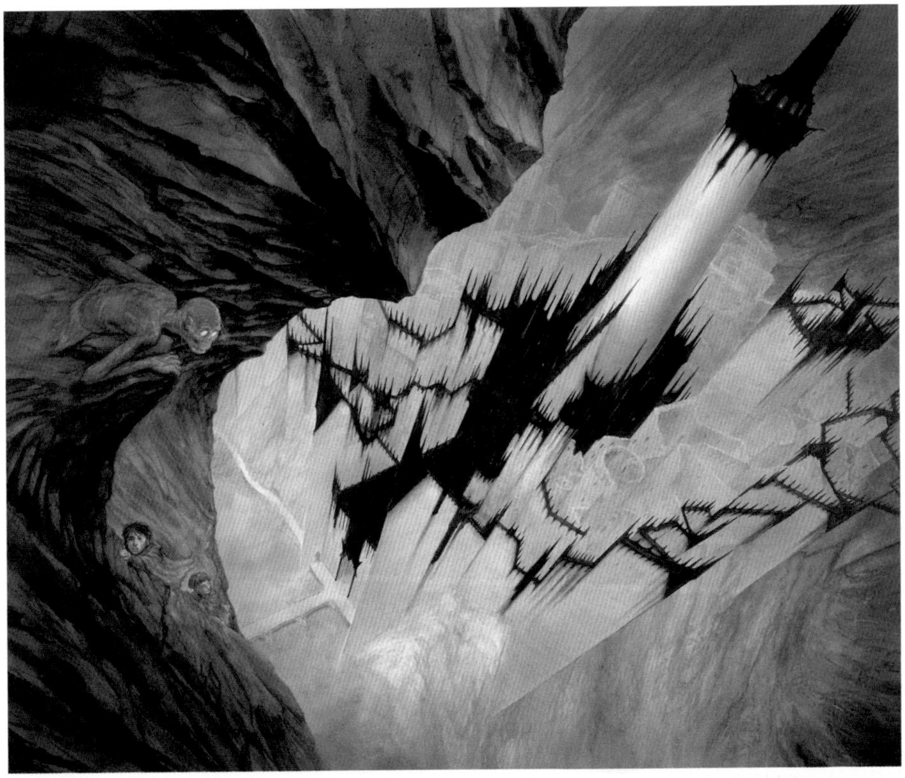

MINAS MORGUL *Watercolor*
"In this painting I was trying to convey the vertigo that affects anyone wearing the Ring, and the horrible sensation of being exposed that the Hobbits have during their climb. The rocks were based on local rock formations to be found around Wellington." *JH*

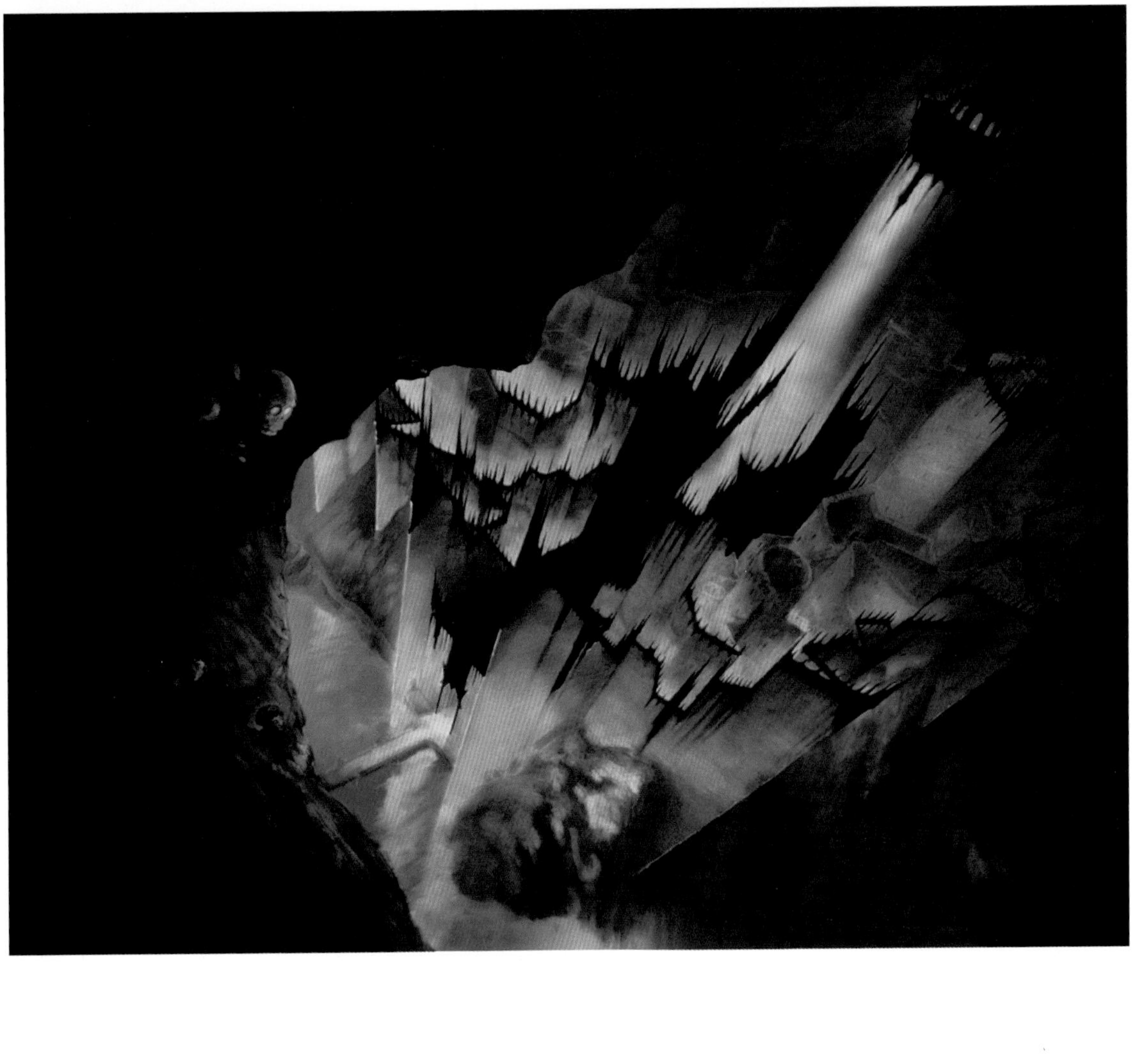

MINAS MORGUL *Watercolor*
"Paul Lasaine reworked the same painting to vividly illustrate the sickly green phosphorescent glow seen in the finished film." *JH*

GROND
Pencil sketch
"An early version of Grond. The wolf's maw was to be filled with burning coals and fire until it would be red hot." *JH*

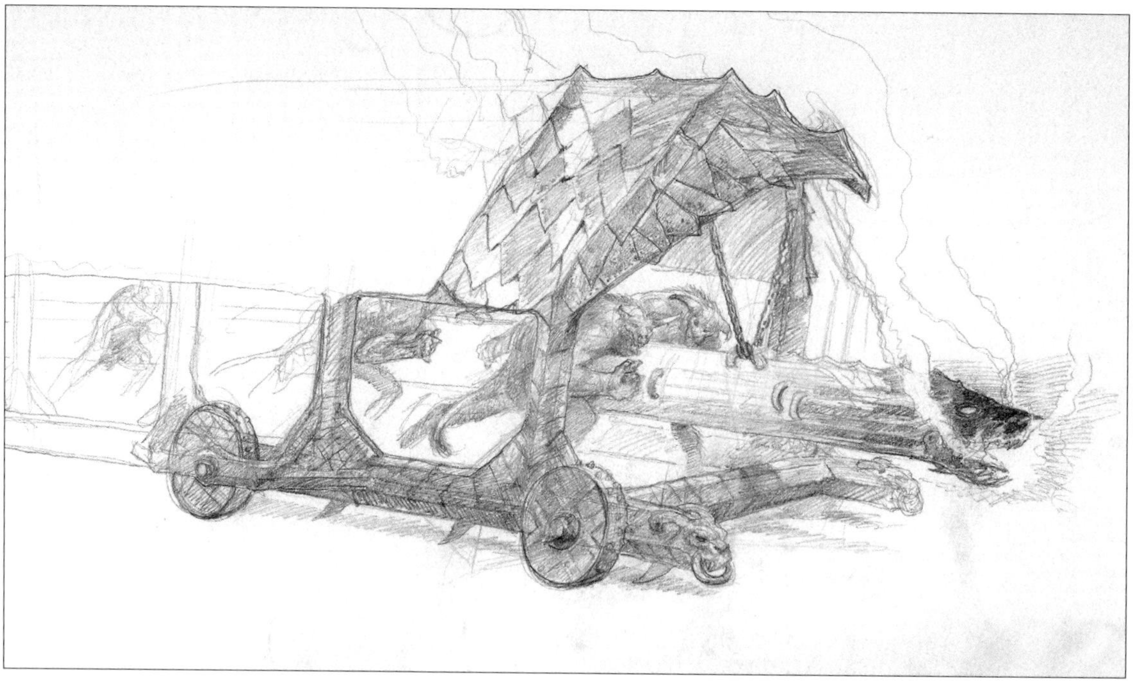

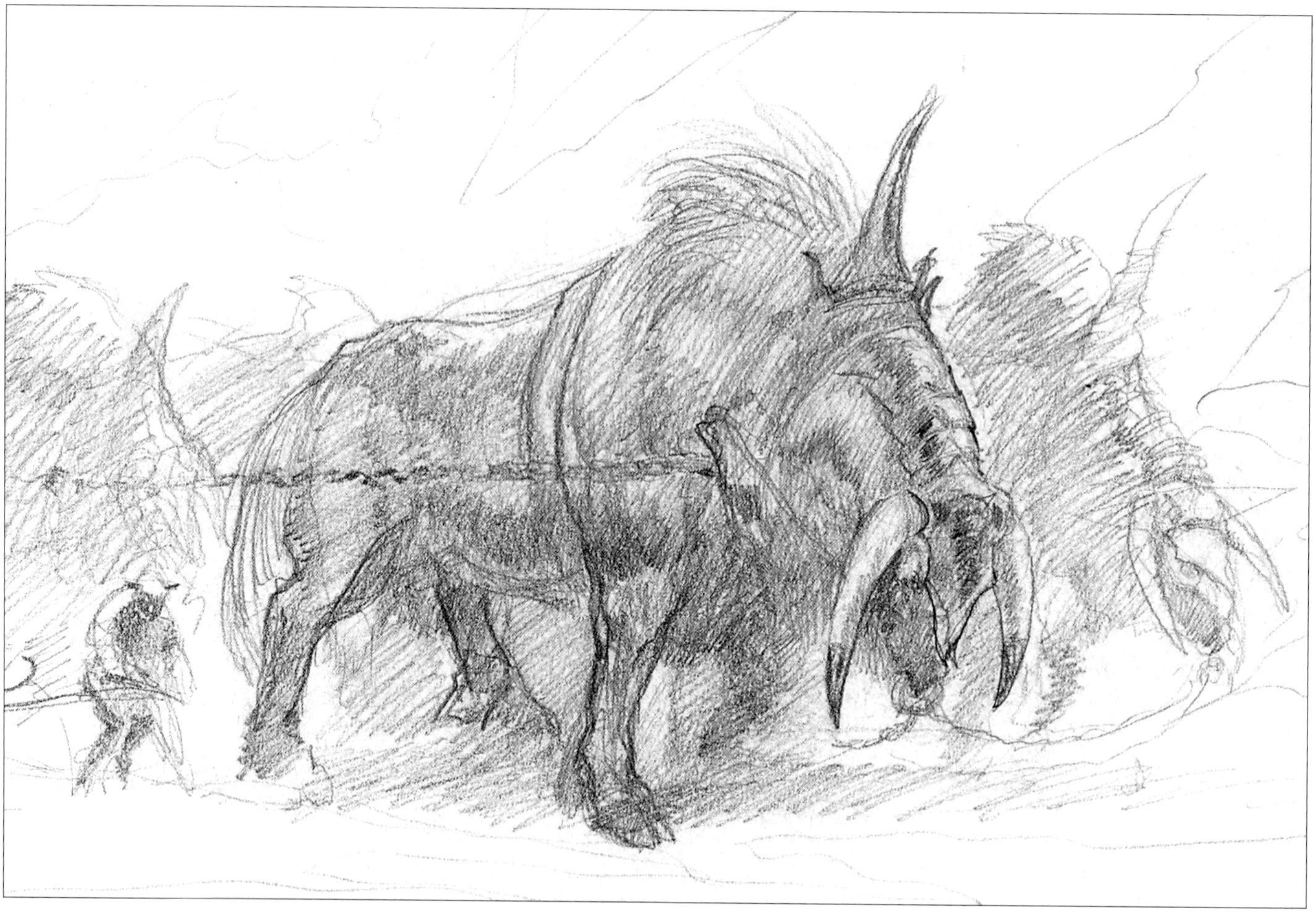

GREAT BEAST ***Pencil sketch***
"An early version of the beasts pulling the great ram, Grond, across the Pelennor Fields toward the gates." *JH*

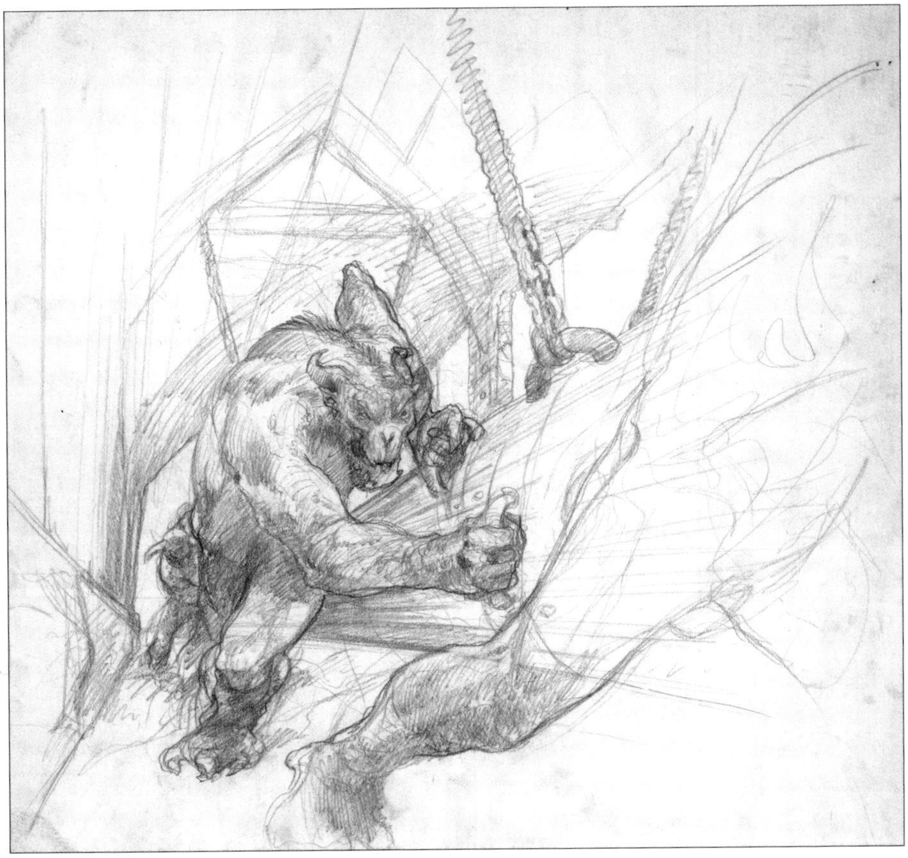

TROLLS *Pencil sketch*
"There were long discussions about the nature of mountain-trolls. I thought they should be somewhat shaggier than their cave-dwelling cousins, and perhaps have horns, like the mountain sheep and goats whose environment they share." *JH*

ROHIRRIM *Pencil sketch*
"The Rohirrim are basically Anglo-Saxons with horses (Tolkien's contribution to alternative history, which would have certainly resulted in a different outcome at Hastings)." *JH*

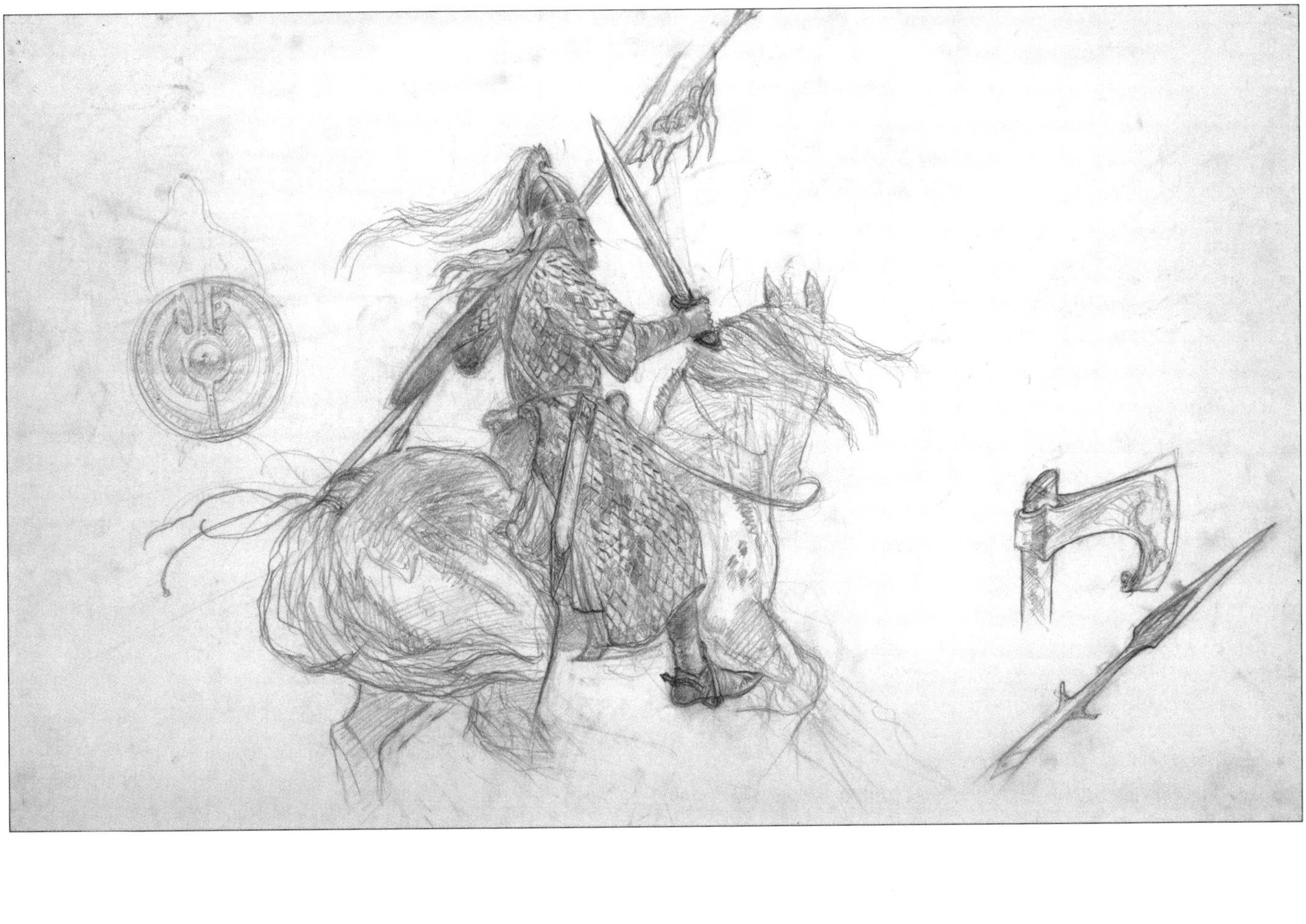

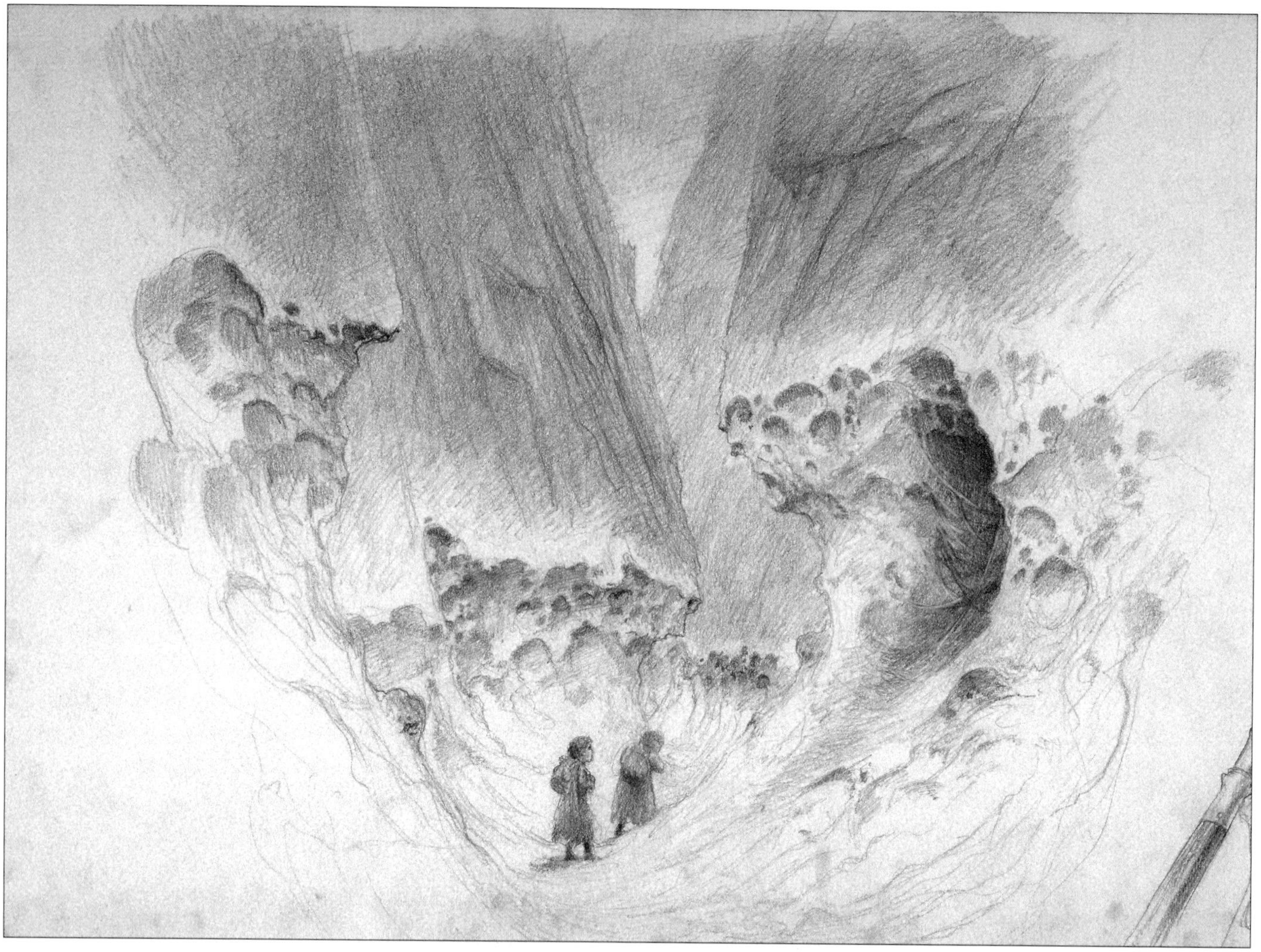

SHELOB'S LAIR ***Pencil sketch***
"In the sketch above you can see numerous disquieting holes above the path through the mountains; the path itself is corroded and eaten away by Shelob's poisonous nature." *JH*

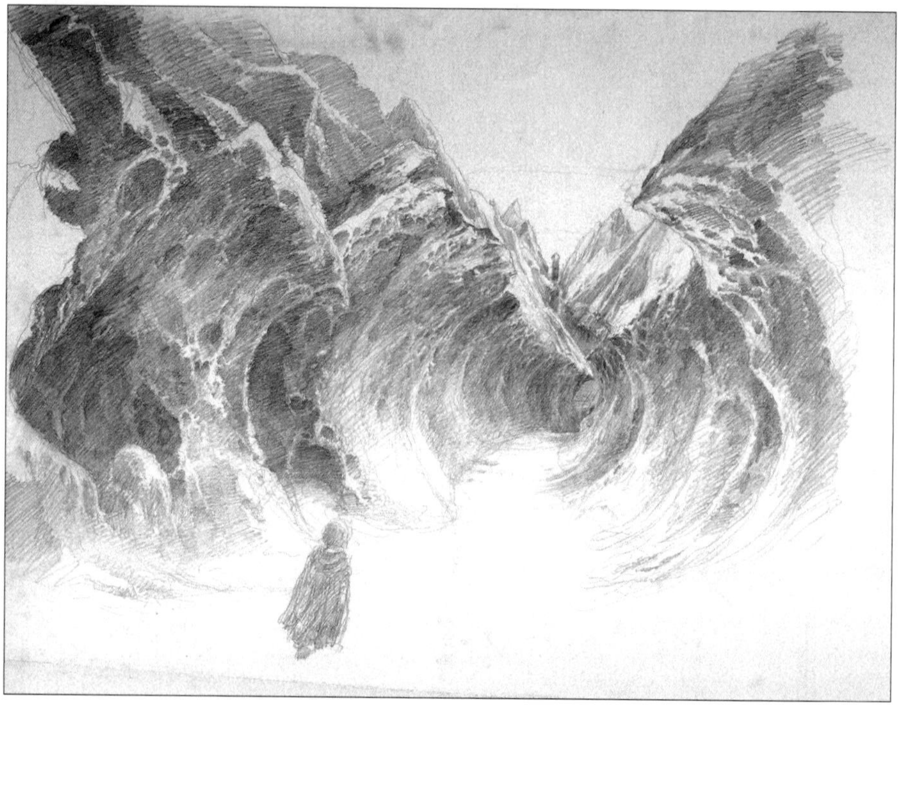

SHELOB'S LAIR ***Pencil sketch***
"The whole environment is eaten away by the consummate evil of Shelob. Rather than following a small path at the bottom of a declivity, the Hobbits find themselves in a horrid avenue of corroded rock, impossible to scale, impossible to escape from." *JH*

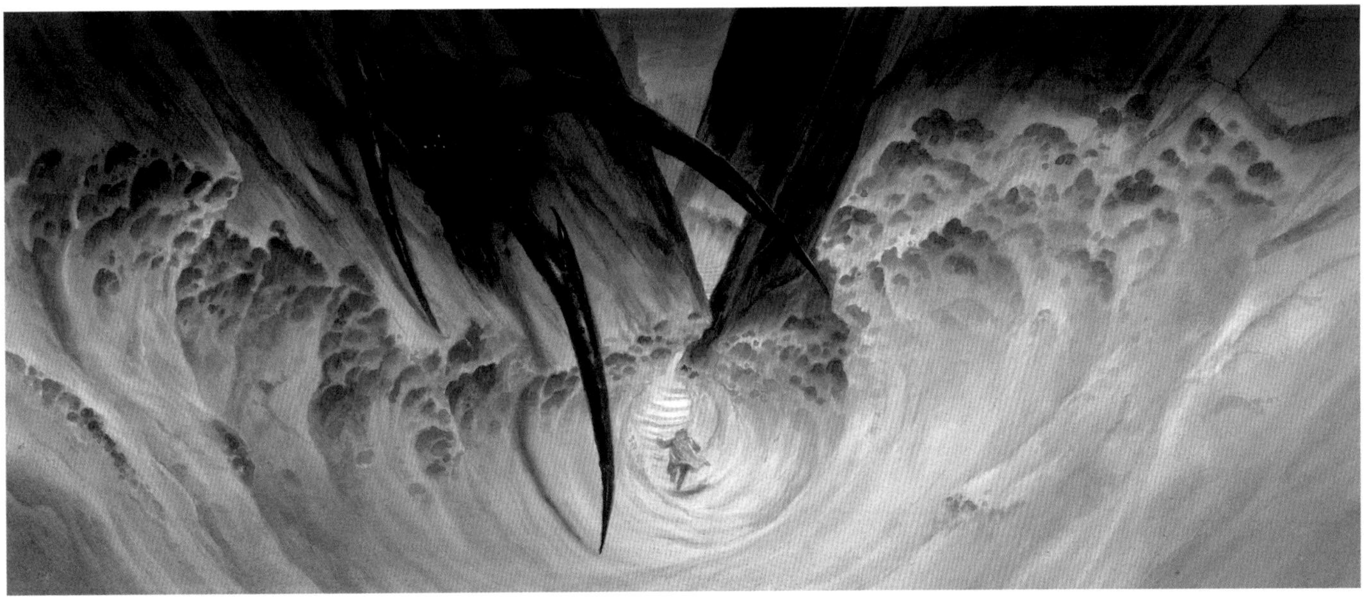

SHELOB'S LAIR *Watercolor*
"Shelob squeezing forth from one of her many back doors. If a raspy dry squelching sound were possible, that's the sound she would make as she eases her belly through the mouth of the tunnel." *JH*

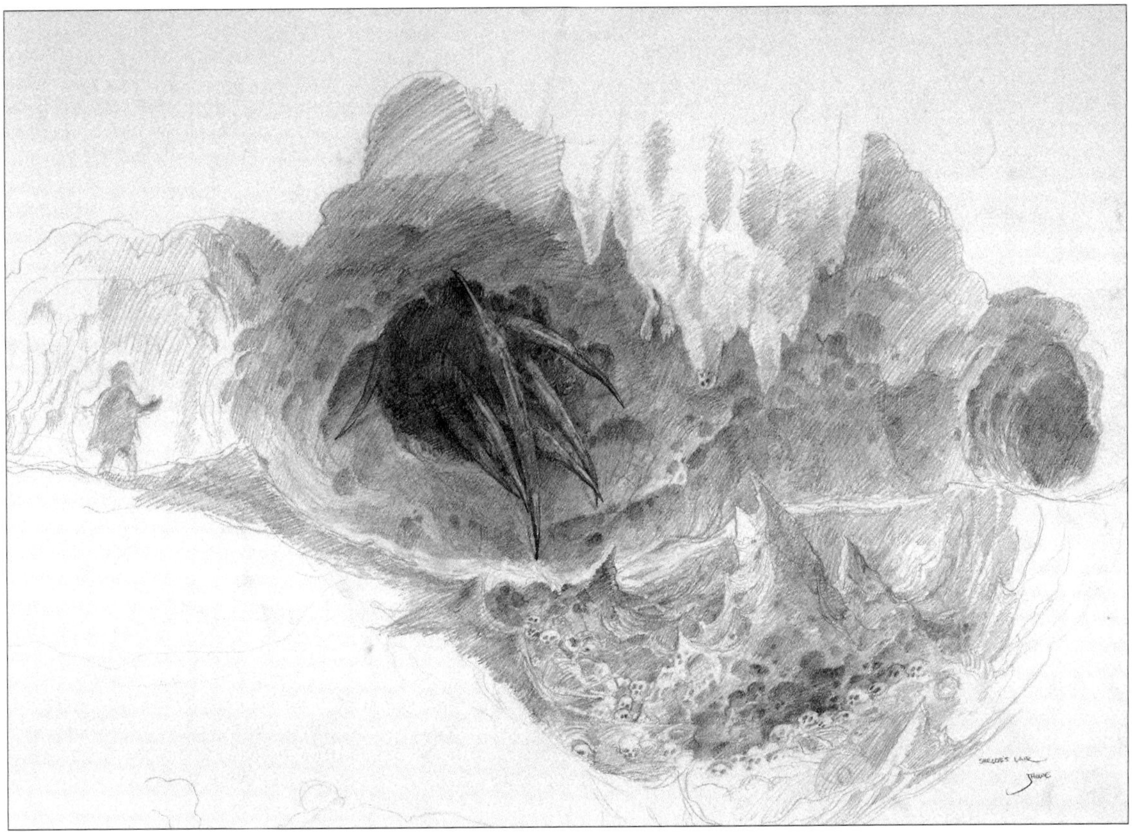

SHELOB'S LAIR *Pencil sketch*
"There's always something incredibly creepy about a spider waiting motionless for its prey. The overhanging corroded rock that the Hobbits have been walking through is an extension of her trap, a trap into which they have been falling ever since being persuaded to climb the Endless Stair." *JH*

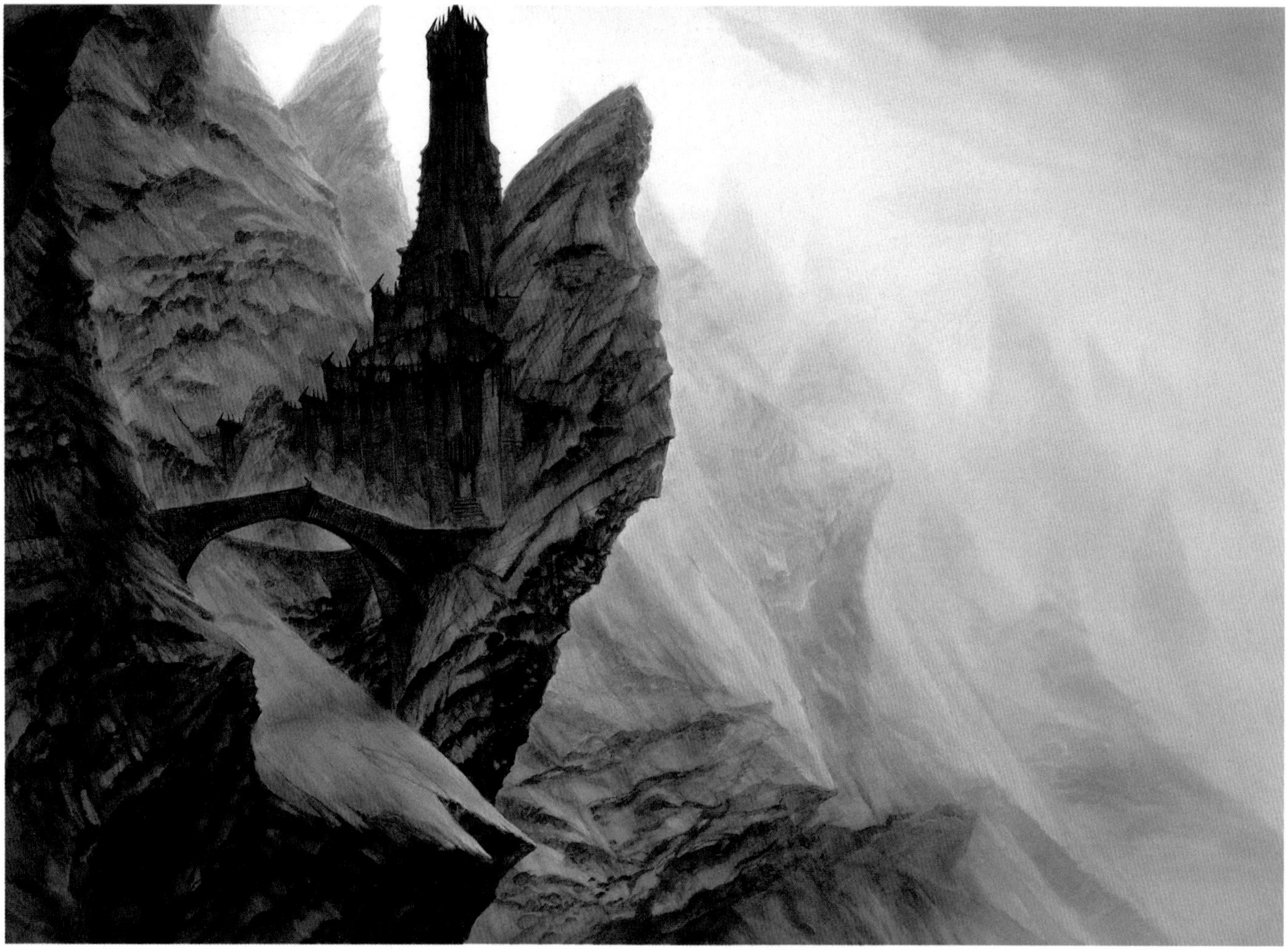

CIRITH UNGOL ***Watercolor and ink***
"Cirith Ungol was originally built to keep Sauron in Mordor, and it has strong Númenórean foundations. Sauron has turned it into a thinly manned, near-forgotten outpost. I imagined it lost in an incredibly tormented wilderness of pinnacles and precipices." *JH*

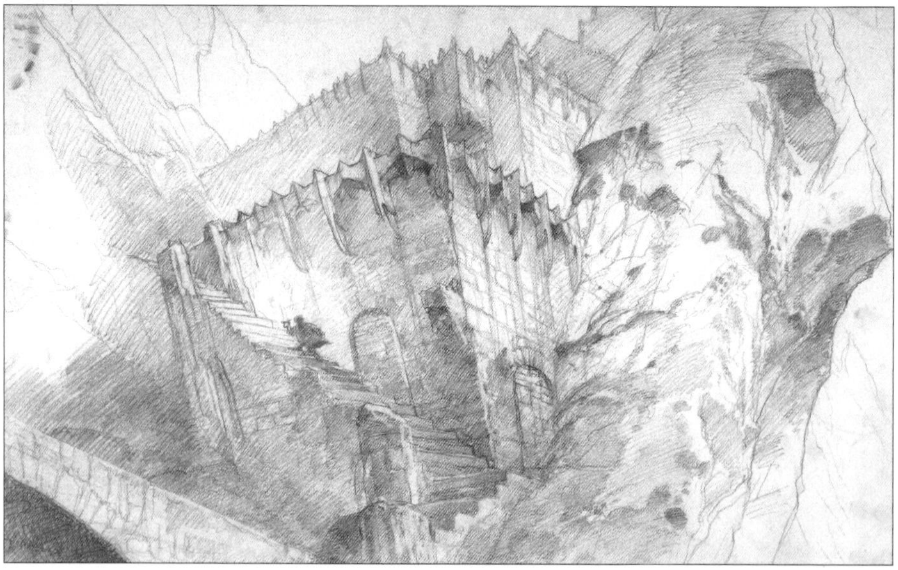

CIRITH UNGOL ***Pencil sketch***
"Cirith Ungol is not a conventional fortress, with its hanging terraces and courts and angles all askew. We wanted to convey the precarious nature of the structure perched on a pinnacle of rock over an abyss. Traces of earlier foundations can be seen beneath the Orcs' more haphazard repairs and 'improvements.'" *JH*

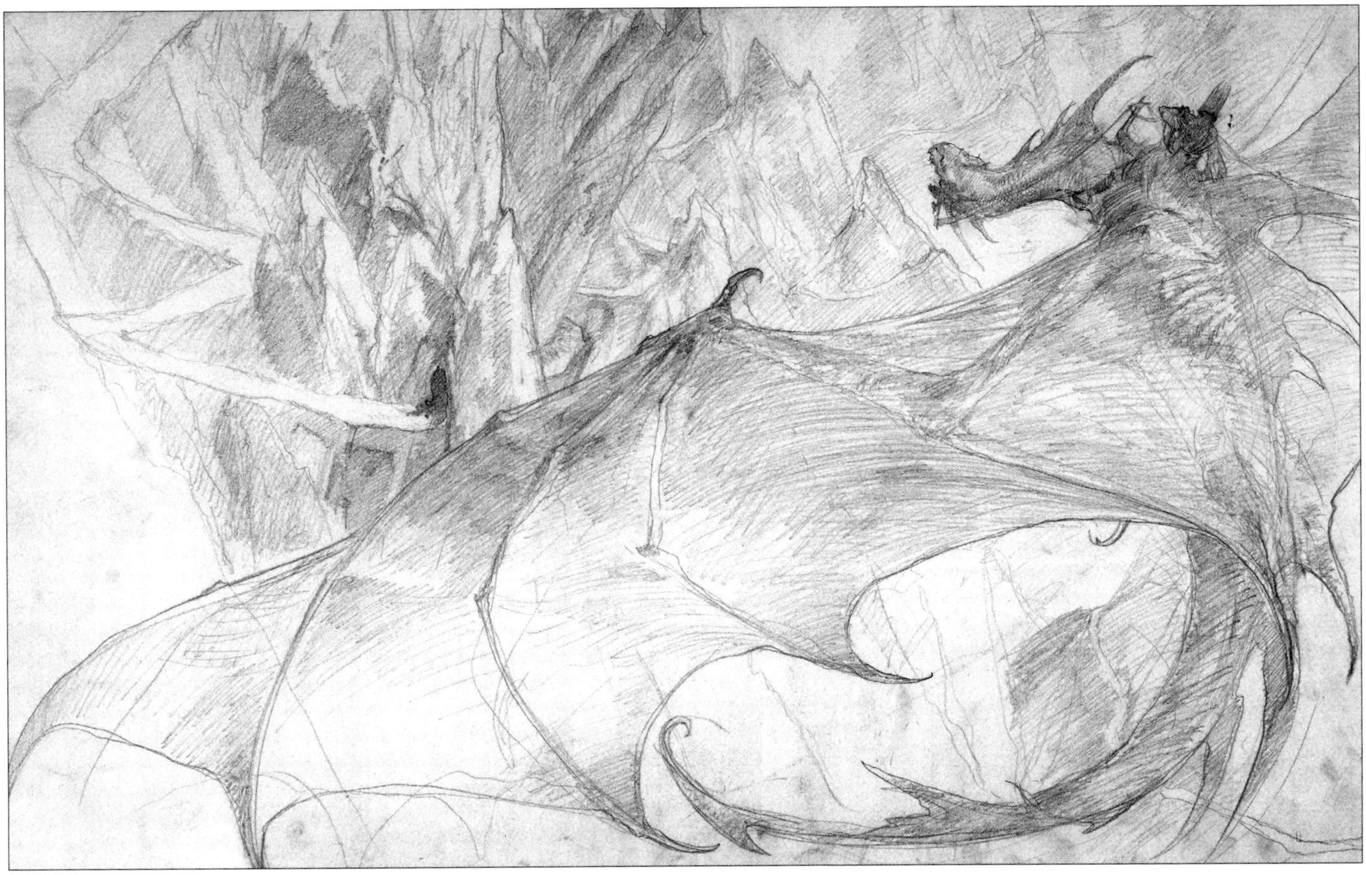

CIRITH UNGOL ***Pencil sketch***
"Above we see Nazgûl patrolling the marches of Mordor. This sketch began as an extension of the sketch below and quickly grew into a rapid study of a fell beast in flight." *JH*

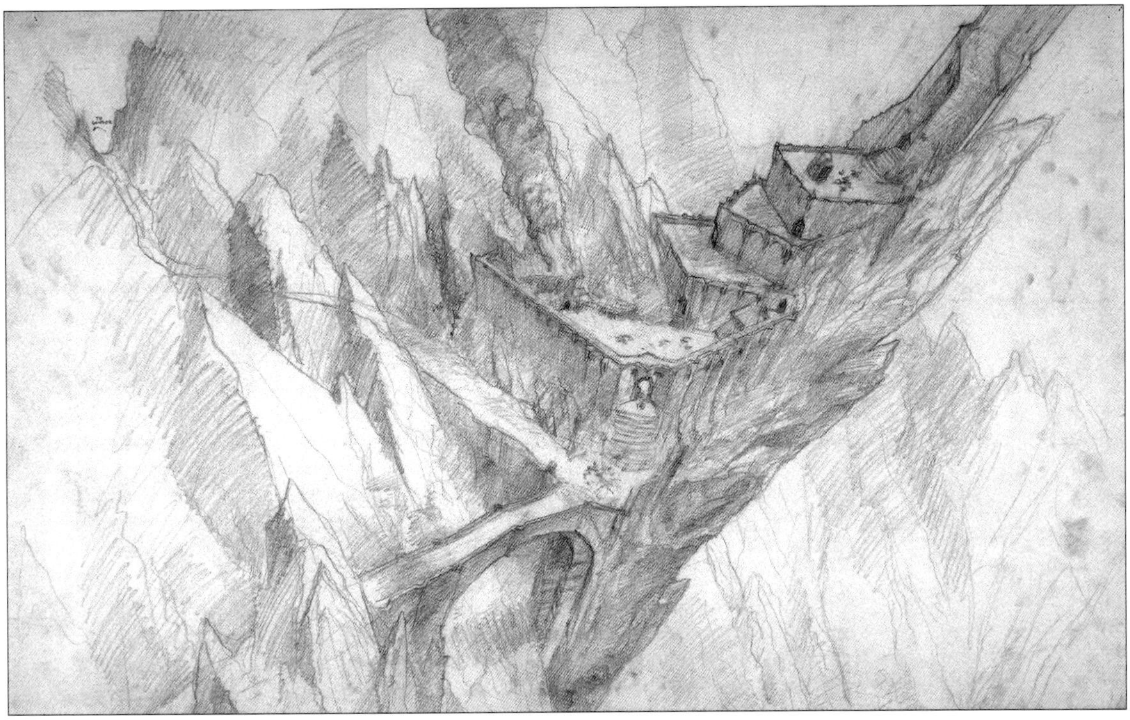

CIRITH UNGOL
Pencil sketch
"It seems all of Mordor induces an underlying disorientation of the senses. The rocks and mountains of Mordor are just too knife-edged and overhanging to be possible in our world. The whole environment is off balance, ready to crumble into ruin with Sauron's demise." *JH*

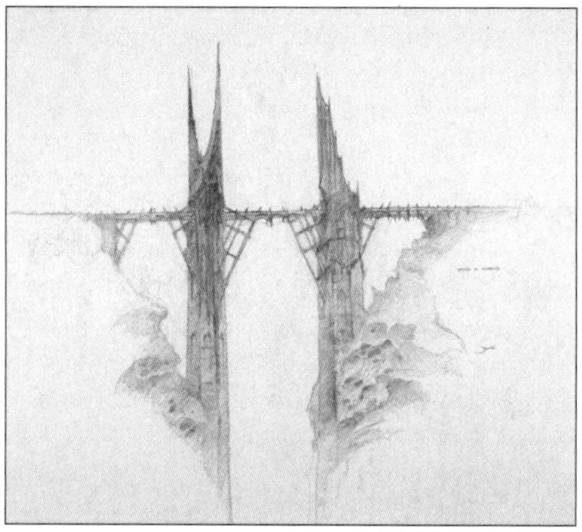

MORDOR ***Pencil sketch***
"Just an idea for a bridge in Mordor. Of all the architects of Middle-earth, Sauron is the most modern, using metals most extensively. With the climate being what it is, Mordor is therefore a land of rust." *JH*

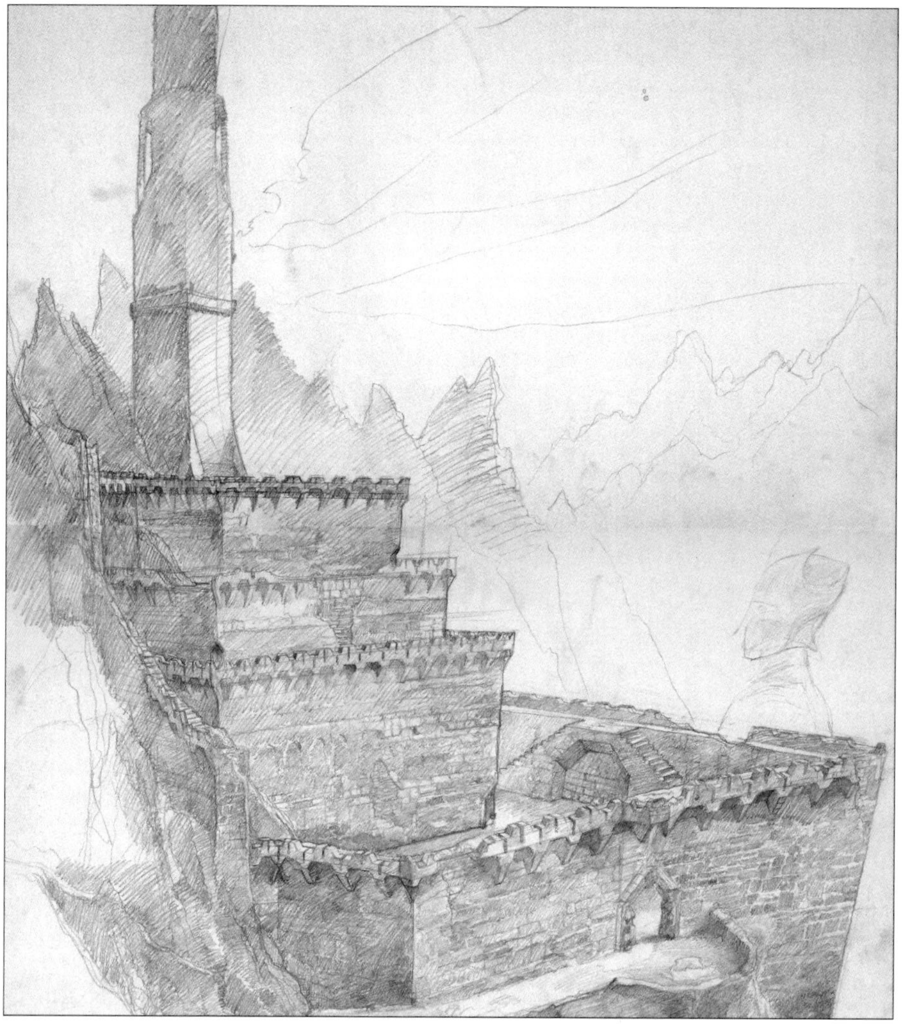

CIRITH UNGOL ***Pencil sketch***
"Initially, I did a fairly straightforward rendering of Cirith Ungol, which went as far as a cardboard mockup before Richard Taylor said, 'Don't you think this is kind of boring?' (in that nice, unassuming way he has). That discussion resulted in a serious revisiting of the fortress, placing it out on a spur of rock and setting each level at an angle from the ones above and below." *JH*

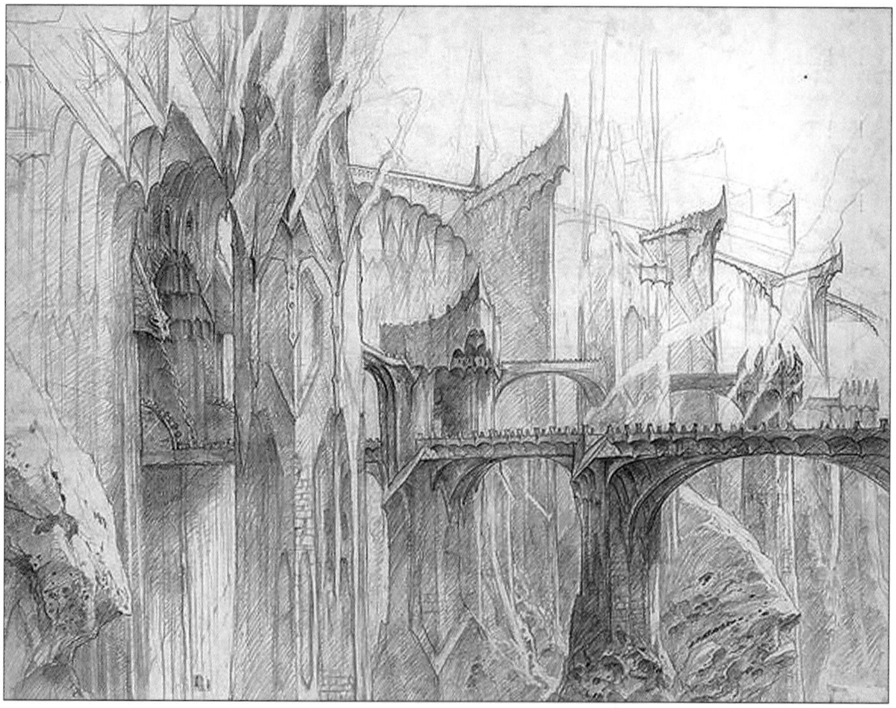

BARAD-DÛR ***Pencil sketch***
"This sketch is big enough to cover half a wall. It's a tribute to the incidental art of concept doodling: start in one square centimeter in the middle (more or less) of a page and let your pencil wander. Your mind tags along; it's like slowly, slowly wiping the fog from a panoramic window to ultimately reveal the landscape outside." *JH*

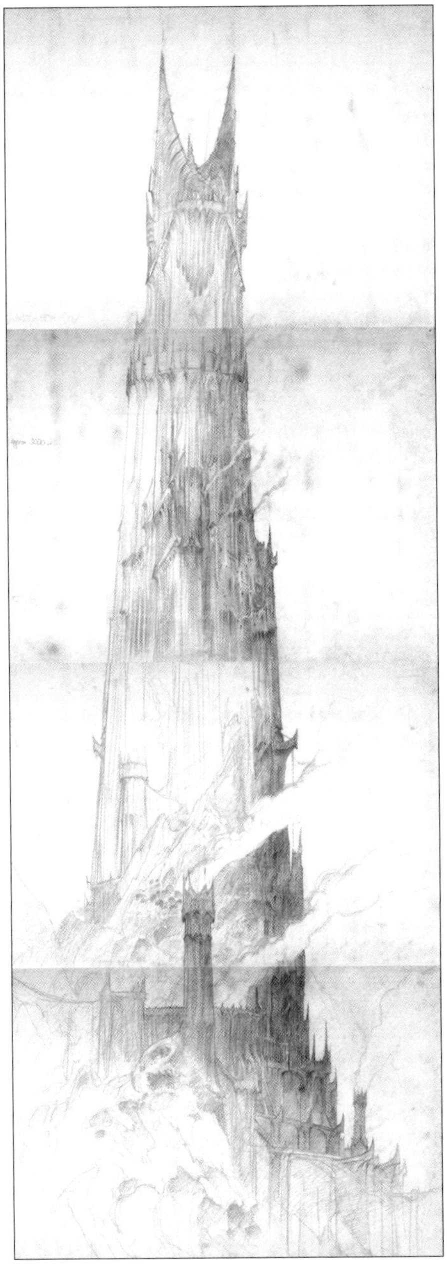

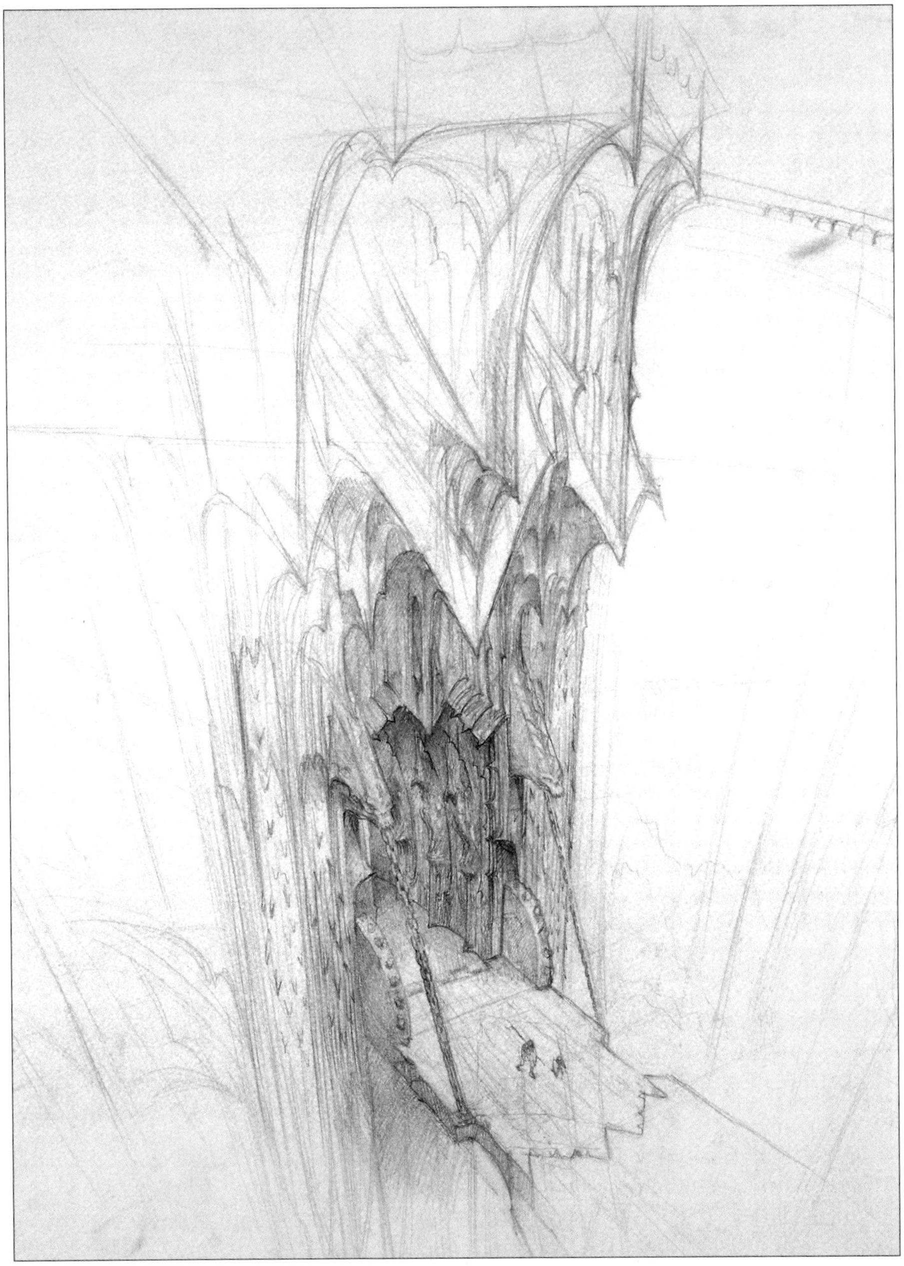

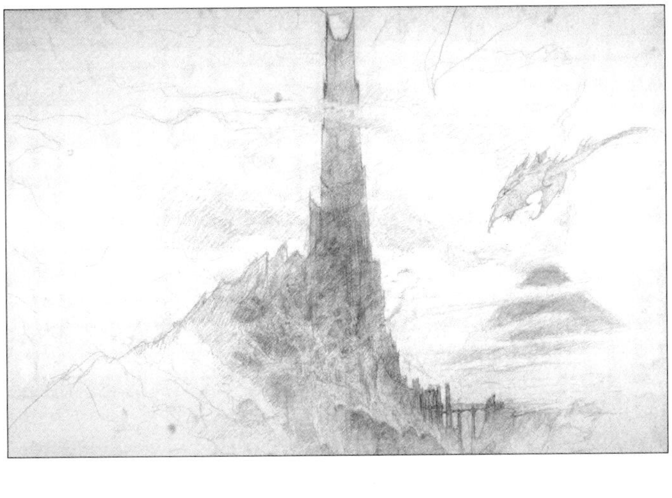

BARAD-DÛR ***Pencil sketches***
"I had already spent time wandering around the base of Barad-dûr, but I was careful never to look up, since what you don't draw is left to the reader's imagination, a much more efficient image generator than pencil or brush. But you can't cloak something like that in cloud for a movie – it has to be built. So I started at the bottom and slowly drew my way upward, not able to decide how the top would look, dallying on the upward climb to give myself more time to decide. Three sheets of paper higher, the two horns designed to cradle the Red Eye finally appeared. Had I procrastinated any longer, it would have been even higher." *JH*

WETA WORKSHOP

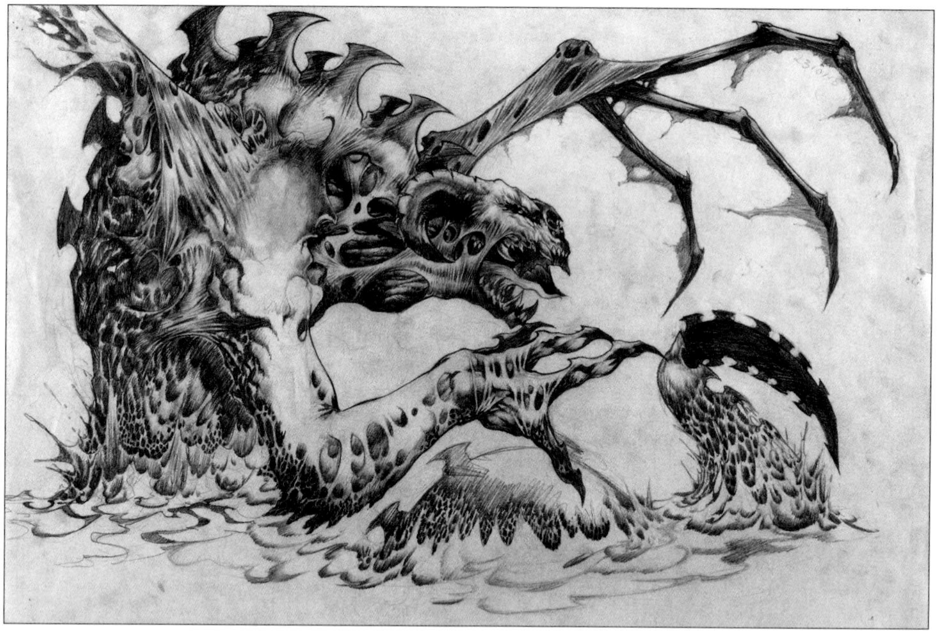

My partner, Tania Rodger, and I set up an effects workshop in Wellington fourteen years ago. Over the years, we've moved around, eventually settling here in the mid-nineties. I think we've got about 65,000 square feet of workshop space, which is pretty good. We operate five departments under one roof, as well as Weta Digital, our digital effects partner. On *The Lord of the Rings* we had 148 people in the workshop and 38 on set, operating over the five departments, in addition to the 200 artists at Weta Digital. There's a very small production staff in our workshop, six people who look after all of the day-to-day ins and outs of both the design, product development, and production side and the on-set operation and post-production requirements.

We started designing *The Lord of the Rings* way back at the tail end of 1997. We've looked after the design fabrication and on-set operation of the special makeup effects and prosthetics, and the creature design and sculpting of the maquettes, including final-stage models used for scanning by our digital arm. Add to this the design, fabrication, and operation of all the armor and weaponry, the building of all the miniature environments, from single towers to complex cities and landscapes, and we think it's the first time that one workshop has looked after so much on one film project. Some may think, "Greedy!" but the fundamental reason that we put our hands up on the first day and said, "Please let us look after so much," is that we knew how important to the integrity of the work a single vision of Tolkien's world would be. It required a singular "Tolkienesque" brush stroke over as much of the work as possible. We felt incredibly passionate about trying to control the look as much as we possibly could from one place, so that the armor looked as if it was worn by the creature who designed it, as if it came from the land it grew up in.

Weta isn't hugely experienced on the world stage, so five years ago it was an immensely ambitious thing to say we could do this. We have now reached the end of the project and are very proud of what everyone has done. We made the conscious decision to employ a number of young New Zealand designers, people who had never worked on feature films before, in order to bring a fresh perspective to the design, which I felt would best serve the old-fashioned innocence of Tolkien's writing. We hunted out

"It was a healthy thing to have a multitude of artists, all creating their vision of the Balrog or a troll or a Nazgûl, or whatever. The Weta team represented diversity – a diversity I encouraged."

PETER JACKSON

people who were passionate about the books and were also awesomely talented, creative people. We put together this team, backed them up with extensive research into appropriate periods of history, and with the much-heralded arrival of John Howe and Alan Lee, who lifted our skill level immensely, we were then able to flesh out this huge and elaborate world and make something we could all be proud of.

Our process basically started with discussions about the subject matter, then research, then sketching, then color illustration, of which we did a comprehensive amount, altogether a phenomenal body of work. Then, after that, I'm a very big fan of three-dimensional maquettes, so we used those to finally capture an image that the director can see in 3D, that he can pick up and actually see in real terms. With some characters and objects, we did only a few, for others we did up to seventy different sculptures before we finally captured the essence of what everyone wanted. We tried to draw most of our design influences first from Tolkien's written word – as a rule of thumb, Weta's policy is always to go back to the written source if ever there isn't a consensus.

For the look of everything, whether it's armor or pennants or general paraphernalia, our primary concern was to ensure that we drew from natural sources. We tried to stay within the palette of the ochers and the natural dyes of the area. To that degree, the first job that we had when we arrived on set, on any location, was to go and dig the soil. We would mix that with wallpaper paste in huge vats, and all of the actors and props were painted down with that particular ocher of the land. It was a conscious decision to try to make the characters look as if they lived off the land and were part of the environment that they'd grown from.

I believe strongly, and many people here agree, that the Fellowship and all the people they encounter are merely players on the surface of the film's most major character, which is Middle-earth, and that this is the story of the evolution of Middle-earth. Therefore, as often as possible, we were trying to make the characters feel as though they were elements of Middle-earth. That was very important to us, and I hope we succeeded.

Richard Taylor
March 2001

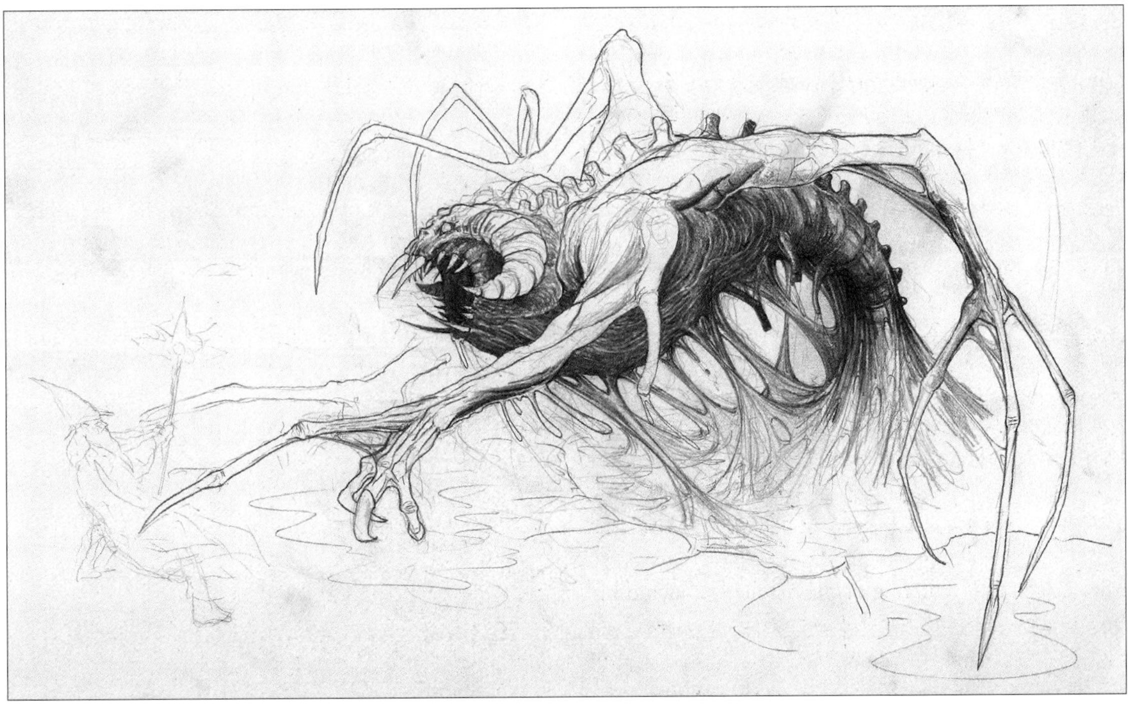

CHRISTIAN RIVERS

I first worked with Richard and Peter before Weta was a company as such. I started working for them in 1991 for *Brain Dead*. I storyboarded it with Peter, and then went on to work for Richard on the special effects crew. Weta was formed during the production of *Heavenly Creatures* in 1993, and I joined full-time a year later as a conceptual illustrator and creature FX technician for shows such as *Hercules* and *Xena*.

When *The Lord of the Rings* project came around, I was one of the first people to do any artwork for the project; I was storyboarding as soon as Peter and Fran started writing. The first storyboards and creature designs were drawn in August 1997 and I've been working on *The Lord of the Rings* ever since.

As far as my background knowledge of the project was concerned, I'd read the books when I was fourteen, but only once, and I didn't remember them that well. However, I was an avid Dungeons and Dragons player, and the sensibilities of the campaigns that I liked to play were very similar in tone to Tolkien's world – very grounded in reality.

When I storyboard Peter's movies, I try not to read the scripts before we start. I know it sounds odd, but I like to get the story straight from Peter's shot-by-shot description of the film. Basically he and I are in a room. I have a drawing board and a stack of panels, and he sits there with the script and describes each shot to me. When we first started, no design work or casting had been done so I was kind of making up the look of the characters and the sets as we went. Of course, they look completely different from the way they look in the film.

Later on, as Alan Lee and John Howe were designing the sets, the art department was making little animatic models for us to use. We had little toy figures for all the characters, which were in scale with the set models, and Peter would create the shots using them and a tiny camera. The camera was hooked up to a monitor and a video board for frame grabbing. Pete would frame the shot he wanted and yell, "Okay, okay . . . grab that frame!" – and I would draw from the screen. Then Pete would reposition the toys and the camera and we'd move on to the next shot. This stage of drawings was very rough, and I would pass off these chicken-scratch sketches to another artist, Andrew Calder, to clean up.

The storyboarding process was basically the first stage of storyboarding the films, which, like any part of the filmmaking process, is ever evolving. We eventually changed the storyboards into 3-D CGI to further assess how we would be able to create the films.

I still find it hard to believe that I was involved in this project. It's incredible to think that I got to work on *The Lord of the Rings* and I didn't have to drive more than fifteen minutes from home to do it.

Christian Rivers
April 2002

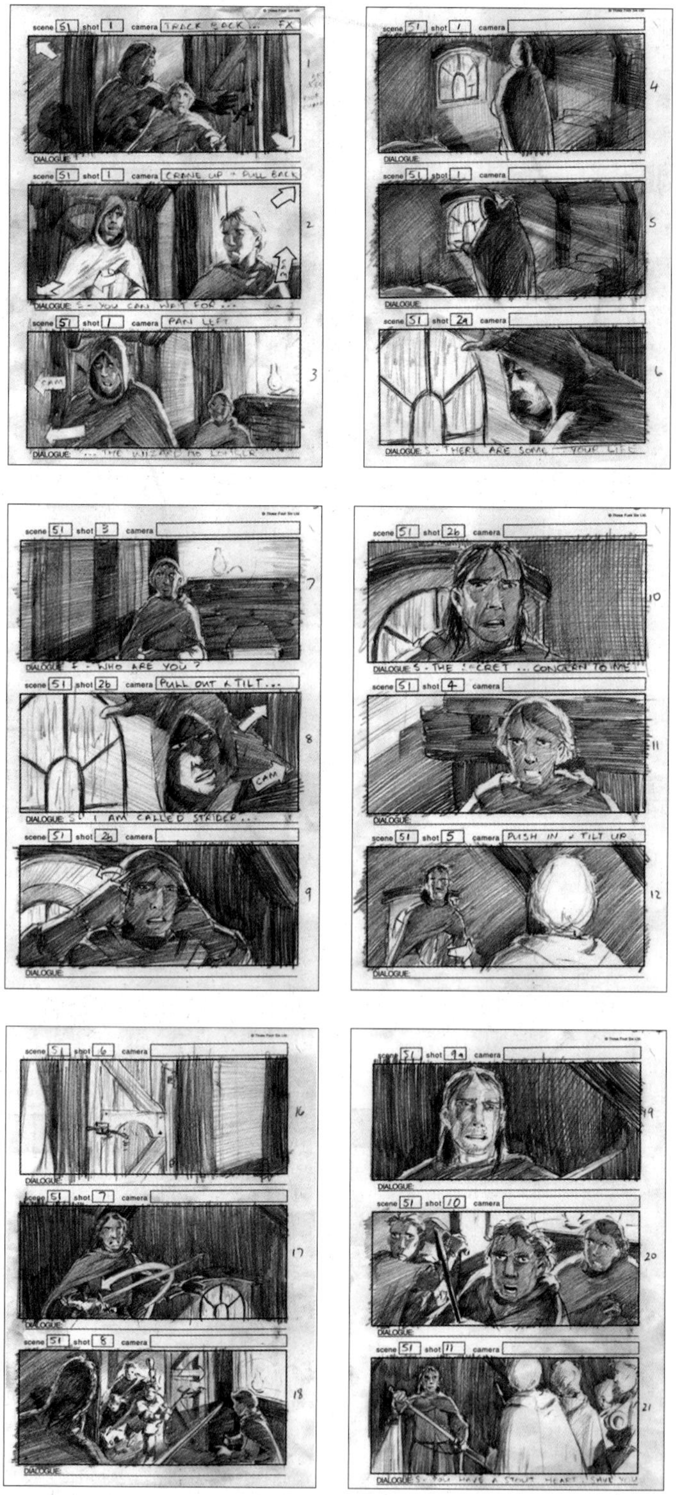

THE PRANCING PONY ***Storyboards***
"This was a sequence of storyboards that I managed to shade in pencil – most storyboards done by myself and Andrew Calder were finished by a group of artists with gray markers. I like this sequence because it was done before any actors had been cast, before the sets were built and, with the exception of a couple of cutaway shots, it is almost the exact sequence in the finished film." *CR*

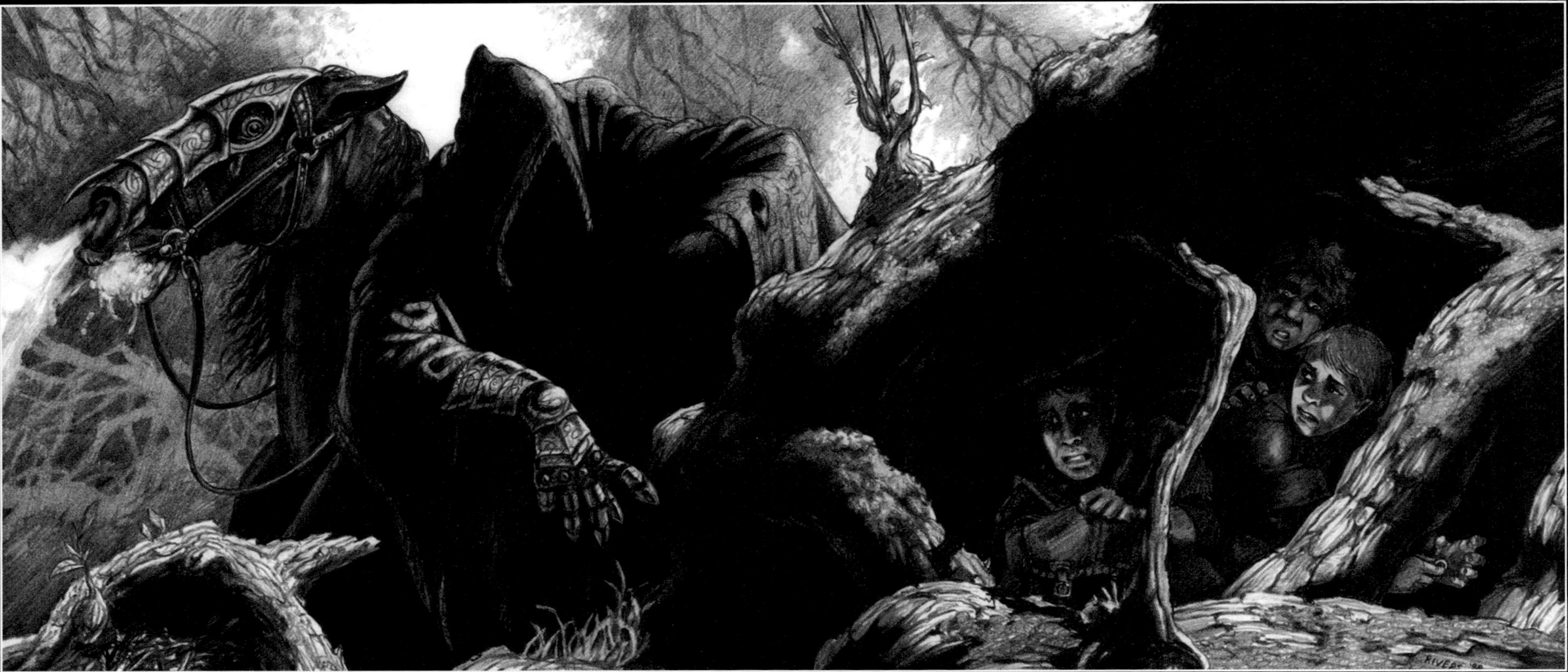

THE BLACK RIDER *Illustration*

"Based on a very early storyboard, I did this purely as an exercise in finishing something. It was done very soon after Alan Lee and John Howe joined us, so I was feeling particularly inspired to do a complete illustration. In an early version of the script, Frodo, Sam, and Pippin meet Merry later at the Brandywine River, which is why there are only three Hobbits hiding under the tree." *CR*

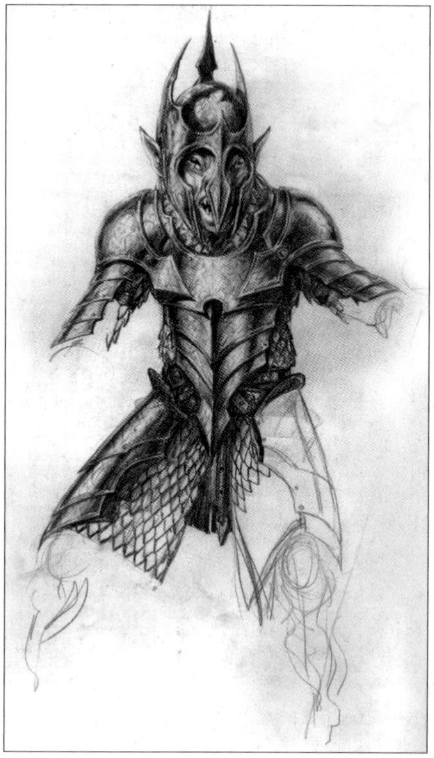

GOBLIN *Armor concept*
"John Howe was always on our backs as designers, questioning how the armor we were drawing was to work, and why we were drawing certain shapes, and what would happen if they were to be made into functioning armor. His input was invaluable in educating us and therefore processing our design of such items. This sketch was done at a stage when I was very aware of what John would have to say if the armor looked as if it wasn't practical." *CR*

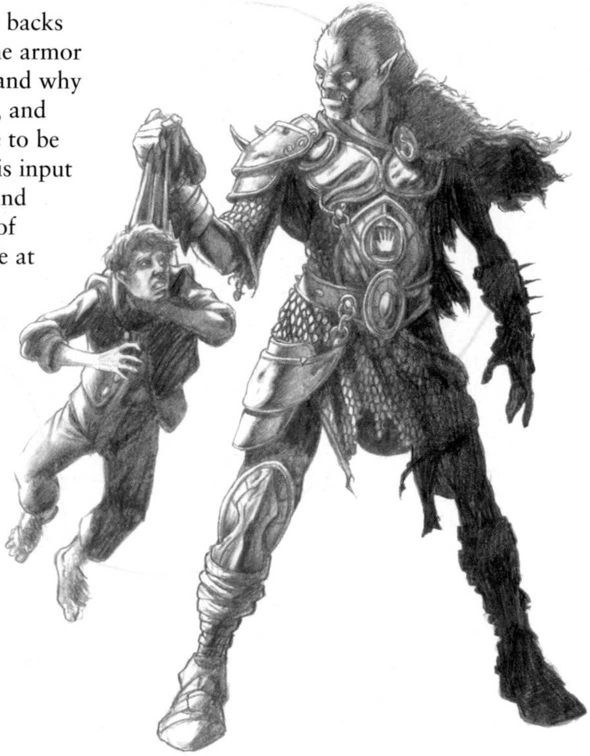

URUK-HAI *Armor concept*
"An early design for an Uruk-hai, seen here menacing a Hobbit, probably Merry or Pippin. The armor design was considered too refined-looking and too evocative of a high-fantasy aesthetic. The design style established for all the races of Middle-earth came to reflect a greater emphasis on historical realism." *CR*

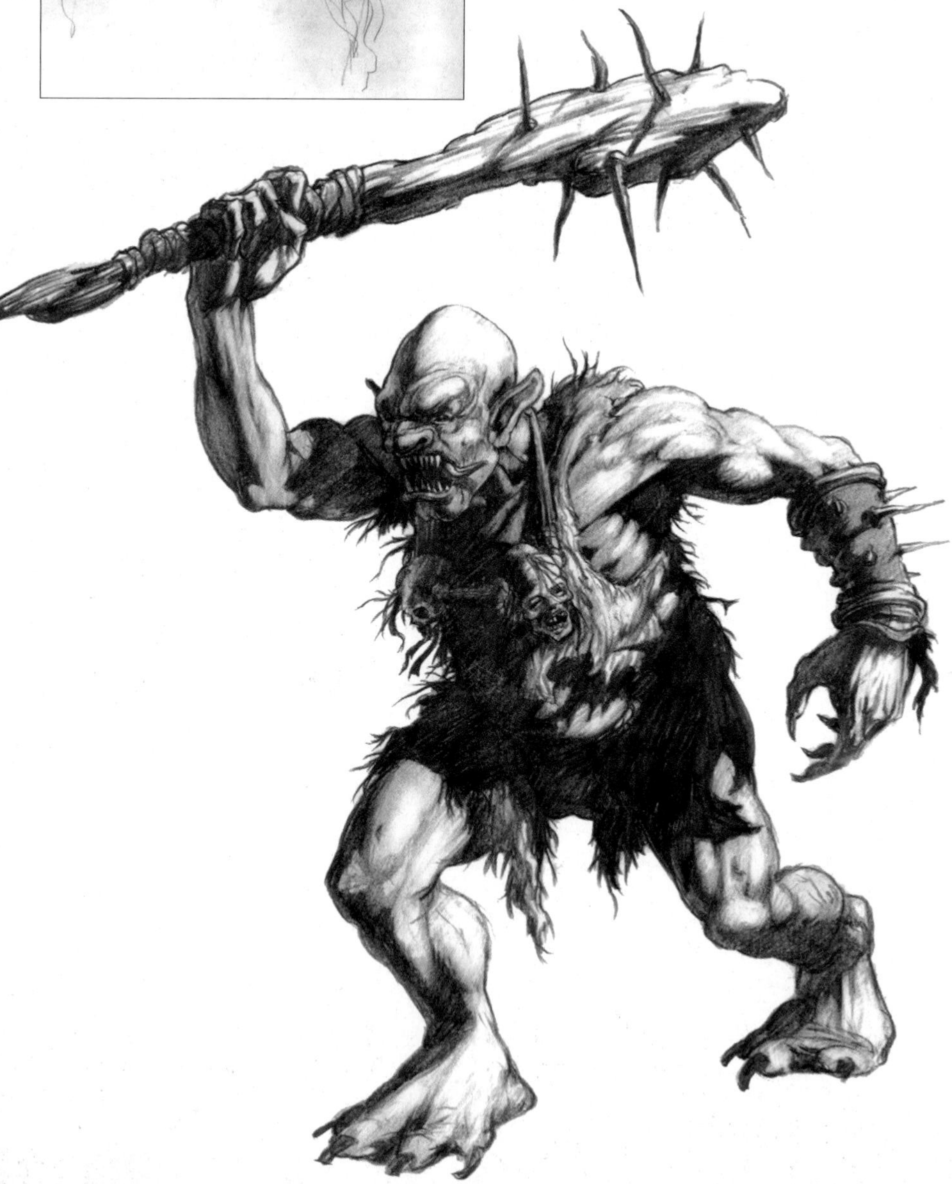

TROLL *Design concept*
"This was one of the first creature designs ever done for *The Lord of the Rings* project. I drew this in August 1997. While I'm still happy with the illustration, it certainly betrays where my design sensibility was at that time. Dungeons and Dragons anyone?" *CR*

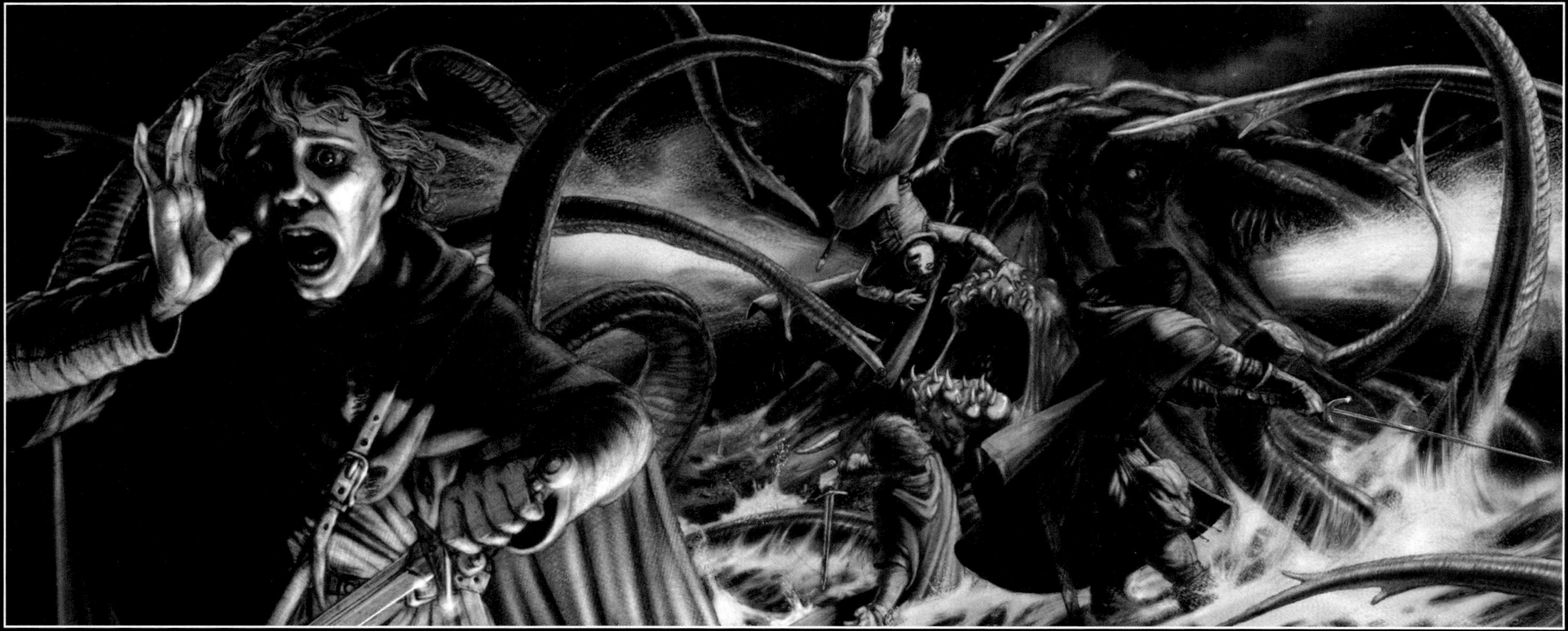

THE WATCHER IN THE WATER *Illustration*
"My first foray into illustrating with Photoshop, though not in color. I can't remember how long this piece took to do, probably longer than it should have, because of the ability to zoom in and scrutinize each pixel. This was done as a production illustration before the Watcher sequence was properly storyboarded." *CR*

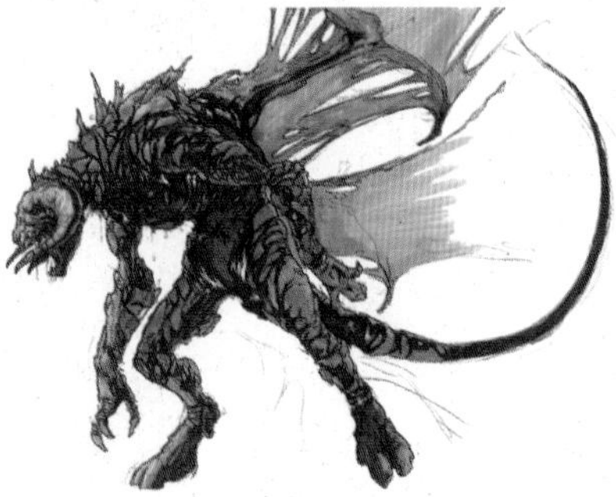

THE BALROG *Color sketch*
"The drawing above was just a concept, really – a different approach from what everyone else was offering Peter. I was a little worried about the Slime Balrog, as a lot of the designs had started taking it in a direction that had it mutating and changing form. I approached him in terms of how a physical creature would look if it were made of lava and dipped in water. As it struggled, its skin would crack and tear as the water tried to cool it – parts of its 'flesh' would be eaten away and hardened. What would be left is this weird, almost scarred, muscular rock." *CR*

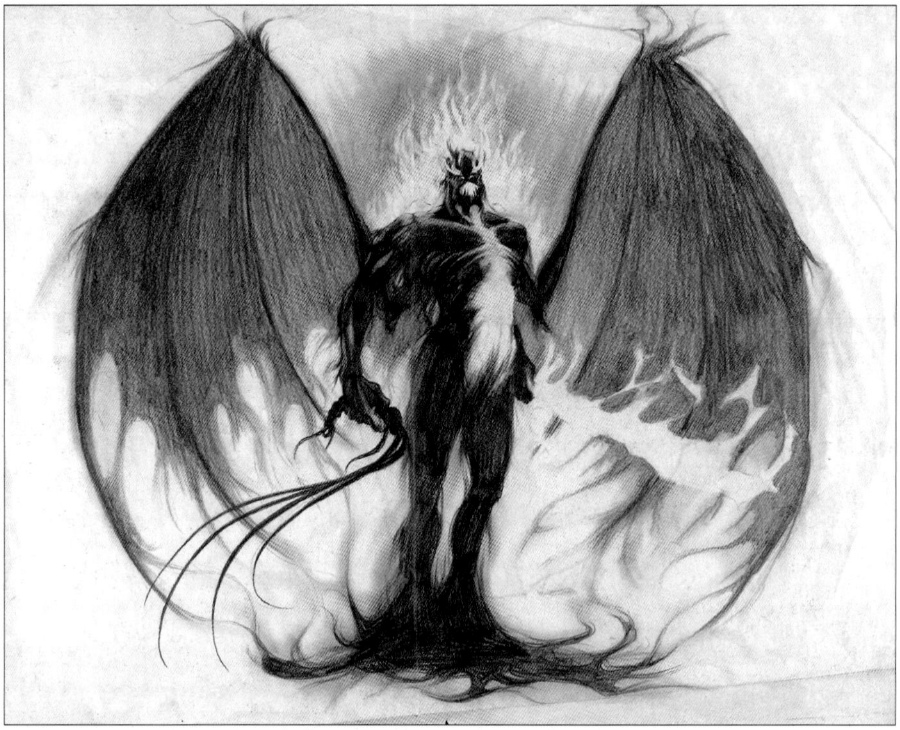

THE BALROG *Conceptual sketch*
One of the earliest ideas for the Balrog. Christian initially went down the route of a man-shaped creature with wings of flame.

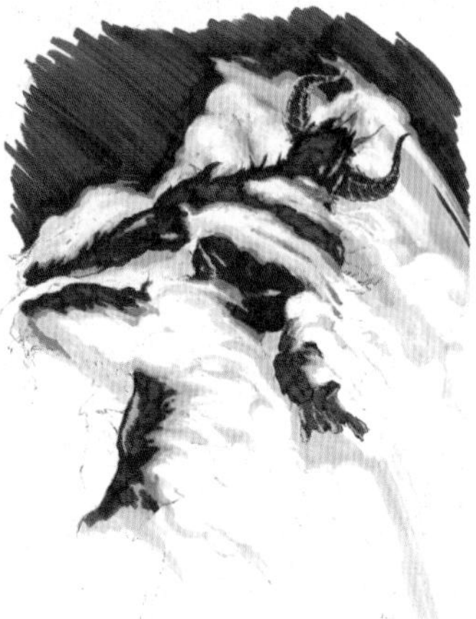

THE BALROG *Color sketch*
"This Balrog was actually drawn before any of the other ones. It was to show him coming out of the water, and he's just erupting in steam and then cooling, like lava or molten metal going into water. You can see fire creeping out, and there's a little bit of fire spitting like blood from his mouth – I wanted to show him really feeling pain." *CR*

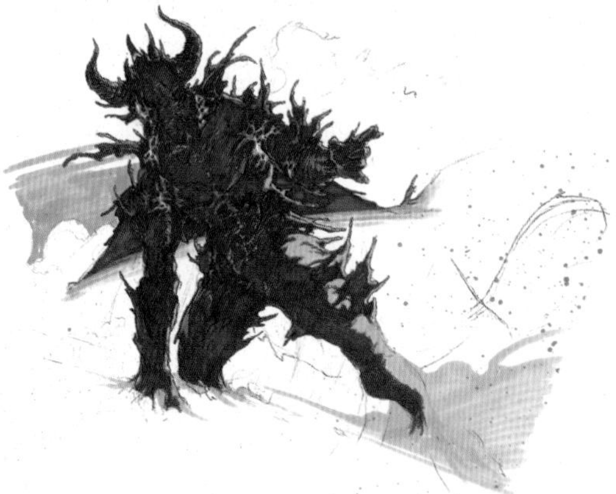

THE BALROG *Color sketch*
"Gandalf's battle with the Balrog at the start of *The Two Towers* picks up from the initial drop down Khazad-dûm into the lake. Then the Balrog comes out slimy and dripping and falling to bits. So I imagined a progression in which he falls into the lake and his fire's extinguished, but there's still this deep hot core of him on fire. And then he emerges and starts changing from having slime dripping off him – which isn't slime; I saw it more as lava cooling through the cracks in his skin. This picture shows where the water has cooled the lava, forming these hard shapes. So this is him as he's cooling and he's starting to crack and then he eventually erupts." *CR*

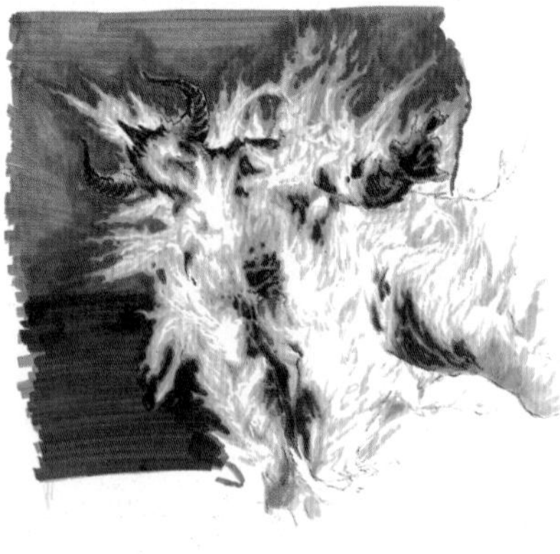

THE BALROG *Color sketch*
"As the Balrog comes out of the water, he's been completely doused and then ripped apart – these are huge gaping holes in him – and, after their climb to the top of Zirakzigil, Gandalf finishes him off. It's taken the Balrog all this time to reignite, but by then it's too late." *CR*

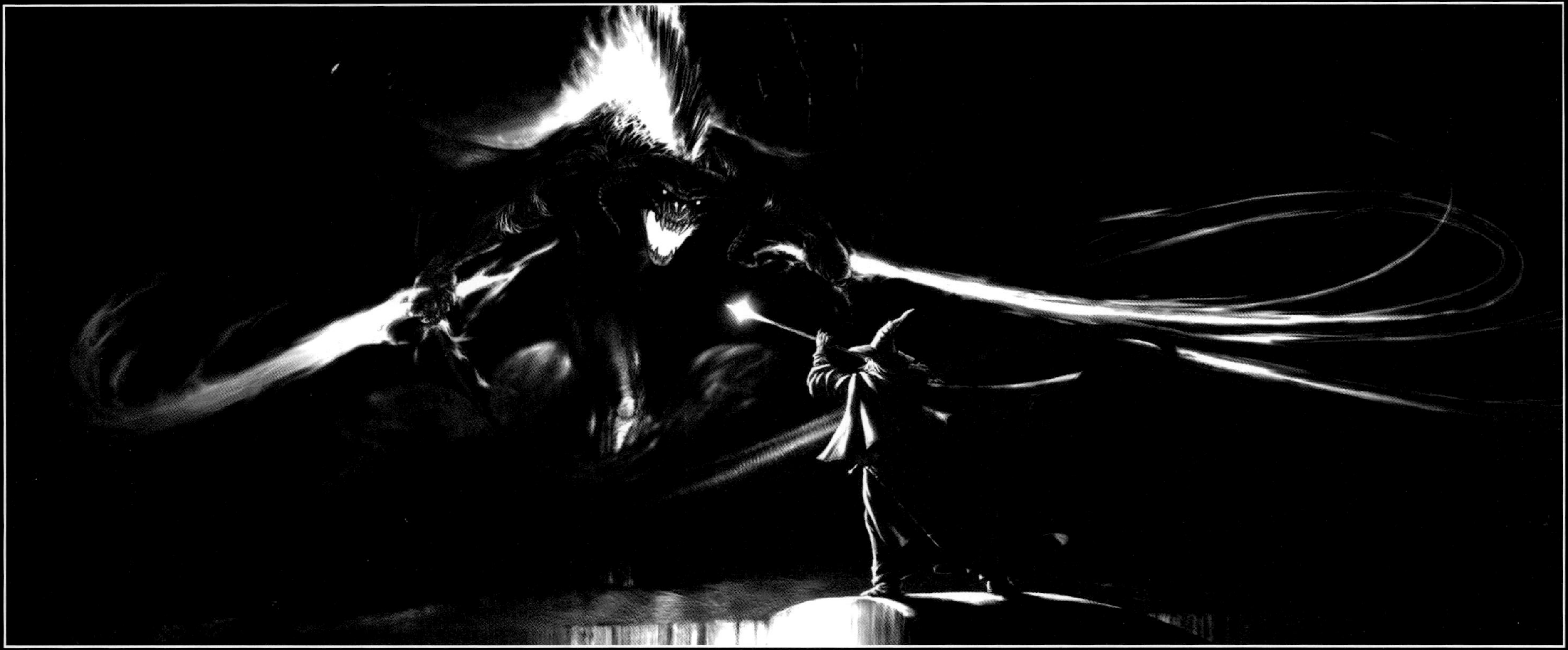

THE BALROG *Illustration*
"Another Photoshop illustration. I would sketch out the picture in pencil, scan it in, and then work up the tones with the paintbrush and the dodge and burn brush. As in the Watcher picture, the curse (and blessing) of the zoom tool probably accounted for this taking twice the time it should have. I did this to show the light play between Gandalf and the Balrog. Also to demonstrate the amount of fire and smoke that should be emanating from him. Like everything on these films, such imagery evolved." *CR*

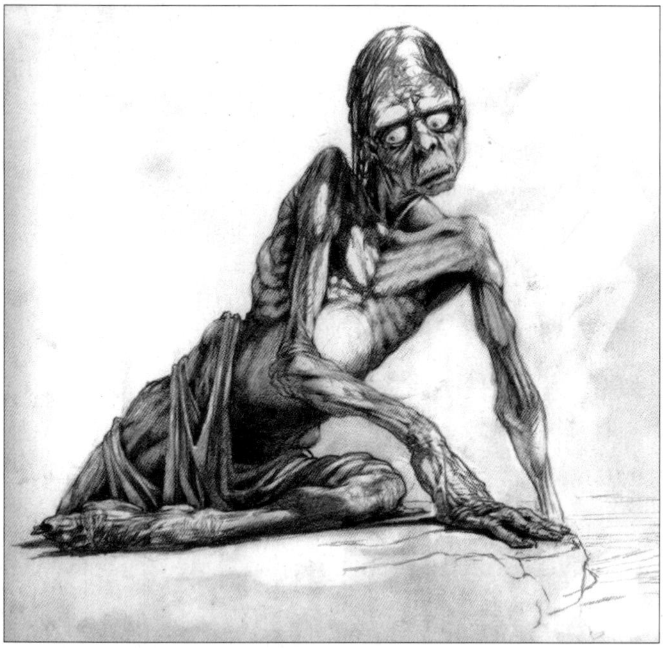

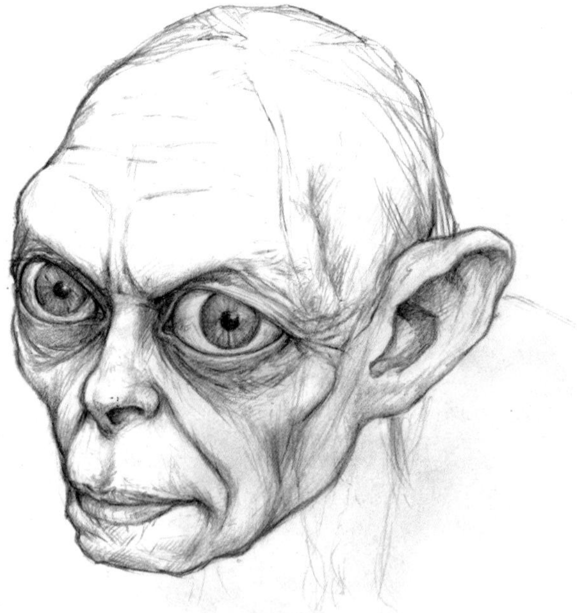

GOLLUM *Pencil sketches*
"Above left is an early sketch of Gollum that is still one of my favorite pieces of work. The design is flawed, the pose doesn't really make sense, and the melancholy and gentleness seem completely out of character, but for some reason I like it. The image above right was done for two reasons: first, to enable Gollum to faithfully and more accurately translate the facial performance of Andy Serkis; and second because Peter Jackson and Fran Walsh actually cast Andy as Sméagol, for the flashback when he and Déagol find the Ring. It became imperative then to change Gollum's design, and that was the motivation for this sketch.
For reference, I used one of Gino Acevedo's makeup archive photos of Andy as Sméagol." *CR*

ENT *Pencil sketch*
"One of the many Ent designs, this one was done at a stage when the actual concepts had not been locked down. Peter had been reacting favorably to a lot of Daniel Falconer's designs, so I took Daniel's lead and did this more as an experiment in pushing the proportions of the body to extremes. I call this design 'Oakbloke.'" *CR*

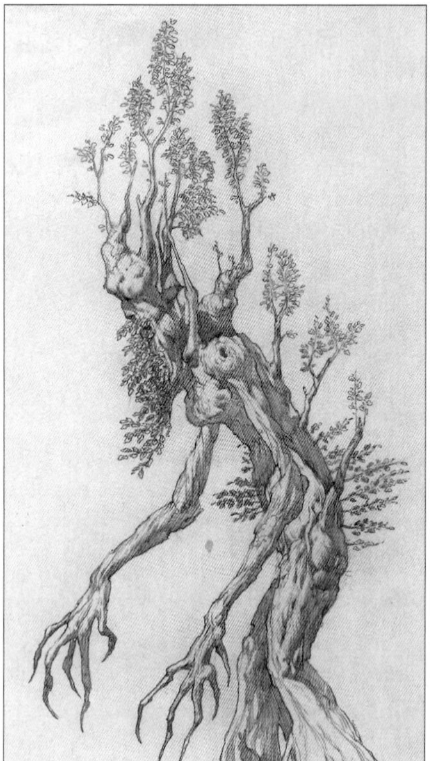

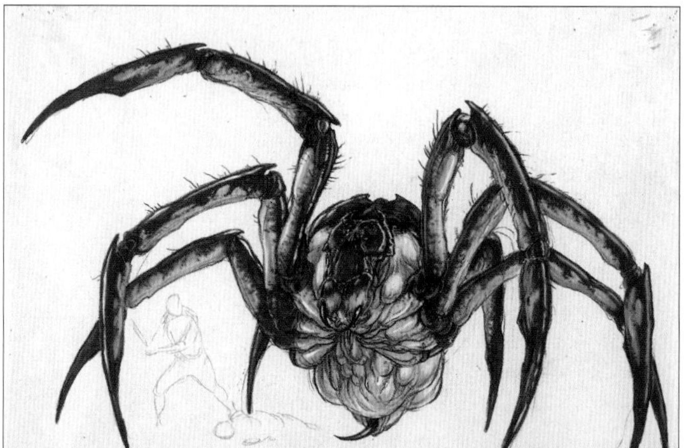

SHELOB *Conceptual sketch*
"This is my favorite Shelob sketch. Even though the design is significantly inferior to the final design used in the film, it was one of my first minor successes with color. I've always been scared of both color and spiders, so it was quite an accomplishment for me to churn this piece out. The design here was a mix of spider and crustacean, making it look a little too 'monsterish.'" *CR*

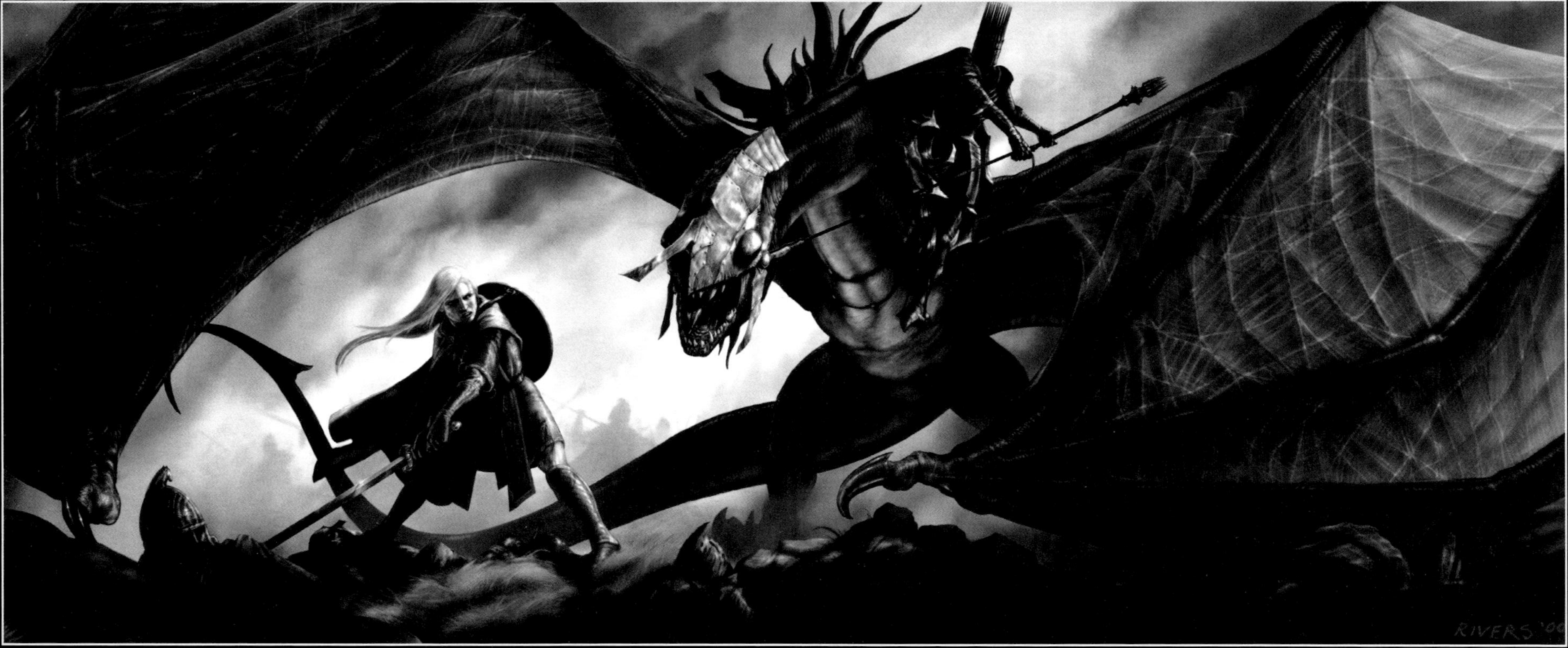

ÉOWYN VERSUS THE WTCH-KING *Illustration*
"One of my most 'retentive' pieces. It was only toward the end of this piece that Paul Lasaine told me to stop using the zoom tool. Wise words they were, too. This was done before I had seen Éowyn and her armor design. The Witch-king's armor is the old design, which was changed to avoid any confusion between him and Sauron." *CR*

DANIEL FALCONER

I think it helped that I am a huge fan of Tolkien's books. It meant I was already very familiar with the material – to the point that, throughout the production, I'd often get calls from people I'd never met saying, "We need this question answered very quickly and we've heard that you're the person who either can answer it or knows where to go and find this information in the books!"

As a reader of the books, I had a visual idea of what everything looked like to me, but I think my ideas were diffused enough not to exclude other ideas and other suggestions. A lot of the time, I found my thoughts weren't entirely dissimilar to what Peter Jackson was asking for. Generally, if he hadn't given us an explicit brief, the first thing I did was think, "I've always imagined it to look like such-and-such" and then go from there. Often, he had quite specific ideas about what he wanted to see, and I would obviously try to deliver what he'd asked for – but also give him options, give him ideas that were maybe more like what I was thinking – and I can't think offhand of any times when they jarred enormously. Which was lucky, I guess.

In a workshop like this we have a system whereby we would give Pete some options to begin with and he'd say, "Okay, yeah, these are kind of nice, but let's throw away all preconceptions here. Let's open up extremely wide. Let's just go for it – from one end of the spectrum to the other." And often he'd push us down a path to some very extreme versions: I mean, there were some ideas for the Watcher in the Water that were big seal-like creatures. There were others that were arthropods . . . and once we'd gone to the absolute limits of imagination, then he'd pull us back and we'd focus. But it's in that exploration that you'll find lots of neat little features that will then be used in the final concept. That's probably why – on the Watcher in the Water, for example – there was quite a range of different ideas drawn up before we nailed it.

There's loads of cross-pollination here. We were all in one big room together, so everybody could feed off each other. And we'd all talk about it while we were working. Everybody brings their own elements to it and what you end up with is so much richer than any one person could ever have conceived of.

So I've been working on this film for five or six years now and it has been phenomenally thrilling for me to be able to see designs that we did nearly five years ago in some cases, appearing on the screen. That is very, very rewarding."

Daniel Falconer
April 2002

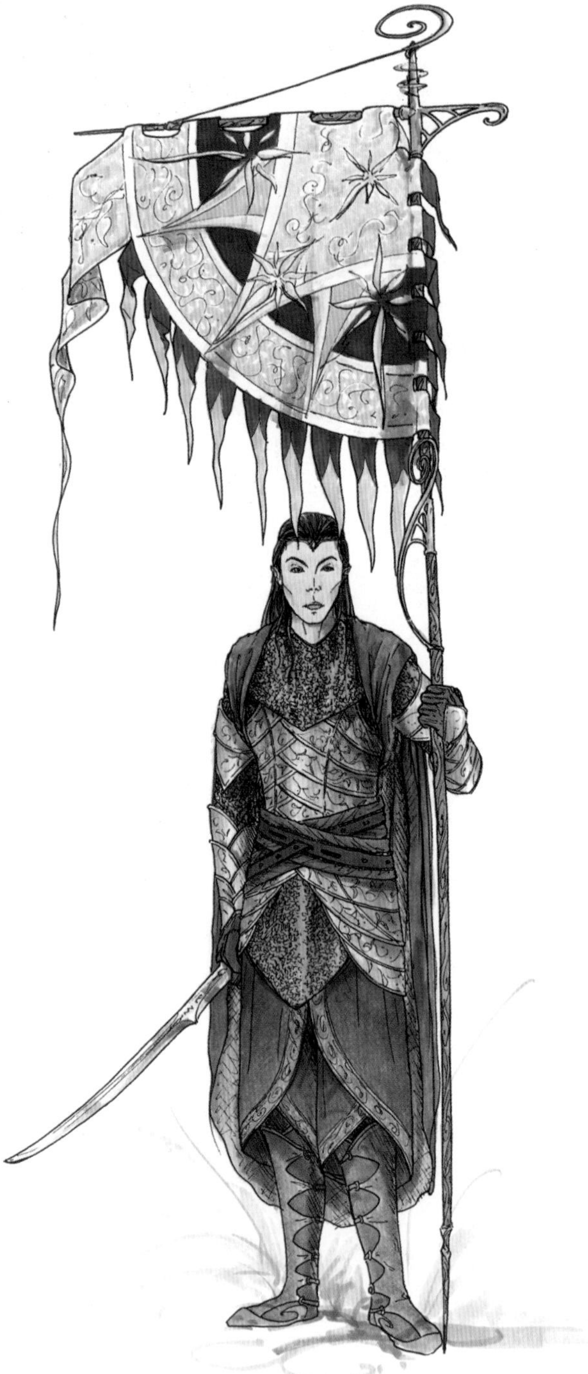

ELROND *Conceptual sketch*
"Based on the standard Elven infantry armor designed by Warren Mahy, I extrapolated and added layers to design Elrond's armor that he wears during the Second Age prologue sequence. There are elements here of ancient Samurai and Grecian design, with a color palette drawn from Gil-galad's heraldry as described and drawn by Tolkien himself." *DF*

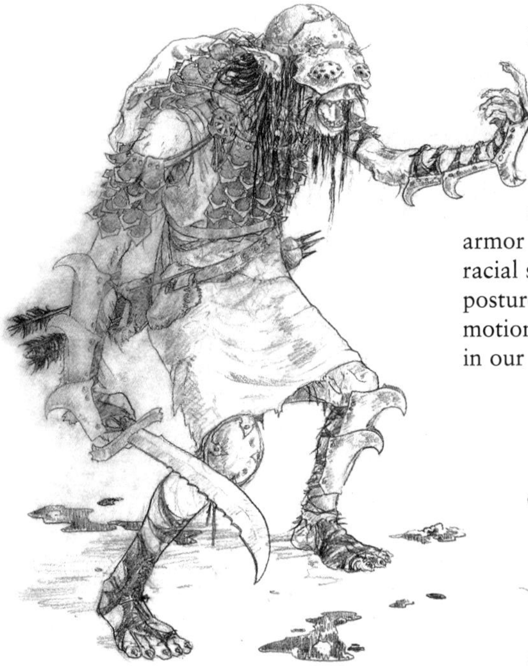

MORDOR ORC ***Conceptual sketch***

"So much of the time, design is about silhouette. In the case of the Orcs, I tried to distort their silhouette and make them less human by raising the shoulders, arching the back, and throwing the head forward and down. A low helmet helps slope the forehead back and make the Orc appear less intelligent and noble in bearing. I brought the back up by adding a rucksack slung high over its back. The hooklike projections on the arm and leg armor were really just to help add menace and, again, differentiate from other racial silhouettes on the battlefield. In the end, however, so much depends on the posture of the performer on the day. Early on, we talked a great deal with the motion coaches, developing ideas together that we would employ in our artwork." *DF*

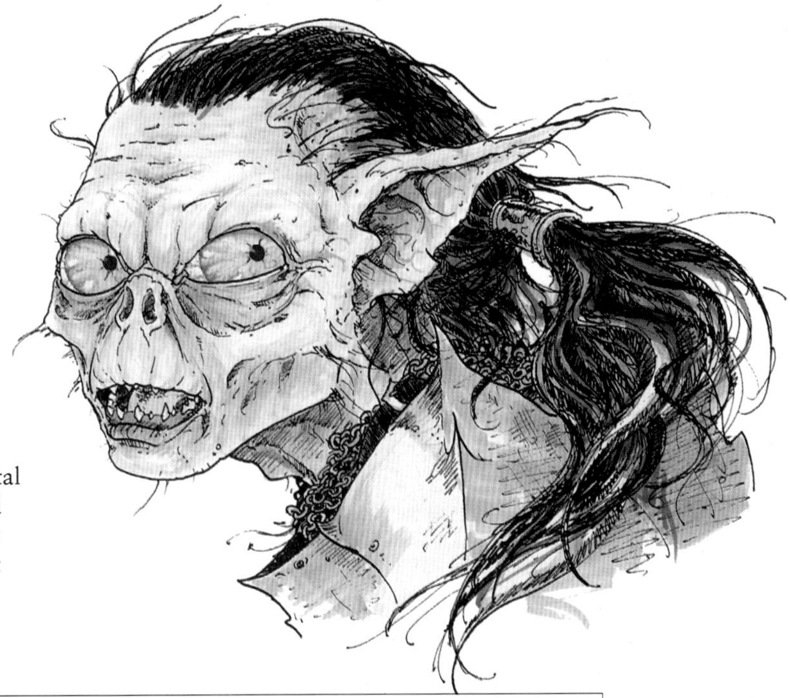

ORCS
Conceptual sketch
This was designed as a face mask for an actor, with digital eye enlargement to be added later. This drawing offered a different eye color from that which was used. Below is a series of potential Orc eye designs. *DF*

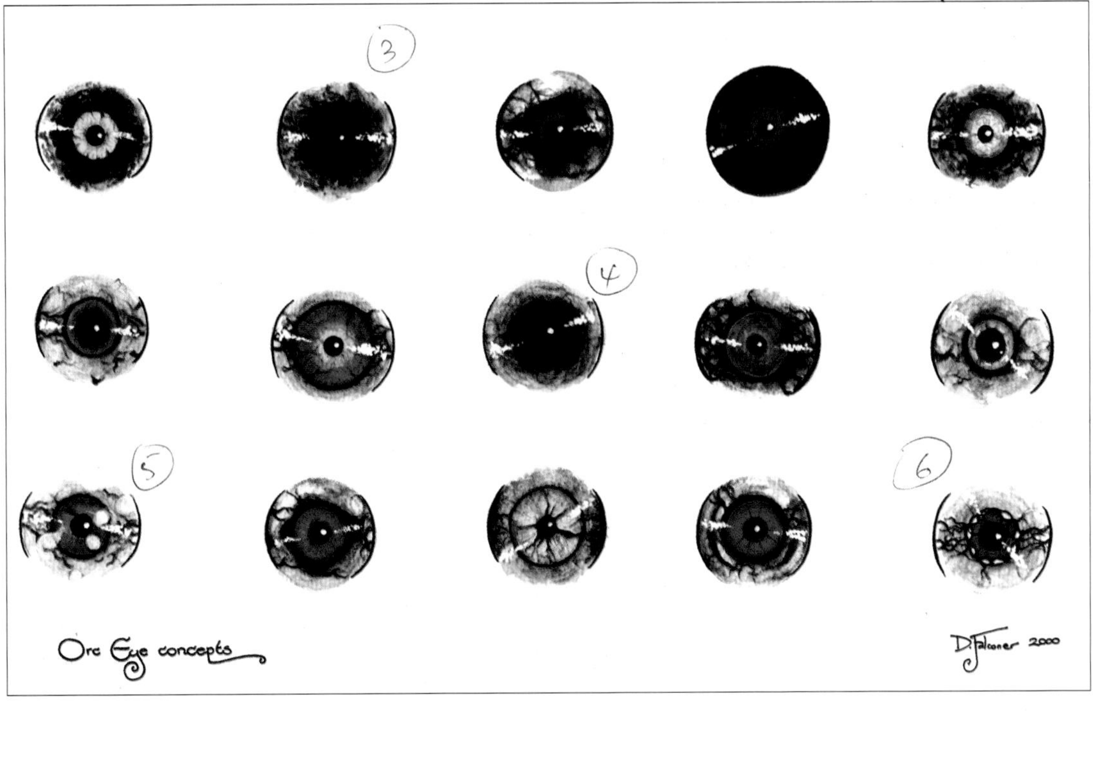

ORCS
Conceptual designs
"One of the ways in which we hoped to differentiate various-featured Orcs was with eye design. The door really was wide open in terms of color and appearance." *DF*

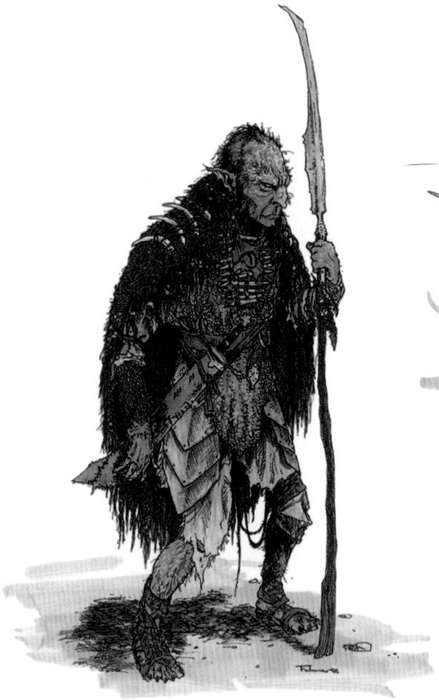

ORCS *Conceptual sketch*
A much later design, this Mordor Orc features many components that would find their way into various Orc costumes.

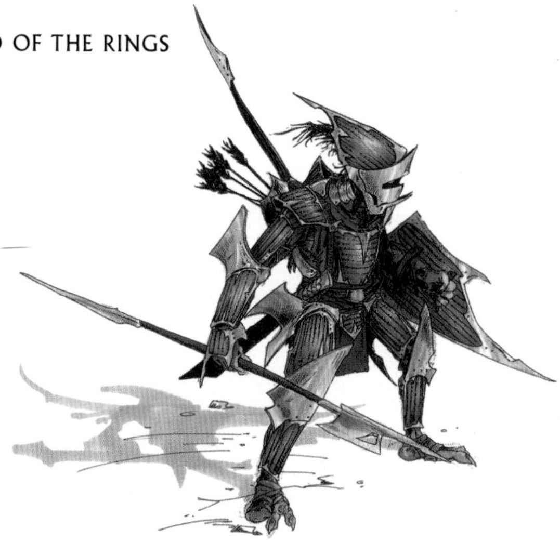

ORCS *Armor design*
For this Moria Orc, Daniel designed armor to be constructed from wood, polished and laid over light steel frames. Lightweight armor, along with unencumbered toes, meant that trees and pillars could be easily climbed.

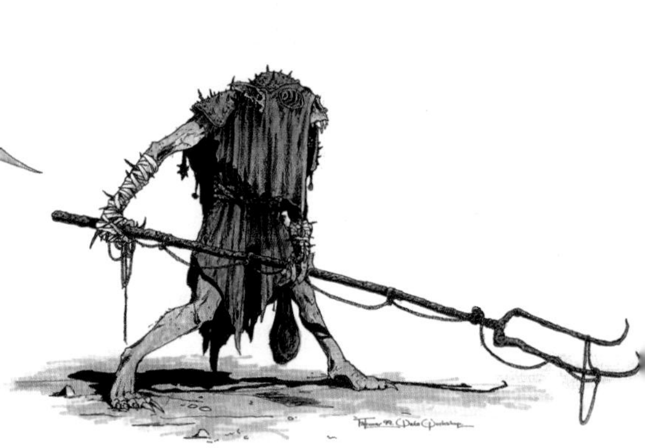

ORCS *Conceptual sketch*
Daniel designed several Moria Orc concepts with a range of varying armor styles. This one carries a weapon designed to snare and tangle foes.

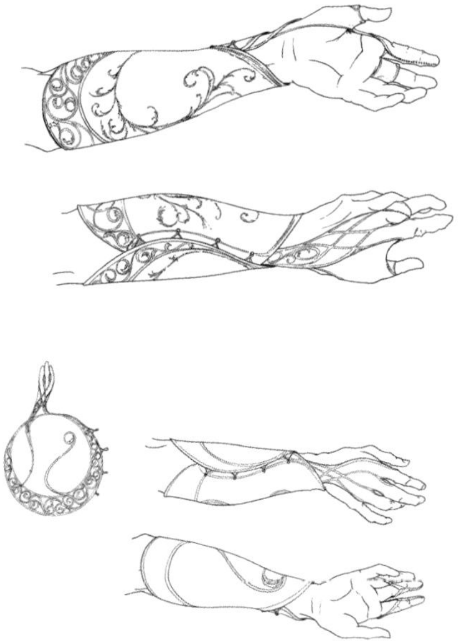

LEGOLAS'S BRACERS
Conceptual designs
"Although ultimately the gloves themselves would be dropped, the designs here for the bracers, or archer's gauntlets, worn by Legolas remained essentially the same. They were designed to be fashioned out of shaped, circular leather wraps that would lace up into a protective arm-guard." *DF*

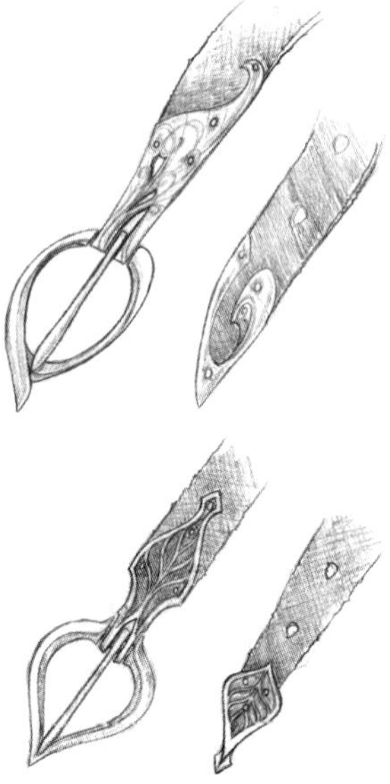

LEGOLAS'S BELT BUCKLE AND CHAPE *Conceptual designs*
"Between his Lothlórien and Mirkwood quivers and his knives, Legolas has probably the largest array of different belt designs. As a result, he needed a pile of buckle concepts. Invariably the inspiration for them came from the natural forms in leaves and seedlings, interpreted in an Art Nouveau style." *DF*

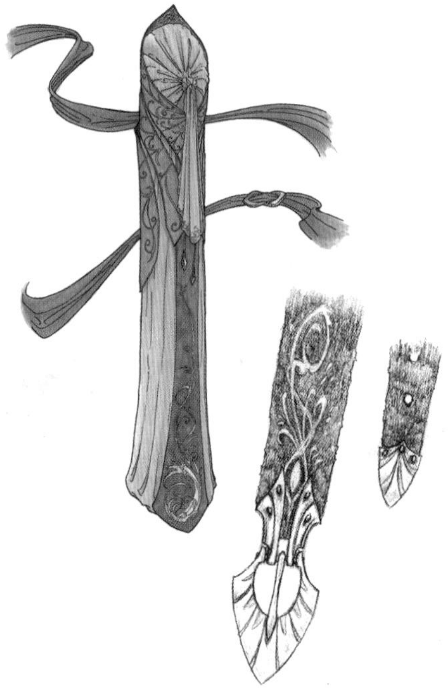

ARWEN'S QUIVER BUCKLE AND CHAPE *Conceptual design*
"Though it never saw use in the movies, we designed and built a complex and quite beautiful quiver for Arwen to wear. I tried to keep the buckle design elegant and feminine, while incorporating shapes from the quiver and bow." *DF*

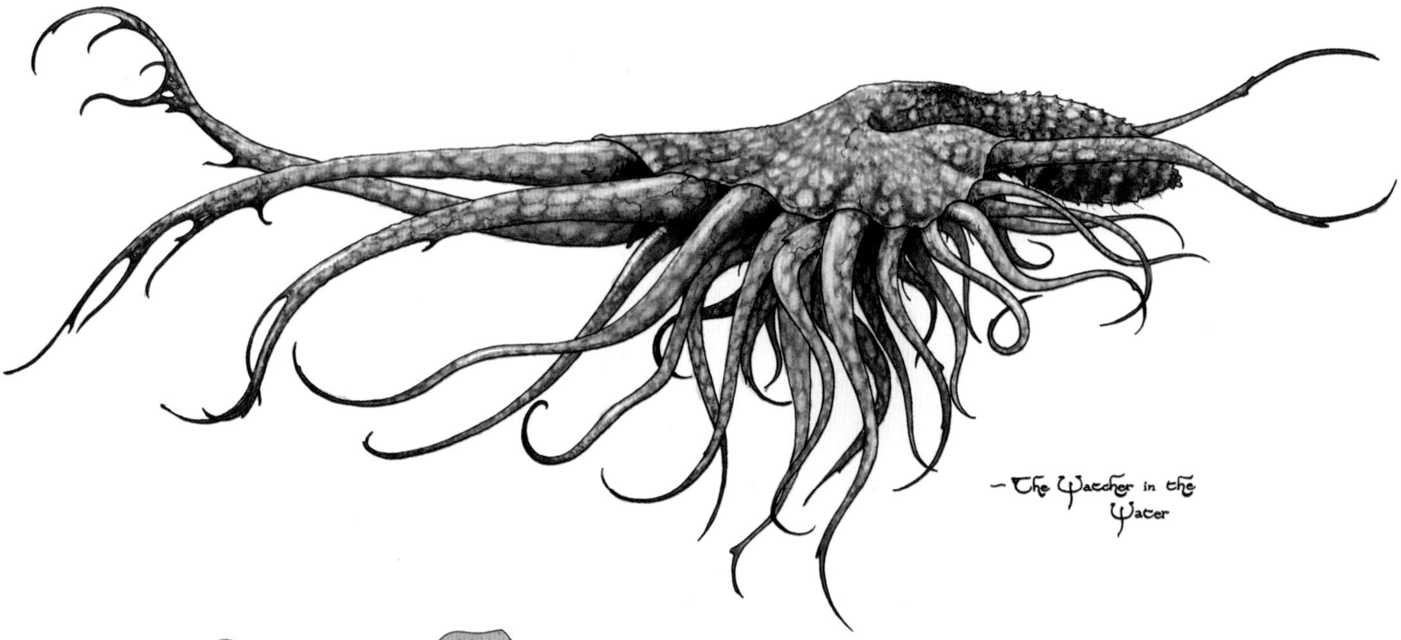

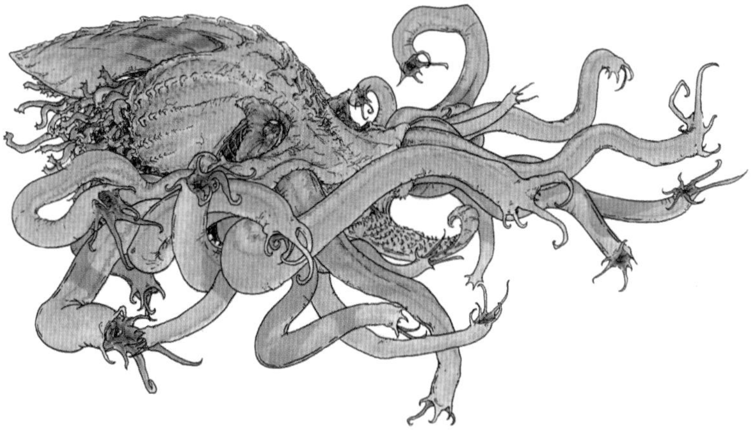

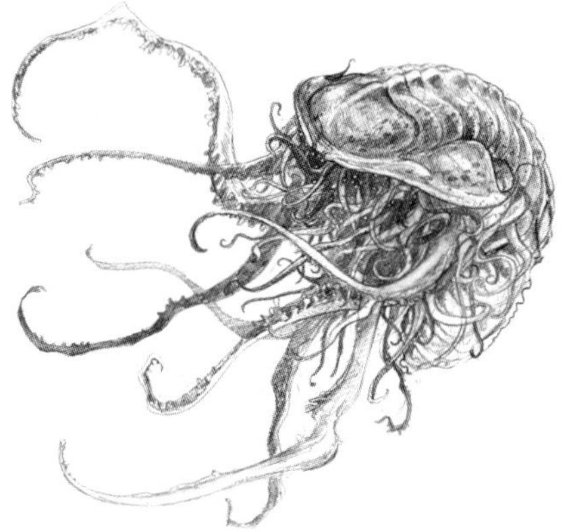

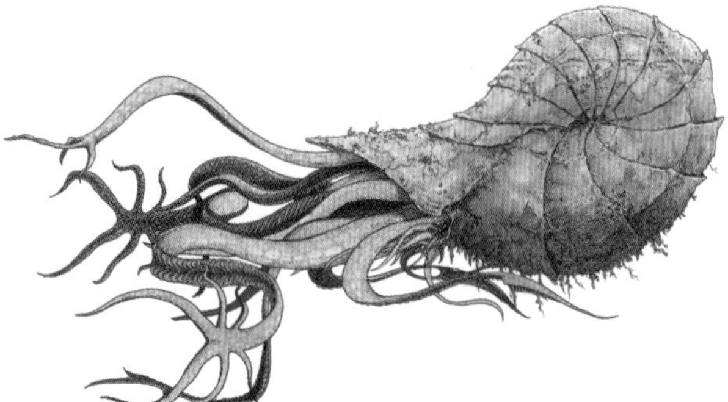

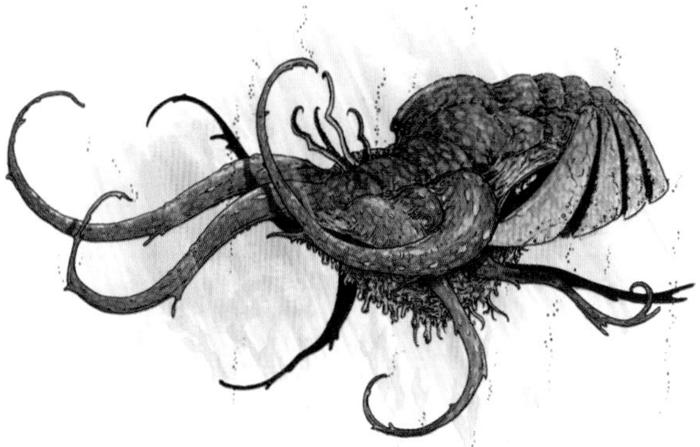

THE WATCHER *Concepual sketches*
"During the 'anything goes' period of Watcher design I came up with many different concepts. The top picture was the first design done and is still one of my favorites: it's too athletic-looking and characterless, but I still enjoy the idea of a huge octopus with hundreds of tiny eyes and tentacles that sprout like hair from underneath its soft, weblike mantle. Of the others, the one center right is a cross between a trilobyte and an octopus. I thought that, as the Watcher is a relic from the First Age of Middle-earth, perhaps drawing from our own prehistory was appropriate.

"Many elements from these wildly disparate designs were pulled together in the final approved look. The drawing above right introduced the riblike gills on the back of the beast, which made it all the way to the final design." *DF*

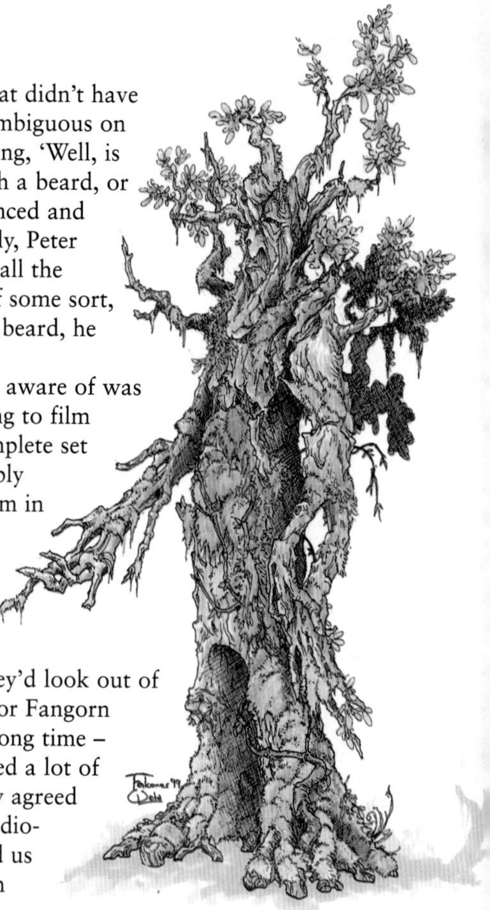

ENTS ***Color sketch***
"I tried to design an Ent that didn't have a beard. The books were ambiguous on this, which left me wondering, 'Well, is Treebeard the only one with a beard, or is his just the most pronounced and unusual-looking?' Ultimately, Peter Jackson liked the idea that all the Ents would have a beard of some sort, so in this case, instead of a beard, he almost has a goatee.

"One of the things I was aware of was that wherever we were going to film these, unless we built a complete set in a studio, we were probably going to end up filming them in a New Zealand forest. It would make no sense to design trees based on exotic woods, as we'd then have to put them in a New Zealand forest and they'd look out of place. The actual location for Fangorn wasn't decided upon for a long time – until well after we'd designed a lot of Ents – and it was eventually agreed that a lot of it would be studio-based. That actually opened us up to going a bit wider with our designs." *DF*

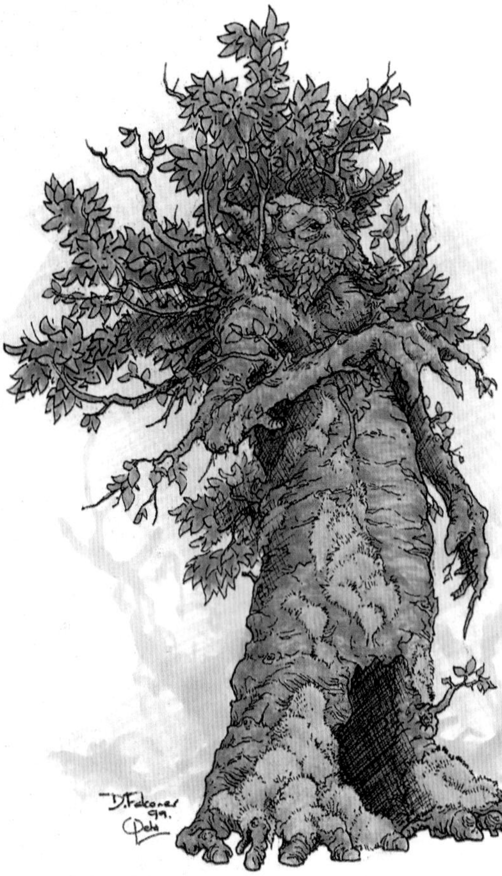

ENT ***Color sketch***
"This one has a very caricatured military look. He's quite a short Ent. I gave him very short, stubby legs – I liked the idea that perhaps he'd wobble around. He has a lot of vegetation, so perhaps he's a younger Ent." *DF*

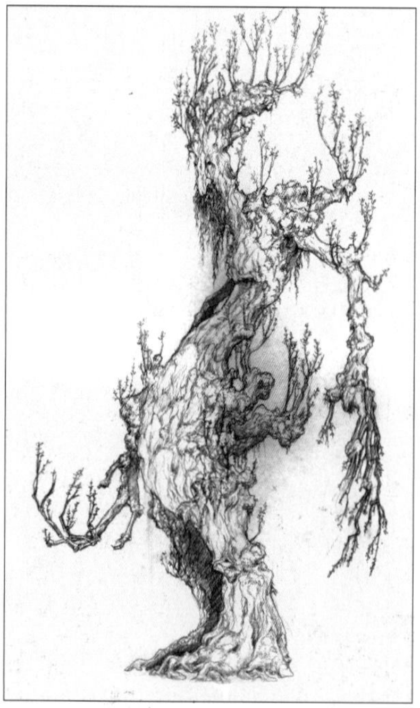

ENT ***Pencil sketch***
"Peter had responded most strongly to the most elderly-looking and twisted of our Ent designs, so this guy was an experiment in trying to twist the body into an extreme 'old gnarled tree' form, trying to break the humanoid form up as much as possible and prevent them from looking like wooden robots." *DF*

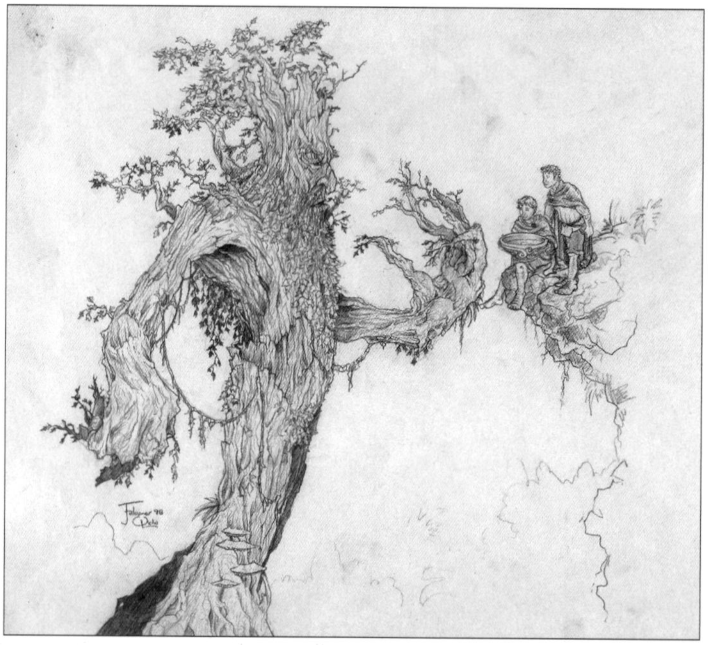

TREEBEARD ***Pencil sketch***
"I really like the idea that the Hobbits are right next to Treebeard and yet have no idea he's there – they just think he's a tree, but he's quietly watching them.

"Putting the Hobbits in gave Peter Jackson an idea of scale. I think this is probably not far off the correct scale." *DF*

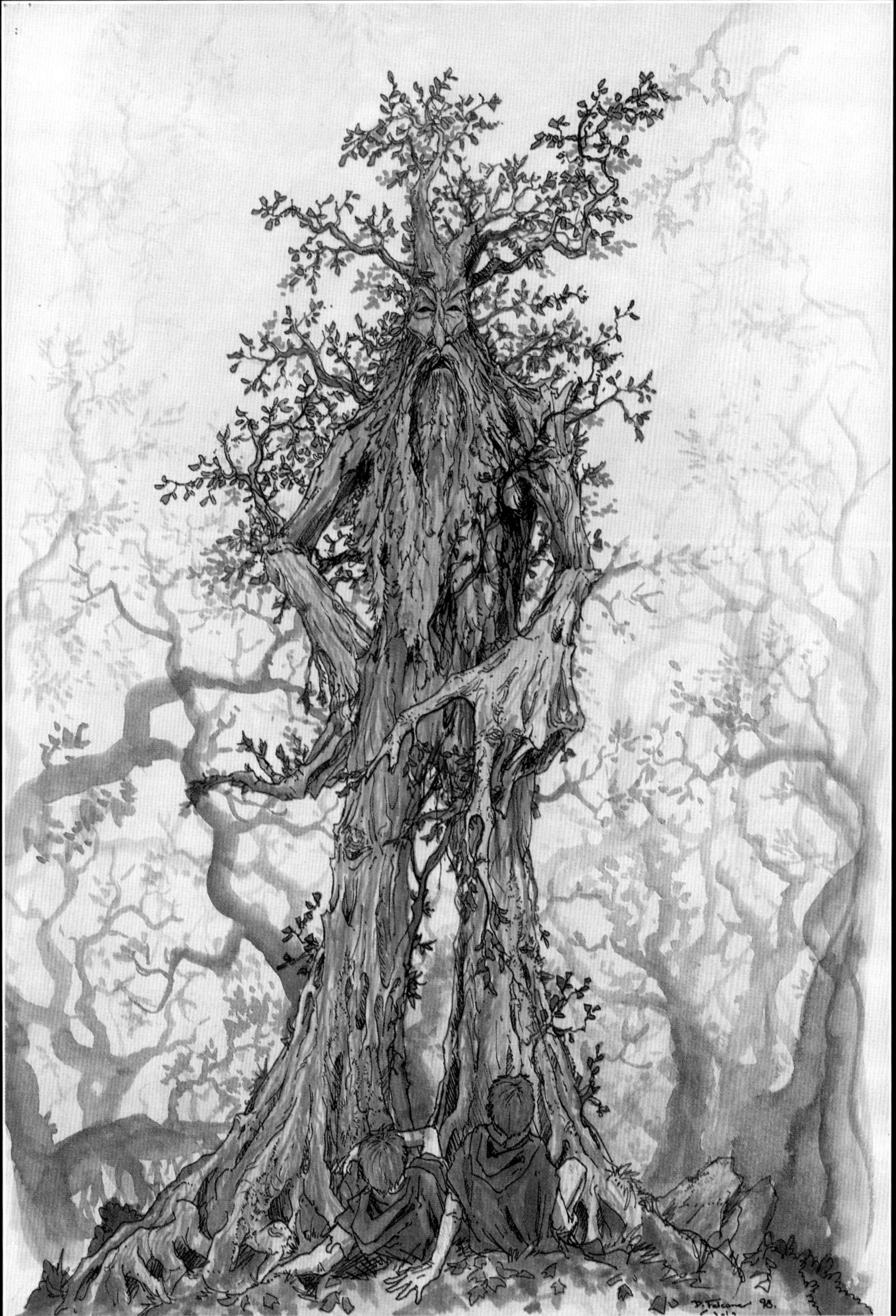

TREEBEARD *Color sketch*

"By this stage, we had really started to lock down what Treebeard would look like, and I thought I'd start playing with the color schemes. His beard is very heavily mossed, quite green. I also liked the idea of his bark being old and gray and gnarled, so that's what we have here.

"He's towering over the Hobbits – I think there's a piece in the book where he looks at them: 'Aah, little Orcs' – thinking that they're actually Orcs, but they say, 'No, no, we're Hobbits! Don't squash us!'

"And there's an interesting idea with the hands, which seem really quite out of proportion, but they're not. It's a perspective thing in this drawing. It wasn't totally successful, but I wanted to give the idea that his head was actually a lot higher up and farther away from where his hands and feet were." *DF*

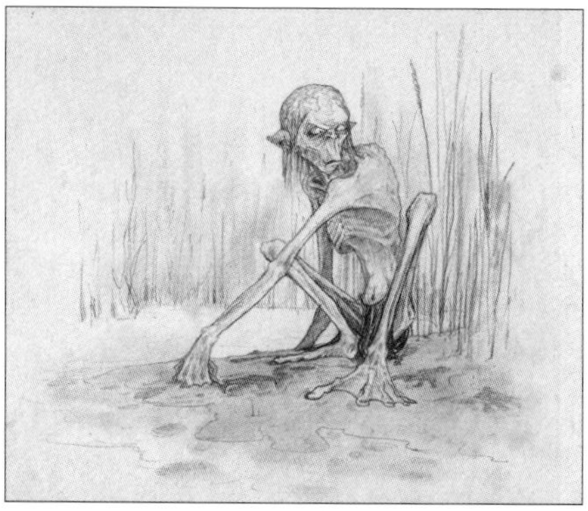

GOLLUM *Pencil sketch*
"It became very apparent quite early on that Jamie Beswarick and Mike Asquith were capturing Gollum quite well with the designs they were doing. This was one of my early versions – too thin and ill-looking." *DF*

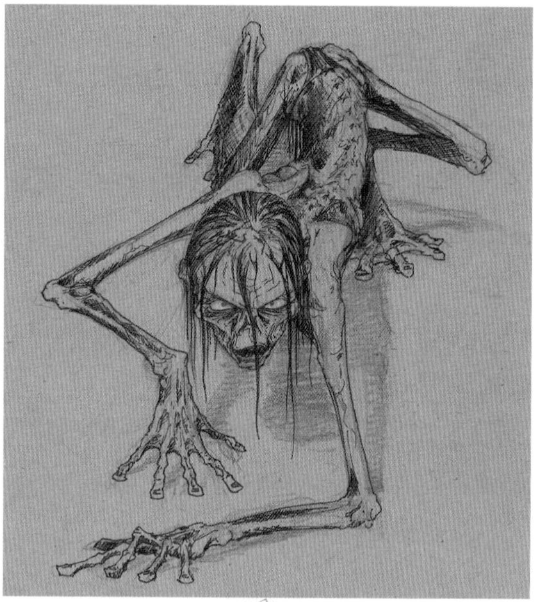

GOLLUM *Design sketches*
"Gollum was always one of my favorite characters when I read the books, but I actually didn't do a great deal on him – in retrospect I think some of my concepts were a little off target, perhaps a little bit too emaciated. In particular these looked less like a Hobbit that has turned into something and more like some kind of new creature entirely. Up until this point, nobody had started looking at the color scheme on Gollum, so I thought I would. In this particular case, the idea was that his skin, while once flesh-toned, has now changed. He's been out in the wilds a long time so it's as if grass stains have almost worn into him from running around in the dirt, and there's very little of the actual flesh tone left. Again, this probably has the effect of making him a little bit too 'monstery.' The final design we went with did actually have a very pale flesh tone, rather than the green." *DF*

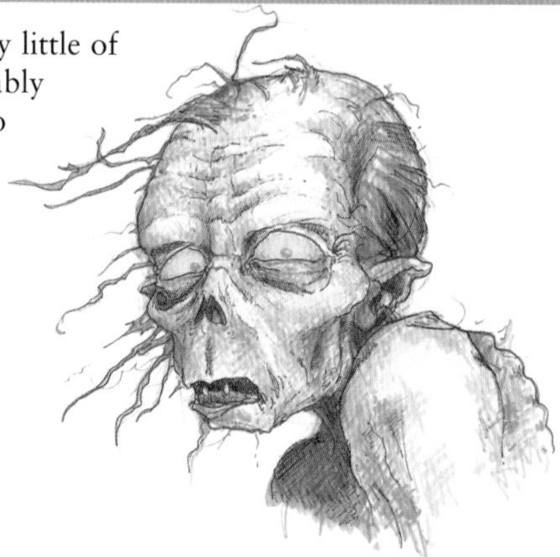

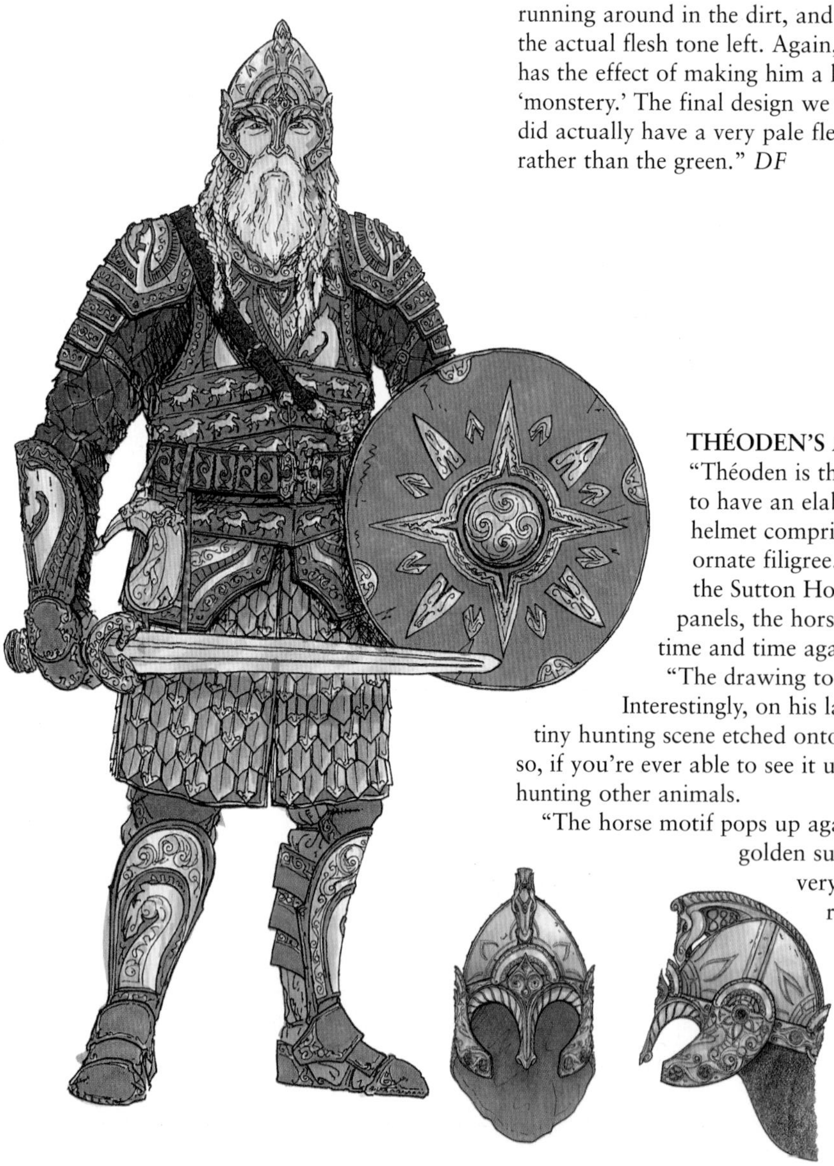

THÉODEN'S ARMOR *Color sketches*
"Théoden is the king, so if any member of the Rohirrim is going to have an elaborate helmet, it should be him; therefore Théoden's helmet comprises three or four different metals. It's also covered in ornate filigree. I looked a lot at the material that was pulled out of the Sutton Hoo burial mound for inspiration. There are little enamel panels, the horse's head, sun emblems, and a Celtic curl that we used time and time again.

"The drawing to the left is very close to the final armor that was made. Interestingly, on his lames, as they crisscross his stomach, there's actually a tiny hunting scene etched onto them. We thought that his armor would tell a story, so, if you're ever able to see it up close, there are little soldiers chasing a boar and hunting other animals.

"The horse motif pops up again and again, so we adopted that and also put the golden sun, which is the flag of Rohan, on the shields. It was very helpful to develop these iconic devices that we would reuse, so that when you see a character in Rohan armor, an audience member, without even questioning it, will think, 'Oh, he's from Rohan,' as opposed to, 'Who's that guy? Where's he from?' There are many peoples and cultures in *The Lord of the Rings,* so it was really important that we had these strong visual styles and color palettes to distinguish each culture." *DF*

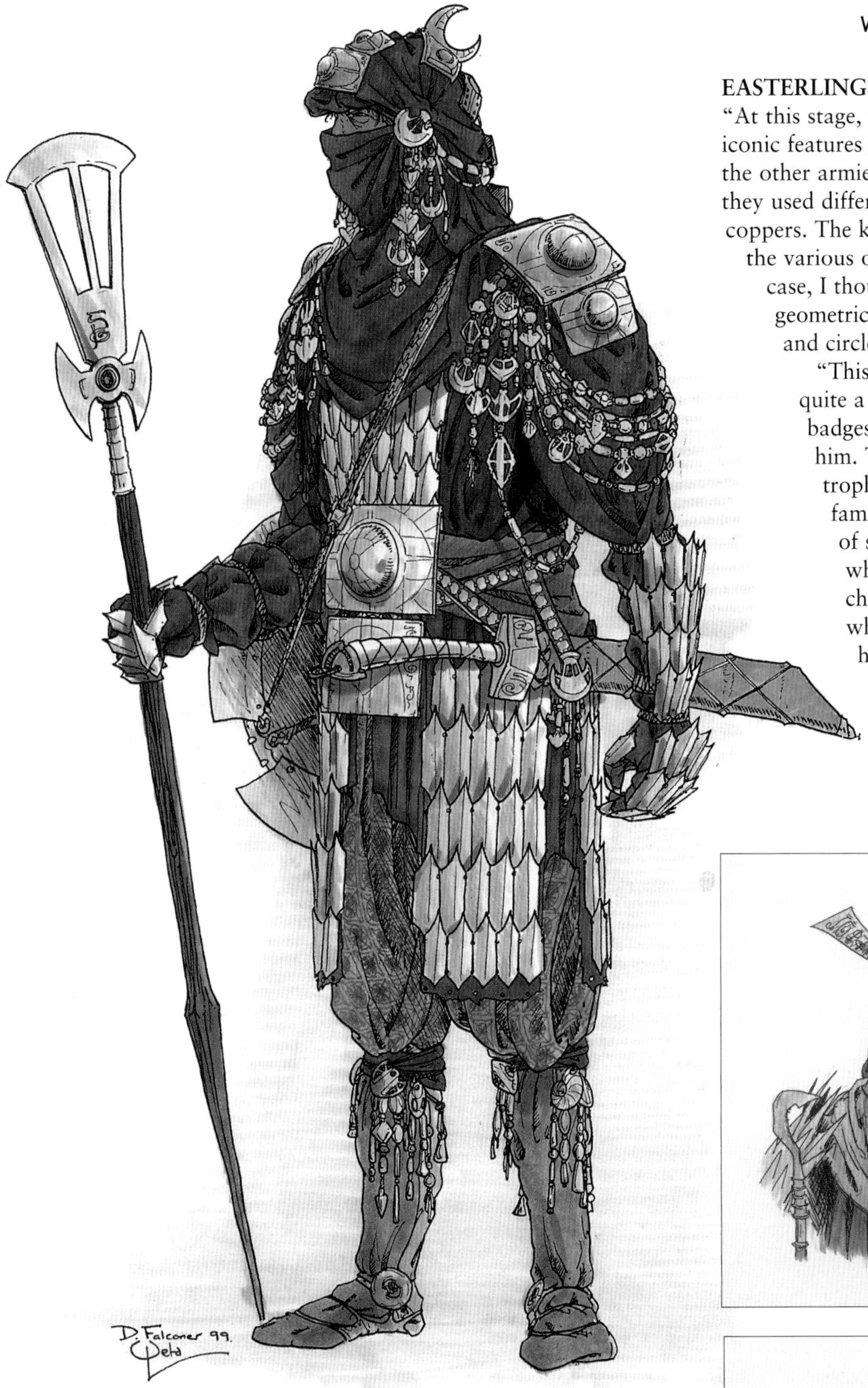

EASTERLINGS *Color sketch*
"At this stage, we were trying to establish very strong iconic features for the Easterlings to differentiate them from the other armies, so one of the things I played with was that they used different metals in their armor – brass, bronze, coppers. The kinds of metals that we haven't seen a lot of in the various other armies, together with new shapes. In this case, I thought it would be interesting to add a strong geometric element to their design, so I used lots of squares and circles.

"This picture introduces the idea that they're actually quite a rich culture, and that each warrior wears the badges of his office and the wealth of his family all over him. They would festoon themselves with either war trophies that they've taken off people they've killed or family heirlooms. He's absolutely covered in this sort of stuff. The pattern for the armor is fairly close to what we finally went with, but there were a few changes. Peter Jackson felt that we needed a helmet, whereas this one has a turban. He believed that a helmet makes him much more warriorlike and again, less obviously from any recognizable culture." *DF*

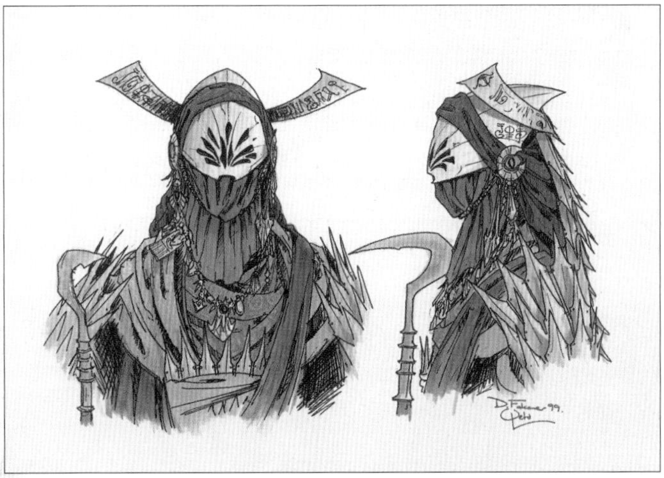

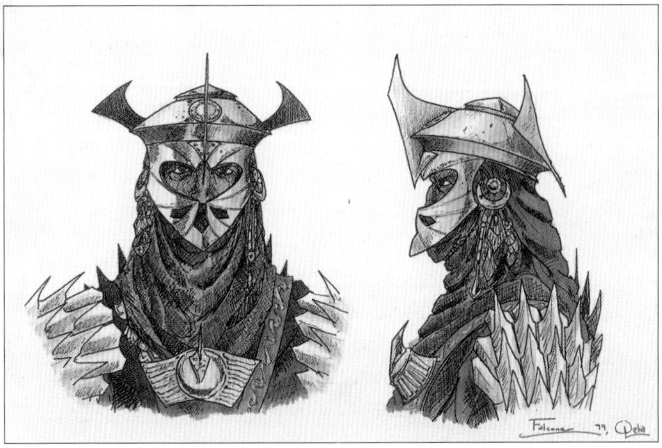

EASTERLINGS *Color sketches*
"Sourisak Chanpaseuth did a great drawing that included a fantastic helmet with the silhouette of two really big blades coming out of it, which Peter Jackson really, really liked. So I began trying different helmet designs that would employ that silhouette. It was something that none of the other races that we'd designed at that stage had. The look of the armor itself had been pretty much locked down, and we also had a very strong idea of what the colour palette would be – ochers, reds, browns, black, and brass." *DF*

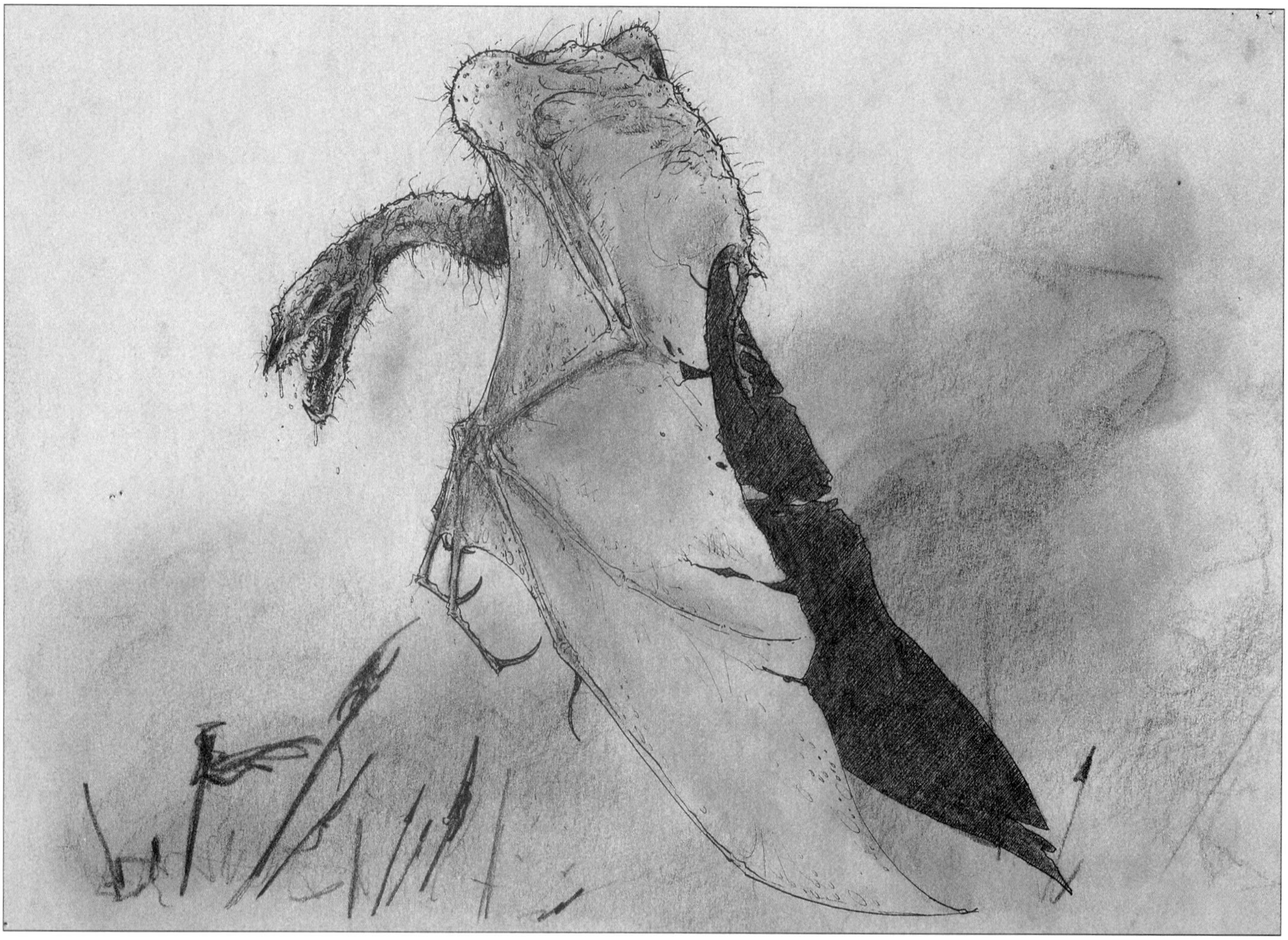

FELL BEAST *Concept*
"Trying to give Peter Jackson a truly repulsive beast, I drew this fell beast concept with the inspiration of vultures, marabou storks, and other carrion-eating species in mind. The creature was almost skeletal in frame, but huge and loathsome. I imagined it would smell as foul as it looked, swooping low over the battlefield." *DF*

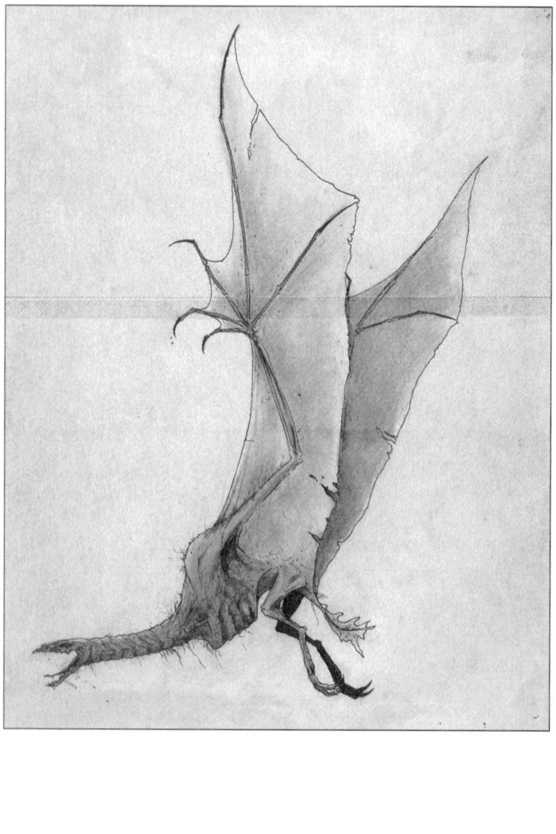

FELL BEAST *Concept*
"The fell beasts were only scantily described in the books, leaving us with quite a bit of latitude when coming up with designs to show Peter Jackson. This drawing was perhaps the most dragonlike that was done. Yet there is something noble about dragons that didn't quite fit. Peter felt they needed to look more repulsive and evil." *DF*

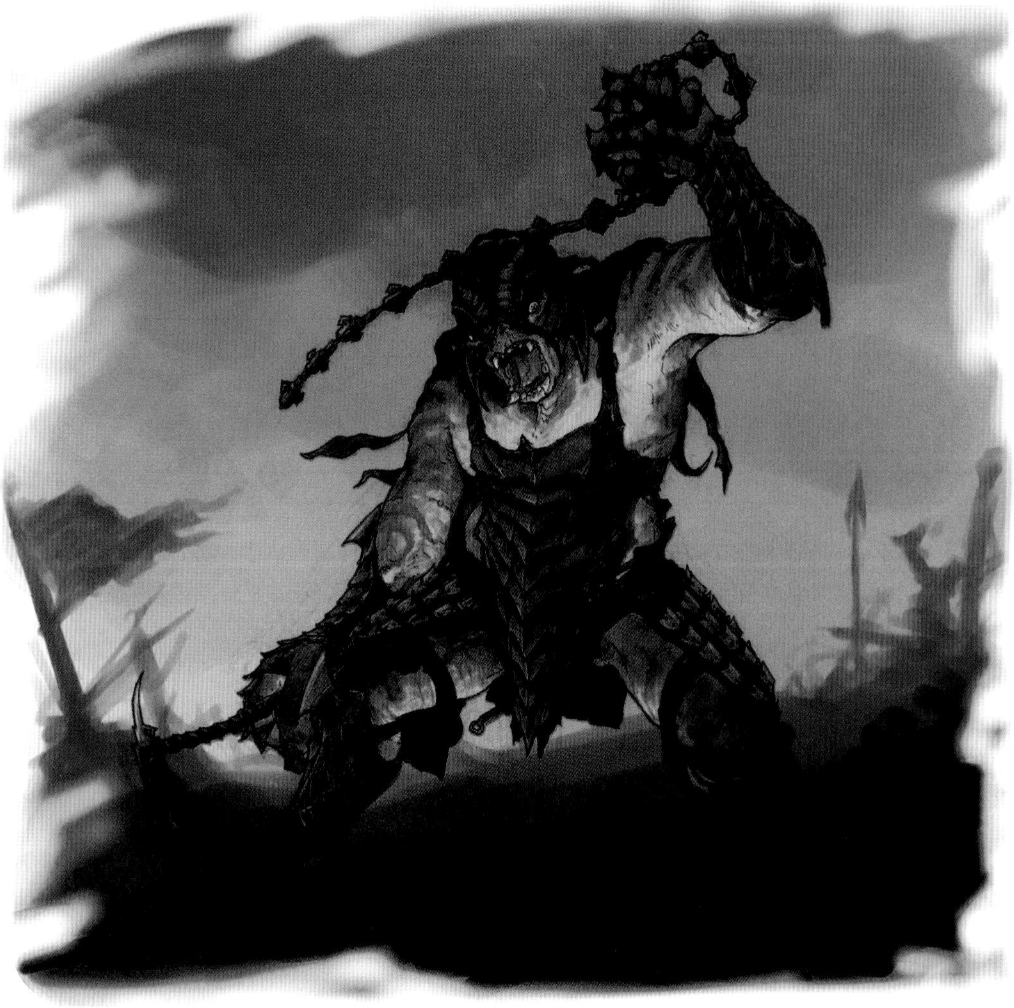

OLOG-HAI ***Helmet concept***
"A variety of different helmet designs were done for the Olog-hai trolls. I was conscious that we needed to create something that didn't resemble Uruk-hai or Orc helmets, such as those we had already seen in the first two films. So I tried some different approaches, using more chain or overlapping scalloped plates, more like Sauron's Second Age armor seen in the prologue to the first film." *DF*

MOUNTAIN-TROLL ***Face concepts***
"Rather than have all our trolls look alike, I explored the possibilities of some level of variation between individuals. These included disease and deformity variants, bug eyes, and the like." *DF*

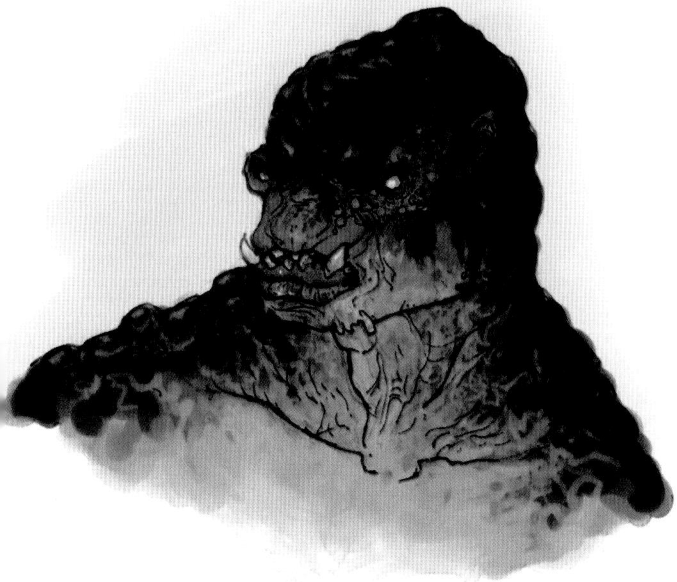

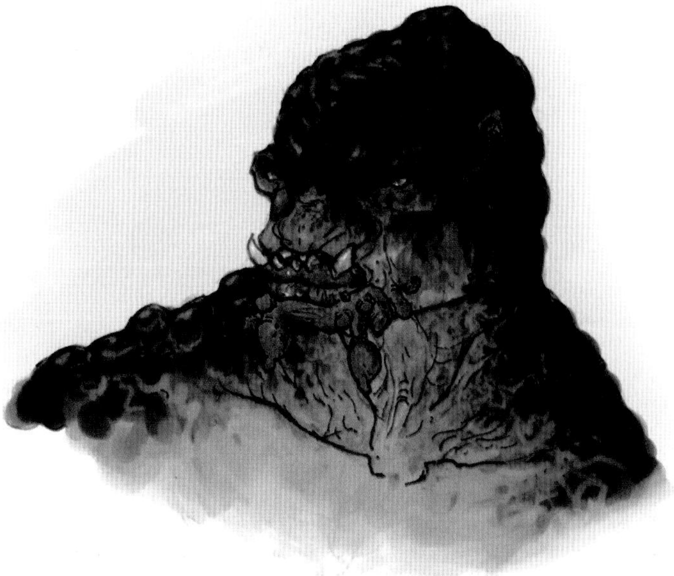

HARADRIM *Armor concept*
"The Haradrim were a human race but under the sway of evil. In *The Two Towers*, we were led to empathize with the young Haradrim boy Faramir's men killed, but in *The Return of the King* we as an audience have to root for the good guys as they fight the Haradrim. That meant dehumanizing the Haradrim when we see them in battle at the Pelennor Fields, something that can be achieved with masks. The moment the human face is taken away, it is easier for an audience to accept a violent death without question or empathy. I tried to imbue the masks the Haradrim wore with menace and cruelty. They are fearsome and brutal, so hopefully the audience will feel comfortable with our heroes slaughtering them." *DF*

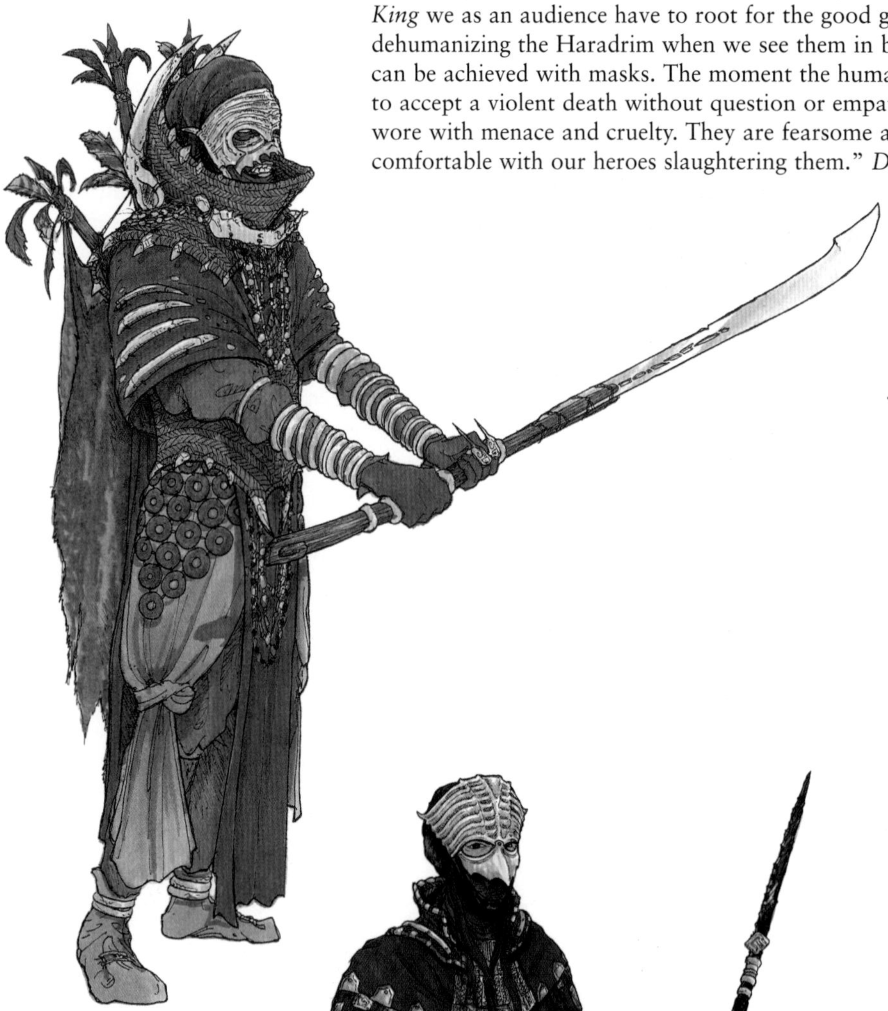

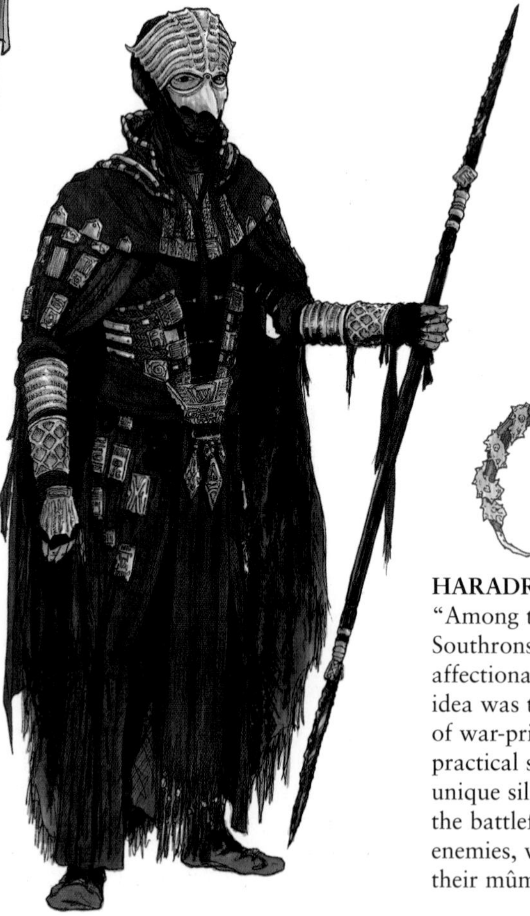

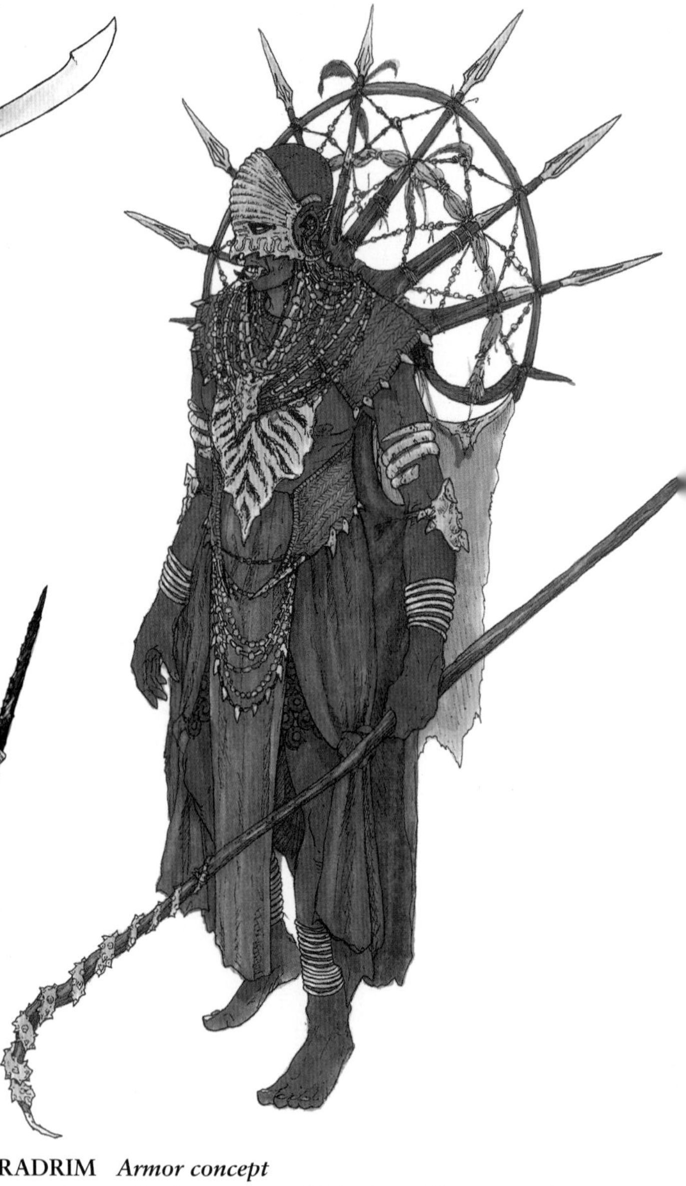

HARADRIM
Armor concept
"The Haradrim were great fun to design because they were highly decorative. I relished the opportunity to include lots of impractical but cool-looking accoutrements and adornment. Their vaguely animalistic headdresses were especially enjoyable to experiment with." *DF*

HARADRIM *Armor concept*
"Among the motifs that were established to differentiate the Southrons was one idea of a ceremonial back-piece that became affectionately known around Weta as 'the dreamcatcher.' The idea was that some of the Haradrim leaders would have the role of war-priests, festooned with items of religious rather than practical significance. The back-piece created an interesting and unique silhouette, which would also help distinguish them on the battlefield. Red body paint, symbolizing the blood of their enemies, was another idea, which would also carry through to their mûmakil mounts." *DF*

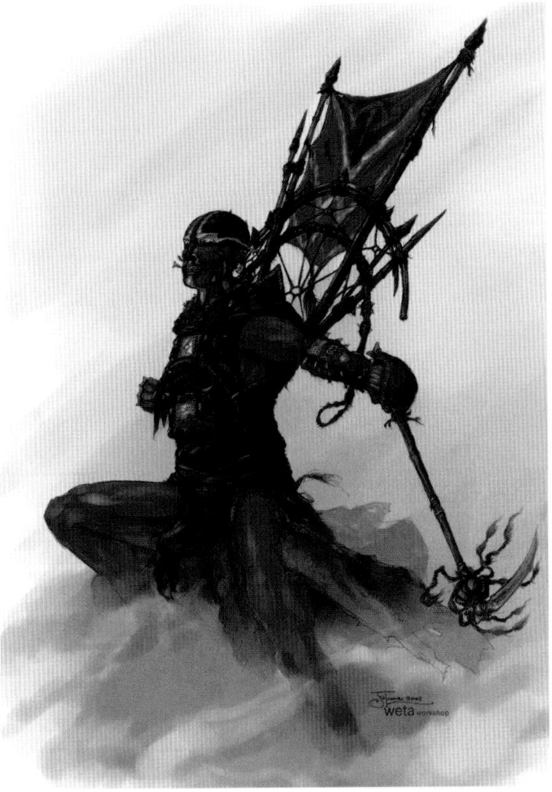

HARADRIM *Conceptual design*
"Almost six years after beginning work on *The Lord of the Rings*, to be able to go back and design into that world again was a true joy. This piece was requested late on as the final round of pick-up photography loomed for *The Return of the King*. By this stage I hadn't done any *LOTR* art for a good while, but it was no trouble to slip back into Middle-earth again. Christian Rivers had done a very loose Photoshop study, which I used as a guide to extrapolate from with this design. It's one of the few drawings I completed on the computer rather than as a pencil or marker drawing. I was very happy with the way it turned out, and the final product on screen looks very much like it, so it was a wonderful note to end on and close the book on *LOTR* for me." *DF*

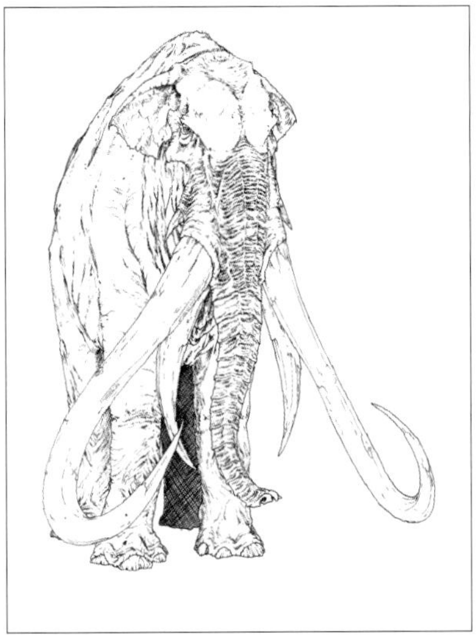

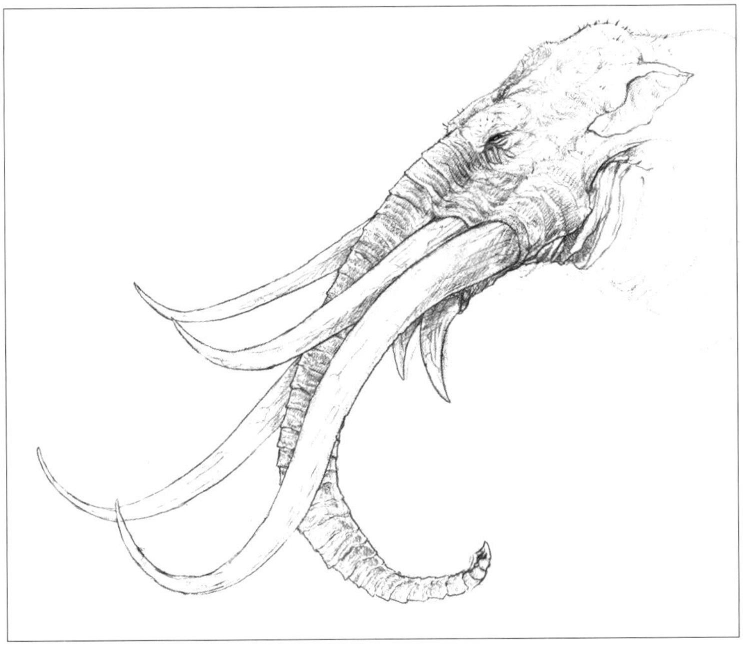

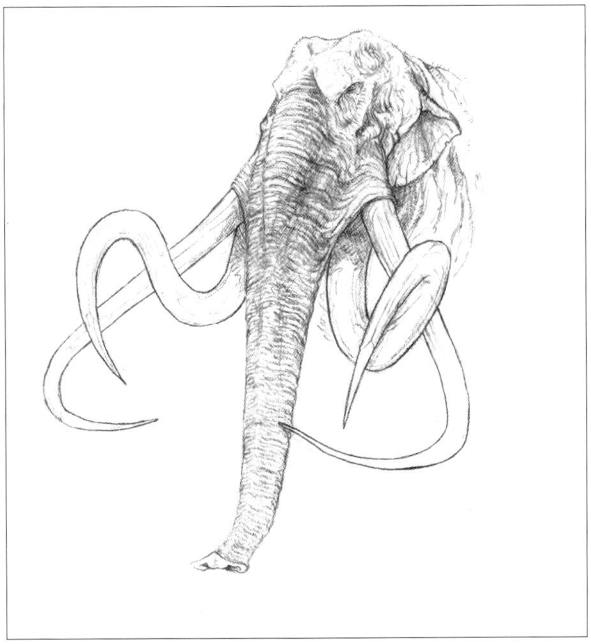

MÛMAKIL *Conceptual designs*
"Designing the mûmakil was great fun, because elephants have such interesting features. I imagined a variety of unusual tusk formations, trying to think about how and why they might have developed. In the drawing above right, I was imagining curved tusks that might be used in bouts of competition between bulls. The points were curved inward to avoid injury to each other, but they would still be a serious threat to smaller creatures and enemies.

"Experimenting with different tusk arrangements, I drew inspiration from prehistoric elephantlike animals. There are elements of mammoth and mastodon in the above concept, with small eyes and ears to help emphasize the huge size of the beast.

"The top drawing was the final approved design, on which we based the final sculpture. It was really an exercise in trying to see how far one could push an elephant in terms of scale, ferocity, and evil while still adhering to principles of reality." *DF*

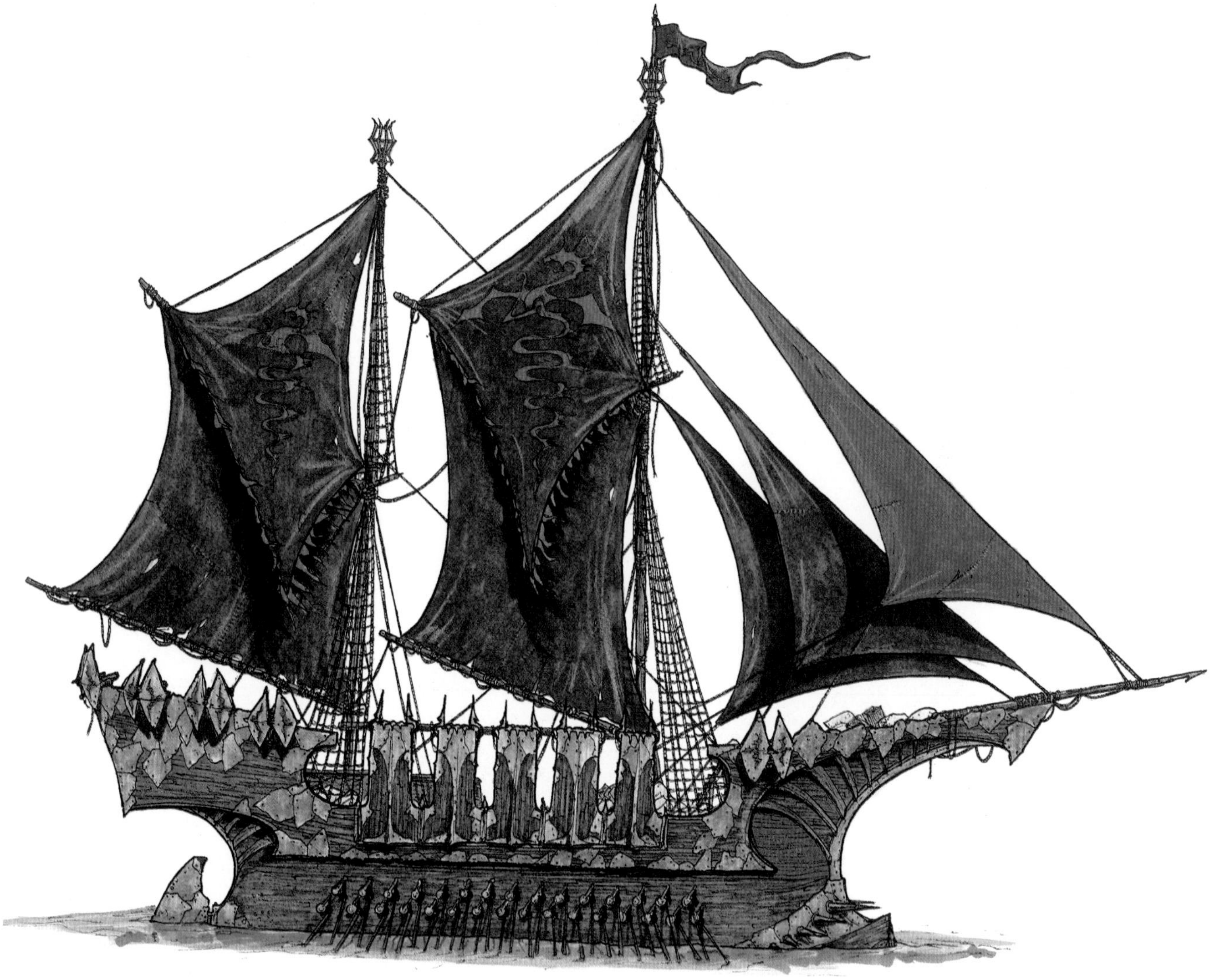

CORSAIR SHIPS
Concepts
"In trying to imagine exciting ways for the Corsair ships to disgorge their cargo of undead onto the docks, I designed the ship above to have five extendable ramps, which would drop from their upright position on the deck, down over the side, and bridge the gap between ship and dock. I imagined that one of the attributes of the Corsairs was to board and seize other ships very quickly because of their ability to land large numbers of their troops in one go with these multiple ramps.

"Although not terribly clear in the illustration opposite top, this concept for a Corsair ship sported a pair of outriggers, making three hulls in total. Apart from its large fan-shaped sail area, the ship would be able to seat many rows of oarsmen in the three hulls, allowing for great bursts of speed. The outriggers' struts also served as boarding ramps for the troops I imagined would be carried on board, with rotating extensions that could be hoisted when traveling and dropped when engaged in boarding. I imagined this would be interesting to see on screen when Aragorn arrives with his undead army. Vertically mounted ballistas also protect the ship fore and aft, and three huge rudders, mounted at the front of the main hull and the end of each outrigger, would increase maneuverability. Beyond that, it was something we had never seen before.

"In an attempt to try to come up with a design for a ship that was both new and interesting, and allow for a dramatic entrance for Aragorn's undead soldiers at the Battle of the Pelennor Fields, I came up with the design opposite bottom. The ship has a low profile, with the masts able to drop to remain unnoticed on the horizon for as long as possible. The sails were based on Pacific designs that I saw while researching at the museum, but in addition the vessel sports two rows of oars down each side of her long hull. I imagined the craft having a shallow draft to allow for beaching maneuvers when conducting coastal raids. The front of the ship would draw up as shallow as possible, and the huge louvered steel doors occupying the front third of the ship would open, allowing her cargo of troops to disembark en masse. I had Aragorn's arrival with the Army of the Dead in mind when designing this, though ultimately this concept went no further." *DF*

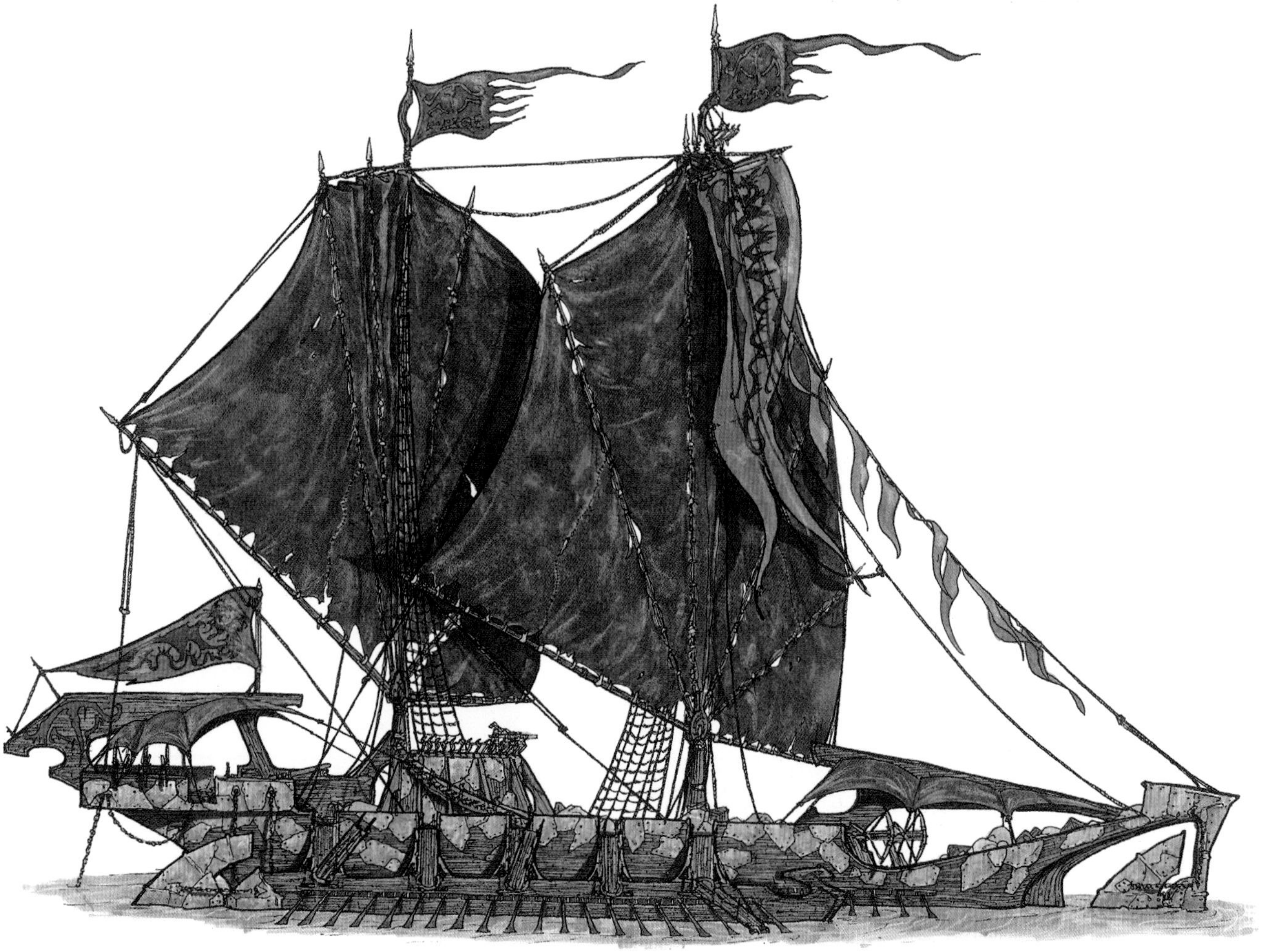

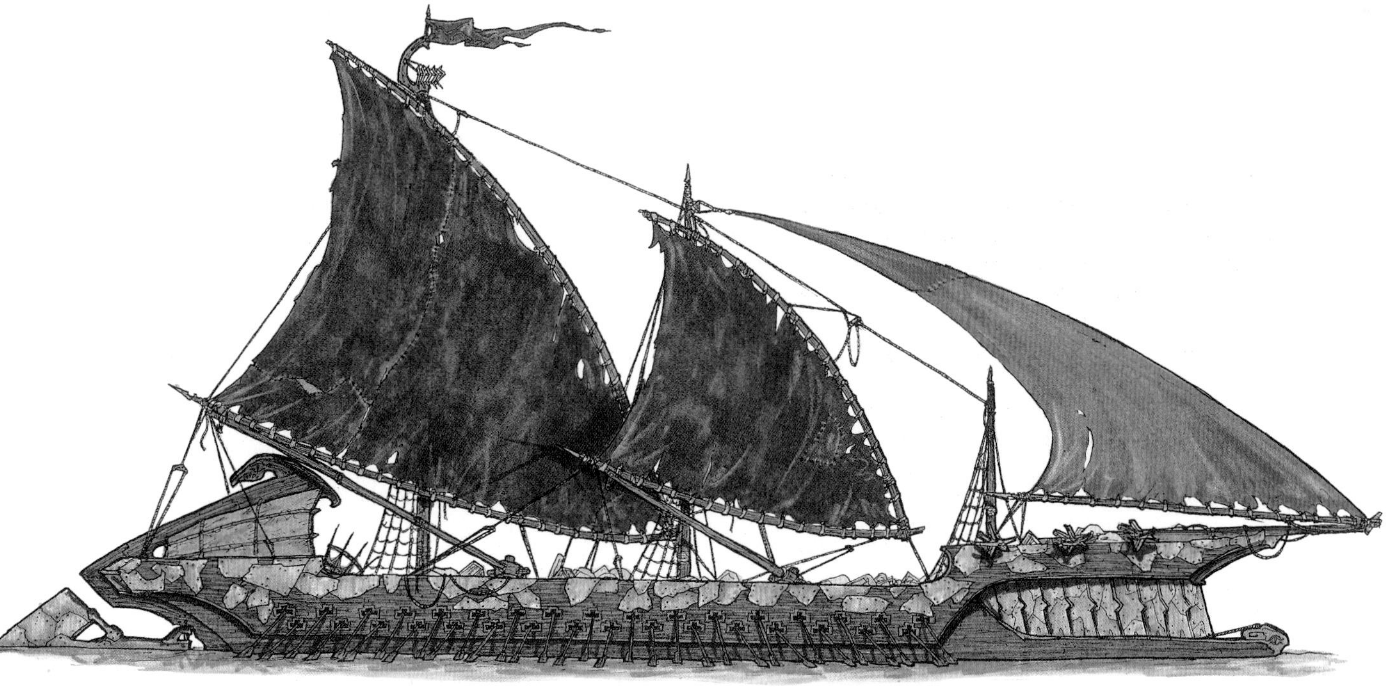

BEN WOOTTEN

I started working at Weta at the same time as Daniel Falconer and Shaun Bolton. I'm a huge fan of the books and couldn't believe we were doing the movies. I went to university in Dunedin, and I had friends down there who were great fans of the books as well. And I remember many late-night talks about what you would do if you were going to make it into a film – whom you'd cast and things like that. And to suddenly find myself, eight years later, designing on the films – it's totally surreal.

John Howe was amazing – I've had his artwork on my walls for ages. So to work with him was fantastic; working from his sketches for the Balrog was probably the most amazing thing.

One of the things that I think makes the design more successful is the fact that we all work together, swapping ideas and information around. No one works in a vacuum. I think that's important – it makes our job not just easier, it makes it far more realistic and far more successful. And far more fun!

Ben Wootten
April 2002

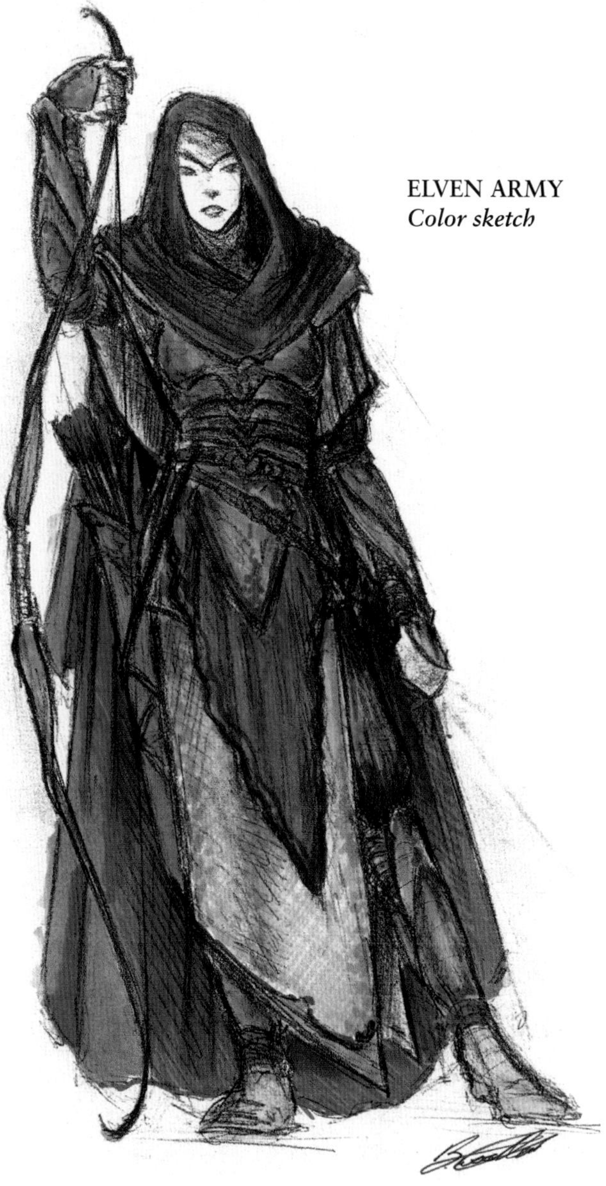

ELVEN ARMY
Color sketch

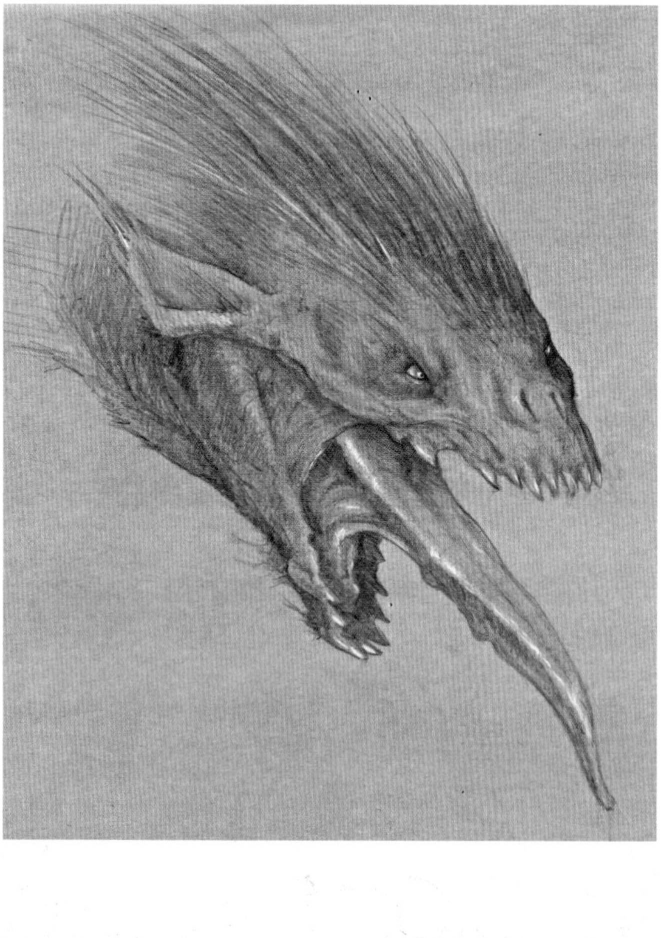

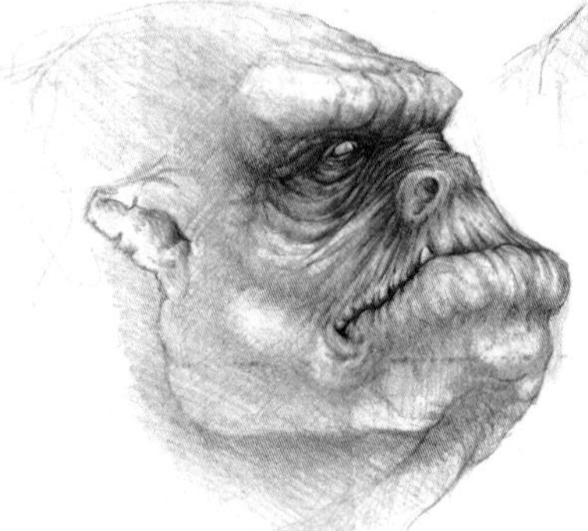

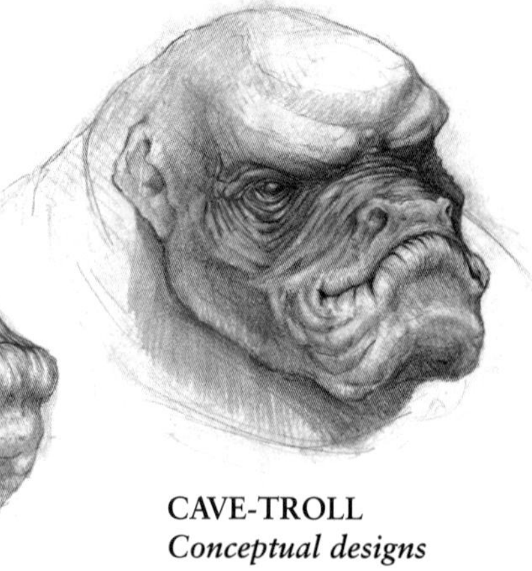

CAVE-TROLL
Conceptual designs

ORCS *Concept sketch*
This early design is entirely animalistic and was intended for digital creation.

THE WATCHER
Conceptual sketch

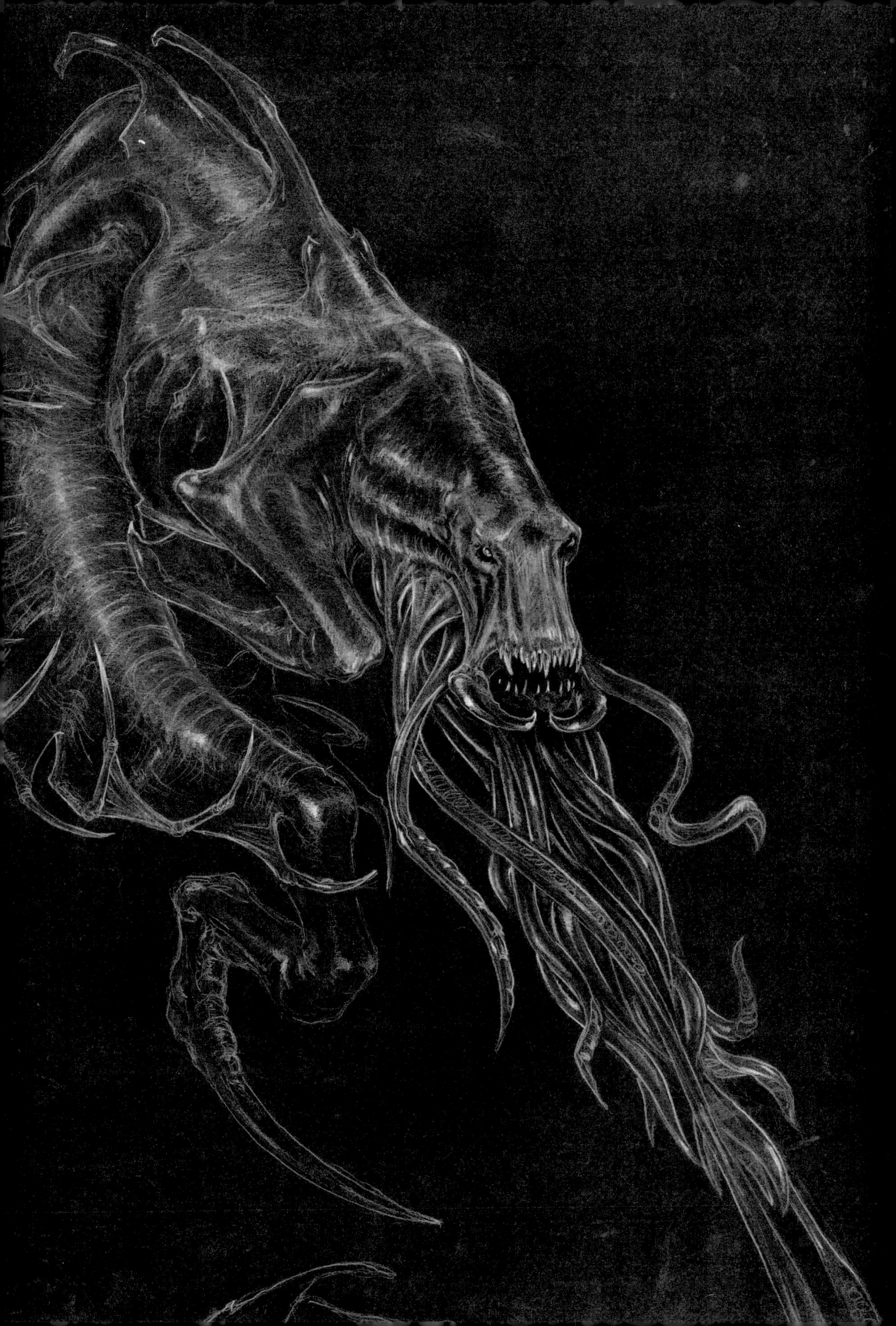

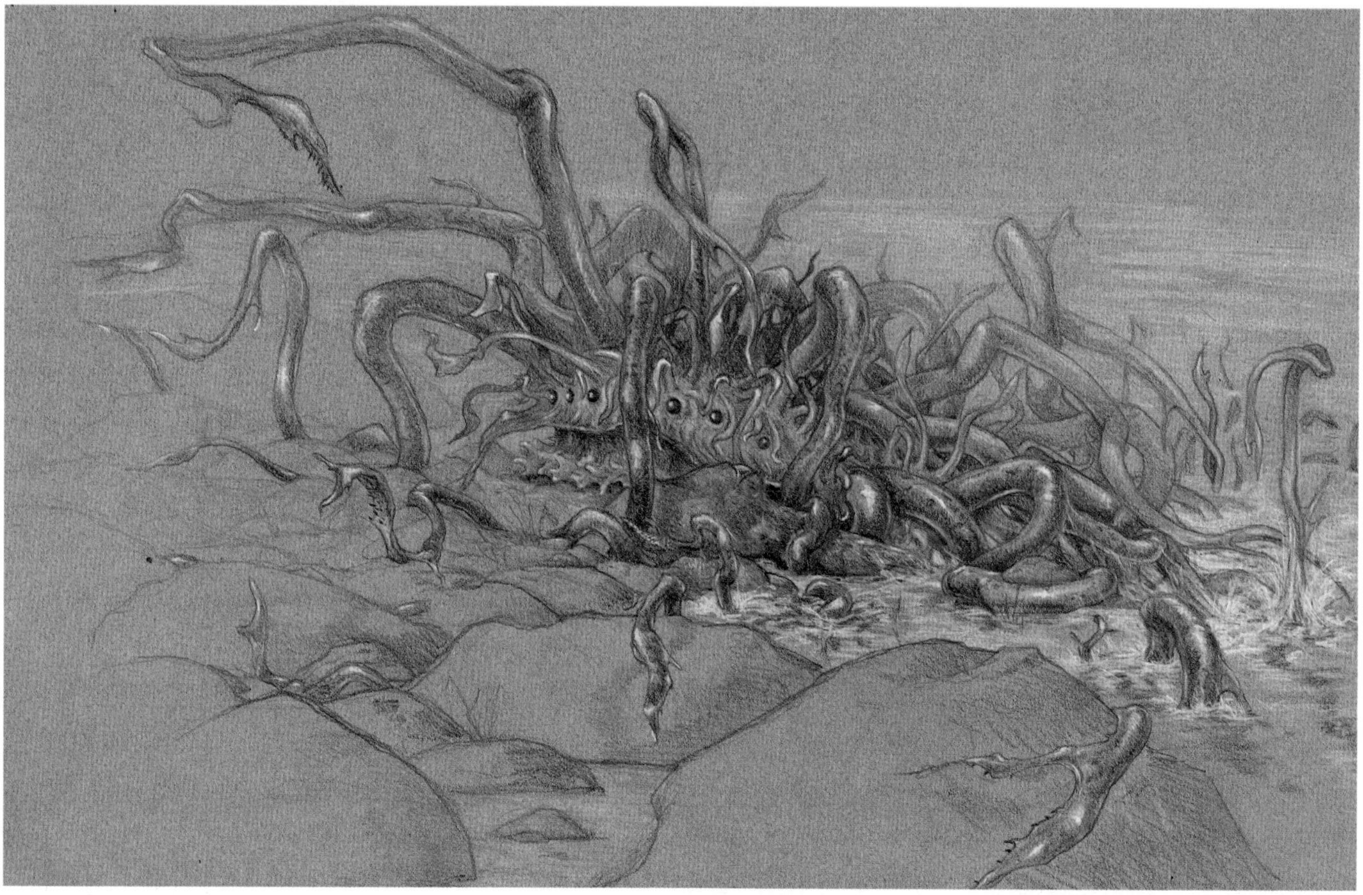

THE WATCHER *Conceptual sketches*
Ben's early Watcher concept, right, was very crustacean-based, while the image above drifted more toward an anemone look.

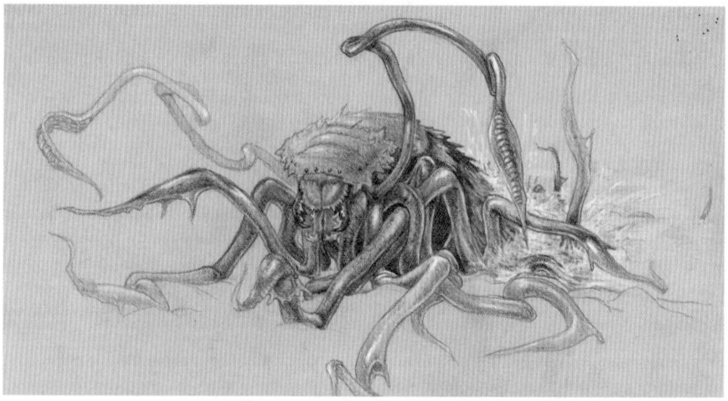

THE WATCHER *Conceptual designs*
The two Watchers below represent ideas that moved away from a more fishlike concept and became more unique to Middle-earth.

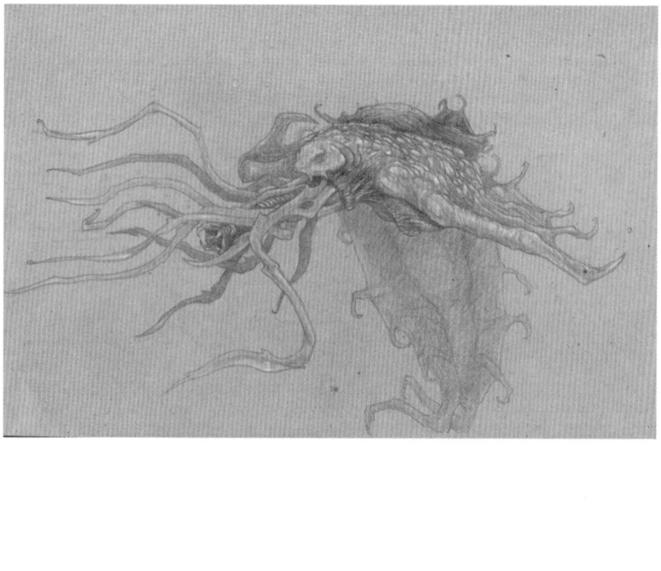

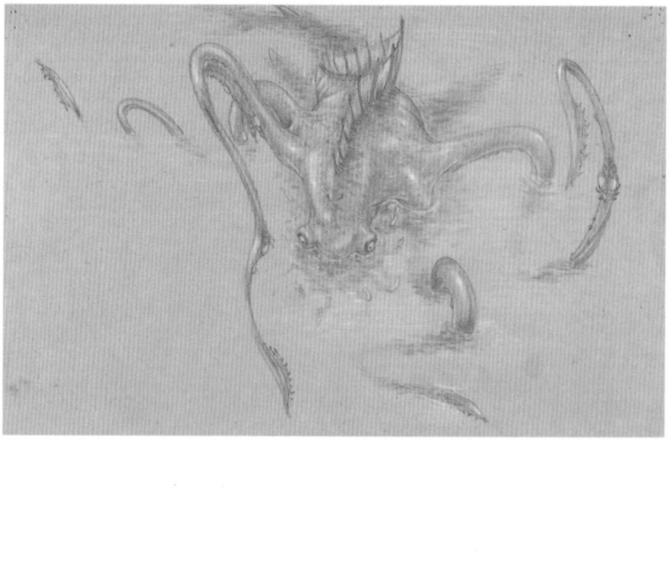

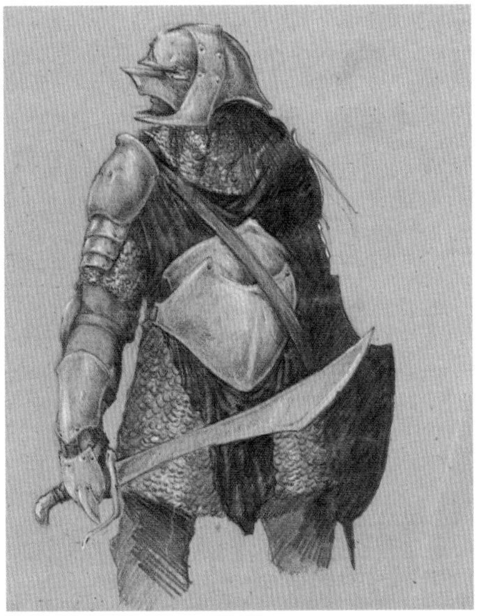

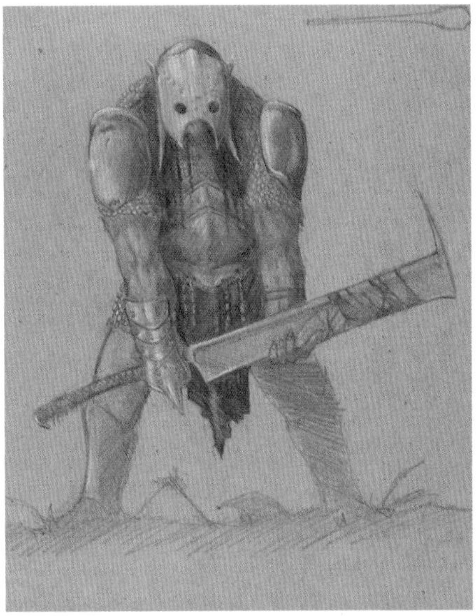

URUK-HAI ARMY *Conceptual sketch*
"Ah, the Berserkers. The heavy shock troops wear masks, and there is that very simple, clean face with just the little eye-holes and the space for the mouth. And there's something kind of creepy about the simplicity of it. It also ties in with the fact that they're easy to make; Uruk-hai armor can be mass-produced. And it's really impersonal, you get no impression of what's going through the mind of your attacker, which is something you use in combat all the time. The thing I like about the weapon is that, for the Uruk-hai, it's such an intuitive-looking weapon; it doesn't look like it needs any skill to wield it. It's just a huge, heavy piece of steel – you can see you don't need fencing lessons!" *BW*

URUK-HAI ARMY *Conceptual sketch*
"With the above sketch we were doing sword design, still resolving how much armor they might be wearing on their arms, and the general cut of the helmet. The swordsman has splints down his arm, which is a very simple but quite an efficient way of stopping your arm getting chopped off, and then there's the shape of the breastplate. We were still trying to establish a look for these guys – straight back, very powerful shoulders, as opposed to the slinky Orcs." *BW*

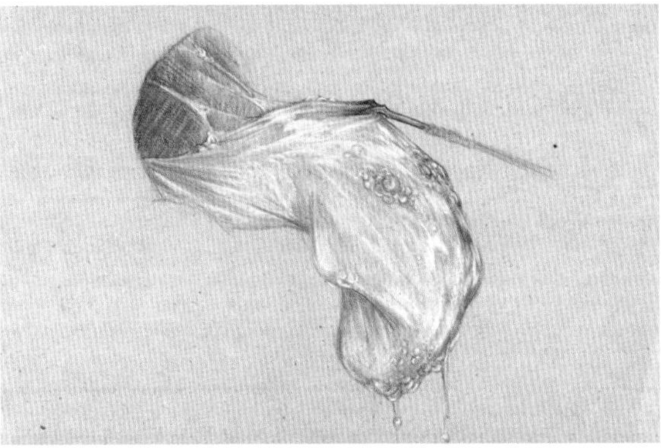

URUK-HAI BIRTHING SAC
Conceptual sketch
Ben's version of the sac itself, seen in the pits beneath Isengard.

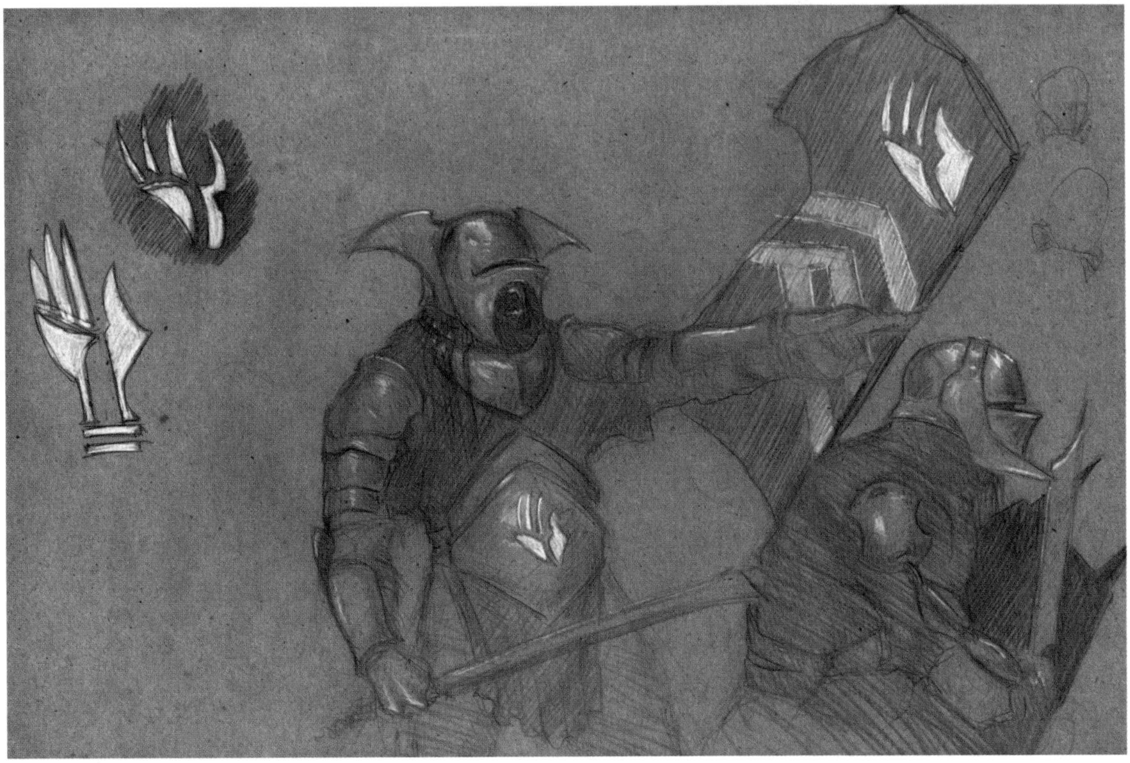

URUK-HAI ARMY
Conceptual sketch

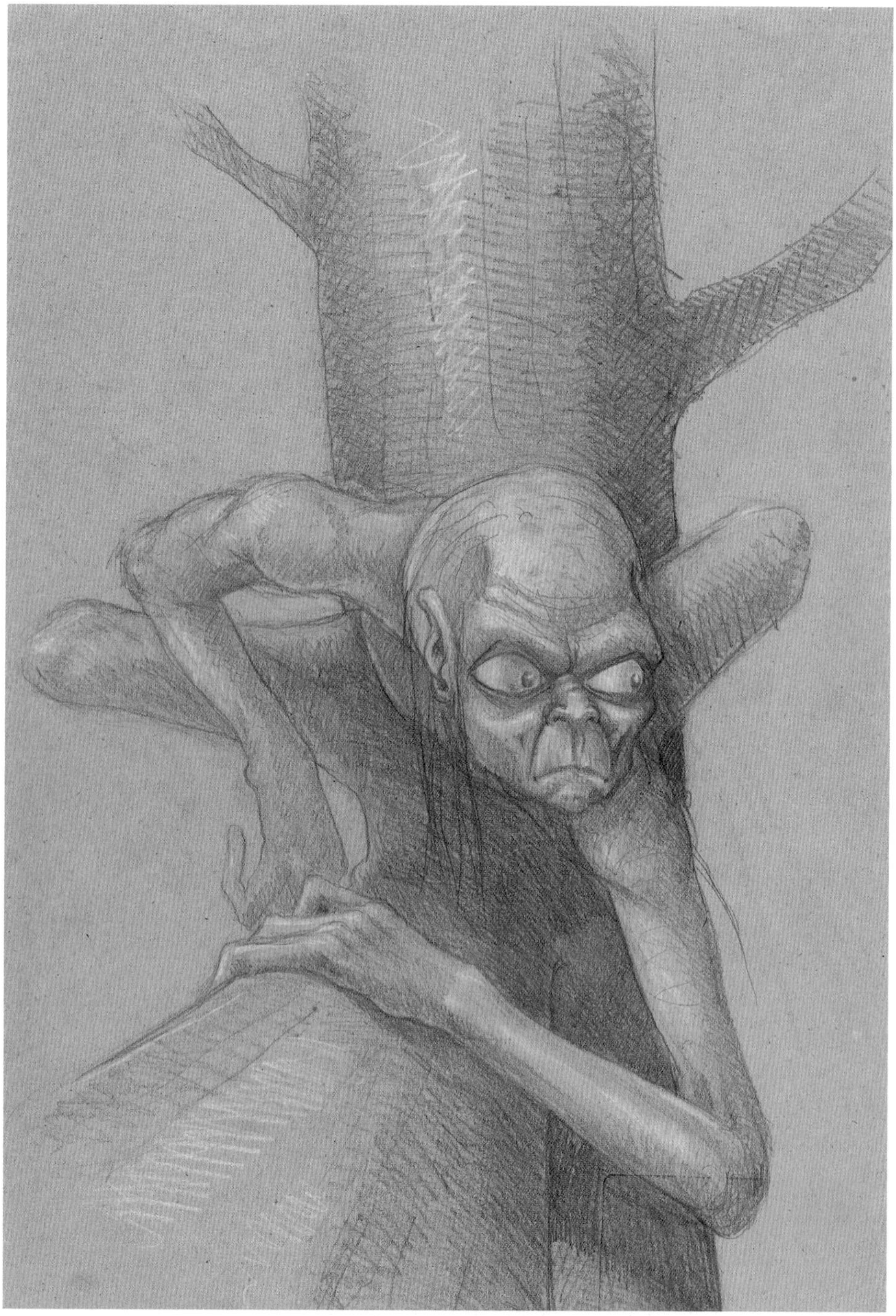

PIPPIN *Armor concept*

"Pippin swears allegiance to Denethor, but instead of being embraced with the same enthusiasm that Merry had been by Théoden, he's billeted out to Beregond. So the armor he ends up with is far more makeshift and hurriedly tailored for him than Merry's. These are basic Gondorian components cut down to his size. The leather tunic with the silver Tree on it and the beautiful little collar could easily be a pageboy's uniform. The chain skirt and sleeves could be trimmed down, and his cut-off breeches and leather armguard are all easily modifiable. It's not as beautiful, but still as logical, as the solution we came up with for Merry.

"Pippin is still wearing the Elven leaf brooch and he's still wearing the gray Elven cloak – a concession mentioned in the book, because they don't have cloaks his size. The helmet, frankly, was harder to justify. It carries the same black feathers as the Citadel Guard design of the time, giving him immediate status in Gondor, although he was still looked upon as a bit of a curiosity." *BW*

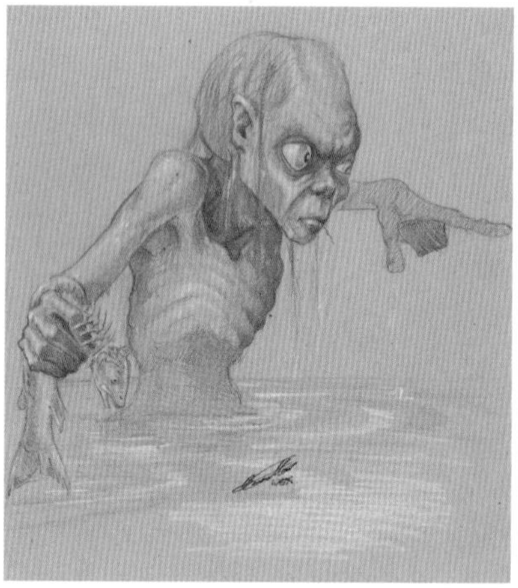

GOLLUM *Design sketches*

"I like this one of him on the tree branch. You can imagine him sneaking around Elven forests, just spying on people. He also looks a lot healthier in this picture. I imagined that it was probably earlier on in Gollum's story, where he's still in reasonably fertile lands, and there's plenty of bird's nests around, plenty of young rabbits, so he's probably quite well fed. Later, of course, when he hasn't eaten for days, and he won't eat the Elven food, he's quite drawn. That's a very strong feeling I took from the book, that toward the end it's sheer force of will that's keeping him alive. Clinically, he's probably dead!

"The idea of designing Gollum was a massive challenge, but I enjoyed taking it on. Because everyone has thought about him, everyone has a preconceived idea, so actually realizing the guy is incredibly difficult. And I think in that respect we were all keen to have a go and get our ideas out there, because obviously we all had differing views on what he looked like. The other thing that is cool about him is that he's probably the most tragic character in all the books. Tolkien doesn't write people's thoughts in his books, it's old saga-style, but you get inside Gollum's head because he's schizophrenic, he talks to himself. He's the only character whose thought processes you see working; I think that draws you to him as well." *BW*

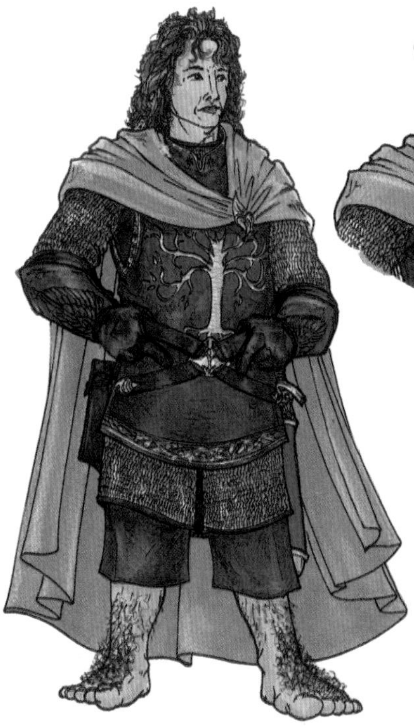

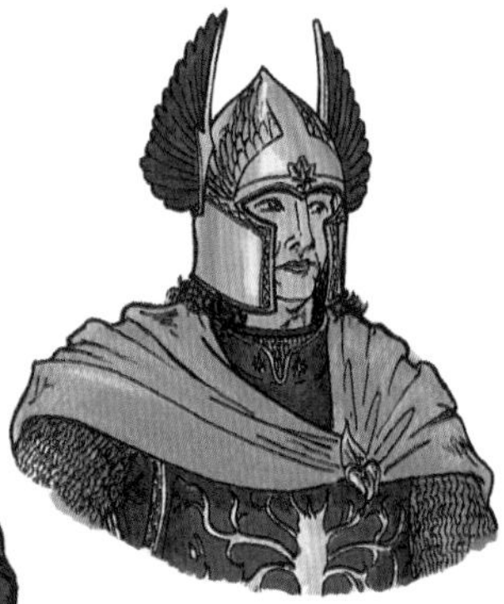

FOUNTAIN GUARD *Armor concept*
"One of the first drawings I did for anything to do with Gondor. It was an ink drawing done on the bus on my way to work. I used to spend an hour a day traveling, my sketching time. There are some ideas here that made it into the final design, such as the heavy shoulder pauldrons over the top of the black robes and the long chain skirt and long lines to the clothing. Lots of blue as well. It's quite a royal color; the pigment for blue is quite hard to find in nature, and without artificial dye, as we have nowadays, it's a very rare color, so it reeks of wealth and a strong civilization that's got the resources to waste on blue dye. It speaks volumes for the age and wealth of the culture." *BW*

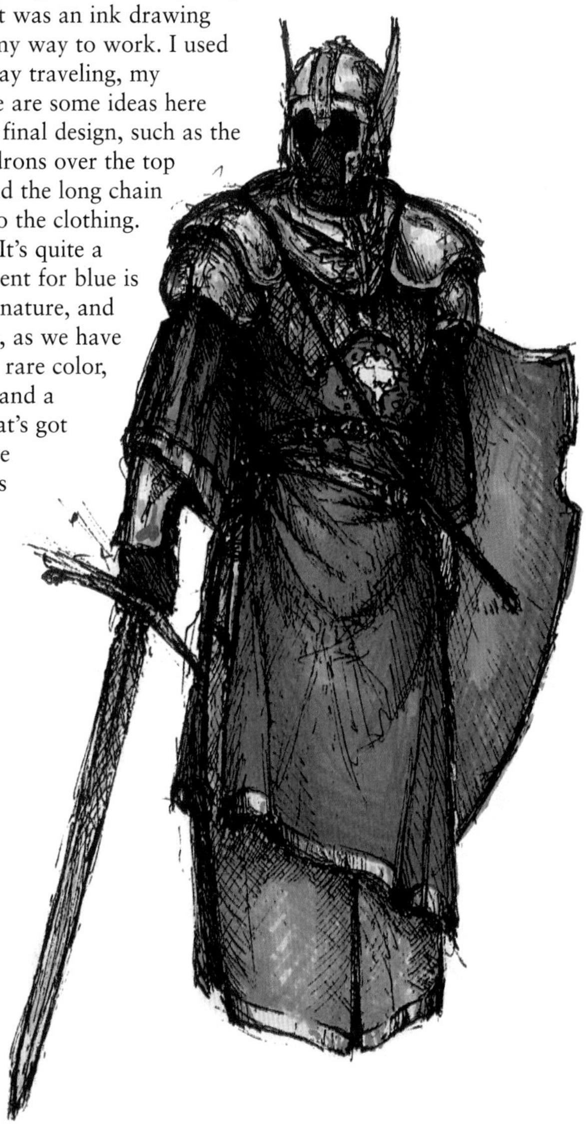

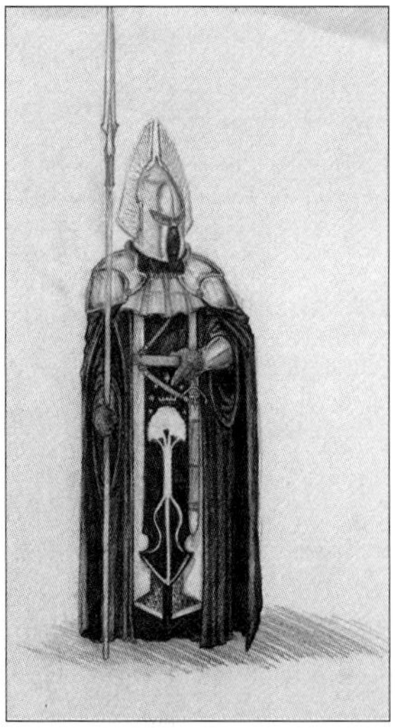

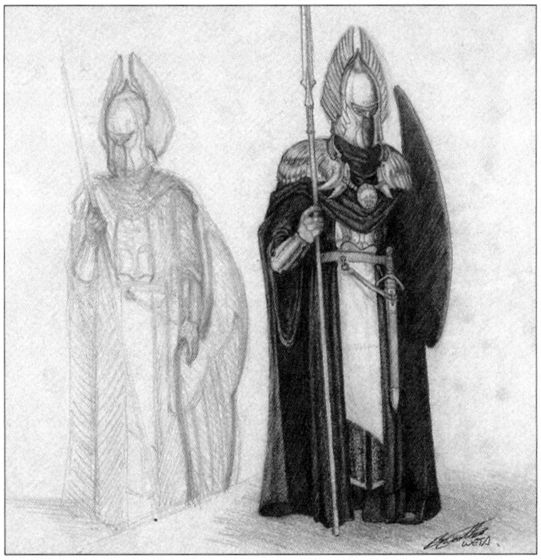

FOUNTAIN GUARD *Armor concepts*
"These later drawings of the Fountain Guard are pretty close to the final design. What works in both of these is the very strong vertical lines: the cloak, tabard, and chain-mail skirt that go right to the floor, obscuring their feet, so we see a pillar of strength in these figures. The heavy silvered pauldrons over the cloak combined with a tall helmet make them appear almost spearlike, or weaponlike, in themselves. Their proud crest of pure white swan feathers is also a bold statement. These men have sworn allegiance to a time gone by that may never return, but this is their job: they're guarding the dead tree, they're guarding the Fountain Court, and they will do so with their lives. We made them even more dangerous and aloof by covering their faces with a black face mask. There is no bargaining with these people; they are like the Beefeaters: they don't move, they don't speak. This is their life; no one is more zealous than these guys.

"I drew them having a short sword. It was nice, as it was different from the longsword you see the other troops carrying and would be used only if someone got past their polearms. However, it was decided it looked a little weak, and so to further complete the vertical line we gave them a longsword, but rather than hanging at an angle like most swords, it hangs straight down at the hip. The shield we can see in the right-hand picture was replaced with a longer, more elegant version of the standard shield, with a different emblem on it. Rather than the wing shape, it is more of a traditional, but taller, Gondorian shield design." *BW*

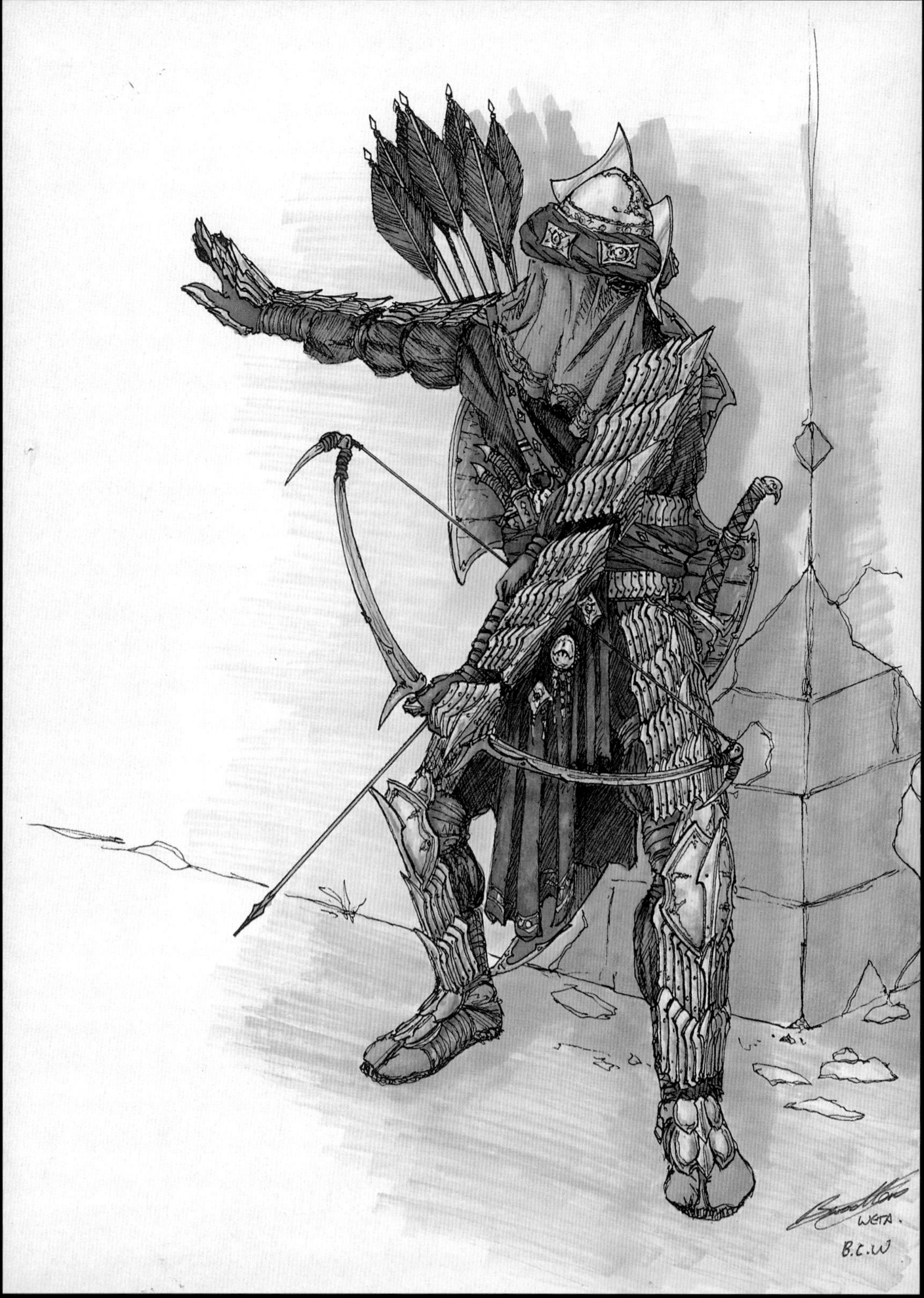

EASTERLING *Color sketch*

"I came in after the initial round of drawings had been done, so there was already a direction that Peter Jackson liked. The heavy-lamed look, the buildup of lots of small lames. He liked the sharp shapes. And he liked the eastern feel. So, it was basically just exploring some of those options – trying some other shapes for the lames and exploring the directions that Pete liked. Going through a lot of the Oriental books I noticed that indigo blue is a color they wear quite a lot. In the book the Easterlings are described as wearing gold and red, which are really easy colors to pick out highlights on, so I just gave them another color that they might wear underneath their gold and red – a pigment that might work well in a desert." *BW*

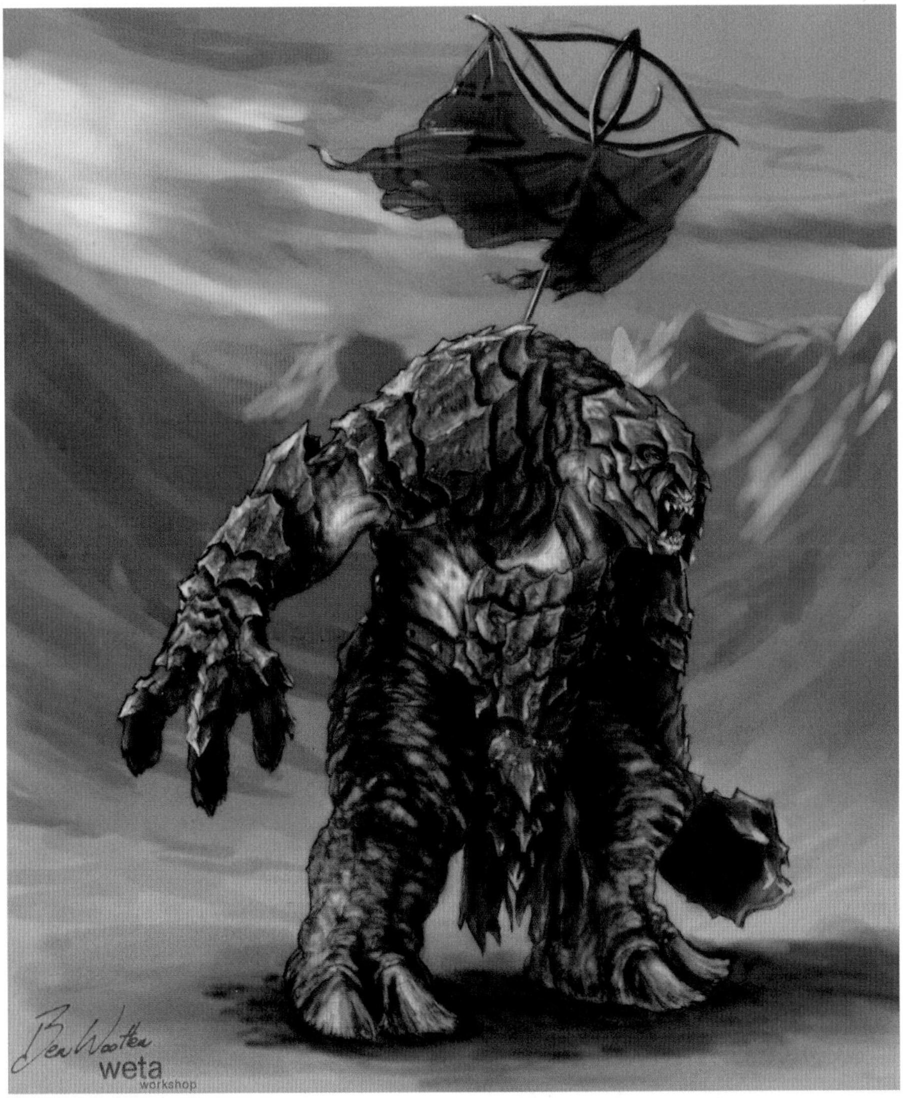

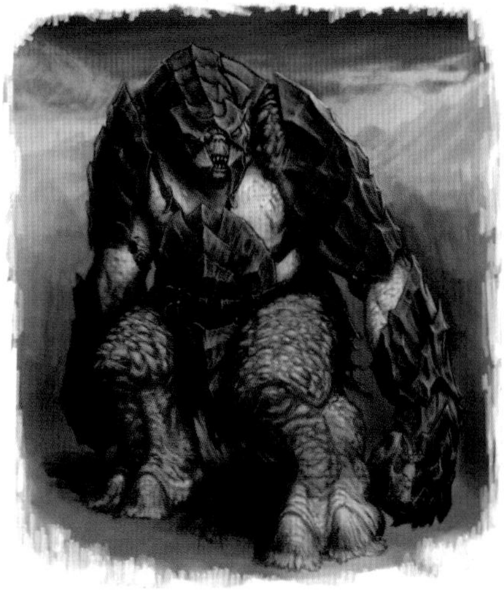

OLOG-HAI *Concepts*
"These were very obviously drawn recently, using digital coloring. It was great to go back and revisit some of our earlier design concepts with a fresher and maybe a slightly more educated mind." *BW*

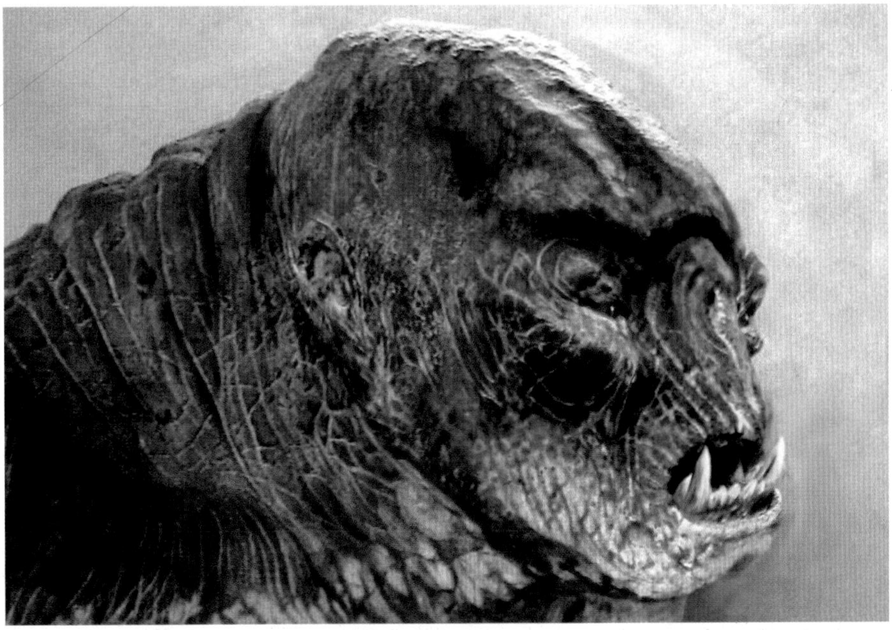

MOUNTAIN-TROLL *Concept*
"We were looking at modifying the trolls slightly from the ones we saw in the first two films to make them bigger and uglier. So this is a Photoshop job, based on a photo of the original cave-troll sculpture. What I've done is resculpt the face in Photoshop, making it more angular, harder, and more dangerous. The eyes are smaller, slightly slanted, and he's got bigger teeth, while the bone structure through the face and the cheekbones and the brow is a lot more severe. I've also darkened him so he looks more rocklike, more like Tolkien's description in the book." *BW*

FARAMIR *Armor concept*
"This was close to the final design of Faramir's armor. It's very similar to the standard Gondor armor, although more ornate and slightly finer in cut. There are more lines in the chest plate, and it has gold trim, but with the very recognizable symbol of the Tree and the seven stars. Faramir's not a man of pomp and ceremony; if he's leading troops he wants armor that's going to protect him. It doesn't have to be flashy. What we did decide is that he has to stand out, and not just for filmic purposes; on the battlefield he has to be able to rally his troops quickly, he needs to be easily seen. So we chose a different color for his cloth, which was green, which suits him in his dual role as captain of the Rangers. Another symbol of Gondor that we adopted as Faramir's personal emblem is the twin ravens: we see these on his greaves, above the noseguard, and on the shield. It's also on the cross-guard of his sword, but we can't see it in this drawing. The armor is beautiful without being complex, because Faramir is all about form and function." *BW*

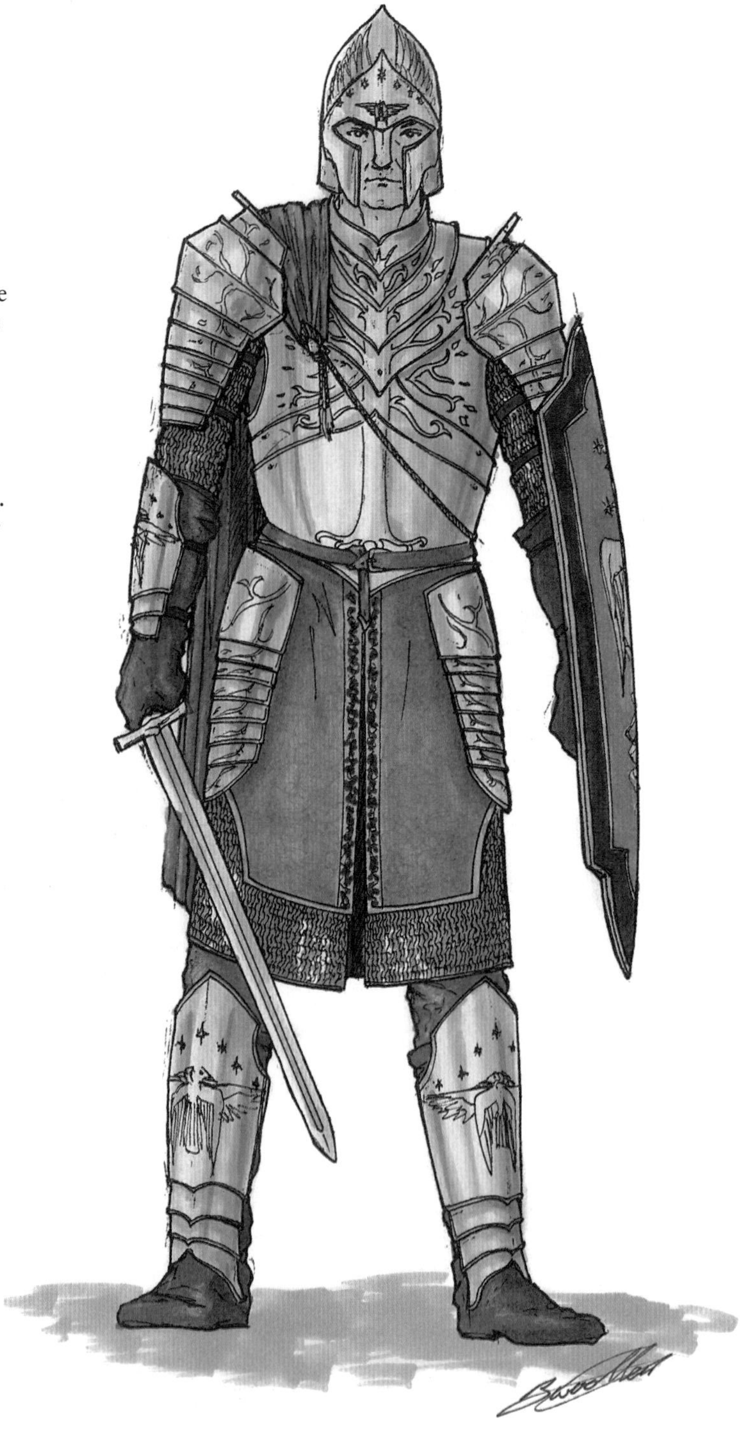

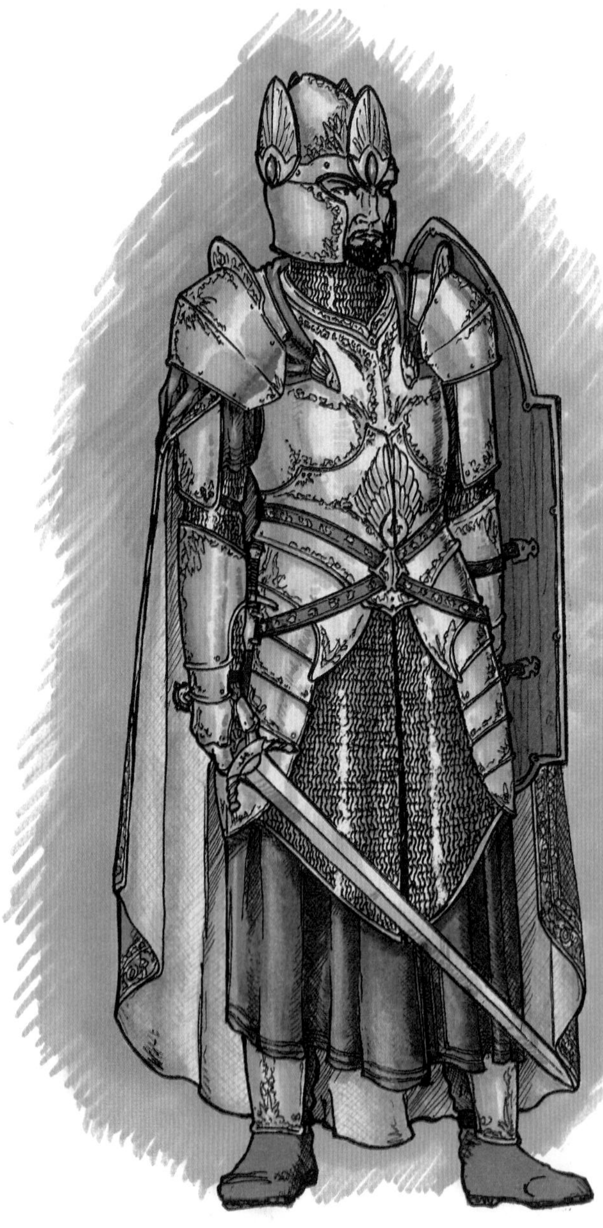

FARAMIR *Armor concept*
"This was originally an unused Elendil design, for the first film, but we considered it again for Faramir's armor. Its lineage from the prologue armor designs is obvious, and because of that we decided it was probably too fancy for Faramir. The edges of the cloak are richly embroidered, which on one level would befit the second son of the Steward of Gondor, but it doesn't suit the character of Faramir. He's not a man of great flourish and show of wealth; he's a simpler, more honest man than that." *BW*

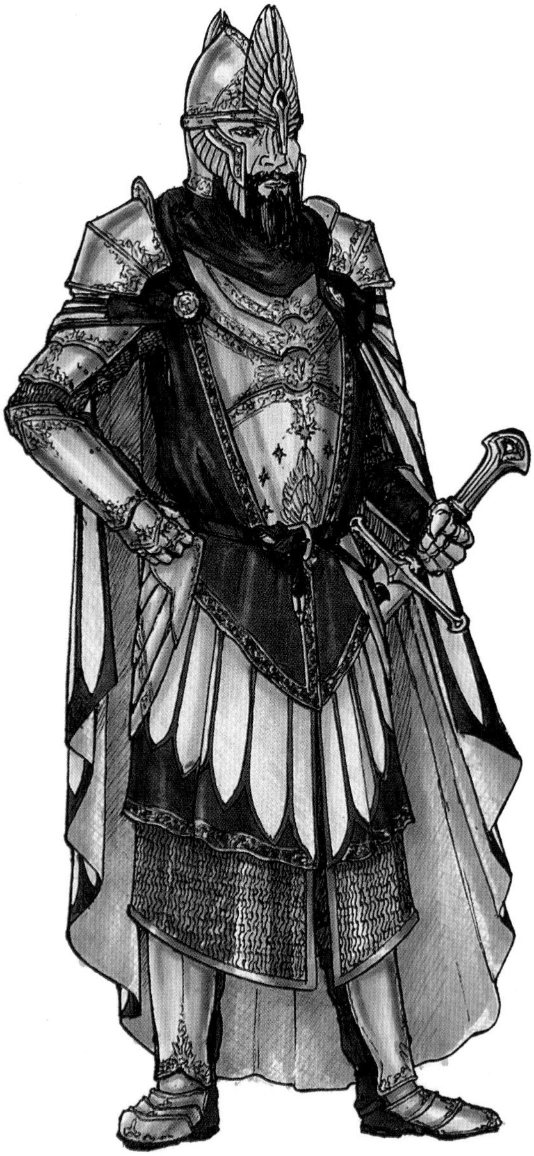

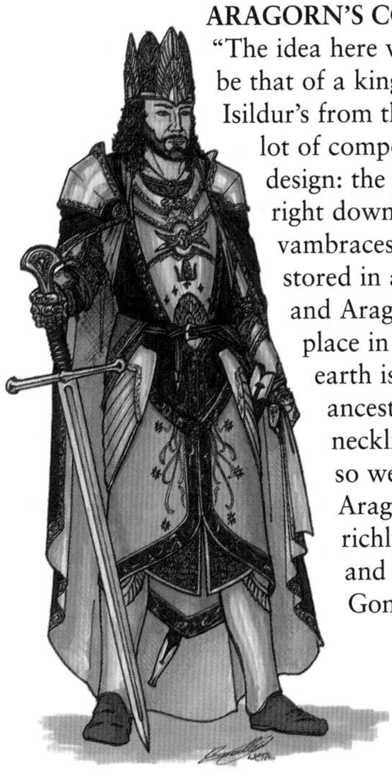

ARAGORN'S CORONATION *Conceptual design*
"The idea here was to cut a figure that could only be that of a king. The crown is the same shape as Isildur's from the prologue. In fact we've used a lot of components from Isildur's armor in this design: the pauldrons, breastplate, tassets, right down to the greaves, gloves, and vambraces. This armor has probably been stored in a vault, maintained and polished, and Aragorn's eventual acceptance of his place in the continuing history of Middle-earth is signified by his wearing his ancestor's armor. We lowered the high neckline of the armor as worn by Isildur so we could see the Evenstar still around Aragorn's neck, and developed some richly embroidered cloth of various cuts and colors, as would befit a king of Gondor." *BW*

ELENDIL *Conceptual design*
Ben adapted an idea by Daniel Falconer that made use of a feathered motif in the cloak to mirror the design of the helmet. Taking this through another couple of stages, he ended up with what was, except for one or two minor costume changes, the final image of Elendil as seen in *The Fellowship of the Ring*. *BW*

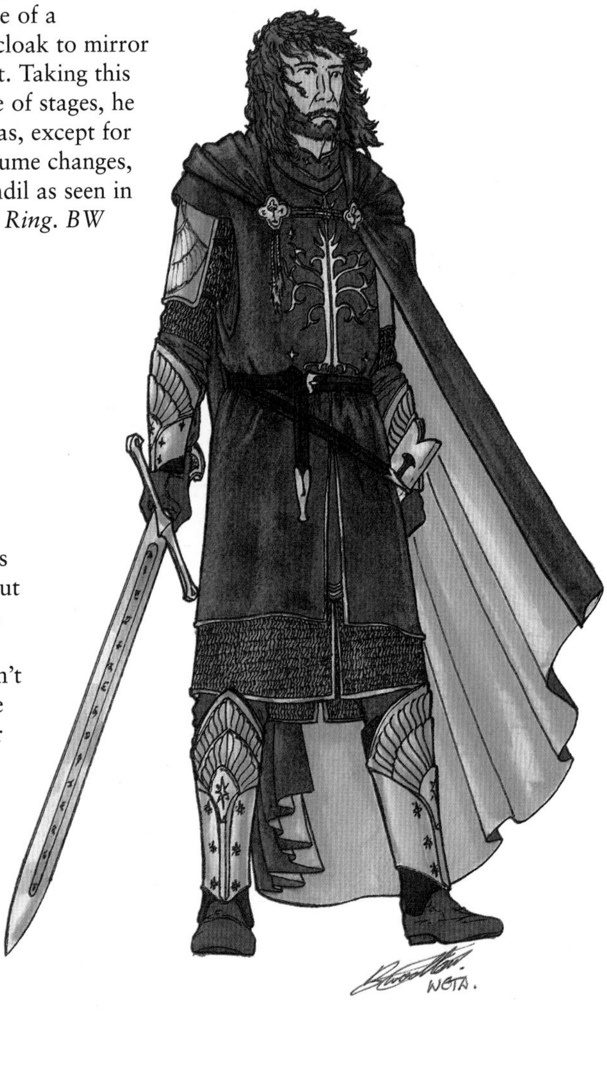

ARAGORN AT THE BLACK GATES *Conceptual design*
"This is the first time that Aragorn is seen as the true commander of his troops, and the first time we recognize him not just as a heroic figure but as the sovereign of Gondor. He has accepted the sword of his ancestors earlier in the film and now he's begun to dress like the king of Gondor. Here we can see the Tree symbol but not the crown – Aragorn still hasn't announced himself as the king, so it's just the seven stars and the White Tree. We can see here familiar imagery from Elendil and Isildur's armor from the Second Age. It's evident in the picture on the right, where we can see in the greaves and the vambraces the familiar wing fluting and almost spearhead-shaped design from Elendil and Isildur's armor. The brooch holding his cloak on is the same shape and design as Elendil's. The color red is also a color we see Elendil and Isildur wearing. So it's the first time we're beginning to see Aragorn as the man he's going to become." *BW*

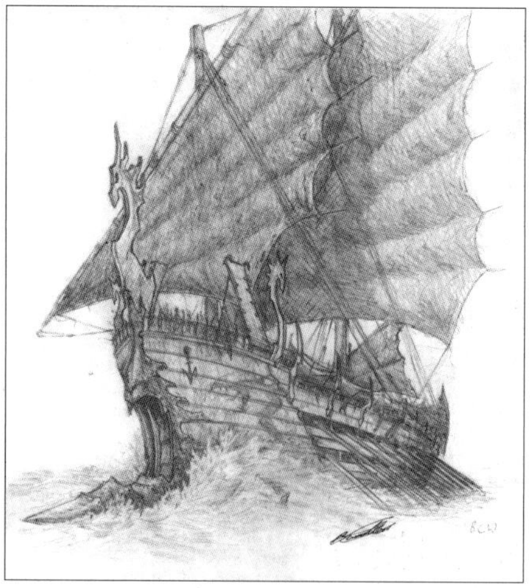

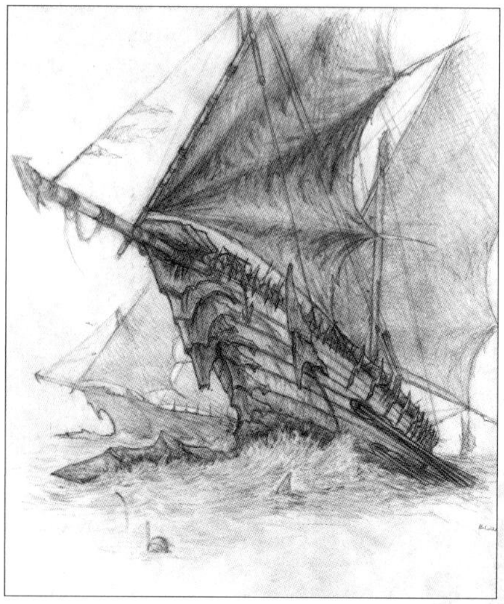

CORSAIR SHIPS *Conceptual designs*
"Peter Jackson liked the design of the sketch at top left; he just wanted to get more of a feel for the size of it, so I drew it from the waterline. Both drawings have a strong mouthlike feel, with the prow overhanging this large ram, making it seem very predatory. If this boat rammed yours, you would be stuck there until it decided you were leaving. It's a pirate vessel, so it needs to look incredibly dangerous, very sleek, and very fast. They carry a huge amount of sail, a Latin design, almost Arabic, but with the sails of a junk to give them a very distinctive silhouette and shape in the wind – almost like shark fins." *BW*

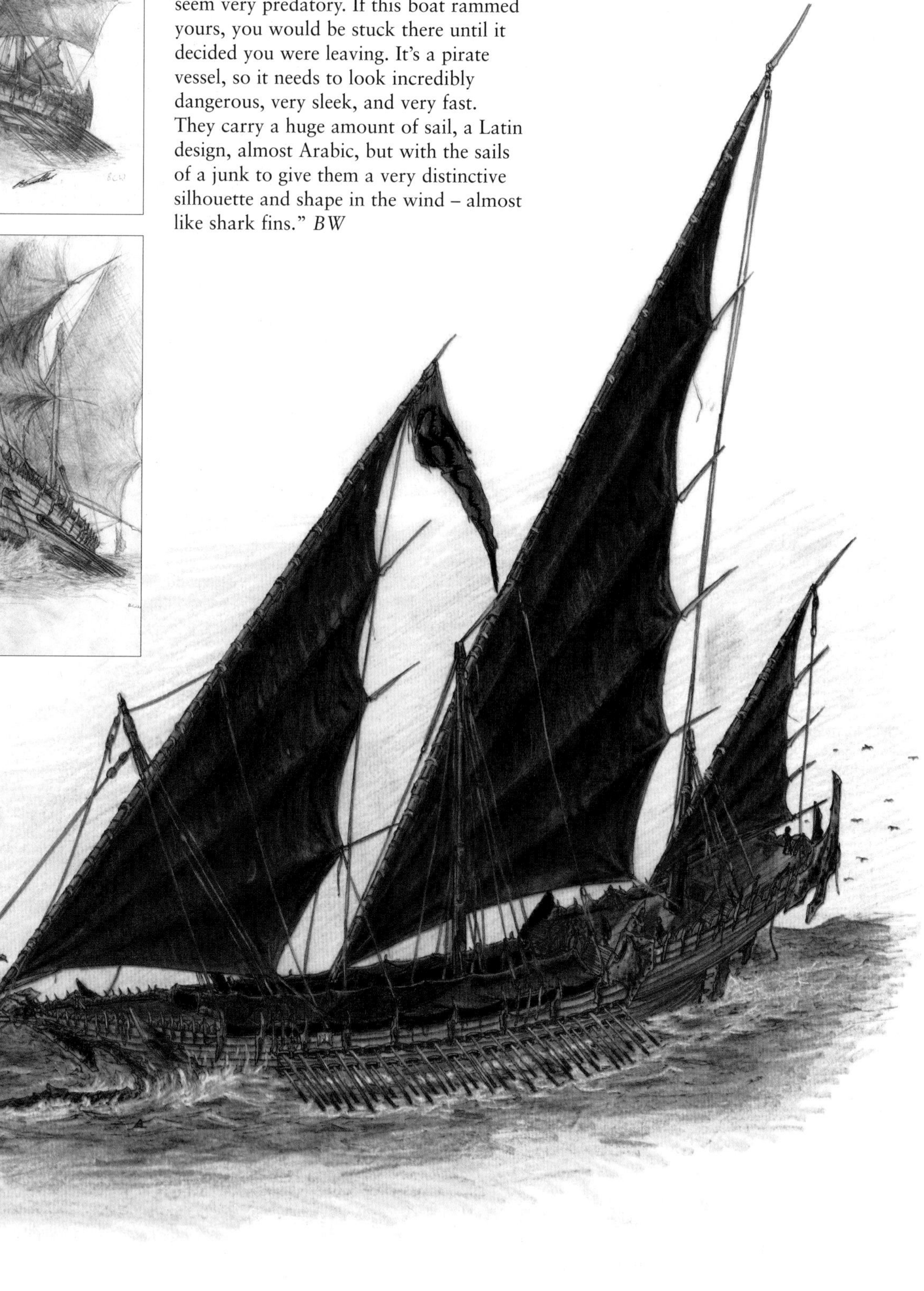

THE WITCH-KING ***Conceptual sketch***
"A very early Witch-king idea. You can see a lot of Dungeons and Dragons influence in the armor design of this. This is definitely pre–John Howe, probably within the first month of design on the project. It's a good piece, though, and there are elements that I think have a nice feeling, but nothing like what we ultimately wanted for *The Return of the King*." *BW*

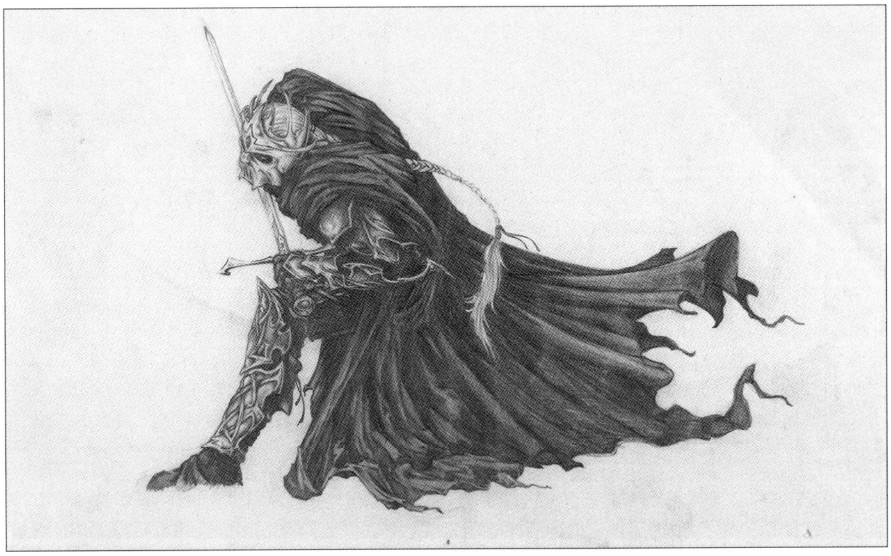

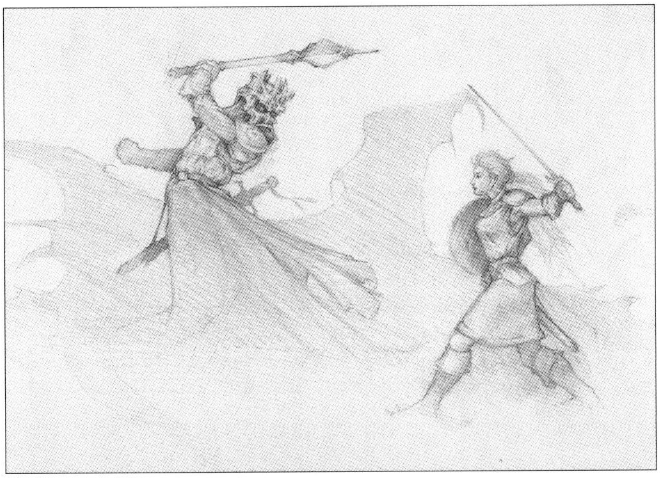

ÉOWYN VERSUS THE WITCH-KING ***Conceptual sketch***
"This was a more illustrative look at the situation, and I think the movement and intent of the Witch-king in this picture are nice. And in the crashed heap of fell beast behind him we can see the wings and ribs splayed up from the wreckage – bear in mind that this is a creature the size of an aircraft. Éowyn looks a little too relaxed for the situation, perhaps because she hasn't quite taken stock of what's going to happen – she could be a bit more dynamic. The fact that he's wielding a mace that size in just one hand and towering above her, unnaturally tall in spite of the bend in his figure, these are elements that I like. At the time I did this, I was quite pleased with it. Now, not so much, but it's still good fun." *BW*

ELVEN SWAN SHIP ***Conceptual design***
"This is a design for an Elven boat found at the Grey Havens. I used an Egyptian influence here with the high bow and stern, and the steering rudders very high up on the little aft deck. This was a larger ship than the one they went with in the end: I was looking at the oceangoing qualities of the vessel, because they're sailing to the Undying Lands, so it's big, with a large sail area, but still graceful. It has a strong swan motif running through it from the curled neck at the bow, almost a figurehead, to the wing shape halfway down the side. I wanted something very elegant and very beautiful, and although it has a Middle Eastern feel it does not seem like a boat of this earth. We can see echoes of Rivendell in the cabin's structure, and if we look closely at midship, just above the wing, we can see a couple of people standing at the rail, giving a sense of its size." *BW*

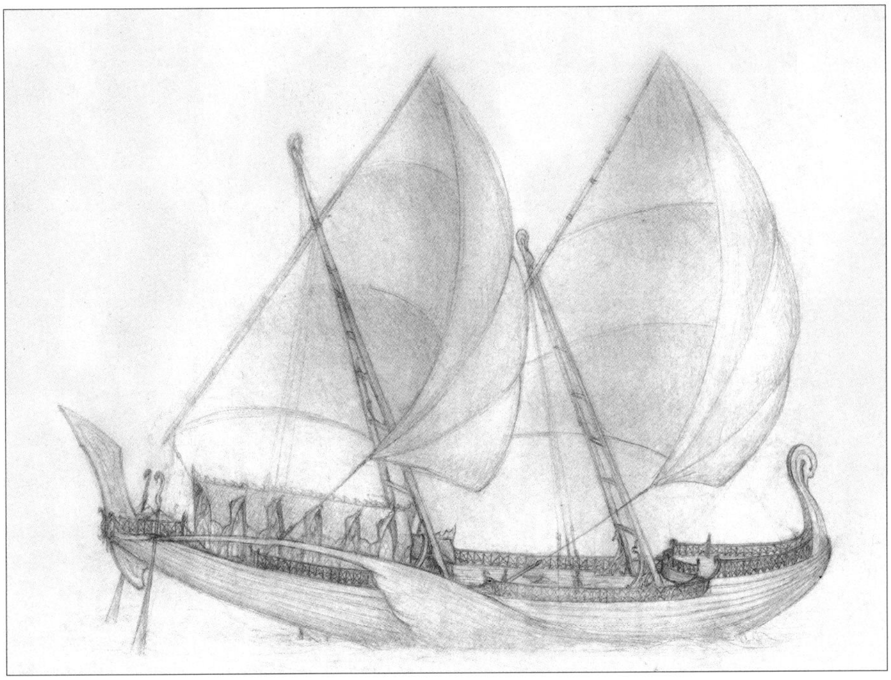

WARREN MAHY

I went to school with Ben Wootten, right from primary school, intermediate, and all the rest of it. Then he went away to university, and I didn't see him for ten years, but one day he contacted me and said there was a project that was happening that I should be involved with. Other than doing stuff at school with Ben, I never trained, didn't go to art school, and in fact I'd ended up being a printer. He said that he thought it was still worth my sending down any work that I had to Richard Taylor here at Weta. So I did, and Richard brought me into the design team. I hadn't read the books for maybe ten years or so – I had read them at school, but as soon as I knew what the project was I read them again.

The great thing about the team here was that, if there wasn't any design work to do, you could do other stuff – Richard would get you fiberglassing, or carving poly, or going out molding trees or picking leaves or something. I've basically had a paid apprenticeship in the last five years – in filmmaking!

Because I was quite happy to be onset as well, just as a set dresser, I spent some time on one of the mountains where they were filming. So if Richard wanted anything designed there, he could grab me; in this way I ended up designing Sauron's sword on top of a mountain, on the back of somebody's call sheet. I remember I was just sitting in the snow, looking down at Richard and Peter Jackson, who had just starting filming, and thinking, "This is cool! This is a good job!"

Warren Mahy
April 2002

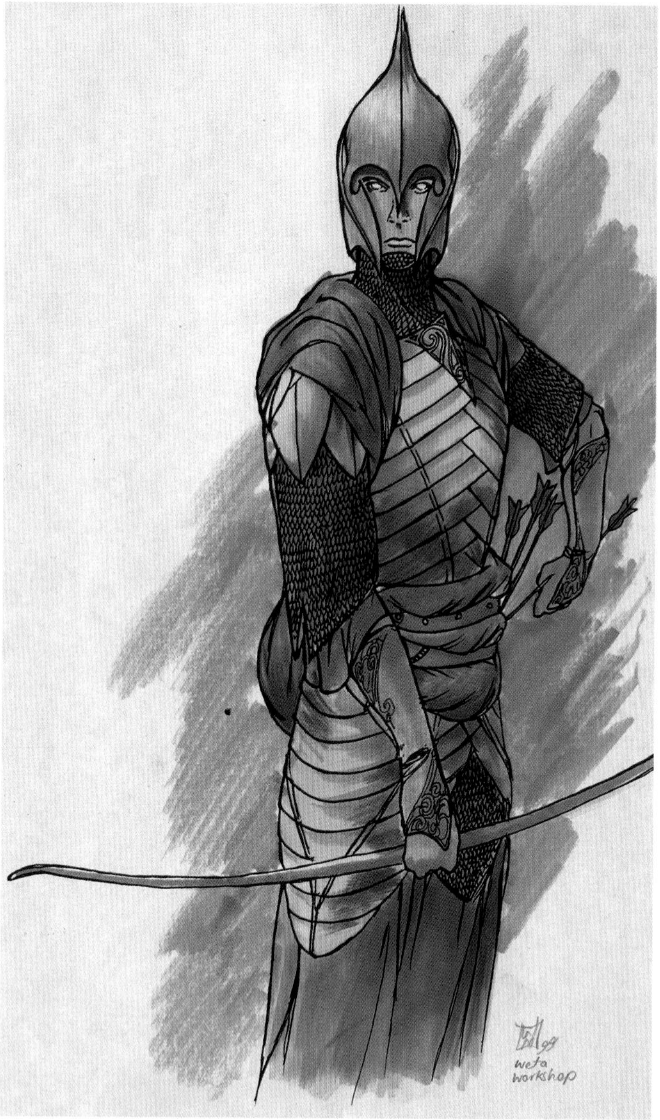

GIL-GALAD *Early conceptual design*
The color scheme was drawn from the heraldry and colors of the generic High-elven armor but was intensified to enable the character to stand out in the battle scenes. Warren created the Second Age weaponry for Gil-galad's troops as well as the encasing armor worn by the army in battle.

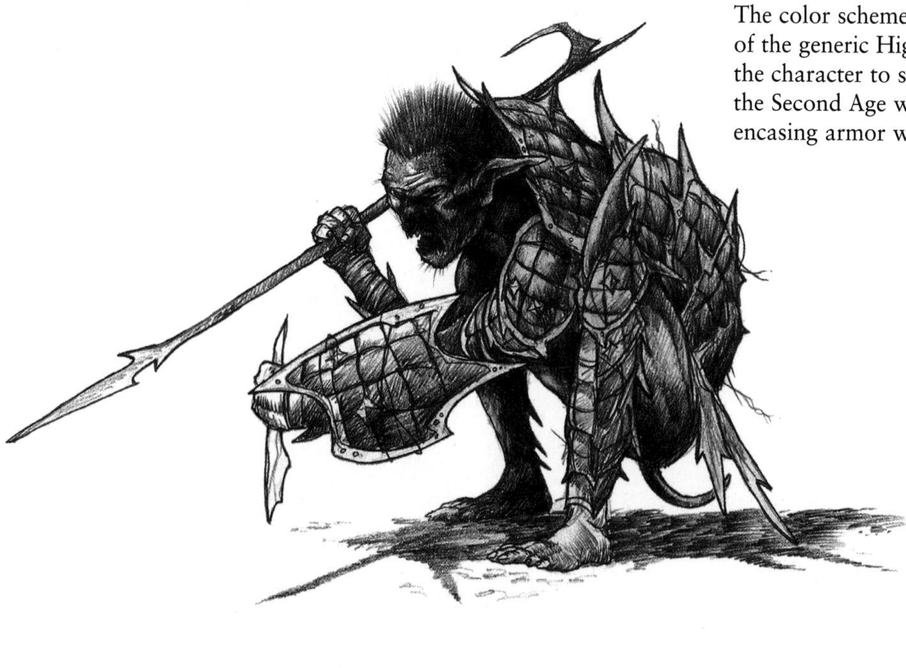

MORIA ORCS *Conceptual sketch*

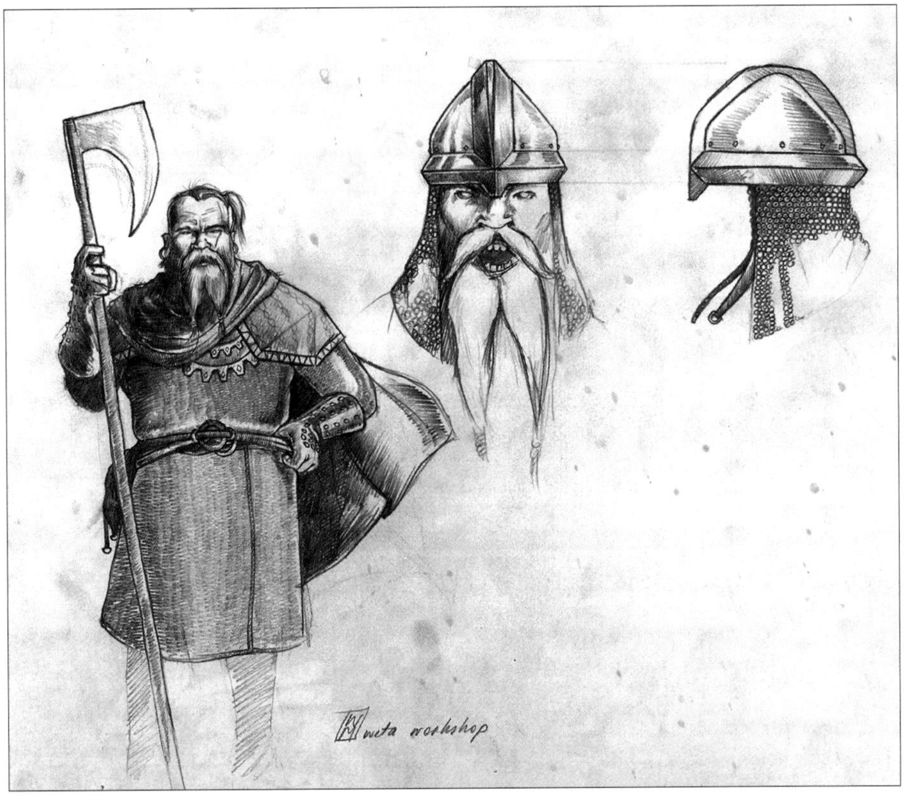

DWARVES *Conceptual sketches*
Warren used a series of geometric shapes to suggest the precision and solidity of the Dwarven armor.

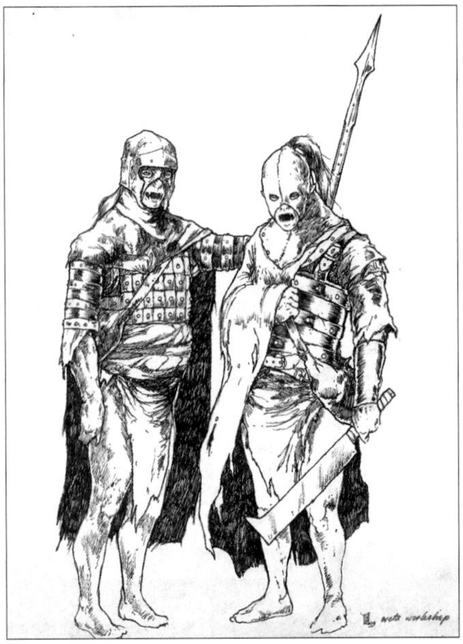

URUK-HAI *Armor sketches*
These are early ideas for Uruk-hai armor, focusing on the covering of their faces.

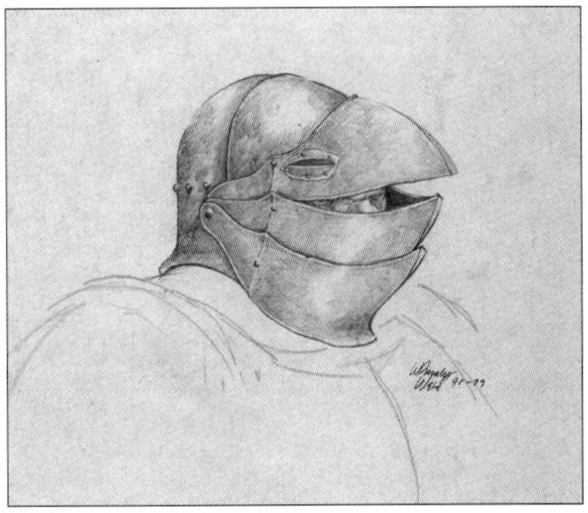

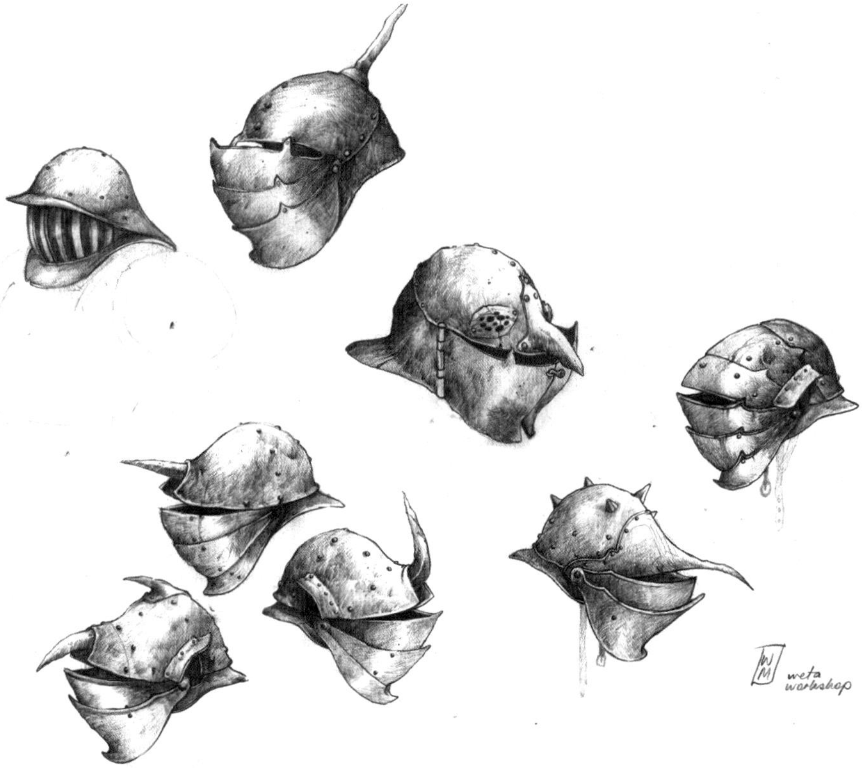

ORC HELMETS *Conceptual sketches*
"There was a big push to do a whole range of Orc helmets quickly, so I had a chance to spend a week or so just designing helmets. I wanted them to be practical, but the ones with the pointed nasal weren't – mainly because the stunt guys could barely see." *WM*

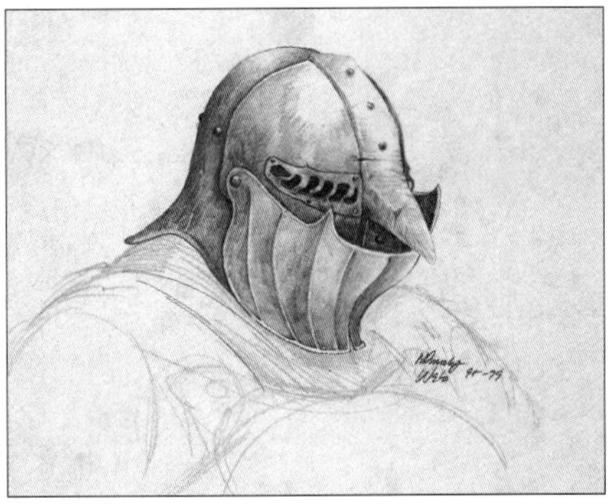

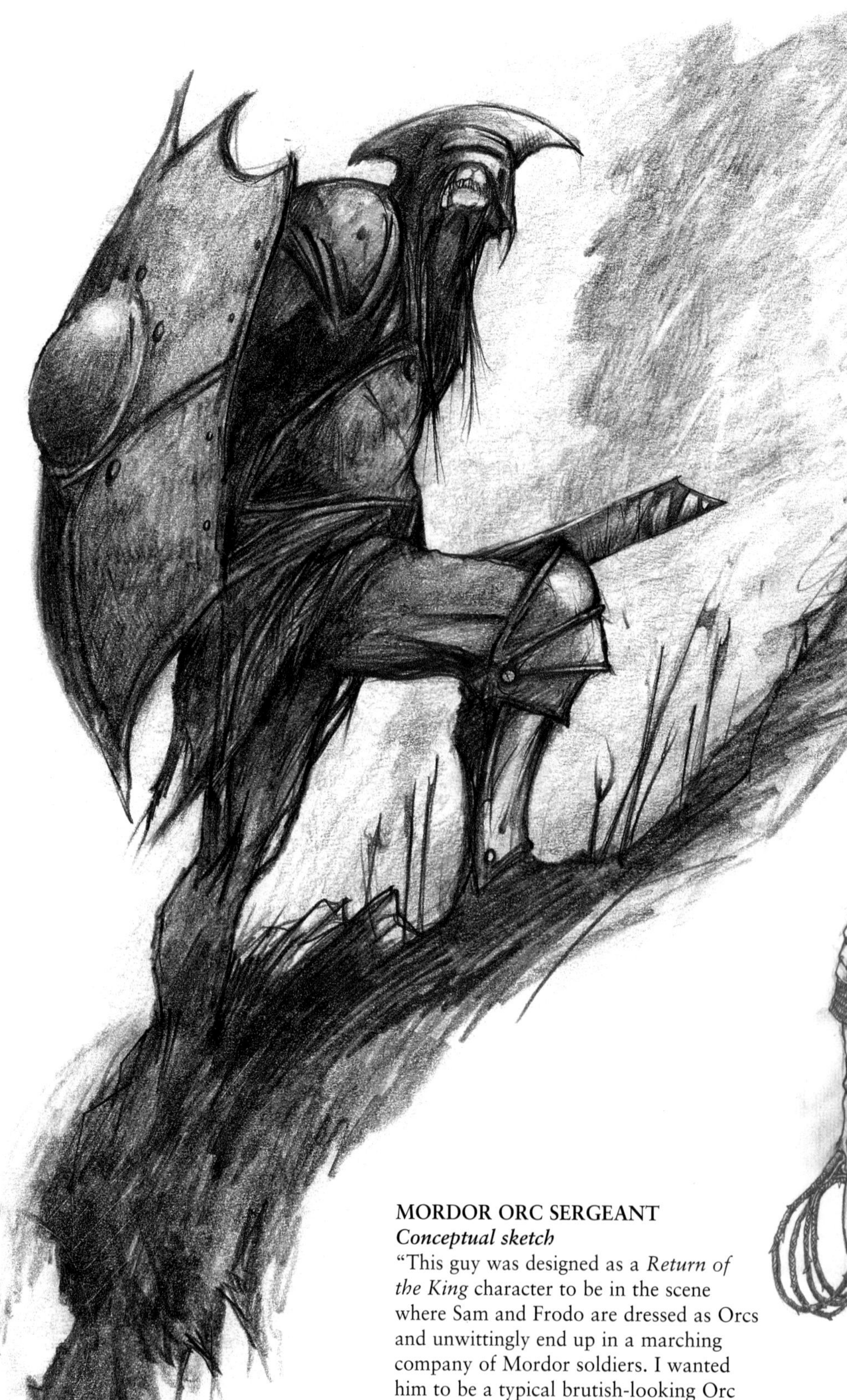

URUK-HAI ARMY
Conceptual sketch
"This is one of the final Uruk-hai drawings I did. I love the concept of the helmet covering the eyes of the Uruk – it's a very scary look." *WM*

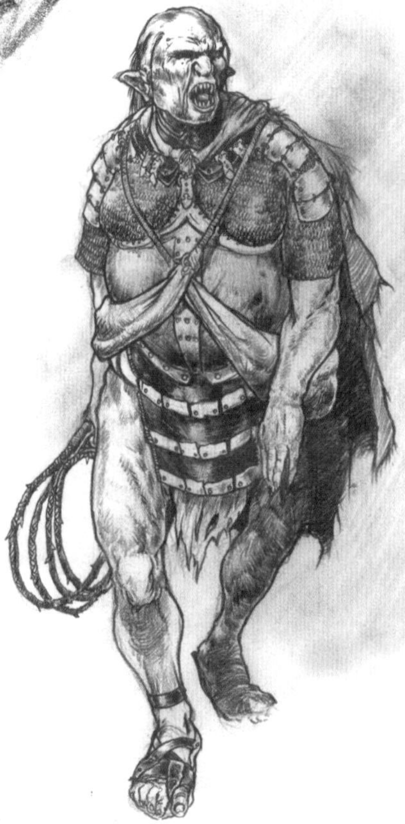

MORDOR ORC SERGEANT
Conceptual sketch
"This guy was designed as a *Return of the King* character to be in the scene where Sam and Frodo are dressed as Orcs and unwittingly end up in a marching company of Mordor soldiers. I wanted him to be a typical brutish-looking Orc who would have no problem using his whip for discussing problems. He ended up being my favorite Orc character in the film trilogy." *WM*

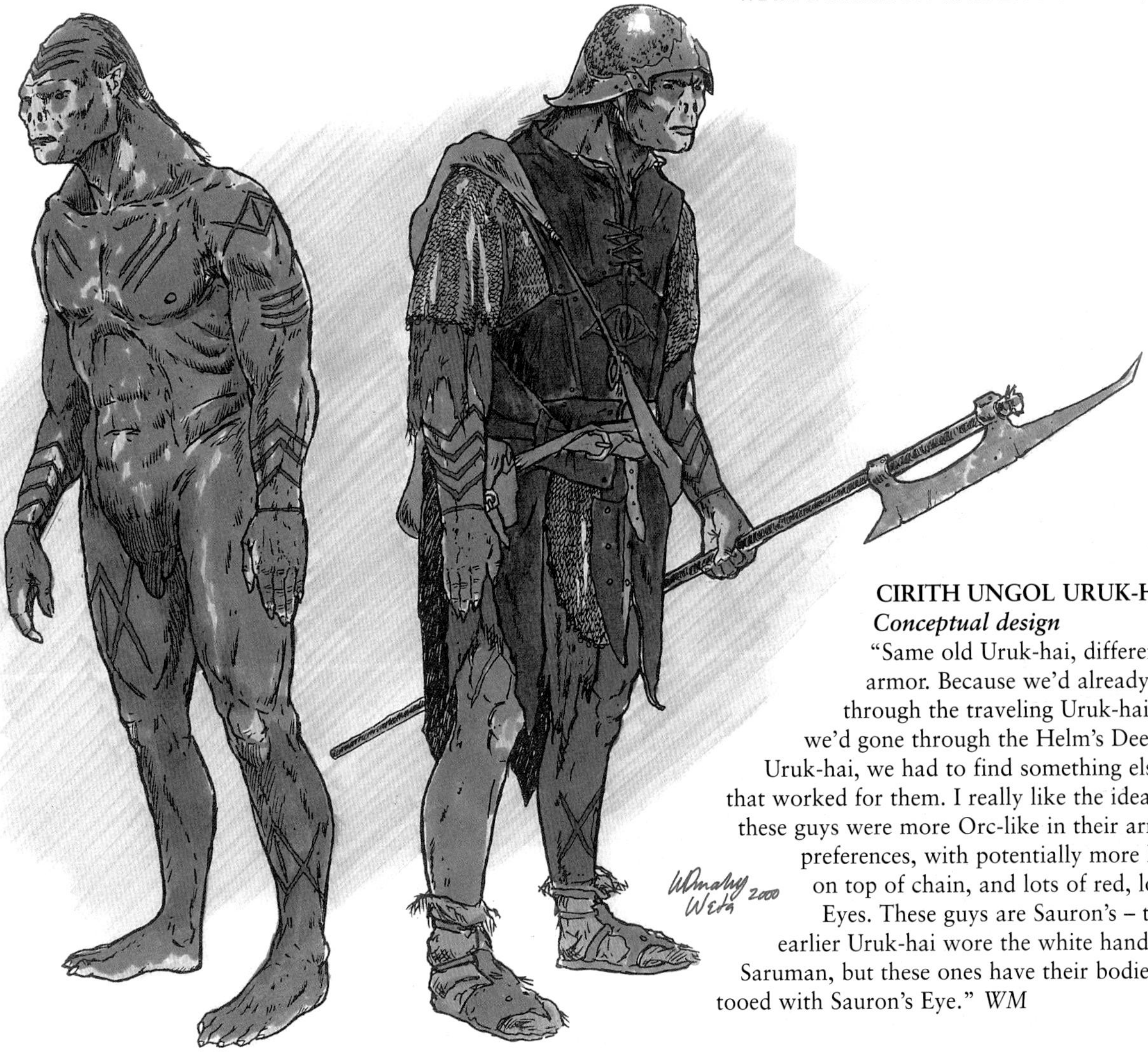

CIRITH UNGOL URUK-HAI
Conceptual design
"Same old Uruk-hai, different armor. Because we'd already gone through the traveling Uruk-hai, and we'd gone through the Helm's Deep Uruk-hai, we had to find something else that worked for them. I really like the idea that these guys were more Orc-like in their armor preferences, with potentially more leather on top of chain, and lots of red, lots of Eyes. These guys are Sauron's – the earlier Uruk-hai wore the white hand of Saruman, but these ones have their bodies tattooed with Sauron's Eye." *WM*

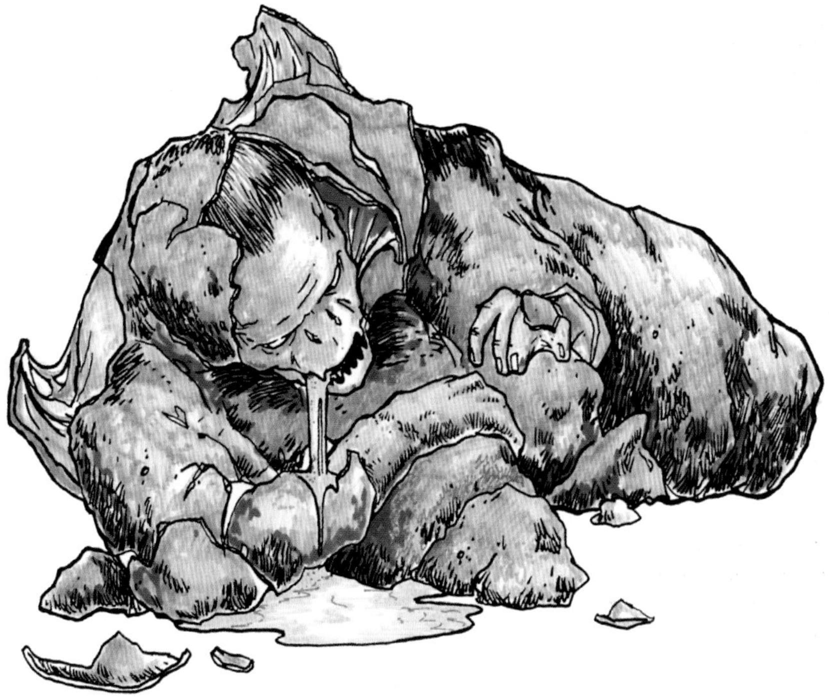

URUK-HAI BIRTHING
Conceptual design
This shows an Uruk-hai emerging from its sac. *WM*

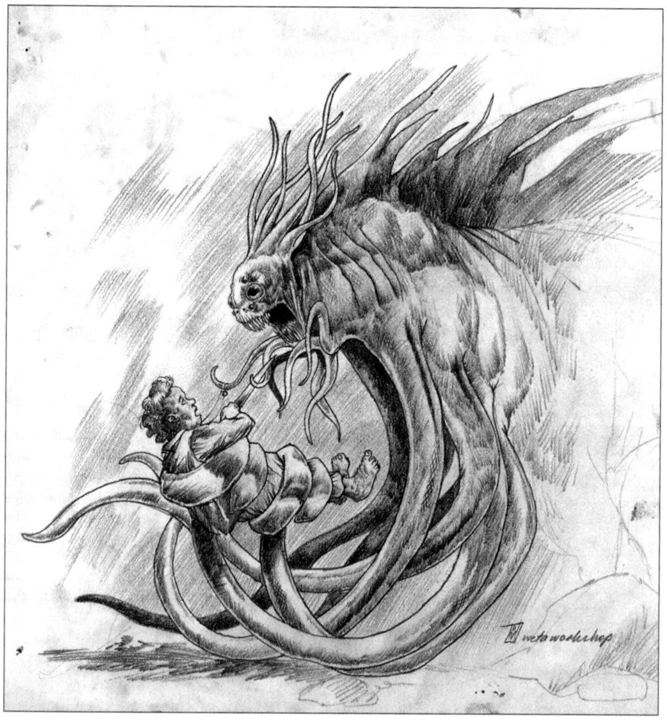

THE WATCHER *Conceptual sketch*
This sketch emphasizes the mouth and tentacles to create a nightmarish vision.

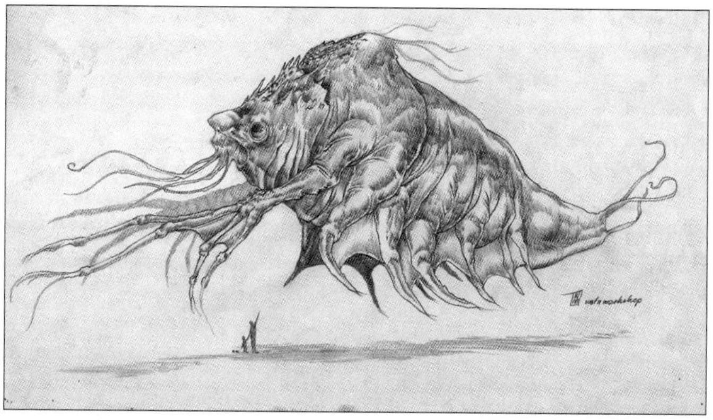

THE WATCHER *Conceptual sketch*
This shows the possible scale of the Watcher against two of the Fellowship underneath.

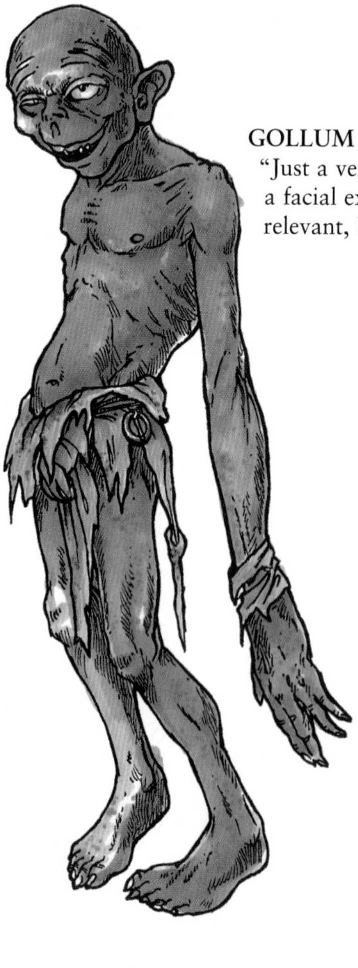

GOLLUM *Conceptual sketch*
"Just a very quick Gollum to show a facial expression – not especially relevant, but still fun to draw!" *WM*

ENTS
Conceptual sketch
"I think I was drawing sketches of the Warg at the time, so I didn't have a lot to do with the Ents, mainly because Dan Falconer had got it so right from the beginning. This one is a very slim-looking Ent." *WM*

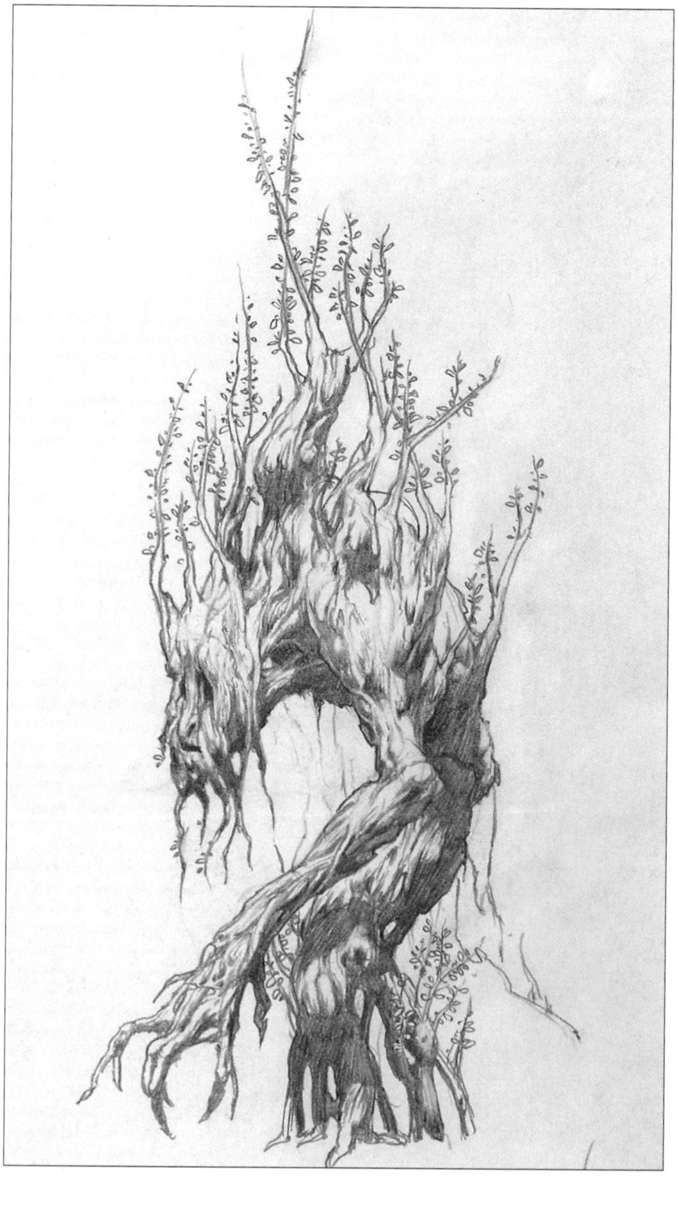

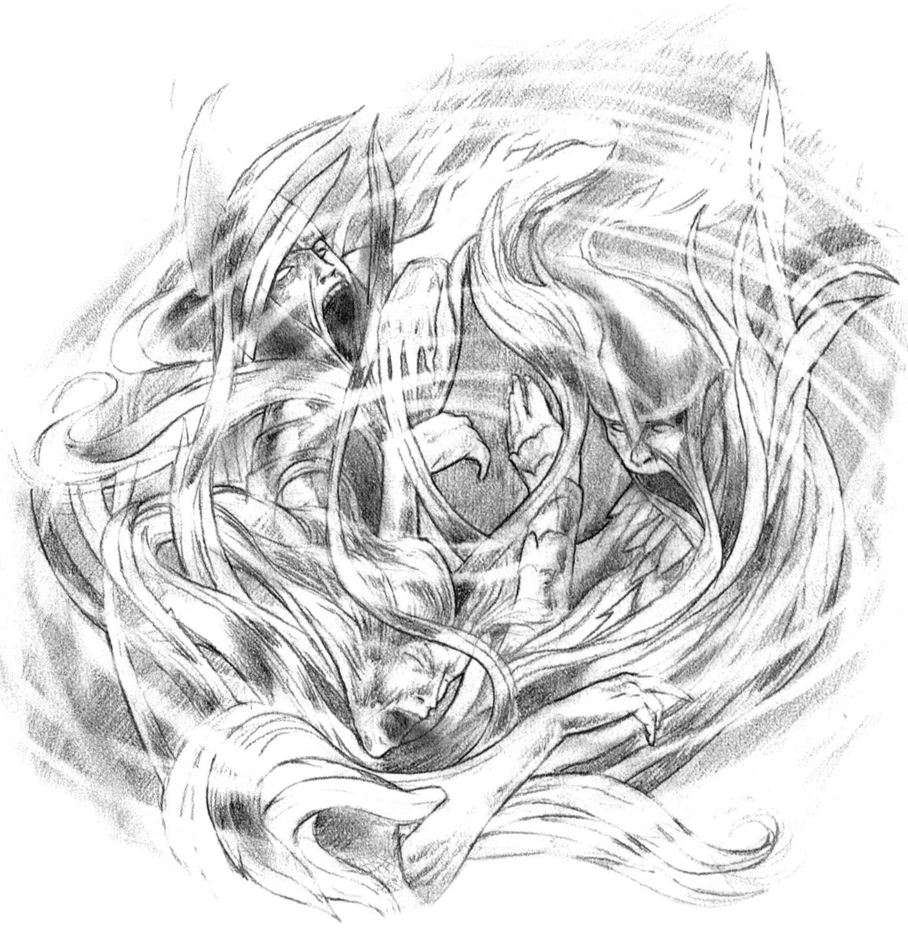

SPECTRAL CORPSES
Conceptual sketch
"Frodo is way down in the reeds, and he's trying to fight his way out, but he's been surrounded by these shapes. I can imagine that the eddies in the water would change the shapes quite often. Potentially at one moment it could be a Gondorian spectral image in front of him, and then it's an Orc, and so on. Actually, that's not true, because Peter Jackson had talked a lot about the fact that he didn't want Orcs in there – he didn't want to confuse people into thinking that the Orcs were chasing him under the water. So we just concentrated on Elven and Gondorian-type characters." *WM*

SPECTRAL CORPSES
Conceptual sketches
"Two sketches that give an idea of the corpses' facial expressions and what it would be like seeing the faces close up. The one below is viewed looking down into the water from the top. Both show how the light would be reflected in the eyes, and the distance to the surface of the water." *WM*

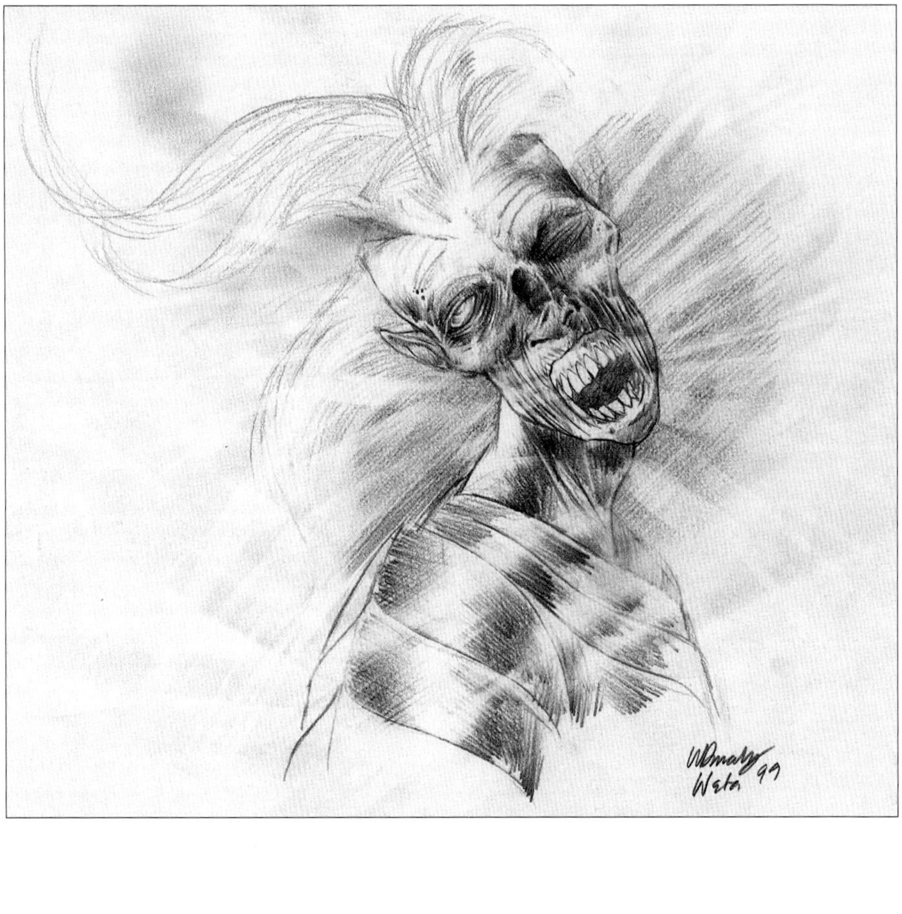

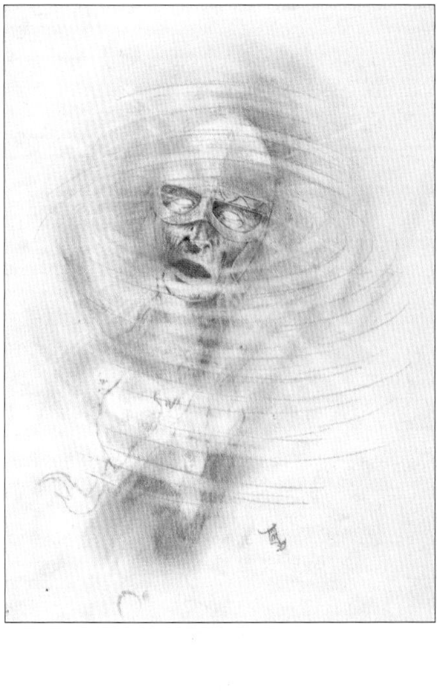

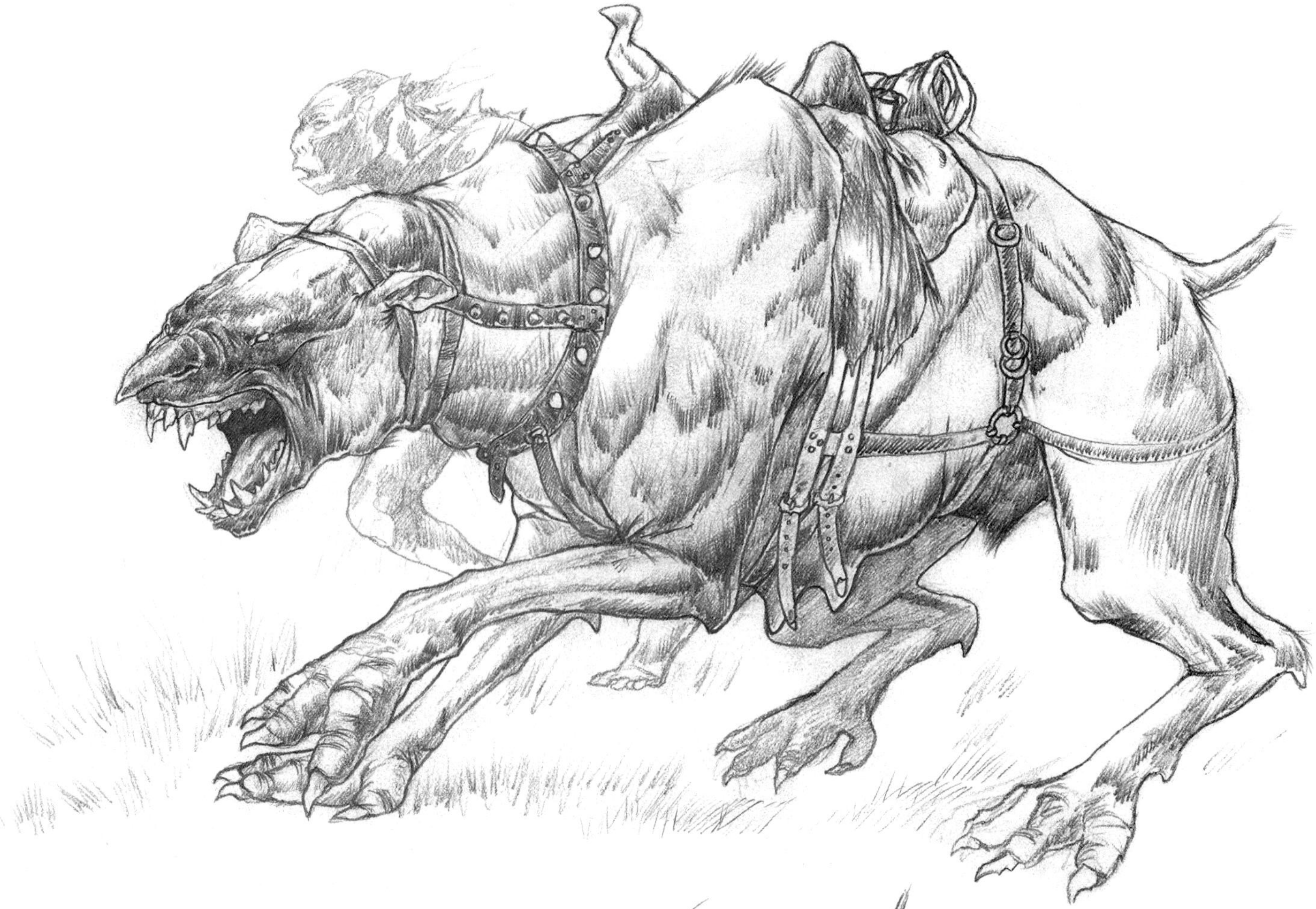

WARGS *Conceptual sketches*
"At the beginning Peter Jackson used a few words that were helpful to us – it was a guide to what he was looking for; he liked the idea of the Wargs being almost reptilian but prehistoric as well. These are definitely more doglike, a mastiff, but strange – with bad anatomy! Then it started drifting more toward a prehistoric doglike creature, only with weird bends and stretches." *WM*

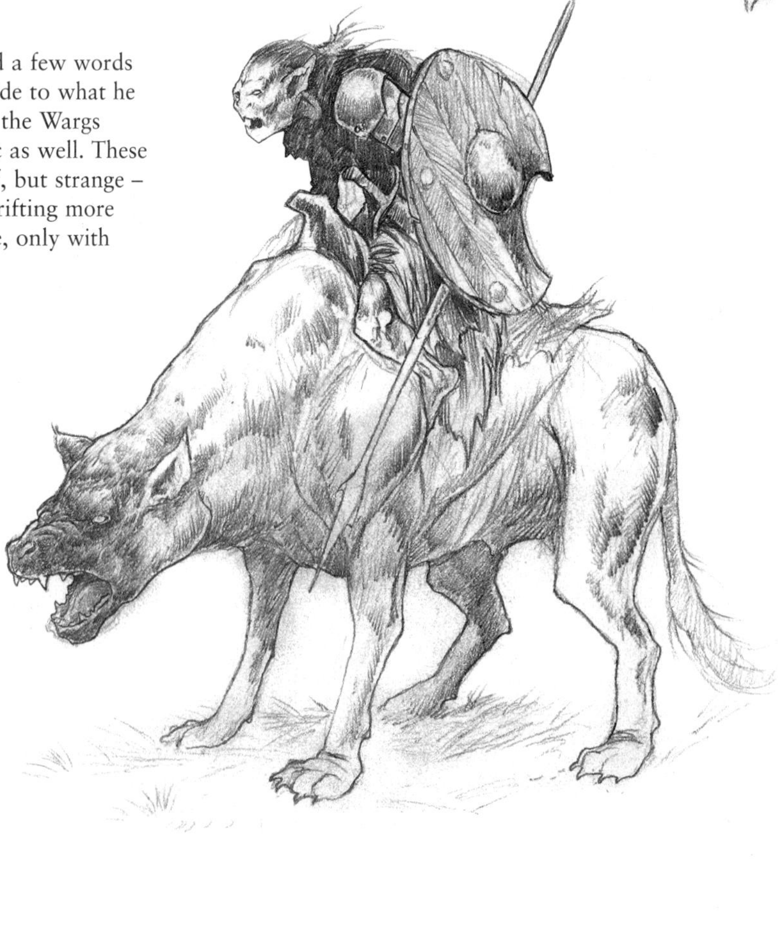

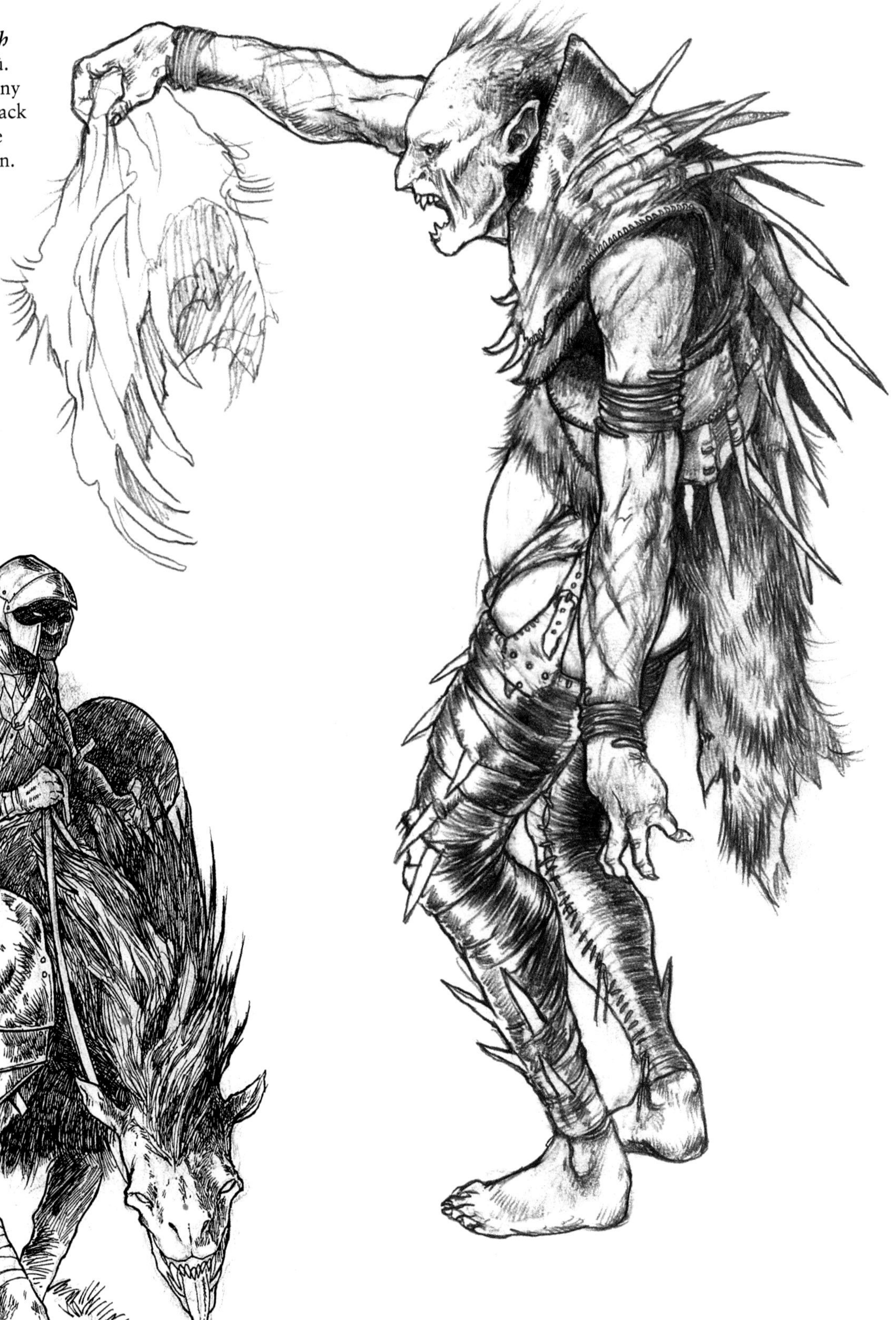

WARG RIDERS *Conceptual sketch*
"This was a later version of Sharkû. There was an illustration that Johnny Brough did that had quite a high back to the leather armor, and Pete quite liked it, so we started adding that in. This is pretty much the starting point for the final costume design. You can see that he's carrying a piece of meat for his Warg. Nice." *WM*

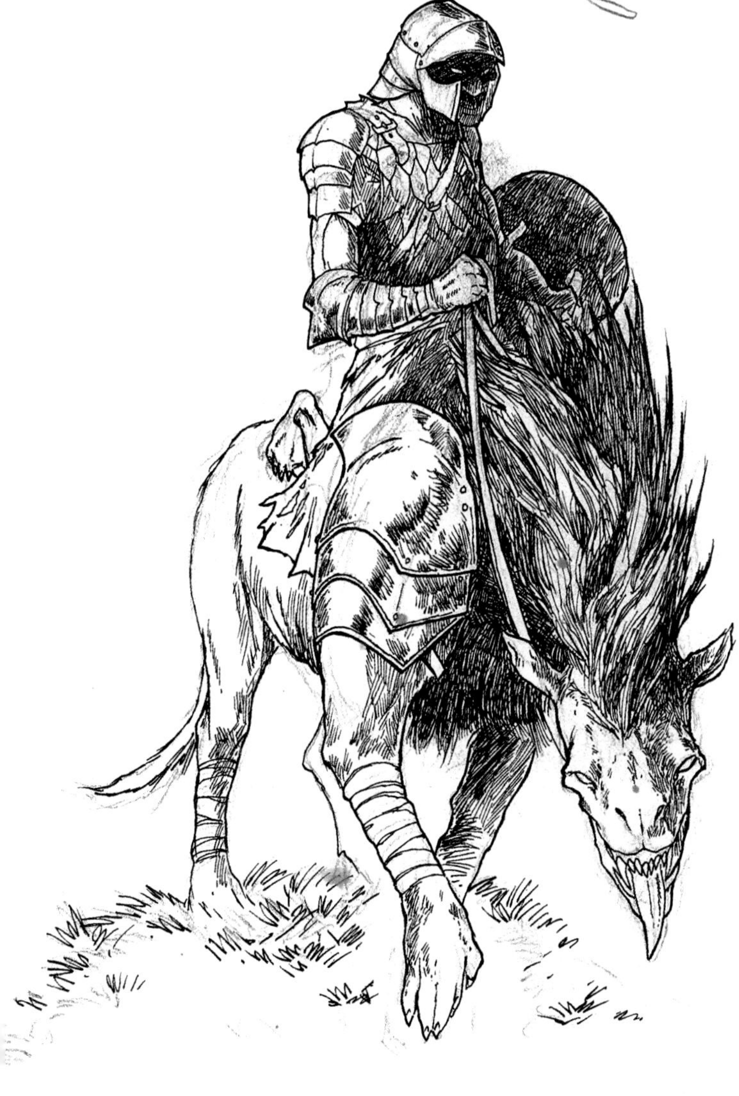

WARGS *Conceptual sketch*
"Moving away from dogs, this one has an almost horselike stature." *WM*

ÉOMER *Conceptual design*
"For Éomer I wanted a royal type of armor – something that was a little more fitting for a prince from the top family. This was unusual for me – I'd never been a drawing-in-color person. I only started doing them when I came to Weta, but I watched Dan Falconer with his marker pens. It was good training, because you could start playing with color quickly by photocopying your drawing, playing around with it. 'Ooh, I've done something terrible!' so you just throw it away and then color up another photocopy." *WM*

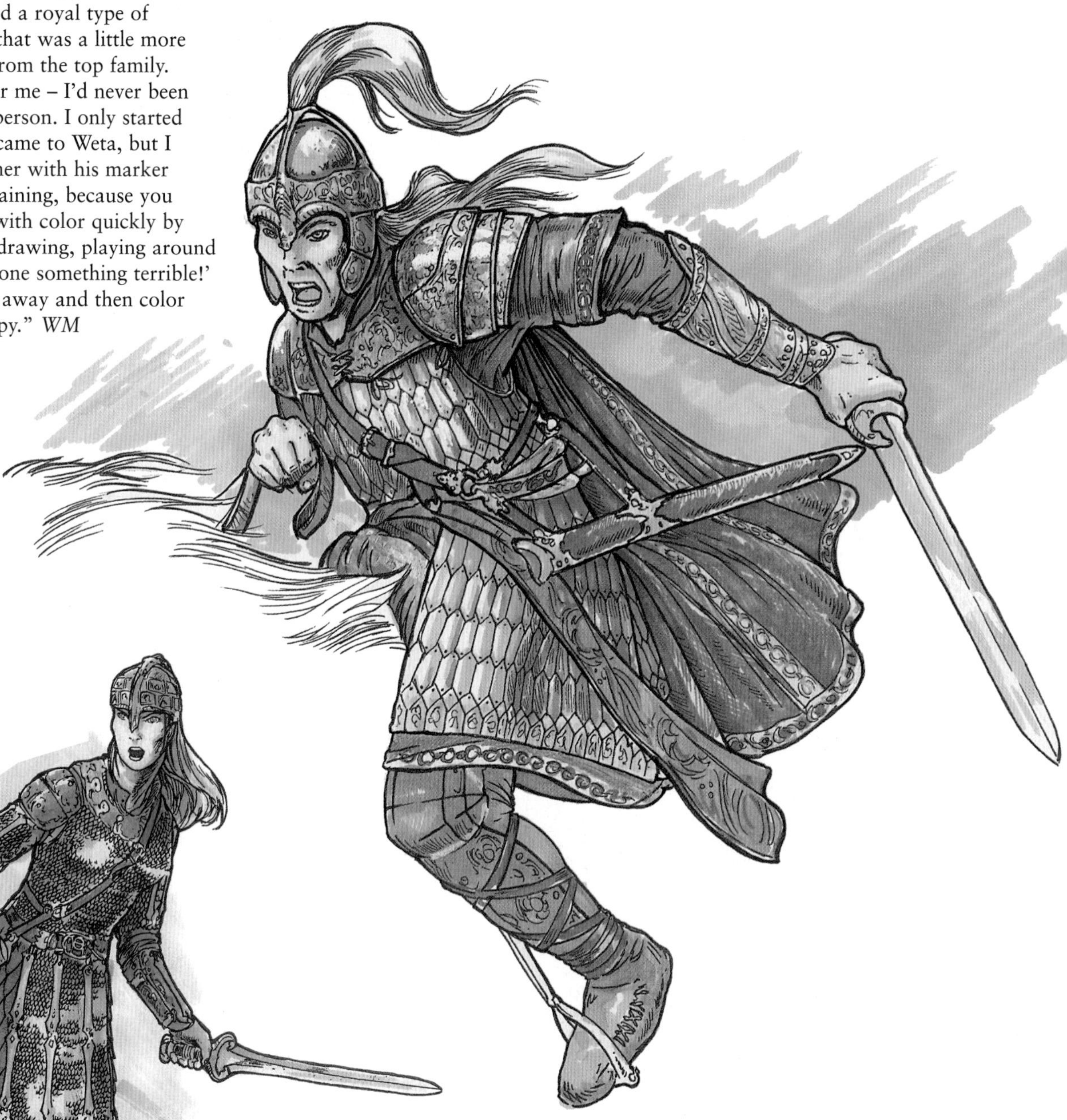

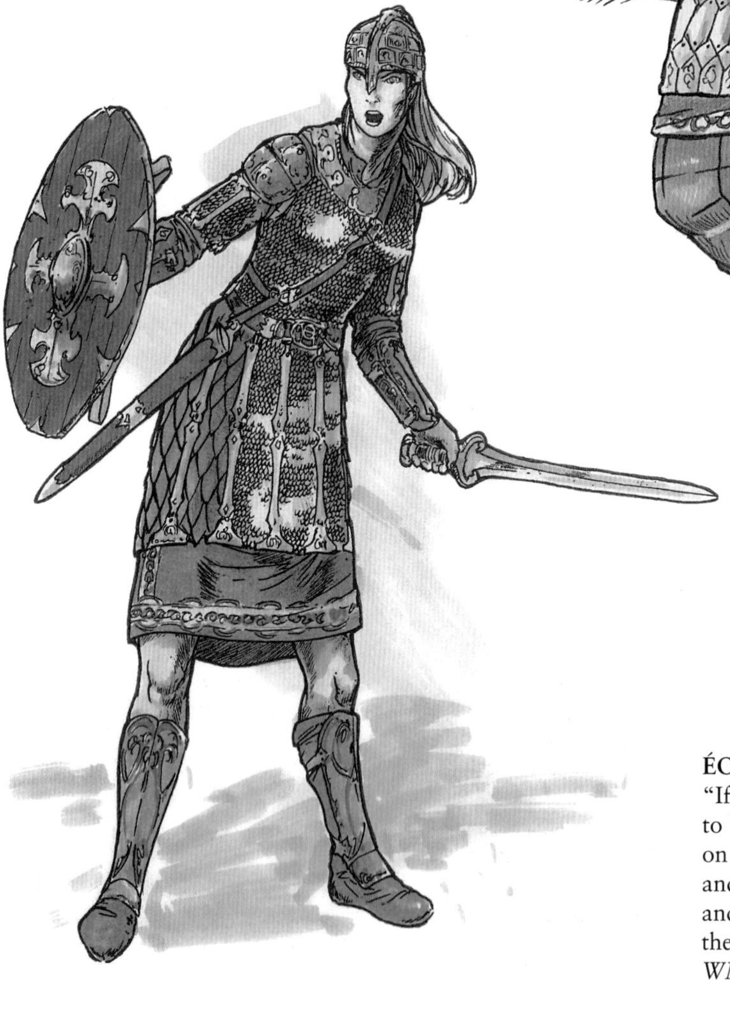

ÉOWYN'S ARMOR *Conceptual design*
"If she was going to be mistaken for a man, Éowyn's armor had to be quite utilitarian. You could imagine the armor she's wearing on just a foot soldier, but hers had to be reasonably form-fitting and accentuate the female form, within reason. It has chain mail and then a splint at the top of it, just for added protection down the arms and down the skirt, and a very basic Rohan shield." *WM*

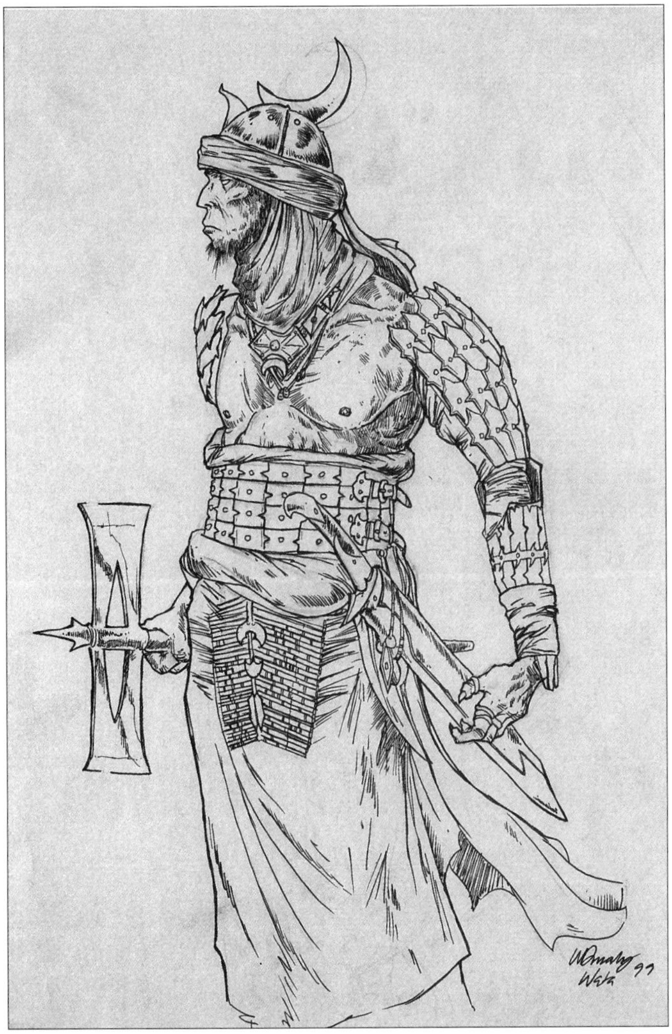

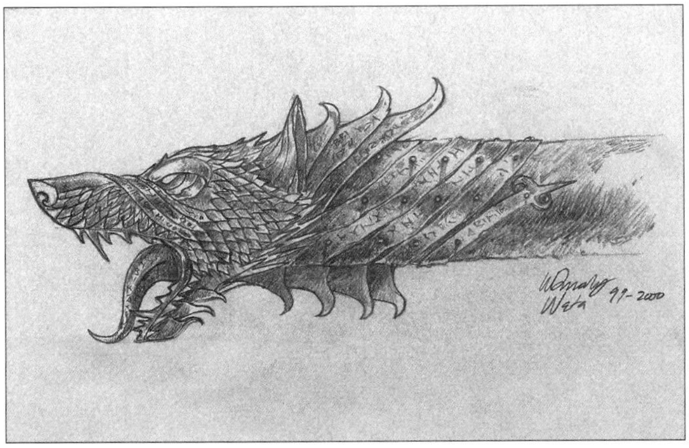

GROND *Conceptual sketch*
"This is a very early pass at Grond's wolf head, which is an idea from the book. Tolken actually described it pretty thoroughly. I think of it as a distant cousin to the Wargs. It was such a strange shape, though, and the end of its nose would work but the rest would be a bit fragile. At this stage, the concept was solely a wolf's head on the end of a battering ram." *WM*

EASTERLING *Conceptual design*
"The great thing about the Easterlings, because they were on the bad side in an alliance with Sauron, was that you could make them more tribal; they could be a bit more raw and a bit more savage. I loved the idea of having exposed skin, a bare chest: he's almost tempting you, 'Come on! I'm armored to a point but, you know, my heart is open! Just try it!'" *WM*

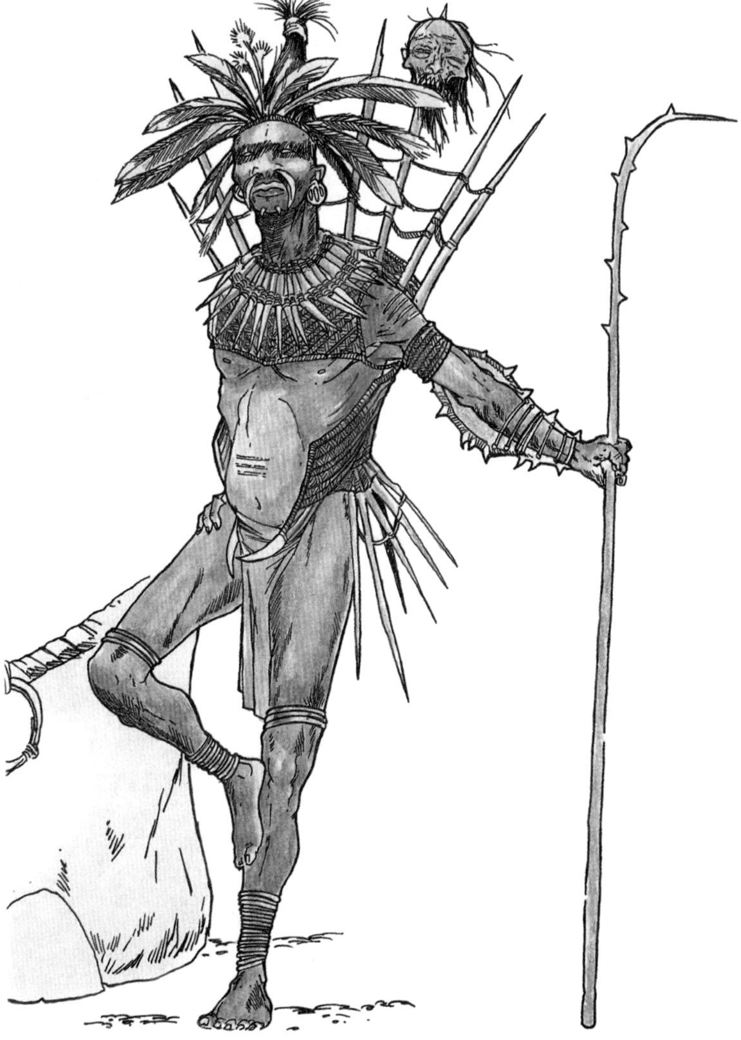

HARADRIM *Conceptual design*
"The brief for the Haradrim was tribal. This guy has a Pacific Island sort of feel. I imagined him being a mûmak driver, with a long spiked driving lance that he uses to steer, pulling the ears or cheek to make the mûmak turn. Everyone was keen on the red body dye as well – paint or blood mixed with earth – to try to get some color into the design.

"One idea that was talked about for the battle scenes was that the Haradrim's victims would be hanging off the mûmakil. See those skulls on spikes? Each head that the driver cut off, he would shove onto a spike. I think the idea got dropped quickly, but I liked it." *WM*

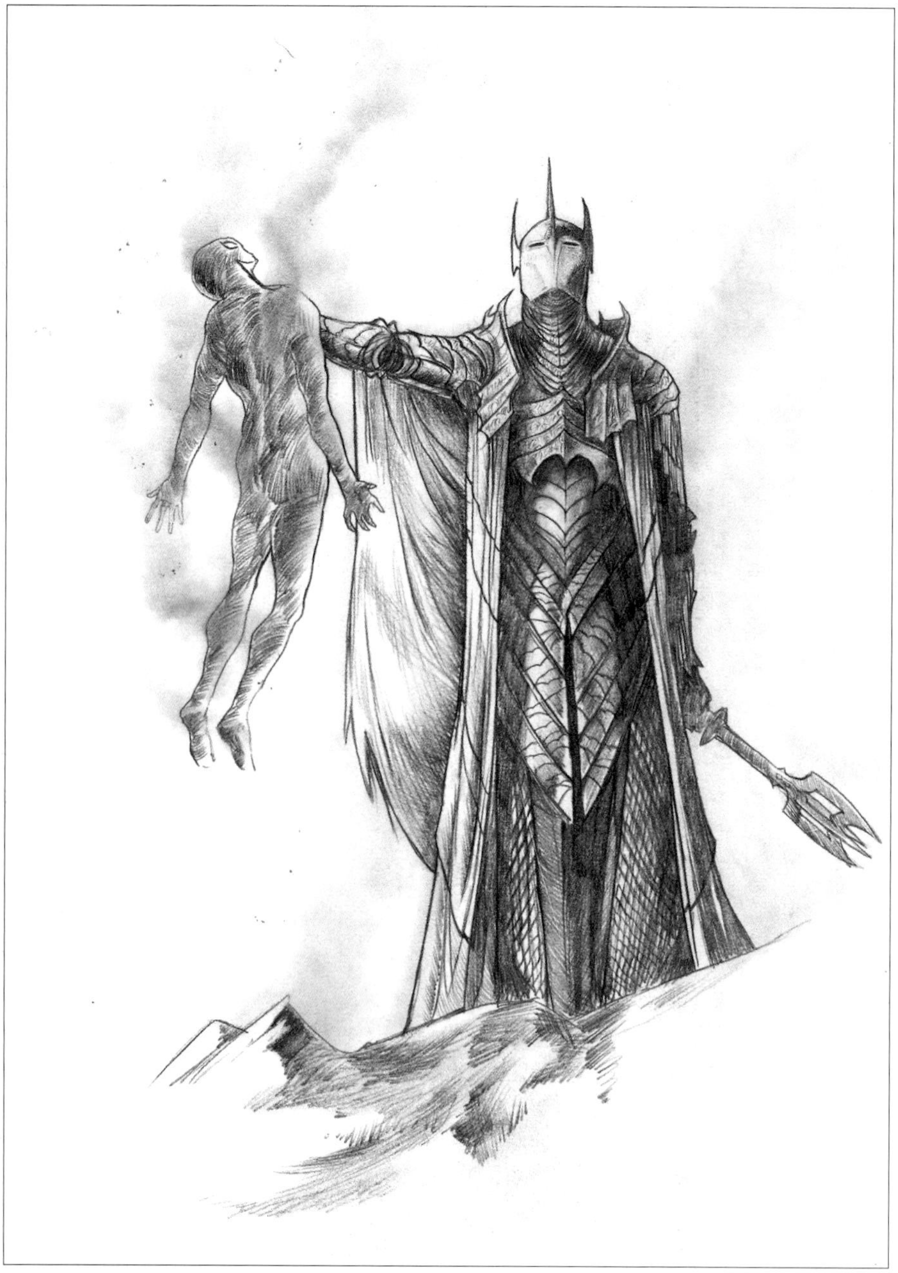

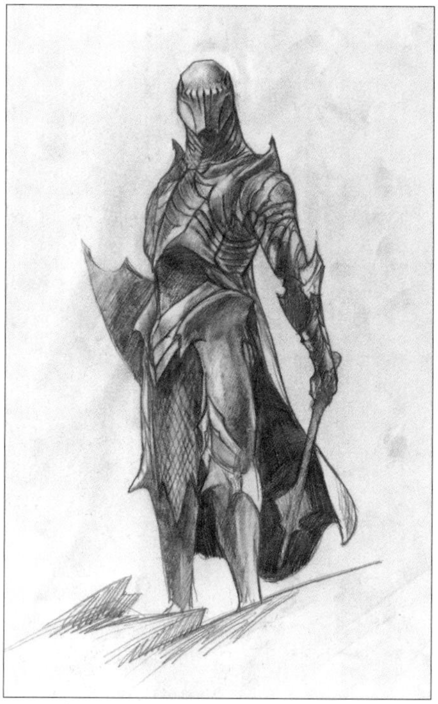

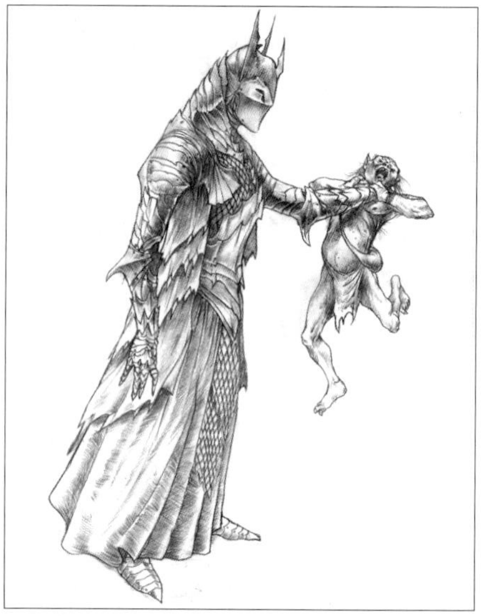

SAURON *Conceptual sketches*
Warren was charged with designing the overall Sauron concepts, such as the helmet, weapons, and armor. Although such a sequence isn't in the story itself, these illustrations showing Sauron throttling an Orc minion and burning Gil-galad were done not only to give an idea of the height of Sauron in his armor, but also to demonstrate the cruel majesty of the character.

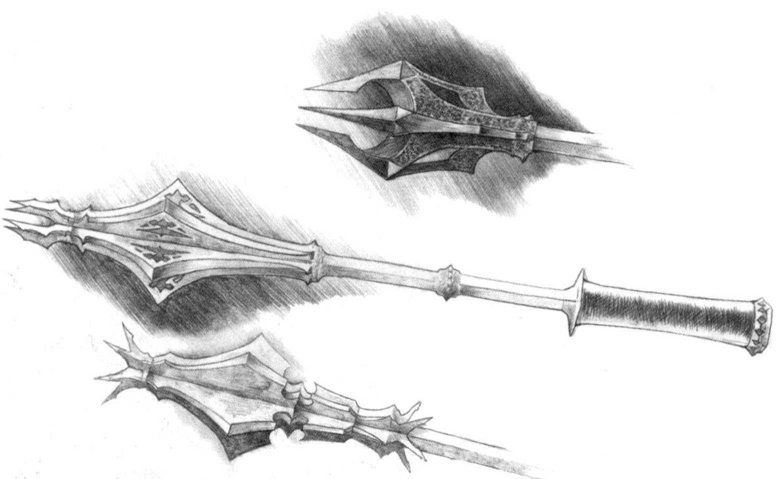

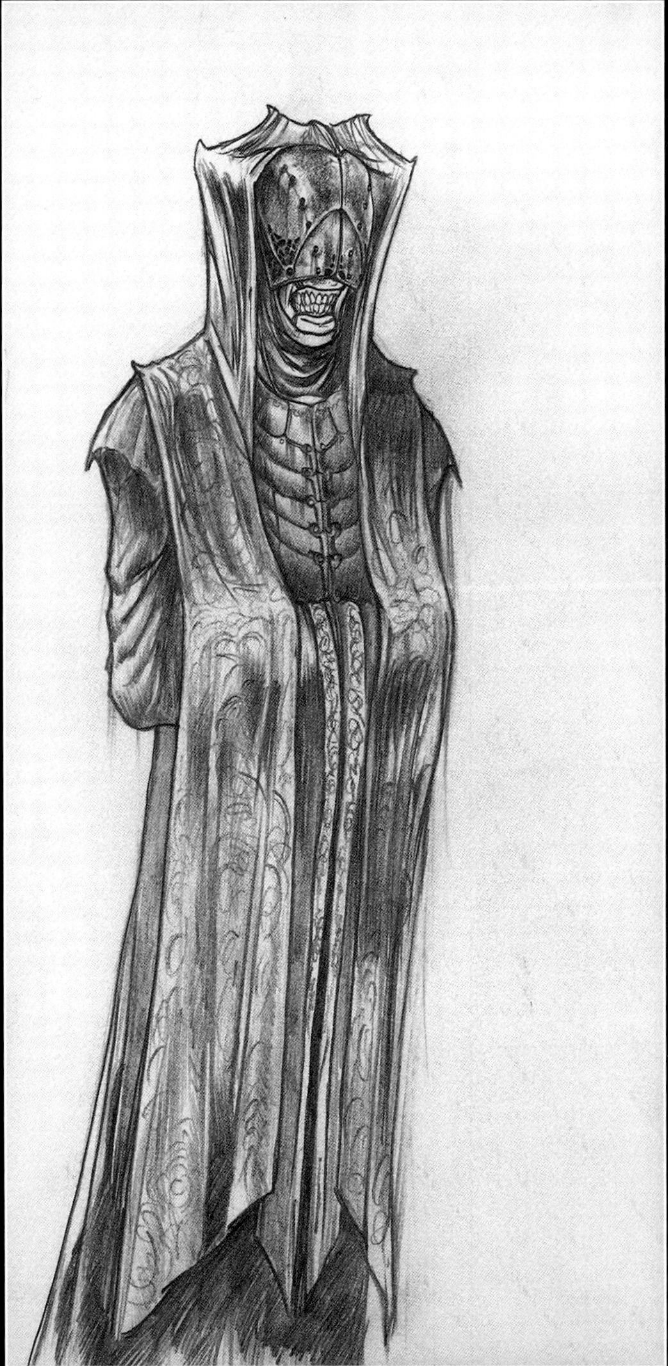

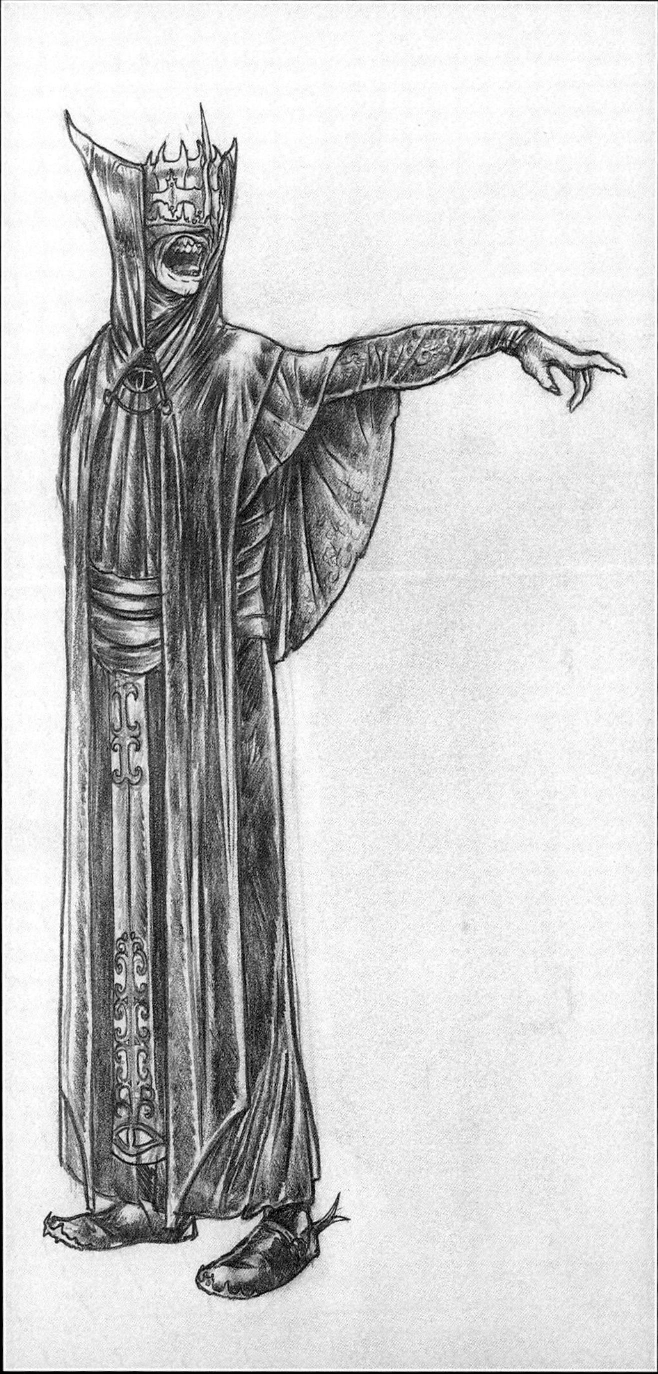

MOUTH OF SAURON *Conceptual sketches*
"The idea was that the Mouth of Sauron was purely that, just the mouth. He couldn't see – well, maybe he could with his mind – but the body was just a tool. There was an idea at one stage, I think it could be this one above left, that parts of his helmet actually had hooks into his mouth that kept his mouth open as well, or pulled his mouth back into a grimace. But it didn't work out that way because Bruce Spence, the actor who plays the Mouth, couldn't talk; he couldn't get his mouth to move. Peter Jackson liked the idea that the robe flowed up onto the helmet, providing the horn shapes out at the sides. I like the way it gives him an almost religious, priestlike look." *WM*

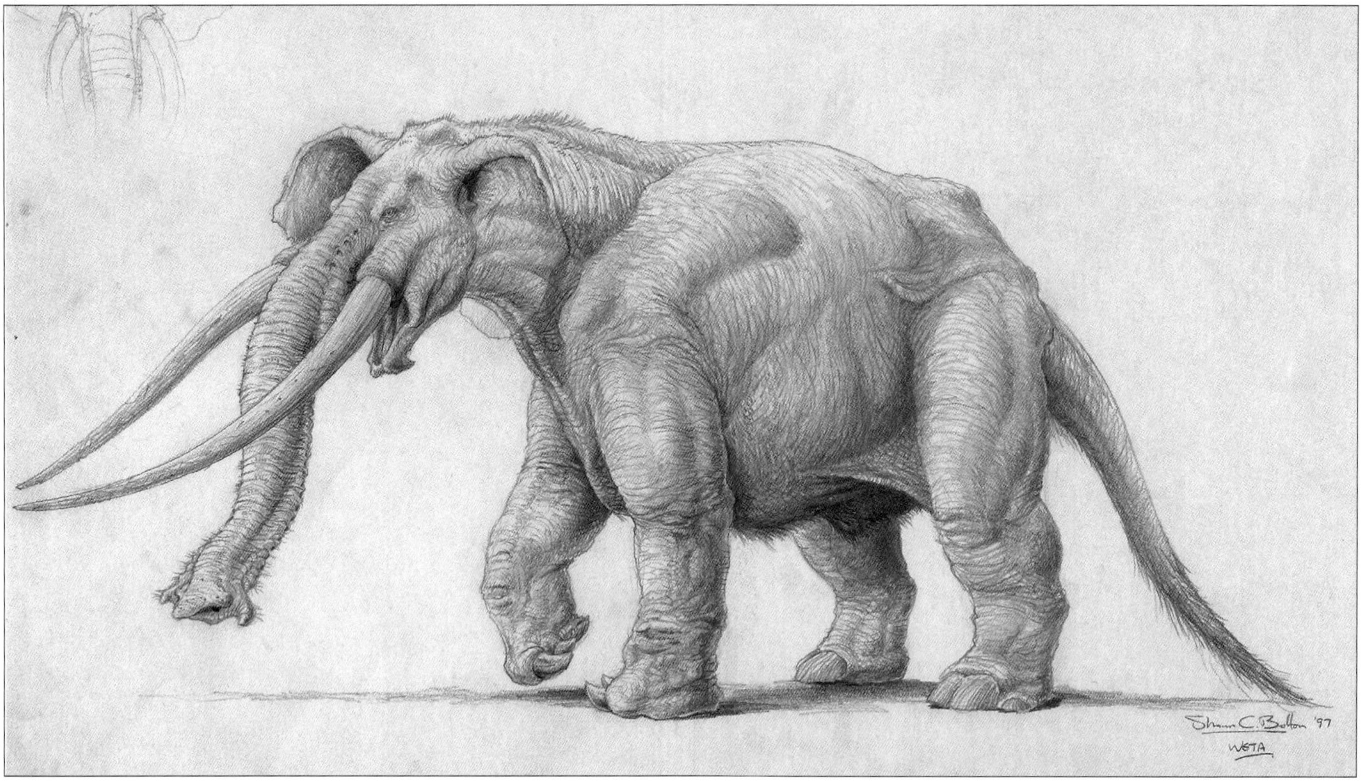

MÛMAKIL *Conceptual sketches*
"I was going for something different with the mumakil, not just giving Peter Jackson a straightforward elephant; you've still got a trunk and tusks, so it still looks like an elephant, but I was trying to alter the proportions to give it that sense of size. I had in mind some of the dinosaurs, with large legs and clawed feet. I quite liked the idea of having the head out on a big thick neck, again giving it that dinosaur look. Since this was at the early stage, whenever we put something on a creature, we hoped it would inspire the scriptwriters to use the creature in a new way. I think we were going for the idea that they were controlled by the Haradrim pulling on the ears, so I gave them substantial ones that could lend some weight to that idea." *SB*

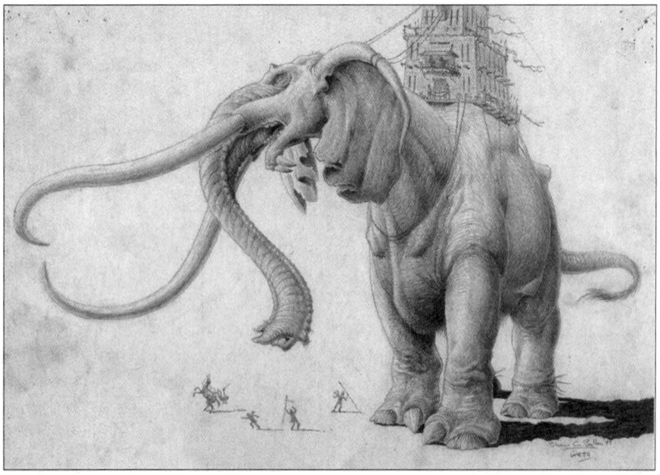

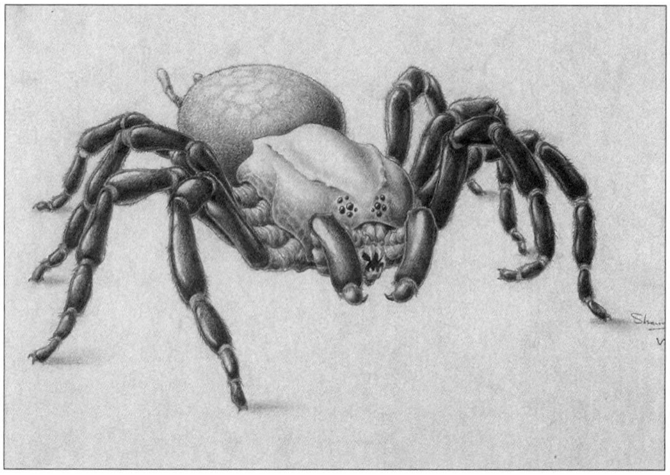

SHELOB *Conceptual sketch*
"I'm not particularly arachnophobic, and people who are all seem to have a different reason for being so – some find the number of legs scary, others the way spiders walk. I confess that one thing I always find creepy in spiders is the multiple eyes. So trying to make a scary spider monster when you're not scared by them was a bit tricky. At this stage, we were trying to keep it more along the lines of a proper spider, rather than Tolkien's description, which is different. His version has horns and jaws and all sorts of things." *SB*

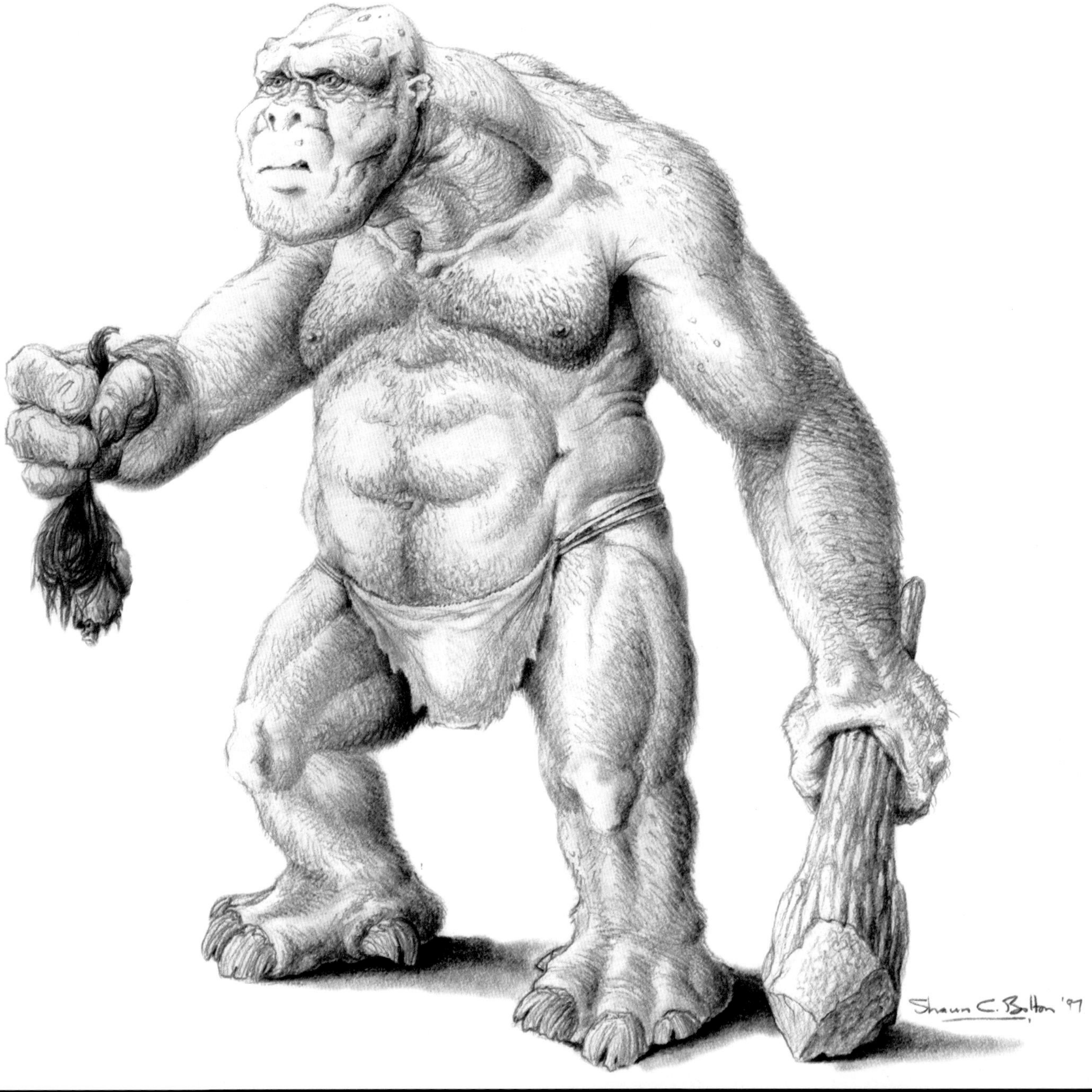

TROLL *Conceptual sketch*
"This was a very early drawing for the cave-troll, possibly my first or second, and was really just a jumping-off point for the design process. Although the design went in a different direction as the look of Middle-earth evolved, the final cave-troll was surprisingly similar in proportions to my 'Neanderthal gorilla' concept." *SB*

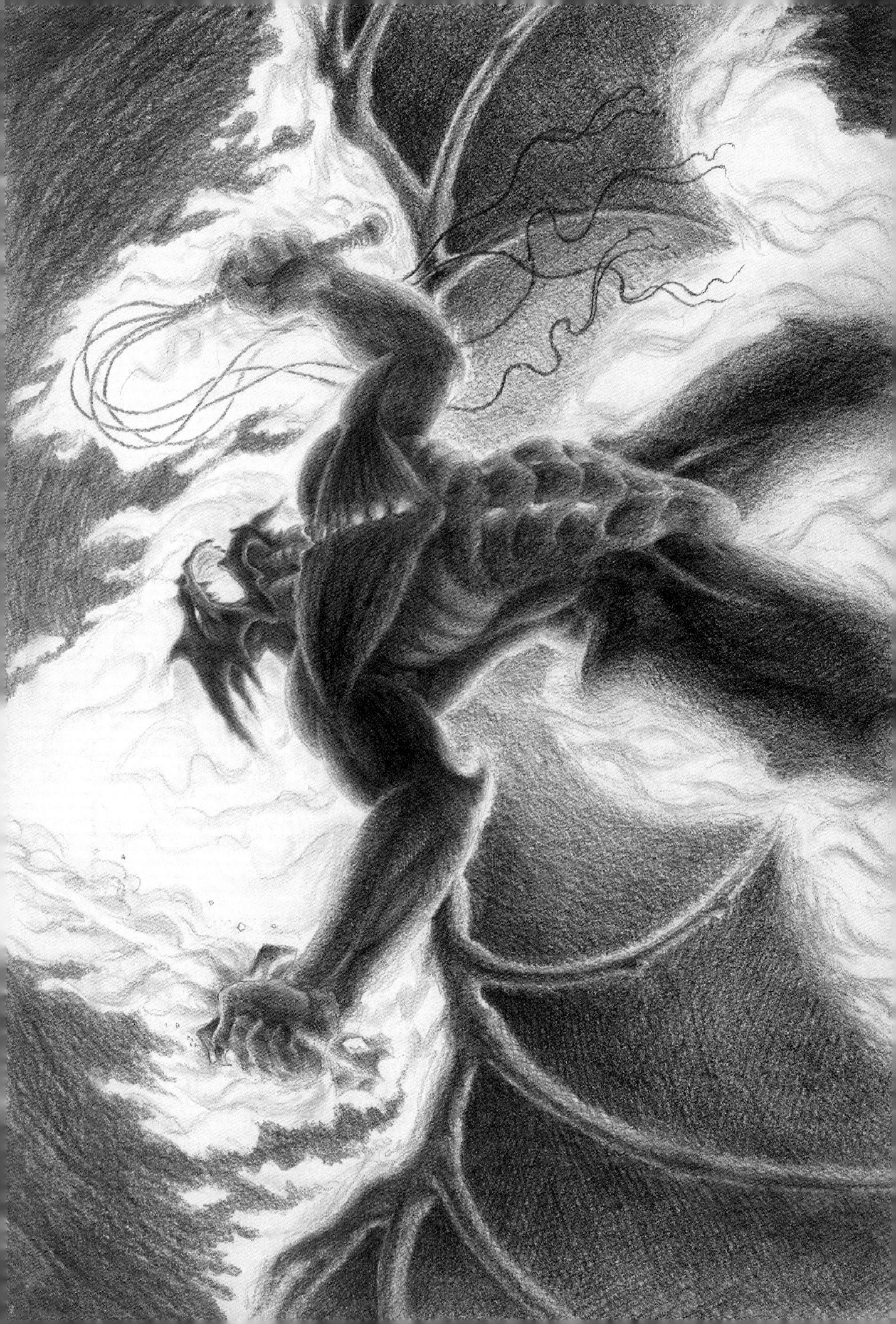

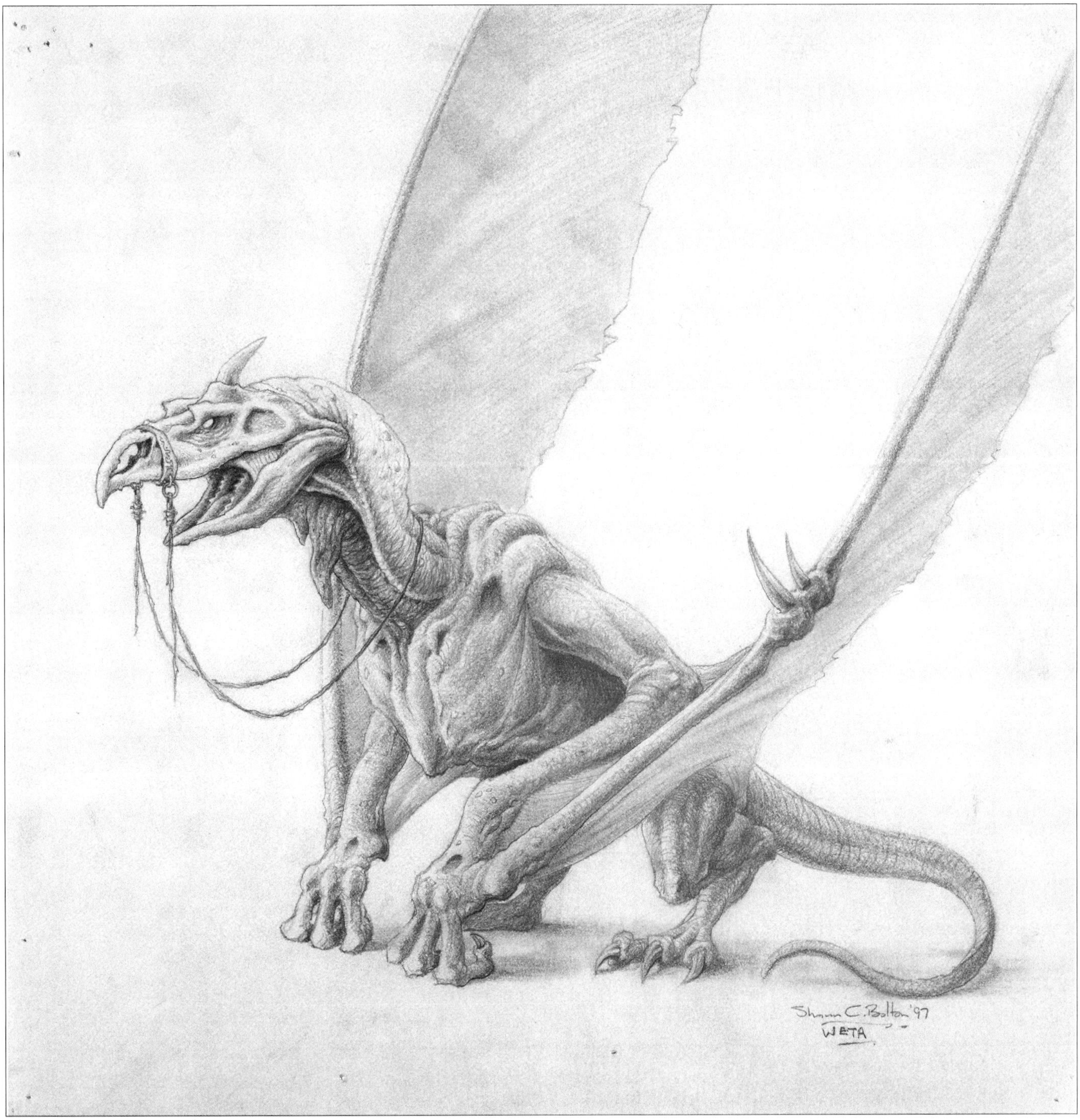

THE BALROG ***Conceptual sketch***
Shaun depicted this early concept for the Balrog wreathed in flame and roaring.

FELL BEAST ***Conceptual sketch***
"I come from a stop-motion background, so I've a big interest in dinosaurs, and you can see that here in this guy. I was trying for something that wasn't a dragon, but not a bird either. I don't think any of us really explored the idea of a feathered fell beast. We were trying for something emaciated, because these creatures aren't well treated. This particular version about how it would look when it's on the ground, how it might walk around, with the bridle, of course, for the rider." *SB*

MAQUETTES

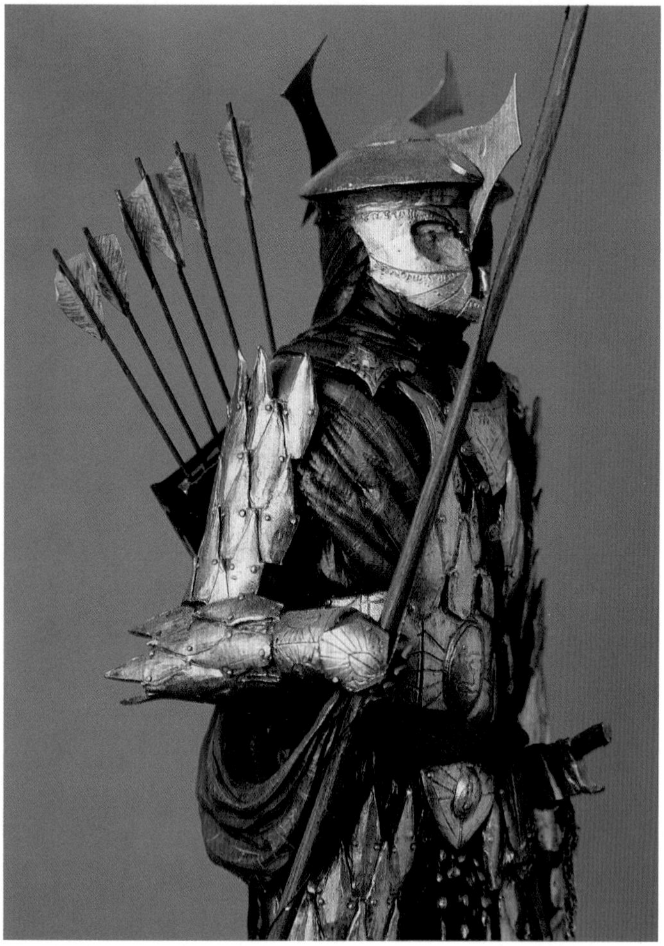

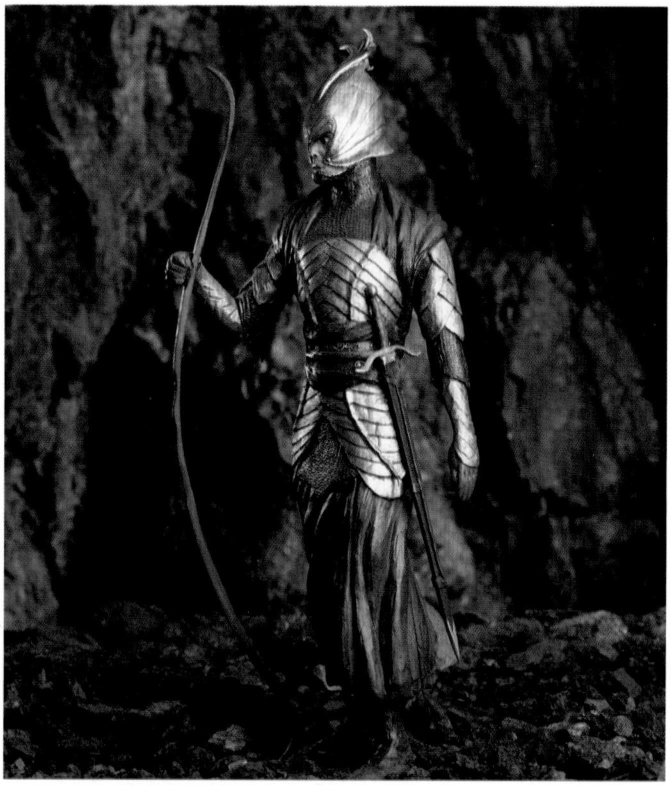

ELVEN ARMOR CONCEPT *Maquette*
Originally designed as an idea for the Elven armor appearing in *The Two Towers*, but ultimately rejected, this maquette was later selected as a strong lead for the armor worn by the Elves in the Second Age, seen in the prologue to *The Fellowship of the Ring*. *WM*

EASTERLING *Maquette*
"I was so pleased to sculpt this. Daniel took the lead on the Easterling designs, but I was lucky enough to realize this design in 3D. It's a great-looking design. I put my own slight spin on it, which is the fan of arrows on his back. They didn't have bows in the end, which is really sad. But other than that, I was just lucky to sculpt a great piece of work from someone else's drawing – that's the whole Weta teamwork thing in action, the culmination of many people's work. It's so cool that almost every drawing or design was produced by the team of artists and designers, rather than just one person. The whole project has been fun because of that." *BW*

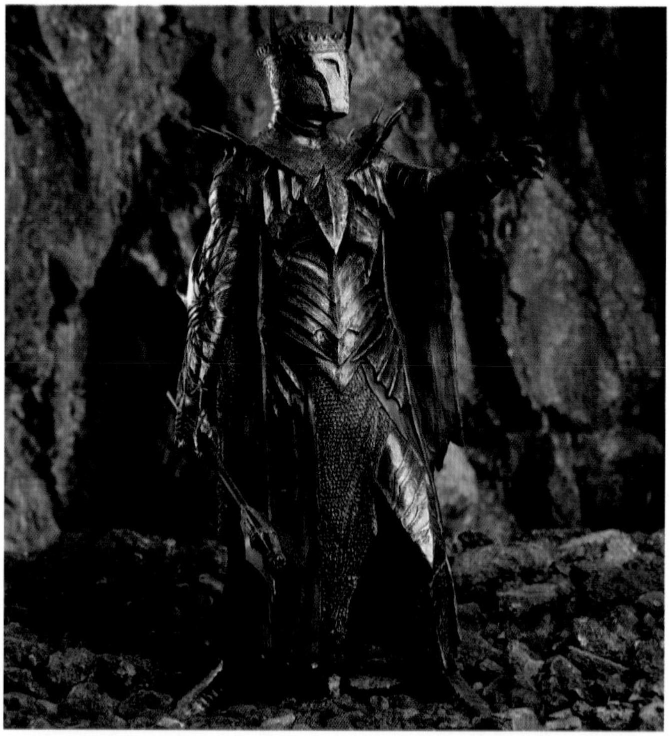

SAURON ARMOR CONCEPT *Maquette*
This is the third and final maquette of Sauron. Peter Jackson responded well to elements from all three of Warren's sculpts – in this one he liked the robes that draped over the armor. *WM*

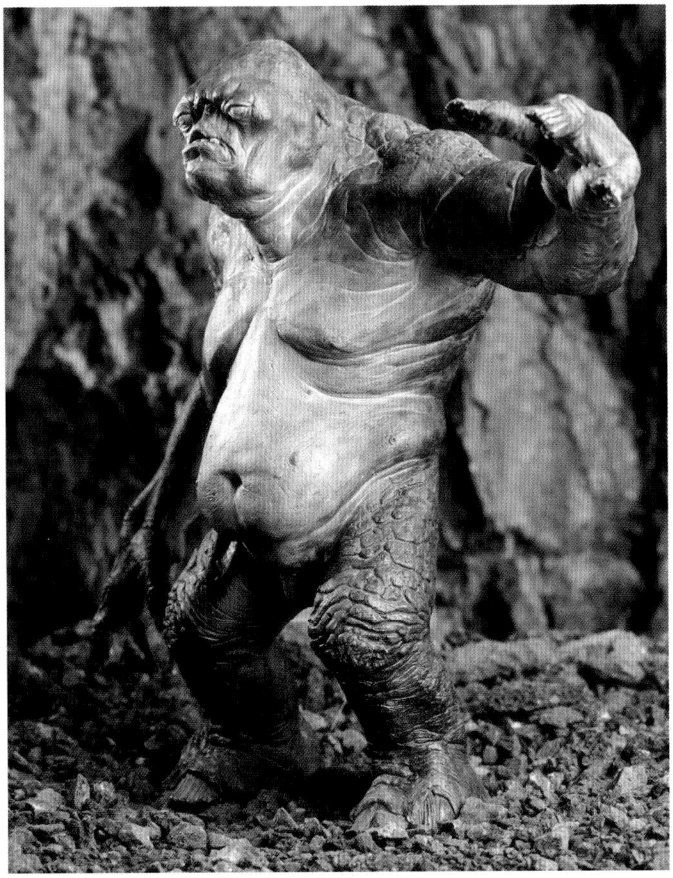

CAVE-TROLL *Maquette*
Jamie's sculpt for the cave-troll, which was then painted by Ben Wootten, was the final approved maquette. *JB & BW*

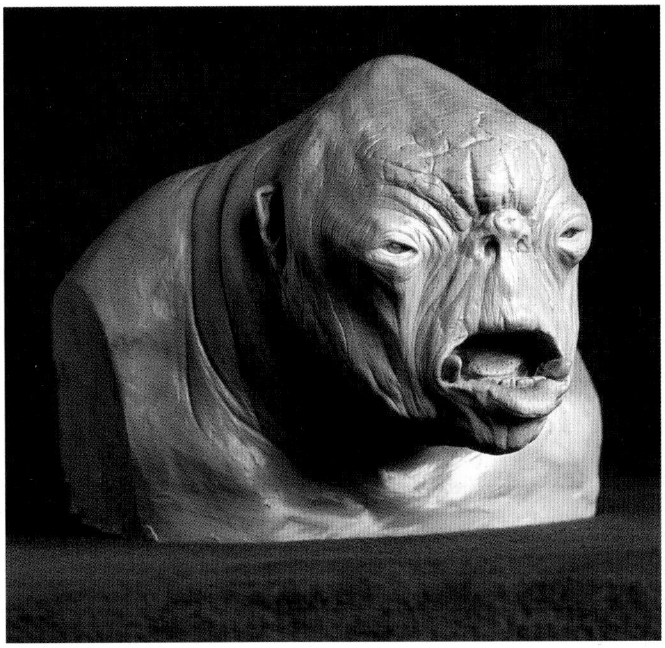

CAVE-TROLL *Maquette*
Ben had already produced a sculpt of the cave-troll's facial design. The above maquette was a refinement of that and was liked by Peter. *BW*

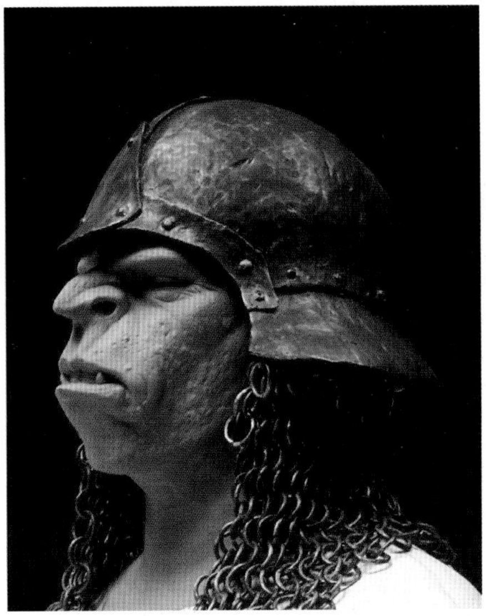

ORC *Maquette*
An early facial sculpt that incorporates a helmet and chain mail made by Weta's armory. *WETA*

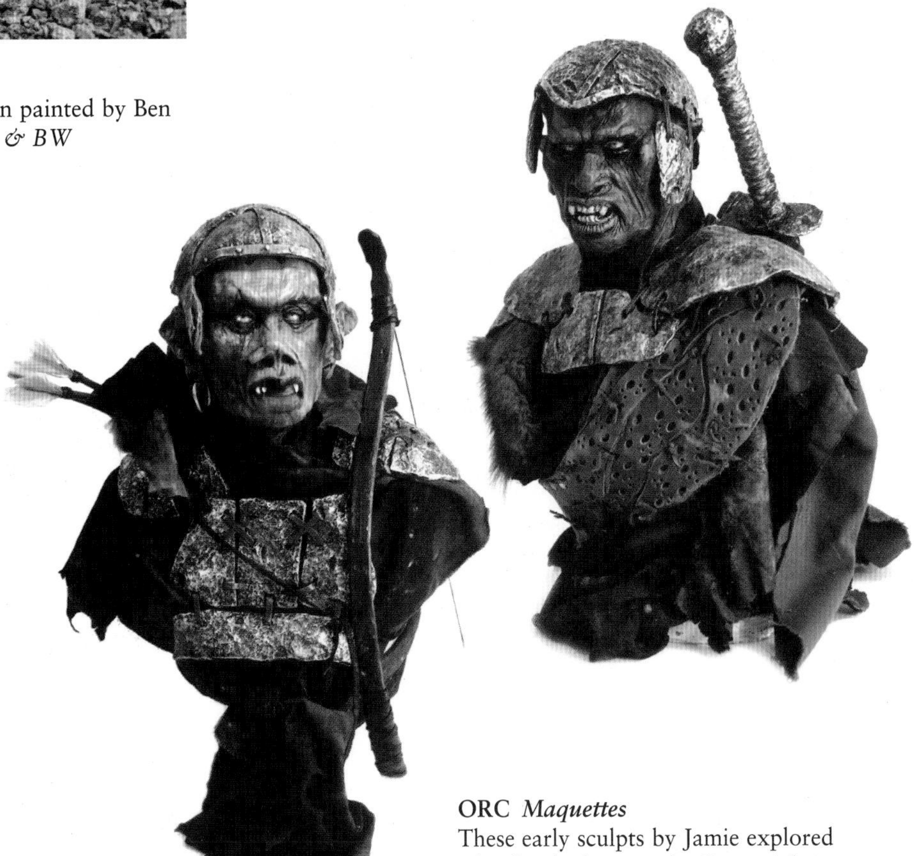

ORC *Maquettes*
These early sculpts by Jamie explored what kind of armor the Orcs might wear. *JB*

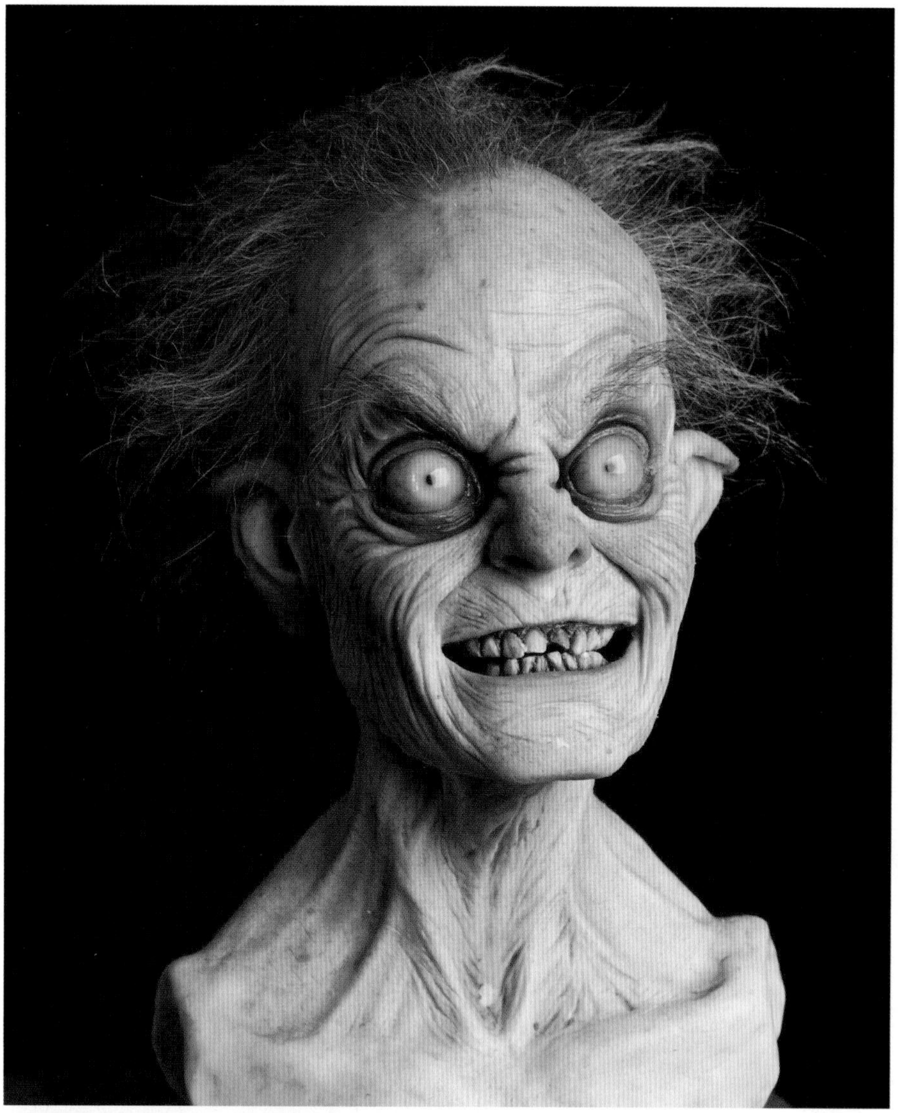

BILBO TRANSFORMATION *Maquette*
This design was produced for the scene at Rivendell where Bilbo's face is seen to briefly transform into a hideous, Gollum-like creature, a kind of "what-if" scenario in which we see what Bilbo might have become had he succumbed to the evil lure of the Ring. *WETA*

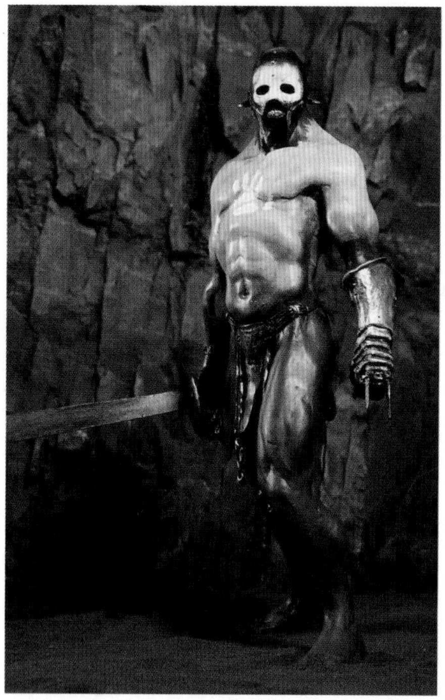

URUK-HAI *Maquette*
JB

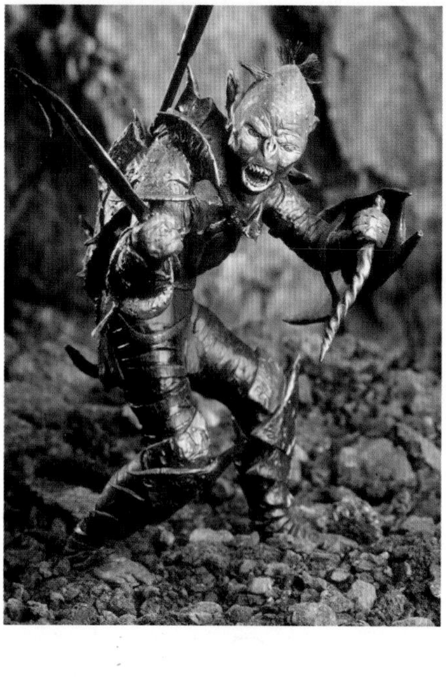

ORC *Maquette*
This sculpture was from very early on in the production, before the design of any part of the Orc had been finalized. *JB*

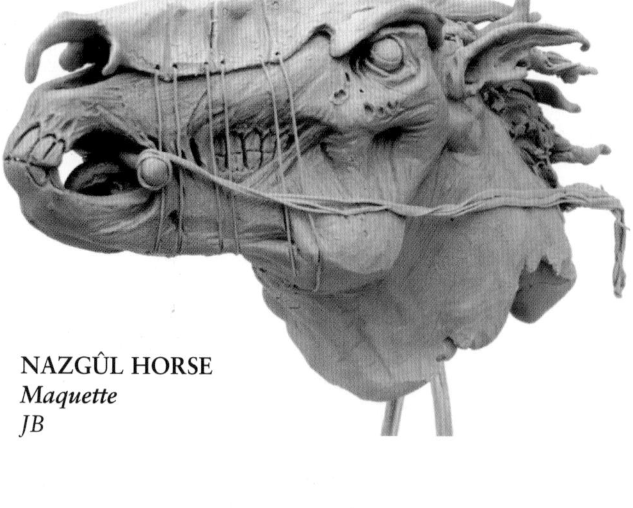

NAZGÛL HORSE
Maquette
JB

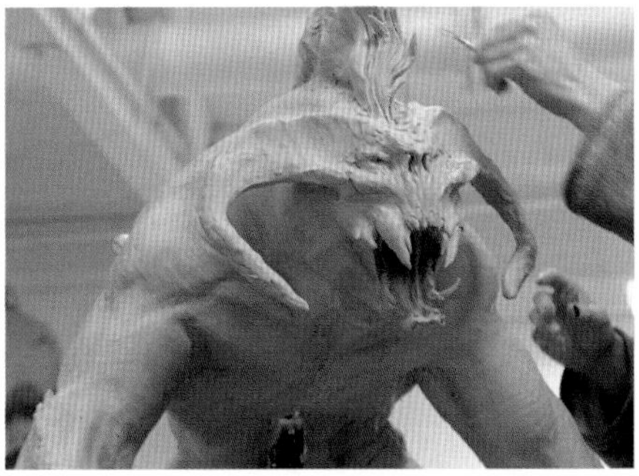

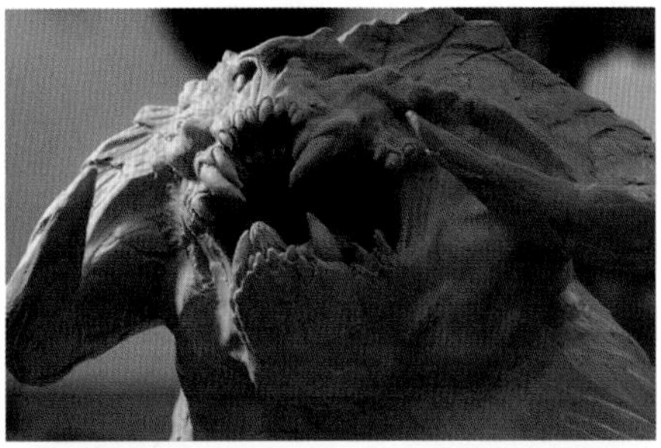

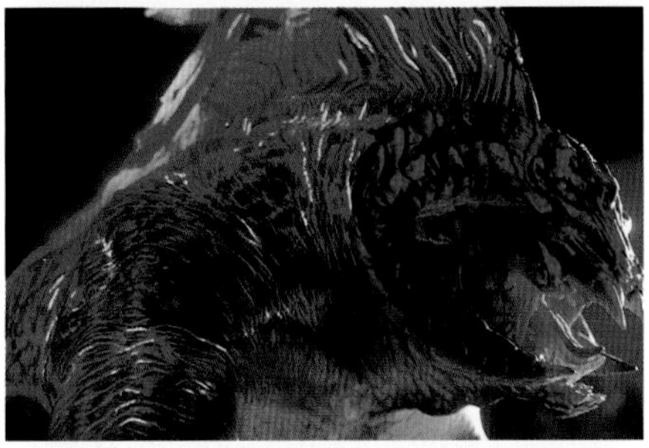

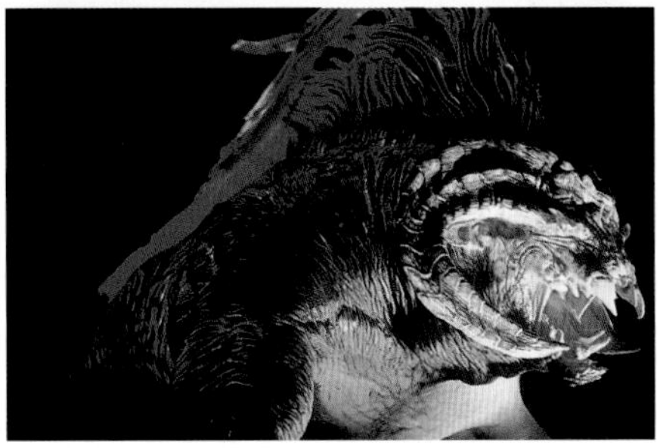

THE BALROG *Maquettes*
Ben's maquette goes through the process from colorless sculpt to the painted and lit creature (main image). Warren's take on the Balrog, bottom right, has a slightly different color scheme.
BW & WM

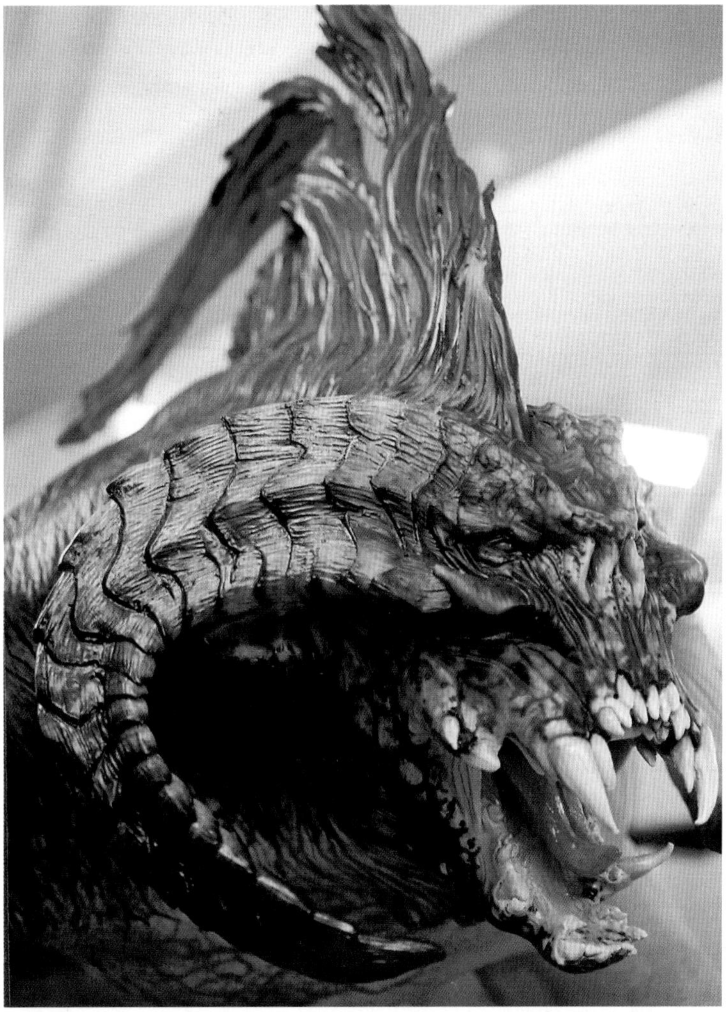

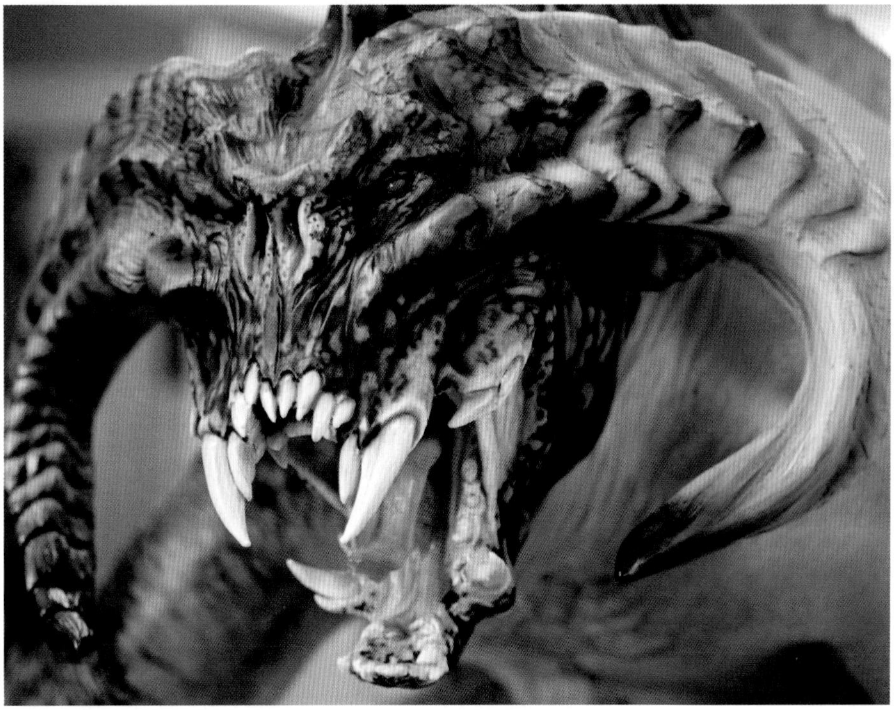

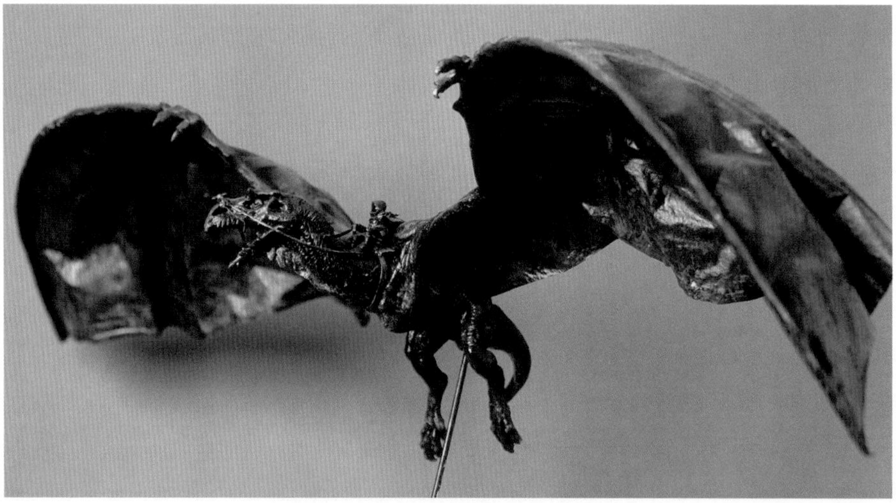

FELL BEAST *Maquette*
"This fell beast was based on my drawings, keeping a dinosaur look. By this stage, I was envisaging it more as a pterodactyl, in terms of its proportions at least. I like working in three dimensions; it's actually a good way to do design, as you can sometimes do a sculpture quicker than you can a drawing. However, drawing in pencil can be equally satisfying, and it's probably quicker to do a lot of detail in pencil as opposed to sculpting a maquette!" *SB*

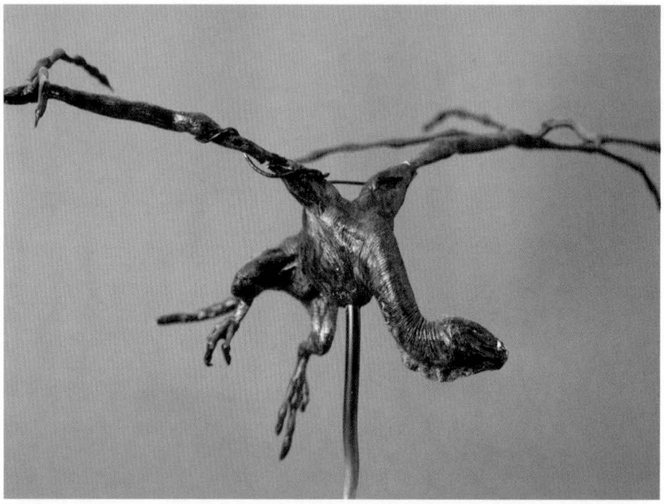

FELL BEAST
Maquette
BW

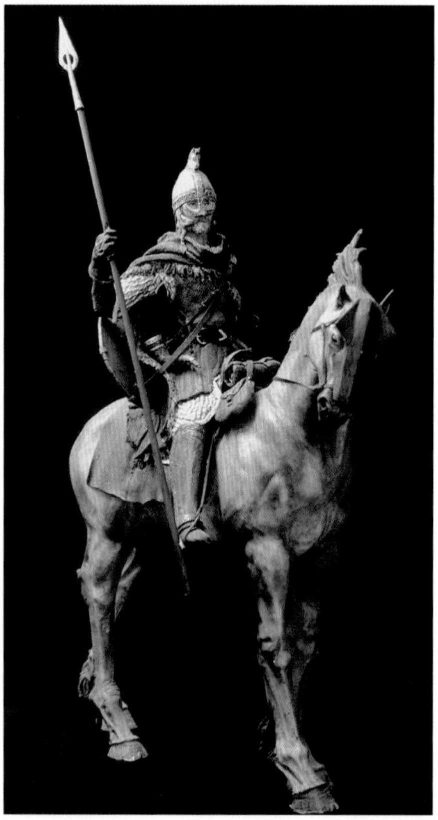

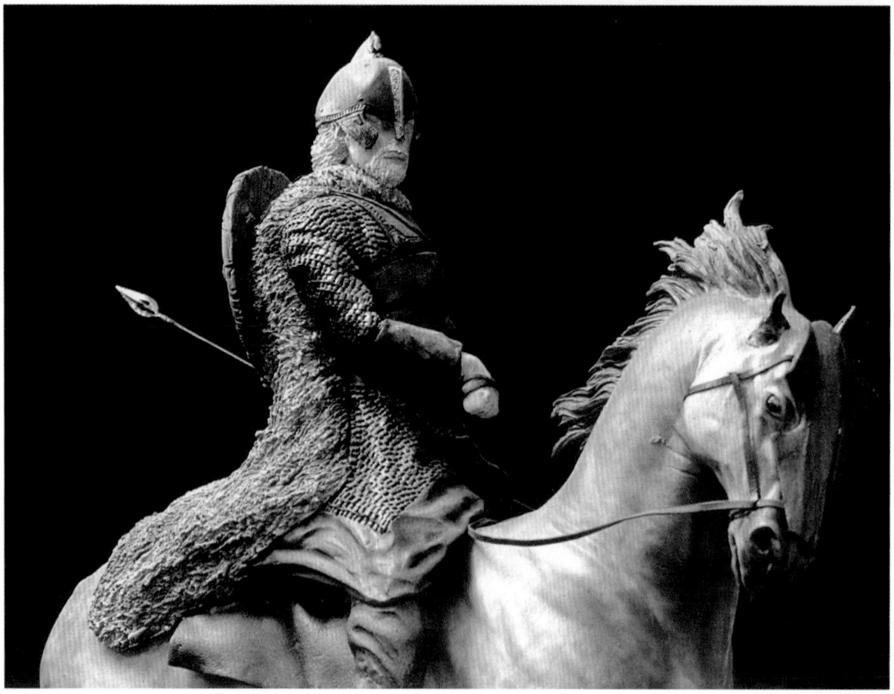

ROHIRRIM *Maquette*
"There was a strong Celtic influence in the Rohirrim designs. We opted for fin-mail – scale mail that tapered to a point – as a point of difference from the chain of the Uruk-hai and Gondorians, and a color scheme dominated by green and gold." *DF*

ROHIRRIM *Maquette*
"The soldier in this maquette has a maroon cloak featuring embroidery on the back. I imagined that his cloak had been passed down through generations from his soldier ancestors." *SL*

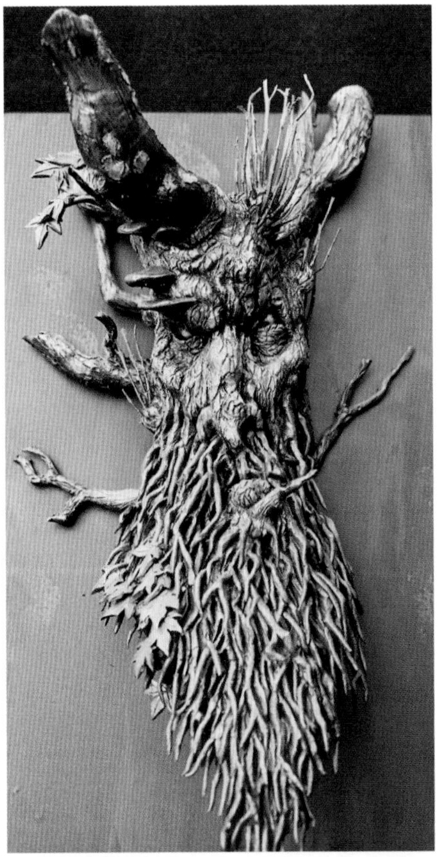

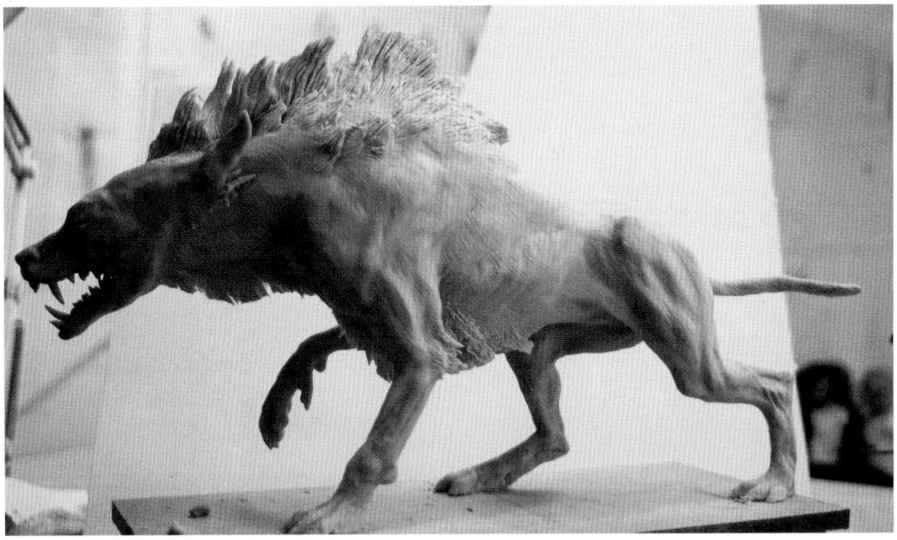

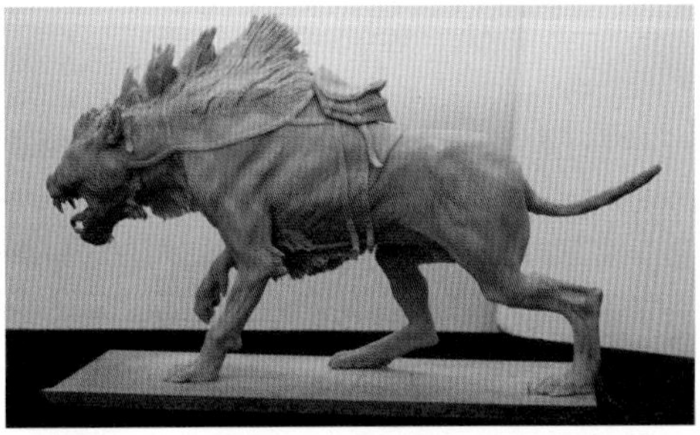

WARGS *Maquettes*
These were created to show the CGI designers how the Wargs looked in terms of size and weight. *WM*

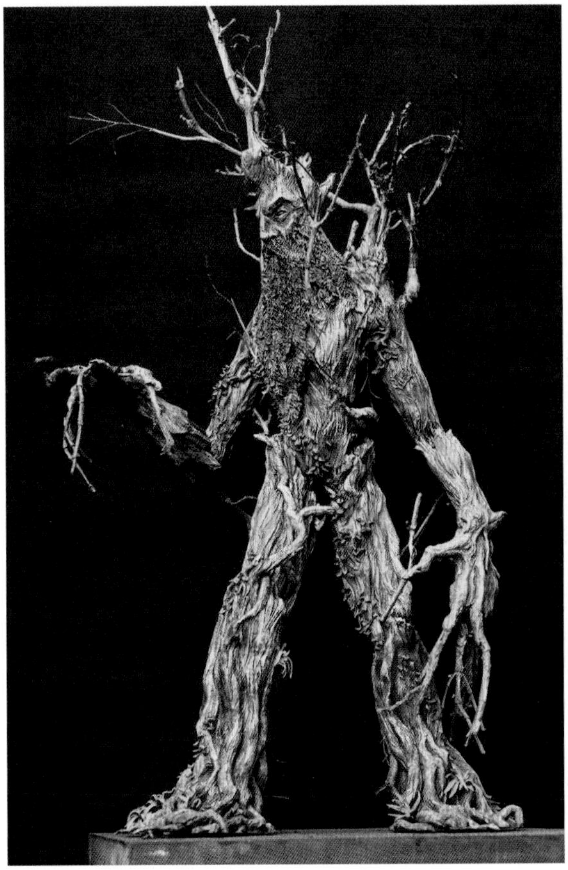

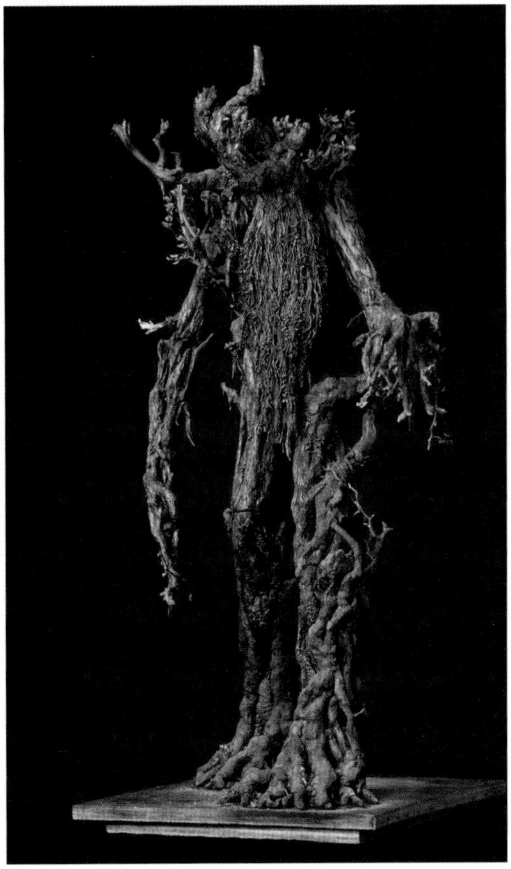

ENTS *Maquettes*
"We experimented with different Ent body proportions, trying to break out of the human form by extending or shrinking their arms and legs. We also explored the balance between how much man and how much tree would make up their final forms. Some were more manlike, but Treebeard (far left) was closer to a tree. Peter Jackson approved this foot-and-a-half maquette and it became the bible reference for Treebeard." *DF*

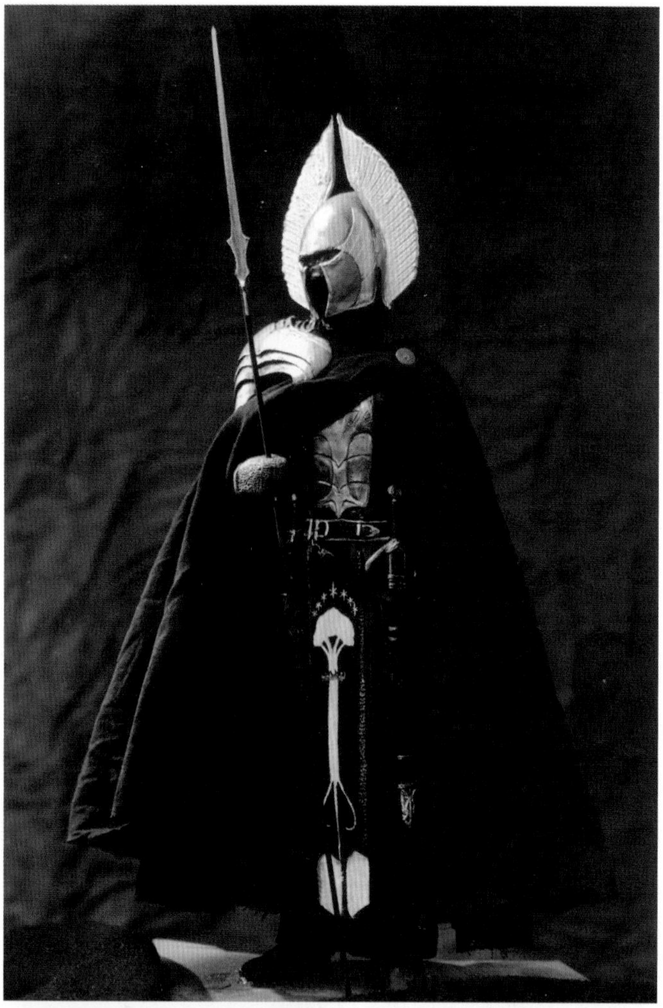

FOUNTAIN GUARD *Maquette*

"This Fountain Guard sculpt is pretty close to the final look. Once Peter Jackson has seen a couple of rounds of drawings, and he's fairly comfortable that the direction we're going in is what he wants, 3D then becomes a requirement – it can be rotated and viewed from all angles. This is so he can confirm it is the look he is after. So the maquette is a realization and a fine-tuning of what he saw in our drawings that he really liked. With the Fountain Guard, we pretty much got the say on how the costumes looked because, on the Fountain Guard and even more on the Gondorian troops, they were far more of a component of the armor. However, there are reversals to that, where costume has more input. Aragorn's Black Gate outfit was more Ngila Dickson's department than ours, so there were concessions made to fit with her designs. As a result, we're unlikely to do a maquette of Aragorn – we tend to do only our own designs when it is something that can't quite be visualized in a drawing. Maquette clothing doesn't give you an accurate representation of texture. A drawing can actually do a better job of clothing than a quick sculpt, whereas a quick sculpt of armor, which is a solid object, is really useful. Also, maquettes were used if there was going to be a digital realization as well. We sculpt special maquettes for digital scanning after the final design has been agreed on, a sculpt that is at least four feet tall. Those are big models!" *BW*

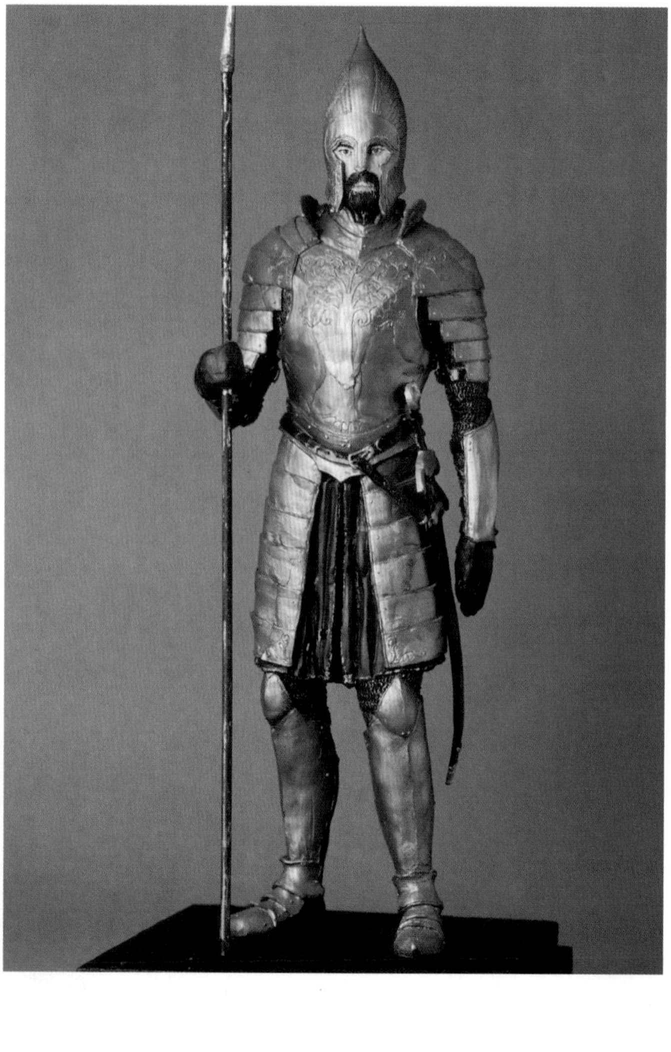

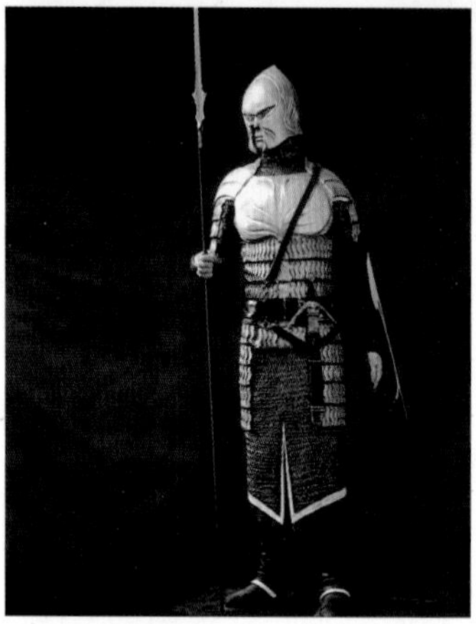

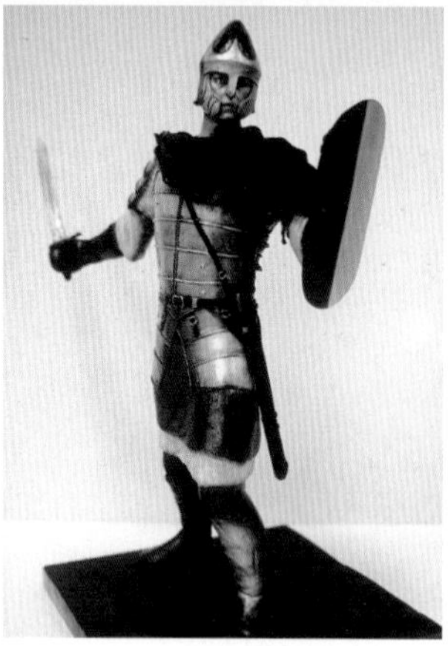

GONDORIAN SOLDIERS *Maquettes*

These three maquettes are some of the many that were produced by Weta as the design of the Gondorian armor progressed toward final approval by Peter Jackson. The one above left is by Ben and shows a Middle Eastern influence, particularly in the long chain skirt. Above right is one of Warren's early sculpts, exploring ideas for armor design. The sculpt to the right was the final Gondorian maquette that Daniel did, and represents the culmination of many people's work. *BW, WM, & DF*

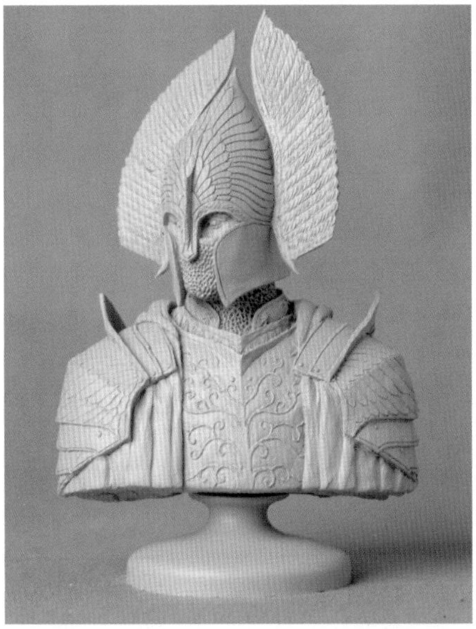

CITADEL GUARD
Maquette
This highly detailed design maquette by Daniel is the final approved design, and was produced for Weta Digital as a scanning model from which to create digital versions of the Citadel Guard figures. *DF*

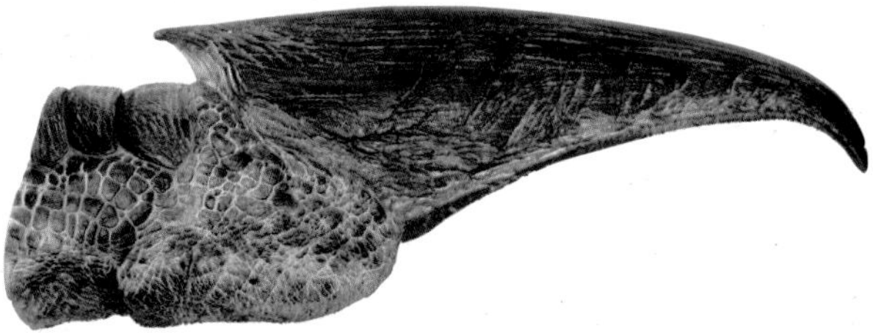

FELL BEAST CLAW *Maquette*
This sculpt of the fell beast's claw by Mike Asquith was done at a large scale for scanning so that the Weta Digital artists could get the textures and colors right for the digital model. Gino Acevedo painted it while demonstrating a technique with plaster of Paris; a cast of the sculpt done in plaster of Paris can be worked up to produce the very hard, crisp feeling that you would get in the actual claw itself. *MA*

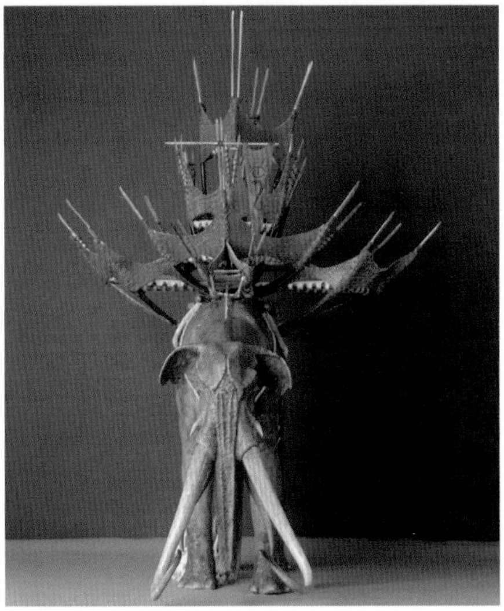

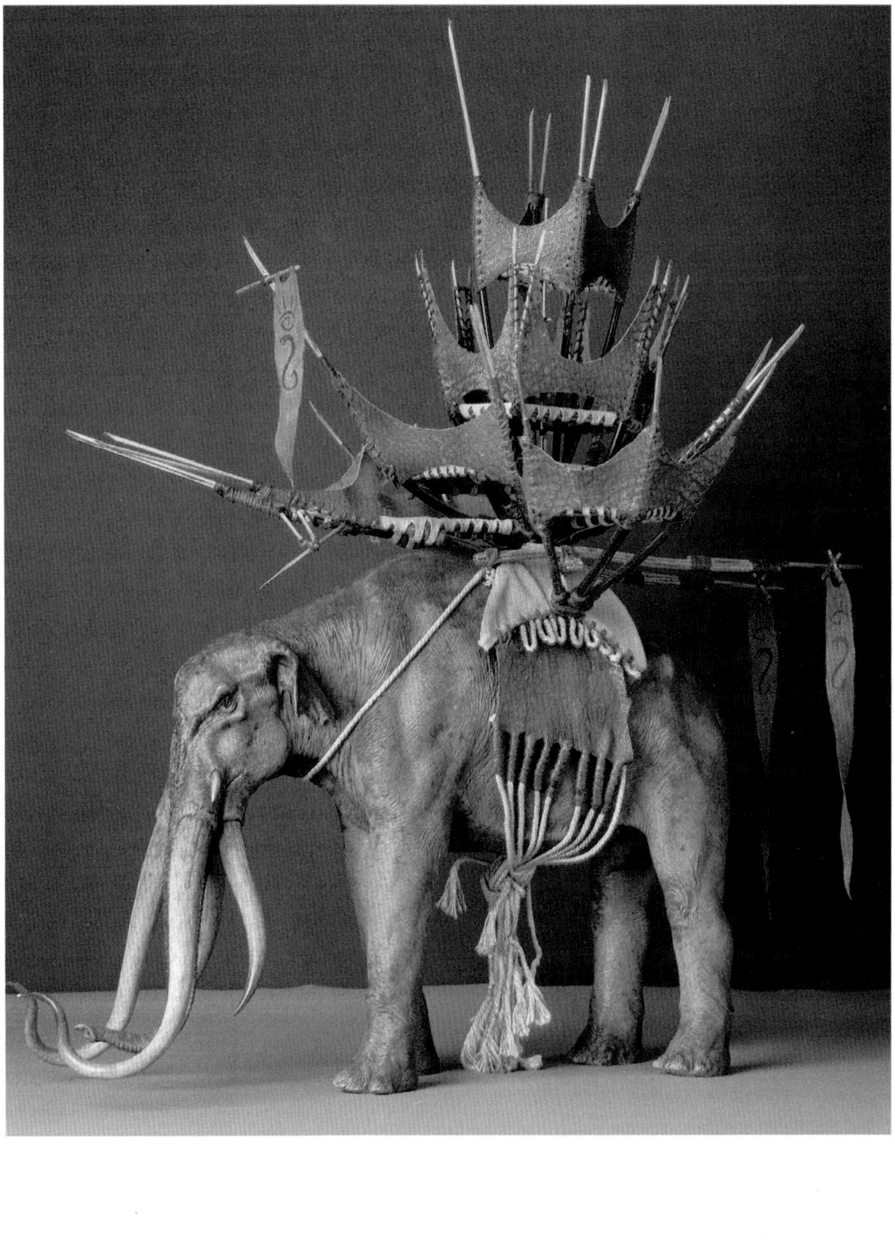

MÛMAKIL *Maquette*
"This maquette was made from a design of Daniel Falconer's that Peter Jackson liked. I just turned it into a three-dimensional creature with a few changes. Because I have a stop-motion background, a lot of my 2D creature designs don't change much as I progress to 3D. At the back of my mind, no matter what I'm drawing, I'm thinking in 3D. It often works out that I pencil it, then sculpt it, but someone else will color it because by that stage I've moved on to something else. I didn't do the tower on the back of this maquette. In fact, that's one of the reasons we had the maquettes in the first place – so that they could try building different structures on its back. I believe this was built by Matt Appleton, but from a design by Johnny Brough." *SB*

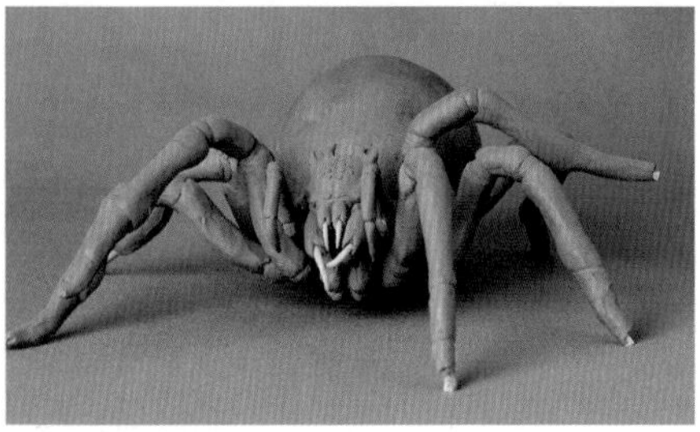

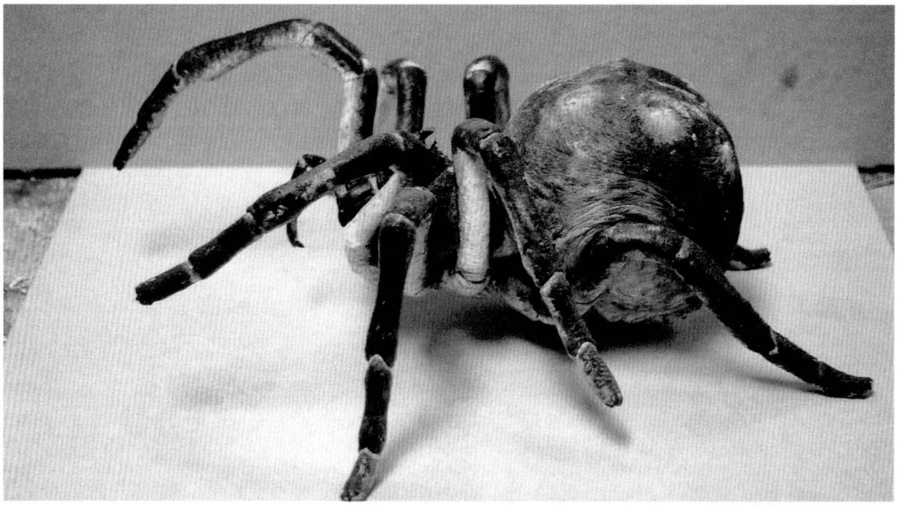

SHELOB *Maquettes*
"In some ways I prefer the sculpt above because it hasn't been painted. With a flat tone, it's easier to study. To the right is the most successful of the three body maquettes that were done – it's about 18 inches in diameter. Some things work well here, such as the immense weight of her abdomen – it's very baggy and wrinkly and we can see that it's actually resting on the back leg, it's so fat. Peter really liked the build of the tunnel web spiders, which have reasonably long but chunky, very strong-looking legs, so we can see that proportion here." *BW*

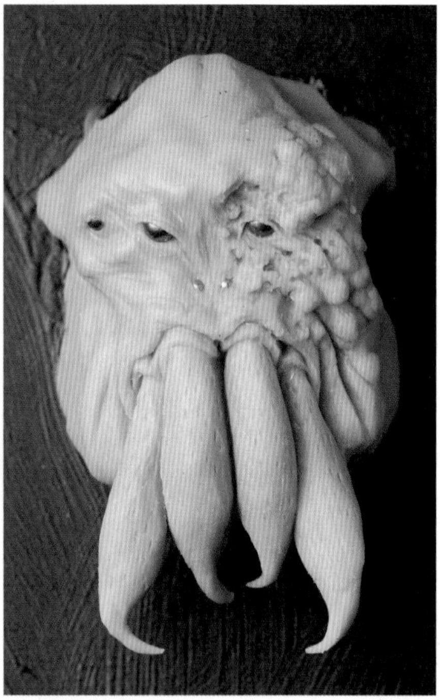

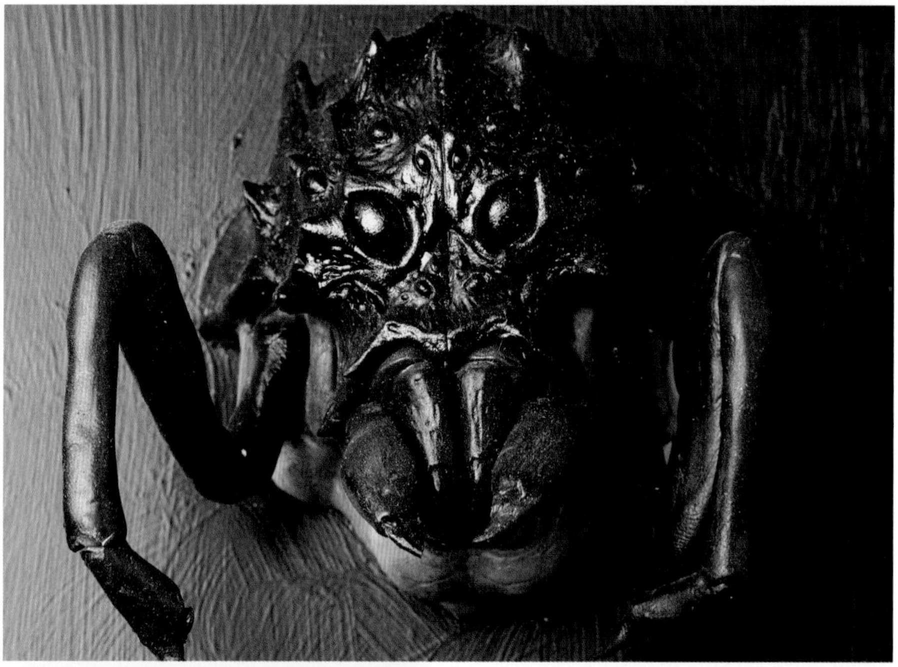

SHELOB *Maquettes*
With so many of the Weta designers working on Shelob, a number of different designs were created, all trying, and in some ways succeeding, to capture the essence of what Peter Jackson envisioned as the ultimate scary spider. The one near right is by Greg Tozer, while the others are by Jamie Beswarick. *GT & JB*

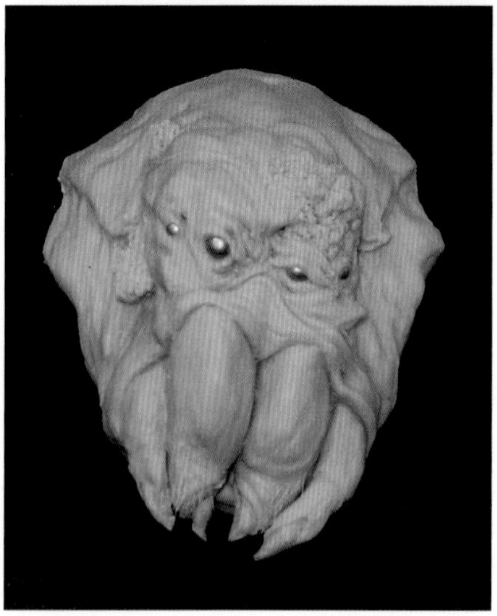

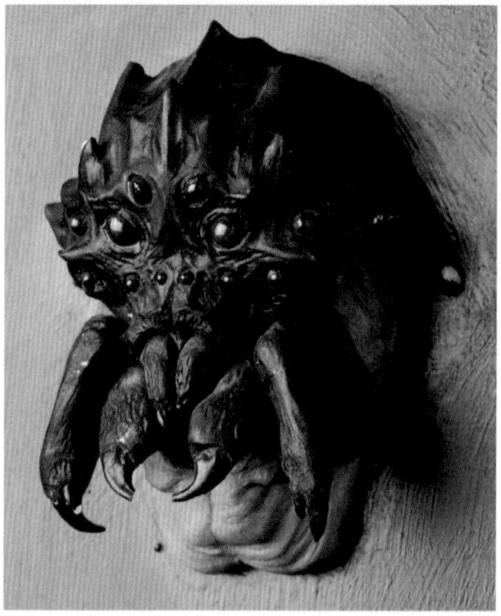

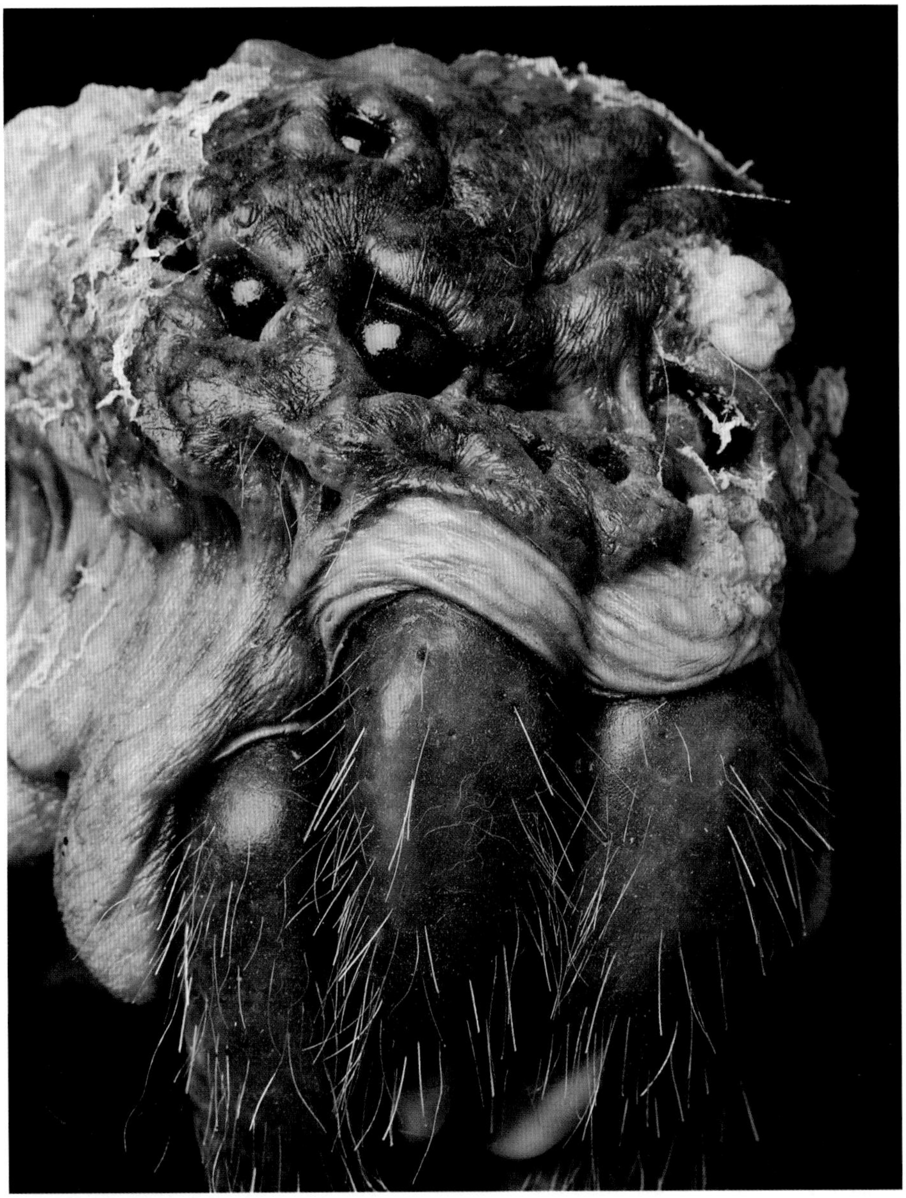

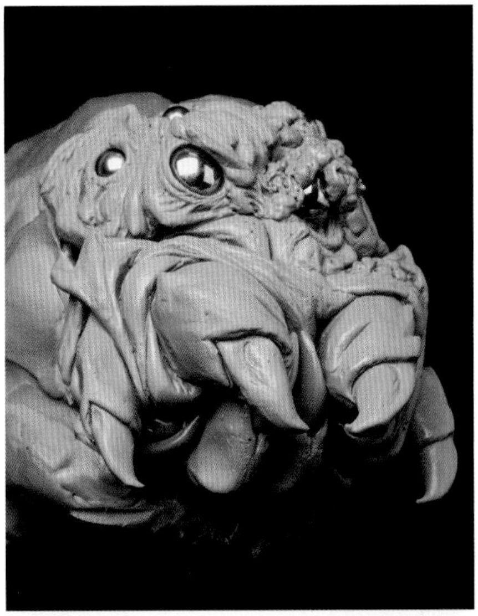

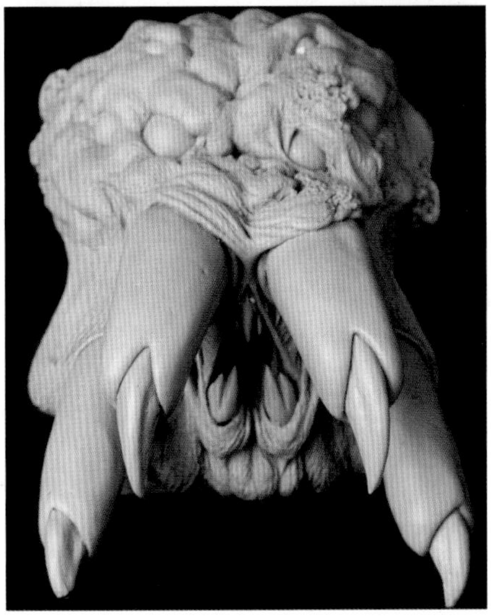

SHELOB *Maquettes*
"After the initial sculpt (top right) had been approved and scanned, Weta Digital quickly realized they would need to have a much more detailed understanding of Shelob's mouthparts in order to create a working digital model. Due to the deadline imposed on the digital animation team, only a day could be spent designing the mouth workings. The quickest way to achieve this was through an augmented version of the original sculpt. We poured a hard Plasticine copy from the existing mold and quickly worked the mouth details into it. The design brief was to the point: scary and disgusting. From memory, I conjured up a combination of the most vile images I could think of and worked them around the existing mandibles: squid beaks, crayfish mouths, and various 'organic apertures' were the main inspiration. The only change Peter made to this design was to remove the large middle tooth at the top of the mouth. The digital team did an amazing job of breathing life into the design (above right). From a static sculpt to a slobbering snapping maw.

"Above is the approved Shelob face sculpt. Designing the paint scheme on an organic-translucent base, Gino Acevedo used this silicone rubber casting of the maquette. Combining elements from Jamie's anatomical spider-face sculpts and Greg's diseased maquettes, opposite, this final version was an attempt to capture all the aspects of design that Peter and Fran warmed to the most. The diseased growths were whittled back to a concentration around the left eye, and a more predatory look was introduced by bringing the alpha eyes closer together. In keeping with the squat nature of the tunnel web spider, Peter had me shorten the length of the face, bringing the eyes and mouthparts closer and creating a more focused creature. Only the size of a fist, this design maquette was to become the scanning model, as the scan technology no longer required large-scale models to achieve high resolution. The resulting scan was so detailed that it perfectly captured an errant thumbprint on the back of the model!" *BH*

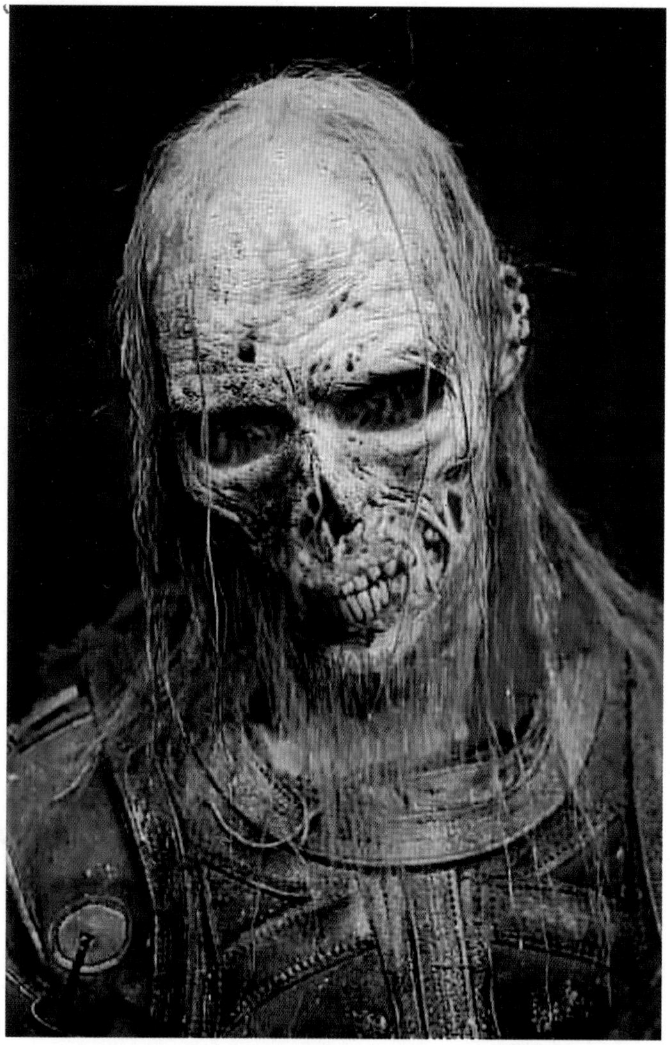

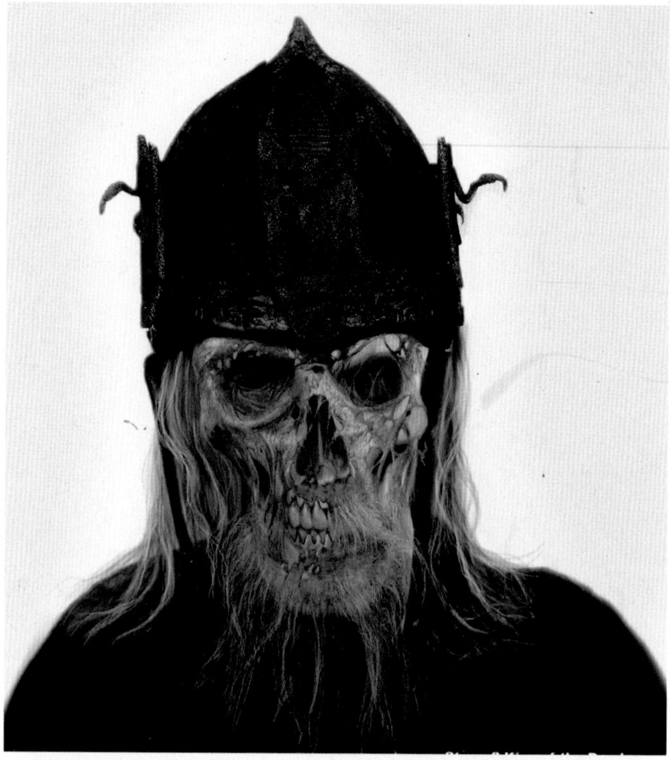

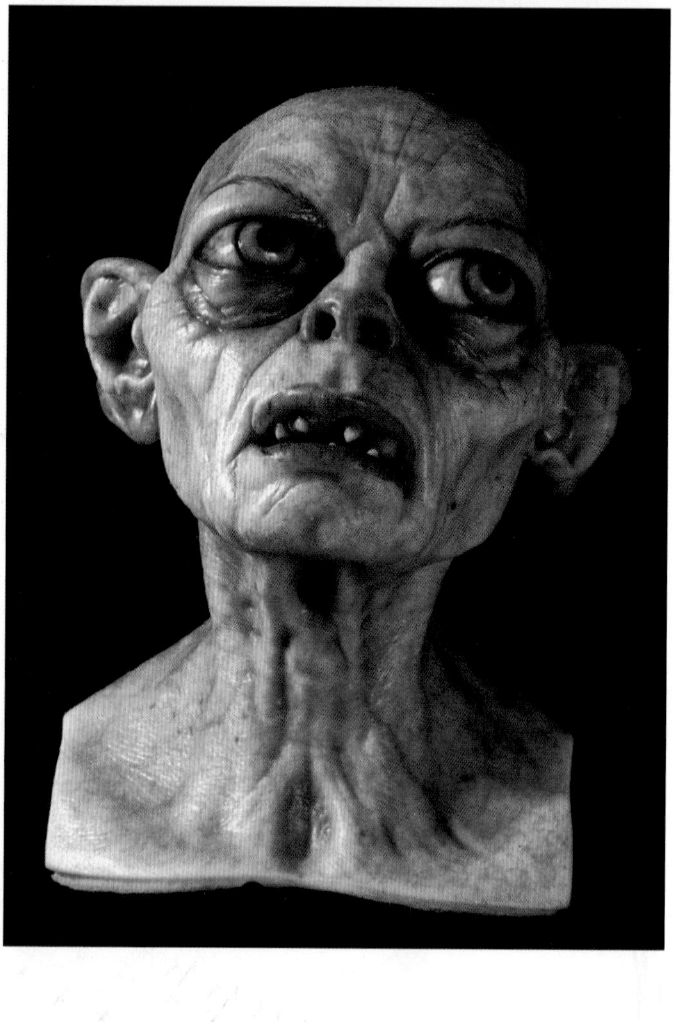

KING OF THE DEAD *Maquette and Photoshop exercise*
"The first stage of the King of the Dead transformation consisted of a full head and facial prosthetic appliance sculpted by Jamie Beswarick (above right). The artwork shown here for the second stage would have to be done digitally to achieve the effect. To achieve this we made a clay copy of the full prosthetic makeup, then sculptor Bill Hunt carved into the appliances until he had sculpted a decomposing skull that would line up perfectly with the makeup, making it possible for Weta Digital composite artist Charlie Tait to complete the ghostly effect of having the skull show through the makeup at times.

"The second stage of the King of the Dead CGI was for the scene in which you see the King during his transformation. Of course, there's also a prosthetic mask on the actor – there's a haze or mist that flows over his face, and as the mist covers him you start to see the deterioration, and begin to see the skull beneath his skin and all the gory detail." *GA*

GOLLUM *Silicone head*
The final head design (right) – designed and sculpted by Jamie Beswarick and painted by Gino Acevedo: "After designing several different paint schemes for Gollum, this is the final 'look' that Peter approved." *JB & GA*

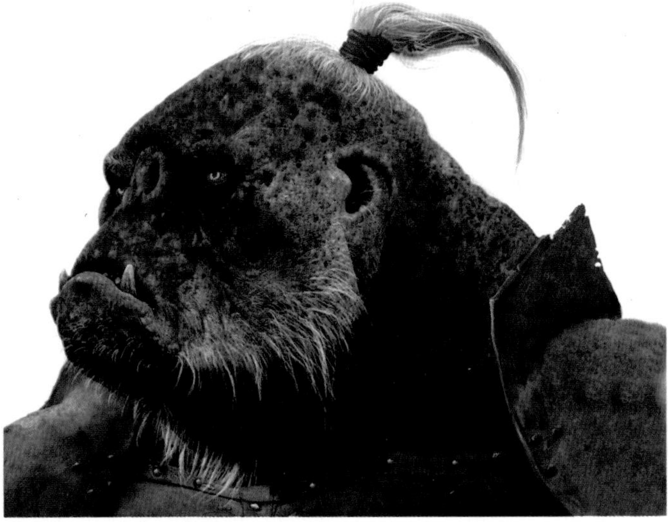

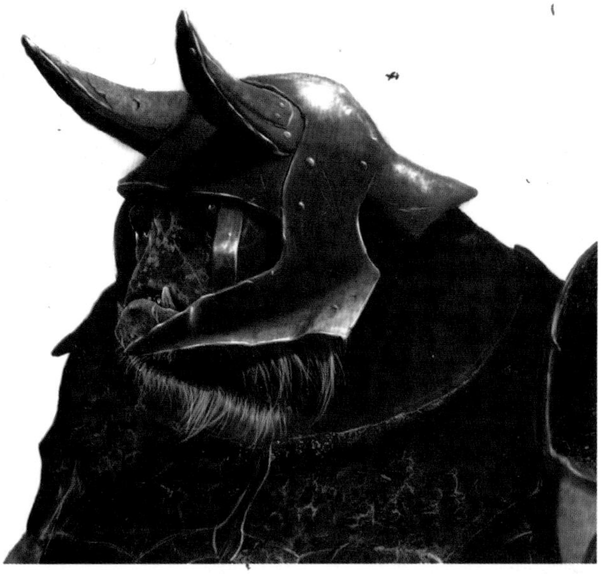

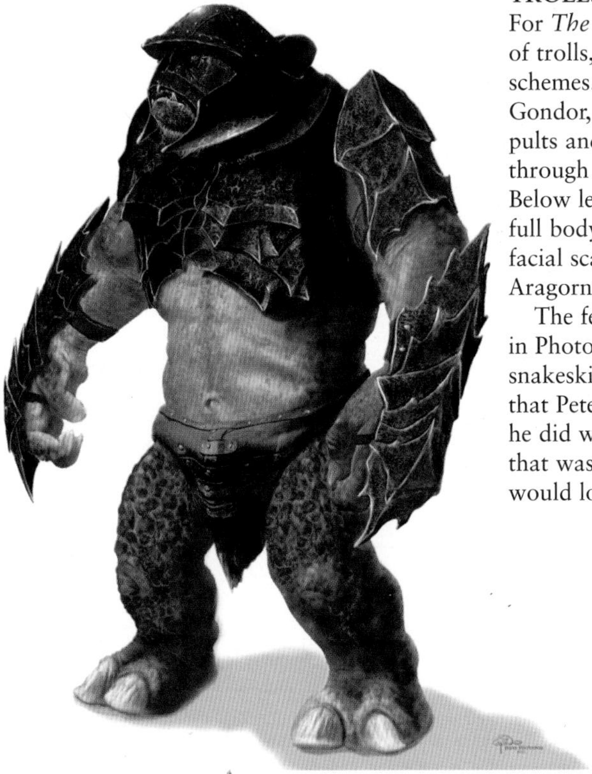

TROLLS AND FELL BEASTS ***Photoshop exercises***
For *The Return of the King*, there were five different types of trolls, all of which required subtly different color schemes. The helmeted ones were for the Siege of Gondor, with the one below loading the catapults and the one above right used to crash through the gate, attacking all in its path. Below left can be seen the Attack Troll in full body armor. The troll above left, with facial scars and sideburns, is the one that attacks Aragorn during the battle at the Black Gates.

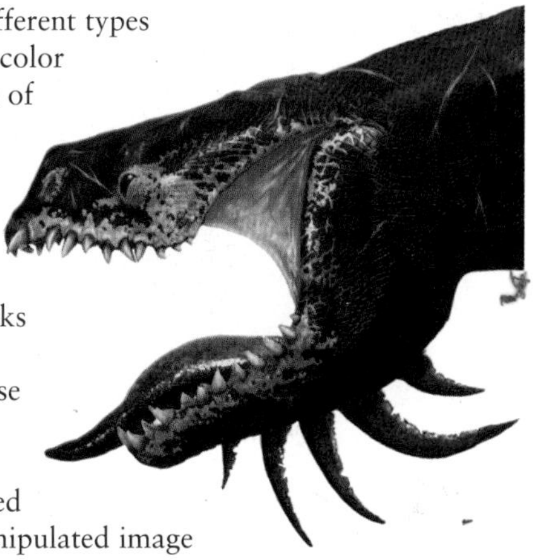

The fell beast image to the right is an exercise in Photoshop, trying to replicate the look of snakeskin and come up with a color scheme that Peter Jackson would approve, which indeed he did with this one. Below it is a digitally manipulated image that was done to show what the inside of a fell beast's neck would look like when the head was removed from the body. *GA*

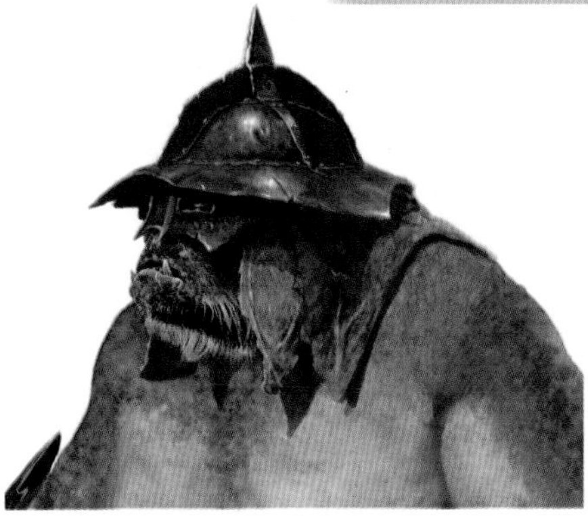

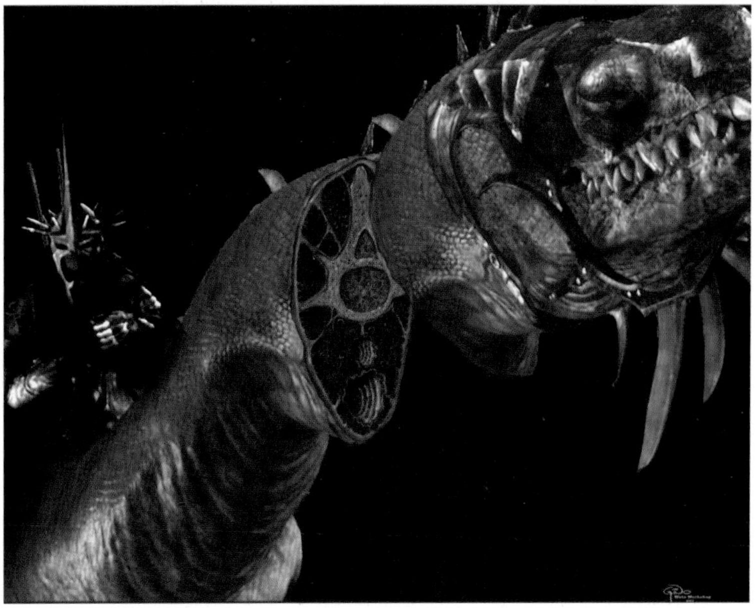

DIGITAL PAINTINGS

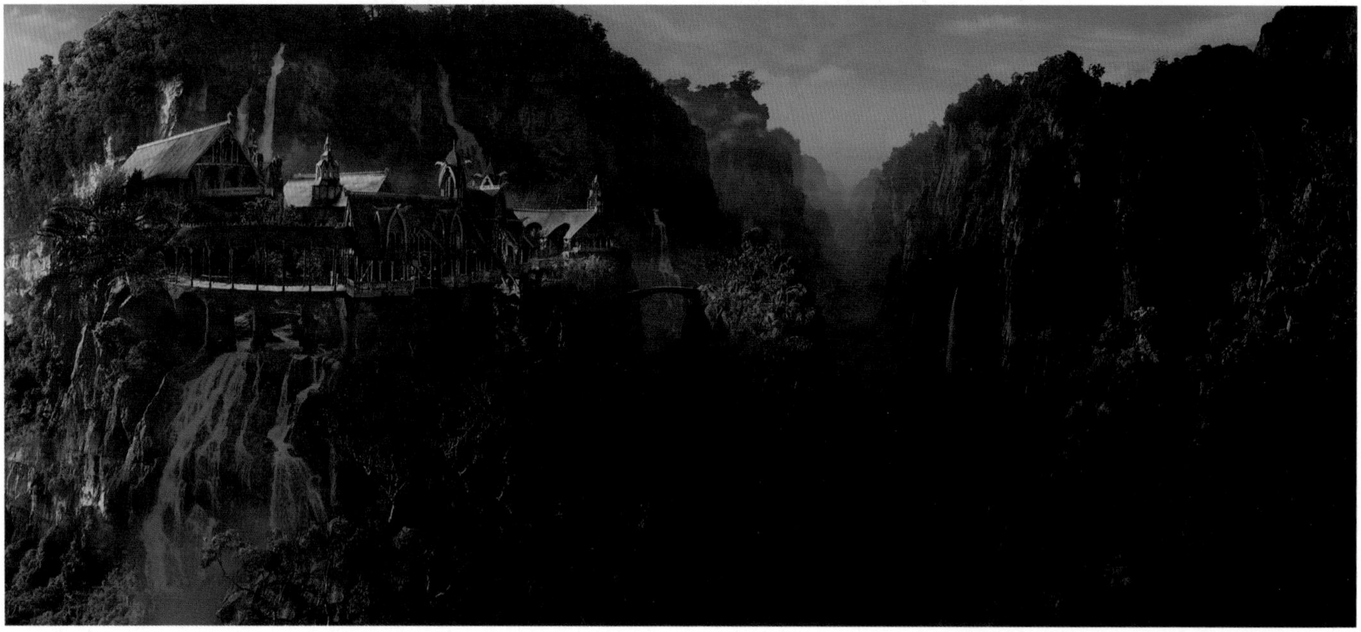

A digital matte artist is a painter first, digital artist second, and quite often that is the approach one had to take when producing matte shots for the films. The world of *The Lord of the Rings* that is being incorporated into the film is based on original art by illustrators such as Alan Lee, so it springs from a very subjective frame of mind. Regardless of the wonderful vistas that New Zealand provides, and that the photo reference sometimes offered, sometimes thrust, into the development of the image, the matte painting is a painting in a very real sense: it has to convey a story. This begins with a sketch by Alan Lee or a quick paint sketch by Jeremy Bennett. Sometimes Gus Hunter will give us a bit more in terms of a Photoshop layout. Once we get the green light (quite often Peter Jackson approves the "feel" of a shot more than anything else) we begin painting, first roughly, to lay the image out accurately and match it to the live plate, then more definitely. Since changing a painting in its later history is not as simple as changing lighting on a shader and rerendering, great care is often taken in making sure that each step is successful. Sometimes we'll even film a rougher painting to see how much more is actually needed. For others we might overpaint – in other words, put in more than will ever be seen, just in case.

Of course, there are paintings that were fairly simple sky replacements, where the matte painter acted like a digital compositor, in a sense using digital tools to replace one image with another without working too hard, but those instances were quite rare. Photos rarely do the trick in and of themselves. The difference between a digital compositor and a matte artist is that they usually have many other concerns (in the case of *The Lord of the Rings*, quite weighty, technical ones) and a variety of tasks to tackle. Our two worlds have a gray area between them, but there is quite a distinction in terms of focus: a simple way to put it would be that one is a photographer on wheels, and the other is a painter, but both can be animators.

Roger Kupelian
May 2003

"Digital painting is a wonderful combination of the oldest artistic technique in the world with the most modern artistic technique. You can manipulate every pixel of a digital picture now to create color and light and shade and so manipulate the data that was shot on the day. But to do that, you go back to the oldest art form, just a brush and pigments and paint to create the look."

PETER JACKSON

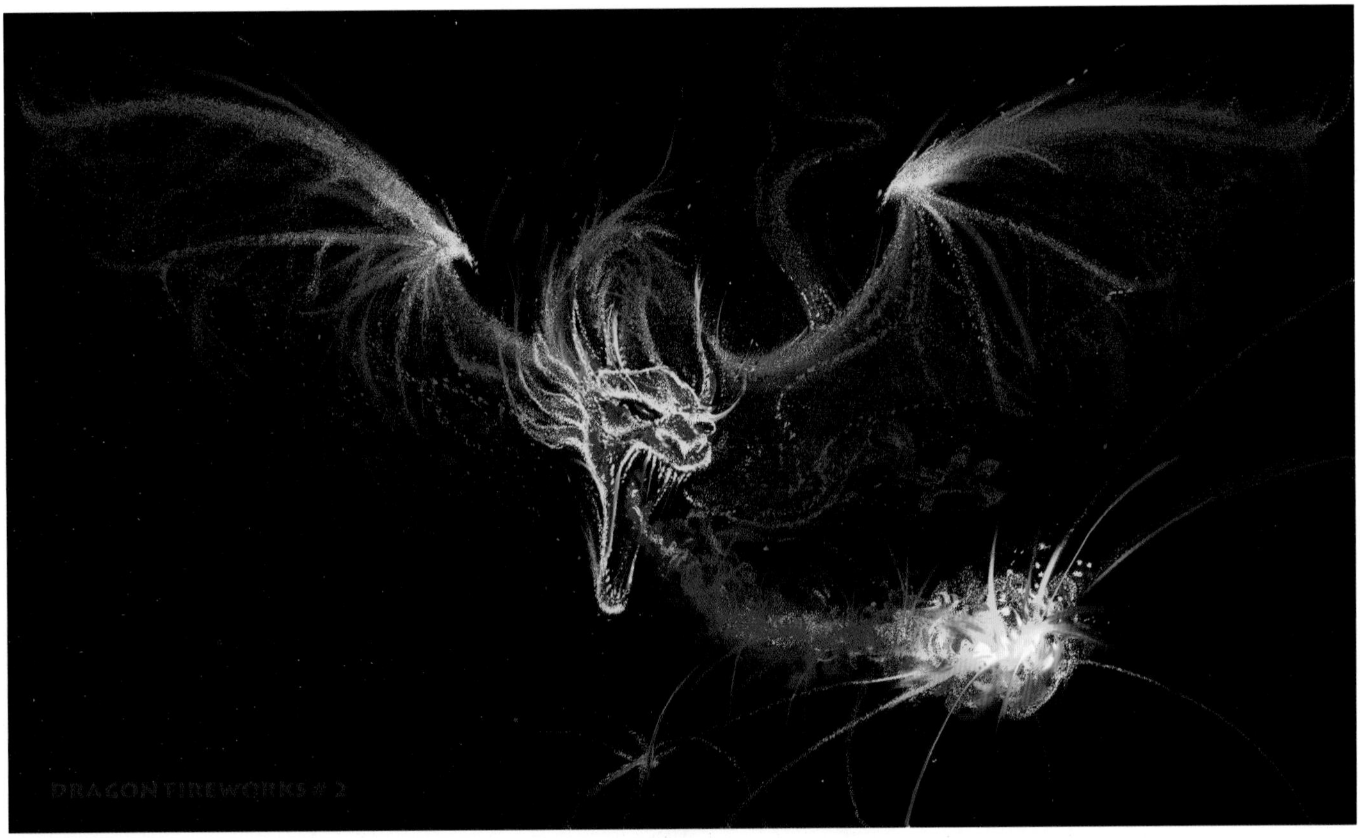

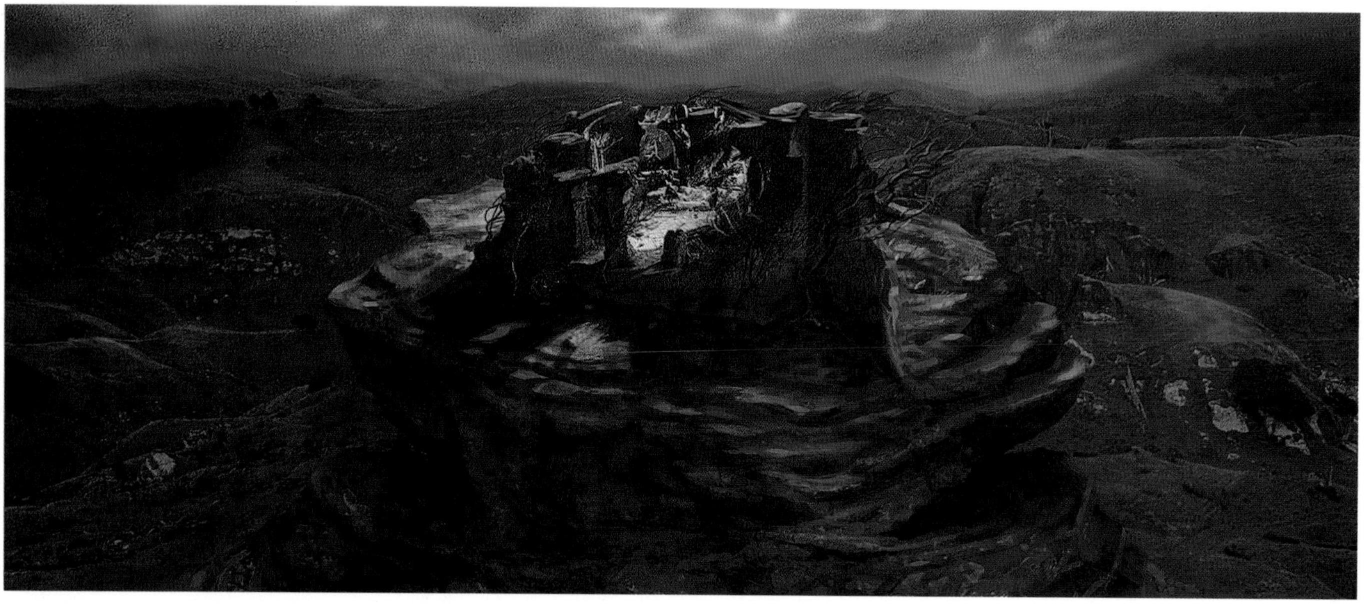

FROM BREE TO RIVENDELL *Weathertop*
"Working from some of Alan Lee and Jeremy Bennett's concept sketches, based upon the actual location footage, this dramatic view was created by adding various background layers and sky elements on the computer." *GH*

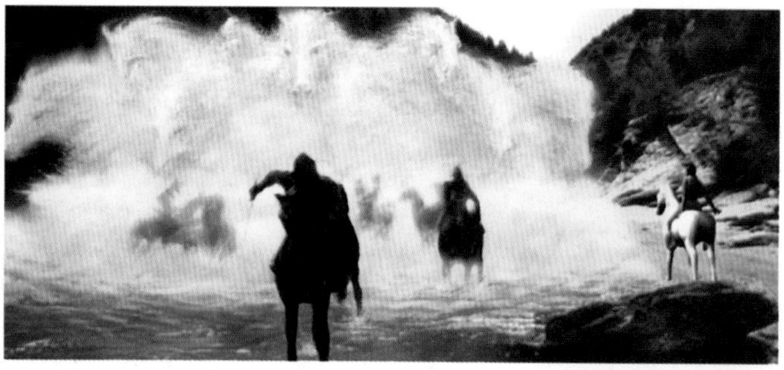

RIVENDELL *The Ford of Bruinen*
"The digital composite to the left was the first illustration of how this spectacular scene would look in the film. It shows the water-based horses – summoned by the power of the Elves – in relation to their environment and to the Ringwraiths and their horses prior to the deluge that washes them away. Arwen on Asfaloth can be seen to the right." *GH*

MORIA *Khazad-dûm*
"Taking Alan Lee's conceptual drawings as a starting point, this painting was created using the miniature stairs built by Weta Workshop. This composite was created to show how much flame and lava are visible in the cavern and to give a feeling of depth, although it was important to hint at the bottomlessness of the chasm. The columns of the stairway actually go down farther than the original frame of the miniature, and the base doesn't show lava so much as flame, rocks, and smoke to imply that it's there somewhere, far beneath the bridge." *GH*

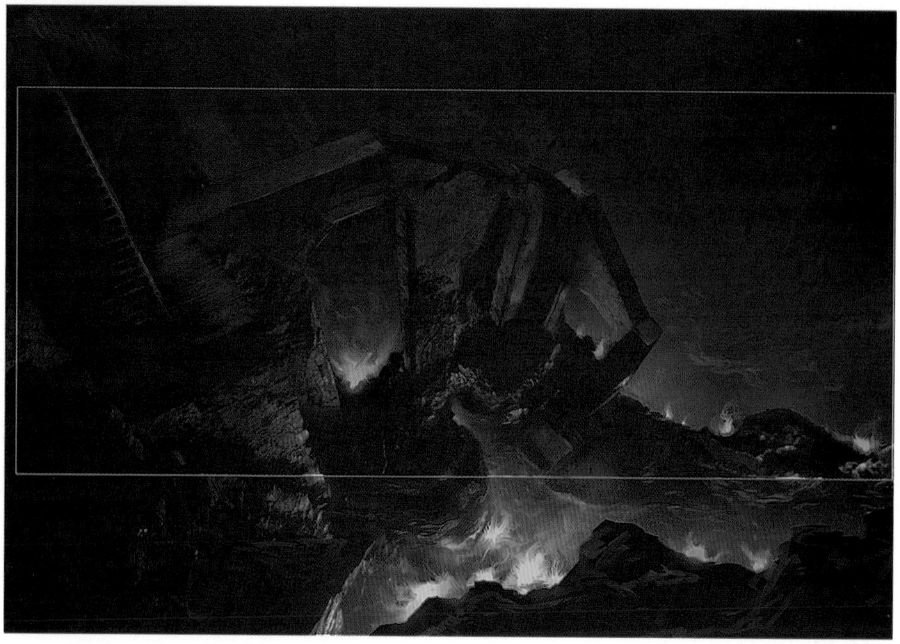

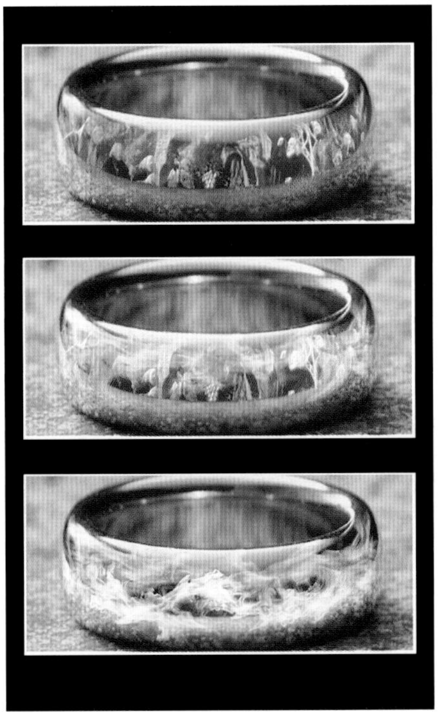

RIVENDELL ***The One Ring***
"This is a study of how we see the fire flow within the Ring. This was used for reference only." *GH*

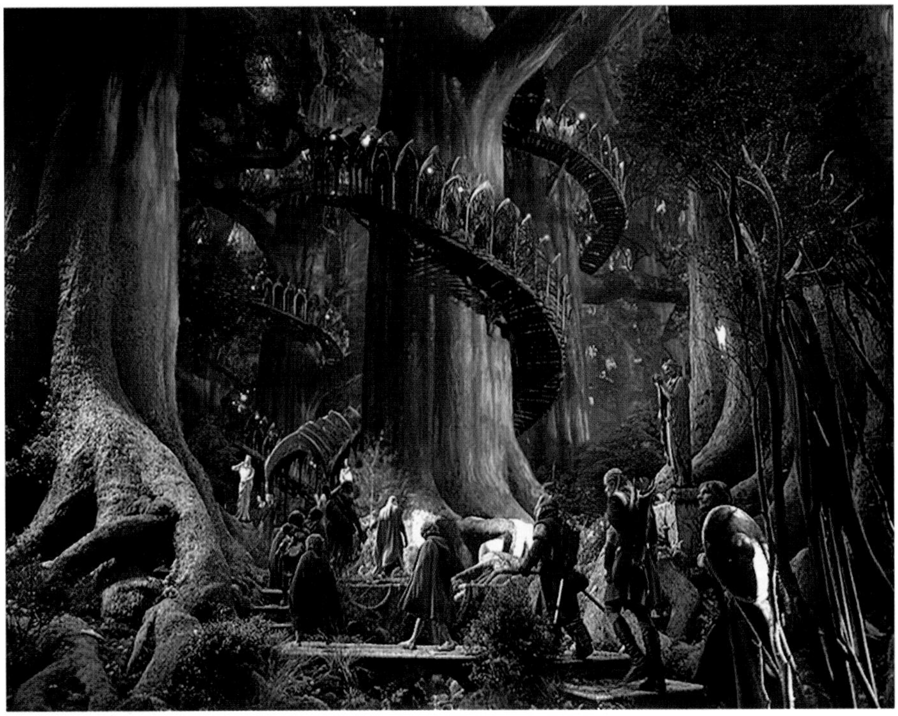

LOTHLÓRIEN ***Caras Galadhon***
"The lower half of the shot was filmed against a blue screen, so the upper part of the shot still had to be designed for the pan-up. The artwork had to include the miniature trees and show the look, mood, and atmosphere." *GH*

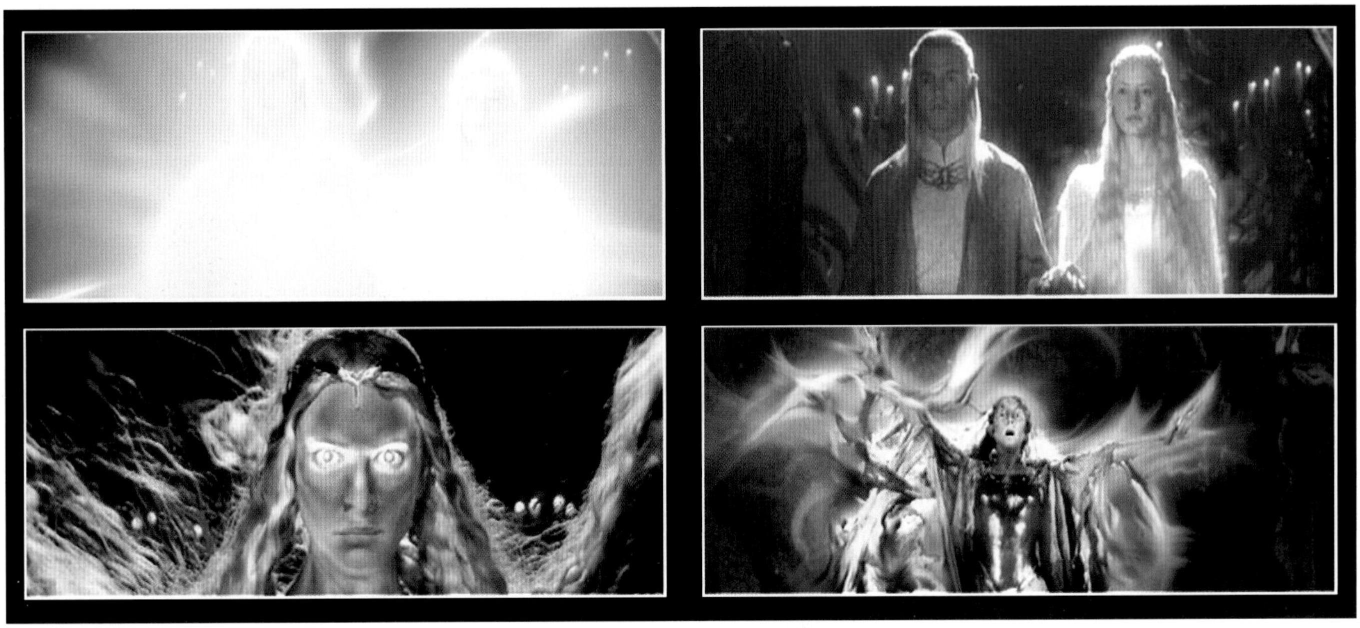

LOTHLÓRIEN ***Galadriel's Glade***
"These are all Galadriel glow studies. Different versions of Galadriel's good, semi-evil, and evil glows were done to show Peter." *GH*

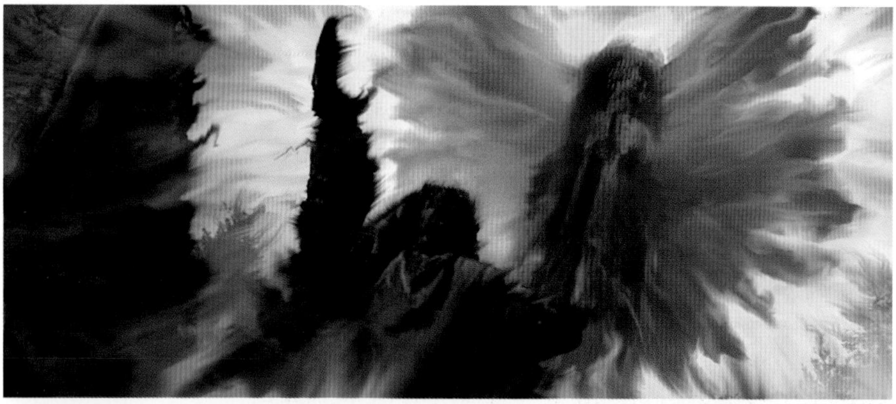

AMON HEN ***Color studies***
"These are the first and last frames of the sequence in which Frodo sees into Wraith World after putting on the Ring. The point of these two designs was to illustrate how the tunnel-vision effect would look on screen to display the sights that emerge. The effect uses tongues of flickering flame, acting like fingers, flowing outward." *GH*

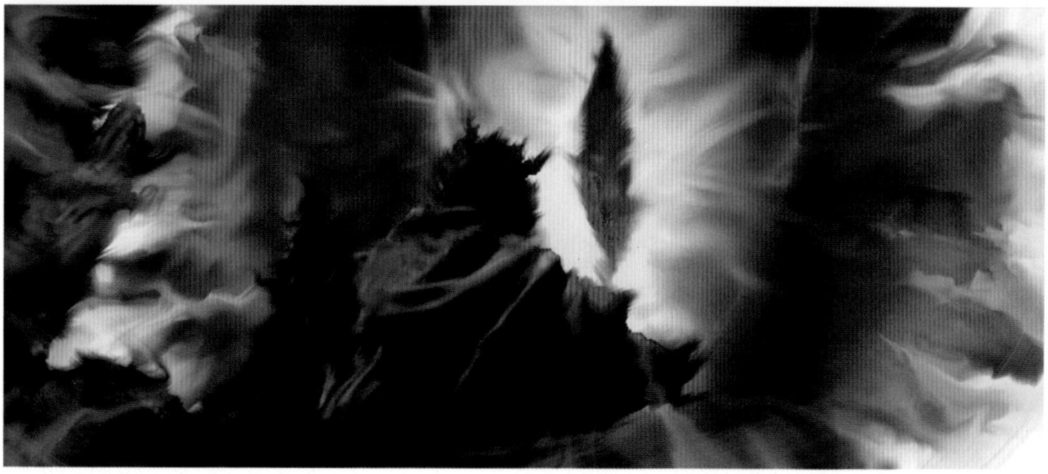

OSGILIATH ***Conceptual design***
"Using a shot from the location footage, below, this is a conceptual design of the view of Osgiliath down below and Minas Tirith in the distance, upon which Roger Kupelian based his final matte painting." *GH*

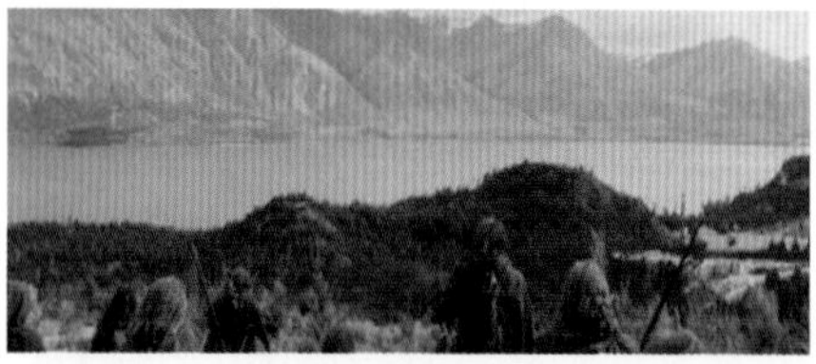

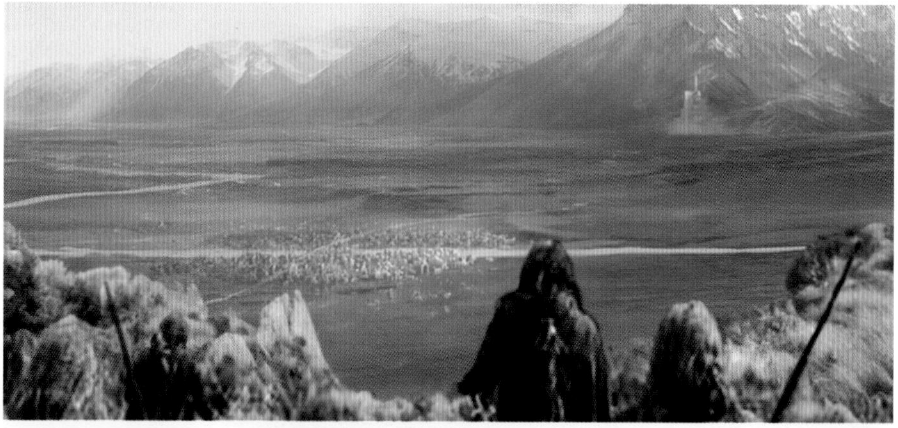

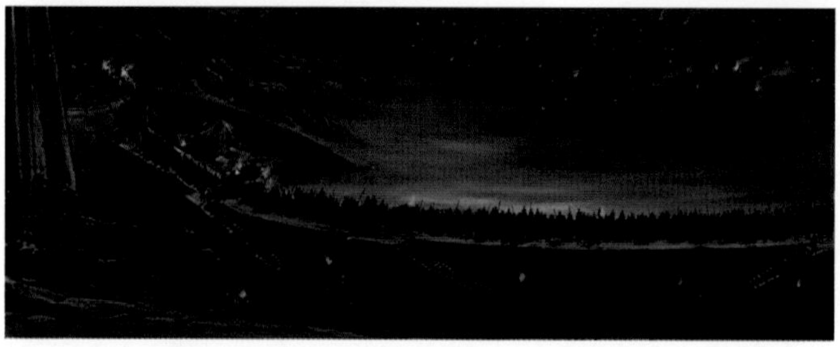

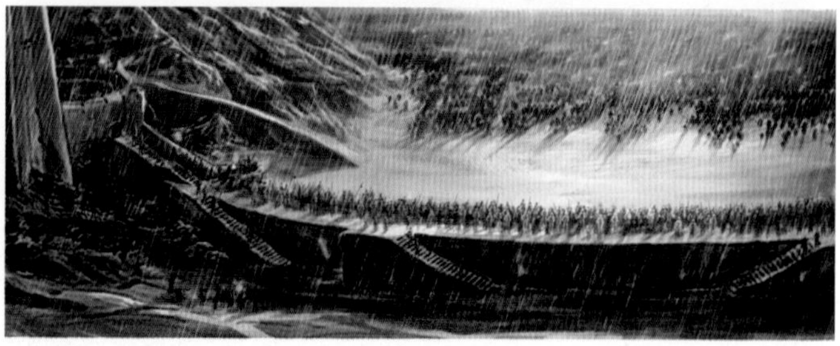

HELM'S DEEP ***Color studies***
"Here are two studies I did that show the before-and-after moment when a flash of lightning finally reveals the huge Uruk-hai that is marching up to Helm's Deep." *GH*

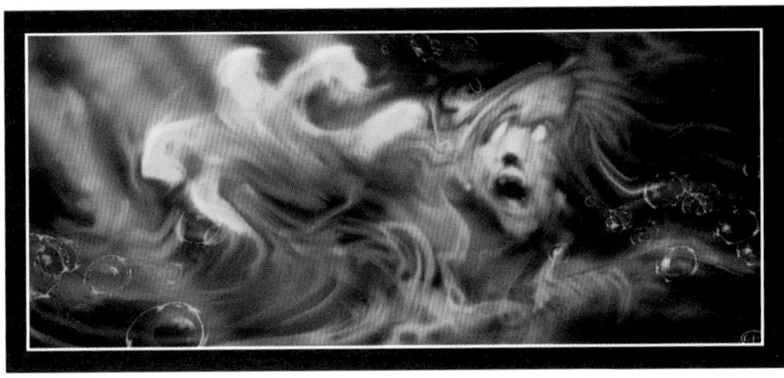

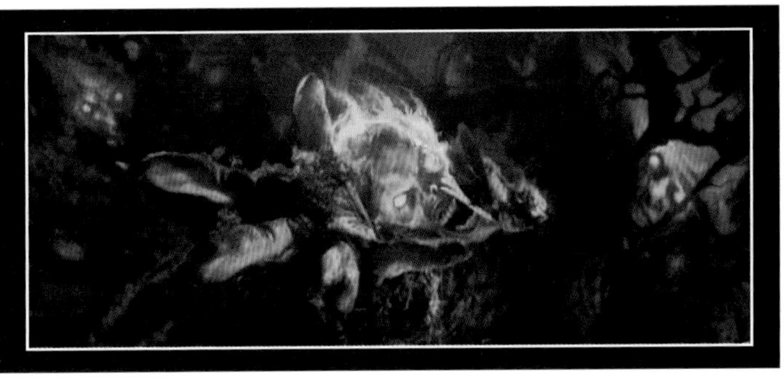

THE DEAD MARSHES *Spectral Corpses*
"These panels show the development from an early painting study of the corpses to combining all the filmed elements together to show what the final look could be." *GH*

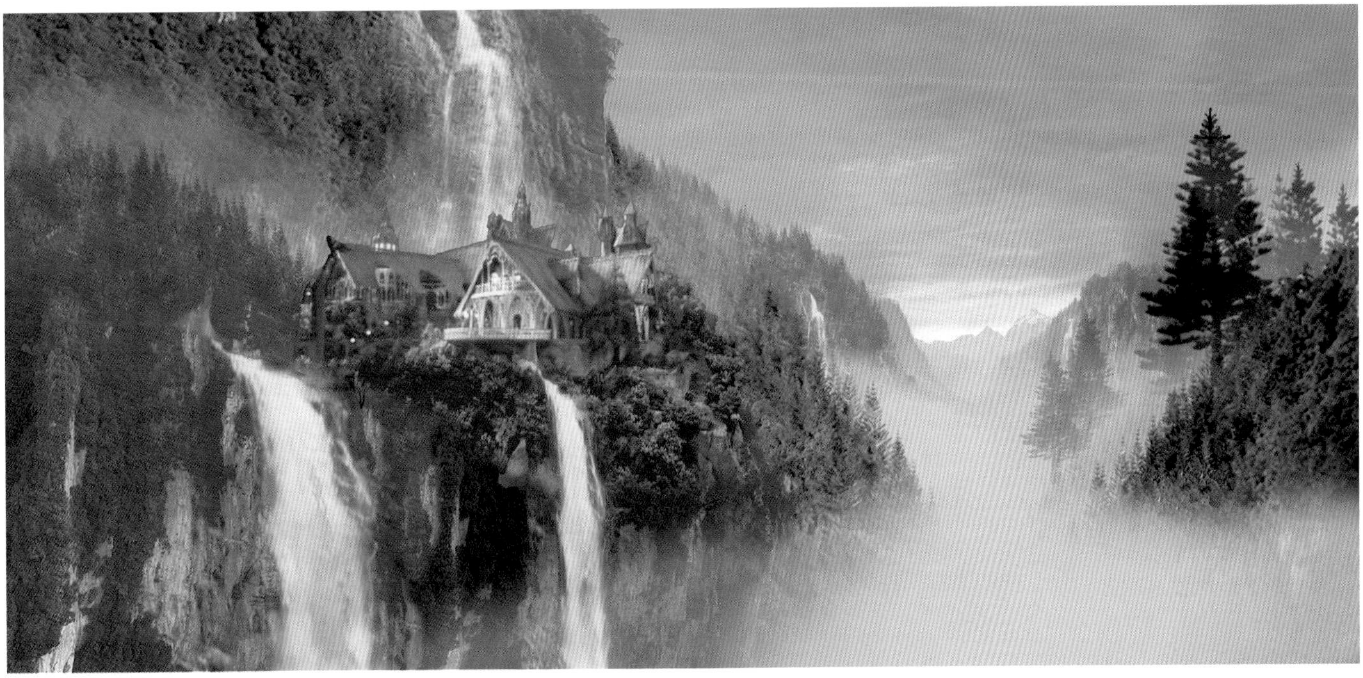

RIVENDELL *Matte painting layouts*
"This layout is for the background behind Arwen and Aragorn during a romantic scene at dusk. Yanick Dusseault based his final matte painting (page 215) on this." *GH*

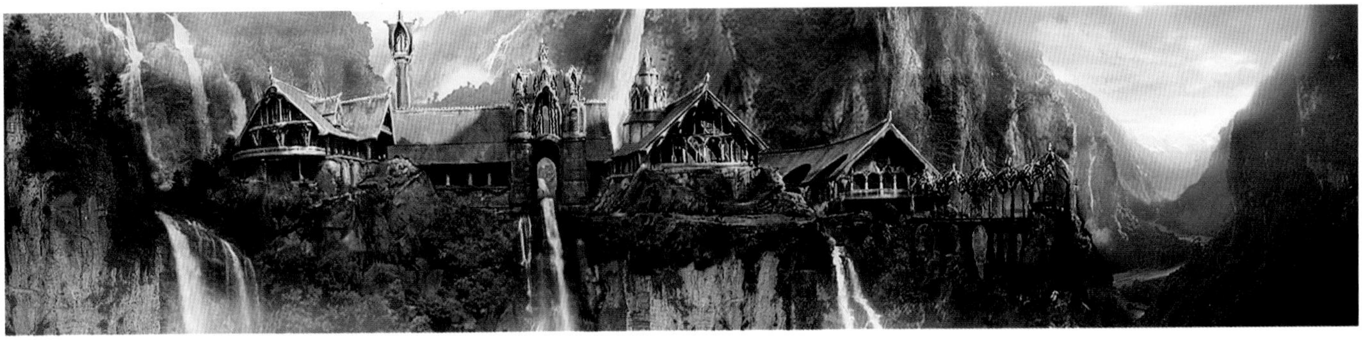

RIVENDELL *Cyclorama study*
"An early matte painting study for when Arwen is talking to Elrond in his chamber. I used subdued blues, greens, and golden colors for the highlights to give it a more melancholic palette." *GH*

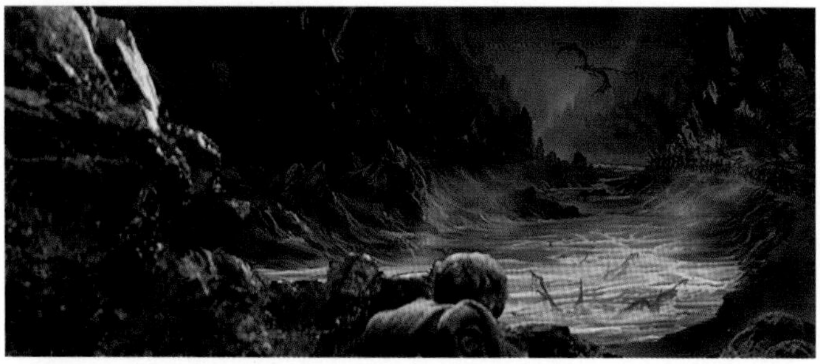

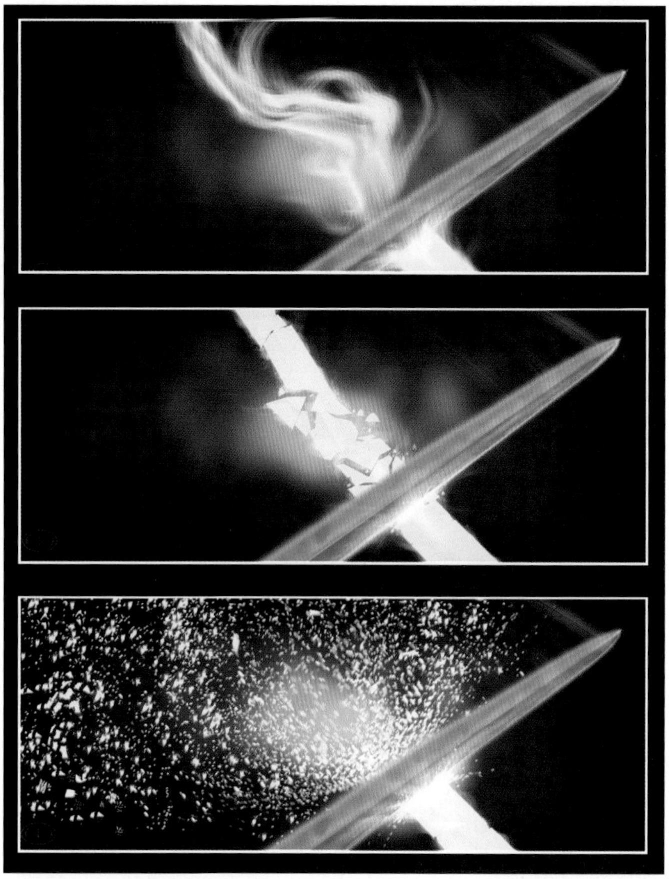

MINAS MORGUL ***Morgul river concept***
"This is a study showing what the Minas Morgul river environment might look like. It was thought that it would be almost like a swamp, sickly green in color and covered in mist. This shot shows Sam and Frodo watching the huge Orc army march away down the very road they have just traveled up, and off to war." *GH*

PATHS OF THE DEAD ***Digital concepts***
"These are concepts showing different ideas of how Narsil might have interacted with the King of the Dead's sword." *GH*

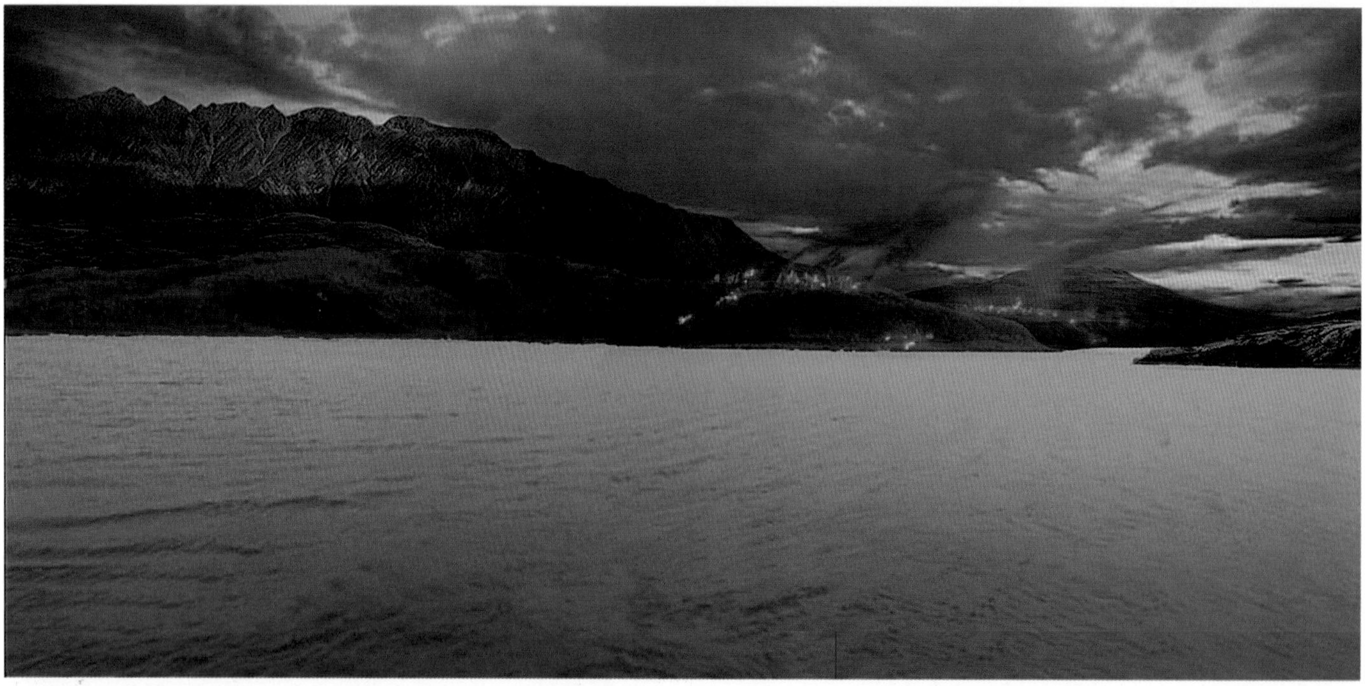

GONDOR ***River Anduin***
"This is a layout of the mid- and background mountains, using three or four photographic elements shot by Craig Potton. Afterward, the burning villages were added and then we put the Corsair ships in the foreground to show what the whole scene would look like." *SL*

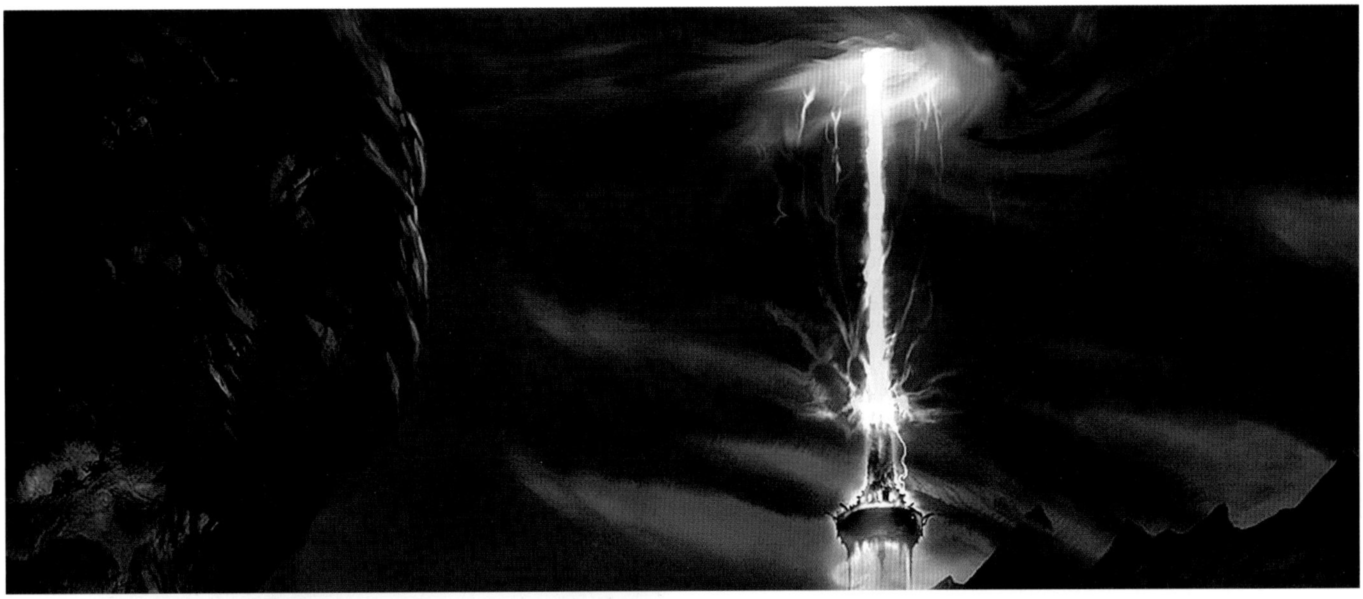

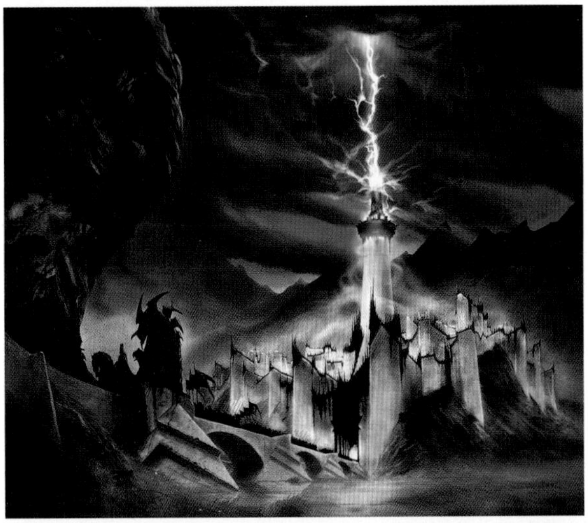

MINAS MORGUL *Lightning-flash concepts*
"Two of a set of conceptual illustrations demonstrating variations of flames shooting up from the beacon tower of Minas Morgul. The one below has been placed over John Howe's illustration from page 129, which has been extended upward and color-corrected to suit approved colors and lighting." *GH*

SHELOB'S LAIR *Phial glow study*
"This is one of two studies that I did, which were a combination of Jeremy Bennett's painting with my Photoshop effects added to show the look of the glowing phial inside Shelob's tunnel." *GH*

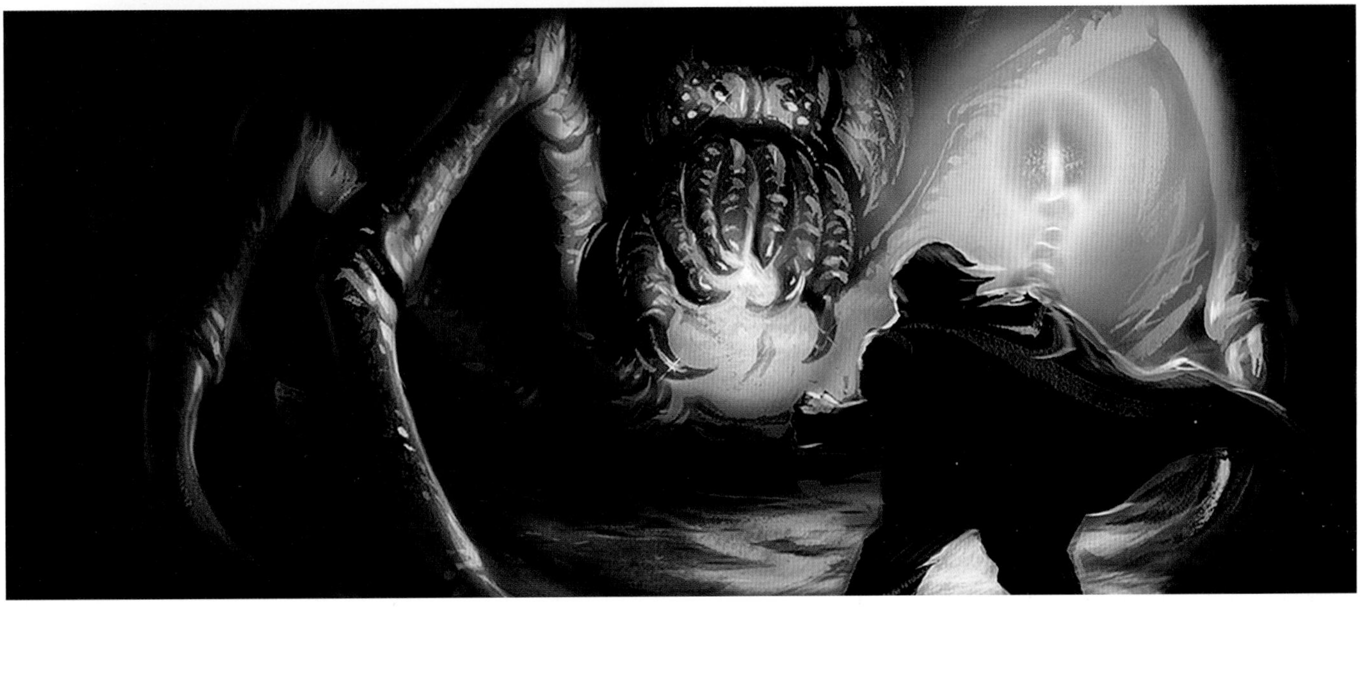

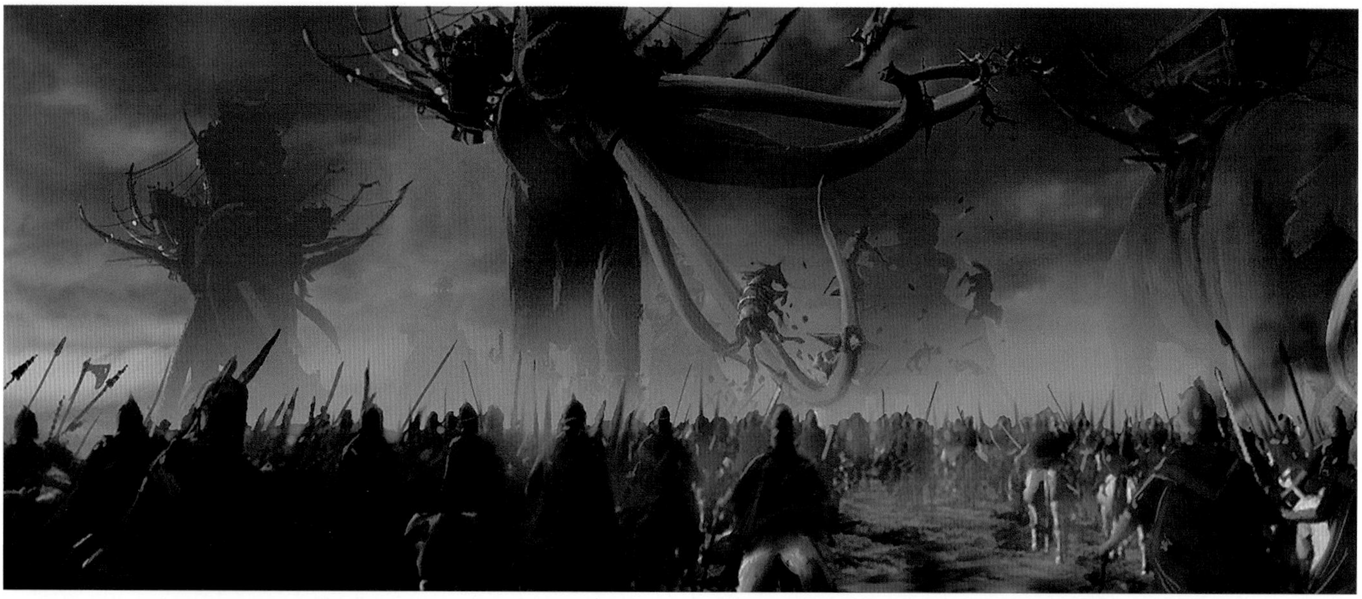

THE PELENNOR FIELDS *Color study*
"This is an early Photoshop concept that shows the mûmakil coming out of the mist and dust toward the Riders of Rohan." *GH*

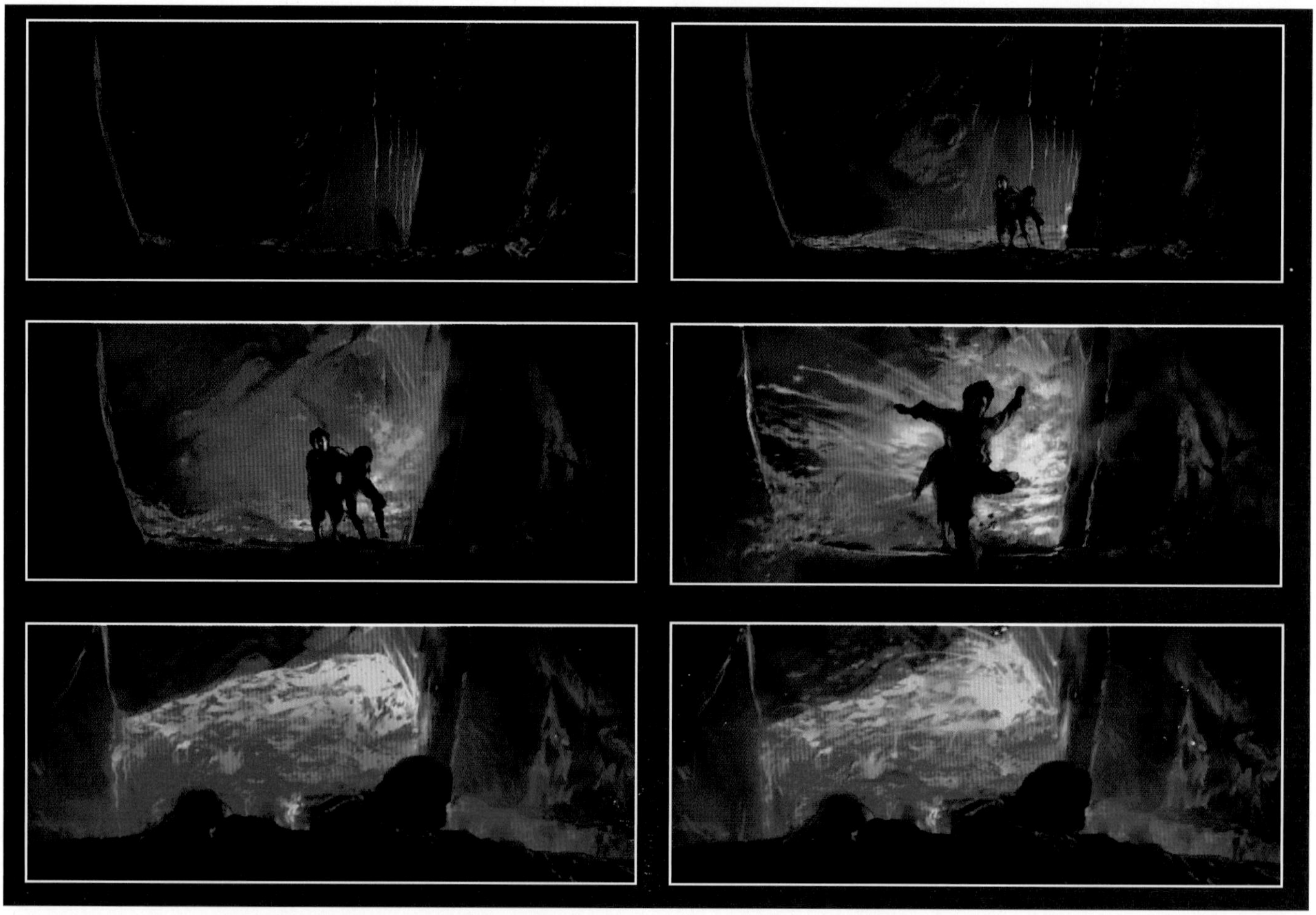

THE CRACK OF DOOM *Color studies and digital artwork*
"These studies were to show the inside of the Mount Doom environment; they are composites featuring the live-action plate in the foreground and the digital painting behind. I was trying to give Peter some options regarding atmosphere, lava, and color palettes." *GH*

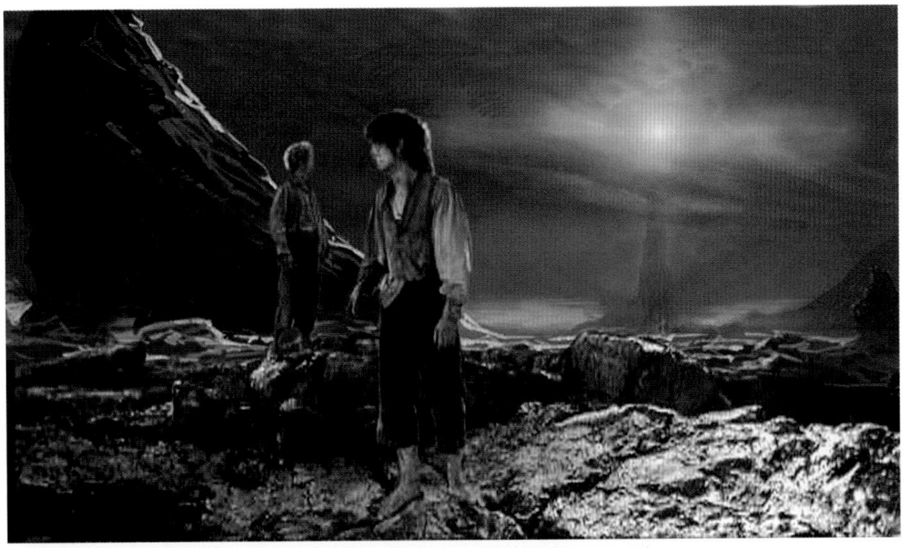

MORDOR *Gorgoroth Plain*
"This establishes the mid and background areas and sky. Jeremy Bennett painted in the Eye of Sauron lighting effects. In the end, we went for a cooler palette to avoid a 'Martian' type of feeling." *SL*

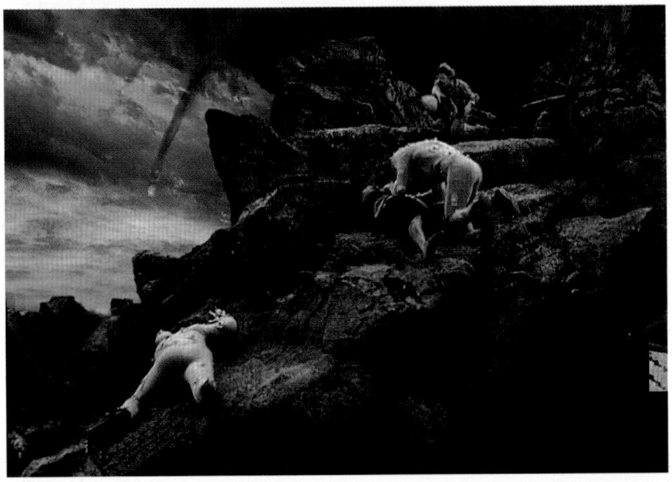

MORDOR *Mount Doom*
"This artwork encompasses the first, middle, and last frames of the shot in which Gollum jumps on Frodo and Sam on Mount Doom. It's pieced together from several skies, rocks from Wellington's south coast, and falling lava bombs." *SL*

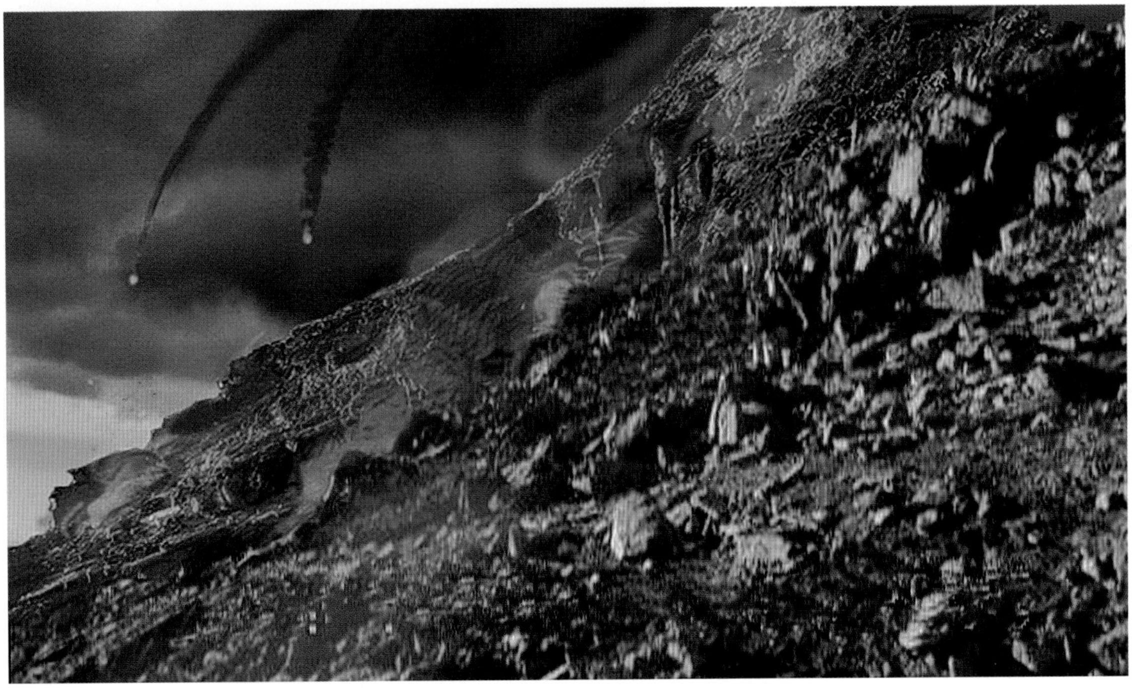

MORDOR
Mount Doom
"Different skies, atmospheres, lava bombs, flowing lava, and rock elements combine to create this particular look up the slopes of Mount Doom." *SL*

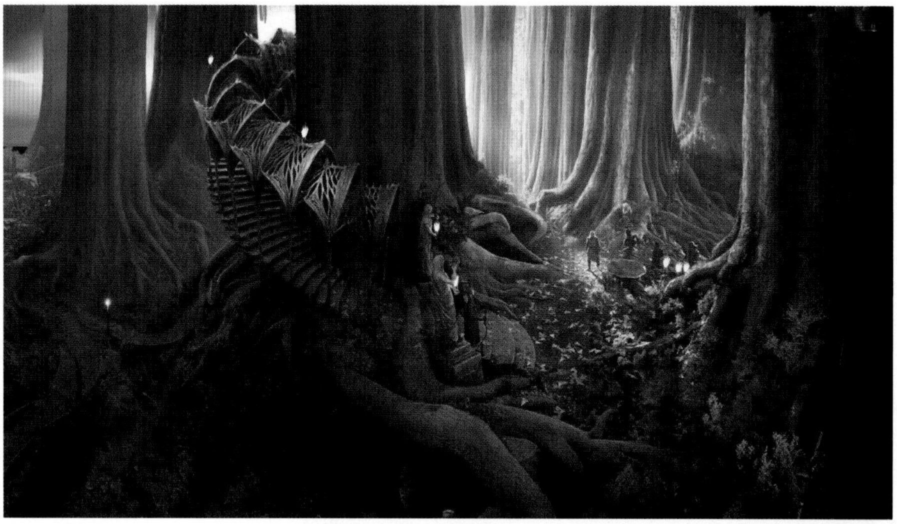

LOTHLÓRIEN ***Caras Galadhon at dusk***
"Unfortunately cut from the final theatrical print, this was a romantic view of the Fellowship being led through the mighty mallorn trees just before they meet Galadriel. The shot became a mixture of miniature mallorns, the live set, and the matte painting." *MD*

LOTHLÓRIEN
Silverlode River
"This painting was for the scene on the banks of the Silverlode River, when the Fellowship make their farewells to Galadriel and Caras Galadhon. This shot required the addition of trees, a major tree extension (note the reflection of the big tree in the water), and also the last views of Caras Galadhon in the early morning mist in the background." *MD*

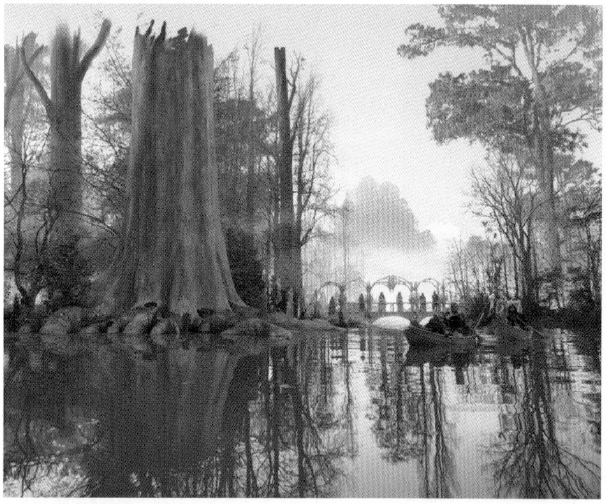

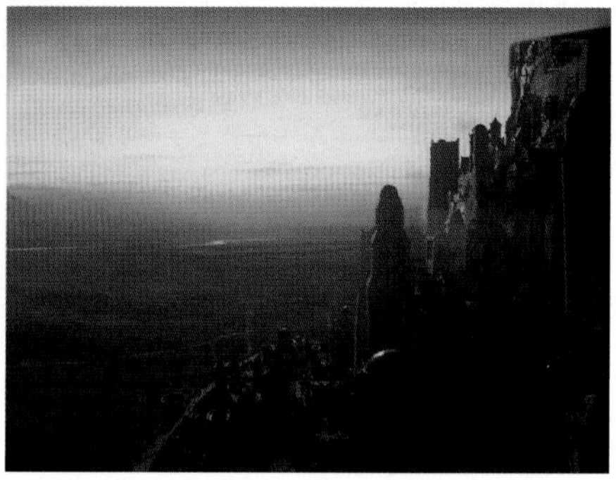

MINAS TIRITH ***Minas Tirith at dawn***
"This was the first big establishing shot of the mighty city of Minas Tirith. It became known as the Istanbul shot; the city was a large-scale miniature composited onto a full painted background. Computer-generated smoke and a scattering of doves were later added." *MD*

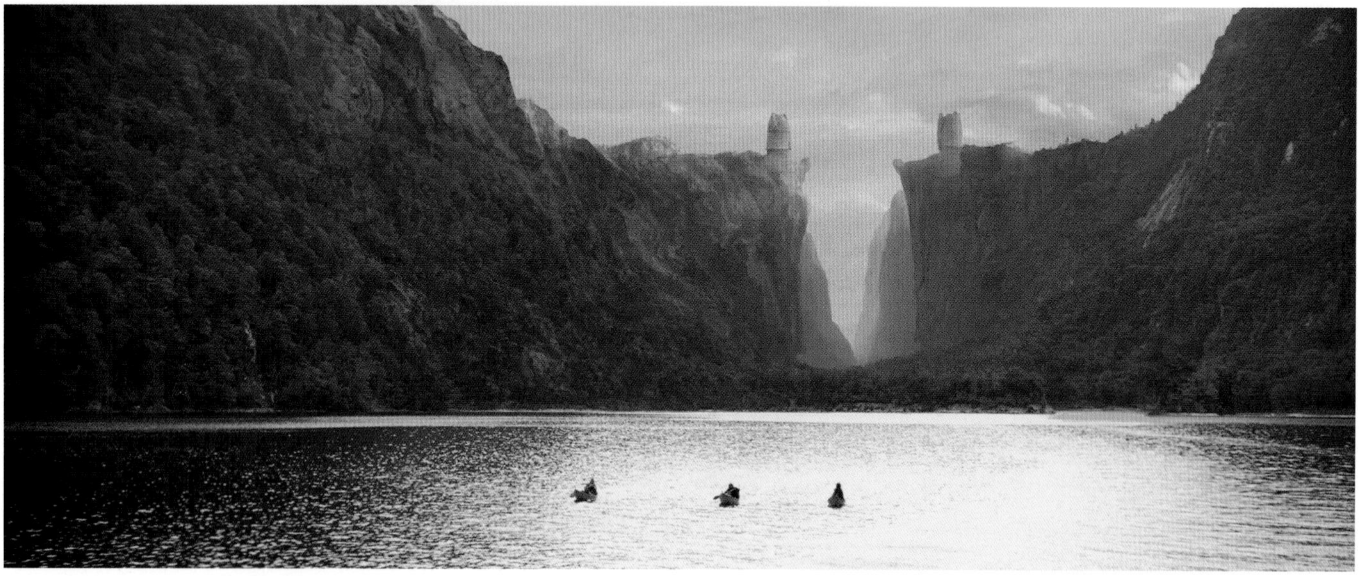

RIVER ANDUIN ***Nen Hithoel***
"This combines the various elements of the location with live footage of the Fellowship heading toward a fateful encounter at Amon Hen." *RK*

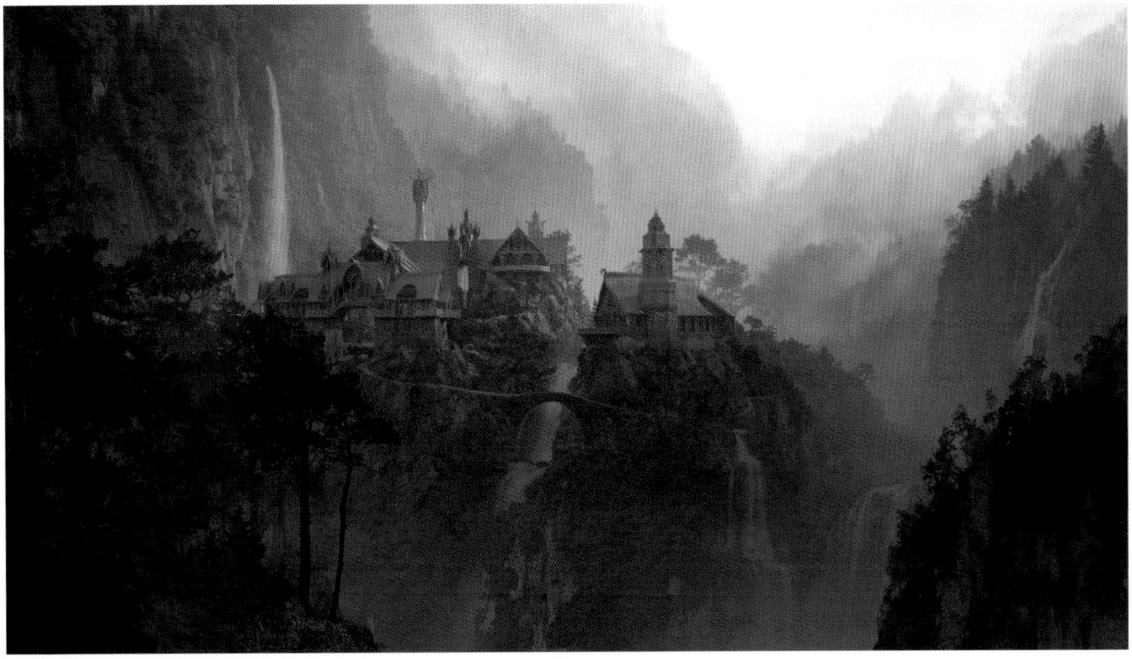

RIVENDELL
Matte painting
"Using Gus Hunter's digital layout (page 209) as a guide, this painting was done in a more monochromatic palette, to convey a slight nostalgic feeling to the romantic sequence between Aragorn and Arwen." *YD*

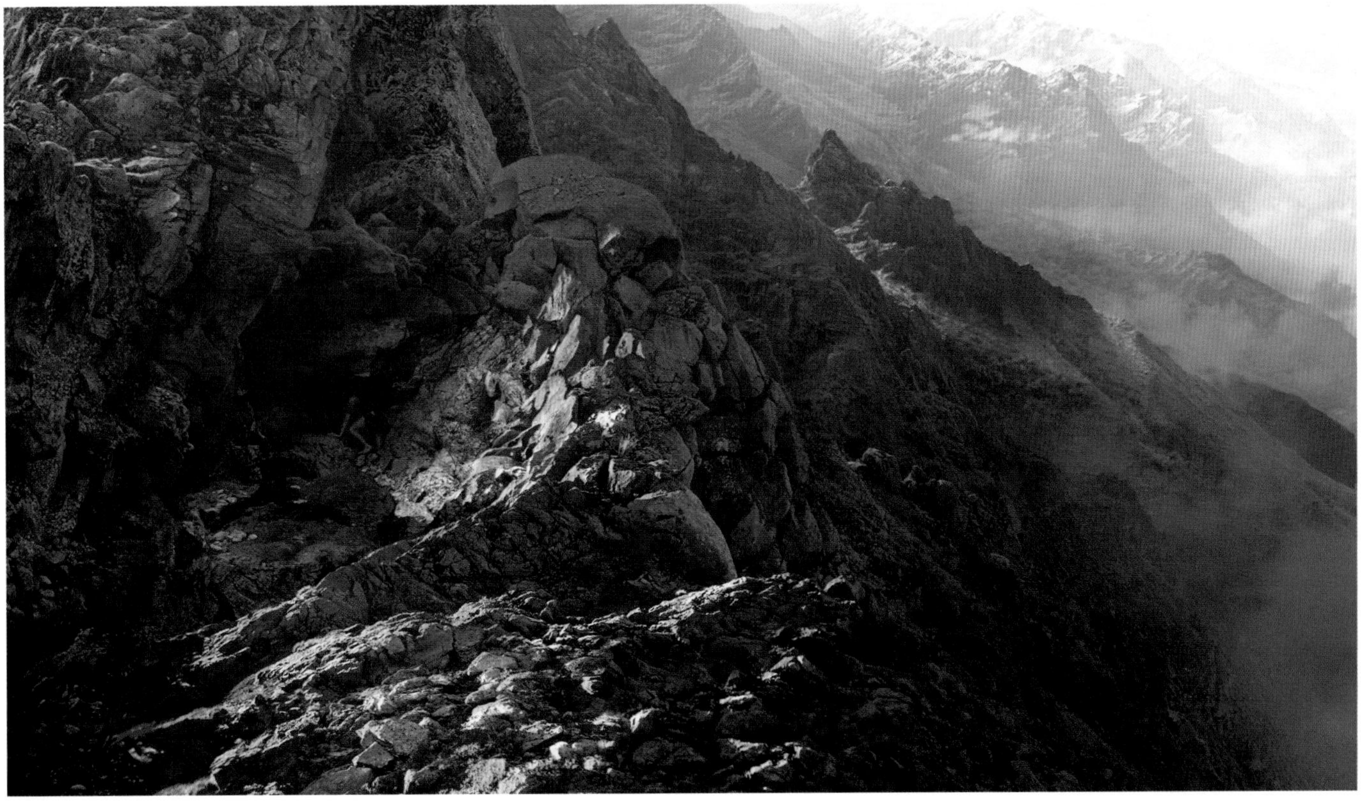

THE MISTY MOUNTAINS *Gollum's cave*
"Alan Lee's preparatory work (page 89) made it very easy for me to complete this painting. He had already produced a detailed sketch and digital painting of the scene; from this, the scene was shot with the actor performing on a small piece of the rock set. From this footage I took a live-action plate of Gollum and inserted it 'behind' the painting. It was then simply a matter of extending the set piece into the vast mountain range." *YD*

THE GLITTERING CAVES
Digital matte painting
"This particular one offered quite a challenge, both technically and artistically. The camera movement had to be digitally extended to reveal the painting filling most of the frame. It was also difficult to find good photographic reference material for the subterranean environment – the result was therefore entirely hand-painted." *YD*

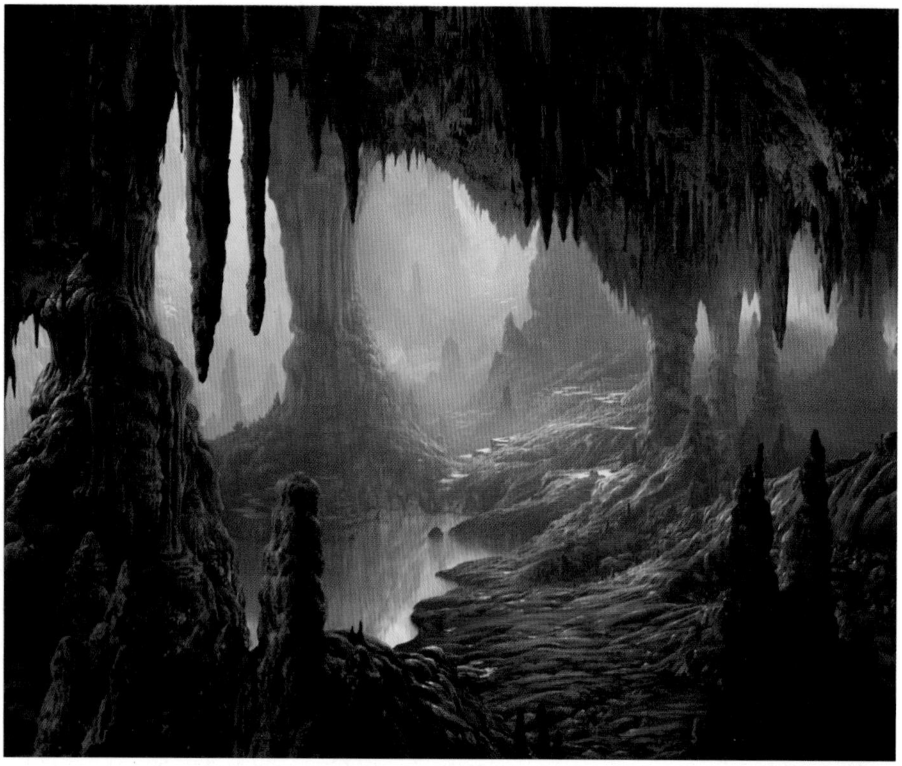

OSGILIATH ***Digital matte painting***
"With this scene, I had to match a live plate with a very specific set of expectations: Ithilien and Osgiliath, with the River Anduin cutting through the plain, as well as Minas Tirith in the distance. There are no plains this vast in New Zealand, so this had to be a painting. Even the miniatures provided had to be completely redressed to suit the feel of the shot. Animation was added as well, in the sky, lighting effects, and minute details within the city, which, by themselves, are barely noticeable. This rendered sequence, an animated matte painting, really, was handed over to Jon Bowen, who then masterfully combined it with the live plate. Because of the vast size of the area it was replacing, this was among the most difficult matte shots produced for the film." *RK*

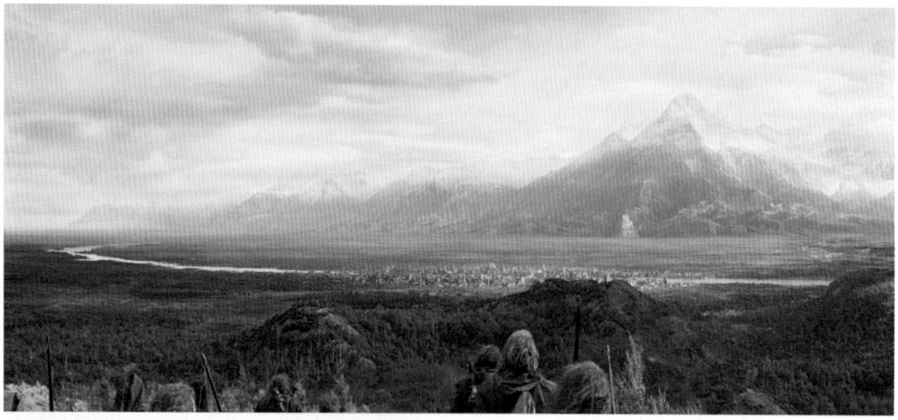

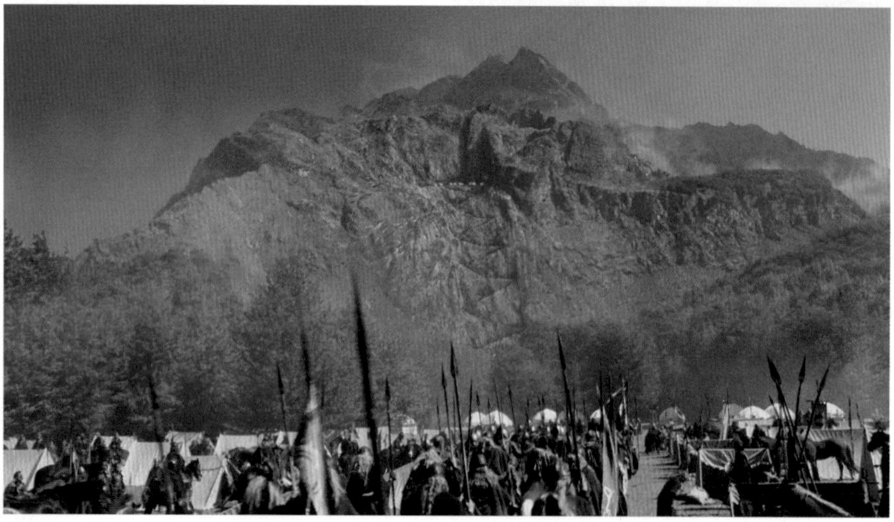

DUNHARROW ENCAMPMENT
Digital matte painting
"This painting is the establishing shot for the Paths of the Dead sequence. It shows the king's camp at Dunharrow and the entrance to the Paths at the top of a precipitous, zigzagging climb. The difficulty in this shot lay in trying to establish both the path and a relatively somber, oppressive mood for what was basically a brightly lit daytime plate." *MD*

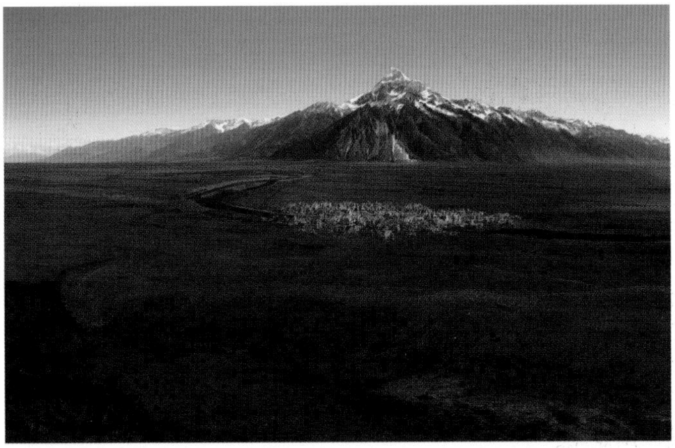

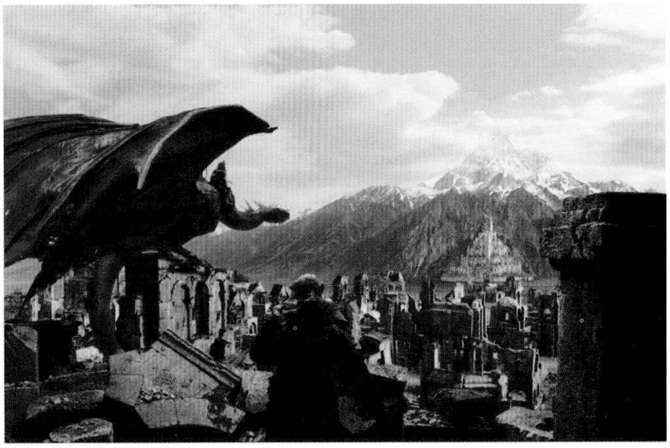

MINAS TIRITH AND THE WHITE MOUNTAINS ***Digital matte paintings***
"Originally I painted this for a shot that was going to show Frodo and Gollum's view from Minas Morgul. It's a huge painting that could be used for multiple shots, such as the one above right. All I had to do each time was tweak the shots by adding different clouds so that it always looked a bit different." *RB*

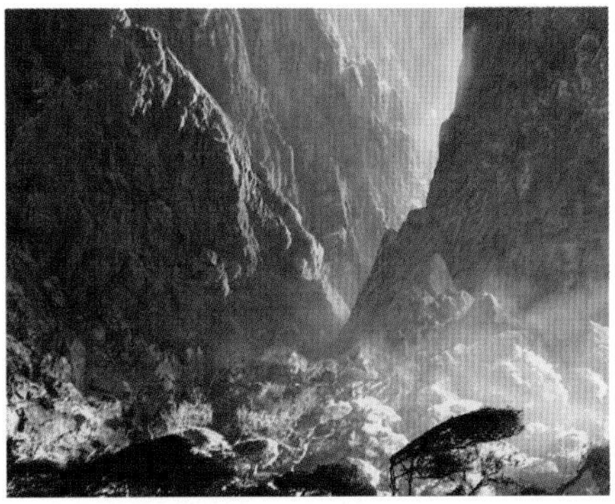

MORGUL VALE
Digital matte painting
"This painting was done for a tilt-down shot that pans down from the Morgul mountains and onto the sleeping Hobbits. Meanwhile, Gollum is having a conversation with himself by a pool." *KdJ*

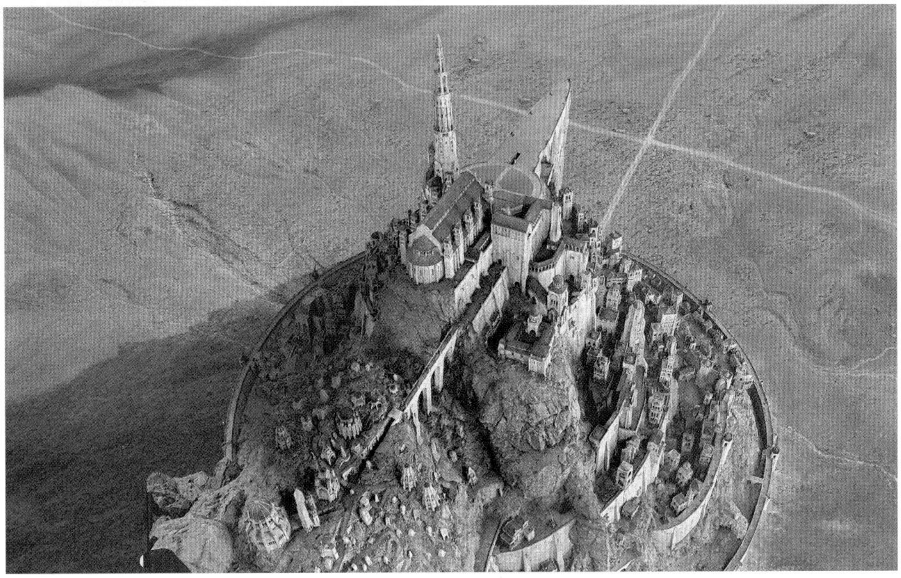

MINAS TIRITH ***Digital matte painting***
"This shot is from a sequence in which Pippin is on his way to light the beacon fire. This view is from just below the beacon on the slopes of Mount Mindolluin. The miniature of the city formed the basis of this painting, but it took some reworking to integrate it into the composition." *DC*

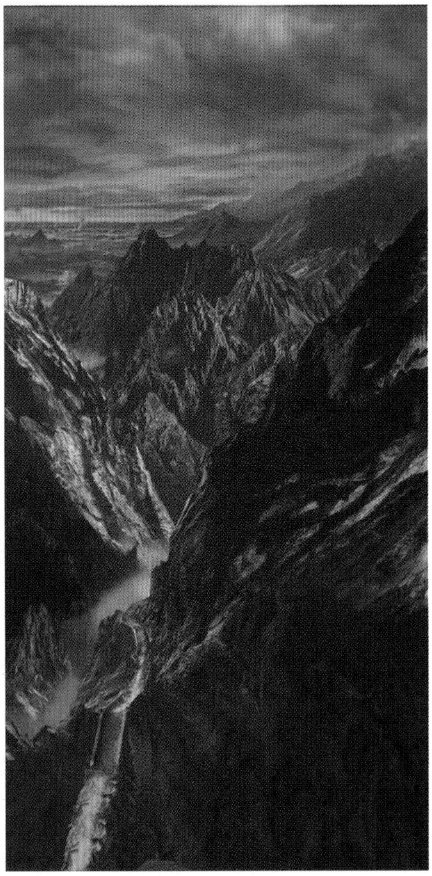

CIRITH UNGOL
Digital matte painting
"This unusually shaped painting, showing the view from the top of the Cirith Ungol tower to the Gorgoroth Plain far below, was designed in this format so that it could follow the tilt-down of the camera, which in turn is following an unfortunate Orc as it falls out of the tower, down to its doom." *RK*

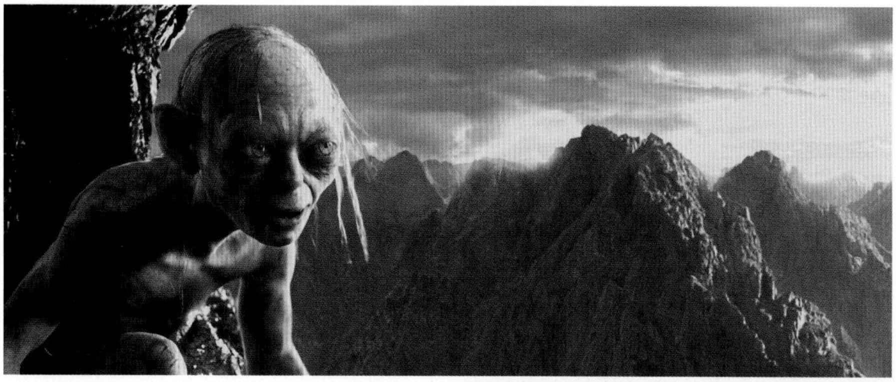

CIRITH UNGOL
Digital matte painting
This painting of the Mordor mountains was combined with the miniature of the entrance to Shelob's Lair and the computer-generated Gollum. All three elements needed to be color-balanced and adjusted to allow for the differing levels of light that would be falling on them. *KdJ*

CIRITH UNGOL *Digital matte painting*
"A broad view of the Cirith Ungol range, looking up toward the sky. This was painted to be a master backdrop, usable in a variety of shots; hence the distorted angles. The final shots were much darker, but this has been presented lighter to show the detail of the painting, which represented more than ten kilometers of mountains. A miniature of the Cirith Ungol tower is included for scale. Because this was used for a number of shots at varying angles, it was projected onto varying complexities of geometry." *RK*

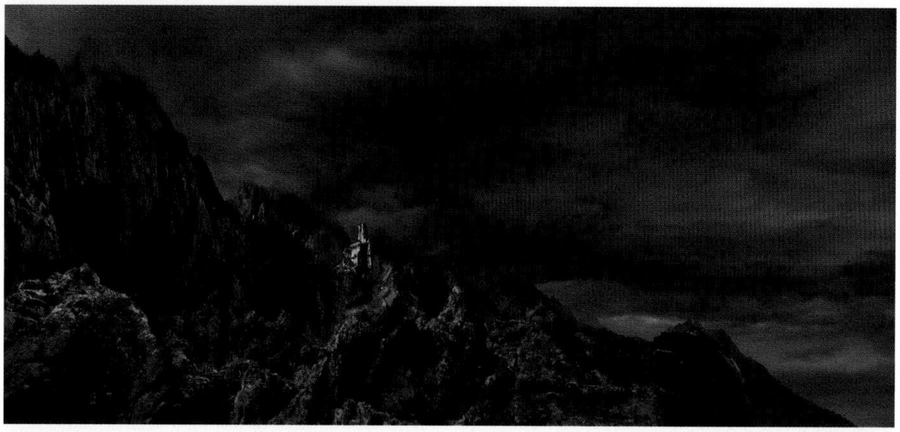

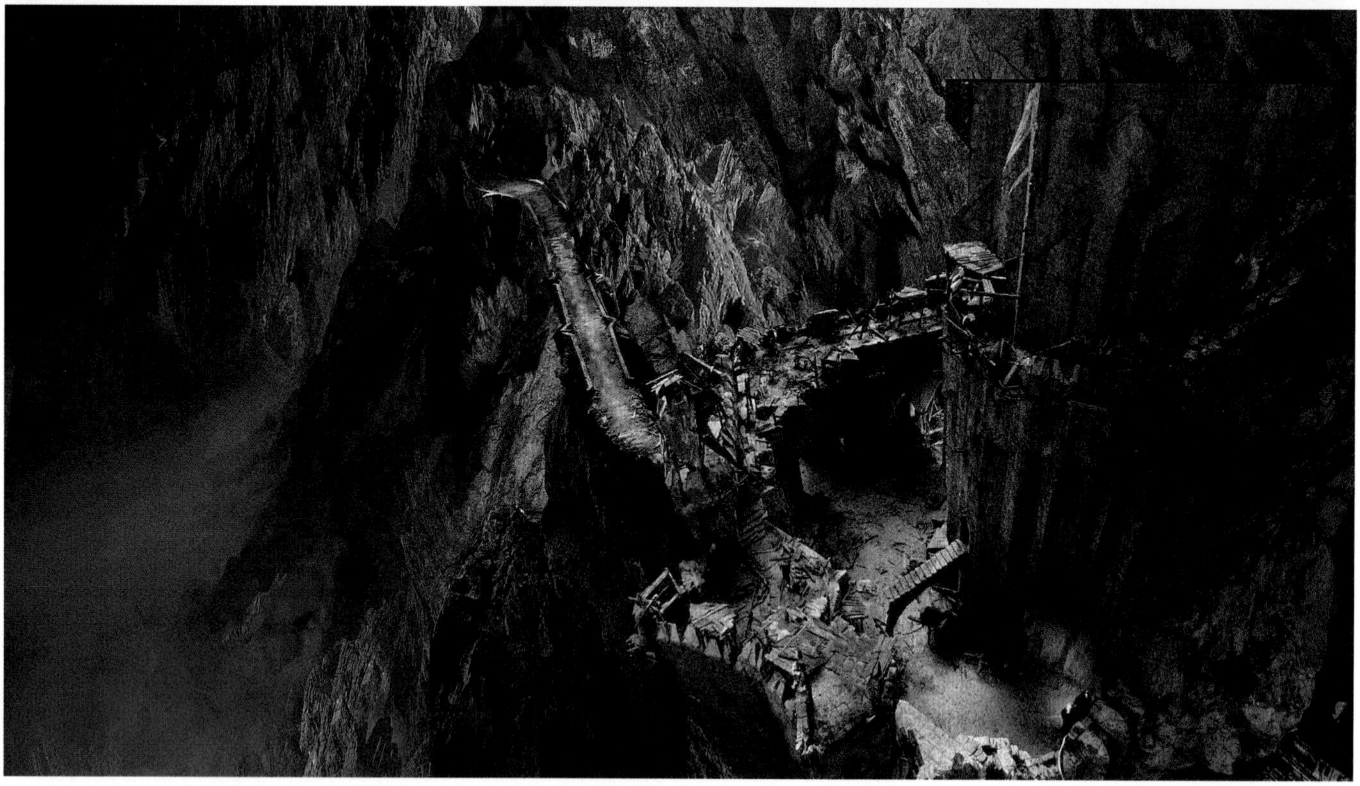

CIRITH UNGOL *Digital matte painting*
"This features the miniature of the Cirith Ungol tower in the foreground, and directly behind it the final matte painting. This was a difficult crane shot, and the pieces had to be overpainted to show parallax." *RK*

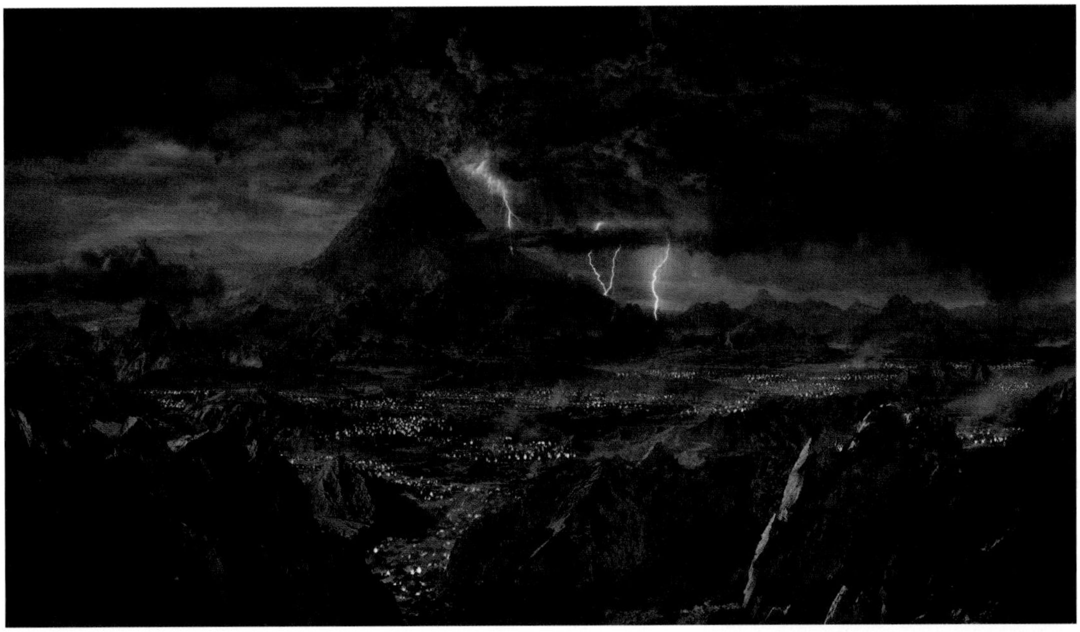

MORDOR ***Digital matte painting***
"This painting reveals the full extent of Mordor's landscape to the two Hobbits as they leave behind the tower of Cirith Ungol and finally enter Sauron's realm. It includes miniatures of Mount Doom and part of the rock set and forms the basis of a wide-pan shot, animated with lightning flashes and the flickering fires of Orc encampments." *RK*

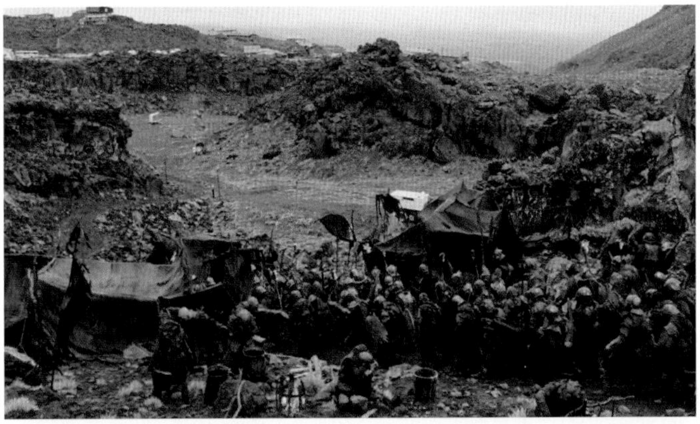

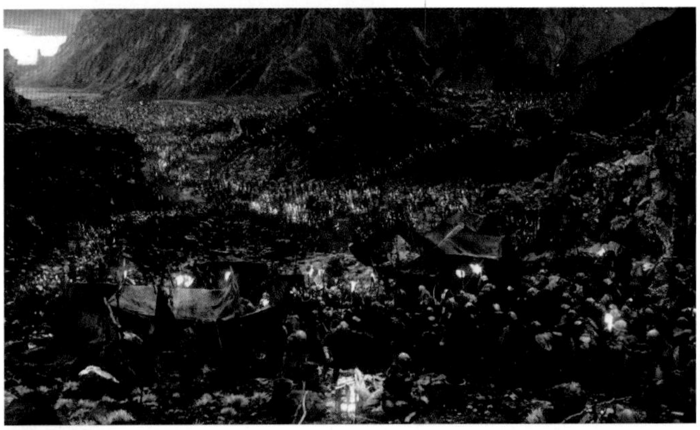

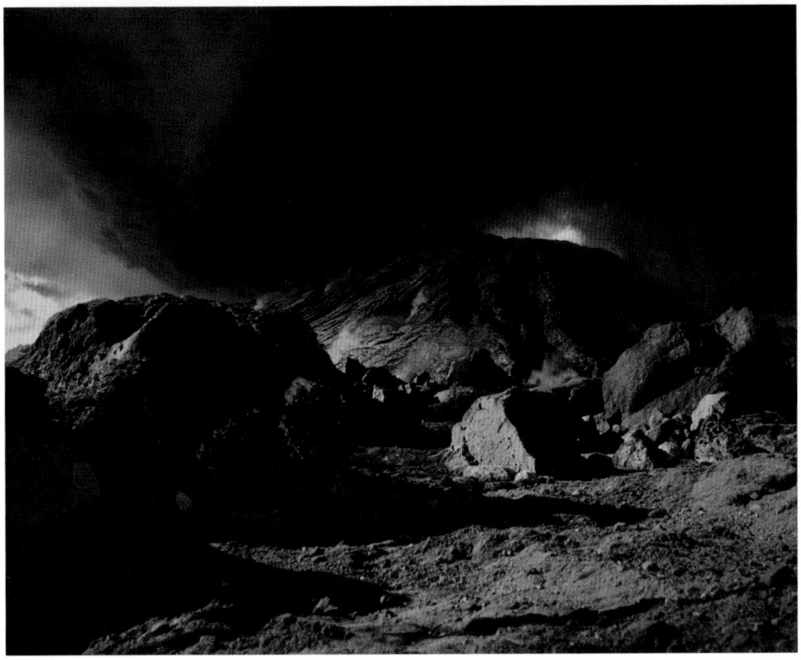

ORC ENCAMPMENT ***Digital matte painting***
"Above is an establishing shot of the Orc hordes as they troop off to battle. It was originally a day shot – as shown in the live-action plate above left – but had to be heavily graded to provide the 'Mordor' feel. The painting starts just behind the mid-ground hill and hints at the vastness and ugliness of the Gorgoroth Plain, and in so doing sets the scene for Frodo and Sam as they continue their journey towards Mount Doom." *MD*

MORDOR ***Mount Doom***
"I really like this shot and think it looked great for the forty frames that ended up on screen! When I started this shot, Jeremy Bennett showed me his painting of Frodo and Sam's view of Mordor, and Yanick Dusseault's wonderful Mordor paintings from the previous films. I felt that in the past some shots of Mordor had made it look rather beautiful, but this shot was going to be really dark. We needed to get a view of the plume of lava that was convincing and not cartoonish." *RB*

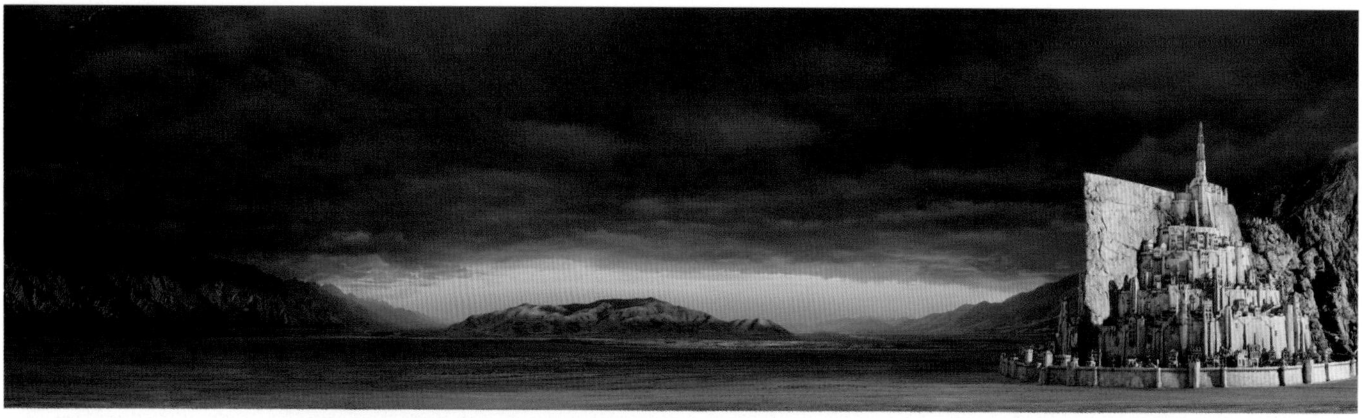

THE PELENNOR FIELDS *Digital matte painting*
"This is a 120-degree view of the Pelennor Fields at dawn and is the vista seen by Théoden as he leads the Rohirrim on their charge into Sauron's Orcs. It was particularly enjoyable to paint the low raking light across the hills and the Mordor range." *DC*

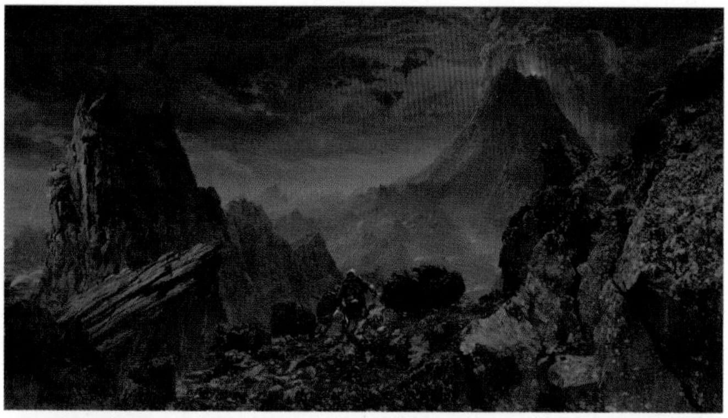

MORDOR *Gorgoroth Plain*
"This shot went through many revisions, from the rough composite using the live plate, left, through many others, until we eventually arrived at the final painting below. This was a much more simplified view of the Gorgoroth Plain, so that we could establish both the desolation and the distance yet to be covered." *DC*

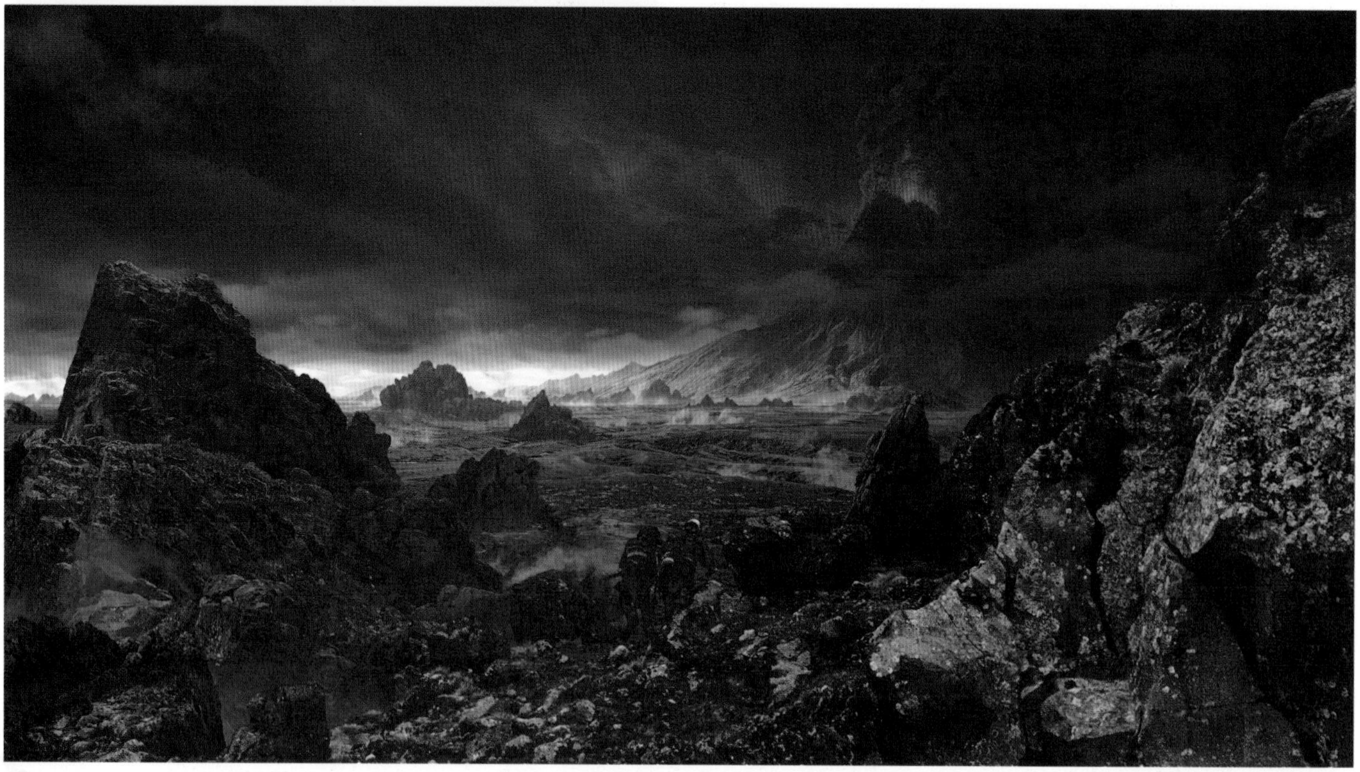

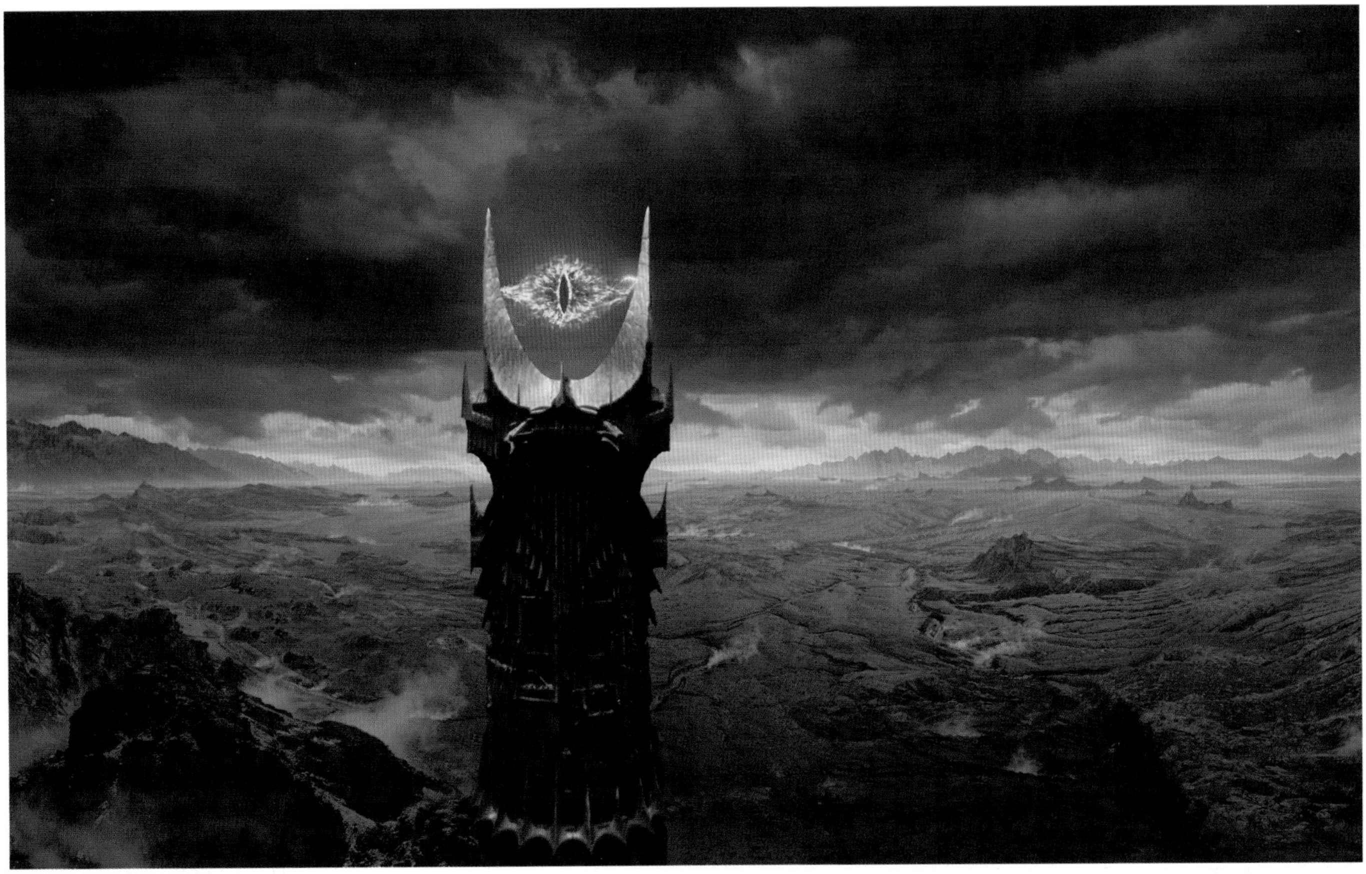

MORDOR ***Barad-dûr***
"For this shot of Barad-dûr and Mordor beyond, the main challenge was to create a sense of height. This was done predominantly by showing the tops of mountains with clinging clouds under Barad-dûr. It is essentially a black-and-white image with the only color being the lava and, of course, the Great Eye. We wanted a sense of scope and scale without taking away from the Eye. The sky was arranged in such a way that the dark part of the tower could be silhouetted against the bright horizon, while the flaming Eye could play against the darker, heavier clouds." *DC*

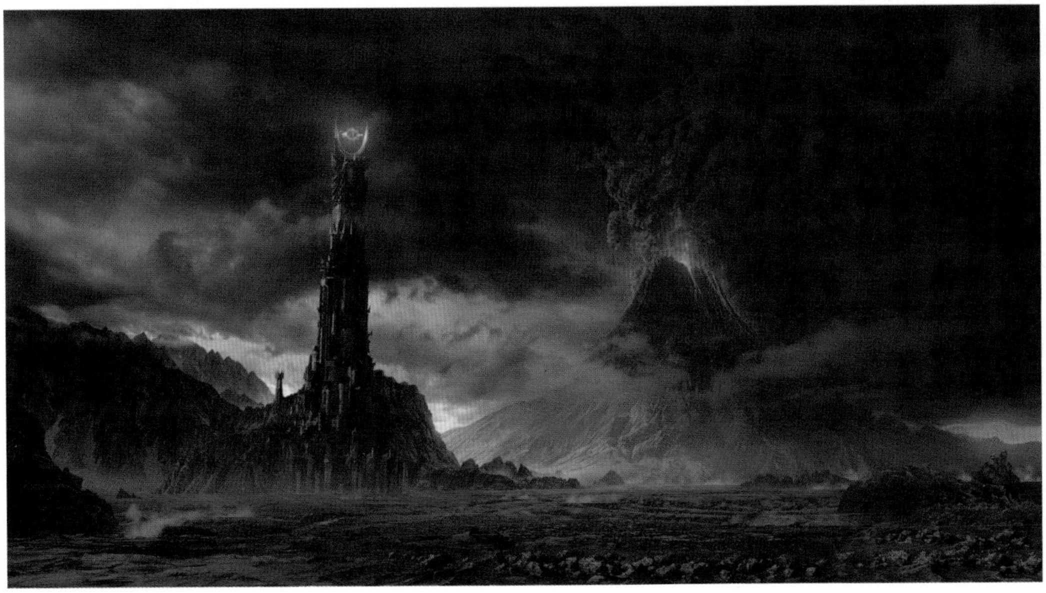

MORDOR ***Barad-dûr***
"We really cheated size and scale for the Barad-dûr destruction shots. Peter wanted Mount Doom large in frame behind the tower to link the destruction of the Ring to the destruction of the tower. It was a challenge to keep the feeling of size and distance for these objects, without obscuring them with haze or making them small. We were also careful to not call too much attention to Mount Doom, so as not to take away from the main focus of the shot, the crumbling tower." *DC*

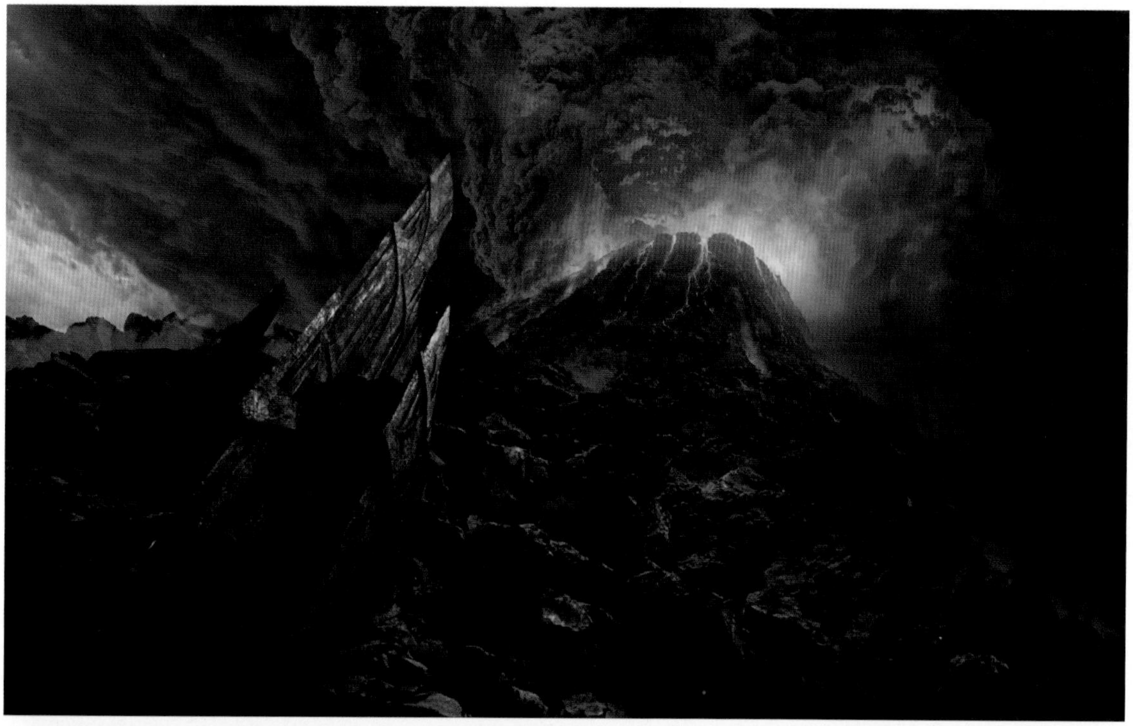

MOUNT DOOM *Sammath Naur*
"This painting is of the view of the top of Mount Doom from the doorway at Sammath Naur. Sam has just followed Frodo into the Crack of Doom. It was a terrific challenge to paint the underside of a pyroclastic cloud." *DC*

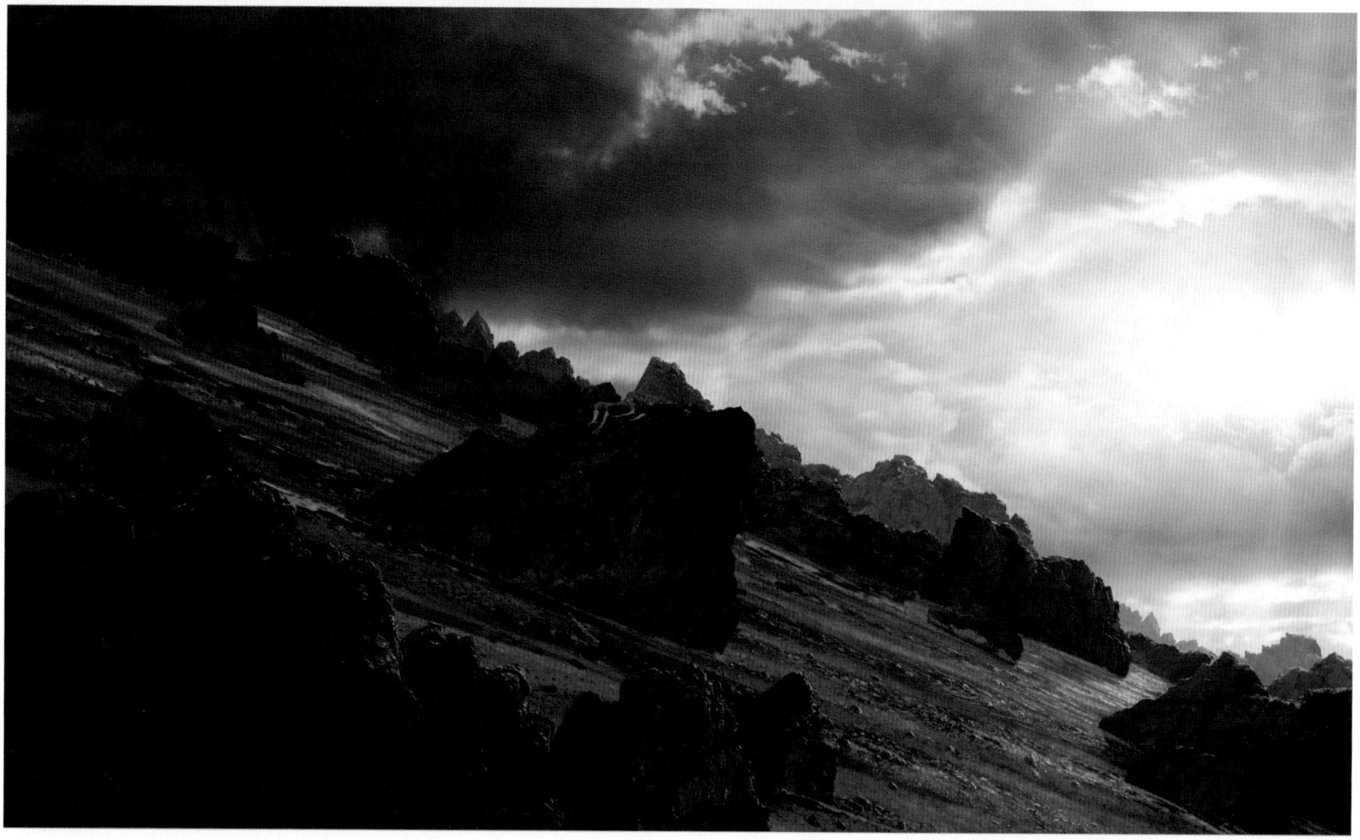

MORDOR *Lava flows*
"For the rescue of Frodo and Sam by Gwaihir, a very dramatic sky was needed, because this is first time that we have seen light break into Mordor. It is a visual relief at the end of a dark journey. In addition to the sky, the rocks and side of the volcano had to be painted. I referenced a lot of rocks found on the coast near Weta, in Wellingon, using their great texture and scale. I was also outside almost daily taking photos of New Zealand skies for inspiration, seeing how the light broke through the cloudy skies." *DC*

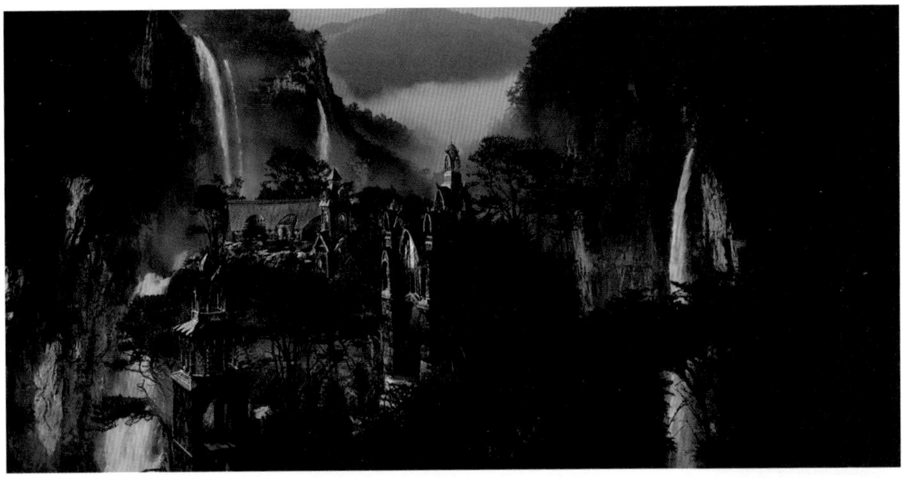

RIVENDELL ***Twilight matte painting***
"Alan Lee described the mood and did a rough concept to show me what was required for this, a nice twilight view out the windows, using the miniatures of a tower and a couple of buildings that were shot a few months previously." *RB*

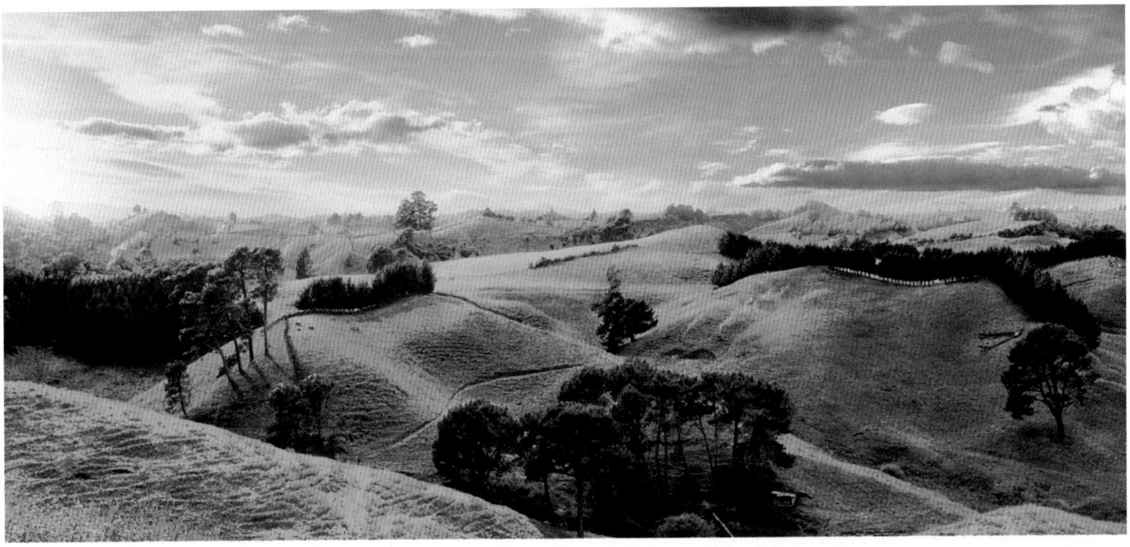

HOBBITON
Digital matte painting
"This takes us back to the green and placid fields of the Shire and Hobbiton. The painting provided a backdrop for a number of shots near the end of the film, when the Hobbits return to the Shire. It is evening time and life remains the same." *MD*

THE GREY HAVENS ***Sunset matte painting***
"This is one of three sunset paintings that I did. I had only a few hours to paint this, and while it would have been great to have had some hi-res sunset photographs, we didn't have any that looked exactly the way Peter Jackson saw this sequence. Alan Lee then found me a photo he had taken on an earlier reference shoot in the South Island, and this was the result." *RB*

CLOSING CREDITS

Peter and Fran had the idea that they would like to mark the ending of the final film in the trilogy by doing something different with the credits. After we did samples and tests on film, the approach chosen was to represent the actors by their portraits, and the rest of the crew by images selected from the huge numbers of drawings and designs by myself and John Howe.

Fran, assisted by VFX art department coordinator Hannah Bianchini, chose frames from the films that represented moments in which each of the characters look the way we would wish to remember them, and I used these as the basis for pencil renditions. Then Jean-Paul Leonard, of Company Wide Shut, who was responsible for the design work on the DVD menus for all three films, and had taken on the task of designing the end credit sequence, carefully composed the images and text and created the elegiac and beautiful look of our final departure from Middle-earth.

Alan Lee
May 2004

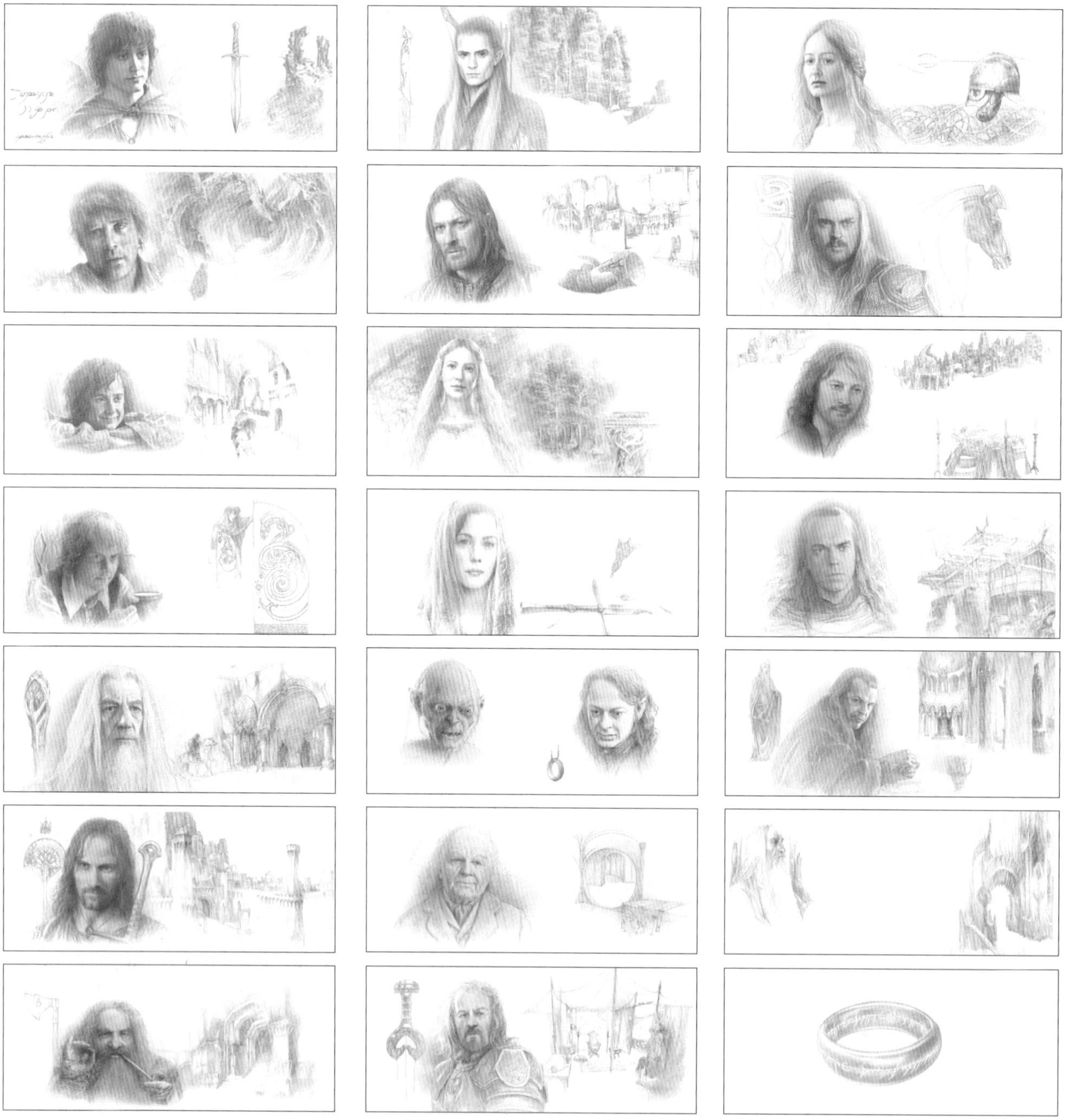